Books and Beyond

Books and Beyond
The Greenwood Encyclopedia of New American Reading

VOLUME 1: A–D

Edited by
KENNETH WOMACK

GREENWOOD PRESS
Westport, Connecticut • London

Library of Congress Cataloging-in-Publication Data

Books and beyond : the Greenwood encyclopedia of new American reading / edited by Kenneth Womack.
   p. cm.
   Includes bibliographical references and index.
   ISBN: 978-0-313-33738-3 (set : alk. paper) — ISBN: 978-0-313-33737-6 (v. 1 : alk. paper) — ISBN: 978-0-313-33740-6 (v. 2 : alk. paper) — ISBN: 978-0-313-33741-3 (v. 3 : alk. paper) — ISBN: 978-0-313-33742-0 (v. 4 : alk. paper)
   1. Books and reading—United States—Encyclopedias. 2. Reading interests—United States—Encyclopedias. 3. Popular literature—United States—Encyclopedias. 4. Fiction genres—Encyclopedias. 5. American literature—History and criticism. 6. English literature—History and criticism. I. Womack, Kenneth.
Z1003.2B64   2008
028'.9097303—dc22   2008018703

British Library Cataloguing in Publication Data is available.

Library of Congress Catalog Card Number: 2008018703
ISBN: 978–0–313–33738–3 (set)
       978–0–313–33737–6 (vol. 1)
       978–0–313–33740–6 (vol. 2)
       978–0–313–33741–3 (vol. 3)
       978–0–313–33742–0 (vol. 4)

First published in 2008

Greenwood Press, 88 Post Road West, Westport, CT 06881
An imprint of Greenwood Publishing Group, Inc.
www.greenwood.com

Printed in the United States of America

The paper used in this book complies with the
Permanent Paper Standard issued by the National
Information Standards Organization (Z39.48–1984).

10 9 8 7 6 5 4 3 2 1

Contents

Preface

Books and Beyond: The Greenwood Encyclopedia of New American Reading offers a multivolume reference work expressly designed to address the shape and nature of contemporary American literature in all of its postwar, print, and post-print cultural manifestations.

Books and Beyond is written to serve the educated general reader, as well as a broad array of high school, college, and university students. The encyclopedia is arranged alphabetically, with more than 70 chapters, or entries, devoted to a wide range of literary areas.

Individual chapters in the encyclopedia provide readers with broad overviews of the topic area, with specific attention and detail afforded to works associated with contemporary popular American literature and culture. Although the chapters often give a historical overview of the genre's development, these entries devote special attention to works published from 1980 to the present.

In addition to establishing a definition of the literary area with attention to its relation to other literary forms, each chapter also offers discussion of major trends and themes, as well as the principal contexts and issues associated with the area. Additional attention is usually given to the genre's reception, including, when possible, criticism, film adaptations, and the relation of the area of literary interest to popular culture in a broader sense.

Each entry provides readers with a discussion of the major authors active in each area, as well as brief analyses of many authors' major works. Helpful cross-references are provided through bolded words in the text, and chapters conclude with bibliographies comprising print and electronic sources related to each rubric; in many cases, a secondary bibliography with suggested works for further reading is provided. At the end of the book, a number of useful features will help users find more about authors and reading in America, with a list of authors active (or recently active) in the field today, arranged by genres, and a list of "Suggestions for Further Reading," which provides material, including Web sites, for more general information about genres and reading. The encyclopedia is fully indexed to afford readers greater ease of use and flexibility.

ACKNOWLEDGMENTS

The editor would like to thank Anne Thompson and George Butler of Greenwood Press for their advice, patience, and steadfast encouragement and professionalism. Special debts of thanks are owed to Amy Mallory-Kani and Susan Yates for their superlative editorial efforts on behalf of the encyclopedia, as well as to Jacki Mowery, Judy Paul, and Aaron Heresco for their good-natured assistance and unflagging generosity of spirit. I am especially grateful to Jeanine Womack for her unerring love and support throughout this project.

Introduction:
Reading in America Today

On any given day, the vast majority of American consumers share in the common language of a popular culture. Whether it be via the latest fast-food craze, video games, hip-hop music, reality-based television, Barbie, and action films, we possess a ready, easily discernible, and shared form of cultural discourse that allows us to converse with one another in an instant. Although the social power of our popular culture clearly has generational boundaries, it often succeeds in transcending the margins of space and time through a perhaps even more powerful and affecting sense of shared nostalgia. Anyone who thinks wistfully of the days of malt shops, big-finned cars, and Marilyn Monroe understands this notion implicitly.

In academic circles, cultural critics have only recently begun to comprehend the significant role of popular culture in our lives and in our systems of social organization, as well as in the evolution of our reading practices. During the early 1950s, for example, we were content simply to understand popular culture as a "low" form of art in contrast with its more austere and presumably more important counterpart, the "high" culture of classical music, ballet, literature, and fine French cuisine. But, of course, that was before the explosion of television, and perhaps even more notably, the advent of cable television and the Internet. Now we commune with one another in a remarkably different fashion. Where once we gathered together on front porches and at summer picnics and spring festivals, we now assemble, many of us, in front of the glowing screens that transport us to *Deal or No Deal*, eBay, and the latest Sony PlayStation. Add to that our vast consumption of communication technologies such as text-messaging, instant-messaging, and e-mail, and the convoluted nature of our language usages and reading experiences becomes even more murky and complex.

The tone of my commentary thus far might suggest the beginnings of a critique of technology and its impact upon our culture—social, economic, reading, or otherwise. This, I shall reassure you, is not that kind of introduction. Technology is merely the means of contemporary popular culture's massive, and nearly instantaneous, dissemination. Perhaps a more interesting and revealing question involves what happens when one nation's popular culture—the popular culture of the United States, for example—is transmitted around the world, erasing and homogenizing the particularities of other cultures across the globe. Although there is little doubt that we import various aspects of other popular cultures into our own—sushi, the River dancing phenomenon, and Harry Potter immediately come to mind the exportation of Americana exists on profound levels that few of us ever genuinely consider.

By any measure, we live in an age of rampant textual instability, and our consumption of popular culture has become inextricably bound with our reading appetites and experiences. There is widespread belief—and ample statistical and anecdotal evidence in support of this notion—that the act of reading itself is on the wane. Yet in an era that demands highly competent reading skills in order to negotiate nearly every avenue of our highly technology oriented contemporary lives, excellence in reading could not be any more significant. As Dana Gioia, chairman of the National Endowment for the Arts, notes in his prefatory remarks for *To Read or Not to Read: A Question of National Consequence* (2007): "Regular reading not only boosts the likelihood of an individual's academic and economic success—facts that are not especially surprising—but it also seems to awaken a person's social and civic sense. Reading correlates with almost every measurement of positive personal and social behavior surveyed. It is reassuring, though hardly amazing," Gioia adds, "that readers attend more concerts and theatre than non-readers, but it is surprising that they exercise more and play more sports—no matter what their educational level. The cold statistics confirm something that most readers know but have mostly been reluctant to declare as fact—books change lives for the better" (6).

WHAT IS A "BOOK"?

But what constitutes a book in our age of rapid textual convolution? And what accounts for "high" and "low" culture in an era in which everyone has access—by virtue of technology and the Internet—to nearly every possible text, as well as the means of producing text on an unheard of scale? The very notion of what makes up a *text* is under reconsideration, and, as the chapters in this encyclopedia demonstrate—with their wide disparity of focuses and disparate textual natures—this is a worthy issue indeed. In truth, we are only just beginning to formulate a critical vocabulary for describing—much less comprehending—the increasingly fluid nature of textuality. How, indeed, do we even begin to understand our cultural artifacts, their popularization, and their reception into the cultural and critical main—especially in a rapidly shifting marketplace in which text, more often than not, does not find its materiality in the pages of a book? As cultural studies continues to challenge our conceptions of the borders of literary and textual studies, issues regarding the nature of what constitutes a text have become increasingly significant in our post-print culture. In addition to involving such controversial subjects as the interrelationships between high and low culture and the component differences between material and nonmaterial texts, the chapters in this encyclopedia explore the manner in which we receive and interpret a wide variety of texts—from works of popular serial fiction and the transhistorical literary imagination to film adaptation and popular music.

As an encyclopedia of contemporary literatures and reading practices in all of their attendant forms, *Books and Beyond* merges conventional forms of text with unconventional ones in a myriad of innovative ways. Attention is devoted to a number of well-honed literary areas, including Adventure Fiction; Children's Literature; Contemporary Fiction; Fantasy Literature; Historical Fiction; Humor; Mystery Novels; Poetry; Romance Fiction; Science Fiction; Spy Fiction; Suspense Novels; Travel Writing; and Western Literature. At the same time, a wide variety of ethnicities and cultures is represented, including Arab American Literature and Native American Literature, to name but a few. Contemporary reading trends are also explored, as evinced by wide-ranging chapters devoted to such areas as Autobiography and Memoir; Biography; Chick Lit; Christian Fiction; Coming of Age Fiction; Erotic Literature; Historical Nonfiction; Inspirational Literature; Legal Thrillers; Literary Journalism; Magical Realism; Military Literature; New Age Literature; Occult/Supernatural Literature; Regional Fiction; Road Fiction; Science Nonfiction; Sea Literature; Self-Help Literature; Series Fiction; Sports Literature; True Crime; Urban Fiction; Utopian Fiction; Vampire Fiction; and Young Adult Literature. Yet in order to demonstrate the breadth and scope of contemporary American literature, attention to a vast range of transcultural and transhistorical forms is also necessary, including chapters devoted to Arthurian Literature; Beat Poetry; Comic Books; Cyberpunk; Dystopian Fiction; Ecopoetry; Film Adaptation; Flash Fiction; GLBTQ Literature; Graphic Novels; Historical Mysteries; Language Poetry; Manga and Anime; Speculative Fiction; Sword and Sorcery Fiction; Terrorism Fiction; Time Travel Fiction; Transrealist Fiction; Verse Novels; and Zines.

But how do we account for the textuality of such a wide array of authorial (and, in some cases, nonauthorial) forms, particularly in terms of the Byzantine nature of their construction, production, and dissemination? Perhaps even more significant, how do educators approach the act of teaching this important aspect of textual theory to new generations of students for whom textuality has become an increasingly diffuse and convoluted concept—a generation for whom textual stability is becoming progressively more irrelevant? For many contemporary "readers," the concept of narrative-driven works of art, whether they be artifacts of high or low culture, concerns the nature and rapidity of its systems of distribution, its value determined almost entirely by the end-user's capacity for negotiating its acquisition, its storage, and the ease of its consumption. A century ago, the textuality of narrative, whether fiction, nonfiction, or news, was delivered to users almost universally via the physical properties of the traditional book, magazine, and newspaper forms. Within a scant few decades, books were joined by the radio airwaves as principal means of textual distribution, to be followed, in short order, by movies and television. The advent of computer technology transformed, in rapid and radical fashion, existing forms of distribution while acting as the catalyst for new eras of textuality as witnessed by the evolution of digital storage media that have irrevocably altered the ways in which we consume not only books, but all manner of music and video in the process.

WHAT IS TEXT?

This incredible shift in the production, distribution, and consumption of our cultural artifacts—our popular textualities, if you will—necessitates an ongoing interrogation of text and its multiplicities of variation. The ideology of text, in and of itself, is deceptively simple. Mikhail M. Bakhtin's working definition of text includes "any coherent complex of signs" (1986, 103). For Roland Barthes, the text exists as a locus of meaning, as a form of discourse rather than as a concrete object. "*The text is experienced only as an activity, a production*," he writes (1977, 157). Texts ask readers to participate in the act of meaning-making, while books take up physical space on a shelf. In this way, readers actively participate in the processes associated with textual production. Yet our post-print theories of textuality must be increasingly enabled to account for the nonphysicality and nonmateriality of digitally-inscribed texts. In *Scholarly Editing in the Computer Age: Theory and Practice*, Peter L. Shillingsburg defines text as "the actual order of words and punctuation as contained in any one physical form, such as a manuscript, proof or book." Shillingsburg astutely recognizes that "text (the *order* of words and punctuation) has no substantial or material existence, as it is not restricted by time and space." Indeed, even in terms of the traditional book format—with its spine, its pages, and its inky print—"the text is contained and stabilized by the physical form but is not the physical form itself" (1996, 46). Hence, textuality enjoys an intrinsically fluid quality, the nature of which can be manipulated by authors, editors, publishers, distributors, and the like with veritable ease, given the relative pliability of electronic storage devices and digital redistribution.

These new ways of thinking about textuality—about the representation of text in our post-print age—mandates a revisioning of our understanding of materiality. Once defined almost exclusively by the brute physicality of the book, text has emerged as an increasingly imaginative and unstable construct. As N. Katherine Hayles shrewdly asks, "What are the consequences of admitting an idea of textuality as instantiated rather than dematerialized, dispersed rather than unitary, processual rather than object-like, flickering rather than durably instantiated?" The answer, Hayles points out, involves a revaluation of text, particularly in terms of what we consider to be its material aspects. "The specter haunting textual criticism," Hayles writes, "is the nightmare that one cannot then define a 'text' at all, for every manifestation will qualify as a different text. Pervasive with electronic texts, the problem troubles notions of print texts as well, for as physical objects they would also differ from one another. But this need not be a catastrophe if we refine and revise our notion of materiality" (2003, 276).

The result of so much variation, as evinced throughout our postwar, post-print culture, is an ongoing and increasingly complex sense of textual instability, particularly as new forms of electronic storage and digital distribution replace earlier storage and delivery methods with a vexing and dislocating rapidity. Philip Cohen describes this concatenation of circumstances as a form of "textual instability" in which "the essence of texts may be their ability to be re-ontologized and re-interpreted endlessly as different textual versions and contexts are employed." Textual instability entails the manner in which "texts are not immune from the flow of history," Cohen writes, as well as the ways in which "they are composed, revised, expurgated, improved, defaced, restored, emended, and circulated as a matter of course" (1997, xxii). As the chapters in this encyclopedia so clearly demonstrate, the analysis of material and nonmaterial texts under these strictures offers prescient reminders about the ways in which we need to approach popular works of literature in our rapidly shifting and expanding digital age. It is nearly impossible to imagine a world in which the formerly conventional strictures of authorship and textual hegemony, or domination, will be restored. As J. Hillis Miller points out, it is always "beneficial to the health of our society to have an abundance of good readers" (1998, 100). Robert Coles takes this notion a step further, writing that "students need the chance to directly connect books to experience." Literary texts, Coles adds, allow educators to "address our humanity with subtlety—conveying the willingness to do justice to our variousness and to the complexities, ironies, and ambiguities that shape our lives" (1994, A64). Indeed, what teachers in society *can* do is provide students with the analytical tools to become experts at getting to the heart of the textual matter, at learning how to sift among the competing texts that they encounter, and to begin establishing a sense of cultural unity and interpersonal growth for themselves. With its wide-ranging emphasis upon the proliferation of material and nonmaterial texts in our increasingly uncertain textual era, *Books and Beyond: The Greenwood Encyclopedia of New American Reading* is one of the first steps in this important direction.

Bibliography

Bakhtin, Mikhail M. "The Problem of the Text in Linguistics, Philology, and the Human Sciences: An Experiment in Philosophical Analysis." In *Speech Genres and Other Late Essays*. Ed. Caryl Emerson and Michael Holquist. Trans. Vern W. McGee. Austin, TX: University of Texas Press, 1986, 103–131.

Barthes, Roland. *Image-Music-Text*. Trans. Stephen Heath. New York: Hill and Wang, 1977.

Cohen, Philip. "Textual Instability, Literary Studies, and Recent Developments in Textual Scholarship." In *Texts and Textuality: Textual Instability, Theory, and Interpretation*. Philip Cohen, ed. New York: Garland, 1997, xi–xxxiv.

Coles, Robert. "Putting Head and Heart on the Line." *The Chronicle of Higher Education* 41 (26 Oct. 1994): A64.

Goodrich, Diana Sorensen. *The Reader and the Text: Interpretive Strategies for Latin American Literatures*. Amsterdam: John Benjamins, 1986.

Hayles, N. Katherine. "Translating Media: Why We Should Rethink Textuality." *Yale Journal of Criticism* 16.2 (2003): 263–290.

Miller, J. Hillis. "Is There an Ethics of Reading?" In *Reading Narrative: Form, Ethics, Ideology*. James Phelan, ed. Columbus, OH: Ohio State University Press, 1988, 79–101.

National Endowment for the Arts. *To Read or Not to Read: A Question of National Consequence*. Research Report #47. Washington, DC, 2007.

Shillingsburg, Peter L. *Scholarly Editing in the Computer Age: Theory and Practice*. 3rd ed. Ann Arbor, MI: University of Michigan Press, 1996.

Worthen, W. B. "Disciplines of the Text: Sites of Performance." In *The Performance Studies Reader*. Henry Bial, ed. London: Routledge, 2004, 10–24.

A

ACADEMIC FICTION

Definition. The campus novel enjoys a long and distinguished history in the annals of literary studies. A review of academic fiction's emergence as a literary form, particularly during the nineteenth century, accounts for its archly satirical manifestations during the latter half of the twentieth century, the era in which academic satire enjoyed its most fruitful period, with forays into a variety of creative spheres, including fiction, poetry, drama, and film. The analysis of exemplary works by Kingsley Amis, Malcolm Bradbury, David Lodge, A.S. Byatt, and Jane Smiley demonstrates the nature of campus fiction's abiding influence.

History. "As a literary genre," Mortimer R. Proctor writes in *The English University Novel*, the academic novel "has always reflected conditions within Oxford and Cambridge far more closely than it has followed any literary trends or movements" (1957, 185). The universal conception of Oxford and Cambridge as unique intellectual societies—in short, the fictive terrain of "Oxbridge"—inspired centuries of fictions devoted to university life, from Chaucer's Clerk of Oxford through the romanticized academic novels of the early nineteenth century. While these narratives poked occasional fun at the ineffectuality of university faculty or the unreality of college life, their plots generally involved sentimental, often melodramatic, portrayals of Oxford and Cambridge. The genre of English university fiction finds its more satiric origins, however, in the various educational reform movements of the mid-nineteenth century, as well as in the admission of women to the sacred groves of Oxford and Cambridge in the latter half of the nineteenth century. During this era, Oxford and Cambridge witnessed a decline in the hegemony of their influence upon English society and culture. Their fictional portrayals, once predicated upon more lofty elements of esteem and erudition, now languished in narratives about "university lecturers who did not lecture, and undergraduates who freely enjoyed all the pleasures of depravity" (Proctor, 11).

The acts of reform experienced by Oxford and Cambridge found their roots in the 1850s, when a series of reports commissioned by the English government revealed a set of institutions that operated on an outmoded classical curriculum and blatantly catered to the needs of the socially privileged. In "From Narragonia to Elysium: Some Preliminary Reflections on the Fictional Image of the Academic," Richard Sheppard notes that for universities this era in English history also marks the shift from their function as clerical institutions devoted to producing educated priests to their emergence as the precursors of our modern research institutions (Bevan 1990, 11). While a set of statutes during the 1870s virtually redesigned the governance of both institutions, reform acts in 1854 and 1856 abolished religious tests at Oxford and Cambridge, respectively, thus providing access to the universities for students outside of the Church of England (Proctor 1957, 56–57). This movement against exclusion ultimately resulted in the momentous events of 1879, when Somerville College first opened its doors to female students at Oxford. As Janice Rossen observes in *The University in Modern Fiction: When Power Is Academic* (1993), the exclusion of women from the university community continues to resonate within the pages of academic fiction. "There has been nothing else like the wholesale resistance to the admission of a particular, coherent group to the University in Britain, and this is part and parcel of the subject," Rossen writes. "The two facts are inextricable—women got into the University, and women were bitterly opposed in their efforts to do so. The powerful initial resistance to their inclusion in the University would certainly have affected how they saw themselves and their place in that community for some time to come" (34).

In addition to increasing the public's interest in the business of higher education, the nineteenth-century reform acts at Oxford and Cambridge succeeded in establishing a social landscape ripe for narrative consideration. "Reform," Proctor observes, "brought new causes to urge, and a new cast of characters to add to the traditional rakes. With reform, it became more plausible to take an interest in the success of scholars; examination halls became the scenes of triumphs and disasters in which good very nearly always triumphed over evil" (1957, 59). As with their English antecedents, American novels about academic life find their modern origins in the nineteenth century, an intense era of social change and industrial growth that destabilized the prodigious cultural influences of privileged institutions of higher learning such as Oxford and Cambridge and, in America, Harvard. The emergence of the American academic novel can be traced to Nathaniel Hawthorne's *Fanshawe*, published in 1828. Set in Harley College in the wilderness of New England during the eighteenth century, Hawthorne's novel—which he later attempted to suppress—explores a number of themes endemic to modern academic fictions, including Hawthorne's depiction of the eccentric Dr. Melmoth, an absent-minded and ineffectual scholar who later becomes the institution's president. In his examination of the American evolution of the academic novel, John Lyons (1962, 4) remarks:

> The advance of industrial capitalism during the nineteenth century is another cause for the popular suspicion of the academy. The mechanical sciences which fathered and made this advance possible were eminently practical ones. It was engineering which laid the rails and built the bridges and designed the mills, not philosophy. And the money which engineering made possible was used to buy and sell engineers, so it was unlikely that the capitalist businessman should even respect the engineer when his knowledge brought him so little power.

The "popular suspicion of the academy" that Lyons ascribes to the industrialized societies of the latter nineteenth century underscores the emergence of the brand of satire endemic to the Anglo-American novels about university life. Satire, by its traditional definition, functions as a critique of the follies of humankind. Yet Lyons astutely differentiates the modern incarnations of satire in university fiction from the texts of the great satirists of the Augustan Age, who invariably situated themselves on the side of "Reason, . . . tempered by humanity and common sense." The satirists of the Augustan era, Lyons notes, often hinted at solutions to the dilemmas depicted in their narratives. Satiric novels of academic life, however, provide no such answers (162–63). Further, in his essay, "Inside Jokes: Familiarity and Contempt in Academic Satire," Brian A. Connery observes that academic satire—in contrast to neoclassical satire, which only attacks the vices and follies of an absent or unknowing target—also aims its satiric barbs at the reader. In this way, he argues, academic novelists deny their readers the ironic, self-congratulatory pleasures of neo-classical satire because the readers themselves, often academics, function as the texts' ultimate targets (Bevan 1990, 124–26).

Trends and Themes. A thematic analysis of various works of postwar academic fiction sheds considerable light on the remarkable rise of the campus novel during the latter half of the twentieth century. Rossen identifies a "dynamics of power" that undergirds postwar manifestations of English and American academic novels during this era. "We should begin to read these novels less in terms of their actual brilliance or success," she argues, "and more in terms of what they reveal about the dynamics of power between the contemporary novelist and his audience" (1993, 188). Rossen's paradigm for interpreting academic fiction's vast output reveals the various structures of power that simultaneously manipulate both the life of the individual scholar and that of the university community. These power structures, she argues, ultimately problematize campus life through their creation of a philosophical paradox that scholars ultimately cannot escape. As Rossen observes, "The scholarly life inevitably consists of life in community, though it is fundamentally predicated on a principle of individualism" (9). Modern universities, by virtue of their tenure and research requirements, maintain, at least in regard to their nontenured members, the explicit threat of expulsion. The ominous power of this vestige of professional affiliation creates "an imposing façade" in favor of the university, Rossen writes, "which suggests a powerful presence through its ability to exclude potential members" (30).

The politics of exclusion—the threat of ultimate severance from the community—functions as a menacing obstacle in the path to institutional success for the individual scholar. For this reason, the nature of academic scholarship receives particular attention in university fictions. As Rossen observes, "All novels about academic life and work exploit the tension between these two poles of idealism and competition, or scholarship as a means to an end and as an end in itself" (140). This tension presents scholars with an emotional dilemma of staggering proportions: in one sense, campus life purports to offer them an arena to engage their colleagues in free intellectual discourse, while in another sense it necessitates that they confront their colleagues in a high-stakes competition based upon the quality and proliferation of their intellectual exertions in order to ensure their professional security. "The emotional dimension of such work can lead to heightened battles between scholars," Rossen remarks, "and in a way which brings their powerful intellectual abilities and skills to bear on what is fundamentally an emotional issue" (145). Rossen's contentions regarding the highly competitive nature of contemporary academic life can be ascribed to the experiences of students as well. Through entrance requirements and performance standards, students endure similar threats of expulsion from the university community. Undergraduates must also conform to a form of communal disruption each term as their lives redefine themselves around new course schedules and holiday breaks. "What undergraduates in all of these novels seem to experience primarily is an intensely intimate, private world with their peers—and one in which they suffer from either ambitions to be included . . . or yearning to find love and acceptance," Rossen observes. "The unique feature of community life for undergraduates is that the small world which they create for themselves vanishes when the students disperse at the end of their University terms" (118). Thus, a number of novels explore the undergraduate experiences of students in the academy, including Martin Amis's *The Rachel Papers* (1973), Clare Chambers's *Uncertain Terms* (1992), and Bret Easton Ellis's *The Rules of Attraction* (1987), among others. Marion Rosen's *Death by Education* (1993) explores student life in a secondary educational institution.

Contexts and Issues. Academic fictions' nostalgia for the ivory towers of their pre-nineteenth-century cultural and social supremacy prevents them from positing solutions in a pragmatic world where the idealism of the academy lacks viability and significance. In the first half of the twentieth century, then, when the world demanded answers to even more complicated social and political predicaments—from the calamities of the First and Second World Wars to the Great Depression and beyond—the academy once again lacked practical answers to the human community's vexing problems. Hence, the interconnections between the satiric ambitions of the Menippean writers and the motivations of twentieth-century academic novelists merit particular attention. As W. Scott Blanchard notes in *Scholar's Bedlam: Menippean Satire in the Renaissance* (1995), "Menippean satire is a genre both for and about scholars; it is an immensely learned form that is at the same time paradoxically anti-intellectual," he writes. "If its master of ceremonies is the humanist as wise fool, its audience is a learned community whose members need to be reminded . . . of the depravity of their overreaching intellects, of the limits of human understanding" (14). In short, modern academic satire began to share in a richly developed and lengthy satiric tradition. And academic novels flourished as never before.

The genre's evolving presence in contemporary British fiction finds its origins in the proliferation of provincial "redbrick" universities, which, like the reform acts of the nineteenth century, undermined the formerly exalted influence of Oxford and Cambridge and expanded appreciably the public's access to institutions of higher education in England. For the first time, academic novels—through their explicit use of satire—seemed to offer solutions for the problems that confront modern readers far beyond the hallowed walls of the university. As Ian Carter remarks in *Ancient Cultures of Conceit: British University Fiction in the Post-War Years*, the answers

---

THE *PROFESSORROMANE*

Campus novels have seen an enormous output in England and the United States since the 1950s. Richard G. Caram usefully describes these works as *Professorromane*, "a term of my own coining, in the tradition of slightly-pompous Germanic scholarship," he writes. "The *Professorroman* has distinctive features that qualify it as a subgenre of literature similar to the *Künstlerroman* or the *Bildungsroman*" (42).

lie in "taking culture seriously, and taking universities to be important bastions of culture. But the notion of what constitutes culture," he cautions, "must be transformed from that typical of British university fiction" (1990, 277). In this way, the academic novel proffers—through its satiric depiction of the institutional states of malaise inherent in its fictive representations of contemporary universities—a means for both implicitly and explicitly advocating positive value systems. In short, contemporary academic novels, by postulating a kind of anti-ethos in their narratives, ultimately seek to enhance the culture and sustain the community through a more ethically driven system of higher education. This anti-ethos, which Kenneth Womack describes as a "pejorative poetics" in *Postwar Academic Fiction: Satire, Ethics, Community* (2001), underscores the satirical motivations of the authors of academic fiction and the manner in which their narrative ambitions function as self-conscious ethical correctives.

Reception. There is little question that the campus novel will continue to resound as one of literature's most satirical genres. While their forebears in the academic fictions of the late nineteenth and early twentieth centuries languished under the specter of "Oxbridge," contemporary academic characters must contend with the whimsy of global economic slumps and university budget cuts, the fashionable nature of structuralist and poststructuralist literary criticism, growing social and racial divisions on college campuses, and an increasingly hostile academic job market, among a range of other issues. Indeed, there seems to be no end to the ways in which the practitioners of Anglo-American university fiction can utilize academic characters and institutional themes as a means for exploring, through the deliberately broad strokes of their satirical prose, the ethical and philosophical questions endemic to their genre that impinge upon such enduringly significant issues as culture, morality, romance, knowledge, and commitment.

Selected Authors. Many scholars attribute the origins of postwar academic fiction to the landmark publication of Kingsley Amis's *Lucky Jim* in 1954. In addition to its widely acknowledged place as the quintessential campus novel of the twentieth century, *Lucky Jim* illustrates the peculiar dilemmas experienced by young scholars in their efforts to achieve selfhood and find acceptance within the larger academic community. Often characterized as an unabashedly comic novel, *Lucky Jim* offers a moral landscape that confronts the novel's protagonist, Jim Dixon, with a variety of ethical predicaments. Amis utilizes the *métier* of comedy in the novel for delivering his judgments regarding the problematic moral state of academic life during the remarkably fractious era in which his novel first appeared. His satiric attacks on the university community find their targets in those privileged individuals who endeavor to maintain the academic status quo in their favor through the exploitation of junior colleagues, and, ultimately, through the threat of expulsion from the seemingly sacred groves of campus life. As Amis's novel so stridently reveals, the very threat of severance from the scholarly community poses as a powerful obstacle in the young academic's path to self-knowledge.

Lucky Jim finds its textual roots in Amis's 1946 visit to the Senior Common Room at Leicester University, although it also owes its genesis to the confluence of three historic moments in twentieth-century British social and literary history: the passage of the Education Act of 1944, the advent of the redbrick university in England during that same era, and the subsequent apotheosis of *Lucky Jim* as the master text of the Angry Young Man movement in the 1950s. In 1946, Amis visited Philip Larkin at Leicester University, where Larkin, Amis's friend from their scholarship days at Oxford, worked as an assistant librarian. "He took me into the Common Room there," Amis later remarked, "and after about a quarter of an hour I said, 'Christ, someone ought to do something about this lot'" (McDermott 1989, 17). Amis's experiences during the late 1940s as a junior lecturer at University College, Swansea, only served to confirm his initial impressions about the ethical inequalities of academic life. In addition to his personal observations of the university community, Amis found the inspiration for his novel in the social and political turmoil that followed the passage of the Education Act of 1944, an article of legislation that, for the first time since the landmark educational acts of the mid-nineteenth century, attempted to undermine the place of university education as an exclusive privilege of the upper classes. The Education Act required students to pursue their primary education to at least the age of 15, while also creating a two-tiered system of free secondary education that consisted of "Grammar Schools" and "Secondary Modern Schools."

During the decades that followed, the Education Act accomplished its intended goal of producing a greater quantity of college-bound working-class students. Accommodating this influx of postsecondary students likewise necessitated the wholesale expansion of the English university system and resulted in the construction of an assortment of provincial redbrick institutions and "new" universities across Great Britain. Despite the Act's intention of assimilating a larger working-class student population into English university life, Philip Gardner observes that the Education Act of 1944 "gave rise to a significant number of deracinated and disoriented young men, no longer at home in their working- or lower-middle-class attitudes and environments, but at the same time not feeling accepted by the social system into which their education appeared to be pushing them" (1981, 24). This culture of alienation in the 1950s ultimately produced the "angry young man," that peculiar social manifestation of cultural angst and intellectual derision depicted in such works as John Wain's *Hurry on Down* (1953), *Lucky Jim*, and John Osborne's *Look Back in Anger* (1956), among others. The figure of the angry young man as a fictive persona reveals himself as a literary character simultaneously oppressed by the hypocritical value system of the same society whose standards and traditions he so desperately strives to oblige.

In *Lucky Jim*, Amis traces the life and times of Jim Dixon, a fledgling academic who must negotiate his way through a maze of ethical choices. In addition to his satiric characterizations of Dixon's senior colleagues, particularly the unforgettable Professor Welch, Amis addresses the perils of scholarly research and publication, as well as the peculiar, unforgiving nature of university politics. Focalizing the narrative through Dixon's working-class eyes allows Amis to dramatize the uneasy relationships that develop between the privileged upper-class denizens of the university community and their disoriented and insecure junior counterparts. A graduate of Leicester University, Dixon secures a temporary adjunct position at an unnamed provincial redbrick university after besting an Oxford candidate at his job interview. Like the other angry young working-class men who struggle to find acceptance and self-sufficiency in the groves of academe, Dixon hungers for job security amidst a world that both bores and bewilders him. A probationary junior lecturer in medieval history—a subject that he detests, yet that seems to offer him the promise of secure employment that he so covets—Dixon confesses in the novel that his policy "was to read as little as possible of any given book" (16–17). He harbors little regard for academic research and scholarly publication, although he realizes their esteemed places in the competitive campus arena.

As one of the most notorious figures in the genre of campus fiction, Professor Welch serves as Dixon's primary nemesis in *Lucky Jim*, as well as the target of many of the novel's satiric barbs. In Welch, Amis proffers a blistering portrayal of academic pretension and indifference, what Gardner calls "a devastating portrait, incidentally, of a certain type of British academic" (1981, 27). For Dixon, Welch represents everything that he finds troubling about academic life—from snobbery and cultural affectation to vocational ineffectuality and self-indulgence. "No other professor in Great Britain," Dixon muses, "set such store by being called Professor" (Amis 1954, 7). Dixon finds himself equally perplexed by the disparity between Welch's academic standing and his vague qualifications: "How had he become Professor of History, even at a place like this?" Dixon wonders. "By published work? No. By extra good teaching? No in italics" (8). Yet, because Welch possesses the power to decide Dixon's ultimate fate at the university, he remains unable to express his dismay at the inequities of his precarious position as a probationary lecturer. For this reason, he accedes to all of the professor's demands for his service, while secretly imagining the violent acts to which he would subject Welch.

When Dixon prods Welch for reassurance regarding the state of his uncertain position in the department, moreover, the professor refuses to show any compassion for his adopted "protégé" and nervously avoids Dixon's glance while stammering unintelligibly. Despite all of his efforts to curry favor with Welch, Dixon essentially lacks any palpable identity in the professor's eyes, for Welch frequently refers to him as Faulkner, the name of a previous temporary assistant lecturer. Counseled by Welch that an effective public lecture on behalf of the department might save his job at the university, Dixon's discourse on "Merrie England" functions as the novel's hilarious climax, as well as Dixon's supreme, inebriated moment of ethical judgment. Well fortified with alcohol, Dixon delivers a protracted and forceful parody of the academy, scholarship, and his senior colleagues. During his "Merrie England" speech, Dixon effects a series of cartoonish faces along with drunken imitations of the voices of Welch, the university principal, and, finally, a Nazi stormtrooper. In this way, he posits his final, blistering attack upon the untenable foundations of the academic world of his experience. When Dixon effects his own expulsion from university life at the novel's conclusion, his sense of humanity soars when he finds solace and acceptance in a bona fide community of genuine friends and truly conscientious mentors. "It is no accident," Rossen argues, "that many of the best University novels are about someone leaving academe at the end of the book" (1993, 188).

Malcolm Bradbury's *Eating People Is Wrong* (1959) provides a tragicomic look at the interpersonal conundrums inherent in academic life. The novel traces the experiences of the inexorably earnest Professor Stuart Treece, the head of an English department at a provincial, redbrick university located—ironically enough—in the city's former lunatic asylum. Through Treece, Bradbury's novel asks complex questions about the nature of liberalism as a philosophy connoting tolerance, decency, and moral liberty. Bradbury complicates this issue via Treece's relationships with two students, including an older, mentally disturbed man, Louis Bates, and Mr. Eborabelosa, an African student who violates academic—indeed, social— decorum at nearly every turn. The manner in which Treece responds to their difficulties leads to disastrous results, especially when he considers his liberal impulses in comparison with the choices that he must inevitably make when confronted with Bates and Eborabelosa's convoluted interpersonal issues. Treece's love affair with

Emma Fielding, a postgraduate student at the university, also suffers from the dichotomy between his liberal ideals and the vexing ethical realities of contemporary life. As the novel comes to its disheartening close, Treece feels utterly betrayed by his value systems—especially his ethical devotion to the precepts of responsibility and goodness—and ends up in a mental hospital with little hope for the future. In this way, Bradbury postulates a damning critique of the academy's capacity for engendering genuine educational and social change when its most cherished principles evince little practical application.

Scholars of academic fiction often identify novelist and critic David Lodge as the genre's most significant practitioner. Lodge's trilogy of academic novels—*Changing Places: A Tale of Two Campuses* (1975), *Small World: An Academic Romance* (1984), and *Nice Work* (1988)—satirizes academe's convoluted nuances with playful abandon. In *Changing Places*, Lodge traces the intellectual and sexual lives of Philip Swallow and Morris Zapp, the academic characters whose professional and social intersections grace each of the narratives in Lodge's academic trilogy. An introverted and ambitionless lecturer at an English redbrick university, Swallow distinguishes himself among his peers at the University of Rummidge because of his superior skills as an examiner, not because of his reputation as a literary scholar. "He is a mimetic man," Lodge writes, "unconfident, eager to please, infinitely suggestible" (1975, 10). In sharp contrast with Swallow's ineffectual scholarly career, Zapp enjoys considerable scholarly renown for his numerous well-received studies of Jane Austen. A full professor of English at the State University of Euphoria in the United States, Zapp plans to embark upon an ambitious critical project that would treat each of Austen's novels from every conceivable hermeneutic perspective: "historical, biographical, rhetorical, mythical, Freudian, Jungian, existentialist, Marxist, structuralist, Christian-allegorical, ethical, exponential, linguistic, phenomenological, archetypal, you name it" (44). In this way, Zapp plans to exhaust Austen's canon of novels for future critical study. "There would be simply *nothing further to say*," Lodge remarks, "periodicals would fall silent, famous English Departments [would] be left deserted like ghost towns" (44–45). Swallow and Zapp's lives collide in 1969 when they agree to participate in an annual professorial exchange scheme that exists between their respective institutions. During their transatlantic experiences, the two scholars not only exchange their students and colleagues, but their wives and families as well. How they literally swap their entire worlds with one another underscores Lodge's satiric critique of his academic characters and the ease and alacrity with which they exchange the emotional and sexual discourses of their respective lives.

As the narrative of *Small World* (1984) unfolds, we find Zapp and Swallow once again ensconced in the comfortable scholarly and interpersonal inroads of their respective worlds. While their private lives seem to follow a rather predictable course—Swallow returns to married life with Hilary and Désirée delivers on her promise to divorce Zapp—the worldwide reinvigoration of their profession in the late 1970s irrevocably alters their academic experiences through the auspices of international conferences and global scholarly trends. "The day of the single, static campus is over," Zapp triumphantly announces in *Small World*, and with its demise arrives a new generation of globe-trotting scholars equally beset by the professional and interpersonal contradictions inherent in academic life (72). In *Small World*, Lodge traces the international scholarly and romantic exploits of Zapp, Swallow, and a wide range of other intellectuals bent on exerting their professional and erotic wills upon one another. A rousing keynote address delivered by Zapp at a conference hosted by Swallow at the University of Rummidge inaugurates the novel's thematic exploration of erotic love and its narrative possibilities for interpersonal fulfillment. Entitled "Textuality as Striptease," Zapp's lecture discusses the inadequacy of language and scholarship as mechanisms for communication. Because it fundamentally encourages the act of interpretation, language necessarily denies itself the capacity to articulate any singular meaning with precision and exactitude. Scholarship suffers from a similar interpretive malady. As Zapp astutely remarks, "Every decoding is another encoding" (29). As with the text, which contains so many convoluted layers of unattainable meaning, the striptease, Zapp argues, entices the viewer with elements of curiosity and desire while ultimately defying possession. This struggle for erotic authority motivates the quests for love embarked upon by Lodge's academics in *Small World*, and its consummate elusiveness challenges their capacity for finding self-satisfaction in the competitive community of scholars.

In addition to detailing once again the sexual and professional exploits of Swallow and Zapp, Lodge traces in *Small World* the erotic quests of such fictive critical luminaries as Arthur Kingfisher and Fulvia Morgana, as well as the romantic experiences of the naïve lover and scholar, Persse McGarrigle, a fledgling young academic from University College, Limerick. In the novel, Persse's search for the elusive independent scholar, Angelica Pabst, functions as a framing device for the erotic quests of Lodge's other intellectual characters. He crisscrosses the globe, exhausting his savings in a wild international pursuit of the evasive Angelica while sporadically encountering Lodge's other protagonists in such disparate locales as Rummidge, Amsterdam, Geneva, Los Angeles, Tokyo, Honolulu, Jerusalem, and finally, New York, where Lodge's entire coterie of academics reconvenes for the annual meeting of the Modern Language Association. Perhaps even more important, Kingfisher acts as Lodge's most corrosive example of academic dysfunctionality. Secluded in his penthouse suite high above Chicago, Kingfisher lies naked in bed with a scattered selection of critical quarterlies and his delectable Korean research assistant, Song-Mi Lee, by his side. An emeritus professor of Columbia and Zürich Universities, Kingfisher spends his days writing reviews of the latest monographs of hermeneutics while watching pornographic movies on television. "A man who has received more honorary degrees than he can remember, and who has at home, at his house on Long Island, a whole room full of the (largely unread) books and offprints sent to him by disciples and admirers in the world of scholarship," Kingfisher, Lodge writes, can unfortunately no longer "achieve an erection or an original thought" (105). Lodge's unsavory depiction of Kingfisher consuming pornography while simultaneously engaging in the act of literary criticism underscores Lodge's exacting critique of the academy via one of its most cherished mechanisms for professional advancement.

As the final installment in Lodge's academic trilogy, *Nice Work* (1988) examines the uneasy relationship that often exists between the academy and the "real world," between the competitive forces of the intellect and the free-market forces of industry. In addition to questioning the relevance of literary theory to the problems that plague the world beyond the halls of the academy, the novel attempts to provide readers with a sense of reconciliation regarding the tenuous relationship between industry and academe through the medium of an erotic affair between the novel's protagonists, Victor Wilcox, the managing director of an engineering firm, and Robyn Penrose, a temporary lecturer at the University of Rummidge. The dramatic consummation of their relationship seems to offer the possibility of mutual under-standing between these remarkably disparate characters, yet the instability of love and language depicted in the novel's closing pages ultimately undermines their gen-uine attempts at ideological compromise. In the novel, Robyn agrees to participate in the "Shadow Scheme" that eventually draws her into Vic's orbit on the advice of Swallow, still chair of the department at Rummidge, although he is beginning to suc-cumb to incipient deafness. The brainchild of the university's vice-chancellor, the shadow scheme endeavors to enhance the university's understanding of the com-mercial world by requiring a faculty member to "shadow" a senior managerial figure in the local manufacturing industry. Swallow believes that Robyn's participa-tion in the exercise might allow her to keep her Rummidge lectureship beyond her current three-year allotment. A gifted and well-published scholar, Robyn remains unable to secure a position in England's depressed academic job market, despite her extraordinary professional credentials.

Vic, Robyn's industrial counterpart and the marketing director of J. Pringle and Sons Casting and General Engineering, harbors disdain for the value of higher edu-cation and views the university as a "small city-state" characterized by its "air of privileged detachment from the vulgar, bustling city in which it is embedded" (Lodge 1988, 14–15). Robyn possesses a similar distrust for members of the private sector and their commercial activities. Her ideological and social differences with Vic likewise manifest themselves on a number of occasions throughout their associ-ation during the shadow scheme. Robyn reacts in horror, for example, when she vis-its the factory's dark, inner recesses: "It was the most terrible place she had ever been in her life," Lodge writes. "To say that to herself restored the original mean-ing of the word 'terrible': it provoked terror, even a kind of awe" (90). Her revul-sion at the squalid conditions in the factory later results in a spontaneous strike after she warns one of the laborers of his imminent dismissal.

The Shadow Scheme reaches its dramatic climax when Robyn agrees to accom-pany Vic on a business trip to Frankfurt, where her knowledge of German allows Vic to negotiate the purchase of a machine for the factory at an exceptional price. Absorbed with the success of their cooperative effort as business negotiators, Robyn and Vic retire to her suite for a sexual encounter: "The captain of industry at the feet of the feminist literary critic—a pleasing tableau," Robyn muses (207). Back in England, their relationship deteriorates rapidly. "When Wilcox screwed you, it was like the factory ravished the university," Robyn's friend Penny observes (212). Robyn and Vic achieve reconciliation only after he visits the university as her "shadow" and after the factory discharges him from his position as managing direc-tor. Using the proceeds of her inheritance from the estate of a recently deceased rel-ative in Australia, Robyn salvages their relationship when she good-naturedly offers to invest in Vic's plans to design a revolutionary spectrometer. In this manner, Vic and Robyn opt for a working relationship over the semiotic and interpersonal strug-gles of romance. Robyn's own professional fortunes eventually soar after Zapp for-tuitously arrives in Rummidge—about to embark upon his annual European conference tour, of course—and negotiates the American rights of her second mono-graph for Euphoric State's university press. The novel's *deus ex machina* conclusion reaches its fruition when Swallow finally, almost predictably, locates the funding to extend Robyn's contract for another year at the University of Rummidge. In this manner, *Nice Work*'s hopeful dénouement allows Lodge to establish a state of reconciliation between industry and academe.

A.S. Byatt's acclaimed *Possession: A Romance* (1990) adopts the detective form in a labyrinthine campus novel about the complicated nature of love and possession, as well as about the primacy of the text in academic circles. In the novel, Byatt narrates the interconnected stories of two, historically disparate couples—Roland Mitchell and Maud Bailey, a pair of contemporary literary scholars on a quest to authenticate a love affair between two Victorian poets; and the poets themselves, Randolph Henry Ash and Christabel LaMotte. As a postmodern *pastiche*, *Possession* features a panoply of textual voices, ranging from scholarly articles and autobiographical texts to Ash and LaMotte's correspondence and verse. While Christine Brook-Rose draws upon the textual nuances of postmodern *pastiche* in her novel *Textermination* (1991), the result hardly compares to the quality and nuance of Byatt's achievement. With *Possession*, Byatt succeeds in both satirizing academic life and yet managing to venerate its capacity for generating viable textual research—and engendering romance, no less—at the same time. Byatt's most exacting critique of the scholarly world emerges via her treatment of Professor James Blackadder, Roland's avaricious employer and the curator of a vast museum of holdings related to Ash's life and work. Byatt similarly derides the unchecked ambitions of two caustic American characters, rival collectors Mortimer Cropper, the representative of a wealthy New Mexico foundation, and Leonora Stern, an influential feminist scholar who longs for Maud's affections, as well as for the fruits of her latest research about LaMotte's clandestine relationship with Ash. In many ways, the most effective aspect of Byatt's satire involves the manner in which Roland and Maud become so obsessed with their subject that they can hardly begin to consummate the romantic feelings that blossom during their time together. Although *Possession* ends by suggesting that they might eventually enjoy a fulfilling romantic connection, Roland and Maud conclude their quest by only solving the mystery of Ash and LaMotte's affair. The novel's sad irony is that they fail to unravel the equally complex and intriguing mystery about the bond that has come to exist between them. The rigors and demands of scholarship, it seems, have established barriers rather than fomenting the interpersonal bridges that the university champions in workaday life.

While Amis's and Lodge's narratives illustrate the vexing world of British higher education, Jane Smiley's *Moo* (1995) focuses a sharp, satiric eye upon the political machinations and ambitions of the administration and faculty of Moo U., a large midwestern university well known for its agricultural department. Rife with social and scholarly intrigue, Smiley's novel admonishes the bankrupt value systems of a powerful American institution of higher learning obsessed with its agenda for technological and financial superiority. Smiley allots conspicuous attention to all of the competing voices comprised in Moo U.'s political maelstrom—from the contentious professoriate in the horticulture and English departments to the institution's dubious administration, an often bemused and vacant student population, and a giant hog named Earl Butz who resides in an abandoned building in the middle of Moo U.'s campus. In addition to her penetrating critique of university life's economic circle—an endlessly negating system of consuming and being consumed—Smiley addresses the interpersonal motivations exhibited by an array of administrative, professorial, and undergraduate characters. Smiley's self-conscious retelling of consumerism's cautionary tale—of what happens when a beast like Moo U. is permitted to gorge itself at the trough of other, ethically dubious creatures—affords us with one of academic fiction's most compelling narratives.

In addition to the aforementioned paradigmatic campus novels by Amis, Bradbury, Lodge, Byatt, and Smiley, the tragicomic world of academic literature increasingly includes works of detective fiction, nonfiction, poetry, drama, film, and textual experimentation. Academic novels frequently employ the conventions of the murder mystery, as evidenced by such texts as Amanda Cross's *Death in a Tenured Position* (1981), P.D. James's *An Unsuitable Job for a Woman* (1972), D.J.H. Jones's *Murder at the MLA* (1993), and Estelle Monbrun's *Meurtre chez Tante Léonie* (1995). In the nonfictional *Masterpiece Theatre: An Academic Melodrama* (1995), Sandra M. Gilbert and Susan Gubar consider the ethical implications of the "culture wars" of the early 1990s by fashioning a loosely veiled account of the political machinations by a host of international academic and political figures. With *Recalcitrance, Faulkner, and the Professors: A Critical Fiction* (1990), Austin M. Wright offers one of the genre's more innovative works. In his quasi-nonfictional study, Wright satirizes contemporary literary criticism through his reproduction of two imaginary essays on Faulkner's *As I Lay Dying* (1930) by a pair of feuding instructors whose students subsequently meet at "Phil's Pub" in order to critique the quality of their professors' divergent arguments. In addition to poet Galway Kinnell's satirical look at literary studies in "The Deconstruction of Emily Dickinson" (1994), the academy receives attention in such plays as Susan Miller's experimental *Cross Country* (1977) and David Mamet's controversial *Oleanna* (1992). Produced as a film in 1994, *Oleanna* concerns a professor and his student's inability to communicate with each other on any genuinely meaningful level. Their utter incapability of comprehending the nature of their obligations and responsibilities, both to each other and to higher education, predicates Mamet's brutal musings on sexual harassment and political correctness. The academic novel reaches its experimental apex in Alexander Theroux's *Darconville's Cat* (1981), a work that features stylistic forays into such genres as blank-verse drama, the sermon, the diary, the fable, poetry, the essay, and formal oration, among a host of others.

Bibliography

Aisenberg, Nadya, and Mona Harrington. *Women of Academe: Outsiders in the Sacred Grove*. Amherst, MA: University of Massachusetts Press, 1988.

Amis, Kingsley. *Lucky Jim*. New York: Penguin, 1954.

Begley, Adam. "The Decline of the Campus Novel." *Lingua Franca* 7 (1997): 39–46.

Bevan, David, ed. *University Fiction*. Amsterdam: Rodopi, 1990.

Blanchard, W. Scott. *Scholar's Bedlam: Menippean Satire in the Renaissance*. Lewisburg, PA: Bucknell University Press, 1995.

Bradbury, Malcolm. *Eating People Is Wrong*. Chicago, IL: Academy Publishers, 1959.

Byatt, A. S. *Possession: A Romance*. New York: Vintage International, 1990.

Caram, Richard G. "The Secular Priests: A Study of the College Professor as Hero in Selected American Fiction (1955–1977)." Diss. Saint Louis University, 1980.

Carter, Ian. *Ancient Cultures of Conceit: British University Fiction in the Post-War Years*. London: Routledge, 1990.

Gardner, Philip. *Kingsley Amis*. Boston, MA: Twayne, 1981.

Inness, Sherrie A. *Intimate Communities: Representation and Social Transformation in Women's College Fiction, 1895–1910*. Bowling Green, OH: Bowling Green State University Popular Press, 1995.

Johnson, Lisa. "The Life of the Mind: American Academia Reflected through Contemporary Fiction." *Reference Services Review* 23 (1995): 23–44.

Kramer, John E., Jr. *The American College Novel: An Annotated Bibliography.* New York: Garland, 1982.

Leonardi, Susan J. *Dangerous by Degrees: Women at Oxford and the Somerville College Novelists.* New Brunswick: Rutgers University Press, 1989.

Lodge, David. *Changing Places: A Tale of Two Campuses.* New York: Penguin, 1975.

———. *Nice Work.* New York: Penguin, 1988.

———. *Small World: An Academic Romance.* New York: Penguin, 1984.

Lyons, John. *The College Novel in America.* Carbondale, IL: Southern Illinois University Press, 1962.

———. "The College Novel in America, 1962–1974." *Critique* 16 (1974): 121–128.

Marchalonis, Shirley. *College Girls: A Century in Fiction.* New Brunswick: Rutgers University Press, 1995.

McDermott, John. *Kingsley Amis: An English Moralist.* London: Macmillan, 1989.

Proctor, Mortimer R. *The English University Novel.* Berkeley, CA: University of California Press, 1957.

Rossen, Janice. *The University in Modern Fiction: When Power Is Academic.* London: Macmillan, 1993.

Siegel, Ben, ed. *The American Writer and the University.* Newark: University of Delaware Press, 1989.

Womack, Kenneth. *Postwar Academic Fiction: Satire, Ethics, Community.* London: Palgrave, 2001.

Further Reading

Bevan, David, ed. *University Fiction.* Amsterdam: Rodopi, 1990; Carter, Ian. *Ancient Cultures of Conceit: British University Fiction in the Post-War Years.* London: Routledge, 1990; Johnson, Lisa. "The Life of the Mind: American Academia Reflected through Contemporary Fiction." *Reference Services Review* 23 (1995): 23–44; Rossen, Janice. *The University in Modern Fiction: When Power Is Academic.* London: Macmillan, 1993; Showalter, Elaine. *Faculty Towers: The Academic Novel and Its Discontents.* Philadelphia, PA: University of Pennsylvania Press, 2005; Womack, Kenneth. *Postwar Academic Fiction: Satire, Ethics, Community.* London: Palgrave, 2001.

KENNETH WOMACK

ADVENTURE FICTION

Definition. What makes an adventure? An adventure is an experience of a situation in which one cannot predict the outcome. It can sometimes be dangerous and chancy, but it can also be thrilling, exciting and fun. The adventures one seeks can also be life-changing events, learning experiences, and good stories to tell. A good adventure story leaves the reader wondering what will happen next. Adventure subgenres include adventurous science fiction stories, and children's adventures like the Harry Potter series by J.K. Rowling, although these novels, originally meant as children's stories, became favorites with adults as well. The Western genre is full of Wild

Many contemporary novels and stories of action adventure often leave any depth of character or plot structure out of the main text. The focus is on action and adventure that involves physical, often violent activity, which is emphasized more than character development, motivation, and overall theme. Fiona Waters says this of Willard Price's adventure series that is also true of many adventure novels and stories: "Nothing gets in the way of the narration, of the boy's exploits and the constant stream of information—no time is wasted on philosophizing or theorizing, all is action and very successful" (Rubinstein 2007).

West adventures, but very seldom do they involve true accounts by the authors who write about them. Spy, thriller, and mystery adventure fall under the same heading, but all belong to different genres because adventure is only a part of the whole story.

History. Traveling the world meant exploration for expanding empires, conquering civilizations, and acquiring new trade routes for new resources. Herodotus in mid-400 B.C.E traveled to Greece, Italy, and northern Africa to learn about its inhabitants and their religions, the native flora and fauna, and the geography. Herodotus is considered one of the first travel writers, and he often gave lectures about his travels. The Vikings may have been adventure seekers and discovered new lands, but their travels also resulted in destruction, as did the different European empires. Colonies of different countries were established around the world, as adventurers claimed new unexplored land in order to acquire their untapped resources such as gold, spices, rubber, and slaves.

Christopher Columbus is one of the world's most famous explorers. He traveled with Marco Polo's journals, convinced that he could find a route to Asia by going west instead of taking the only known route to the East that sailed south of Africa and around India via the Indian Ocean. He failed to find the route he was looking for, but he did succeed in finding what is today known as Cuba, setting European sights on new land and resources. He also succeeded in inspiring other explorers to seek their own adventures. Although the accounts of his travels are not always accurate or factual, his stories contain the key elements of traveling: excitement, intrigue, wonder and amazement, and most important, adventure.

Taking the grand tour began in the 1600s and gained in popularity through the 1800s and 1900s. Termed as the *le grand tour* by the French, the grand tour was especially popular with young men, and eventually young women, of wealthy families. The voyage was for many a rite of passage, signaling their transformation from school-aged children to young adults. At first, the mode of transportation was the steamships that sailed across the oceans, until the arrival of the steam train in the mid-1800s that enabled passengers to travel over land. The young traveler was accompanied by a tutor or other adult guardian and was taught the history of the countries visited, as well as their cultural aspects, such as fencing, language, dancing, horseback riding, manners, and fashion. These lessons helped shape the travelers in their everyday life, preparing them for the social life that was expected of persons of their class and wealth; often, these experiences gave young men the foundation for leadership positions in the military.

Writings of these voyages came by letter to family and friends at home.

The destination of these journeys was often the colonies of the empires of which they were citizens. Subjects of the colonizing empires were guaranteed entry without special passports or visas. The presence of English travelers was extremely common in India from the early 1600s until the World War II in 1945. One example of the grand tour novel is *A Passage to India,* published in 1924, by author E.M. Forster. The novel captures the sense of adventure of a British woman traveling to India to meet her fiancé who works for the British raj, a form of British government in India. In 1908, Forster also published *A Room with a View* about a young woman traveling through Italy, and in 1905, his other Italian novel, *Where Angels Fear to Tread*, was published. Forster, a traveler in his own right and a British subject, used his experiences of traveling to both India and Italy to provide the background scenes and ideas for many of his novels. Another example is Louis-Ferdinand Céline's novel *Journey to the End of the Night,* published in 1934.

It is the story of a young French man who travels to the different French colonies of Africa and, ultimately, to America. The characters reflect their society; they were able persons with financial means traveling and experiencing the adventure of other countries and cultures. Both novels, *Journey to the End of Night* and *A Passage to India*, explore the racial tensions between colonizer and colonized, bringing depth to the characters and providing political commentary while creating excitement for the reader.

Other adventure novels that emerged in the beginning of the century told a story of travel, but they dealt with the characters' development as a reflection of mankind. Mark Twain is another novelist who used his personal travels as the basis for his narratives. His classic novels, *The Adventures of Tom Sawyer* (1876) and *Adventures of Huckleberry Finn* (1884), and his nonfiction book *Old Times on the Mississippi* (1876), are taken from Twain's experience on the steamboats of the Mississippi River.

Trends and Themes. Outdoors adventures are real stories about real people creating their adventures by traveling the world and beyond. Some examples of outdoor adventures are Heinrich Harrer's *Seven Years in Tibet* (1953), Norman MacLean's *Young Men and Fire* (1992), Jonathan Raban's *Old Glory* (1981), travel writer Bill Bryson's *A Walk in the Woods* (1998), Alexandra David-Neel's *My Journey to Lhasa* (1927), Ian Frazier's *Great Plains* (1989), Thor Heyerdahl's *Kon-Tiki* (1950), Joe Kane's *Running the Amazon* (1989), Bernard Moitessier's *The Long Way* (1971), Eric Newby's *A Short Walk in the Hindu Kush* (1958), journalist Jon Krakauer's *Into Thin Air* (1997) and *Into the Wild* (1996), journalist Tim Cahill's *Jaguars Ripped My Flesh* (1987), Piers Paul Read's *Alive* (1974), Sebastian Junger's *The Perfect Storm* (1997), Antoine de Saint-Exupéry's *Wind, Sand, and Stars* (1939), Peter Matthiessen's *The Snow Leopard* (1978), novelist Graham Greene's *Journey Without Maps* (1936), James Tobin's *To Conquer the Air* (2003), Nathaniel Philbrink's *Sea of Glory* (2003), Apollo 11 astronaut Michael Collins's autobiography *Carrying the Fire* (1974), naturalist John Muir's *My First Summer in the Sierra* (1911), F.A. Worsley's *Endurance* (1931), Ernest Shackleton's autobiography *South* (1919), and mountaineer Reinhold Messner's *The Crystal Horizon* (1982). Maurice Herzog's *Annapurna* (1952) inspired many mountain climbers such as Reinhold Messner and Ed Veisters who chronicled his own adventures of climbing all 14 of the world's highest peaks in his 2006 autobiography *No Shortcuts to the Top*. Apsley Cherry-Gerrard's *The Worst Journey in the World* (1922) is considered to be the National Geographic's number one adventure book, followed by Meriwether Lewis and William Clark's *Journals* (1814). Women also played the role of adventurers, detailed in such accounts as Osa Johnson's *I Married Adventure* (1940); Arlene Blum's *Annapurna: A Woman's Place* (1980), an autobiography of the ascent of Annapurna, by a team of women, two of whom died; Isabella L. Bird's *A Lady's Life in the Rocky Mountains* (1879); and Mary Kingsley's *Travels in West Africa* (1897).

Alive and *The Perfect Storm* were both made into blockbuster movies in 1993 and 2000, respectively, as was Harrer's *Seven Years in Tibet* in 1997 starring Brad Pitt. Isak Dinesen's novel *Out of Africa* (1937) was also made into a movie starring Robert Redford and Meryl Streep in 1985. The movie won seven Academy Awards, including Best Picture in 1986. *Endurance,* based on Ernest Shackleton's journey to Antarctica, was developed in 2002 as an A&E Channel miniseries entitled *Shackleton* starring British actor Kenneth Branagh. Mountaineer Joe Simpson's *Touching the Void* (1988) was made into a documentary film in 2003.

Context and Issues. In nonfiction adventure, the author as the main character usually comments on ideas and experiences that contribute to their personal identity, as well as developing skills of travel and survival through the adventure. Often authors, or their critics, describe their writings as outlets for their personal and spiritual development, as can be seen Peter Matthiessen's *The Snow Leopard* (1978).

Many nonfictional accounts of adventure begin as a quest, as the author develops a route of travel that has a purpose, either of exploration, self-discovery, sport, or a combination of all three. Jon Krakauer utilized all three of these aspects when he was first propositioned for a journey to Mt. Everest in 1996. A mountaineer and a journalist, Krakauer has written several articles and books about his experiences at a high altitude. His experience on Everest in the spring of 1996 also became a soul-searching endeavor, as he witnessed one of the worst death tolls on the mountain. Eventually adventure becomes a commodity—adventure for a price. Armchair travelers have, at their advantage, movies and television that takes them to places they have never been, doing things they may never do. Average people do not need to go anywhere to experience the beauty of a different country, but they do miss out on the true culture, the true nature of people. Essentially, they miss out on the experience, the thrill and the excitement. "Without the possibility of death," said mountaineer and author Reinhold Messner, "adventure is not possible" (Alexander 2006, 44).

Messner is first a mountaineer, and second a writer. He penned the story of his adventures in *The Crystal Horizon* (1982), which is filled with danger, excitement, life, death, and rebirth. He embodies the real-life hero of adventure, knowing the risks involved with climbing mountains, sometimes alone and without bottled oxygen. But when Mount Everest, the tallest mountain in the world, has been conquered, explorers look to what is beyond the planet and explore the stars as Apollo 11 Command Module Pilot Michael Collins details in his autobiography *Carrying the Fire* (1974). In a 1923 interview with *The New York Times*, mountaineer George Mallory made famous, , the phrase "because it's there" (Knowles 2001), meaning that the mountain was there to climb, the moon was there to explore, and adventure is all around for us to experience.

Reception. Action novels are becoming increasingly popular, and many movies have been made because of the theatrical success of the original action adventure films, such as *Star Wars* (1977–2005), the *Indiana Jones* trilogy (1981–1989), the *Mummy* trilogy (1999–2005), *The Lord of the Rings* trilogy (2001–2003), *The Pirates of the Caribbean* trilogy (2003–2007), and The *Harry Potter* films (which began in 2002). Other adventure movies include *The Treasure of the Sierra Madre* (1948), *The Crimson Pirate* (1952), *The African Queen* (1951), *Romancing the Stone* (1984), *The Goonies* (1985), *National Treasure* (2004), multiple remakes of *King Solomon's Mines* (1937, 1950, and 1985), *The Lord of the Flies* (1963 and 1990) based on the novel by William Golding, and *Sahara* (2005) based on the novel by Clive Cussler.

Many successful action and adventure films are based on best-selling thriller novels. Both *The Lord of the Rings* and the *Harry Potter* movies were originally based on best sellers. The second book in C.S. Lewis's *The Chronicles of Narnia* series, *The Lion, the Witch, and the Wardrobe* (1950), was developed into a highly successful film in 2005. The popularity of the film version of adventure books has been overwhelming. The films are easily accessible, and the visual effects are often elaborately planned and well executed. Examples of movies based on such novels include John Grisham's *The Pelican Brief* (1992), *The Client* (1994), *The Firm*

(1991), and *The Rainmaker* (1995); Robert Ludlum's *The Bourne Identity* (1980), *The Bourne Supremacy* (1986) and *The Bourne Ultimatum* (1990); and Michael Crichton's *Jurassic Park* (1990) and *The Andromeda Strain* (1969). Each movie contains a popular actor or actress to enhance the film's marketability, along with special effects and continuous action throughout the film. Other novels that were turned into popular films include Edgar Rice Burroughs's *Tarzan of the Apes* (1921), which spawned numerous movies and television shows; Forster's novels *A Room with a View* (1908) and *A Passage to India* (1924); and Ian Fleming's famous character James Bond, also known as 007, originally created in 1952 and turned into such movies as *Dr. No* (1962), *Goldfinger* (1964), and *Live and Let Die* (1973). After Fleming's death, other authors have kept the Bond name alive with new adventures in novels and such blockbuster movies as *The World Is Not Enough* (1999) and *Die Another Day* (2002). *Casino Royale*, based on Fleming's 1953 novel, was released in 2006.

Authors and Their Adventures. Adventure travel writers differ from adventure fiction writers in that the travel writers write about their own adventures, whereas fiction adventure writers write about an adventure that happened to fictional characters that has been embellished to create a sense of heightened excitement and intense anticipation. Adventure travel writers, however, have written harrowing adventures that are based in reality; and, for the reader, knowing that the story is true creates a different kind of excitement. The reader usually experiences anxiety and concern for the characters, who are often the authors themselves, and because they know that the story is true, they often experience empathy for the author, the people involved in the story, and the land and the culture as well. Not every adventure turns out fine, as it does in adventure fiction. Examples are Robert Ludlum's *The Bourne Identity* (1980) and Michael Crichton's *Jurassic Park* (1990).

Selected Authors

Mark Twain (1835–1910). Mark Twain was one of the first American authors to be considered a travel writer, basing most of his work throughout his life on the journeys he had taken in the United States and Europe. Born Samuel Langhorne Clemens, Mark Twain began his writing career writing articles for local newspapers and magazines about his traveling experiences. As a young man in 1851, he worked as a typesetter at the *Hannibal Journal,* owned by his brother Orion Clemens, in his hometown of Hannibal, Missouri. There he was given the opportunity to contribute articles to the paper. Twain also worked as a printer in various cities including Cincinnati, St. Louis, New York, and Philadelphia, but it was the steamboats of the Mississippi River that he loved. Twain studied the maps of the Mississippi River's 2,000-plus miles over the course of several years, earning his steamboat piloting license in 1959, and he continued to work on the ships until 1861 when the Civil War began, which immediately halted the travel and the trade of the steamboats along the river.

In 1863, he and his brother Orion traveled for two weeks across the Great Plains and the Rocky Mountains, finally settling in Virginia City, Nevada. These travels would become the basis for his nonfiction book *Roughing It* (1872) and his short story *The Celebrated Jumping Frog of Calaveras County,* published in the *New York Saturday Press* on November 18, 1865, and finally as a novel in 1867. Twain was also given the opportunity to travel to the Sandwich Islands (Hawaii) to write about his experience for the *Sacramento Union* newspaper based in California. In the summer of 1867, Twain took a trip on the cruise ship *Quaker City*. His compilation of travel letters, published as *Innocents Abroad* in 1869, was written during this time as he traveled though Europe, the Mediterranean, and the Middle East. *A Tramp Abroad,* published in 1880, is based on a second trip to Europe. In 1875, Twain published a series of essays titled *Old Times on the Mississippi* in the *Atlantic Monthly,* which he eventually turned into a nonfiction book titled *Life on the Mississippi* in 1883.

The Adventures of Tom Sawyer, published in 1876, was one of Twain's first works of fiction. It was closely based on Twain's own life as a boy in Hannibal, Missouri. Another novel to follow took Tom Sawyer's friend, Huckleberry Finn, on his own adventures with a runaway slave named Jim. The story was set during the 1850s when slavery was still legal. *Adventures of Huckleberry Finn,* published in 1884, became more successful than *Tom Sawyer.* The book was well received with the public, cheering Huck's sense of rightness and his refusal to conform to the prejudices of society just because they were the popular belief. Although the book was banned in many schools in the latter half of the 1900s because of language considered by today's standards as vulgar, *Adventures of Huckleberry Finn* proved that adventure novels can have depth; instead of just exploring the landscape. The character, too, can grow to reflect society.

Willard Price: The Adventure Series (1887–1983). Willard DeMille Price wrote many stories based on his travels around the world, including his work editing for the journals *Survey* and *World Outlook.* From 1920 to 1967, Price traveled for the National Geographic Society and for the American Museum of Natural History. In 1949, he wrote a series of children's adventure novels.

> My aim in writing the 'Adventure' series for young people was to lead them to read by making reading exciting and full of adventure. At the same time I want to inspire an interest in wild animals and their behavior. Judging from the letters I have received from boys and girls around the world, I believe I have helped open to them the worlds of books and natural history. (Rubinstein 2005)

Price wrote 14 Adventure Series books from 1949 until 1980: *Amazon Adventure* (1949), *South Sea Adventure* (1952), *Underwater Adventure* (1954), *Volcano Adventure* (1956), *Whale Adventure* (1960), *African Adventure* (1963), *Elephant Adventure* (1964), *Safari Adventure* (1966), *Lion Adventure* (1967), *Gorilla Adventure* (1969), *Diving Adventure* (1970), *Cannibal Adventure* (1972), *Tiger Adventure* (1979), and *Arctic Adventure* (1980).

Fellow children's author Fiona Waters said of Price's novels: "The exploits may be fiction, but the facts and settings could only have come from real life; Price's tales are based on his own tumultuous and action-packed life" (Rubinstein 2005).

His passion was for traveling and learning about different cultures and geography. His travel books *Rivers I Have Known* (1965), *Key to Japan* (1946), *Adventures in Paradise, Tahiti and Beyond* (1955), and *The Amazing Amazon* (1952), all contain photos, maps, and sketches made by Price during his travels.

Price also wrote nonfiction stories based on his own life adventures, such as *Ancient Peoples at New Tasks* (1918, for the Missionary Education Movement), *Japan Rides the Tiger* (1952), *Japan's Island of Mystery* (1944), *The Japanese Miracle and Peril* (1971), and *My Own Life of Adventure: Travels in 148 Lands*

(1982). Price also wrote articles for *Harper's Magazine* from 1935 to 1942, exploring territorial expansion of the islands of the Pacific as well as military policy and the political situations of Japan, Korea, and China.

Enid Blyton 1897–1968. In contrast to Price, Enid Blyton wrote several children's books for the British Publications Adventure Series. Blyton also wrote many tales of adventure for television and movie production. Her adventure series consists of the novels *The Island of Adventure* (1944), *The Castle of Adventure* (1946), *The Valley of Adventure* (1947), *The Sea of Adventure* (1948), *The Mountain Adventure* (1945), *The Ship of Adventure* (1950), *The Circus of Adventure* (1952), and *The River of Adventure* (1955). Two of these novels were made into movies for British television: *The Island of Adventure* in 1982 and *The Castle of Adventure* in 1990 (IMDb.com 2007).

Blyton also wrote many other novels for children, about 300 titles in all, but later in life, she was accused of having a limited vocabulary, even for younger readers and it was said that her stories were rife with sexism, racism, and English snobbishness (Stoney 2006). Unlike Price who had really had adventures, Blyton had stayed for most of her life in England, writing stories from her imagination rather than from real travel experience.

National Geographic Society (1888–). Started in 1888 by 33 explorers and scientists, the National Geographic Society began as a way to learn more about the geography of the world. The first president of the society was Gardiner Greene Hubbard. Upon his death in 1897, Hubbard's son-in-law, Alexander Graham Bell, became his successor. In turn, Bell's son-in-law, Gilbert Hovey Grosvenor, became the first editor of the *National Geographic* magazine in 1889. Grosvenor incorporated photographs and stories of travel and adventure to add to the intrigue of geography, and published studies of the people and cultures of different countries. The magazine also features maps, is published quarterly, and has been translated into 31 different languages. From 1919 until 1975, the National Geographic Society distributed a monthly newsletter for schools. The school newsletter's title was changed to *National Geographic World* in 1975 and again in 2001 to *National Geographic Kids.* Other publications include *National Geographic Traveler,* created in 1984, and *National Geographic Adventure* in 1999. The society also publishes many atlases, maps, travel guidebooks, and other larger photography books about specific travel destinations.

In 1964, the society began a television program in conjunction with CBS. The program moved to ABC in 1973, and in 1975 made its final move to PBS. In 1997, National Geographic launched its own cable channel, appropriately titled the National Geographic Channel. The channel gives viewers 24-hour access to the programs that originated in the 1970s and continues to make groundbreaking discoveries on Earth and in space exploration. The society also produces feature-length films and documentaries such as the adventure film *K-19: The Widowmaker* (2002) and *March of the Penguins* (2005), which won an Academy Award in 2006.

The National Geographic Society also awards grants for research. Among the more famous recipients of these grants are Lewis Leakey and his wife Mary, who in the latter half of the twentieth century spearheaded primate research in Africa and Indonesia. His researchers included Jane Goodall who studied chimpanzees in northern Africa, Dian Fossey who studied mountain gorillas in Rwanda and Uganda, and Biruté Galdikas who studied the orangutan in Indonesia. Leakey, along with his wife Mary and son Richard, made a name for his family and for the society as a physical anthropologist, uncovering many of the historical archeological digs in British East Africa, Nairobi, and Kenya and at the now-famous Olduvai gorge, where Mary Leakey made her most important discovery of an early hominid skull that she named Zinganthropus, which was dated at from 1 to 1.75 million years old.

Leakey helped create the growing interest in the National Geographic Society, filming many television specials that ran in the 1970s in prime time. In addition to the famous Leakey projects, the National Geographic Society also funded expeditions Ian Baker's exploration of the legendary "hidden waterfalls" of the Tsangpo Gorge in Tibet in 1998 and 1999, Robert Bartlett's arctic exploration from 1925 to 1945, Hiram Bingham's 1911 excavation of Machu Picchu in Peru, and Jacques-Yves Cousteau's many underwater explorations and television specials.

Tim Cahill (1943–), Road Fever *(1991) and* Lost in My Own Back Yard *(2004)*. Tim Cahill is considered one of the foremost adventure writers by Outside magazine, the National Geographic Society, and fellow travel writer Bill Bryson, who said, "Partly the reason Tim Cahill is adventurous is because he's an adventurous kind of guy. He's more inclined than the rest of us to do adventurous and brave things, partly because he knows he can write it very skillfully, but also because he's drawn to those types of things. He's in his element in those situations" (Shapiro 2004, 135). Cahill became a journalist for the San Francisco Examiner and Rolling Stone magazine in the early 1970s. In 1976, he started Outside magazine with friends Michael Rogers and Harriet Fier. Today it is one of the leading outdoors adventure magazines.

Cahill has been around the world collecting sources for his stories, often including more than one continent in a book. For example, in *Road Fever: A High Speed Travelogue* (1991), Cahill and friend Garry Sowerby drive 15,000 miles, starting at the southernmost tip of Tierra del Fuego, the main island south of Chile in South America, and ending at Prudhoe Bay in Alaska, a trip made in only 23½ days. "Adventure is physical or emotional discomfort recollected in tranquility. An adventure is never an adventure when it's happening. An adventure is only an adventure when you've had time to sit back and think about it" (Shapiro 2004, 10). This adventure includes humor juxtaposed alongside their everyday troubles, which include the weather conditions, revolution, and stale food.

Cahill's other books include *Jaguars Ripped My Flesh: Adventure Is a Risky Business* (1987), *A Wolverine is Eating My Leg* (1989), and *Pass the Butterworms: Remote Journeys Oddly Rendered* (1997). In 2004, Cahill was given the opportunity to explore one of his favorite spots, Yellowstone National Park. *Lost in My Own Back Yard: A Walk in Yellowstone National Park,* published in 2004, was written with permission from his editors, even though an abundance of travel books about that area had been written in previous years. Cahill claims that he must have had "the capacity to see it with fresh eyes" (Shapiro 2004, 12).

Peter Matthiessen (1927–), The Snow Leopard *(1978) and* In the Spirit of Crazy Horse *(1983)*. Peter Matthiessen is a naturalist and author of historical nonfiction as well as fiction. He was one of the founding fathers of a literary journal called *The Paris Review* in 1953; some claim the journal was just a cover for his involvement in the CIA. Besides writing for *The Paris Review,* Matthiessen also wrote for *The New Yorker* magazine and for the *Atlantic Monthly*. His novel *At Play in the Fields of the Lord* (1965) was nominated for a National Book Award and in 1991 was made into a film of the same name.

His first two novels *Race Rock* (1954) and *Partisans* (1955) were published to little acclaim, and it wasn't until his nonfiction environmental piece *Wildlife in America* (1959) that Matthiessen discovered what his real passion.

> My earliest nonfiction book, *Wildlife in America,* was about wildlife and the environment, and I've always been concerned with it. A parallel concern was traditional people who are also threatened, their languages and their culture, and they too show up in *Wildlife in America*. One cannot really separate those concerns, the environment and biodiversity and social justice. They're all tied in very closely together. (Shapiro 2004, 347)

Matthiessen's 1983 nonfiction story, *In the Spirit of Crazy Horse*, shows his passion for the environment, native culture, and social justice. The main story is about Leonard Peltier, a member of the 1970s American Indian Movement (AIM), who was allegedly involved in the deaths of two FBI agents during a standoff between several members of AIM and the FBI near Wounded Knee, South Dakota, in 1975. Of the four members of AIM that were indicted, Peltier was the only one to be convicted and is currently serving several consecutive life sentences. Matthiessen delves into the controversy surrounding the case as well as the overall treatment of Native Americans on the Pine Ridge reservation in South Dakota, the poorest reservation in the United States.

Adventure novels were once written without much character development, but as the authors of such novels started to do more exploring and research for their works, the criteria for the characters of the books also changed. One such example lies within the text of Matthiessen's nonfiction book *The Snow Leopard* (1978), which won the contemporary thought category of the National Book Award in 1979. In 1995, freelance writer Amanda Jones was stranded in Calcutta, India, when she was given a copy of Matthiessen's book as a gift from her Sherpa. She was drawn to the book because it mirrored much of her own travel at the time, but she was also drawn to the personal journey Matthiessen experienced that helped form the thesis of his book.

> A year prior to the trip, the writer's wife had died of cancer. *The Snow Leopard* is an excruciatingly beautiful and honest account of what turned into a tough spiritual and physical journey. With the energy that great travel writers have coursing through their veins, Matthiessen walked me, pace by pace, over those mountain passes, through the precepts of Buddhism and the valleys of his soul. (Jones 2007)

Inspired by his travels, Matthiessen devoted his life to the study of Zen Buddhism. For him, travel is a spiritual journey, and the evidence is found throughout *The Snow Leopard*. Matthiessen began this journey at the invitation of naturalist and zoologist George Schaller to join him in his study of the Himalayan blue sheep in the Dolpo region of the Nepalese Himalayas. This expedition would give Matthiessen, who was studying Buddhism at the time, a prime opportunity to visit with ancient Tibetan Buddhist monks living in a remote and isolated area of Nepal, and to "possibly glimpse the most elusive of all great cats, the ice-eyed snow leopard" (Jones 2007). Matthiessen did not see a snow leopard, but he did meet with his Buddhist mentors and continued his practice, becoming a Buddhist teacher in the late 1990s.

Jon Krakauer (1954–), Into the Wild *(1996),* Into Thin Air *(1997).* Jon Krakauer received a degree in environmental studies at Hampshire College in Massachusetts. He began his writing career with articles in magazines such as the *American Alpine*

Journal and later *Outside* and *Playboy*. He began mountain climbing in 1974, which helped give him an edge in outdoor adventure journalism. His familiarity with the Brooks Range in Alaska, and later the Stikine Icecap region of Alaska, would help him develop articles leading to the publication of *Eiger Dreams* (1990), a compilation of articles detailing his success and failures with mountain climbing. He was also able to identify with the subject of his book *Into the Wild* (1996), a story about Christopher McCandless, who, after graduating from Emory University, gave away all of his money and possessions, changed his name, and set out to live alone in the Alaskan wilderness. Krakauer could understand McCandless's need for isolation because he has searched for isolation in the mountains. Several months after McCandless's disappearance, his body was discovered near an abandoned bus. His only possessions were a .22 caliber rifle, a camera, and literature by authors Leo Tolstoy, Henry David Thoreau, and Jack London.

Krakauer's best-known work is the 1997 book *Into Thin Air*, a nonfiction work about his experience climbing Mount Everest in May 1996 and the tragedy that occurred. He found that, with travel to high places more reachable, the top of the world became more quickly accessible. The summit of Mount Everest was once an exclusive club for only the most experienced and adventurous climbers, but now it could be bought for the right price:

> The slopes of Everest did not lack for dreamers in the spring of 1996; the credentials of many who'd come to climb the mountain were as thin as mine, or thinner. When it came time for each of us to assess our own abilities and weigh them against the formidable challenges of the world's highest mountain, it sometimes seemed as though half the population at Base Camp was clinically delusional. But perhaps this shouldn't come as a surprise. Everest has always been a magnet for kooks, publicity seekers, hopeless romantics, and others with a shaky hold on reality. (88)

Krakauer describes the ascent and descent of two of the climbing parties that ventured to the summit on May 10, 1996, led by Rob Hall and Scott Fischer. Krakauer was sent to the mountain on assignment for *Outside* magazine in March of the same year, slated to be on New Zealander Rob Hall's team. Around 1 P.M. on May 10, a storm approached the mountain, but as Krakauer noted, teams were still heading up the mountain to the summit rather than heading back down to shelter. "Why did veteran Himalayan guides keep moving upward, ushering a gaggle of relatively inexperienced amateurs—each of whom had paid as much as $65,000 to be taken safely up Everest—into an apparent death trap?" (6). Six people would lose their lives that day because of the storm. On record as one of the worst climbing tragedies in Everest history, the season itself went on record with 15 deaths, making it the deadliest year ever for climbers.

Bill Bryson (1951–), A Walk in the Woods *(1998)*. Prior to becoming a travel writer, Bryson wrote columns for a British newspaper, often resubmitting the same travel story to several papers in both England and the United States, but his adventures were what people were to read about. Michael Shapiro claims that "Reading one of (Bryson's) books feels like visiting with an old friend who spins the most amazing tales; you laugh, you learn, you long for more" (Shapiro 2004, 130).

Bryson didn't originally set out to be a travel writer, but when he started to write with a humorous twist about the places he had been, he found that he had a talent for writing about these experiences and adventures. In an interview with Michael

Shapiro, Bryson said: "I had no desire to become a travel writer, in fact it never occurred to me to think of myself as that" (Shapiro 2004, 134). His first book, *The Palace Under the Alps and Over 200 Other Unusual, Unspoiled, and Infrequently Visited Spots in 16 European Countries* (1985), was written about one of his many trips to Europe. *Neither Here nor There: Travels in Europe* (1991) also documented his early travels in Europe.

After returning to the United States, with his wife whom he met in England on one of his first journeys through Europe, Bryson wrote *The Lost Continent: Travels in Small-Town America* (1989). In 1989, Bryson returned to the United States after living in England for many years, settling in New Hampshire. Of this experience Bryson wrote *I'm a Stranger Here Myself: Notes on Returning to America After Twenty Years Away* (1998) and *A Walk in the Woods: Rediscovering America on the Appalachian Trail* (1998). In *I'm a Stranger Here Myself,* he describes how, even though he was born in the United States, he still felt out of place returning to this country after being away for so long. "It's weird in the United States because it's all changed—three years later it's not recognizable . . . It's so hard in the States to find anything the way it used to be. In Europe it's exactly the opposite—you can go back and nothing has changed. It's the same café and still the same old waiter" (Shapiro 2004, 139–140).

His most popular travel book is *A Walk in the Woods,* which spent many weeks on *The New York Times* best-seller list in 1998 and again in 1999 when the paperback edition was released. When he told his family and friends that he had decided to walk the greater part of the Appalachian Trail from New Hampshire to Georgia, not everyone was enthusiastic about his new adventure:

> Nearly everyone I talked to had some gruesome story involving a guileless acquaintance who had gone off hiking the trail with high hopes and new boots and come stumbling back two days later with a bobcat attached to his head or dripping blood from an armless sleeve and whispering in a hoarse voice, 'Bear!' before sinking into a troubled unconsciousness. (5)

The story relates the adventures of Bryson and his friend Stephen Katz, who had made an appearance in Bryson's earlier book *Neither Here nor There.* Katz, as he is called, provides much of the entertainment for the trip as Bryson describes hiking across miles of trails, though rain, sleeping out in tents, and finding salvation in a gas station convenience store. Bryson also describes the scenery in detail, expressing his concern about the trees that are disappearing due to climate change and the garbage people leave along the trail. He also explores how Americans can become more environmentally conscious about their national parks and nature in general.

Paul Theroux (1941–), The Great Railway Bazaar (1975). Adventure novelist Paul Theroux traveled the world for inspiration and stories for his many novels and travel essays. As a contributor to *The Smithsonian* magazine, *The New Yorker,* and *Time Asia,* Theroux gained experience writing about his travels for scholarly journals, giving him the freedom to be honest about his discoveries, even if he found things to be unpleasant. In an interview with Theroux, author Michael Shapiro asked him what his worst experience traveling was, to which Theroux replied: "There are no 'worst' in the negative sense. There are only experiences which are the very stuff of my books" (Shapiro 2004, 158). His travel experience fed his passion for writing, and as a result he authored many fictional and nonfictional books about traveling and adventure. "Even if I were not a writer I would be a traveler" (Shapiro 2004, 154). In reference to the travel narrative of *The Great Railway Bazaar* (1975), Shapiro claimed, "(Theroux) eschewed florid prose in favor of unvarnished observations, peppered with abundant dialog" (Shapiro 2004, 150). Theroux loved overland travel as can be seen in his two other railroad-themed novels, *The Old Patagonian Express* (1979) and *Riding the Iron Rooster* (1988), but *The Great Railway Bazaar* would become his best known work, detailing Theroux's trip by train through Great Britain, western and eastern Europe, the Middle East, south and southeast Asia and Japan, and Russia. "The only worthwhile trip is what you call a challenging trip" (Shapiro 2004, 154). Theroux's other nonfiction books include *Sunrise with Sea-monsters* (1985), *The Happy Isles of Oceania* (1992), and *The Pillars of Hercules* (1995). His fiction novels include *Waldo* (1967), *Sinning with Annie* (1972), *The London Embassy* (1982), *My Other Life* (1996), and *Blinding Light* (2006).

Theroux was also a part of the Peace Corps in Malawi, Africa, from 1963 to 1965, and he later moved to Uganda to teach at Makerere University, basing his novel *Dark Star Safari* (2002) on his experiences there. Theroux comments: "Travel is a form of autobiography. This book is not about Africa—this is a book about my trip through Africa—this book is, I suppose, about me" (Shapiro 2004, 151). Theroux gives rich descriptions of the people and places that he experiences, giving them almost larger-than-life characteristics in his books, which also made them perfect for film adaptation. Theroux's 1973 novel *Saint Jack* was made into a movie by director Peter Bogdanovich in 1979; the novel *Doctor Slaughter* (1984) was adapted to become the film *Half Moon Street,* released in 1986; and *The Mosquito Coast* (1981) was made into a film in 1986, starring Harrison Ford, Helen Mirren, and River Phoenix.

Bibliography

Adams, P.G. *Travelers and Travel Liars 1600–1800.* New York: Dover, 1962.

Adler, J. "Origins of Sightseeing." *Annals of Tourism Research* 16 (1989): 7–29.

Alexander, Caroline. "Murdering the Impossible." *National Geographic Magazine* 5 (November 2006): 42–67

Ashworth, G.J., and Tunbridge, J.E. *The Tourist—Historic City.* London: Belhaven Press, 1990.

Bassett, Jan, ed. *Great Southern Landings: An Anthology of Antipodean Travel.* Melbourne: Oxford University Press, 1995.

Broc, Numa. *La géographie des philosophes: Géographes et voyageurs français au XVIIIe siècle.* Thèse: Université de Montpellier, 1972.

Bryson, Bill. *A Walk in the Woods: Rediscovering America on the Appalachian Trail.* New York: Broadway Books, 1998.

Burgess, Anthony, and Haskell, Francis, *Le Grand Siècle du Voyage (1967).* Paris: Albin Michel, 1968.

Céline, Louis-Ferdinand. *Journey to the End of the Night.* New York: New Directions, 1934.

Colins, Michael. *Carrying the Fire.* New York: Ballantine, 1974.

Coupland, Douglas. *Generation X: Tales for an Accelerated Culture.* New York: St. Martin's, 1991.

Debord, Guy. *The Society of the Spectacle.* Trans. Donald Nicholson-Smith. New York: Zone, 1995.

Devitt, Amy J. *Writing Genres.* Carbondale, IL: Southern Illinois University Press, 2004.

Forster, E.M. *A Passage to India*. London: Arnold, 1924.

Fussell, Paul, ed. *The Norton Book of Travel*. New York: W.W. Norton & Co., 1987.

Hanbury-Tenison, Robin. *The Oxford Book of Exploration*. Oxford University Press, 1993.

Ghose, Indira. *Memsahibs Abroad: Writings by Women Travelers in Nineteenth Century India*. New Delhi: Oxford University Press, 1998.

Helterman, Jeffrey, and Lyman, Richard. *Dictionary of Literary Biography*. Detroit, MI: Gale, 1978.

Hibbert, Christopher. *The Grand Tour*. London: Thames Methuen, 1987.

IMDb. "Enid Blyton." March 16, 2007. http://www.imdb.com/name/nm0090067/.

Jones, Amanda. "Wander Lust, Peter Matthiessen." *Salon.com*. 8 July 1997. http://www.salon.com/july97/wanderlust/matthiessen970708.html.

Knowles, Elizabeth. "World of Words: A Quote from George Leigh Mallory." Ask Oxford.com. 2007. http://www.askoxford.com/worldofwords/quotations/quotefrom/mallory/?view=uk.

Krakauer, Jon. *Into Thin Air*. New York: Random House, 1997.

Leed, Eric J. *The Mind of the Traveler: From Gilgamesh to Global Tourism*. New York: Basic Books, 1991.

MacCannell, Dean. *The Tourist: A New Theory of the Leisure Class*. Berkeley: University of California Press, 1999.

Matthiessen, Peter. *In The Spirit of Crazy Horse*. New York: Penguin, 1983.

———. *The Snow Leopard*. New York: Penguin Nature Classics, 1987.

Messner, Reinhold. *The Crystal Horizon*. Seattle, WA: Mountaineers, 1982.

Pettinger, Alasdair. *Always Elsewhere: Travels of the Black Atlantic*. London: Cassell, 1999.

Poole, Robert M. *Explorers House: National Geographic and the World It Made*. New York: Penguin, 2004.

Price, Willard. *Adventures in Paradise, Tahiti and Beyond*. New York: John Day Co., 1955.

———. *The Amazing Amazon*. New York: John Day Co., 1952.

———. *Key to Japan*. New York: John Day Co., 1946.

———. *Odd Way Around the World*. New York: John Day Co., 1969.

———. *Rivers I Have Known*. New York: John Day Co., 1965.

Robinson, Keith. "Enid Blyton." *Enid Blyton.net*. 2004. http://www.enidblyton.net/index.html.

Rojek, Chris, ed. *Touring Cultures: Transformations of Travel and Theory*. New York: Routledge, 1997.

Rubinstein, Matt. "Adventure Adventure." June 11 2005. http://mattrubinstein.com.au/?p=78.

Shapiro, Michael. *A Sense of Place*. Berkeley: Publishers Group West, 2004.

Smith, Valene L. *Hosts and Guests: The Anthropology of Tourism*. University of Pennsylvania Press, 1989.

Stoney, Barbara. *Enid Blyton: The Biography*. London: NPI Media Group, 2006.

Twain, Mark. *Adventures of Huckleberry Finn*. New York: Webster, 1884.

———. *The Adventures of Tom Sawyer*. New York: American, 1876.

———. *Innocents Abroad*. New York: Atlantic Monthly, 1869.

———. *Life on the Mississippi*. Boston, MA: Osgood, 1883.

———. *Old Times on the Mississippi*. Toronto: Belford, 1876.

———. *Roughing It*. New York: Harper, 1872.

———. *A Tramp Abroad*. London: Chatto & Windus, 1880.

Further Reading

Adams, P.G. *Travelers and Travel Liars 1600–1800*. New York: Dover, 1962; Fussell, Paul, ed. *The Norton Book of Travel*. New York: W.W. Norton & Co., 1987; Hanbury-Tenison, Robin. *The Oxford Book of Exploration*. Oxford University Press, 1993; Ghose, Indira. *Memsahibs Abroad: Writings by Women Travelers in Nineteenth Century India*. New Delhi: Oxford University Press, 1998; Hibbert, Christopher, *The Grand Tour*, London: Thames Methuen, 1987;

Leed, Eric J. *The Mind of the Traveler: From Gilgamesh to Global Tourism.* New York: Basic Books, 1991; MacCannell, Dean. *The Tourist: A New Theory of the Leisure Class.* University of California Press, 1999; Pettinger, Alasdair. *Always Elsewhere: Travels of the Black Atlantic.* London: Cassell, 1999; Smith, Valene L. *Hosts and Guests: The Anthropology of Tourism.* University of Pennsylvania Press, 1989.

ANNE BAHRINGER

AFRICAN AMERICAN LITERATURE

Definition. African American literature is the verbal organization of experiences into oral forms, such as spirituals, work songs, blues, and sermons; and into written forms, such as autobiography, poetry, fiction, drama, essay, and letter (Henderson 1973, 4). Produced by writers of African descent, the oral and written genres are closely tied to African Americans' ways of life, their needs, their aspirations, and their history—in short, their culture (Henderson 1973, 4). Since the mid-twentieth century, African American literature has gained an ever-increasing celebratory and scholarly status in the United States. As editors and critics contend, it is rare to find a library that does not collect or a bookstore that does not market literary works by African Americans. Even in the academy, African American writers, particularly those who have earned the prestigious honors of the National and American Book Awards, the Nobel Prize in Literature, and the Pulitzer Prize are increasingly included in newly reconstituted curricula in American literature, American studies, women studies, and ethnic studies. What must not be lost in this literary paean for African American arts and letters is that African American writing *as* literature has been a long time coming in the United States (Andrews, Foster, Harris 1997), and today's writers stand on the shoulders of writers from ages beyond, whose roles have been complexly accommodating, apologetic, and experimental.

History

Accommodation and Protest. During the Slave and Reconstruction eras in the United States, African American writers produced accommodating works that said what seemed acceptable to their largely white audiences (Davis and Redding 1971, 5). The most notable accommodating writers of the eighteenth century include Lucy Terry, Jupiter Hammon, Phyllis Wheatley, and George Moses Horton. In 1746, with the ballad "Bar's Fight," Lucy Terry published the first literary work in African American arts and letters. As an exemplary genre, "Bar's Fight" (1997), however, does not emulate a structural form from African American culture. Instead of relying on multiple meters, improvisation, or call and response that are found in African American spirituals or work songs, Terry's work preserves the standard rhymed tetrameter couplet:

> The Indians did in ambush lay,
> Some very valiant men to slay, (Stanza 1, lines 3–4)

The content of Terry's ballad also reflects the accommodating trend in African American arts and letters in the eighteenth century. Set in 1745, in the regional meadows of Deerfield, Massachusetts, the African American writer's work focuses on an Indian ambush of two notable white, New England families.

Some 20 years after Terry's "Bar's Fight," writer Jupiter Hammon emerges as yet another accommodating artist of the eighteenth century. Throughout his lifetime, with support largely from Quaker abolitionists, Hammon publishes a number of essays, including "A Winter Piece: Being a Serious Exhortation, With a Call to the Unconverted"; "A Short Contemplation on the Death of Jesus"; "An Evening's Improvement, Showing the Necessity of Beholding the Lamb of God"; and "An Address to the Negroes of the State of New York." Appearing first in anti-slavery periodicals also are Hammon's essays that understandably promote an anti-slavery sentiment: "An Evening Thought: Salvation by Christ, with Penetential (sic) Cries" and "Salvation Comes by Christ Alone." Critics cannot agree on what makes the works of Jupiter Hammon African American. Enthusiasts such as Sandra O'Neale argue that when using choice words such as "my brethren," "Africans by nation," and/or "Ethiopians," Hammon is coding his writings with protest of African American life in the 1800s (Hammon, 72–73). Earlier critics such as Arthur P. Davis and Sterling Brown, however, are adamant in their critiques of Hammon's protest writings. Both contend Hammon's protest comes in the form of subtle irony that is overshadowed by his use of "common-metre hymn doggerel" (Davis and Redding, 5):

Lord turn our dark benighted Souls;
Give us a true Motion,
And let the Hearts of all the World,
Make Christ their Salvation. (Stanza 1, lines 45–48)

The sermonic language of Hammon's "An Evening Thought" and "Salvation Comes by Christ Alone" suggests the role of the writer in his works is that of folk preacher. Expectantly, he is to help move African American life toward a sense of spiritual wholeness (Hubbard 1994, 383). But, after close scrutiny, Hammon's performance seems reminiscent of evangelical preachers of the Great Awakening in early history in the United States. Undeniably, Hammon counsels fellow slaves to expect "salvation," "freedom," and "equality" after death.

Phyllis Wheatley publishes her first poem "On Messrs. Hussey and Coffin" in 1767. Six years later, she publishes *Poems on Various Subjects, Religious and Moral,* the first collection of writings by an African American. Unlike her African American literary peers of the eighteenth century, Wheatley's style is sophisticated in meter and elegant in control. Like her literary peers, however, as a writer, Wheatley is accommodating to her audience. She models her work after neoclassical writer Alexander Pope who insisted on displaying respect for structure and rules by way of his structural use of the heroic couplet; his admiration for reason and judgment via his classical allusions; and his striving for desirable human qualities that are intimated in his achievement of neatness and precision (Cuddon 1991, 578). Like the neoclassical writer in general, in her poetry, Wheatley models being intensely moralistic and religious, and she maintains lyrical restraint that is regarded as one of the highest of virtues (Davis 1971, 4).

A number of critics who have looked beyond Wheatley's accommodating poetics recognize in her poems a subversive tone of protest via her duality of meaning. For instance, the masking of protest in "To Maecenas" is reminiscent of multiplicity of meaning often demonstrated in the spirituals and work songs. In African American oral genres such as the spirituals and work songs, creators drew attention to their circumstances via repeated personal situations. Wheatley saturates her poem with personable situations while simultaneously she draws attention to her questioning of her situations as "partial grace." She asks why she is unable to succeed as a serious poet, or why the African American race is unable to succeed as a group? In "On Imagination," Wheatley offers her work to literary scrutiny. The poet allows her imagination to wonder in order to question the inhumanity of slavery in the eighteenth century. Ironically, attention is drawn to Wheatley's protest when her lines invoke Samuel Johnson's warning to classical writers to avoid "letting the imagination run away with one" (Cuddon 1991, 578).

George Moses Horton is perhaps the most versatile of the accommodating writers of the eighteenth century. Like his literary peers, Horton's poetry is predetermined: It is formulaic (Davis 1971, 4). But, unlike his peers, Horton's poetry is influenced by varied personal experiences other than slavery. For instance, for a time at The University of North Carolina at Chapel Hill, Horton was a servant to several college students. The students often commissioned him to write lyrical verses of love. For a time, Horton also traveled in North Carolina with the Union Army. For his patron, William H. S. Banks, Horton commemorated in writing a number of northern and southern leaders.

Because of Horton's associations with abolitionists, it was easier for him to get into print many of his anti-slavery poems such as "Liberty and Slavery," "The Slave's Complaint," and "On Hearing of the Intention of a Gentlemen to Purchase the Poet's Freedom." Like his literary peer Hammon, Horton's freedom comes in his unbridled opportunity to write and to publish poetry. Horton's style, however, is far superior as demonstrated in "The Slave's Complaint" (1998):

> Must I dwell in Slavery's night,
> And all pleasure take its flight,
> Far beyond my feeble sight,
> Forever? (Stanza 2, lines 5–8)
> Or, in "On Liberty and Slavery":
> Say unto foul oppression, Cease:
> Ye tyrants rage no more,
> And let the joyful trump of peace,
> Now bid the vassal soar. (Stanza 5, lines 17–20)

Writing in the introduction to *The Norton Anthology of African American Literature* (1997), editors Henry Louis Gates, Jr. and Nellie Y. McKay summarize best the legacy left by the eighteenth century writers: Their "mastery of language, the essential sign of a civilized mind to the European, implicitly qualified [the] black writer, and by analogy those whom he or she represented, for self-mastery . . . " (128).

Critic Sterling Brown, writing in *The American Negro* (1969) has called poet Paul Laurence Dunbar and fiction writer Charles Waddell Chesnutt pioneering writers of the nineteenth century (78–79). In their respective genres, Dunbar and Chesnutt lead the way in *adapting* aspects of African American life to purposes of an African American literary tradition (Brown 1969, 78–79). Both writers consciously introduce a range of "matter and mood" of African American culture, particularly at a time in American history when African American life had become largely disenfranchised and stereotyped. Following the Civil War, known also as Reconstruction, African Americans made significant political, economic, and social gains, particularly in the South. These gains, however, were short-lived and forcefully reversed. In what would be called the Plantation Tradition of the nineteenth century, largely white southern writers such as Joel Chandler Harris, Thomas Nelson Page, Thomas Dixon, and Irwin Russell, sought to recover forms of power and racial order that had been dismantled by the war. Created by these writers were idealized African Americans who wished to return to the southern days when whites provided, among other things, housing, work, clothing, and food in exchange for servitude. Created by the writers of the plantation school are stereotypical sketches of African Americans who were content with their status or happy-go-lucky slaves. Writers of the plantation school also created sketches of African Americans who objected to returning to an idealized world of servitude: the wretched freedman, the brute, or the tragic mulatto. The dialect of all of these characters in plantation literature solidified a perception of the African American as incapable of reasoning and of self-governance (Brown 1969, 78–79). Adapted by mainstream America during Reconstruction are these ideological constructs of plantation literature.

The challenge for the nineteenth century writers Paul Laurence Dunbar and Charles Chestnutt was how to portray the humanity of African Americans and to express an African American literary tradition of perseverance and survival, especially when the largely white patrons preferred the characterization of African American as contented slave, tragic mulatto, and brute, to name a few. In Dunbar's poem "Worn Out," he insists on conveying to his largely white patrons that the African American had become weary of his disempowered status in the United States. Unlike several of Dunbar's African American literary predecessors from the eighteenth century whose protest was very subtle, Dunbar is direct and detailed. He uses sophisticated meters in his lyrical expressions to convey his protest on behalf of disenfranchised African Americans in the 1900s:

> You bid me hold my peace
> And dry my fruitless tears,
> Forgetting that I bear
> A pain beyond my years. (Stanza 1, lines 1–4)

Dunbar also exceeds his predecessors Hammon and Horton in style and language when in poems such as "Ere Sleep Comes Down to Soothe the Weary Eyes," "Sympathy," and "Negro Love Song," he skillfully emulates the unnamed creators of the spirituals and uses repetition "to personalize" the African American experience.

Intimated in several of Dunbar's poems, particularly "Ode to Ethiopia," are also vertical movements of the African American folk sermon. Performing like an African American folk preacher, Dunbar regenerates the spirits of a downtrodden and conveys their sense of endurance and survival through his lyrics (Hubbard 1994, 383). In general, the folk sermon moves from complication, rising action, denouement, and cathartic release. Dunbar begins the "Ode" with complication: "I know the pangs which thou didst feel,/When slavery crushed thee with its heel/With they dear blood all gory" (Stanza 1; lines 4, 5, 6). His poem then rises in action: "The forests flee before their stroke,/Their hammers ring, their forges smoke . . . " (Stanza 3, lines 16–17). As the poem moves toward its end, Dunbar tells his subjects, the slaves of Africa, that, "Thou has the right to noble pride./Those spotless robes were purified/By blood's severe baptism." (Stanza 6, lines 33–35). Unlike Hammon in "An Evening Thought" or "On Salvation," who tells his audience that happiness or freedom for the slave comes after death, in "Ode to Ethiopia," Dunbar allows his audience to release pent-up emotions and to achieve a spiritual connection to an ontological life force here on earth:

> Go on and up! Our souls and eyes
> Shall follow the continuous rise;
> Our ears shall list thy story

From bards who from the root shall spring,
And proudly tune their lyres to sing
Of Ethiopia's glory. (Stanza 8, lines 44–48)

Dunbar's experimentations with African American oral structures such as spirituals and sermon, of free verse, and of conventional dialect convey a versatile style. But, in the nineteenth century, the art of capturing African American life via, for instance, dialect and music, proved to be liabilities for the writer and for African American literature. Regrettably, Dunbar's realism of African American life is overshadowed by his audiences' desire to be entertained by the familiar sketches of the plantation tradition. In his own reflections of this turn of events in his career in "The Poet," Dunbar laments that while "he sang of life/ serenely sweet,/ With, now and then, a deeper note," (Stanza 1, lines1–2) his audience preferred "A jingle in a broken tongue" (Stanza 2, lines 8).

Conventional dialect poetry of the nineteenth century is popularized by the writers of the plantation school and by Dunbar in poems such as "Negro Love Song," "When Malindy Sings, or "Little Brown Baby." Criticism of dialect in African American literature in the 1900s is found in James Weldon Johnson's Preface to *The Book of American Negro Poetry* (1921), the first anthology of African American literature complied by an African American. In this work, Johnson (1969) calls for poets who follow Dunbar to refrain from the use of conventionalized dialect. His regrets are as follows:

> [It] is based upon the minstrel traditions [or fictionalized plantation traditions] of Negro life that had but slight relation—often no relation at all—to actual Negro life, or is permeated with artificial sentiment. It is now realized both by the poets and by their public that as an instrument for poetry the dialect has only two main stops: humor and pathos. (4)

Southern writers of the plantation school reinforced their sketches of the contented slave, the primitive, or the wretched freeman via tales narrated by African Americans who speak in conventionalized dialect. Unlike African or African American lore that draw from African American experiences and is intended to instruct, to protect, to entertain, or, as Zora Neale Hurston writes, "to laugh to keep from crying" (Hemenway 1977, 157), stories by Thomas Page, Joel Chandler Harris, or Irwin Russell help to retain "the good Negro" and to reserve other vital markers of a nurturing slave culture.

In his 1899 collection *The Conjure Woman*, Charles Chesnutt sets out to revise the African American stereotypes of plantation lore. The writer introduces a trickster figure from African lore whose role is to outmaneuver foes of the African American community with guile, wit, and charm (Smith 1997, 736–737). There is a duality in the language of the trickster figure. Within his story there is always an inner plot that provides subversive opportunities to redress a power imbalance or neglect to basic human needs (Smith 1997, 736–737). In the *Conjure* stories, Chesnutt's trickster figure is Uncle Julius McAdoo. The McAdoo character is intended to counterbalance the likes of the stereotypical Uncle Remus from Joel Chandler Harris' *Uncle Remus: His Songs and His Sayings* or the likes of Sam from Thomas Nelson Page's "Mar's Chan." The fact that Uncle Julius is a descendent of Africa's Yoruba's trickster, who would demonstrate an art of multiplicity in language and performance, gets lost in Chesnutt's familiar expressions of dialect, superstitions, and free-wheeling lifestyle of his freedmen. The above are core elements of plantation literature. Also, because Chesnutt's Uncle Julius shares the inner plot of his stories with his white patron John, critics claim Uncle Julius and Chesnutt too often limit the abilities of author and character to affirm African American life.

Widely anthologized is Chesnutt's short story "The Goophered Grapevine" that first appeared in *The Conjure Woman*. The structural presence of Uncle Julius in the short story is to intimate his power and control over his white patrons John and Annie, and over his own fate, but in this story and others, audiences of the nineteenth century fail to recognize Uncle Julius' cultural distinction. The strength of the trickster figure is overshadowed by the degrading weaknesses of familiar sketches of African Americans from plantation literature and by audiences' expectations of the sketches. Like Dunbar, Chesnutt attempts to adapt African American life to an African American cultural tradition and purpose in his literature, but his efforts are compromised. The largely white audiences of the nineteenth century expect a continuation of sentimental African American life and characters, institutionalized by the school of plantation literature (Johnson, 1969, 9). The legacy left by Dunbar and Chesnutt is the actual attempt by writers to return to the folk culture for poetic symbols.

Trends and Themes

Modernism and Postmodernism. Writing in *Modernism and The Harlem Renaissance* (1987), Critic Houston Baker calls attention to the seminal moments of "Afro-American modernism" presented in the works of Harlem Renaissance writers Jean Toomer, Langston Hughes, and Sterling Brown. He reminds critics and readers that because the southern African American life had been distorted in nineteenth century plantation literature by Thomas Dixon and his school, writers such as Toomer, Hughes, and Brown transformed sentimental characters in order to reveal the realistic, modern conditions of "black sufferers of marginalization and dispossession" (Baker 1987, 95)—that is, alienation, fragmentation, a lack of social identity, and a lack of historical continuity. In particular, Toomer's *Cane*, which "embodies the tensions of modern science and folk tradition, of psychoanalytic technique and Afro-American music, [and] of mysticism and Afro-American spirituality" (Bell 1987, 96), focuses on the psychology of the characters Ralph Kabnis, Bona, and even Karintha who attempt throughout their journeys "to reconcile [themselves] . . . to the blood and soil that symbolize [their] ethnic and national identities" (Bell 1987, 99). In Langston Hughes' autobiography *Big Sea*, particularly in the early pages, the writer focuses on dealing with his search for literary and racial identities against the backdrops of three continents. In *Southern Road*, Sterling Brown gives voice to the displaced traveling blues man and blues woman of rural America who redefine their fragmented identities by overcoming limiting circumstances.

In the 1940s, 1950s, and 1960s major writers, such as Richard Wright in *Native Son*, Ann Petry in *The Street*, Ralph Ellison in *Invisible Man,* and Melvin Tolson in *Harlem Gallery,* communicate in their works concerns "[about] the plight of the individual in the modern world" (Hogue 2003, 30). As W. Lawrence Hogue, writing in *Race, Modernity, and Postmodernity* points out, *pervading* the fiction and non-fiction of these writers, in particular, are existentialism, secularism, rationalism, and individualism (Hogue, 30). Although these writers experiment with cultural forms in their works—circularity, improvisation, call and response—they consciously move beyond the values of wholeness, transcendence, and historical continuity (Hogue 31) that were evident in a number of the general works of Hughes and Hurston. Instead, Bigger Thomas in *Native Son* and Lutie Johnson in Ann Petry's *The Street* succumb to their environments or, as in Ellison's *Invisible Man,* the individual succumbs to invisibility.

The shift from modernity to postmodernity in African American literature is marked by works such as James Baldwin's *Another Country,* Toni Morrison's *Sula* and *Song of Solomon,* David Bradley's *The Chaneyville,* Ishmael Reed's *Mumbo Jumbo,* Clarence Major's *All-Night Visitors,* John Edgar Wideman's *A Glance Away,* Doris Jean Austin's *After the Fall,* and Andrea Lee's *Sarah Phillips.* Not only is there *the* "blurring of the boundary between history and fiction and the cross of the line from modern to postmodern aesthetics, but these writers, Morrison in particular, are concerned also with the atypical aspects of postmodern aesthetics. They are concerned with the 'collective' that existed before African Americans were integrated into the American modernization process" (Hogue). These writers, Morrison in particular, are concerned with reintroducing African Americans, and readers in general, to an African American collective and historical past—a past where rejuvenation of the spirit toward wholeness and other racial traditions become solutions to alienation and fragmentation. Central to the individual or to the community is a sense of spiritual survival. In the twenty-first century, there are a number of contemporaries who stand on the shoulders of postmodern writers like Morrison, Lee, Wideman, Reed and others. Like their predecessors, these writers revisit the cultural values and norms of the racial past that existed before African Americans were integrated into the American modernization process. Among others, included in this group are Edward P. Jones and his Pulitzer Prize winning fiction *The Known World* and his collection of short stories *Lost in the City* and *All Aunt Hager's Children;* James McBride and his *Song Yet Sung;* and Albert French and his *Billy.*

Context and Issues

Apology and Propaganda. In 1921, in the Preface to *The Book of American Negro Poetry* (1969), the first anthology of African American literature compiled by an African American editor, James Weldon Johnson instructs African American writers on what to retain from the legacies of nineteenth century writers Paul Laurence Dunbar and Charles Chesnutt: "form[s] that [would] express the racial spirit [of African Americans] . . . from within" (41–42). Johnson also instructs writers on what to abandon from the period writers: conventionalized dialect and any symbols "from without" that had become reminiscent of the degrading stereotypes found in the Plantation literature of the century (41–42). African American writers of the early twentieth century comply, but they also initiate a challenge to the national mental attitude regarding the African American by creating what Sterling Brown called apologetic or propagandistic literature that suggest genteel African Americans are not so vastly different from any other American, just distinctive (Brown 1969, 105). Examples of apologetic literature include W.E.B. Du Bois's *The Quest of the Silver Fleece,* Jesse Fauset's *There Is Confusion* and *Plum Bun,* and even James Weldon Johnson's *The Autobiography of an Ex-Colored Man.* In general, these writers revise earlier stereotypes, focusing on the psychology of individual characters, their choices in life, and the ideology of gender and class. For instance, in *The Quest of the Silver Fleece* (1969), an allegorical novel, Du Bois portrays characters that are consumed by their economic survival—that is, cotton or the fleece.

Eventually, Du Bois's characters such as Elspeth and Zora learn that "without intelligence and training and some capital it is the wildest nonsense to think you can lead your people out of slavery" (137). In *There is Confusion* (Fauset, 1989) rewrites the tragic mulatto character. Her characters Joanna Marshall and Peter Bye in *Confusion* overcome color prejudice and achieve success by committing themselves to education, hard work, respectability, and each other (Bell 1987, 107). Thematically, *Confusion* explores middle-class attitudes, and it stresses the significance of family and origin. In *The Autobiography of an Ex-Colored Man* (1960), Johnson also rewrites the tragic mulatto. He confronts his narrator's double consciousness or sense of two-ness (American and African American) as he attends college, travels abroad, and even passes for white. In the end, the narrator permanently adopts a white American identity. His explanation is that he deservedly should have "every possible opportunity to make a white man's success" (147).

While the nineteenth century southern white writers of the plantation school use literature to effect change in national politics, African American writers of the early twentieth century use literature to challenge the national mental attitude regarding African American life and characters. Aesthetically, the role of the writer as apologist and the function of literature as propagandistic equate to what Sterling Brown, writing in *The American Negro,* calls "race-glorification"(1969, 103). As Brown concludes in the same work, "it was natural that [African American] novelists [of the early twentieth century] . . . should write as apologists. His objection is, however, that writers such as Du Bois, Johnson, Fauset, and others kept the charge *instead* of a story to be told (105).

Reception

Contemporary African American Literature and Pop Culture. In 1990, Terry McMillan published the best-selling *Breaking Ice: An Anthology of [African American] Contemporary Fiction.* According to McMillan, the writers of her collection are a "new breed," standing on the shoulders of past African American writers: "We are a new breed, free to write as we please, in part because of our predecessors . . . " (1990, xxi). As Trey Ellis reminds us in "The New Black Aesthetics," important also to remember is that unlike their predecessors, the present generation of "new black artists [are no longer] shocked by racism as were those of the Harlem Renaissance, nor are [they] preoccupied with it as were those of the Black Arts Movement. For [this group of contemporary writers] racism is a hard and little-changing constant that neither surprises nor enrages" (1989, 234). With all said, the publications of the "new breed" of African American writers are "personal response[s]. What [writers] want to specify. What [writers] see. What [writers] feel" (McMillan 1990, xxi). In essence, contemporary writers are individuals "trying to make sense of ourselves to ourselves" (McMillan, xxi). With such criteria for the writer, the role of the writer and the function of African American literature become exhaustive.

In the preface to *Breaking Ice,* John Wideman reminds the contemporary writer of James Weldon Johnson's charge of 1921. He reminds the writer of the following within African American arts and letters:

A long-tested view of history is incorporated in the art of African-American people, and our history can be derived from careful study of forms and influences that enter our cultural performances and rituals. In spite of and because of marginal status, a powerful, indigenous vernacular tradition has survived, not unbroken, but unbowed, a magnet, a focused energy, something with its own logic, rules, and integrity connecting current developments to the past. An articulate, syncretizing force our best artists have drawn upon, a force sustaining both individual talent and tradition.

If what a writer wants is freedom of expression, then somehow that larger goal must be addressed implicitly/explicitly in our fictions. A story should somehow contain clues that align it with tradition and critique tradition, establish the new space it requires, demands, appropriates, hint at how it may bring forth other things like itself, where these others have, will, and are coming from. This does not mean defining criteria for admitting stories into some ideologically sound, privileged category, but seeking conditions, mining territory that maximizes the possibility of free, original expression. (1990, vi–vii)

For the contemporary writer, free and original expressions have translated into an exhaustive list of memoirs, short and long fiction, and independent films that are, to pull from Susanne B. Dietzel's "The African American Novel and Popular Culture," relatively unexplored terrain[s] in African American literary history and criticism (2003, 100). Reasons for this exclusion or oversight range from academic practices and aesthetic standards that qualify a text for inclusion in the African American literary canon—practices and standards that are traceable over the centuries to ancestral African American writers who strived to keep in place a division between literary and commercial forms of literature that rendered expressions of African American life and culture.

Selected Authors

Experimentations with Form. Regarded as an architect of the Harlem Renaissance, James Weldon Johnson reprints in his collection *The Book of American Negro Poetry* (1969) a number of writers who published in the nineteenth and early twentieth centuries. In the preface to this collection, Johnson instructs writers to experiment with form in their works and to express a "racial flavor" of African American life "from within" (41–42). After all, Johnson firmly believes the following: "The status of the [African American] in the United States is more a question of national mental attitude toward the race than of actual condition. And nothing will do more to change that mental attitude and raise his status than a demonstration of intellectual parity by the [African American] through the production of literature and art (41–42). With such directives, Johnson refocuses discussions of African American arts and letters, particularly the role of the African American writer and the function of African American literature. In the 1920s, Alain Locke, writing in the introduction to *The New Negro,* and Langston Hughes, writing in his 1926 essay, "Negro Artist and the Racial Mountain," embrace the idea of experimenting with form, but they go a step further. Unlike the apologists who preferred to portray the most genteel of African Americans, Locke and Hughes want writers to return to the masses and to create "an art of the people." They urge writers to use inherent expressions of African American life for "themes and treatment of [structure]" (qtd. in Ervin 1999, 50). These themes include identity, dreams, journey, freedom, endurance, and survival. The inherent structures were to be found in the culture's spirituals, blues, jazz, and so forth. (qtd. Ervin 1999, 131).

Major writers of the 1920s, who returned to the African American masses for their themes and to African American musical traditions, such as the spirituals and blues for their structural forms, include, among others, Jean Toomer, Langston Hughes, Zora Neale Hurston, Claude McKay, and Sterling Brown. In a number of their poems, there also is evidence of experimentation with traditional verse lines such as heroic couplet and with stanzaic forms such as free verse, the sonnet, and the ballad. As instructed by Johnson, these writers also are successful in deepening their understandings of the intricate rhythms and repetitions of the spirituals and blues as forms that give a racial voice to the urban and rural working class in their works. By way of his instructions and others, the writer gives rise to "an art of the people." Although it is clear that these writers did not *fully* understand the inherent structural techniques that are traceable to West African provinces—for example, multiplicity of meaning (Yoruba); syncopation (Mande); call and response (Ejagham); improvisation (Yoruba); circularity (Dohomean); and mysticism (Kongo)—(Thompson), their work offers ample evidence in terms of experimentation with form.

In his poem "Song of the Son," from *Cane* (published in 1923), Toomer reveals his attempt to add "racial flavor" to his writing "from within." In the last two sentences of each of the first three stanzas of the poem, Toomer employs repetition and syncopation, as found in the spirituals, to personalize the connection of the African American soul to the southern landscape. For example, in the first stanza of "Song of the Son," he writes:

> Pour O pour that parting soul in song,
> O pour it in the saw dust glow of night,
> Into the velvet pine-smoke air to-night
> And let the valley carry it along
> And let the valley carry it along (Stanza 1, lines 1–5)

The intended structure of the first three verses is the standard iambic pentameter—that is, five iambs of an unaccented syllable followed by an accented syllable. The last two lines of the poem, which have fewer words, resemble lines in a spiritual where the author must employ the West African form of syncopation. The last two lines require the writer/reader to lengthen out a few syllables in order to fill one metrical foot. Toomer also explores the West African form of improvisation. *Cane* consists of the "integration of song and movement" via poems and fiction, always returning to recurring themes.

In "The Weary Blues" (1997) Hughes returns to the classic blues *aab* structure to add "racial flavor" from within to the poem. Providing the name of his collection *The Weary Blues,* the poem begins as follows:

> Droning a drowsy syncopated tune, (*a*)
> Rocking back and forth to a mellow croon, (*a*)
> I heard a Negro play.(*b*) (Stanza 1, lines 1–3)

Like the genre that allows spiritual escape for some readers and, for others, a dramatization of cultural vitality and rebelliousness, Hughes' blues musician endures and escapes the routine: "He slept like a rock or a man that's dead."

Sterling Brown experiments with African American oral forms such as the blues and the work song. From the rural community, he adapted local African American heroes to the proportion of national heroes—for example, John Henry, Stackolee, and Casey Jones.

Like Langston Hughes, he also attempts to use language and humor as vehicles for determining the diversity as well as the complexity of African American life. In the poem "Long Gone," the reader meets "a railroad man,/ With a itch fo' travelin'" (Stanza 2, lines 2–3) and in the poem "Slim Greer," the reader meets the "Talkinges' guy/An' biggest liar" (Stanza 2, lines 1–2) who moved around and left "only echoes/ Of his tune." These men, like others, exert control in an often hostile world through their music and mobility.

More so than other writers of the early twentieth century, Claude McKay experiments with the standard stanzaic sonnet, particularly the Shakespearean sonnet. A verse form that consists of 14 lines and is usually written in iambic pentameter, the Shakespearean sonnet has three quatrains, each of which explores a theme, and a concluding couplet that offers resolution. By literary standards and focus, the sonnet represents high or elegant art. McKay uses such a form to obtain the attention of his readers and, then, he renders his criticism of the plight of the African American race (e.g., "The White House," "Enslaved," and "If We Must Die").

In the 1940s and 1950s, writers/critics such as Richard Wright, writing in "Blueprint for Negro Writing"; James Baldwin, writing in his essay "Many Thousand Gone"; and Ralph Ellison, in his interview "The Art of Fiction," return to James Weldon Johnson's charge to express a "racial spirit" by way of symbols of the larger things" (Wright 1994, 1) and a "sensibility [of an African American tradition]" (Baldwin, 36). Speaking in 1955 in "The Art of Fiction," which is collected in Ralph Ellison's *Shadow and Act* (1964), Ellison looks back to the complex roles of earlier writers and ahead to the role of the modern writer when he elucidates Johnson's charge:

> Too many books by Negro writers are addressed to a white audience. By doing this the authors run the risk of limiting themselves to the audience's presumptions of what a Negro is or should be; the tendency is to become involved in polemics; to plead the Negro's humanity. You know, many white people [and by now some middle class black people] question that humanity but I don't think that Negroes can afford to indulge in such a false issue. For us the question should be, what are the specific *forms* of that humanity, and what in our background is worth preserving or abandoning. (171–172)

Like James Weldon Johnson, Alain Locke, Langston Hughes, and others, Ellison is calling for what bell hooks later called "an aesthetic of blackness" (hooks 1990, 113) in African American literature. For Ellison, the genre manifests itself already in the oral structures of black music and in black speech. In his major work *Invisible Man*, there is evidence of experimentation with structures adapted from the oral forms: multiplicity of meaning, circularity (the end is the beginning and the beginning is the end), and improvisation. The language and actions of the narrator in *Invisible Man* are used to help him achieve self definition as he moves from being gullible to "recognizing my invisibility."

James Weldon Johnson's instructions to writers to capture the "racial flavor" of African American life in African American literature is realized as late as the 1960s via the writers of the Black Arts Movement and later in the 1970s and 1980s via women writers such as Gloria Naylor, Alice Walker, and Toni Morrison. In the 1960s, co-editors LeRoi Jones (Amiri Baraka) and Larry Neal of *Black Fire: An Anthology of Afro-American Writing* (1988) detail how the poet of the Black Arts Movement is to capture the "racial flavor" of African American life: "[T]he poet must become a performer the way James Brown is a performer—loud, gaudy, and racy. . . . He must learn to embellish the context in which the work is executed; and where possible, link the work to all usable aspects of the music—that is, largely jazz" (655). For Baraka and Neal, the context of the work is as important as the work itself. According to Neal, poets must learn to sing, dance, and chant their work, tearing into the substance of their individual and collective experiences (655). To demonstrate the expectations of African American writers of the 1960s (i.e., as performer, a presenter of "various selves" in unconventional ways, and capturer of usable improvisation of the African American musical tradition, namely jazz), there was, among others, Baraka's poem "Dope." In it, ignoring all conventions for writing poetry, Baraka teaches writers how to chant and sing the lines.

Following the Blacks Arts Movement, writers moved beyond debating a politically narrow and limiting role of the writer and functions of the literature. In the late 1970s, there is a shift in discussions of African American literary aesthetics. As Houston Baker points out in his essay "Generational Shifts and the Recent Criticism of Afro-American Literature" (1981),

> [A] new and resplendent nation of Afro-Americans invested with Black Power . . . gave way in the late seventies to a new . . . group of intellectuals . . . [willing] . . . to separate the language of criticism from the vocabulary of political ideology. . . . Their proclaimed mission was to "reconstruct" the pedagogy and study of Afro-American literature so that it would reflect the most advanced thinking of a contemporary universe of literary-theoretical discourse. (80)

One of the voices that "reconstruct[s]" discussions of an African American literary aesthetics, first called for by James Weldon Johnson in 1921, is Toni Morrison in her 1984 essay "Rootedness: The Ancestor as Foundation." While echoing earlier writers who pull from West African structural patterns such as multiplicity of meaning, circularity, call and response, and improvisation, Morrison adds *ancestor* to the discussion. According to Morrison, in our literature, ancestors are grandparents as in Ralph Ellison's *Invisible Man* or healers like Minnie Ransom in Toni Cade Bambara's *The Salt Eaters*. The important point is that ancestors are "timeless people whose relationship to the characters (and perhaps readers) are benevolent, instructive, and protective (1980, 339–345). Ancestors also provide a certain kind of wisdom and, often in conjunction with the language and the overall structure of the work, they help to regenerate spiritual aspects of African American life toward some sense of spiritual wholeness (Hubbard 1994, 383) and ancestral truths. In Morrison's own works, there are often females who guide members of the younger generation in some way: M'Dean and Aunt Jimmy in *The Bluest Eye;* Ondine and Sydney in *Tar Baby;* Baby Suggs in *Beloved;* and even the shadowy female images that haunt Jadine Childs in *Tar Baby*. The most known ancestor in Morrison's work is Pilate Dead in *Song of Solomon*. In Gloria Naylor's *Mama Day,* the ancestor is Mama Day. In Alice Walker's *The Color Purple,* often the ancestor is a community of women who remember and proscribe their existence by bonding with one another.

In the late 1980s, experimentations with form shift yet again. As Trey Ellis points out in his 1989 essay "The New Black Aesthetic," a new generation of novelists, poets, screenwriters, critics, and curators called for a "new black aesthetics" (NBA) that was more individualistic (but not in the mold of art for art's sake and not without social and political responsibility). In essence, the NBA artists sought to communicate what Greg Tate in "Cult-Nats Meet Freaky Deke" called "the complexities of our culture" (5). Echoing this young generation, Ellis writes as follows:

> [The New Black Aesthetic icons included] Ishmael Reed, Clarence Major, Toni Morrison, and John Edgar Wideman; George Clinton with his spaced-out funk band Parliament/Funkadelic; conceptual artist David Hammons who has hung empty Thunderbird bottles and spades from trees; Richard Pryor with his molten parodies of black life on his early albums and short-lived television show. (234)

At another point in his essay, Ellis describes the NBA artists as culturally eclectic:

> Young blacks [are] getting back into jazz and the blues; [or] the only one you [saw] at punk concerts . . . [or] who admit liking both Jim and Toni Morrison . . . Eddie Murphy, Prince, and the Marsalis brothers. (234)

In the twenty-first century, a few twentieth-century icons have been replaced with more contemporary hip hop ones, but the role of the NBA artists remains the same: culturally eclectic and individualistic but not without social and political responsibility.

Bibliography

Andrews, William L., Frances Smith Foster, and Trudier Harris, eds. *The Oxford Companion to African American Literature.* New York: Oxford University Press, 1997.

Baker, Houston, Jr. "Generational Shifts and the Recent Criticism of Afro-American Literature." *Black American Literature Forum* 15, no. 1 (Spring 1981): 3–21.

———. *Modernism and the Harlem Renaissance.* Chicago, IL: University of Chicago Press, 1987.

Baldwin, James. "Many Thousand Gone." *Notes of a Native Son.* Boston, MA: Bantam, 1972, 13–36.

Bell, Bernard W. *The Afro-American Novel and Its Tradition.* Amherst, MA: Massachusetts University Press, 1987.

Brown, Sterling. *The American Negro: His History and Literature.* New York: Arno Press, 1969.

Cuddon, J.A. *Dictionary of Literary Terms and Literary Theory.* New York: Penguin, 1991.

Davis, Arthur P., and Saunders Redding, eds. *Calvacade: Negro American Writing From 1760 to the Present.* Boston, MA: Houghton Mifflin, 1971.

Dietzel, Susanne B. "The African American Novel and Popular Culture." *The Cambridge Companion to the African American Novel.* Maryemma Graham, ed. New York: Cambridge University Press, 2003.

Du Bois, W.E.B. *The Quest of the Silver Fleece: A Novel.* 1911. Reprint. Miami, FL: Mnemosyne Publishing Co., 1969.

Dunbar, Paul Laurence. "Worn Out." *The Norton Anthology of African American Literature.* Henry Louis Gates, Jr. and Nellie Y. McKay, eds. New York: W. W. Norton & Company, 887–888.

———. "Ode to Ethiopia." *The Norton Anthology of African American Literature.* Henry Louis Gates, Jr. and Nellie Y. McKay, eds. New York: W. W. Norton & Company, 886–887.

Ellis, Trey. "The New Black Aesthetic." *Callaloo* 12 (Winter 1989): 233–243.

Ellison, Ralph. "The Art of Fiction: An Interview." In *Shadow and Act* by Ralph Ellison. 171–172. New York: Signet Book, 1964.

Ervin, Hazel Arnett. *African American Literary Criticism, 1773 to 2000.* New York: Twayne, 1999.

Fauset, Jesse. *There Is Confusion.* Boston, MA: Northeastern University Press, 1989.

Gates, Henry Louis and Nellie Y. McKay, eds. *The Norton Anthology of African American Literature.* New York: W. W. Norton & Company, 1997.

Hammon, Jupiter. "An Evening Thought: Salvation by Christ with Penetential [sic] Cries." *Call and Response: The Riverside Anthology of the African American Literary Tradition.* Patricia Liggins Hill, Bernard W. Bell, Trudier Harris, William J. Harris, R. Baxter Miller, and Sondra A. O'Neal, eds. Boston, MA: Houghton Mifflin, 1998.

Hemenway, Robert E. *Zora Neale Hurston: A Literary Biography.* Champaign, IL: University of Illinois Press, 1977.

Henderson, Stephen E. *Understanding the New Black Poetry: Black Speech and Black Music as Poetic References.* New York: William Morrow, 1973.

Hogue, Lawrence. *Race, Modernity, Postmodernity: A Look at the History and the Literatures of People of Color Since the 1960s.* Albany, NY: State University of New York Press, 2003.

hooks, bell. "'Homeplace': A Site of Resistance." In *Yearning: Race, Gender, and Cultural Politics,* 411–450. Boston: South End Press, 1990.

Horton, George Moses. "On Liberty and Slavery." *Call and Response: The Riverside Anthology of the African American Literary Tradition.* Patricia Liggins Hill, et al., eds. Boston, MA: Houghton Mifflin, 1998, 373.

———. "The Slave Complaint." *Call and Response: The Riverside Anthology of the African American Literary Tradition.* Patricia Liggins Hill, et al., eds. Boston, MA: Houghton Mifflin, 1998, 372.

Hubbard, Dolan. *The Sermon and the African American Literary Imagination.* Columbia, MO: University of Missouri, 1994.

Hughes, Langston. "Negro Artist and the Racial Mountain." In *African American Literary Criticism, 1773 to 2000.* Hazel Arnett Ervin, ed. New York: Twayne, 1999, 44–48.

———. "The Weary Blues." *The Norton Anthology of African American Literature.* Henry Louis Gates and Nellie Y. McKay, eds. New York: W. W. Norton & Company, 1997, 1257.

Johnson, James Weldon. The *Autobiography of an Ex-Coloured Man.* 1912. Reprint. New York: Hill and Wang, 1960.

———, ed. *The Book of American Negro Poetry.* New York: Harcourt, Brace, 1922. Rev. ed. San Diego, CA: Harvest Books, 1969.

Locke, Alain. "Art or Propaganda?" In *African American Literary Criticism, 1773 to 2000.* Hazel Arnett Ervin, ed. New York: Twayne, 1999, 49–50.

McMillan, Terry. Introduction. *Breaking Ice: An Anthology of Contemporary African American Fiction.* Terry McMillan, ed. New York: Penguin, 1990, xv–xxiv.

Morrison, Toni. "Rootedness: The Ancestor as Foundation" (1980). In *African American Literary Criticism, 1773 to 2000.* Hazel Arnett Ervin, ed. New York: Twayne, 1999, 198–202.

Neal, Larry. "And Shine Swam On." In *Black Fire: An Anthology of Afro-American Writing.* LeRoi Jones and Larry Neal, eds. New York: William Morrow and Co., 1988, 638–656.

O'Neale, Sandra. "Jupiter Hammon." *Call and Response: The Riverside Anthology of The African American Literary Tradition.* Patricia Liggins Hill, et al., eds. Boston, MA: Houghton Mifflin, 1998, 69.

Rodgers, Carolyn. "Uh Nat'chal Thang—The WHOLE TRUTH—US." *Black World* 60 (September 1973): 4–14.

Smith, Jeanne. "Plantation Literature." *The Oxford Companion to African American Literature.* William L. Andrews, Frances Smith Foster, and Trudier Harris, eds. New York: Oxford University Press, 1997, 736–737.

Tate, Greg. "Cult-Nats Meet Freaky Deke." *Voices Literary Supplement* (December 1986): 5–8.

Terry, Lucy. "Bar's Fight." *The Norton Anthology of African American Literature*. Henry Louis Gates and Nellie Y. McKay, eds. New York: W. W. Norton & Company, 1997.

Thompson, Robert Farris. *Flash of the Spirit, African and Afro-American Art and Philosophy*. New York: Random House, 1984.

Toomer, Jean. "A Song of the Son." *Cane*. 1923. Reprint. New York: Perennial Classic, 1969.

Wideman, John Edgar. Preface. *Breaking Ice: An Anthology of Contemporary African American Fiction*. Terry McMillan, ed. New York: Penguin, 1990, x–v.

Wright, Richard. "A Blueprint for Negro Writing." (1937). In *The Portable Harlem Renaissance Reader*. David L. Lewis, ed. New York: Viking Press, 1994.

Further Reading

Andrews, William L., Frances Smith Foster, and Trudier Harris, eds. *The Oxford Companion to African American Literature*. New York: Oxford University Press, 1997; Dickson-Carr, Darryl. *The Columbia Guide to Contemporary African American Fiction*. New York: Columbia University Press, 2005; Gabbin, Joanne V. *Furious Flower: African American Poetry from the Blacks Arts Movement to the Present*. Charlottesville, VA: University of Virginia Press, 2004; Graham, Mary Emma, ed. *The Cambridge Companion to the African American Novel*. Boston, MA: Cambridge University Press, 2004; Hogue, Lawrence. *Race, Modernity, Postmodernity: A Look at the History and the Literature of People of Color Since the 1960s*. Albany, NY: State University of New York Press, 2003; Major, Clarence. *Calling the Wind: Twentieth Century African American Short Stories*. New York: Perennial, 1992; McMillan, Terry. *Breaking Ice: An Anthology of Contemporary African American Fiction*. New York: Penguin, 1990; Miller, E. Ethelbert. *Beyond the Frontier: African American Poetry for the Century*. Baltimore, MD: Black Classic Poets, 2002; Nelson, Emmanuel S. *Contemporary African American Novelists: A Bio-Bibliographical Critical Sourcebook*. Westport, CT: Greenwood, 1999; Ostrom, Hans, and J. David Macey. *The Greenwood Encyclopedia of African American Literature*. Westport, CT: 1990; Quashie, Kevin Everod, R. Joyce Lausch, and Keith D. Miller, eds. *New Bones: Contemporary Black Writers in America*. Upper Saddle, NJ: Prentice Hall, 2000.

HAZEL ARNETT ERVIN

ARAB AMERICAN LITERATURE

Definition. Arab American literature was already growing by leaps and bounds in the late 1990s, but the Sept. 11, 2001, hijacking attacks fueled an upsurge of interest in all things Arab and Muslim and helped broaden the mainstream appeal of poetry and prose by American authors of Arab descent and the work of Arab immigrants who have settled in the United States. The early years of the twenty-first century have seen the publication of a spate of new works of Arab American fiction and poetry, autobiographical memoirs, anthologies, and a growing body of literary criticism of this emerging body of work. Anti-Arab and anti-Muslim racism has continued to limit the number and range of works that have been published, prompting increasing numbers of Arab Americans to create venues of their own to present works of literary and cultural production.

The definition may change as this emergent genre matures, but for now, it includes poetry and prose by Arab immigrants residing in the United States and American writers of Arab descent, regardless of the "Arabness" of the content. That includes writers such as Mona Simpson and Samuel Hazo who are of Arab descent but whose work does not significantly touch on "Arab" themes.

History. Contemporary Arab American writers are heirs to a group of poets active in the 1920s that was known as Al-Mahjar or "the immigrant poets," which included writers from Lebanon and Syria such as Gibran Kahlil Gibran, Ameen

Rihani, and Mikhail Naimy. Some wrote in Arabic but collaborated closely with their translators. Others wrote in English, embracing more fully the culture and language of their adopted country. Together as a group, these writers are credited with sparking an interest in immigrant writing among the mainstream American audience (Abinader 2001). Rihani, whose works include *The Book of Khalid* (1911), *The Green Flag* (1911), *The Quatrains of Abul-'Ala'* (1903), *Myrtle and Myrrh* (1905), and *A Chant of Mystics and Other Poems* (1921), is often described as the "father of Arab American literature," and one of his most notable accomplishments was to introduce free verse to the formulaic and traditional Arab poetic canon around 1905 (Abinader 2000, 1).

Gibran, who was prominent among the early Arab American writers and kept company with U.S. literary figures such as the poet Robinson Jeffers and playwright Eugene O'Neill, eventually became one of the most popular authors in the United States. Gibran was born in Bsharri, Lebanon, in 1883 and emigrated to the United States in 1895, living first in Boston and later in New York. His works include *The Madman, His Parables and Poems* (1918), *The Forerunner* (1920), *Sand and Foam* (1926), and *Jesus, The Son of Man* (1928). His opus, *The Prophet* (1923), has been translated into more than 40 languages and has remained a top seller for Alfred A. Knopf, Inc., for more than half a century. For many years, it was the best-selling book in the United States after the Bible, with some eight million copies in print (Abinader 2000, 2; Orfalea and Elmusa 1988, xvi). The U.S. Congress recognized Gibran's contribution to American arts and letters in 1990 by authorizing creation of the Kahlil Gibran Memorial Poetry Garden in Washington, D.C., which was dedicated by then President George H.W. Bush in 1990. It remains the only park dedicated to a writer in the nation's capital.

Despite Gibran's immense popularity, the first serious anthology of American poetry to include his work was *Grape Leaves: A Century of Arab-American Poetry,* published in 1988. He remains revered by ordinary people and literary critics in the Arab world, but Gibran has been scorned and dismissed by the literary establishment in the United States. This may change after the release of a feature film about Gibran's life being made by Arab American writer Rana Kazkaz, whose screenplay has already won a national prize.

From the late 1940s through the early 1980s, there was little self-identification by writers as Arab American, although strong independent poets and writers such as Samuel Hazo, D.H. Melhem, and Etel Adnan established their reputations in this time period. Elmaz Abinader, an award-winning writer herself, says these writers "distinguished themselves initially as writers independent of ethnic categorization

Although there is a centuries-old tradition of Arab letters and philosophy, it has remained largely outside Western consciousness. When these works are available in English translation, Arab literary and religious classics are often grouped with Third World literature, emergent literature, and post-colonial literature, something Fedwa Malti-Douglas describes as a "grave injustice" given their rich history (Malti-Douglas 1994, 226). One of the few Arab writers with a strong publishing record in the United States was Egyptian writer Naguib Mahfouz, but his works became readily available only after he won the Nobel Prize for Literature in 1988, the first and only Arab to achieve that honor.

(and) later donned the cloak of the Arab American identity" (Abinader 2000, 3). She describes them as a bridge between the two generations, as well as between Arab American writing and the American literary canon. For instance, Melhem, the author of the first comprehensive study of African American poet Gwendolyn Brooks, helped mainstream Arab American literature by organizing the first Arab American poetry reading at the annual meeting of the Modern Language Association in 1984 (Abinader 2000, 3). Adnan created her own publishing company, The Post-Apollo Press, which has helped ensure publication and distribution of many works by Arab American writers (Abinader 2000, 3). She also served for years as president of the Radius of Arab American Writers, Inc., a writers' group founded in the early 1990s.

Several important anthologies and periodicals have helped generate interest in Arab American literature over the past decade, including *Grape Leaves: A Century of Arab-American Poetry,* published in 1988 by Gregory Orfalea and Sharif Elmusa, and *Food for Our Grandmothers: Writings By Arab-American and Arab-Canadian Feminists,* an anthology of unusually frank essays and often jarring poetry published by Joanna Kadi in 1994. Kadi's anthology gave voice to a community she dubbed "the most invisible of the invisibles" and paved the way for candid discussions by and about Arab American women.

Post Gibran: Anthology of New Arab American Writing (1999) showcased poetry and prose by recognized writers and introduced a host of newer writers, including Hayan Charara, Mohja Kahf, and Suheir Hammad. The editors encouraged cross-genre experiments, asking poets to send in fiction, and essayists their attempts at drama: "We wanted to know what adjustments Arab American writers are making, both in their own self-image and the understanding of their Americanness, now that their Arabness has become more visible and is gaining a seemingly lasting presence" (Khaled and Akash 1999, xiii).

Poet Nathalie Handal's collection, *The Poetry of Arab Women: A Contemporary Anthology* (2001), was published by Interlink Publishing and has sold more than 10,000 copies. Michel Moushabeck, who founded Interlink in 1987 to introduce more Arab writers to the U.S. public, described sales of Handal's anthology as a "phenomenal" achievement for a book of poetry in the difficult U.S. market (Shalal-Esa 2007).

Another important collection, *Dinarzad's Children: An Anthology of Contemporary Arab American Fiction,* followed in 2004, published by Mattawa and co-editor Pauline Kaldas. In addition, the work of an increasing number of Arab Americans has also found its way into broader anthologies of women's writing and other postcolonial collections.

Barbara Nimri Aziz, a journalist, also deserves credit for establishing Radius of Arab American Writers, Inc., or RAWI, in the early 1990s. The organization has grown immensely since its inception and now includes over 100 Arab American writers and maintains a Web site that features member profiles and original writing. In 2000, writers D.H. Melhem and Leila Diab compiled an anthology of the work of RAWI members, and the group has begun hosting annual literary conferences to further promote Arab American literary production.

Playwright Kathryn Haddad founded the award-winning journal *Mizna: Prose, Poetry and Art Exploring Arab America* in 1999, facilitating publication of the work of hundreds of Arab American writers and visual artists whose work might not otherwise have seen the light of day. In addition, the new Arab American

National Museum in Dearborn, Michigan, has also begun hosting annual conferences on Arab arts and culture, another important venue for discussion about and presentation of Arab American literature.

Together these efforts have contributed significantly to the emergence of a rich and growing body of Arab American literature, and they are making this literature increasingly accessible to scholars and students in disciplines such as English, comparative literature, American studies, and women's studies. In addition, these collections have helped to create a national community of Arab American writers, many of whom had felt isolated within their own regional communities. The emergence of this community has helped fuel more collaborative projects and remains a key driver behind conferences and other events that showcase and encourage Arab American literary production.

Trends and Themes. Major themes in the works of contemporary Arab American writers include heritage, family, food, hybridity, gender, exile, assimilation, alienation, nationalism, displacement, and the horrors of war. Although many of the earliest Arab American writers were men, including the famed poet and artist Gibran Kahlil Gibran, many of the emerging contemporary writers are women, and the entire body of current work is clearly influenced by feminism, postmodernism, and a deep sense of connection to other communities of color.

Twentieth-century Arab American writers focused mainly on the genre of poetry; they were led by such writers as Naomi Shihab Nye, Lawrence Joseph, D.H. Melhem, and Samuel Hazo. These writers were followed in the 1990s by Hayan Charara, Nathalie Handal, Suheir Hammad, and David Williams. In *Dinarzad's Children: An Anthology of Contemporary Arab American Fiction* (2004), co-editors Pauline Kaldas and Khaled Mattawa cite a sense of isolation felt by Arab American writers even within their own communities and suggest that the lyric poem afforded writers a safer "way to speak as individuals to individuals" rather than representing a larger bloc (Kaldas and Mattawa 2004, xi). In a climate of negative stereotyping about Arabs and hypersensitivity to any criticism of Israel, many Arab American writers may have found it easier to express themselves in the abstracted way that poetry makes possible. Majaj notes that the poetic compression of the lyric mode favors vignettes rather than narratives and "moments of insight over sustained analysis" (Majaj, "New Directions" 1999, 70).

Poetry remains popular, but Arab American writers have increasingly turned to prose narratives and plays to tell their stories. Burgeoning cultural production by Arab American writers may also have come as a reaction to an increasingly hostile environment characterized by anti-Arab and anti-Muslim racism spurred by the 9/11 attacks and the continuing war in Iraq. The political and social situation of Arab Americans in general has worsened since 2001, civil liberty violations are up, and stereotypical representations of Arabs and Muslims in Hollywood films and the media are more prevalent than ever. Long invisible on the American literature scene, Arab American writers are now responding to growing interest in their lives and simultaneously trying to set the record straight. Increasingly, that includes performances on the stage. For instance, San Francisco-based playwright, screenwriter, and actor Betty Shamieh has written over 15 plays, including *Roar,* and Iraqi American Heather Raffo won wide acclaim for *9 Parts of Desire,* which has been performed around the world.

Although earlier literary works were haunted by a deep sense of nostalgia, contemporary Arab American writers are wielding their pens to chronicle decades of racism, oppression, and marginalization in the United States, and to begin uncovering the particularities of their own ethnic histories. They are also beginning to address conflicts within a beleaguered ethnic community. These conflicts were largely ignored during the ethnic identity politics of the 1970s that focused mainly on a trinity of **African American, Asian American,** and **Latino** writers.

Collectively, Arab Americans have been subject to decades of racism, discrimination, negative stereotyping, and hostility in the United States, a phenomenon which has made some Arab American writers wary of discussing issues that could deepen already debilitating stereotypes about Arabs in America. For many years, the real or perceived need for unity among a beleaguered minority has hampered an honest discourse by Arab American writers about patriarchal structures, arranged marriage, and other controversial topics. Stereotypes are still prevalent, even in the academy. Amal Amireh and Lisa Suhair Majaj published a collection of essays on the transnational reception of Third World women writers, a project that grew out of their frustration about just this phenomenon. They noted that even when they were invited to panels, certain discursive, institutional, and ideological structures preempted their discourse and determined what they could and would say. Any critique of Arab society or culture they seemed to utter would confirm the audience's vision about "the patriarchal, oppressive nature of Third World societies," but when they challenged these stereotypes, they were accused of defensiveness and their feminism was questioned (Amireh and Majaj 2000, 3).

Reaction from within the Arab American community can also be fierce if it perceives any kind of attack or challenge to its prevailing social and familial structures, especially from one of its "own." Many fear that candid discussions of problems within the community could be further used against Arabs in the United States. At the same time, mainstream publishers have tended to encourage what critic Steven Salaita calls "stories of escape" and other plotlines that reinforce existing stereotypes while remaining skeptical about the marketing prospects for more complex tales that do not fit into such neat categories (Shalal-Esa 2007).

Context and Issues. Contemporary Arab American writers are concerned with dispossession, exile, loss, and grief, but rather than sinking into an abyss of introspection, they envision possibilities for taking action, seizing power, and building alliances with other groups. One thread that unites these newer writers is a conscious decision to identify as—and with—communities of color. They claim the margins as their native soil and honor the inherent contradictions of their identities. Their works see identity not as a fixed essence but a social construction, a product of the multiple and overlapping forces of geography, historical moment, gender, ethnicity, age, and class.

Memoirs. The past decade has also seen the publication of several important memoirs by Arab American writers, including Edward Said's remarkable 1999 autobiography *Out of Place*, a moving story of exile, displacement, and an identity forever torn between languages, places, and even ways of thinking. Said embarked on the writing of the memoir after being diagnosed with cancer, and his writings represented a deliberate attempt to reclaim and record his brilliant memories of the lost landscapes and communities of his childhood, many of which literally no longer exist. The book gives the reader an intimate look at the forces that shaped one of the most important intellectuals in recent memory, narrating his often painful experiences as an immigrant, an exile, and ultimately, an outsider.

Naomi Shihab Nye's book, *Never in a Hurry: Essays on People and Places* (1996), Suheir Hammad's *Drops of This Story* (1996), and Diana Abu-Jaber's food memoir, *The Language of Baklava* (2005), further illuminate the rich diversity of Arab American lives.

Literary Criticism. Aside from selected individual reviews, it was only in the 1990s that one could identify any serious tradition of Arab American literary criticism, aided largely by the work of a few "pioneers," including Lisa Suhair Majaj, Therese Saliba, Nathalie Handal, Evelyn Shakir, Mohja Kahf, and Elmaz Abinader. One excellent example of the serious scholarship emerging is *Etel Adnan: Critical Essays on the Arab-American Writer and Artist* (2002), which provides a comprehensive look at Adnan's literary and artistic accomplishments through analysis and close readings. Its authors, Lisa Suhair Majaj and Amal Amireh, have elevated the genre of Arab American writing to a secure place within U.S. academic circles and helped situate it for English-speaking readers. In addition, their work to gather and disseminate secondary sources has helped spawn public appetite for more Arab American writing.

Another notable book is *Ameen Rihani: Bridging East and West: A Pioneering Call for Arab-American Understanding* (2004), a book of scholarly essays compiled by editors Nathan Funk and Betty Sitka to explore the work of this prolific early Arab American writer.

The U.S.-based journal, *Al Jadid: A Review & Record of Arab Culture and Arts*, launched in 1993 by Elie Chalala, has also been an important force facilitating the study of Arab and Arab American texts. *Al Jadid* includes timely book reviews, translations, and a host of original articles on topics ranging from music to theatre, books to journals, fiction to fine art, poetry to performing arts. It provides a forum for continuing scholarship and acts as an important bridge connecting Arab American artists to the Arab world.

Selected Authors

Naomi Shihab Nye. Naomi Shihab Nye, born in St. Louis to a Palestinian father and an American mother, is an accomplished poet and essayist who has also published several children's books and two novels for young adults, *Habibi* (1997) and *Going, Going* (2005). Nye has also played an important role in showcasing the work of Arab writers and artists in various anthologies, including *The Space Between Our Footsteps: Poems and Paintings from the Middle East* (1998).

Although her Arab heritage is an important factor in her work, Nye's writing draws on and reflects a wide variety of cultural contexts and sources, including the American Southwest where she lives and the many places she has traveled. Saddeka Arebi, a Saudi Arabian scholar, has also done important work to claim a positive and separate space for Arab women writers, citing an important Islamic concept of "middleness" or *Wasat,* and concluding that being in the middle "does not have to mean 'between-ness,' being torn or on shaky ground, but can be a firm and advantageous position from which one can see both sides more clearly" (Arebi 1994, xi). Nye has inherited this sense of empowerment present in the concept of "middleness," and it pervades her work. In contrast to some Arab Americans who feel fragmented because of their bicultural identities, Nye developed a feeling even as a young child that her "difference" was "always a strength. You were free" (Nye 2000).

This sense of detachment calls to mind Abdul JanMohamed's use of the term "specular border intellectual," a person he defines as being equally familiar with two cultures but unwilling or unable to be "at home" in these societies, subjecting the cultures to analytic scrutiny rather than combining them (JanMohamed 1990, 97). For instance, Edward Said, the late Palestinian American scholar, wrote that he always felt he belonged to both the Arab and the Western worlds, "without being completely *of* either one or the other" (Said 1993, xxvi). Nye's poetry often gives one exactly this sense of standing somehow apart. In a poem entitled "Over the Fence," she addresses the lack of fit that sometimes plagues people with a bicultural or multicultural heritage, staging the poem as a dialogue that takes place between two neighbors over the fence that divides their properties and lives. Nye yearns for the steadiness of having lived one's whole life in one town, perhaps even one house, as her neighbor has. But the neighbor sees Nye's life as far more exciting than the yawning tedium of her own, with each day marked only by her husband's departure, when "the world clicks shut/like a little dead door" and with the endless cycle of dirty dishes to wash (Nye 1986, 69). Even the plants seem more glamorous on Nye's side of the fence, where purple iris "float their silken heads"; on her side, the neighbor sees her rose as "a stick forever" (Nye 1986, 69). For her part, Nye refuses to be put on some pedestal for her worldliness, concluding that she would gladly "take one tongue if it fit me." She doesn't consider herself any more fortunate than her neighbor. "I say no one is lucky. We have faces, they get old," she writes, reminding them both of their common frailty as human beings (Nye 1986, 69).

Although Nye chafes at "voices chiding me to 'speak for my people,'" her Palestinian American heritage informs earlier poems such "The Man Who Makes Brooms" (Nye 1986, 36), while her outrage about the war in Iraq looms large in more recent poetry. In one poem, an ode to "The Sweet Arab, the Generous Arab," Nye implores, "Please forgive everyone who has not honored your name." She paints a portrait of the "Arabs I know, generous to a fault, welcoming, with the same wish for a safe daily life as millions of other people around the world. Who packed the pieces, carried them, to a new corner. For whom the words rubble and blast are constants" (Nye 2005, 57).

Despite the frustration and grief apparent in her newer poems, Nye holds fast to a sense of agency and empowerment. Her heroine in *Going, Going* is a courageous teenage girl who rallies her friends and neighbors to boycott the growing corporate influences on her community and fight to save small local businesses. The overall theme is a metaphor for Nye's own effort to salvage the particularities of our rich divergent histories and avoid the generalizations and homogenization that Wal-Mart represents.

Diana Abu-Jaber. Diana Abu-Jaber is a novelist and essayist who has broken into the mainstream media market through several novels and a food memoir. Her 1993 novel *Arabian Jazz,* about an Arab immigrant and his two daughters, received excellent reviews in the mainstream U.S. press, although it was controversial within the Arab American community, mainly due to its discussion of sensitive topics such as arranged marriage, racism, abject poverty, female infanticide, and incest. Using multiple narrators and continually blurring the lines between the past and the present, the book provides a potent materialist critique of America while casting an equally skeptical eye on the patriarchal vestiges of the Arab world. It tracks the journey of Jemorah, one of the main characters as she begins to develop a clear view of the racism that surrounds her.

Abu-Jaber's second novel, *Crescent* (2003), delves further into the issues of exile and hybridity as the central character, Sirine, an Arab American chef, learns a new appreciation for her own tangled identity through her relationship with an exiled

Iraqi literature professor. The book also examines the lives of other so-called hybrids, people who navigate between borders, countries, languages, and ethnicities, providing an interesting mosaic of the many ways there are to be Arab, American, or some combination of the two.

Abu-Jaber says writing gave her a way to imagine herself in the world, a "way to say the deepest sorts of truths that I had been taught it was not polite or reasonable for a young woman to speak out loud" (Abu-Jaber 2004, 123). In *Arabian Jazz,* she used comedy and hyperbole to portray her characters and the difficult situations they encountered, but this approach backfired with the Arab American community. Mainstream reviewers loved the book, but Arab Americans felt betrayed by Abu-Jaber's farcical tone. In her food memoir *The Language of Baklava* (2005), she writes about the "betrayed" readers of *Arabian Jazz,* who wrote her letters complaining about a "sense of being unfairly cast, unrepresented, their unique stories and voices . . . unheard and ignored." She empathizes, acutely aware of feeling alone in a country where "the only media images of Arabs are bomb throwers and other lunatics." But at the same time, these critical voices leave Abu-Jaber feeling vulnerable and a bit exiled herself, cut off from family, home, and her cultural community— the very people she had hoped would provide her with a sense of acceptance and connection.

In her short story, "My Elizabeth," Abu-Jaber explores what she describes as "deep cultural ambivalences," weaving the tale of an Arab American girl who is brought to live with relatives in Wyoming after the suicide of her father (Abu-Jaber 2005, 235). Her great aunt Nabila, known as Great-aunt Winifred, gives her a new American name and instructs her sternly, "Never, ever speak Arabic. . . . Wipe it out of your brain. It's clutter, you won't need it anymore" (Abu-Jaber, "My Elizabeth" 2004, 297). Estelle, as she is now called, becomes friends with a Native American girl named Elizabeth. The two girls both lack fathers, have secret names, and are haunted by the duality of shuttling between public and private languages. "We were descended from nations that no map had names or boundaries for," writes Abu-Jaber in this poignant story of friendship, the jagged edge of memory, and the pain of growing up (Abu-Jaber, "My Elizabeth" 2004, 299).

Suheir Hammad. Strengthening the connections among marginalized populations is also a priority for spoken-word poet Suheir Hammad. Hammad draws inspiration from her poor, working-class childhood in Brooklyn, where she grew up mostly among Puerto Rican children, went to terrible public schools, and experienced first-hand what it means to be poor and of color in America. Hammad's poetry is filled with images of violence, sexuality, and rage, as well as compassion for the nation's dispossessed and wrongly imprisoned.

DEF POETRY JAM

Suheir Hammad's most recent poetry collection, *ZaatarDiva,* was published in late 2005 by Rattapallax Press, but she has also won great acclaim and public recognition as a cast member of the award-winning *Russell Simmons Presents Def Poetry Jam* on Broadway, as well as a regular participant in HBO's "Def Poetry Jam." Hammad adopts a direct and combative style in her poetry, which is written to be delivered orally. Her poetry throbs with the rhythm of urban life, a hip-hop beat pulsating to the words as they damn oppression, racism, fascism, and violence in any form—in the war zones of our families, streets, and nations.

She locates herself proudly as a woman of color, as evidenced by the title and content of her first book of poetry, *born Palestinian, born Black* (1996). Its title is taken from "Moving towards Home," a poem that African American poet June Jordan wrote in response to the massacre of Palestinians in Lebanon in the Sabra and Shatila refugee camps after Israel's 1982 invasion. In that poem, Jordan proclaims: "I was born a Black woman/and now/I am become a Palestinian" (Jordan 1989, 143). Hammad, writing in the foreword to *born Palestinian, born Black*, says that line of Jordan's changed her life: "I remember feeling validated by her statement. She dared speak of transformation, of re-birth, of a deep understanding of humanity" (Hammad, *born Palestinian* 1996, xi).

Uncovering racism and sexism in her essays and poetry, Hammad urges women of color to accept themselves as they are. In her poem, "bleached and bleeding," Hammad catalogs the misery of young women living under the yoke of these Westernized ideals of beauty: in the end, after decimating and reshaping our bodies, *"we hate ourselves/we kill ourselves"* (Hammad, *born Palestinian*, 1996, 75–76). Only by accepting themselves as they are can women of color finally be free, Hammad argues in a poignant vignette about women "bleaching their hides to reach an impossible shade of porcelain," when their skin was so beautiful in its natural state. "Don't need blush, even on sallow days . . . This beauty is of earth; ain't no plastic here" (Hammad, *Drops* 1996, 90).

Risking the wrath of the conservative Arab community, Hammad also begins to expose sexual abuse and harassment of women—within her family, the Arab community, and the larger world. In "letter to anthony (critical resistance)," a letter poem to a friend in prison, Hammad writes about working on poetry with women in prison: in the end, *"every home she has ever inhabited,"* the poet writes, has been broken into and exploited, *"starting with her body"* (Hammad 2005, 65).

Mohja Kahf. Sexuality is also a critical concern for Mohja Kahf, a Syrian-born poet, novelist, and scholar, who writes a regular column, "Sex and the Ummah," for the Web site www.muslimwakeup.com, which examines sexuality from a Muslim perspective through advice and short stories. In one story, a Saudi woman Wedad confesses to her sister as they leave the mosque after praying together that she was praying for an orgasm—something she hasn't experienced in four years. A blunt discussion ensues, in which the sister, Hamida, advises Wedad that she is responsible for her own body and pleasure. "There's fingers and mouths and things, darling," Hamida said. "There's more to a man than one body part, for heaven's sake. And then there's technique to consider, and positions that can help you on your merry path . . . Point being, take responsibility for your pleasure, ya sheikha. Take your orgasm into your own hands!" (Kahf 2005).

Kahf, who teaches literature at the University of Arkansas, argues that Islam includes many positive teachings about sex and that it "can be a form of ibada (worship) like any other act" (Mack 2007). She sees her writing as being connected to a rich literary tradition in the Middle East that includes often racy stories from *1001 Arabian Nights* as well as Sufi poetry. Her poem, "More than One Way to Break a Fast," pays homage to the dark, datelike lips of her lover, and captures the anxious waiting for dusk and the ritual breaking of the Ramadan fast, after a long day of doing without food, drink, and sex.

Kahf's first book of poetry, *E-mails from Scheherazad,* addresses the discomfort of being a Muslim woman in America, including a series of poems about the damning— and sometimes liberating—consequences of wearing a hijab, or head scarf. Another poem relates the story of Kahf's Syrian grandmother washing her "well-groomed" feet in the sink of the ladies' room at Sears to prepare for a Muslim prayer—and the shocked reactions of the white American women, who consider the act "an affront to American porcelain,/a contamination of American Standards/by something foreign and unhygienic/requiring civil action and possible use of disinfectant spray" (Kahf 2003, 26). The incident ends with Kahf holding the door open for all the women as they lose themselves "in the great common ground/of housewares on markdown" (Kahf 2003, 28).

Kahf's first novel, *The Girl in the Tangerine Scarf* (2006), examines the life of Khadra Shamy, who grows up in a devout Syrian Muslim family in the middle of Indiana. The book draws on some of Kahf's own experiences growing up in Indiana, but it is not primarily autobiographical. This coming-of-age novel presents an array of Arab American characters and perceptions but also transcends the immigrant story to examine friendships, family, racism, violence, and the realities of life in the contemporary United States.

Nathalie Handal. Poet, playwright, and scholar Nathalie Handal has played a central role in the renaissance of Arab American literature, contributing her own sensual, luscious poetry and plays, directing plays and performances, and anthologizing the work of Arab women poets and young Arab writers from all over the English-speaking world. "It's very much a question of eradicating invisibility and bringing awareness to who we are as Palestinians and Arabs," says Handal (Handal 2006), whose works of poetry include *The Neverfield* (1999) and *The Lives of Rain* (2005) and two CDs combining poetry and music, *Traveling Rooms* (1999) and *Spell* (2006).

Handal defies categorization. She hails from a big Palestinian family from Bethlehem, but was born in Haiti and spent years in the Caribbean, Latin America, the United States, and Europe. She writes in English but slips fluidly from English to Arabic to French in conversation. Her poetry is also peppered with Spanish words because so much of her family lives in Latin America that these experiences also inform her life and work.

Like many other contemporary Arab American writers and poets, Handal grapples with the U.S. wars in Iraq and Afghanistan, as well as Israel's continued occupation of Palestinian territories captured in the 1967 war. In some ways, one could say current U.S. military engagements are a defining issue for younger writers in a manner not unlike the role the Vietnam War played in defining the generation of the 1960s. In her poem "Twelve Deaths at Noon," Handal writes poignantly of "the prisons in our souls" and the voices of the murdered sons and husbands echoing "like drumbeats in our ears" (Handal 2005, 15). She meticulously records the deaths of civilians, including "a dead man, perhaps thirty/with a tight fist, holding some sugar for morning coffee" and "coffee cups full/left on the table/in a radio station/beside three corpses" (Handal 2005, 15). In "Jenin," a poem for the Palestinian city where more than 50 people were killed during a massive Israeli incursion in April 2002, Handal chronicles the devastation.

Hayan Charara. Violence is also a central theme in the poetry of Hayan Charara, an Arab American poet and scholar who grew up in Detroit and first attended college at age 13. The author of two poetry books, *The Alchemist's Diary* (2001) and *The Sadness of Others* (2006), Charara's poetry chronicles the full gamut of death and violence, including the rape of a fellow student, the death of two young Arab engineers killed in an apparently intentional gas explosion, suicides, the death of his mother, and even the stampede of a herd of cattle. His earlier work focused heavily on narrating his experience as a Muslim growing up in Detroit, a town he describes as "a shithole, it's where/you were pulled from the womb/into the streets" (Charara

2001, 13). For Charara, it is a city "where boys are manufactured into men/where you learn to think in American" (Charara 2001, 13). It is the place where he and his friends swam in a dammed river, daring each other to go over the edge, despite the drowning of a boy from a neighboring town. "We stood in line, hesitant,/until someone shouted 'pussy'/or 'chicken-shit'/and we knew what we had to do" (Charara 2001, 58). It is also the place where his mother died and his father was held up at gunpoint by a thief—a criminal "who believed himself/a failure, pulled back/the pistol in his hand,/and said as he left,/"This is your lucky day, camel jockey" (Charara 2001, 25–26).

Rabih Alameddine. Rabih Alameddine delves into issues of violence, death, AIDS, sexual identity, racism, and homophobia in his writing. His writings include *Koolaids: The Art of War* (1998) and a book of short stories, *The Perv* (1999). These were followed in 2001 by an experimental novel in first chapters, *I, The Divine*, which uses a fragmented, nonlinear approach to examine the ravages of the Lebanese civil war and the life of Sarah Nour El-Din, a Lebanese immigrant in the United States, who remains haunted by Lebanon even after she flees to America. "In Lebanon, during the war, however, all unhappy families were not unhappy in their own way. They suffered because at least one family member was killed. It did not matter why a family was unhappy before; death became the overpowering reason," she writes in one of her many tantalizing unfinished attempts to start a novel or memoir (Alameddine 2001, 63). Alameddine told one interviewer the civil war "permeates every corner of my life. I can't seem to write about anything else. The war taught me how to deal with impermanence, how to sharpen my sense of the absurd, and how to function in a chaotic world" (Devlin 2002).

Like Kahf, Alameddine candidly explores the sexuality of his characters and the pain of living with HIV. In one passage of *Koolaids*, Samir, the main character, receives a letter from his 93-year-old great-uncle, who explains that he too is gay, although he married and had children and "had a good life," while another relative died a bitter man because his homosexuality was never accepted. The great-uncle tells Samir he regrets "not having shared my bed with a man even once, but after a while, even those feelings dimmed" (Alameddine 1998, 129).

Laila Lalami. In her debut novel *Hope and Other Dangerous Pursuits*, Laila Lalami, a Moroccan American writer and critic, traces the story of four desperate Moroccans caught among love for their homeland and families, the quiet desperation of their lives in Morocco, and their unflinching efforts to build a better life in Spain. Translated into five languages, the novel has won critical acclaim for its spare but elegant prose exposing the ravages of globalization and the trials of refugees everywhere.

Grappling with 9/11. Clearly the events of Sept. 11, 2001, left huge marks on the U.S. psyche and particularly on Arab Americans. The hijacking attacks and their aftermath

---

RECEPTION

Blogging on Arab American literature, politics, and culture

Laila Lalami, educated in Morocco, Britain, and the United States, also writes a well-designed and substantive blog—www.moorishgirl.com—that covers a wide range of topics, including reviews of current literature, movies, events, essays on Arab American issues and politics, information about her publications, recommendations of "underappreciated books," guest columns, "All Things Moroccan," and more. Archives extend back to October 2001.

figure prominently in several of the recent works discussed—and prompted a swathe of new poems and essays. Naomi Shihab Nye appealed to "would-be terrorists" to "find another way to live. Don't expect others to be like you. Read Rumi. Read Arabic poetry . . . Plant mint" (Nye 2002, 287–91). D.H. Melhem, a lifetime resident of New York City, described "cloud messages/from the plume of hell,/I breathe you, taste the mist—/concrete dust, chairs, shoes,/files, photos, handbags, rings, a doll,/upholstery, breakfast trays,/body parts and parting words/and screams" (Melhem 2005, 165). Poet Lawrence Joseph, who works as a lawyer, struggles to make sense of the attacks in "Why Not Say What Happens," describing the lingering trauma of the attacks as well as the city's efforts to move forward. He captures individual vignettes from the day of the attacks, including, "one of Garfinkle's patients/tripped over a severed foot while evacuating/the Stock Exchange," as well as the sentiment of a policeman who doesn't want to talk about it at all (Joseph 2005, 25–26). But Joseph and Melhem also see the need for renewal and rebuilding, capturing the city's resilience in myriad ways. Joseph describes a sunset over the Hudson, evoking the promise of tomorrow for the city, its people—and perhaps for Arab Americans specifically: "The sky blue, dark blue/yet pure in color, not blackened/or tarnished, above the low, old/buildings, like a painting of something/solid rather than the solid thing itself,/a high and low composition. But what/light there is in that landscape . . ." (Joseph 2005, 32).

And what light there is in this landscape of Arab American literature. Each passing year brings more works to relish, every word helping to create a more complex, rich, and vibrant mosaic of the real and imagined lives of this growing and increasingly vocal minority.

Bibliography

Abinader, Elmaz. "Children of the Al-Mahjar: Arab-American Literature Spans a Century." 2000. http://usinfo.state.gov/journals/itsv/0200/ijse/abinader.htm.

Abu-Jaber, Diana. *Arabian Jazz*. New York: Harcourt Brace, 1993.

———. *Crescent*. New York: W.W. Norton, 2003.

———. *The Language of Baklava*. New York: Pantheon, 2005.

———. A Life of Stories. In *Scheherazade's Legacy: Arab and Arab American Women on Writing*. Susan Muaddi Darraj, ed. Praeger, 2004: 121–129.

———. My Elizabeth. In *Dinarzad's Children: An Anthology of Contemporary Arab American Fiction*. Pauline Kaldas and Khaled Mattawa, eds. Fayetteville: University of Arkansas Press, 2004: 295–312.

Alameddine, Rabih. *I, the Divine: A Novel in First Chapters*. New York: W.W. Norton, 2001.

———. *Koolaids: The Art of War*. New York: Picador, 1998.

Amireh, Amal. Writing the Difference: Feminists' Invention of the 'Arab Woman.' In *Interventions: Feminist Dialogues on Third World Women's Literature and Film*. Bishnupriya Ghosh and Brinda Bose, eds. New York: Garland Publishing, 1997: 185–211.

Amireh, Amal, and Majaj, Lisa Suhair. Introduction. In *Going Global: The Transnational Reception of Third World Women Writers*. Amal Amireh and Lisa Suhair Majaj, eds. New York: Garland Publishing, 2000: 1–25.

Arebi, Sadeeka. *Women and Words in Saudi Arabia: The Politics of Literary Discourse*. New York: Columbia University Press, 1994.

Darraj, Susan Muaddi, ed. *Scheherazade's Legacy: Arab and Arab American Women on Writing;* Westport, CT: Praeger, 2004.

Devlin, Kieron. "A Conversation with Rabih Alameddine." *Mississippi Review Online* 8.2. (Spring 2002). http://www.mississippireview.com/2002/leilani-devlin-alameddine.html.

Hammad, Suheir. *born Palestinian, born Black*. New York: Harlem River Press, 1996.

————. *Drops of This Story*. New York: Harlem River Press, 1996.

————. "Interview with Nathalie Handal. Drops of Suheir Hammad: A Talk with a Palestinian Poet Born Black." In *Al Jadid: A Record of Arab Culture and Arts* 3.20 (Summer 1997): 19.

————. *ZaatarDiva*. New York: Rattapallax Press, 2005.

Handal, Nathalie. *The Lives of Rain*. Northampton, MA: Interlink, 2005.

————. *The Neverfield*. Sausalito, CA: Post-Apollo Press, 1999.

————. *Spell*. Northampton, MA: Interlink, 2006.

————. Poetry as Homeland: A Letter to Lisa Suhair Majaj. In *Post-Gibran: An Anthology of New Arab American Writing*. Khaled Mattawa and Munir Akash, eds. Syracuse: Syracuse University Press, 1999: 139–144.

————, ed. *Poetry of Arab Women: A Contemporary Anthology*. New York: Interlink, 2001.

JanMohamed, Abdul. "Worldiness-Without-World, Homelessness-as-Home: Toward a Definition of the Specular Border Intellectual." In *Edward Said: A Critical Reader*. Michael Sprinker, ed. Cambridge: Blackwell, 1992. 96–120.

Jawdat, Nameer Ali. "Melvina and Jemorah in a Promised Land." Review of *Arabian Jazz* by Diana Abu-Jaber. *The Washington Post* 13 June 1993: X6.

Jordan, June. *Naming Our Destiny*. New York: Thunder's Mouth Press, 1989.

Joseph, Lawrence. *Into It*. New York: Farrar, Straus and Giroux, 2005.

Kadi, Joanna, ed. *Food for Our Grandmothers: Writings by Arab-American and Arab-Canadian Feminists*. Boston: South End Press, 1994.

Kahf, Mohja. *E-Mails from Scheherazad*. Gainesville: University of Florida Press, 2003.

————. *The Girl in the Tangerine Scarf*. New York: Carroll and Graf, 2006.

————. "Wedad's Cavalry." *Muslim Wake Up* website. Apr 10, 2005. http://www. muslimwakeup.com/sex/archives/2005/04/wedads_cavalry_1.php.

Kaldas, Pauline, and Khaled Mattawa, eds. *Dinarzad's Children: An Anthology of Contemporary Arab American Fiction*. Fayetteville: University of Arkansas Press, 2004.

Lalami, Laila. *Hope and Other Dangerous Pursuits*. Orlando: Harcourt, 2005.

Mack, Mehemmed. "Sex and the Freethinker." *LA Weekly* 3 Jan. 2007. http://www.laweekly. com/news/features/sex-and-the-freethinker/15330/.

Majaj, Lisa Suhair. Arab American Literature and the Politics of Memory. In *Memory and Cultural Politics: New Approaches to American Ethnic Literatures*. Amritjit Singh, Joseph Skerrett, and Robert E. Hogan, eds. Boston: Northeastern University Press, 1996. 266–90.

————. The Hyphenated Author: Emerging Genre of 'Arab-American Literature' Poses Questions of Definition, Ethnicity and Art." In *Al Jadid: A Review and Record of Arab Culture and Arts* 5 (Winter 1999): 26. http://leb.net/~aljadid/features/0526majaj.html.

————. New Directions: Arab American Writing at Century's End. In *Post-Gibran: An Anthology of New Arab American Writing*. Khaled Mattawa and Munir Akash, eds. Syracuse: Syracuse University Press, 1999. 67–77.

————. "Two Worlds Emerging: Arab-American Writing at the Crossroads." *Al Jadid: A Review and Record of Arab Culture and Arts* 3.16 (March 1997): 8–9.

————, Paula Sunderman, and Therese Saliba, eds. *Gender, Nation, and Community in Arab Women's Novels*. Syracuse: Syracuse University Press, 2002.

Malti-Douglas, Fedwa. Dangerous Crossings: Gender and Criticism in Arabic Literary Studies. In *Borderwork: Feminist Engagements with Comparative Literature*. Margaret Higgonet, ed. Ithaca: Cornell University Press, 1994: 224–26.

Mattawa, Khaled, and Munir Akash. Introduction. In *Post-Gibran: An Anthology of New Arab American Writing*. Khaled Mattawa and Munir Akash, eds. Syracuse: Syracuse University Press, 1999: xi–xiii.

Mehlem, D.H. *New York Poems*. Syracuse: Syracuse University Press, 2005.

Mehlem, D.H., and Leila Diab, eds. *A Different Path: An Anthology of the Radius of Arab American Writers*. Detroit: Ridgeway Press, 2000.

Nye, Naomi Shihab. "Bread." *Sycamore Review* 3:1. http://www.sla.purdue.edu/sycamore/v31-e2.html.

———. *Fuel.* Rochester: BOA Editions, 1998.

———. *Going, Going.* New York: Greenwillow, 2005.

———. The Gravities of Ancestry. In *Grape Leaves: A Century of Arab-American Poetry.* Gregory Orfalea and Sharif Elmusa, eds. New York: Interlink Books, 2000: 266.

———. *Never in a Hurry: Essays on People and Places.* Columbia: University of South Carolina Press, 1996.

———. Personal interview. June 6, 2000.

———. *Red Suitcase.* Brockport: BOA Editions, 1994.

———. *Sitti's Secrets.* New York: Four Winds Press/Macmillan, 1994.

———. "This Crutch That I Love: A Writer's Life, Past and Present," U.S. State Department. http://usinfo.state.gov/products/pubs/writers/nye.htm.

———. *Words Under the Words.* Portland, OR: Eighth Mountain Press, 1995.

———. *Yellow Glove.* Portland: Breitenbush Books, 1986.

———. *You & Yours.* Rochester, NY: BOA Editions, 2005.

———, comp. *The Space Between Our Footsteps: Poems and Paintings from the Middle East.* New York: Simon & Shuster Books for Young Readers, 1998.

———, comp. *This Same Sky: A Collection of Poems from Around the World.* New York: Four Winds Press/MacMillan, 1992.

———, comp. *What Have You Lost?* New York: Greenwillow, 1999.

Orfalea, Gregory, and Sharif Elmusa, eds. *Grape Leaves: A Century of Arab-American Poetry.* New York: Interlink Books, 2000

Said, Edward. *Culture and Imperialism.* New York: Alfred A. Knopf, 1993.

———. *Out of Place: A Memoir.* New York: Afred A. Knopf, 1999.

Shakir, Evelyn. "Arab American Literature." In *New Immigrant Literatures in the United States: A Sourcebook to Our Multicultural Literary Heritage.* Alpana Sharma Knippling, ed. Westport, CT: 1996: 3–18.

———. *Bint Arab: Arab and Arab American Women in the United States.* Westport, CT: Praeger. 1997.

Shalal-Esa, Andrea. "One Book at a Time." *Saudi Aramco World* 58.6 (2007). http://www.saudiaramcoworld.com/issue/200706/one.book.at.a.time.htm.

———. "Arab American Writer Is Ambassador to Middle East." December 19, 2006. *Reuters.*

Williams, David. *Far Sides of the Only World.* Durham, NC: Carolina Wren Press, 2004.

Further Reading

Arida, Holly, and Anan Ameri, eds. *Etching our Own Image: Voices from the Arab American Art Movement.* Newcastle: Cambridge Scholars Press, 2006 (forthcoming); Darraj, Susan Muaddi, ed. *Scheherazade's Legacy: Arab and Arab American Women on Writing;* Westport, CT: Praeger, 2004; Kaldas, Pauline, and Khaled Mattawa, eds. *Dinarzad's Children: An Anthology of Contemporary Arab American Fiction.* Fayetteville: University of Arkansas Press, 2004; Majaj, Lisa Suhair. "Of Stories and Storytellers." In *Saudi Aramco World.* March/April 2005: 24–35; Orfalea, Gregory. *The Arab Americans: A History.* Northampton, MA: Olive Branch Press, 2006; Radius of Arab American Writers Inc. Web site. http://rawi.org/index.html.

ANDREA SHALAL-ESA

ARTHURIAN LITERATURE

Definition. Arthurian tradition is like a mighty river: long, and wide, and deep.

It is long in that it stretches far back into the mists of time, some one and a half millennia, to when a military leader named Arthur (or some such variant spelling) may (or may not) have fought to preserve Britain against the invaders who came to plunder and settle after the departure of the Roman legions in the fifth century A.D. Moreover, many tributaries have flowed into this river, reaching back into even earlier eras. The love story of Tristan and Isolde and the Grail legend appear to have had an independent existence before they attached themselves to Arthurian tradition; and the stories told of Arthur and many of his warriors, as well as the figures themselves, may have sources in historical events and legends from Celtic lands and beyond, through continental Europe and the Middle East, and deep into the steppes of Asia (Lacy 1996, 17–21, 396–97).

It is wide in that it has found expression in most of the languages of Europe, and a few even beyond, and it has been carried throughout the world, wherever these languages are now spoken. It remains, however, one of the great ironies of a tradition that preserves many ancient cultures and tongues that it should find its strongest and most persistent voice in English, the language spoken by the tribes that were Arthur's most determined foes.

It is deep in that it has expanded into a bewildering range of literary forms, genres, and subgenres; it has yielded reams of scholarship and commentary, some scrupulously learned and some wildly speculative, some concerned only with historical "facts" and some with mystical significance; it has ventured into nonliterary forms of creative activity as well, including art, music, and games; and although the Arthurian element may be minor in some works, in many the legend is exhaustively re-created.

History

Early Development—The Middle Ages. The earliest references to Arthur and his champions appear in Latin chronicles and in Welsh poems and heroic tales during the Dark Ages. Four major developments, however, propelled the legend onto a wider stage. The first was Geoffrey of Monmouth's *History of the Kings of Britain,* a Latin chronicle composed around 1138. This includes the first extended account of Arthur's wars: defeating invaders at home; then conquering parts of Europe; and finally falling in the Battle of Camlann against his nephew Mordred, who had usurped the throne in his absence. This account proved very popular, and it spread the legend throughout Europe.

This international attention coincided with the evolution of a new literary form, the medieval romance, and the success of Arthurian legend was guaranteed when the greatest French master of the form, Chrétien de Troyes, made it the subject of his major poems in the latter part of the twelfth century. His example encouraged other poets to compose their own Arthurian romances, not only in French, but also in other languages, especially German. In the thirteenth century, romances also were written in prose, developing into great cycles. The romances switched attention from military campaigns and battles to the adventures of individual knights as they rode throughout Arthur's realm, jousting with adversaries, dining at castles, and righting wrongs. They also introduced two of the great themes of Arthurian romance: love, as exemplified by figures such as Tristan and Isolde, Lancelot and Guenevere; and the Grail quest, which inspired knights like Perceval and Galahad.

The third development was the emergence of Arthurian legend in English literature in the fourteenth century. The chronicles viewed Arthur as an English warrior-hero; the romances focused upon the exploits of his knights, especially his nephew Gawain. He is the hero of arguably the finest Arthurian romance, *Sir Gawain and the Green Knight.*

The fourth development was Sir Thomas Malory's *Morte d'Arthur* (completed about 1470). Not only did this work present the complete Arthurian story in very readable prose, but it had the good fortune not only to be written in an accessible dialect of English, and it was also one of the first works printed by William Caxton in 1485. It thus could reach a much wider audience than romances copied by hand.

Sixteenth to Nineteenth Centuries. As the Middle Ages gave way to the Renaissance, interest shifted to new literary forms, and the Arthurian legend, like its major vehicle the romance, fell out of favor. It languished until it was rediscovered in the nineteenth century during the Arthurian Revival. Alfred Lord Tennyson's poem *Idylls of the King* achieved wide popularity, and the legend was adapted, with mixed results, into the new forms of drama and opera. Its appearance in prose fiction, however, most notably Mark Twain's *A Connecticut Yankee in King Arthur's Court* (1889), marked the direction that it was destined to pursue with greatest success in the next century.

Twentieth Century. As the twentieth century advanced, the focus of Arthurian legend shifted from poetry and drama to prose fiction. Initially, the favored genre was historical fiction, in which Arthur was presented as either a sixth-century war leader or a monarch in the high medieval setting made popular in the romances. The great surge in the popularity of fantasy in the second half of the century, however, much of it written for younger readers, proved a boon to Arthurian tradition, for it permitted the inclusion of the magical elements that marked some of its best-loved figures and stories, such as Merlin and the Lady of the Lake, the Sword in the Stone, and the last voyage to Avalon.

The legend also spread into various other byways: it turns up in such subgenres asscience fiction, mystery fiction, historical romance, and time-shift novels; plays have rarely aroused much interest, but films for both cinema and television, sometimes animated, often with special effects to portray magic, have reached a wide audience; art is found most frequently as illustrations in books for children or in comics and graphic novels; games have followed fashion shifts, from board games, to role-playing games, and now interactive computer games (Lacy 1996, 97–98, 174–176, 590; Lacy and Thompson 2001, 204–205, 218; Thompson and Lacy 2005, 111–113).

Although the legend attracted some attention in other languages, particularly German, it has attained by far its greatest popularity in English, and increasingly that popularity has been created by North American authors. In part, this reflects the size of the American market. Moreover, a number of authors have been transplanted across the Atlantic in both directions, so that their national affiliation is ambivalent. It is well to remember, however, that trends within Arthurian literature may be initiated or augmented by authors who are from Britain, Australia, and elsewhere in the English-speaking world, as well as by translations from other languages; and these trends do influence authors in North America. For the legend it matters little, for Arthur's return from Avalon in the pages of literature ignores national distinctions.

Trends and Themes. Although the rise and fall of Arthur's kingdom remains a central concern, increasingly authors focus attention upon one figure in an attempt not only to impose some unity upon events, but also to reinterpret them from a fresh perspective. One of the ways to achieve this has been to give a voice to characters who might be considered overlooked or unjustly maligned in earlier accounts, and one such group is women. Moreover, because many Arthurian authors are themselves women, it is no surprise that they should wish to give a voice to their sisters.

Guinevere has achieved considerable popularity in recent years as a number of authors rally to the defense of the queen often blamed for the fall of the Round Table (Brewer 1991). Their books include not only Nancy McKenzie's *Queen of Camelot,* but also *The Dragon Queen* (2001) and *The Raven Warrior* (2003) by Alice Borchardt, and *Sword of the Rightful King* (2003) by Jane Yolen. Reflecting modern preferences, all three authors depict Guinevere as high spirited, independent, and noble minded: McKenzie makes her a skilled horsewoman as well as kind and modest; Borchardt portrays her as a mighty warrior and powerful Pictish queen; and Yolen has her travel to Arthur's court in the guise of a young boy so that she can avenge her heartbroken sister. There she becomes Merlinnus's assistant and the king's trusted advisor before foiling Morgause's plot to prevent Arthur from drawing the Sword from the Stone. When her true identity is revealed, she agrees to marry Arthur. Sara Maitland, by contrast, offers a more conventional portrait in "Foreplay" (2003), although the queen speaks her mind with a modern frankness. After failing to conceive an heir, Guinevere recognizes bitterly, "I had been the perfect wife for nothing" (Maitland 2003, 86), and she initiates an affair with Lancelot: "It was not love . . . it was lust" (79).

Nor has Guinevere been the only woman to attract the attention of authors. Sarah L. Thomson tells the Arthurian story from four points of view in *The Dragon's Son* (2001), and three of them are women: the wife of Myrddin (Merlin), Arthur's half-sister and wife Morgan, and a maidservant of another half-sister. Elsewhere, Morgan, the narrator of *I Am Morgan le Fay* (2001) by Nancy Springer, describes her early years, during which she developed both her supernatural powers and her enmity to Arthur (Thompson 1992, 231); Anna, Arthur's sister in the medieval chronicles, is the protagonist in *The King's Sister* (2000) by Kate Schafer; in Judith Tarr's "Finding the Grail" (2001), Beaumains turns out to be the disguise, not of Gawain's younger brother but his sister Elaine, and she finds the Grail among the holy women of the Isle of Avalon; and in Cabot's *Avalon High,* the witty narrator and female hero turns out to be none other than a modern reincarnation of the Lady of the Lake, much to everyone's surprise (including her own).

Men have, of course, continued to attract attention. Merlin is the protagonist of novels by King and Barron, and he plays an important role in many other novels and short stories (Goodrich 2002). For example, in Guler's *In the Shadow of Dragons,* he is a druid who helps his father and uncle (Ambrosius and Uther) against the plots of their enemies; in Mallory's *Merlin* trilogy, he helps Arthur to become king; and in Keith Taylor's "A Spear in the Night" (2002), he makes use of his foresight to trap an ambitious king who tries to poison the child Arthur. He also frequently makes a brief appearance as a convenient magic worker: in Jernigan's *Christmas in Camelot,* for example, he turns up in time to heal the mortally wounded hero and so allow a happy ending.

The encounters between Arthur's nephew Gawain and both the Green Knight and the Loathly Lady have proved a fruitful source of inspiration not only for Mitchell's free-wheeling retelling, but for other authors who have drawn upon them to initiate a series of novels. The former is the basis for *Ride South to Purgatory,* the first novel in Work's Keystone Ranch saga, and for Meredith Lahmann's *Sir Gawain and the Green Knight: The Quest* (2003). Lahmann includes the latter story in *Sir Gawain's Challenge* (2004), her second novel. In his *Squire's Tales* series, Morris reverses the sequence: the hero meets the Loathly Lady in his opening novel, *The Squire's Tale* (1998), and the Green Knight in his second, *The*

Squire, His Knight, and His Lady (1999). In later novels in the series, Gawain reappears, and he almost invariably displays kindness and good sense to those he meets; as in the medieval verse romances upon which most are based, he serves as an encouraging mentor and friend to the young protagonists, both male and female. Zettel also includes both motifs in *In Camelot's Shadow*. To these authors Gawain is an admirable figure, the noblest knight at Arthur's court despite Lancelot's preeminence. By drawing upon the medieval verse romances, they offer a welcome defense of a hero too long maligned in the prose romances of Sir Thomas Malory and his predecessors (Thompson 2006).

Gawain's half-brother and Arthur's nemesis, Mordred, has also proved a fascinating figure recently, not only to British authors such as Beric Norman in *Mordred's Version* (2005), but also to Nancy Springer, who wrote *I Am Mordred* (1998), and to Douglas Clegg, whose *Mordred, Bastard Son* (2006) announces itself as Book One of the *Mordred Trilogy*, a dark fantasy. Most fiction portrays Mordred as evil, driven by ambition and a desire for revenge, as does *The Book of the Stone* (2000), the fourth and concluding book of Diana Paxson's series *The Hallowed Isle*. Increasingly, however, authors try to present a more balanced view of his conduct, either by emphasizing his efforts to resist an inexorable fate or by shifting blame onto others, a tradition begun by Mary Stewart in *The Wicked Day* (1983). In Wein's *Coalition of Lions,* he even fights for, not against, Arthur at the last, fatal Battle of Camlann.

In *Grail Prince,* McKenzie thoughtfully reinterprets the story of Galahad's quest for the Grail and Spear, although it is only after he learns compassion and humility and seeks the forgiveness of his beloved (the sister of Perceval) and their child that he finally succeeds. He chooses, however, not "the glory of Britain," but "the loving embrace of his wife and child, the kingdom that awaited him, and the responsibilities that went with it . . . and without looking behind him, slipped back into the warmth of the world" (McKenzie 2003, 510). In *The Quest of the Fair Unknown* (2006), Morris adopts a humorous approach to Galahad's story. These two novels humanize the figure of Galahad, whose unswerving virtue on the quest for the Holy Grail irritates most modern readers. A typical response is found in "Me and Galahad" (2001) by Mike Resnick and Adrienne Gormley, who transpose the story to the American West: here an arrogant and sanctimonious Galahad fails to recognize the Grail when it is offered to him by a woman he considers inferior.

The love story of Tristan and Isolde attracted relatively little attention in fiction during the second half of the twentieth century, in part because it was "largely neglected by fantasy," the most prolific genre of Arthurian literature (Thompson 1985, 125). This situation changed at the beginning of the twenty-first century, however, when their love story inspired several works: the film *Tristan and Isolde;* the *Tristan and Isolde* trilogy by British author Rosalind Miles (2003–2004), and two works by American authors. In *Prince of Dreams,* McKenzie integrates the version found in the medieval prose romances with the characters and Dark Age setting she created in her earlier novels. By contrast, in his novella "The King in the Tree" (2003), Steven Millhauser draws upon verse tradition as he re-creates the intensity of the psychological impact of the lovers' affair on Mark (Lacy 1996, 463–465).

Less prominent figures have also sprung into the limelight in this century. Morris relates the adventures of Parsifal in *Parsifal's Page* (2001) and of Dinadan in *The Ballad of Sir Dinadan* (2003); and he amusingly reinterprets the story of how Gareth rescues Lyonesse in *The Savage Damsel and the Dwarf* (2000), how Lancelot rescues Guinevere in *The Princess, the Crone, and the Dung-Cart Knight* (2004), and how Ywain rescues Laudine in *The Lioness and Her Knight* (2005). Ywain's story also inspired Work's *Ride West to Dawn* and *Ride to Banshee Cañon*. Sarah Zettel imaginatively adapts the tale of Geraint and Enid in *For Camelot's Honor* (2005), her second Arthurian novel, and that of Gareth and Lynet in her third, *Under Camelot's Banner* (2006).

Sometimes, however, the narrator or central figure is invented rather than traditional. Guinevere provides Arthur with a spirited daughter in both Kemp's *Firebrand* (and a forthcoming sequel *The Recruit*) and Wein's *Coalition of Lions;* Karr relates the adventures of a minor knight of Arthur's realm in *The Follies of Sir Harald;* and in "The Fall of the Kingdom" (2001) by Mary Soon Lee, Guinevere's nursemaid confesses that it was she who told Arthur about her mistress's affair with Lancelot because she was angered by Guinevere's long years of self-centeredness.

Wein is not alone in carrying on the Arthurian story through survivors and successors: in "The Shadow of a Sword" (2000) by Ed Greenwood, Constantine refuses to give Excalibur to Morgan le Fay, returning it to the lake as Arthur ordered; in *Albion: The White Phantom* (2000) by Patrick McCormack, Bedwyr searches for Gwenhwyvar after Arthur's death; in *Rexcalibur* (2001) and *Eternity's Hope* (2001) by Mitzi Kleidon, descendants of the knights of the Round Table fight dark forces in an attempt to restore Camelot.

However, the links can stretch even farther. In *Kingdom of the Grail* (2000), Judith Tarr blends Arthurian legend with the story of Charlemagne when she makes Roland a shape-shifting descendant of Merlin and Nimue. After the disaster at Roncesvalles, he is taken to the Grail Castle to lead its warriors in the Grail War. Irene Radford has written an ongoing series entitled *Merlin's Descendants* (1999–), and Bertrice Small has written *The Dragon Lord's Daughters* (2004) about three descendants of an illegitimate son of Arthur. As events grow more distant in time, the Arthurian links in these historical romances become more tenuous.

Context and Issues

Poetry and Drama. Poetry on the Arthurian legend has dwindled over the years. Long poems have become rare, often confined to the pages of limited-run chapbooks or print-on-demand publications, such as *The Song of Sir Rod the Long* (2000) by Larry Howard, which describes itself as a rowdy, ribald novel in verse with a gay twist. Short poems do appear in poetry magazines, for example, Pamela Constantine's "The Royal Dream" (2001), and in such collections as Guy Gavriel Kay's *Beyond the Dark House* (2003), but they are few and far between. A favorite topic is love, both its dangers and delights.

Play scripts also continue to be written, but they are usually intended for children and performed in schools. More ambitious was the ballet *Merlin,* performed by the Atlantic Ballet Theatre of Canada in 2003, but drama only reached a wide audience in the form of film and television. Sometimes the Arthurian elements are no more than borrowings of objects such as Excalibur or characters such as Merlin, who appears, along with Morgan le Fay and reincarnations of Guenevere and Mordred, in the television series *Guinevere Jones* (2002). This Canadian/Australian co-production is set in a high school, as is Neil Mandt's *Arthur's Quest* (2000), in which Arthur is sent to the modern era through Merlin's magic. More often, however, modern figures return to the past, a tradition inspired by Mark

Twain's *Connecticut Yankee:* in Gil Junger's *Black Knight* (2001), after falling into a moat at a medieval theme park, a maintenance man resurfaces in medieval England and there encounters Perceval; in Derek Hayes's *Otherworld* (2002), when three teenagers in modern Wales investigate an underwater island, they find themselves reliving events drawn from several medieval Welsh tales.

The grittily imagined Dark Ages are the setting for three more ambitious films: a two-part telefilm *The Mists of Avalon* (Turner Television, 2001), *King Arthur* (Touchstone Pictures, 2004), and *Tristan and Isolde* (Twentieth Century Fox, 2006). The first is based upon Marion Zimmer Bradley's popular fantasy, while the other two offer what are intended to be historically plausible accounts of Arthur's rise to power after the withdrawal of the Roman legions and the doomed relationship of the lovers, respectively. Reviews have been unenthusiastic. Television series have also spawned novelizations, such as James Mallory's trilogy *Merlin* (1998–2000) based on the miniseries of the same name.

Prose Fiction. By far the most prolific literary form of Arthurian legend since the nineteenth century is prose fiction, in the form of the short story and novel. The former has received a substantial boost since 1988 from the publication of anthologies specifically devoted to the legend (Thompson and Lacy 2005, 100), and although the trend seems to be waning, it has continued into the twenty-first century with *The Doom of Camelot* (2000) and *Legends of the Pendragon* (2002), both edited by James Lowder, and *Out of Avalon* (2001), edited by Jennifer Roberson. Novels remain as popular as ever, thanks in part to the development of print-on-demand publication. Moreover, authors who treat the legend are increasingly likely to expand to a trilogy, as did Bernard Cornwell in his Grail Quest series (2000–2003), or to embark on an even longer series. Jack Whyte's Arthurian cycle eventually extended to nine long novels (1992–2005); the Squire's Tales series by Gerald Morris numbers nine and counting (1998–); and although the Arthurian element is usually confined to the frame for the protagonists' adventures, Mary Pope Osborne's popular Magic Tree House series of first-chapter books for early readers currently extends to 36 books.

Retellings. Prose fiction can be divided into various categories (Thompson 1985, 4–6). Retellings, usually for children, adapt and abbreviate the familiar stories from Malory and the romances into modern, often simplified, English. Many of those currently available are reprints, but new versions continue to appear as publishers seek to tap fresh markets—by providing lavish illustrations, as does *King Arthur's Knight Quest* (2005) by Andy Dixon, with full-page illustrations by Simone Boni, and by employing language considered suitable for particular age groups, as does Jane Bo Mason's *King Arthur* (2005) from Scholastic Press, which is aimed at readers aged 9 to 12. Sometimes the Arthurian stories are set within a frame provided by a figure from the past, such as Merlin or Arthur, who tells his story to modern children. In *The Dragon Stone* (2001) and *A Cup of Kindness* (2003) by John Conlee, however, the story is told by Cabal, Arthur's dog. In *Sir Gawain's Little Green Book* (2000), which is intended for adult readers, Mark J. Mitchell allows Gawain considerable freedom to comment upon his feelings and conduct when he tells us about his encounters with both the Green Knight and the Loathly Lady.

Realistic Fiction. Realistic fiction introduces the Arthurian story into the modern world without recourse to fantasy, and it is divided into two main groups: mystery thrillers and modern transpositions. The former are rare, but Amy Myers does include descendants of King Arthur in her short story "The Rightful King of

England" (2002). Brown's *The Da Vinci Code* is constructed around a modern quest for the Holy Grail, although it turns out to be the bloodline of Jesus through his offspring with Mary Magdalene (Lacy 2004).

Interestingly, the twenty-first century has seen the sudden emergence of transpositions of Arthurian legend in the form of American westerns. James C. Work sets his ongoing Keystone Ranch saga in Wyoming, where Art Pendragon and his wife Gwen, owners of the biggest ranch in the territory, dream of order and justice in the West. *Ride South to Purgatory* (1999) recasts the English fourteenth-century romance *Sir Gawain and the Green Knight*; *Ride West to Dawn* (2001) and *Ride to Banshee Cañon* (2002) deal with the story of Yvain/Owain; *The Dead Ride Alone* (2004) is based upon Tennyson's poem "The Lady of Shalott"; and *Riders of Deathwater Valley* (2005) adapts from the twelfth-century poem *Lancelot* by Chrétien de Troyes the tale of Guenevere's abduction. In *Code of the West* (2001), Aaron Latham focuses on the figure of Arthur himself and includes many familiar motifs: he is fostered by Indians, taught by the tribal shaman (Merlin), draws an ax (sword) from an anvil, and acquires a wife and a first hand (Guinevere and Lancelot), whose love is disclosed by a man (Mordred) claiming to be his son by his cousin. His second novel, *Cowboy with the Tiffany Gun* (2003), is a very loose adaptation of the story of Percival's quest for the Holy Grail. Although much of the interest in these novels lies in the ingenuity with which they adapt traditional Arthurian material to a new context, both authors are careful to maintain the credibility of the setting.

Historical Fiction. As these novels demonstrate, American authors are understandably interested in their own history, but this focus has led them to pay less attention to that of others. As a consequence, historical novels about King Arthur are more likely to be written by authors from Britain or elsewhere in Europe. The two most prolific authors of Arthurian historical fiction in this century are Bernard Cornwell and Jack Whyte. The former, who wrote the Warlord Chronicles (1995–97) and the Grail Quest series (2000–2003), is English, although he now lives part of the time in the United States; the latter, who wrote an Arthurian cycle (1992–2005), was born in Scotland and only emigrated to Canada as an adult. Cornwell's Grail Quest trilogy follows the adventures of an English archer during the Hundred Years War against France. The search for the Holy Grail is less important, to both the hero and the author, than the campaigns against the French and the Scots, although it forms a useful narrative link for his adventures. Whyte's first six novels tell the history of the post-Roman colony of Camulod, mainly through the eyes of Merlyn; *Uther* (2000) revisits and expands upon part of the story from the point of view of Uther, the father of Arthur; in *Clothar the Frank* (2003, published in the United States as *The Lance Thrower*, 2004) and in *The Eagle* (2005), Clothar (Lancelot) brings the sprawling narrative to a conclusion. The novels offer plenty of battle scenes and fast-paced action, but the care with which both authors construct their settings is indicative of their attention to historical research into each period.

When American authors do explore Arthurian legend through historical fiction, they are inclined to introduce elements of fantasy into the story. This is the case with Nancy McKenzie's trilogy: two earlier novels about Guinevere, *The Child Queen* (1994) and *The High Queen* (1995), were revised and published as a single volume, *Queen of Camelot* (2002); *Grail Prince* (2003) deals with Galahad's quest for the Grail and Spear; *Prince of Dreams* (2004) tells the tragic story of the love between Tristan and Essylte. Into what is essentially historical fiction, McKenzie introduces features such as Merlin's second sight, Galahad's mystical visions of the Grail and

Arthur, and the magical love potion that binds Tristan and Essylte. Throughout the trilogy, McKenzie examines the vulnerability of women in a violent and patriarchal society, where those who lack protectors may be beaten and raped, by brutal husbands as well as lustful suitors. Debra A. Kemp presents an even darker picture of the suffering of female slaves in *The Firebrand* (2003), which describes the savage mistreatment of King Arthur's daughter at the hands of Morgause and Modred. In *A Coalition of Lions* (2003) by Elizabeth Wein, however, Arthur's daughter finds a kindly welcome when she journeys to the African kingdom of Aksum (Ethiopia). Kathleen Cunningham Guler also adds supernatural elements, such as her heroine's gift of visions, into her ongoing Macsen's Treasure series (1998–), which is set in the years before Arthur's reign. In the author's notes to the second novel, *In the Shadow of Dragons* (2001), she defends the use of this "bit of mysticism" as part of the beliefs of the age, although she admits, "To some, the visions may represent an element of fantasy" (11).

Science Fiction. Although Arthurian legend is, by and large, unsuited to treatment as science fiction (Thompson 1985, 77), it does figure occasionally in two types of stories: those that provide alien origins for some of its elements, and those that involve time travel. Robert Doherty has written Area 51, an action-packed series about the struggle of humanity against predatory aliens. In *Area 51: The Grail* (2001) and *Area 51: Excalibur* (2002), it is revealed that the Grail and Excalibur are powerful devices of alien origin; in *Area 51: The Truth* (2003), Arthur and Mordred are discovered to represent rival alien factions; and *Area 51: Legend* (2004) follows the lives of the two characters known to later ages as Gawain and Morgana, from their extraterrestrial origins and voyage to Earth, through the fall of Atlantis, down the millennia to the Battle of Camlann. Their longevity is preserved by an alien device that transfers their personalities to new bodies grown from their own DNA.

In *For King and Country* (2002) by Robert Asprin and Linda Evans, the fifth novel in their Time Scout series, a captain in the British special forces follows an Irish Republican terrorist and an Ulster Protestant extremist back in time to the sixth century in order to prevent them disrupting history and changing present conditions. There the three find themselves sharing with the original characters the bodies of Ancelotis (Lancelot), Morgana, and the minstrel Lailoken, respectively. Ancelotis and Morgana form an alliance to help Artorius against the plotting of his half-sister Morguase and her protégé Corianna Nim (Nimue) that culminates at the Battle of Badon.

Fantasy. By far the most popular genre for Arthurian fiction is fantasy. That this should prove the case is no surprise given the tenacity of such supernatural elements as Arthur's sword Excalibur, the Grail, and the love potion that binds Tristan and Isolde; and the magical powers of Merlin, Morgan le Fay, and the Lady of the Lake. Throughout the pages of medieval romance, moreover, lurk giants and dragons, shape-shifters and talking beasts, sorcerers and faery folk from the Other World, waiting to test the mettle of Arthur's knights as they ride forth from the Round Table in search of adventure.

Amid so many works, it is helpful to subdivide the genre further into three categories: mythic, ironic, and heroic.

Mythic Fantasy. In mythic fantasy. the primary battle is waged between the forces of good and evil, often represented as light and dark. A striking example of this category is J. Robert King's trilogy, *Mad Merlin* (2000), *Lancelot du Lethe* (2001), and *Le Morte d'Avalon* (2003), in which the war between their followers mirrors the war between the gods, with the Norse gods and the more malevolent older gods of Britain ranged against most of the Celtic gods and nature spirits. Merlin himself is none other than a fallen Jupiter who has lost most of his power.

T.A. Barron's *The Lost Years of Merlin* (1996–2000), a series for younger readers, also presents a clash between good and evil. The series recounts the untraditional adventures that befall Merlin during his childhood years in the legendary Isle of Fincayra, and in the fifth and concluding novel, *The Wings of Merlin* (2000), evil is at last vanquished by the sacrifice and love of the Fincayrans, who put their mutual hostilities aside in order to battle the external threat. Merlin's experiences enable him to develop both the magical powers and wisdom that will serve him later when he meets Arthur. Barron's trilogy *The Great Tree of Avalon* (2004–2006) continues the struggle between good and evil in the world of Avalon, but Arthurian figures such as Merlin and the Lady of the Lake make only infrequent appearances.

Ironic Fantasy. The high-minded ideals of Arthur and his knights, although admirable, do have their comical side, and when this perception dominates the approach to the material, the fiction falls into the category of ironic fantasy. American humorists have enjoyed deflating the pretensions of the Arthurian aristocracy since Twain's *Connecticut Yankee,* and Thomas Berger's *Arthur Rex* (1978) was one of the finest Arthurian novels of the last century. In this century, American authors have followed in their predecessors' footsteps. Esther M. Friesner has written many humorous short stories, and in 2000 she collected several in *Up the Wall,* including "Articles of Faith." Here the Grail's inherent virtue frustrates a demonic plot to steal it, but a later story, "In Days of Old" (2002), offers a scurrilous account of the deception that leads to the Quest for the Holy Grail; in *The Follies of Sir Harald* (2001), Phyllis Ann Karr explores the humor inherent in the conventions of medieval romance; and in *The Squire's Tales,* a series for younger readers, Morris continues to find a rich source of comedy in such romance conventions as love and chivalry. By contrast, it is not Arthurian romance but the attitudes of teenage high-school students that Meg Cabot mocks in *Avalon High* (2006).

Heroic Fantasy. Most Arthurian fantasies belong to this category in which the heroes, as in medieval romance, prove their worth by overcoming various challenges. Sometimes these figures are traditional, whether a major character such as Guinevere or Merlin, or one who is less well known, such as Arthur's sister Anna or the sister of Gawain. Often, however, the characters are invented by the author to serve as convenient narrators or to experience adventures in their own right. These adventures may occur within Arthur's court or at a distance, both in space and time. Occasionally, the latter are set before the establishment of Arthur's realm, preparing for what will happen, but more often they take place later, involving descendants and reincarnations of Arthurian figures, or artifacts such as Excalibur and the Grail.

One popular subgenre of heroic fantasy is the romantic novel (Thompson 2004; Romance, 467). Sometimes the story is set in Arthur's day, as in *Christmas in Camelot* (2002) by Brenda K. Jernigan and in Sarah Zettel's *In Camelot's Shadow* (2004); sometimes the story is set in the present and features characters who are reincarnations of their Arthurian predecessors, as in Cabot's ironic fantasy *Avalon High.* The conventions of the genre follow the Cinderella pattern: the quest of the heroine is "to dodge her father, and if not kill at any rate pretty severely neutralise her mother, and make it possible for her man to get her" (Brewer 1980, 9). Although the father and mother figures may be displaced and their role played by others, their control must be broken and obstacles overcome if the heroine is to find true love

---

KING ARTHUR IN THE TWENTY-FIRST CENTURY

Arthurian literature in America is alive and well in the twenty-first century. Some authors are as likely to owe a debt to a role-playing game or a film as they are to a medieval romance; others may have been inspired by John Waterhouse's nineteenth-century painting of the Lady of Shalott, or by *Camelot,* the 1960 musical by Frederick Loewe and Alan Jay Lerner; and Dan Brown, author of the best-selling novel *The Da Vinci Code* (2003), makes use of theories about the Holy Grail that were articulated in *Holy Blood, Holy Grail* (1982), a speculative history by Michael Baigent, Richard Leigh, and Henry Lincoln.

Nor has Arthurian literature shown signs of losing its popularity. Indeed the proliferation of new literary genres and subgenres, as well as the advent of electronic media (especially the computer), has spurred creative activity in the field of publishing and in forms such as films and games, including the 2004 movie *King Arthur* and the continued popularity of *Monty Python and the Holy Grail* (1975) (Thompson and Lacy 2005, 100).

---

with the partner of her choice. This pattern does, in fact, underlie virtually all Arthurian fiction that includes romantic love, but in romantic fiction the conventions are more noticeable, sometimes even formulaic.

Reception. Arthurian literature in this century continues developments that emerged in the last, including the focus on prose fiction and filling in the gaps in earlier accounts. This entails a fuller description of both the cultural and geographical setting (Thompson 2004; Sense), for although medieval genres like the romance usually paid scant attention to background details, readers of the novel have different expectations. They also expect a fuller and more realistic characterization of both major and minor figures. Servants and peasants must be people with feelings, not a shadowy presence; villains must have motivation; women and children must be both seen and heard. One result is a more critical assessment of the dominant hierarchy of Arthur's realm, as those excluded from power are given a voice. Another is the projection of modern social values onto figures in the past: women are much more likely to be active rather than passive figures, as the proliferation of warrior queens attests, and although they still welcome worthy partners, they are ready to go out and find them, not quietly accept their parents' choice; heroes reveal a sensitive as well as an aggressive side, readily deferring to their talented partners; children give witness to neglect or abuse and to its consequences later in life; heroes are flawed, and villains struggle against their darker impulses (Thompson 2002, 97).

This may distort history, but it is a pattern that Arthurian literature has adopted throughout the ages, shaping itself to reflect prevailing attitudes and concerns. It is, moreover, the main reason that the legend has continued to appeal to each generation, despite the changes that have transformed the world since its inception.

Selected Authors

Quests. Another device through which authors extend the range of Arthurian legend is the quest for artifacts, the most famous of which are Excalibur and the Grail. The former appears before it comes into Arthur's possession in Barron's *Wings of Merlin,* Doherty's Area 51 series, and Valerie Frankel's "Tea and Company" (2002), in which Merlin promises to return and live with Niniane under her lake if she will give Arthur the sword and scabbard. In "Metal and a Man of Good Heart" (2002),

Lee Martindale describes the forging of both the sacred sword and chalice during the Roman era. In *The Anvil Stone* (2006), Kathleen Cunningham Guler makes the sword one of the five ceremonial symbols used by the high kings of Britain and sets the quest to find it before the birth of Arthur.

The Grail has yielded even more fiction (Thompson 2000; Lupack 2002), most famously perhaps Brown's *The Da Vinci Code*. As an artifact rather than a bloodline, however, the Grail has been sought in many places throughout the ages: in the Middle East during the Crusades in Stephen R. Lawhead's *The Mystic Rose* (2001); in France and England during the Hundred Years War in Cornwell's Grail Quest series; and in the American West during the nineteenth century in "Me and Galahad" by Resnick and Gormley.

Sometimes the quest can be for a place rather than an object. Avalon is sought not only in short poems, in which it is conceived as an ideal place removed from the stress of a busy world, but also in fiction. In *Priestess of Avalon* (2001) by Marion Zimmer Bradley and Diana L. Paxson, the protagonist trains in Avalon as a priestess long before Arthur's day; in "The Heart of the Hill" (2001) by the same two authors, Morgaine recalls an episode in her early training there; and in "Avalonia" (2001) by Kristen Britain, an American tourist's visit to Glastonbury inspires her own work as a biologist at a wildlife refuge in a modern Avalon. Barron, meanwhile, has completed *Great Tree of Avalon* (2004–2006), another fantasy trilogy for younger readers set in the world of Avalon.

Timeslip Fiction. Since Twain's *Connecticut Yankee,* authors, like filmmakers, have played with the idea of sending a character from the present back to Arthur's day. Asprin and Evans accomplished the journey by means of a mechanical device, but more often supernatural powers are invoked. In "A Connecticut Welshman in Artognov's Court" (2001) by Peter T. Garratt, a young American physicist of Welsh descent travels back to Arthur's time and tries to alter history by helping fight the Saxons; Angelica Harris sends an American woman and her family to the Arthurian past in *The Quest for Excalibur* (2001) and *Excalibur and the Holy Grail* (2002); in Osborne's Magic Tree House series, Morgan le Fay and Merlin use their magic to send two children on exciting learning adventures in different places and ages, including Arthur's Camelot in *Christmas in Camelot* (2001).

Sometimes the journey is goes forward in time, as characters from the past travel to the future. In *Charmed: The Legacy of Merlin* (2001) by Eloise Flood, a novel based on the television series, modern druids bring Merlin's son into the twenty-first century. More often, however, characters from the Arthurian past appear in modern times because they are either magically long-lived or else reincarnations. Magical powers preserve Morgan le Fay and Merlin (who lives backwards in time) in Peter David's *Knight Life* (2002) and its sequel *One Knight Only* (2003); in a series of short stories, including "The Final Score" (2000), which is set at a medieval fair in Oklahoma, Bradley H. Sinor transforms Lancelot into a vampire who does not age (the vampire from whom he contracted the condition was, we are told in an earlier story, none other than Guinevere herself).

Reincarnation is the most common device for making characters from the past available to a later era. In David's two books, the other Arthurian characters, who include Arthur and Guinevere, Lancelot and Percival, are all reincarnations; as part of the cycle of their eternal return, several Arthurian figures appear in Renee Bennett's "The Fey" (2000); a modern Guinevere is the central figure in Andre Norton's "Ravenmere" (2001); in Trevor Denyer's "Glastonbury" (2000), Joseph of Arimathea is reincarnated to prepare for the return of the king; and in "Artie's Angels" (2001) by Catherine Wells, Arthur and Morgan, reborn into a post-apocalyptic future, start a bicycle gang dedicated to protecting their community.

Fiction for Younger Readers. One of the most entertaining books that make use of Arthurian reincarnations is Cabot's *Avalon High,* which is written for a teenage audience, and a large proportion of Arthurian fiction is, in fact, directed at younger readers: illustrated retellings for the youngest; stories, both old and new, in simplified language for early readers; and exciting adventures for the adolescent market. The presence of young protagonists, the often explicit effort to instruct readers about conditions in the past and right conduct in any age, and the avoidance of difficult issues such as incest, are some of the traits of this material, which has been helpfully surveyed in *Adapting the Arthurian Legends for Children* (Lupack 2004). Because they focus on the childhood years of the characters, these books have filled in an area neglected in medieval accounts, which jump from birth to early adulthood.

Bibliography

Asprin, Robert, and Evans, Linda. *For King and Country.* Riverdale, NY: Baen, 2002.

Barron, T.A. *The Wings of Merlin.* New York: Philomel Books, 2000.

Brewer, Derek. *Symbolic Stories: Traditional Narratives of the Family Drama in English Literature.* London: Brewer, 1980.

Brewer, Elisabeth. The Figure of Guenevere in Modern Drama and Fiction. In *Arturus Rex: Acta Conventus Lovaniensis 1987.* Willy Van Hoecke, Gilbert Tournoy, and Werner Verbeke, eds. Leuven: University Press, 1991. Reprinted in *Arthurian Women: A Casebook.* Thelma S. Fenster, ed. New York: Garland, 1996.

Brown, Dan. *The Da Vinci Code.* New York: Doubleday, 2003.

Cabot, Meg. *Avalon High.* New York: HarperCollins, 2006.

Doherty, Robert. *Area 51: Legend.* New York: Bantam Dell, 2004.

Goodrich, Peter H. Merlin in the Twenty-First Century. In *New Directions in Arthurian Studies.* Alan Lupack, ed. Cambridge: Brewer, 2002; 149–162.

Gormley, Adrienne, and Resnick, Mike. "Me and Galahad." *Out of Avalon.* Jennifer Roberson and Mark H. Greenberg, eds. New York: ROC, 2001; 209–219.

Guler, Kathleen Cunningham. *In the Shadow of Dragons.* Steamboat Springs, CO: Bardsong, 2001.

King, J. Robert. *Le Morte d'Avalon.* New York: St. Martins, 2004.

Lacy, Norris J., et al., eds. *The New Arthurian Encyclopedia.* New York: Garland, 1996.

———. *The Da Vinci Code:* Dan Brown and the Grail That Never Was. *Arthuriana* 14.3 (2004): 81–93.

———, and Raymond H. Thompson, eds. Arthurian Literature, Art, and Film, 1995–1999. In *Arthurian Literature XVIII.* Keith Busby, ed. Cambridge: Brewer, 2001.

Latham, Aaron. *Code of the West.* New York: Simon and Schuster, 2001.

———. *Cowboy with the Tiffany Gun.* New York: Simon and Schuster, 2003.

Lupack, Alan. "A Very Secondary Position": Perceval in Modern English and American Literature. In *Perceval/Parzival: A Casebook.* Arthur Groos and Norris J. Lacy, eds. New York: Routledge, 2002.

Lupack, Barbara, ed. *Adapting the Arthurian Legends for Children: Essays on Arthurian Juvenilia.* New York: Palgrave Macmillan, 2004.

Maitland, Sara. Foreplay. In *On Becoming a Fairy Godmother.* London: Maia, 2003.

Malory, Thomas. *Le Morte d'Arthur.* London: Cassell Illustrated, 2003.

McKenzie, Nancy. *Grail Prince.* New York: Ballantine, 2003.

Thompson, Raymond H. *The Return from Avalon: A Study of the Arthurian Legend in Modern Fiction.* Westport, CT: Greenwood, 1985.

————. The First and Last Love: Morgan le Fay and Arthur. In *The Arthurian Revival*. Debra Mancoff, ed. New York: Garland, 1992.

————. The Grail in Modern Fiction: Sacred Symbol in a Secular Age. In *The Grail: A Casebook*. Dhira B. Mahoney, ed. New York: Garland, 2000.

————. Darkness over Camelot: Enemies of the Arthurian Dream. In *New Directions in Arthurian Studies*. Alan Lupack, ed. Cambridge: Brewer, 2002.

————. The Sense of Place in Arthurian Fiction for Younger Readers. In *Adapting the Arthurian Legends for Children: Essays on Arthurian Juvenilia*. Barbara Lupack, ed. New York: Palgrave, 2004.

————. Twentieth-Century Arthurian Romance. In *A Companion to Romance: From Classical to Contemporary*. Corinne Saunders, ed. Oxford: Blackwell, 2004.

————. Gawain in Post-Medieval English Literature. In *Gawain: A Casebook*. Raymond H. Thompson and Keith Busby, eds. New York: Routledge, 2006.

————, and Norris J. Lacy, eds. The Arthurian Legend in Literature, Popular Culture, and the Performing Arts, 1999–2004. In *Arthurian Literature XXII*. Keith Busby and Roger Dalrymple, eds. Cambridge: Brewer, 2005.

Mckenzie, Nancy. *Queen of Camelot*. New York: Ballantine, 2002.

————. *Grail Prince*. New York: Del Ray, 2003.

Mitchell, Mark J. *Sir Gawain's Little Green Book*. Philadelphia, PA: Xlibris, 2000.

Osborne, Mary Pope. *Christmas in Camelot*. New York: Random House, 2001.

Tarr, Judith. *Kingdom of the Grail*. New York: ROC, 2000.

Whyte, Jack. *The Eagle*. New York: Forge, 2007.

Work, James C. *Ride South to Purgatory*. Unity, ME: Five Star, 1999.

Zettel, Sarah. *In Camelot's Shadow*. New York: Luna, 2004.

Further Reading

Harty, Kevin J., ed. *Cinema Arthuriana: Twenty Essays*. Jefferson, NC: McFarland, 2002; Lupack, Alan C. "Merlin as New-World Wizard." In *Merlin: A Casebook*. Peter H. Goodrich and Raymond H. Thompson, eds. New York: Routledge, 2003, pp. 230–249; Lupack, Alan, and Barbara Tepa Lupack. *King Arthur in America*. Cambridge: Brewer, 1999; Thompson, Raymond H. "The Enchanter Awakes: Merlin in Modern Fiction." In *Merlin: A Casebook*. Peter H. Goodrich and Raymond H. Thompson, eds., pp. 250–262; Thompson, Raymond H. "Rationalizing the Irrational: Merlin and His Prophecies in the Modern Historical Novel." *Arthuriana* 10.1 (Spring 2000); 116–126.

RAYMOND H. THOMPSON

ASIAN AMERICAN LITERATURE

Definition. Asian American literature refers to writings in English by Americans with cultural and ethnic origins in East Asia, South Asia, and Southeast Asia. The term *Asian American* was coined during the civil rights movement of the 1960s. During that movement, Asian ethnic community activists and college students strove to unify isolated Asian ethnicities into a political and cultural solidarity for racial equality and social justice in the United States. The term "implies that there can be a communal consciousness and a unique culture that is neither Asian nor American, but Asian American" (Wei 1993, 1). Emerging as a distinctive genre in the wake of the civil rights movement, Asian American literature is primarily defined as "published creative writings in English by Americans of Chinese, Japanese, Korean, and Filipino descent" (Kim 1982, xi). However, like its modifier "Asian American," which initially designated national origins in such East Asian countries as China, Japan, and Korea but has now been widely used to accommodate other Asian ethnic groups from South and Southeast Asian countries, Asian American literature has "broadened to include writings by Americans of Bangladeshi, Burmese, Cambodian, Chinese, Filipino, Japanese, Korean, Indian, Indonesian, Laotian, Nepali, Pakistani, Sri Lankan, Thai, and Vietnamese descent" (Cheung 1997, 3). This expansion is in response to the development of Asian American communities as a result of the influx of immigrants from those countries in the past three decades or so.

In addition to representing multicultural Americans' lives, especially those of the underrepresented, Asian American writers, from their earliest manifestations to contemporary expressions, have inevitably confronted their cultural origins and presented perspectives that are foreign to the American mainstream. Yet, writing about different racial memories and ethnic experiences of Asian immigrants as well as their second, third, or even fourth and fifth generations in the United States should be considered part of American literature, which is, or should be, multifaceted and is supposed to reflect the pluralistic American society. Indeed, Asian American literature has battled to be recognized as part of American literary tradition. Maxine Hong Kingston, one of the most celebrated Asian American writers, for example, once asserted a strong resistance to being considered as writing stories of the "other":

> Actually I think that my books are much more American than they are Chinese. I felt that I was building, creating myself and these people as American people. . . . Even though they have strange Chinese memories, they are American people. Also, I am creating part of American literature, and I was aware of doing that, of adding to American literature. The critics haven't recognized my work enough as another tradition of American literature. (qtd. in Rabinowitz 1987, 182)

A branch of American literature now, Asian American literature is taught in American educational institutes and studied in scholarships as such. Moreover, recently the rubric of Asian American literature has actually stretched to denote writings in English by Asian diasporic residents in North America, including Canada (Ty and Goellnicht 2004, 2) and Hawaii (Lim and Ling1992, 4). For the sake of clarity, however, discussion of Asian American literature in this chapter is basically confined to writings in English about existential experiences in the United States by Americans with cultural and ethnic origins in East Asia, South Asia, and Southeast Asia, and in accordance with current practice in the field, writings exclusively on non-American experiences by Asian Americans, such as Ha Jin and Nien Cheng, are not included.

History. Although defined in the 1960s, the origin of Asian American literature can be traced to the turn of the twentieth century. Edith Maude Eaton, a Eurasian also known as Sui Sin Far, is generally regarded as the first Asian American writer. Writing about Chinese American lives in a social context of intense Sinophobia in the early twentieth century, Eaton's autobiographical and fictional writings manifested racial oppression in her contemporary American society. Moreover, the issue of ethnic identity, an issue frequently recurring throughout Asian American literature, was embedded unavoidably in her writing. The fiercely racist environment presented in Eaton's works and those of other early Asian American writers, such as Younghill Kang, a Korean American, continued to appear in mid-century Asian American writings when the demographics and numbers of Asian Americans were limited due to restriction policies of the United States government on immigration (Lawrence and Cheung 2005, 15). Two representative writers of this period are Carlos Bulosan, a Filipino American, and John Okada, a Japanese American. Both lived and wrote in the period of the Great Depression through World War II and the Cold War, and they attempted to confront American society through their oft-gendered exploration of identity and depiction of psychological wounds of racial violence and discrimination.

Along with the emergence of an Asian American consciousness during the 1960s and an influx of immigrants from the Philippines, China, Korea, and India in the post-1960s due to the relaxation of immigration laws (Lowe 1996, 7), the 1960s and 1970s witnessed a distinct and prolific development of Asian American literature. Louis Chu's 1961 novel, *Eat a Bowl of Tea,* is an authentic portrayal of the Chinatown culture in which he grew up. In the 1970s, a few distinctive collections of Asian American creative writings were published, such as *Asian-American Authors* (1972), edited by Kai-yu Hsu and Helen Palubinskas, which comprises works by two generations of Chinese, Japanese, and Filipino American writers, and *Aiiieeeee! An Anthology of Asian American Writers* (1974), edited by Frank Chin, Jeffery Paul Chan, Lawson Fusao Inada, and Shawn Wong, a collection of works by American-born Asian Americans. However, other works reflected the Asian American experience of the time, such as Frank Chin's play entitled *The Chickencoop Chinaman* (1972) and Maxine Hong Kingston's influential work, *The Woman Warrior: Memoirs of a Girlhood among Ghosts* (1976). In depicting lives of their contemporary Asian Americans who still "share common experiences of immigration, discrimination, acculturation, conflict, and generational strains," and whose "originating cultures set then apart from the dominant Euro-American ones" (Lim and Ling 1992, 4), writings by these Asian American writers either interrogate or seek answers to problems of ethnicity. To a great extent, particular issues such as ethnic or cultural identities, which Amy Ling theorizes as "between worlds," are strongly and sensitively represented by these writers (Ling 1990, v). Moreover, in reifying this identity, most authors and their characters adopted strategies of resistance rather than accommodation.

Landmarks of Asian American Literature. Following are principal works by influential Asian American writers whose works were published before the 1980s.

Edith Eaton's "Leaves from the Mental Portfolio of an Eurasian" (1909). Edith Maude Eaton (1865–1914) was born in England to an English father and a Chinese mother. She traveled widely first with her family, who moved in 1872 from England to New York then to Montreal, and later by herself mainly between Canada and many cities in the United States.

Published under the pen name Sui Sin Far (meaning "Chinese lily"), Edith Eaton's literary output was small. Yet of her fictional and biographical works, the 1909 autobiography titled "Leaves from the Mental Portfolio of an Eurasian" has drawn critical attention. In this seven-or-so-paged autobiographical essay that chronicled her experiences from age four to forty, Eaton provided the reader with sincere and straightforward sketches of her life, which included experiences with racist bigotry and prejudice in a hostile social environment. From her childhood, Eaton frequently involved herself in direct confrontation of racism. The word "battle" is often used in the autobiographical essay, as Amy Ling notes, and is "initially in a literal sense and later figuratively" (Ling 1990, 35): "They pull my hair, they tear my clothes, they scratch my face, and all but lame my brother; but the white blood in our veins fights valiantly for the Chinese half of us" (qtd. in Ling 1990, 35). Although often suffering pain as a Eurasian woman who was neither Chinese nor Caucasian and who would try to be "'invisible' and attempt to 'pass,'" or preferably be mistaken, as a lady of the more fortunate Japanese (White-Parks 1995, 81; 39), Eaton took her mixed heritage and diverse readership as advantages. She strongly sensed the middle space between her Europeanness and Chineseness, no matter how insignificant it might be for others, and made efforts to connect the two by building a bridge over it. Furthermore, in her autobiographical writing Eaton embraced her Chinese heritage and established an ethnic consciousness and pride. The Chinese, as she wrote in the essay, were grateful for her efforts in asserting and defending her Chinese ethnicity in her writing: "My heart leaps for joy when I read one day an article signed by a New York Chinese in which he declares 'The Chinese in America owe an everlasting debt of gratitude to Sui Sin Far for the bold stand she has taken in their defense'" (qtd. in Ling 1990, 32).

Writing half a century before distinctive Asian American writers such as Louis Chu and Maxine Hong Kingston, Eaton offered an early voice to Asian American literature—in doing so, she was sometimes joined by her younger sister Winnifred Eaton (1875–1955), who, writing under a Japanese pseudonym Onoto Watanna, was a very successful writer of popular stories with Asian themes.

Younghill Kang's The Grass Roof *(1931) and* East Goes West: The Making of an Oriental Yankee *(1937).* Younghill Kang (1903–1972) received his early education in Chinese classics in his hometown of Song-Dune-Chi in Korea and youth education in modern science and Western culture in Japan. At the age of eighteen he immigrated to North America and thereafter completed his English education with a B.S. from Boston University and an M.A. from Harvard.

Kang's major works, *The Grass Roof* and *East Goes West,* are regarded by critics as autobiographical novels. Told in the voice of a Korean young intellectual Chung-pa Han, the two novels sequentially portray the narrator-author's quest for Western civilization in America. As a pioneer Korean writer who wrote in English and represented Korea and early Korean Americans in these novels, Kang is regarded as the founder of Korean American literature.

The Grass Roof, a recollection in nostalgia, tells of Chung-pa Han's origin in Korea, his upbringing in a Korean village, and extended stories of the Han clan. Set entirely in Korea with memorized and fictionalized exotic events and people, the autobiographical novel attracted a great deal of critical attention. However, it served mainly "as a necessary psychological bridge to *East Goes West,* the record of his experience in America and Canada as a displaced person" (Yun 1999, 172). It is thus *East Goes West* that deserves more attention in terms of Kang's literary reflections of early Asian immigrants in America.

East Goes West narrates Chung-pa Han's life, as well as the lives of a few other Korean Americans, in the urban United States during the 1920s and 1930s, starting from the protagonist's arrival in the United States in 1921, three years before the 1924 anti-Asian Immigration Act. Although written in an oft-humorous style and cautiously, the novel presents a critical portrayal of the Korean intellectuals who are rejected by arrogant and ignorant Americans, and who experience brutality, loneliness, and even hunger. On their path to "enter into the economic life of Americans," or "to the West to find a new beauty, a new life" (Kang 1937, 277; 178), the protagonist and the other major characters only encounter a complete shutout from American social and intellectual life by societal prejudice and discrimination. Even so, Chung-pa Han does not seem to give up his seeking the American Dream. King-Kok Cheung remarks:

> *East Goes West* ends with Han's dream of being locked in a dark cellar with some blacks, as torch-bearing white men are about to set them all on fire. His only hope is a Buddhist interpretation of the dream: that he will be reincarnated to a better life. (Cheung 1997, 159–160)

Instead of taking the reader on an immigrant's journey from penniless foreigner to successful citizen, *The Grass Roof* and *East Goes West* interrogate U.S. history and American nationalist narratives of progress, equality, assimilation, and upward mobility. If the first novel "is a justification of Han's departure from Korea" (Kim 1982, 34), the second novel, considered to be more mature in style and highly developed in content, offers American readers access to Korean immigrants' endless struggles for inclusion and assimilation during the 1920s and 1930s.

Carlos Bulosan's America Is in the Heart: A Personal History *(1946)*. The Filipino American writer Carlos Bulosan (1911–1956) was born in a small village in the Philippine Islands. He immigrated to the United States in 1930, soon after California had set up restrictions on the flood of East Asian immigrants, and spent most of his immigrant life on the West Coast among Filipino field and cannery workers before he died of poverty and illness.

Compared to Younghill Kang who spoke basically for himself and a small elite group of individuals, Bulosan wrote about the poor and the oppressed Asian Americans with consciousness: "What impelled me to write? The answer is—my grand dream of equality among men and freedom for all. To give literate voice to the voiceless one hundred thousand Filipinos in the United States, Hawaii, and Alaska" (Bulosan 1995, 216). His many published works of prose and poetry reflected the Depression and Filipino immigrants' frustrated and disappointed feelings, their experiences of racism and economic inequality in American society, and their painful memories of the homeland, but his most famous work is the fictionalized recounting of Bulosan's personal history in the United States titled *America Is in the Heart: A Personal History*.

Considered by critics as "a composite portrait of the Filipino American community, a social document from the point of view of a participant in that experience" (Kim 1982, 48), *American Is in the Heart* narrates the life story of a male Filipino immigrant variably called Carlos, Carl, or Allos. For his American Dream, the narrator of the book comes to the United States from his hometown of Binalonan. Like the author himself, the narrator works as both a migrant worker in the fields of California and a cannery worker in Alaska and Seattle, and together with many other Filipino workers, he encounters filthy working conditions and violent racism. Moving among drunks and criminals in different episodes, the narrator witnesses poverty, fear, assaults, and merciless murders, experiencing the ugly side of his American Dream.

In Bulosan's opinion, the social problems that bedeviled Filipino Americans did not come out of man's nature, rather, they were caused by racial oppression and economic exploitation. In relation to this oppression and exploitation, Bulosan portrays Carlos and his Filipino American folks as "men of subordinate masculinities," who were denied politically and materialistically "the roles, privileges, and accomplishments of hegemonic masculinity" in American society (Nguyen 2002, 67). Even though the narrator expresses his disappointment and disillusionment and conveys a confrontational critique of the inequality of American society, he is still of the conviction that America has the potential for man's ideals and democracy:

> My faith in America . . . was something that had grown out of my defeats and successes, something shaped by my struggles for a place in this vast land . . . something that grew out of the sacrifices and loneliness of my friends, of my brothers in America and my family in the Philippines—something that grew out of our desire to know America, and to become a part of her great tradition, and to contribute something toward her final fulfillment. (Bulosan 1973, 327)

John Okada's No-No Boy, a Novel *(1957).* John Okada (1923–1971) was born to Japanese immigrant parents in Seattle, Washington. After receiving a B.A. in English and library science from the University of Washington, he went to Columbia University, where he graduated with an MA in English. Like many other Japanese Americans, Okada and his family were evacuated and interned at Minidoka of Idaho during the Second World War. Yet, he served in the U.S. Air Force and was discharged in 1946.

As Okada's only published work, *No-No Boy* is about confusion, loss, and the quest for self-identity. It starts with Ichiro Yamada, the protagonist, returning to the Japanese American community in Seattle at the end of World War II from a prison term at McNeil Island Federal Penitentiary in Washington for refusing to join the armed forces. Caught up in a war involving the country of his citizenship, the United States, and the country of his ancestry, Japan, Ichiro lost his identity; after two years in prison, he is still uncertain about why he answered "No-s" to the two key questions on the loyalty oath known as "War Relocation Authority Form 126 Rev.":

> *Question No.* 27: Are you willing to serve in the armed forces of the United States on combat duty whenever ordered?
> *Question No.* 28: Will you swear unqualified allegiance to the United States of America and faithfully defend the United States from any or all attack by foreign or domestic forces, and forswear any form of allegiance or obedience to the Japanese emperor, to any other foreign government, power or organization? (qtd. in Fujita 1992, 240)

Yet, being labeled a "no-no boy," isolated from his ethnic community, and severely excluded from the country he loves, he sees his past actions as a fatal judgmental lapse and wishes to be redeemed from them. On his two-week journey of "redemption," in which the fictional story takes place, Ichiro compares himself to other Japanese Americans he knows and examines his relationships with his family. For instance, tracing his childhood within the family headed by a mother with an "unreckoning force" (Okada 1979, 20) helps Ichiro find the formation of his being a no-no boy: "There was a time when I was your son. There was a time. . . . You used to smile a mother's smile and tell me stories. . . . [W]e were Japanese with Japanese feelings and Japanese pride and Japanese thoughts" (Okada 1979, 15). Identifying with his mother, who claimed to be loyal to the Japanese emperor and called those Japanese Americans enlisting in the U.S. military "traitors," Ichiro acted according to her will and refused the draft.

Like Carlos Bulosan's *America Is in the Heart*, Okada's novel also tackles the issue of "subordinate" masculinities in American society; for Ichiro, being a middle-class man with access to commodities would signify the American "dominant" masculinity. Moreover, written during the Cold War, *No-No Boy*'s thematic disloyalty and insecurity are connected by critics to the domestic Cold War environment of the country: "In *No-No Boy*, two modes of disloyalty are in operation: the original disloyalty of the no-no boy and the invisible, overarching presence of the communists and other 'un-American' types who presumably infested America at the time of *No-No Boy*'s writing and publication" (Nguyen 2002, 65).

Foreshadowing the lesson many Americans learned during the McCarthy era, Ichiro's "plight as a suspected traitor and the consequences he suffers of exclusion, isolation, imprisonment, paranoia, and stigmatization . . . can also be read as an implicit commentary on the domestic Cold War" (Nguyen 2002, 74).

No-No Boy did not receive serious attention during the author's lifetime. But the novel was revived in 1976 by the Combined Asian American Resources Project in Seattle and then republished by the University of Washington Press in 1979. Within the Japanese American public the novel was rejected because of its topic of the internment camps, which most Japanese Americans wanted to forget, and because of its representation of Japanese Americans as "tormented, uncertain, and incapacitated by self-hatred" and "violently distorted by racism" (Kim 1982, 156).

Louis Chu's Eat a Bowl of Tea *(1961).* Louis Chu (1915–1970) was born in China. In 1924, the year when the National Origins Law banned all subsequent immigration from Asia, he immigrated to the United States with his parents. He graduated from Upsala College in New Jersey with a B.A. in English and sociology and then worked in New York City's Department of Welfare before enlisting for military service in which he was dispatched to China for a year in 1945. After the war, working as the director of a social center, serving as executive secretary for an association in New York's Chinatown, and hosting a radio program called "Chinese Festival," Chu witnessed many Chinese Americans' sociopolitical and economic dislocations and displacements, which he inevitably used as rich sources for his only book, the novel *Eat a Bowl of Tea.*

From an insider's perspective, *Eat a Bowl of Tea* approaches the issue of ethnicity through depiction of the racial, patriarchal, and familial tensions experienced by a father, Wang Wah Guy, and his son, Wang Ben Loy, in New York's Chinatown. Wang Wah Guy is made a Chinatown bachelor by the 1924 National Origins Law that prohibits the entry of Chinese wives into the United States, and he is too old to change his bachelor lifestyle when those immigration restrictions are lifted in 1943. His son Ben Loy, following the footprints of many Chinese bachelors in the late 1940s, has to go back to China to find a wife. After returning to New York City, Ben Loy works long hours at a restaurant, leaving his bride Mei Oi at home alone, leading to Ben Loy's impotence and Mei Oi's adultery. Their marriage is in danger; and this damaged relationship critically reflects the problematic "bachelor society" created by restrictive immigration policies.

Although set in New York's Chinatown in 1947, the novel represents the social and economic marginalization of the Chinese in the United States in the larger context of sociopolitical problems, including the consequence of nineteenth-century anti-miscegenation laws and the impact of McCarthyism. Jinqi Ling pointed out the following:

> As a university-trained sociologist working for government welfare agencies, Chu could not have failed to notice bureaucratic indifference toward Chinatown's continued marginal existence both before and during the cold war. And certainly as a

member of New York's Chinatown community in the 1950s and 1960s, he could not have been unaffected by the consequences of the relentless anticommunist campaigns, the widespread distrust of people of Chinese origin or descent. (Ling 1998, 57)

In depicting Chinese bachelors' poverty, isolation, and struggle in New York's Chinatown as an ethnic community, Chu chose a spare, realistic style. The novel's explicit sexuality and frankness about sexual problems, such as impotence and prostitution, are unusual for its theme and era. Yet perhaps because of this, and because of its unlikeness of "rags-to-riches prototype in many immigrant memoirs" (Hsiao 1992, 158), the novel unfolds before the reader an authentic portrayal of Chinatown culture in which male Chinese American immigrants, and especially their sons, are frustrated with the confines of patriarchal tradition, unfulfilling marriages and relationships, and racism. The novel was not seriously reviewed by major American newspapers and magazines after its publication, probably due to the literary Eurocentric bias then. However, the advent of new Asian American literary sensibilities and consciousness in the late 1960s and 1970s reclaimed the importance of the novel. The novel was also adapted into a movie in 1989 by the Asian American film director Wayne Wang.

Frank Chin's The Chickencoop Chinaman *(1972).* Frank Chin was born in Berkeley, California, in 1940 to a Chinese immigrant father and a fourth-generation Chinese American mother. While attending the University of California at Berkeley, Chin began publishing as a contributor to the University of California, Berkeley's humor magazine, the *California Pelican*. From 1959 to 1960 he served as the associate editor for the magazine and as its editor later in 1960. Some of Chin's literary characters, as well as his upsettingly humorous style and singular ethnic sensibility, can be traced back to his early short writings published in the magazine.

Appearing Off Broadway at the American Place Theatre in 1972, Chin's first play *Chickencoop Chinaman* manifested the identity crisis in Asian American masculinity and evoked an authorial gender politics. The plot of the play revolves around a Chinese American filmmaker named Tam Lum. Struggling with the historical and cultural falsification and distortion of Asian male imagery in America, the protagonist undergoes a search for a metaphorical replacement of his absent, "emasculated" father who, according to Tam Lum himself, was "an old dishwasher," wearing his underpants in the bath due to his fear of the peek through the keyhole by those "old toothless goofy white ladies" (Chin 1981, 16; 17). Disdainful of his own father, Tam rallies several other father figures, including Ovaltine Jack Dancer, a professional boxer, and Charley Popcorn, a black fatherlike trainer of boxers, who gives a different version of Tam's father as a lover of boxing with a fierce sense of dignity.

Mainly through humor, deliberate self-irony, voices of other ethnic males, such as the black boxing trainer, wordplay, and presentation of interethnic and intergenerational conflicts, Chin interrogates the historical and cultural consequences of the "emasculation" of the Chinese American father and foregrounds an ethnic masculinity that he would ultimately call "Chinaman." In empowering the masculine image of the Asian American man, Chin situates Tam's "authentic" ethnic identity in languages of synthesis and hybridity:

I am the natural born ragmouth speaking the motherless bloody tongue. No real language of my own to make sense with, so out comes everybody else's trash that don't conceive. . . . I am a Chinaman! A miracle synthetic! Drip dry and machine washable. . . .

> I speak nothing but the mother tongues bein' born to none of my own, I talk the talk of orphans. (Chin 1981, 7–8)

Thus, the play acknowledges the multifaceted identities of Asian Americans and their synthetic and hybrid cultural and genealogical inheritances. Tam's "Chinaman" has a history of myth, theft, Sierra railroad, and Oakland Chinatown.

The play concludes with Tam's monologue on the issue of language, a recurring focus of the play: just as the Asian American heroic tradition is invisible, the Asian American man lacks a proper cultural expression. "For Chin," as Jinqi Ling notes,

> the crisis in masculinity is bound up not only with the Asian American man's socially inflicted "emasculation" but also with the crisis in language facing the artist; his ultimate hero therefore becomes not only the idolized ancestral Chinese American male . . . but also the emerging Asian American artist, who must not only envision and connect with an Asian American heroic tradition but also fight to make his voice effective in the present. (Ling 1997, 318)

Frank Chin emerged on the Asian American literary scene in the early 1970s and, as reflected in the mixed responses to the tone of *The Chickencoop Chinaman* and its challenges to ethnic minority writers, has remained a prominent and contentious figure in contemporary Asian American literature and Asian American literary studies. On the one hand, his resistance to the externally imposed image of Asian American men and his construction of Asian American male subjectivity have significantly contributed to the development of Asian American literature and the field of ethnic literary studies. On the other, as critics have pointed out, his literary formation of Asian American cultural identity, which is based on American birth and effectively neglects women, "conceals rather than accentuates the emerging multiple agendas and the changing ethnic composition of the Asian American communities" (Ling 1997, 319).

Maxine Hong Kingston's The Woman Warrior: Memoirs of a Girlhood among Ghosts *(1976)*. Born in Stockton, California, in 1940 to first-generation Chinese immigrant parents, Kingston started showing her talents in writing by the time she attended high school. While majoring in English at UC Berkeley, she wrote for the university newspaper. She graduated from UC Berkeley in 1962 with a B.A. in English and earned her teacher's certificate from the same university in 1965. Together with her husband, fellow Berkley graduate and stage actor Earll Kingston, Kingston was active in anti-Vietnam War movements and efforts protecting freedom of speech during the 1960s.

In 1976, right after it was published, *The Woman Warrior* became an immediate popular and critical success—it was a long-standing bestseller for paperbacks until 1989 and won Kingston the National Book Critics Circle Award for non-fiction in 1976. The book is catalogued as an autobiography, but it is actually a mixture of personal and communal facts, elements of fantasy and mythology, newly created fiction, as well as folktales and familial history.

The Woman Warrior is about the life of a young Chinese American girl who lives between two different cultures, between reality and fantasy, and in face of racial and sexual prejudices in America. Kingston fantasizes of becoming Fa Mu Lan (Hua Mulan), the fearless, celebrated Chinese legendary warrior woman who, in man's armor, avenges her father and brother by attacking an evil baron and beheading the emperor. Besides this fantasized legendary swordswoman who empowers the author spiritually, Kingston also identifies herself intellectually and more realistically with another powerful ancient woman Ts'ai Yen (Cai Yan), a Chinese princess who was kidnapped by northern barbarians but expressed her lonely, sad feelings through self-created Chinese songs with the barbarians' reed pipes.

Revolving around her family stories and oral histories, Kingston creates an autobiographical text that crosses boundaries of genres to simultaneously incorporate myths and fictionalizations, weaving and meshing undistinguished characters and events: "Night after night my mother would talk-story until we fell asleep. I couldn't tell where the stories left off and the dream began, her voice the voice of the heroines in my sleep. . . . At last I saw that I too had been in the presence of great power, my mother talking-story" (Kingston 1976, 20).

This unconventional style establishes her intent to probe the Asian American identity effectively and raise questions about various cultural definitions. Metaphorically subverting the socially constructed stereotypical identity of Chinese Americans, for example, Kingston draws a similarity between herself and the Chinese legendary warrior woman:

> The swordswoman and I are not so dissimilar. May my people understand the resemblance soon so that I can return to them. What we have in common are the words at our backs. The idioms for revenge are "report a crime" and "report to five families." The reporting is the vengeance—not the beheading, not the gutting, but the words. And I have so many words—"chink" words and "gook" words too—that they do not fit on my skin. (Kingston 1976, 53)

Like the legendary warrior woman, who refused to act in accordance with her appointed gender role and gained respect from her family and community by avenging the wrong-doing against them, Kingston deconstructs and subverts the racial, ethnic, and gender definitions by voicing loud her opposing point of view about the stereotypical images and perceptions of Chinese Americans.

Kingston's creative amalgamation, on the one hand, has become the benchmark against which Asian American writings are measured:

> The Woman Warrior remained the first text to both enter the arena of national culture and arrest American public imagination. Its appeal to the shared category of gender produced a heterogeneous readership beyond ethnicity; its postmodern play of the folk fanned commercial interest in the future publication of Asian American texts; and its extensive review and study by critics of legitimate cultural affiliations also enabled the scholarly excavation and preservation of Asian American literary tradition. (Li 1998, 44)

On the other hand, it has problematized the generic boundary between fiction and nonfiction, as well as the legitimate representation of Asian American culture and community. Nevertheless, the book made Kingston the most studied Asian American writer of the twentieth century, as evidenced by the MLA's 1991 publication of *Approaches to Teaching Kingston's The Woman Warrior*. After *The Woman Warrior*, Kingston produced two other important, award-winning texts, *China Men* (1980), which won the American Book Award, and the John Dos Passos Prize-winning *Tripmaster Monkey: His Fake Book* (1989).

Trends and Themes. Correspondingly, apart from literature by writers with initially designated national origins such as China, Japan, and Korea, the rubric of Asian American literature has broadened to bring out writings by authors of Southeast

Asian descent, such as the Vietnamese American writer Le Ly Hayslip, and South Asian descent, such as the Indian-born Chitra Divakaruni. Moreover, because veteran writers; younger American-born authors, such as Chang-rae Lee; and writers from the recent immigrant influx have all been making their imprints on the contemporary Asian American cultural milieu, it has become more problematic to distinguish the recently arrived Asian immigrants from those native-born Americans of Asian origins. This indistinctness has challenged the constructions of Asian and American, and in part has conceptually complicated the Asian American identity and identification. As Elaine Kim notes in her 1992 forward to *Reading the Literatures of Asian America*:

> As the world has changed, so have our conceptions of Asian American identity. The lines between Asian and Asian American, so important in identity formation in earlier times, are increasingly been blurred. . . . The notion of either as monolithic and homogeneous dissolves when placed against the multiplicitous identities and experiences of contemporary Asian Americans. (Lim and Ling 1992, xiii)

As part of post-modernist American literature, which is characterized with conflict and contradiction, contemporary Asian American literature has assumed various attitudes and perspectives toward issues regarding the immigrant experience in America, such as assimilation, ethnicity, and multiculturalism. On the one hand, Asian American texts, such as those by Hisaye Yamamoto and Amy Tan, continue to retain or build a distinct ethnic or cultural identity both by focusing on gender roles and family relations, as well as through a discourse that resists and disrupts the lingering marginalization of minority ethnics by the mainstream. On the other hand, many Asian American writers with different ethnic and cultural backgrounds either approach issues of ethnicity in different tones and shifted narratives, such as Jessica Hagedorn and David Henry Hwang, or espouse to be accepted as Americans, such as Gish Jen, and no longer see Asian American identities simply as orbiting around vacillation between Asian and American or conflict between the core and the peripheral, but as more universal human issues. Subjectivities in writings by the latter camp of Asian American writers, thus, "are forged upon numerous interstices involving variables such as economic and social status, religious affiliation, physical ability, gender and sexuality, degree of linguistic competence, and acceptance and integration into Western capitalist and consumer culture" (Ty and Goellnicht 2004, 5).

The development of a diverse, heterogeneous Asian American literature that features a great variety of genres, themes, and styles, enacts both a continuation of and a departure from previous Asian American literature.

Context and Issues. Since the 1980s, "Asian American writers have been extremely productive," and all types of their writings, such as novels, poems, stories, plays, memoirs, and autobiographies have drawn attention from and been published by mainstream presses, "often garnering national awards and international recognition" (Lim and Ling 1992, 3). The rapid growth and wide recognition of Asian American literary production in the last quarter of the twentieth century through the cusp of the twenty-first century, have not only made the voice of Asian American literature heard loud and clear but have also helped break the conventional thematic, generic boundaries of this literature. As Maxine Hong Kingston once hoped (Rabinowitz 1987, 182), Asian American writing is now, like its earlier

African and Native American counterparts, assuming an undisputable and undeniable position in contemporary American literature.

The coming-of-age of Asian American literature flourishes in response to changing patterns of Asian immigration. In reality, the Asian groups embraced by the rubric "Asian America" encompass not a static list but a dynamic collection of immigrant communities. According to some census statistics, the Chinese American community is the largest, which also includes the largest percentage of American-born members. The Filipino community is the second largest group, and next to it is the Japanese community with many of its members born in the United States. The most recent Asian immigrants to the United States are the Southeast Asians, such as Vietnamese, Cambodians, and Laotians, and South Asians, comprising peoples from Pakistan, India, Bangladesh, Sri Lanka, Nepal, Bhutan, and the Maldives.

Reception. The changes and maturity in Asian American literature have been witnessed by and reflected in critical studies. Scholars and critics of Asian American literature have been raising significant questions, varying from those about immigration, assimilation, and acculturation to those concerning gender conflicts, stereotypes, the relations between Asian American and mainstream American literature, and aesthetics. As King-Kok Cheung aptly elaborates,

> A significant switch in emphasis has also occurred in Asian American literary studies. Whereas identity politics—with its stress on cultural nationalism and American nativity—governed earlier theoretical and critical formulations, the stress is now on heterogeneity and diaspora. The shift has been from seeking to "claim America" to forging a connection between Asia and Asian America; from centering on race and on masculinity to revolving around the multiple axes of ethnicity, gender, class, and sexuality; from being concerned primarily with social history and communal responsibility to being caught in the quandaries and possibilities of postmodernism and multiculturalism. (Cheung 1997, 1)

Before we turn to the selected representative writers in contemporary Asian American literature since the 1980s, it is worth mentioning that a few anthologies of Asian American literature published at the beginning of the twenty-first century have made contribution to the expanded representation of this literature: Shirly Geok-lin Lim's *Asian-American Literature: An Anthology* (2000), *Bold Words: A Century of Asian American Writing* edited by Rajini Srikanth and Esther Y. Iwanaga (2001), and Victoria Chang's *Asian American Poetry: The Next Generation* (2004).

Selected Authors. Hisaye Yamamoto (1921–), one of the most-studied Asian American short story writers, was born in Redondo Beach, California, to *issei* parents (first-generation immigrants from Japan). In her early teens Yamamoto started writing, and her experience of the Japanese American internment during 1941–1945 became an important source for her fictional writing later. After Los Angeles's Excelsior High School, she attended Compton Junior College, where she graduated with an associate of arts degree in European languages and Latin.

Yamamoto's first and only collection of short fiction, *Seventeen Syllables: 5 Stories of Japanese American Life*, was published in Tokyo in 1985; through its republications in newer, revised, and enlarged editions in 1988 by Kitchen Table, Women of Color Press, and in 1994 and 2001 by Rutgers University Press, this book has become her most celebrated work. Throughout the latter half of the twentieth century, Yamamoto's works appeared in such noted journals as *Kenyon Review* and

Arizona Quarterly and were anthologized in books such as *Best American Short Stories* (1950) and *Charlie Chan Is Dead: An Anthology of Contemporary Asian American Fiction* (1993). Recognizing her contribution to Asian American literature, Yamamoto was awarded the American Book Award for Lifetime Achievement by the Before Columbus Foundation in 1986.

Yamamoto's most famous short stories in her collection, the title story "Seventeen Syllables," "Yoneko's Earthquake," and "The Legend of Miss Sasagawara," are critical retrospective ones; they are about Japanese Americans' life experiences in California farmlands before World War II and in the concentration camps during the war. With Japanese American women at the center, these stories often weave complicated issues of gender, domestic relationships, and ethnic identity into double or multiple plotlines. In "Seventeen Syllables," the familial and farm life of a Japanese American couple is narrated from the point of view of their teenage daughter, Rosie Hayashi. Mrs. Hayashi's attempt to pursue her artistic talents by writing *haiku* is objected by her husband, a traditional-minded farmer, whose ideas about his wife's role stick to the constricting boundaries of daily necessity. Sophisticatedly "[using] the *haiku* as a submerged structuring device" (Grice 2002, 89), the story connects its exploration of female ethnic subjectivities with issues of language and sexuality through the paralleled plots:

> Rosie, on the brink of adulthood, undergoes the process of sexual awakening; her mother, throughout the story, becomes more and more focused on writing her haiku. Sexuality and art are closely associated, connected through their relation to language and silence. (Yamamoto 1999, 170)

Similarly, in "Yoneko's Earthquake," which is about the orange-growing Hosoume family, female subjectivities, especially maternal subjectivity, are explored via parallel situations of Yoneko, the ten-year-old daughter, and Mrs. Hosoume, her mother. The haunting story "The Legend of Miss Sasagawara" is set in an Arizona Japanese American internment camp and depicts another type of family relationship. The girl narrator suffers both neglect from her father, a Buddhist minister, and rejection from her community because of her unpredictably strange behaviors, even though she has musical and writing talents and is religiously loyal to her father. In 1991, "Seventeen Syllables" and "Yoneko's Earthquake" were adapted for a PBS movie titled *Hot Summer Winds* for *American Playhouse*.

Born in Los Angeles and raised in a middle-class Chinese American family, David Henry Hwang (1957–) graduated from Stanford University with a B.A. in English in 1979. During his undergraduate years, he developed a strong interest in drama and started writing his first play *FOB*, which premiered in 1980 and won him an Obie Award. Hwang's training in drama included a playwriting program at the Yale University School of Drama in 1980–1981.

Since the early 1980s, Hwang has produced, co-produced, and published numerous plays, such as *The Dance and the Railroad* (1983), *The Sound of Voice* (1984), *Trying to find Chinatown* (1996), *Golden Child* (1998), *Flower Drum Song* (2003); and *Yellow Face* (2007), and most of these plays have drawn critical and popular attention. Besides plays, Hwang also writes opera librettos, books for musicals, and motion picture and television screenplays. Among his many honors and fellowships are a Rockefeller Foundation playwright-in-residence grant and a National Endowment for the Arts Artistic Associate Fellowship.

Among Hwang's plays, *M. Butterfly* (1988) is the most celebrated and studied work. It was the first Asian American play to be performed on Broadway and won the Outer Critics Circle Award and the Tony Award for best play of 1988. Centering on a dramatic interplay of perception, misperception, and deception in the relationship between the Chinese male spy Song Liling, who masquerades as a female, and the French diplomat Rene Gallimard, *M. Butterfly* foregrounds what is at the heart of many of Hwang's works: the harsh split between the images of Chinese/Asian Americans represented in the dominant culture and what really exists and a subsequent subversion of those stereotypes that accompany ethnicity, gender, and sexuality. Tina Chen noted the following:

> Hwang suggests that the stereotype about and practice of Asian subterfuge is emblematized by the figure of the Asian/American spy. Song Liling's flamboyance as a secret agent . . . ; his ability to impersonate a female Chinese opera singer contingent not only on his skill in deception but on the willingness of his partner, Rene Gallimard, to believe in the fantasy of the submissive Asian woman that he exploits. . . . Because Hwang's play attempts to deconstruct the stereotype of the submissive Asian woman, particularly as it was represented in Puccini's opera *Madame Butterfly*, Song's spying does predominantly act as a metaphor through which issues of desire, secrecy, and racial in/visibility can be explored. (Chen 2005, 261–262)

A poststructuralist, postcolonial dramatic work, *M. Butterfly* undoubtedly problematizes a series of contemporary issues, such as racism, colonialism, sexism, homosexuality, and East-West relations, and, its use of masquerade, as noted by critics, holds rich implications and of which a single interpretation can impossibly convey its whole meaning (Li 1998, 154–164). The play was adapted in 1993 into a movie of the same title by David Cronenberg.

Amy Tan (1952–) was born in Oakland, California, to Chinese parents John and Daisy Tan. She attended San Jose State University, earning a B.A. in English and linguistics in 1973 and an M.A. in linguistics in 1974.

One of the most significant women writers in contemporary Asian American literature, Tan has enjoyed popular as well as critical success since the publication of her first novel, *The Joy Luck Club*, in 1989. This novel was on *The New York Times* hardcover best-seller list for about ten months, sold more than four million copies, was translated into twenty-five languages, and was adapted for a movie (1993) by Asian American director Wayne Wang; it also received glowing critical reviews, and its honors and awards included finalist for the National Book Award and the National Book Critics Circle Award and winner of the Bay Area Book Reviewers Award for Best Fiction, the American Library Association Best Book for Young Adults Award, and the Commonwealth Club Gold Award. *The Joy Luck Club* addresses issues regarding displaced immigrant individuals in America, dual cultural identities as healing devices, mother-daughter relationships, and generational, intercultural gaps. These thematic concerns are repeated over and over, though in different plots and narrative modes, in her other major novels: *The Kitchen God's Wife* (1991), *The Hundred Secret Senses* (1995), and *The Bonesetter's Daughter* (2001). Life stories of Tan's parents and those she heard from relatives were the main sources for some of her novels.

The Joy Luck Club is about the ethnic malaise of four families in San Francisco. Focusing on four pairs of mothers and daughters in the four families, the novel tells sixteen inter-related short stories about these women told by them in nonlinear narration. The ethnic malaise depicted here is manifested in the relationship between the four Chinese immigrant mothers, who have formed a *mahjong* group called the Joy Luck Club; their cherished ideologies of old China; and their four American-born daughters who believe in modern American individuality and independence. The generational and intercultural gap between mothers and daughters unfolds with the daughters getting confused and angry toward their mothers while growing up.

The conflict in the relationships between the Chinese mothers and American daughters is the dilemma that many immigrants are faced with: living between worlds. Also, the novel structurally devotes equally two chapters to each of the mothers and daughters, who tell their stories therein, and thus places equal weight on both sides of the Chinese American—the mothers being portrayed as representatives of traditional Chineseness and daughters as Americanness. By giving equal weight to both sides, Tan, from a feminist standpoint, makes these Chinese-born mothers' experiences comparable to that of their American daughters in order to blur "the distinction between the progressive (Euro-American) woman and the traditional Asian woman" and polemically record "the marginalization and disempowerment of all women within patriarchal institutions—whether in China or America" (Schueller 1992, 78–79). Tan's idea of this universalized female identity is emphatically reflected in the mother-daughter bond in the second part of the novel. Jing-mei June Woo's (one of the daughters) returning to China at the end of the novel and seeing the resemblance among herself, her two lost sisters, and their dead mother can be read as a trope for a return to cultural origins: "And now I also see what part of me is Chinese. It is so obvious. It is my family. It is in your blood. After all these years, it can finally be let go" (Tan 1989, 331). By connecting with the larger family of China, the rupture in an ethnic American family is eventually healed.

Le Ly Hayslip (1949–) was born on a rice farm in Vietnam. She lived in the United States for many years before returning to Vietnam to live and oversee her philanthropic projects there.

Hayslip published two autobiographical books in which her life in wartime Vietnam and in the United States is remarkably recorded. The first book, *When Heaven and Earth Changed Places* (1989), alternates between narration of her youthful life in Vietnam and her return to Vietnam in 1986. Memories of being caught in the war, struggling for a living in the big city, being impregnated by a rich employer, and married to an American civilian who took her to the United States in 1971 juxtapose her concerns about her reentering Vietnam as a rich capitalist at a risky time. The second book, *Child of War, Woman of Peace* (1993), is a more linear narrative structure that follows her life chronologically in the United States from 1972 to 1986 and then her travels back and forth between Vietnam and America after 1986.

Hayslip is the first Vietnamese American writer to receive significant attention from reviewers and critics:

> For American readers, Hayslip has become representative of those anonymous millions of Vietnamese in whose name the Vietnam War was fought by both sides. Through her extraordinary personal story, she not only symbolically bears their collective pain but also bears the victim's burden of forgiveness. (Nguyen 2002, 108)

Another testament to the influence of her Vietnam stories was the release in 1993 of Oliver Stone's movie, *Heaven and Earth*, based on Hayslip's autobiographical writing. Hayslip's texts, however, are often ambivalent or even contradictory in their politics. Yet, this also best reveals her hybrid encounters. As Viet Thanh Nguyen points out, "In rewriting this victimized body and making it her own, she is caught, to use her own expression, 'in between'—Viet Nam and the United States, war and peace, hell and heaven, and . . . the needs of 'representation' and those of 'reconciliation'" (Nguyen 2002, 109).

Jessica Hagedorn (1949–), the Filipino American poet and fiction writer, dramatist, multimedia artist, performance artist, and singer, was born in Manila. Influenced by her mother and grandmother, Hagedorn showed at an early age strong interests in art and writing. Along with her youthful absorption of multiple types of cultural media and her studies at the American Conservatory Theater in San Francisco, those interests developed into a hybrid sensibility and multifarious literary and artistic accomplishments.

Hagedorn's contribution to Asian American literature lies mainly in her poetic and fictional writings. Her representative poems were collected in such anthologies as *Pet Food and Tropical Apparitions* (1981), which won the American Book Award in 1983. Her first novel, *Dogeaters*, published in 1990 and nominated for the National Book Award, is mainly about the hierarchical Filipino society under the Marcos regime and yet provides an "authenticity . . . of the exiled voices . . . with competing identities" (Davis 1997, 117). *Dogeaters* was followed by two more novels: *The Gangster of Love* (1996) and *Dream Jungle* (2003), a story about sexual abuse and a mother's anguish over the loss of her child in the backdrop of the Philippines.

Hagedorn's depiction of ethnicity is enriched with her wide-ranging experiences in music and drama, reflecting a postcolonial literary sensibility. For example, *The Gangster of Love* is based on her experience in the New York City music circle. The narrator-protagonist Raquel "Rocky" Rivera, "a mixed-race woman of Chinese, Filipino, and Spanish descent who matures into adulthood after immigrating from the Philippines with her mother and brother to the U.S.," forms a rock band with her friends traveling across the United States—searching for "a sense of home, identity, and community amid the contradictions of American postmodern capitalism" (Santa Ana 2004, 37). Along with the band's musical experiments and disbandment, Hagedorn depicts a disenchanted American society, where the reader is led to encounter street people, prostitutes, and poor artists like Rocky who are faced with drug abuse, political corruption, denigration of women, and "a dialectical struggle between her desire for the hybridity of consumer individualism and her ties to family and the Filipino immigrant underclass" (Santa Ana 2004, 37). In subverting the mainstream's racial stereotyping of Filipino Americans, however, Hagedorn comically uses the toy yo-yo in her story,

> because I have this fascination with the Filipino yo-yo champions who used to do the exhibitions. . . . To me, they were a kind of matinee idol, running around the country showing off. Yet, underneath, there was this horrible tension because they had to travel to places where segregation was imposed and they were attacked. (qtd. in Lawsin 2000, 36)

The Korean American novelist Chang-rae Lee was born in South Korea in 1965 but brought up in the United States from three years old. Besides a B.A. in English from Yale in 1987, Lee also earned an M.F.A. in creative writing from the University of Oregon in 1993.

Lee's first novel, *Native Speaker* (1995), was very well received by American read-ers. It won first-time novelist laudatory reviews and literary awards, including the PEN/Hemingway Award for Best First Fiction, the American Book Award, and the Barnes and Noble Discover Award. His second novel, *A Gesture Life* (1999), also garnered vibrant reviews and honorable awards, such as the Anisfield-Wolf Prize and the Myers Outstanding Book Award. In 2004 Lee surprisingly introduced to his readers a Caucasian protagonist in his third novel *Aloft*.

Native Speaker has been Lee's most acclaimed work. The novel narrates the suf-fering of a crisis of both professional and personal faith by a Korean American spy, Henry Park, who works for a company specializing in racial and ethnic matters. Interrogating the politics of ethnicity in American culture and society, Lee "cleverly incorporates the stereotype of the inscrutable Asian into his plot and uses it to dis-mantle traditional notions of the benefits of assimilation" (Hawley 1997, 189). As the novel's protagonist tells

> I think my father would choose to see my deceptions in a rigidly practical light, as if they were similar to that daily survival he came to endure, the need to adapt, assume an advantageous shape. My ugly immigrant's truth, as was his, is that I have exploited my own, and those others who can be exploited. This forever is my burden to bear. But I and my kind possess another dimension. We will learn every lesson of accent and idiom, we will dismantle every last pretense and practice you hold, noble as well as ruinous. (Lee 1995, 297)

Likewise, *A Gesture Life* continues the revelation of the problems of immigration and assimilation through the various life phases of its principal character, Franklin "Doc" Hata, from a native Korean to a Japanese soldier and then to a medical sup-ply store owner in the United States. The layers of Hata's constant displacement and problematic assimilation in his host countries are best peeled through the trope of naming in the novel:

> Doc Hata's Americanized name is Franklin Hata and the transit of his name symboli-cally maps his journey toward U.S. citizenship and identity formation. Franklin is an assumed name; his Japanese name is Jiro; and Hata is a shortening of Kurohata, his Japanese last name. This typical immigrant renaming is further complicated when the reader discovers that Doc Hata, who is of ethnic Korean ancestry, was adopted as a boy and that Jiro Kurohata is not his original name. . . . Arguably, this absence of origins is precisely what Hata hopes to overcome in his transit to U.S. citizenship. (Carroll 2005, 597)

Born in 1956 and raised in Calcutta, India, in a traditional middle-class family, Chitra Banerjee Divakaruni obtained an M.A. in English from Wright State Univer-sity in Ohio in 1977 and earned a doctorate in English at UC Berkeley in 1984.

With topics closer to her life experiences as an immigrant and woman, Divakaruni started her writing career in poetry; her first collection of poems is *Dark Like the River* (1987). Following that, she published two volumes of short stories: *Arranged Marriage* (1995), which won the 1996 Before Columbus Foundation American Book Award and the PEN Oakland Josephine Miles Award, and *The Unknown Errors of Our Lives* (2001). But Divakaruni is more prolific with novels: *The Mistress of Spices* (1996), chosen by the *Los Angeles Times* as one of the best books of 1997, *Sister of My Heart* (1999), and *The Vine of Desire* (2002).

Divakaruni's writing is thematically concerned with South Asian women immigrants dealing with issues of violence, marriage, and family and the sociocultural inequities and injustices concerning South Asian men immigrants. However, as a prolific writer at the turn of the century and a member of the "new set of South Asian American authors" (Rajan 2006, 105), Divakaruni's fictional subjects are not simply presented in traditional narratives that attempt to evoke sympathy for ethnic or cultural malaise and convey ideological messages; rather, they are freshly probed through a sort of "feminist ethics." In other words, she portrays her subjects and situations that become memorable

> by invoking other kinds of aesthetic responses, something akin to brief or fleeting but pleasurable instances of shared cultural reminiscences or poignant memories of loss as they grapple with new realities. . . . The formal devices . . . create a space between readers and texts to locate one's aesthetic responses in the dynamic gap, where one encounters crises in the narratives and formulates a reaction that is based upon assessing the risk factor in not acting ethically. (Rajan 2006, 105)

Moreover, her fiction challenges the current transparency of gender and sexuality concerning South Asian Americans and has evoked hot debates in the Asian American literary circles (Srikanth 2004, 127–128).

Born in 1955 to Norman and Agnes Jen, immigrants from China in the 1940s, Gish Jen was raised in Scarsdale, New York. Jen graduated from Harvard in English in 1977; she completed the M.F.A program at the University of Iowa in 1983.

A critically acclaimed author of fiction, Jen began her writing career with short fiction. Her talent in this genre is evidenced by many short stories published in ethnic and mainstream American journals and magazines, and some collected in anthologies, such as *The Best American Short Stories: 1988,* and *The Best American Short Stories of the Century* (1999). However, as reflected in her collection *Who's Irish?: Stories* (1999), Jen does not confine herself to representing the Asian American experience only; some stories deal with Americanization of other ethnic or hyphenated Americans. Among her numerous awards are a National Endowment for the Arts Award (1988), a Lannan Literary Award for fiction (1999), and a Strauss Living from the American Academy for Arts and Letters (2003).

Jen is widely known for her novels. Although still probing contemporary issues of immigration, ethnicity, and cultural dilemma, these novels are written in such different ways that they convey something "beyond . . . 'typical' themes of cultural dislocation, generational conflict, and immigrant success" (Lee 2000, 215), and they exhibit a group of characters who are much more than Asian American stereotypes. *Typical American* (1991), her first novel, depicts the pursuit of the American dream by a Chinese immigrant family with humor and comedy. In the novel, things are temporary and changing; "America's glorious promise to the (soon-to-be-disabused) immigrant is symbolized by a joy ride in a commandeered convertible" (Wong 1993, 120).

Mona in the Promised Land (1996), more comical than the first novel and with an even lighter tone, continues the ethnic American theme but in a larger context. What is more significant is that the novel complicates the issue of identity in the postmodernist American society through the title character Mona's attempt to convert to Judaism. "In a way, I've tried to contribute to the process of boundary crossing, to painting pictures that are little less black and white—a little more complicated" (qtd. in Lee 2000, 229). If in her homecoming toward the end of *Mona in the Promised Land* Mona is "symbolically 'homeless' . . . because [her] embrace of multiple ethnic affiliations results in a loss of family identification" (Ho 2005, 146), in her third novel *The Love Wife* (2004), Jen moves one step further to launch an exploring yet more ironic inquiry into complicated issues involving America's multi-ethnicity and multiculturalism. With a story centering on the happiness, discrimination, vacillation, and identity problems of the members of an "American family" consisting of white Americans and Asian Americans, the novel tackles not only the problematic Americanization of Asian Americans but also, more important, essential human issues in the pluralistic American society.

Bibliography

Bulosan, Carlos. *On Becoming Filipino: Selected Writings of Carlos Bulosan*. Philadelphia, PA: Temple Unversity Press, 1995.

———. *American Is in the Heart: A Personal History*. Seattle, WA: University of Washington Press, 1973.

Carroll, Hamilton. Traumatic Patriarchy: Reading Gendered Nationalisms in Chang-rae Lee's *A Gesture Life*. *Modern Fiction Studies* 51 (3) (2005): 592–616.

Chang, Victoria, ed. *Asian American Poetry: The Next Generation*. Urbana, IL: University of Illinois Press, 2004.

Chen, Tina. "Recasting the Spy, Rewriting the Story: The Politics of Genre." In *Native Speaker* by Chang-rae Lee. In *Form and Transformation in Asian American Literature*. Zhou Xiaojing and Samina Najmi, eds. Seattle, WA: University of Washington Press, 2005, 249–267.

Chin, Frank, et al., eds. *Aiiieeeee! An Anthology of Asian American Writers*. Washington, D.C.: Howard University Press, 1974.

Chin, Frank. *The Chickencoop Chinaman* and *The Year of the Dragon*. Seattle, WA: University of Washington Press, 1981.

Chu, Louis. *Eat a Bowl of Tea*. Seattle, WA: University of Washington Press.

Davis, Rocio G. "Ninotchka Rosca's *State of War* and Jessica Hagedorn's *Dogeaters*: Revisioning the Philippines." In *Ideas of Home: Literature of Asian Migration*. Geoffrey Kain, ed. Michigan State University Press, 1997, 115–127.

Divakaruni, Chitra Banerjee. *The Palace of Illusions: A Novel*. New York: Doubleday, 2008.

———. *The Vine of Desire*. New York: Doubleday, 2002.

———. *Sister of My Heart*. New York: Doubleday, 1999.

———. *The Mistress of Spices*. New York: Doubleday, 1996.

———. *Arranged Marriage*. New York: Doubleday, 1995.

Eaton, Edith Maude. *Mrs. Spring Fragrance and Other Writings*. Chicago, IL: University of Illinois Press, 1995.

Fujita, Gayle K. "Momotaro's Exile: John Okada's *No-No Boy*." In *Reading the Literatures of Asian America*. Shirley Geok-lin and Amy Ling, eds. Philadelphia, PA: Temple University Press, 1992, 239–258.

Grice, Helena. *Negotiating Identities: An Introduction to Asian American Women's Writing*. Manchester: Manchester University Press, 2002.

Hagedorn, Jessica. *The Gangster of Love*. Boston, MA: Houghton, 1996.

Hawley, John C. Gus Lee, Chang-rae Lee, and Li-young Lee: The Search for the Father in Asian American Literature. In *Ideas of Home: Literature of Asian Migration*. Geoffrey Kain, ed. Michigan State University Press, 1997, 183–195.

Hayslip, Le Ly, and Jay Wurts. *When Heaven and Earth Changed Places*. New York: Doubleday, 1989.

Hayslip, Le Ly, and James Hayslip. *Child of War, Woman of Peace*. New York: Doubleday, 1993.

Ho, Jennifer Ann. *Consumption and Identity in Asian American Coming-of-Age Novels.* New York: Routledge, 2005.

Hsiao, Ruth Y. Facing the Incurable: Patriarchy in *Eat a Bowl of Tea.* In *Reading the Literature of Asian America.* Shirley Geok-lin and Amy Ling, eds. Philadelphia, PA: Temple University Press, 1992, 151–162.

Hsu, Kai-yu, and Helen Palubinskas, eds. *Asian American Authors.* Boston, MA: Houghton Mifflin, 1972.

Hwang, David Henry. *Trying to Find Chinatown: The Selected Plays.* New York: Theater Communication Group, 2000.

———. *FOB and Other Plays.* New York: New American Library, 1990.

———. *Broken Promises: Four Plays.* New York: Avon Books, 1983.

Jen, Gish. *The Love Wife.* New York: Knopf, 2004.

———. *Who's Irish?: Stories.* New York: Knopf, 1999.

———. *Mona in the Promised Land.* New York: Knopf, 1996.

———. *Typical American.* Boston, MA: Houghton Mifflin/Seymour Lawrence, 1991.

Kang, Younghill. *East Goes West: The Making of an Oriental Yankee.* New York: Charles Scribner's Sons, 1937.

———. *The Grass Roof.* New York: C Scribner's Sons, 1931.

Kim, Elaine H. *Asian American Literature: An Introduction to the Writings and Their Social Context.* Philadelphia, PA: Temple University Press, 1982.

Kingston, Maxine Hong. *Tripmaster Monkey: His Fake Book.* New York: Alfred A. Knopf, 1989.

———. *China Men.* New York: Alfred A. Knopf, 1980.

———. *The Woman Warrior.* New York: Alfred A. Knopf, 1976.

Lawrence, Keith, and Floyd Cheung, eds. *Recovered Legacies: Authority and Identity in Early Asian American Literature.* Philadelphia, PA: Temple University Press, 2005.

Lawsin, Emily Porcincula. "Jessica Hagedorn." In *Words Matter: Conversations with Asian American Writers.* King-Kok Cheung, ed., Honolulu: University of Hawaii Press, 2000, 21–39.

Lee, Chang-rae. *Aloft.* New York: Riverhead, 2004.

———. *A Gesture Life.* New York: Riverhead, 1999.

———. *Native Speaker.* New York: Riverhead, 1995.

Lee, Rachel. "Gish Jen." In *Words Matter: Conversations with Asian American Writers.* King-Kok Cheung, ed., Honolulu: University of Hawaii Press, 2000, 215–232.

Li, David Leiwei. *Imagining the Nation: Asian American Literature and Cultural Consent.* Stanford: Stanford University Press, 1998.

Lim, Shirley Geok-lin, and Amy Ling, eds. *Reading the Literatures of Asian America.* Philadelphia, PA: Temple University Press, 1992.

Lim, Shirly Geok-lin, ed. *Asian-American Literature: An Anthology.* Lincolnwood, IL: NTC Publishing Group, 2000.

Ling, Amy. *Between Worlds: Women Writers of Chinese Ancestry.* Elmsford, NY: Pergamon Press, 1990.

Ling, Jinqi. *Narrating Nationalisms: Ideology and Form in Asian American Literature.* New York: Oxford University Press, 1998.

———. "Identity Crisis and Gender Politics: Reappropriating Asian American Masculinity." In *An Interethnic Companion to Asian American Literature.* King-kok Chueng, ed. Cambridge: Cambridge University Press, 1997, 312–337.

Lowe, Lisa. *Immigrant Acts.* Durham: Duke University Press, 1996.

Nguyen, Viet Thanh. *Race and Resistance: Literature and Politics in Asian America.* Oxford: Oxford University Press, 2002.

Okada, John. *No-No Boy.* Seattle, WA: University of Washington Press, 1979.

Rabinowitz, Paula. "Eccentric Memories: A Conversation with Maxine Hong Kingston." *Michigan Quarterly Review* 26 (1) (1987): 177–187.

Rajan, Gita. "Poignant Pleasures." In *Literary Gestures: The Aesthetic in Asian American Writing*. Rocio G. Davis and Sue-Im Lee, eds. Philadelphia, PA: Temple University Press, 2006, 104–120.

Santa Ana, Jeffrey J. "Affect-Identity: The Emotions of Assimilation, Multiraciality, and Asian American Subjectivity." In *Asian North American Identities Beyond the Hyphen*. Elenor Ty and Donald C. Goellnight, eds. Bloomington, IN: Indiana University Press, 2004, 15–42.

Schueller, Malini Johar. "Theorizing Ethnicity and Subjectivity: Maxine Hong Kingston's *Tripmaster Monkey* and Amy Tan's *The Joy Luck Club*." *Genders* 15 (1992): 72–85.

Srikanth, Rajini. *The World Next Door: South Asian American Literature and the Idea of America*. Philadelphia, PA: Temple University Press, 2004.

Srikanth, Rajini, and Esther Y. Iwanaga, eds. *Bold Words: A Century of Asian American Writing*. New Brunswick, NJ: Rutgers University Press, 2001.

Tan, Amy. *Saving Fish from Drowning*. New York: Putnam, 2005.

———. *The Bonesetter's Daughter*. New York: Putnam, 2001.

———. *The Hundred Secret Senses*. New York: Putnam, 1995.

———. *The Kitchen God's Wife*. New York: Putnam, 1991.

———. *The Joy Luck Club*. New York: Putnam, 1989.

Ty, Eleanor, and Donald C. Goellnicht, eds. *Asian North American Identities Beyond the Hyphen*. Bloomington, IN: Indiana University Press, 2004.

Wei, William. *The Asian American Movement*. Philadelphia, PA: Temple University Press, 1993.

White-Parks, Annette. *Sui Sin Far/Edith Maude Eaton: A Literary Biography*. Urbana, IL: University of Illinois Press, 1995.

Wong, Sau-ling Cynthia. *Reading Asian American Literature: From Necessity to Extravagance*. Princeton, NJ: Princeton University Press, 1993.

Yamamoto, Hisaye. *Seventeen Syllables and Other Stories*. Revised and Expanded Edition. New Brunswick, NJ: Rutgers University Press, 2001.

Yun, Chung-Hei. "Beyond 'Clay Walls': Korean American Literature." In *Asian American Writers*. Harold Bloom, ed. Philadelphia, PA: Chelsea House Publishers, 1999, 171–185.

Further Reading

Bloom, Harold, ed. *Modern Critical Views: Amy Tan*. Philadelphia, PA: Chelsea House, 2000; Chueng, King-kok, ed. *Words Matter: Conversations with Asian American Writers*. Honolulu: University of Hawaii Press, 2000; Chueng, King-kok, ed. *An Interethnic Companion to Asian American Literature*. Cambridge: Cambridge University Press, 1997; Cheung, King-Kok. *Articulate Silences: Hisaye Yamamoto, Maxine Hong Kingston, Joy Kogawa*. Ithaca: Cornell University Press, 1993; Chu, Patricia P. *Assimilating Asians: Gendered Strategies of Authorship in Asian America*. Durham: Duke University Press, 2000; Davis, Rocio G., and Sue-Im Lee, eds. *Literary Gestures: The Aesthetic in Asian American Writing*. Philadelphia: Temple University Press, 2006; Duncan, Patti. *Tell This Silence: Asian American Women Writers and the Politics of Speech*. Iowa City: University of Iowa Press, 2004; Eng, David L. and Alice Y. Horn, eds. *Q & A: Queer in Asian America*. Philadelphia, PA: Temple University Press, 1998; Kain, Geoffrey, ed. *Ideas of Home: Literature of Asian Migration*. Michigan State University Press, 1997; Lim, Shirley Geok-lin, et al., eds. *Transnational Asian American Literature: Sites and Transits*. Philadelphia, PA: Temple University Press, 2006; Palombo-Liu, David. *Asian/American: Historical Crossings of a Racial Frontier*. Stanford: Stanford University Press, 1999; Pao, Angela. The Critic and the Butterfly: Sociocultural Contexts and the Reception of David Henry Hwang's *M. Butterfly*. *Amerasia Journal* 18 (3) (1992): 1–16; Simmons, Diane. *Maxine Hong Kingston*. New York: Twayne Publishers, 1999; Singh, Amritjit, et al., eds. *Memory and Cultural Politics: New Approaches to American Ethnic Literatures*. Boston, MA: Northeastern University Press, 1996; Skandera-Trombley, Laura E, ed.

Critical Essays on Maxine Hong Kingston. New York: G. K. Hall & Co, 1998; Yamamoto, Traise. *Masking Selves, Making Subjects: Japanese American Women, Identity, and the Body.* Berkeley, CA: University of California Press, 1999; Yin, Xiao-huang. *Chinese American Literature since the 1850s.* Urbana, IL: University of Illinois Press, 2000; Xiaojing, Zhou, and Samina Najmi, eds. *Form and Transformation in Asian American Literature.* Seattle, WA: University of Washington Press, 2005.

LI ZENG

AUTOBIOGRAPHY AND MEMOIR

Definition. Autobiography and memoir are personal narratives of an individual's life experiences, either written by that individual or "as told to" another writer, as distinct from **biography**, in which a writer researches and recounts the events of another person's history. An autobiography is a life history; memoir spans only a certain portion of that life. Often they are a look into another culture and time—by such notables as Maya Angelou, Richard Wright, and Frederick Douglass—and portions of these works are often anthologized. Autobiographies have been written by such diverse persons as Bill Clinton and Bob Dylan, Sylvia Plath and Carol Burnett, Adolf Hitler and Benazir Bhutto.

In a 2005 *Poets & Writers* article, Sven Birkerts, editor of *AGNI* and author of six books including a memoir, *My Blue Sky* (2002), and a book on memoir, *The Art and Time of Memoir: Then, Again* (2006), discusses the function and importance of the genre. "For whatever story the memoirist may tell, she is at the same time modeling a way to make sense of experience. . . . Reading the work of memoirists, we borrow their investigative energy and contemplate similar possibilities of access to our own lives. . . . The contemporary memoir, then, assumes that the path to self-awareness makes a universally relevant story that we, as readers, can apply as a supple screen to our very different experiences" (2005, 26).

History. Early autobiography included historic or political events, or philosophical viewpoints. "At one time the actual memoirist was considered insignificant to the memoir," writes Barrie Jean Borich, author of the memoirs *My Lesbian Husband: Landscapes of a Marriage* (1999) and *Restoring the Color of Roses* (1993) on her Web site.

> When a soldier described a battle, for instance, it was the battle that mattered, not the soldier. Public events were considered historical, while private life was seen as inappropriate to the written word, unless you were a person considered of singular historic importance, Winston Churchill, or a Kennedy, for instance.
>
> All of this has changed in our postmodern day-to-day. Feminism has privileged the personal, changing the paradigms of what is worthy of cultural notice and recovering the stories of lives previously absent from history. Identity and cultural politics redirected attention to people of color, gays and lesbians, the disabled, and anyone else who was up to that point missing from the public record. (Borich 2008)

"One of the first great Western autobiographies was written by St. Augustine . . . describing his lustful and dissolute ways. . . . Its title was *Confessions.*" Further, "Confession (always linked to redemption) remained the model for autobiographical writing for more than a thousand years until the Renaissance when entertainment became more popular than redemption," says Steve Zousmer, author of *You Don't Have to be Famous,* a how-to on autobiography writing, (2007, 185).

Because so much excellent work exists within the genre, it is not possible to cover all of it here. A brief survey follows.

Early Americans read the *Autobiography of Benjamin Franklin* and huge blocks of history involving the slave narrative, including such titles as *Narrative of the Life of Frederic Douglass, an American Slave* in 1845, Booker T. Washington's *Up from Slavery* in 1901, and *Incidents in the Life of a Slave Girl* by Harriet Jacobs (1862).

Henry David Thoreau wrote *Walden* in 1854, Helen Keller *The Story of My Life* in 1903, and Mark Twain his *Mark Twain's Autobiography* in 1917. Mahatma Gandhi's *The Story of My Experiments with Truth* appeared in 1927 and was reprinted in 1929. *Black Elk Speaks* by Black Elk and John J. Niehardt, Gertrude Stein's *The Autobiography of Alice B. Toklas,* and William Butler Yeats's *Autobiography* were written in 1931, 1933, and 1936, respectively. The Holocaust era produced a wealth of literature. Anne Frank's *Diary of a Young Girl*, which recorded her life in hiding from June 12, 1941, to August 1, 1942, and Elie Wiesel's *Night* are two of the better known.

Among classic African American autobiographies are Amiri Baraka's *The Autobiography of LeRoi Jones/Amiri Baraka* (1984), Zora Neale Hurston's *Dust Tracks on the Road* (1942), and Richard Wright's *Black Boy* (1945).

The civil rights and women's liberation movements and the Vietnam War era produced autobiographies by Martin Luther King, Jr., Malcolm X, and Rosa Parks, to name a few. Maya Angelou's 1969 *I Know Why the Caged Bird Sing*s expanded into a six-volume autobiography with later installments published in 1974, 1976, 1981, 1986, and 2002, including *Gather Together in My Name, Singin' and Singin' and Getting' Merry Like Christmas, The Heart of a Woman, All God's Children Need Traveling Shoes*, and *A Song Flung Up to Heaven*. Other notable titles include Audre Lorde's *Zami: A New Spelling of My Name* (1982), John Edgar Wideman's *Brothers and Keepers* (1984), and Henry Louis Gates's *Colored People: A Memoir* (1994).

In 1993, *A Child Called "It,"* Dave Pelzer's memoir about an abusive childhood, shocked its readers and stayed on the *New York Times* bestseller list for five years. It was followed up by *The Lost Boy* and *A Man Named Dave*.

Feminist memoir includes the work of Simone de Beauvoir, Adrienne Rich, and Alice Walker, among many others.

Included in the abundant work of the Gay, Lesbian, Bisexual, Transgendered, and Queer (GLBTQ) community are classics such as Gertrude Stein's *The Autobiography of Alice B. Toklas,* May Sarton's work, and the writing of Adrienne Rich. Later works include Lance Bass's (of the pop music group 'N Sync) autobiography, *Out of Sync,* and a memoir by Greg Louganis, *Breaking the Surface*.

Other notable memoirs and autobiography have been written by Eleanor Roosevelt, Annie Dillard, Gore Vidal, Virginia Woolf, bell hooks, Joseph Stalin, Jimmy Carter, and Sidney Poitier.

Trends and Themes. Literature tends to cluster around events of historical significance or events that affected large segments of humanity. As mentioned, Holocaust literature, literature exposing racial injustice, works concerning the Vietnam War, the civil rights, and feminist movements, and GLBTQ voices have been popular. No doubt we will soon see works by American soldiers in Iraq that will tell the rest of us what it is like to be a person who has lived through that situation. As Maya Angelou so aptly puts it, "I speak to the Black experience, but I am always talking about the human condition" (Comley et al. 2007, 43).

Although recent efforts have concentrated more on private lives, these works have also spoken to the human condition. Recent books about alcohol/substance abuse and recovery, and others speaking candidly about sexuality, are breaking taboos and telling stories that have seldom been heard in the past.

A first memoir often leads to a series and a movie, as happened with Frank McCourt's *Angela's Ashes,* (Paramount/Universal, 1999) and Augusten Burroughs' *Running with Scissors* (Sony, 2006). McCourt followed up with *'Tis* (1999) and *Teacher Man* (2005); Burroughs with *Dry* (2003), *Magical Thinking* (2004), and *Possible Side Effects* (2006), not to mention an earlier novel, *Sellevision* (2000).

In addition, the current popularity of the genre has created a real market for courses and books on how to write one's own autobiography or memoir. For example, the Writers Digest Book Club offers works such as *Writing Life Stories* by Bill Roorbach and *You Don't Have to Be Famous* by Steve Zousmer.

Context and Issues. One issue to be dealt with is the difference between escapist literature and interpretive literature, sensationalism and serious social or personal statement. Laurence Perrine in *Literature: Structure, Sound and Sense,* a standard volume, defines escapist literature as that which is "written purely for entertainment," whereas interpretive literature "illuminates some aspect of human life and behavior" and "helps us to understand our world, our neighbors, ourselves" (1988, 4). Other functions of the artist are to make the personal universal and to speak for those who can't (or won't) speak for themselves.

Works such as Richard Wright's *Black Boy* and Black Elk's *Black Elk Speaks* (with John J. Neihardt) have given us insights into the struggles of race. Nguyen gives a first-person account of Amerasian children left behind by American fathers in the Vietnam War era, writing of the results of the prejudice he experienced due to his mixed race, the terrors of war, and tyrant regimes. Joan Didion gives a less sweeping but certainly affecting glimpse into living with grief. Augusten Burroughs, Carolyn Knapp (*Drinking: A Love Story*), and Pete Hamill (*A Drinking Life*) portray the reality of the alcoholic or addict.

By contrast, a culture of television voyeurism is certainly at work in today's society, and that can create an atmosphere of sensationalism for sensationalism's sake. "This is, after all, a time when you can turn on afternoon television to see people confessing to astonishingly shameless and sordid behavior, usually sexual or violent or both" (Zousmer 2007, 186). Borich (2008) partially concurs. "The negative view of these cultural changes suggests that we are interested in the private story and the personal vantage point only because we are held hostage by talk show and tabloid culture." But she goes on to say, "I believe that these phenomena are coupled with what has become a healthy intellectual and emotional curiosity about the world as it actually exists" (Borich 2008).

Birkerts quips, "Were you abused, neglected, discriminated against; did you turn your pain into pills, drink, or satanic cults? Write a memoir!" (2005, 22). But he then defends the genre.

> The fact of a boom in rampant sensationalism must not be allowed to obscure another fact, which is that recent decades have seen the flourishing of a sophisticated and quietly vital mode of literary expression . . . In the last quarter century or so, it has refurbished itself in a contemporary way, and that tall stack of books marks a genuine contribution to our literature. (2005, 22)

Coupled with this is the fact that the border between other types of writing and memoir, originally a nonfiction genre, is often blurred—for instance, in the cases of

Maxine Hong Kingston, whose works blend fiction and nonfiction, and by Tim O'Brien, who calls his *The Things They Carried* "auto fiction"—or they may be out-and-out violated (allegedly) by writers such as Stephen Frey, who is quoted in *Smoking Gun* as saying "events 'were embellished for obvious dramatic reasons'" (Wyatt 2006). Burroughs admits that his time frame was often compressed for story-telling purposes.

Several writers have addressed this issue. Gore Vidal makes this distinction in *Palimpsest*: "A memoir is how one remembers his own life, while an autobiography is history, requiring research, dates, facts double-checked" (1995, 3). In his poem "Dangers," Rodney Jones tells us, "Memory, at best, retrieves maybe 6 percent in studio light" (Jones 1989: 13). Barrie Jean Borich writes on her Web site, "Writing about a subject inevitably changes the way we know a subject" (Borich 2008). Sara DeLuca sums it up beautifully in the acknowledgments of *Dancing the Cows Home: A Wisconsin Girlhood*: "Memory is fragile and fluid. Sifted through layers of time and experience, some edges soften. Others reveal themselves with increased clarity. Disjointed happenings continue to shift and warp and seek out new connections" (DeLuca 1996, ix).

The problem then remains for the audience to decide how much of this "shifting and warping" is a legitimate difference between the perspective of the memoirist and the perspective of the human subjects, and if and where the line is crossed from non-fiction to fiction.

Concerning a recent lawsuit, Augusten Burroughs "acknowledge[s] that the family members portrayed recall the past differently" (Deahl 2007). In his "Preface to This Edition" of *A Heartbreaking Work of Staggering Genius*, Dave Eggers states, "For all the author's bluster elsewhere, this is not, actually, a work of pure nonfiction. Many parts have been fictionalized in varying degrees, for various purposes" (Wheeler 2002, ix). James Frey, however, makes no such disclaimer, and his work has been called into question. However, "one fan who identified herself only as Julie [on Frey's Web site] wrote, 'Even if his story is fake, he opened up the eyes of so many people'" (Wyatt 2006).

Reception. In 1997, Frank McCourt's *Angela's Ashes* won the Pulitzer Prize for Literature and topped the best-seller list for more than two years. *'Tis* and *Teacher Man*, however, met with mixed reviews. The *Austin Chronicle* praises *'Tis*, "He has the nerve to write what he felt. This makes the difference between a real writer and a merely good storyteller. . . . You miss his voice once the book has been completed" (Stacy Bush), while the *Washington Post* accuses it of being filled with "mawkish self-pity" (Ron Charles), and the *Herald Tribune* calls it "sour, resentment-filled" (Michiko Kakutani). Of *Teacher Man*, *USA Today* says this "is as good as writing" gets about teaching and learning and finding yourself through writing (Minzesheimer), and *Publishers Weekly* says, "It should be mandatory reading for every teacher in America." In contrast, the *San Francisco Chronicle* complains that it "seems listless, forced, . . . its sporadic moments of passionate brilliance only reminding the reader of how disengaged the rest of the book seems" (Skloot). "Those looking for an involving story will be disappointed, as will those hoping for a fresh look at teaching," says Brendan Halpin of the *Boston Globe*.

The film version of *Angela's Ashes* (Paramount/Universal, 1999) was billed as "Rotten Tomatoes" by the *Minneapolis Star Tribune*. *The New York Times* accused it of presenting "a quaintly romantic view of poverty. The film isn't wrenching enough to do [the pain in the novel] justice. The family's suffering . . . is curiously unreal," and "even the father's drunkenness is somehow sugar coated" (Maslin 1999).

Similarly, the film *Running with Scissors* (Sony, 2006), based on Burroughs's memoir of an abusive childhood, doesn't fare well with critics. Justin Chang of *Variety* notes, "This rudderless adaptation never gets a firm grip on the author's deadpan tone or episodic narrative style." He calls the film "more of a crazy-quilt . . . than a cohesive drama. It's a messy, discursive piece of work."

The book *Dry*, though, receives kind attention. *Entertainment Weekly* described it as "a stylish memoir about a messy life" (Emma Forrest). A medical doctor noted in the *Permanente Journal*, "Dry is the alarmingly open and shockingly honest autobiography of . . . an alcoholic man who . . . just might provide the insight we physicians need to understand the complexity surrounding alcoholism." Gregorio D. Saccone claims that the "brief-but-helpful glimpse into the life that preceded [the alcoholism]" shows "the importance of dealing with these [childhood] events and the emotions they birthed" (Saccone).

Kein Nyugen enjoys nothing but praise from the literary world. Douglass Brinkley, director of the Center for American Studies at the University of New Orleans, says, "*The Unwanted* is a haunting memoir of both nightmarish agony and redemptive self-discovery destined to become a literary classic" (2007). *The Minneapolis* Star *Tribune's* Richard C. Kagan exclaims, "Kien's story deserves a place with the best memoirs of immigration and exile" (2007). *Publishers Weekly* also praises Nguyen's *The Tapestries*, calling it "a daringly complex and vividly imagined debut novel." He has won the 2005 NCM Pulitzer award for ethnic writers and was nominated for the 2004 Grinazne Cavour Prize.

Likewise, Joan Didion's *The Year of Magical Thinking* is immensely popular. A *Time* magazine a reviewer calls it "an act of consummate literary bravery, a writer known for her clarity narrating the loss of that clarity" (Lev Grossman). "Didion has written a lacerating yet peculiarly stirring book," says *The Washington Post*. It is "a work of surpassing clarity and honesty . . . a journey into a place none of us can fully imagine until we have been there" (Yardley). "The writing is exhilarating," says Robert Pinsky of *The New York Times*.

Selected Authors. Because an abundance of fine literature exists within this genre, it will be necessary to examine only a few works.

In *The Unwanted* (Little, Brown, 2002), Kien Nguyen exposes the plight of Amerasian children abandoned by their American fathers in 1970s Vietnam. The memoir spans his life from before the 1975 fall of Saigon, when he and his family watched from the top of the American Embassy as U.S. Army helicopters left without them, until his immigration 10 years later. Nguyen skillfully illustrates major issues in prose so natural and vibrant it feels as if you were reading a novel for pleasure.

He first hears the term *half-breed* from his own cousins, and at one point his mother, in a fit of disgust or fright, pours liquid black dye over her two blonde sons' heads.

Nguyen portrays a mother so vain and cruel that the reader feels little sympathy when the Communists strip her of her wealth and status—that is, until it's made clear that the new regime is every bit as corrupt and power and money hungry as the capitalists to whom they claim superiority. Of this woman who gave his puppy to his cousins to use as a football until it was dead, he says, "Her heart had no room for any relationship stronger than a detached friendship," and "she despised anyone beneath her" (Nguyen 2001, 15). When Loan, the maid who cared for Kien and his brother Jimmy, boarded the van in which the family escaped the mansion and " . . . bow[ed] down to press her face to my mother's hands, my mother pulled away as if touched by fire. Her face darkened, and her eyes burned at the girl with hatred. With a swift movement that startled everyone, my mother struck a hard blow across Loan's left cheek" (Nguyen 2001, 18).

Although it takes over half of the 339-page memoir, Madame Khoun finally redeems herself. Reduced from her position as a powerful and prosperous banker, she takes on the lowest form of employment—trafficking in the illegal marketplace—and goes on to finally sell both her body and her blood to feed the family. Her situation encapsulates the fate of many of that time who were seen as "capitalists."

The Unwanted takes the reader into a world where citizens are so afraid of their government that they are eager to report anything in their comrades' past that might be deemed counterrevolutionary for the reward of "earning up to 30 points [that] would exempt [them] from a day of volunteer work in the jungle" (Nguyen 2001, 110).

Another aspect of repressive Communist rule is shown when a favorite teacher disappears. The leaders have deemed that she is not worthy of concern. At morning assembly, the dean tells the schoolchildren, "You are all curious about her absence. My advice to you is: don't be . . . It is none of your business. It is an act of opposition for anyone to continue probing this matter" (Nguyen 2001, 144–145).

It is learned that Miss San was shot trying to escape the country on a boat. Due to Nguyen's similar attempt later, the audience is "treated" to a description of a reeducation camp—actually a concentration camp. The first stop for the "criminals" is a dark pit where they stand in stagnant water for several hours. Some prisoners are driven to insanity.

> She clutched a child of about six or seven years old against her naked chest. . . . Hold her please, the mother said . . . I accepted the heavy child from her mother. In my arms, her head fell backward like that of a broken toy. The wet blanket dropped from her face and my fingers came into contact with her clammy skin, as wrinkled and rough as a piece of leather. I could feel her lips, which were swollen to the size of two filled leeches on her small lifeless face. (Nguyen 2001, 248)

Yet throughout his harsh life, Nguyen doesn't forget the universal aspects of childhood anywhere: family love, friendship, jealousy, bullying, and first love. The book begins with Nguyen's first and happiest memory, his fifth birthday, where "chefs stood around an enormous table, decorating a gigantic white cake with bunches of red roses, brown vines, and green leaves made from heavy whipped cream and food coloring" (Nguyen 2001, 6), making an effective contrast to the scenes of deprivation and horror to come.

Nguyen's other books are the novels *The Tapestries* and *Le Colonial* (2002; 2004).

Augusten Burroughs writes *Dry* (2003) in the immediacy of the present tense. Throughout are scenes of alcoholic dysfunction. In one particular scene, he starts out with his drinking buddy, Jim, at 9 o'clock in the evening and, at 4:15 in the morning, he is

> standing on a stage at a karaoke bar somewhere in the West Village. The spotlights are shining in my face and I'm trying to read the video monitor in front of me, which is scrolling the words to the theme from *The Brady Bunch*. I see double unless I close one

eye, but when I do I lose my balance and stagger. Jim's laughing like a madman in the front row, pounding the table with his hands. The floor trips me and I fall. (Burroughs 2003, 7)

After less than two hours of sleep, he showers, eats breath mints, and even sprays cologne on his tongue, but the odor of alcohol seeps from his pores so strongly that it is entirely noticeable to his coworkers at the ad agency where he works. In a similar instance, he misses entirely a meeting with one of the firm's most important clients, arriving at noon just when everyone else is packing up their briefcases. This behavior precipitates an intervention on the part of the staff.

Scenes of early rehab present his denial of the extent of his addiction. Hearing others' stories in group therapy, he says to himself, "Car accidents, facial lacerations, paralyzed mothers . . . I am definitely in the wrong place. This is for hard-core alcoholics. Rock-bottom, ruined-their-lives alcoholics. I'm an Advertising Alcoholic" (Burroughs 2003, 52). Finally, he comes to a slow realization of the extent of his problem when he admits in therapy that in order to drink his liter or more of Dewars nightly he had to down 10 to 15 Benadryl because of an allergy that was so severe that he'd often have difficulty breathing. His therapist asks him, "And the recommended dose? What is that?' But she's not really asking me about the dosage, she's asking me if I recognize insane when I see it" (Burroughs 2003, 58).

This could be almost any alcoholic's or addict's story. Honest and gutsy, it is at once painful and funny—as life can often be.

Against the horrors of addiction, the author's internal monologue can be hilarious. The memoir also gives a glance into gay lifestyle, with a surprisingly beautiful love story, (surprising because of his previously going out to "get some penis" at bars). He's dealing with an ex-lover's AIDS and cross-addicting to an unhealthy relationship with a sometimes-recovering crack addict. After an account of a relapse so serious that he suffers from alcohol poisoning, Burroughs's book ends with the chapter "One Year Later" and his successful sobriety.

He is at work on a new memoir about his father—*A Wolf at the Table*.

A key theme in Joan Didion's *The Year of Magical Thinking* (2005) is this: "One thing I noticed during the course of those weeks at UCLA was that many people I knew . . . shared a habit of mind usually credited to the very successful. They believed absolutely in their own management skills. They believed absolutely in the power of the telephone numbers they had at their fingertips, the right doctor, the major donor, the person who could facilitate a favor at State or Justice. . . . I had myself for most of my life shared the same core belief in my ability to control events" (Didion 2005, 98).

This is a memoir of attempting to deal with death and loss. Home from visiting their seriously ill daughter in the hospital, Didion and her husband, John Gregory Dunne, sit down to dinner at which he collapses and dies as a result of a heart attack. Throughout the text, Didion repeats this haunting chorus: "*You sit down to dinner and life as you know it ends.*" Didion's mourning is delayed because Quintana, once released from the hospital, is stricken again and hospitalized for several months. The work recounts Didion's search for meaning. She turns to psychiatric texts to understand the process of grief, to medical texts to try to grasp the reasons for both John's death and Quintana's illness, to poetry, even to Emily Post.

Surprising facts are uncovered in her research. She cites Melanie Klein's, *Mourning and its Relation to Manic-Depressive States* (1940), and Freud's *Mourning and*

Melancholia (1917). "'The mourner is in fact ill . . . ,'" states Klein, and Freud says, "'It never occurs to us to regard it [mourning] as a pathological condition and refer it to medical treatment'" (Didion 2005, 34). This disordering of the mental functions is the reason for the book's title. "There was a level on which I believed that what had happened remained reversible" (Didion 2005, 32). "Survivors look back and see omens, messages they missed. They remember the tree that died, the gull that splattered onto the hood of the car. They live by symbols" (Didion 2005, 152). "Had I not misread the meaning of the red flashing light in 1987, would I be able to get in my car today and drive west on San Vicente and find John at the house in Brentwood Park? Standing by the pool?" (Didion 2005, 132).

When the organ bank calls after she had been cleaning out her husband's closet and couldn't force herself to give away the rest of his shoes, she wonders, "How could he come back if he had no organs, how could he come back if he had no shoes?" (Didion 2005, 41).

There is a beautiful if mournful quality to the writing and the subject matter that sometimes gives way to almost aggravatingly technical medical terminology. This, however, is not so strange in such a situation. It accentuates the alienation one must feel when confronted by a situation this large, in hospital settings where all the language seems foreign. She copies medical explanations meticulously, especially after Quintana's second hospitalization. Perhaps this is the way for her to understand. The idea that knowledge is power, wanting to control the outcome (with knowledge) and knowing that she can't, she feels her helplessness. She explains, "In time of trouble, I had been trained since childhood, read, learn, work it up, go to the literature. Information was control" (Didion 2005, 44).

Hers is a story that anyone who has experienced grief will recognize. She writes of coming home from places with news to tell John, then remembering there is no John to tell.

For other works by Joan Didion, please see the "Bibliography" section.

Angela's Ashes (McCourt 1999), originally published by Scribner in 1996, recounts a poverty-stricken childhood in Ireland. Frank, Malachy Jr. and Margaret, the children of Irish immigrants Angela and Malachy Sr., were born in the Bronx.

Due to the Depression and the death of baby Margaret, their parents return with them to Ireland. There his alcoholic father rarely worked, blaming it on the prejudice of the southern people against the northern Irish, (which was truly present), but McCourt Senior had a habit of drinking his wages over the weekend and being absent from work on Mondays. After going on the dole, he drinks that money as well, ignoring the need for groceries. When World War II breaks out, the senior McCourt goes to England because there is work there. After that, the family only sees the father twice, he sends wages home only once, and he finally disappears entirely by the end of the memoir.

The family lives in damp cold quarters, and at one place they were not able to inhabit the downstairs portion of their rented home due to floods carrying sewage from the one lavatory on the lane. McCourt includes scenes of neighborhood boys chasing rats out of their homes with sticks almost as if it were a game.

Due to substandard living conditions and lack of proper nourishment, twin younger brothers die—as well as an infant at birth. Frank will contract typhoid and later conjunctivitis for the same reasons. The conjunctivitis is the most heartbreaking ailment to him because it deprives him of a job (and the pay) of which he was so proud—helping a neighbor deliver coal. Because of the father's inability to support the family, the mother, Angela, frequently endures shame and verbal abuse going to St. Vincent de Paul Society, then while receiving public assistance, and finally she is seen, after the abandonment by the elder Malachy, by the 11-year-old Frank begging with others at the back door of the rectory for food the priests have left over from their meal.

At times *Angela's Ashes* reads like a novel by Dickens or Bronte. When Angela applies for public assistance, one of the workers enjoys torturing her. (There is a curious lack of quotation marks around dialogue in the book.)

> He didn't send us a penny in months, Mr. Kane.
>
> Is that a fact? Well, we know why, don't we? We know what the men of Ireland are up to in England. We know there's the occasional Limerickman trotting around with a Piccadilly tart, don't we?
>
> He looks out at the people on the queue and they know they're supposed to say, We do, Mr. Kane, and they know they're supposed to smile and laugh or things will go hard with them when they reach the platform. They know he might turn them over to Mr. Coffey and he's notorious for saying no to everyone. (McCourt 1999, 326)

Schoolmasters and certain church officials also enjoy torturing children. Because Brendan Quigley asks too many questions in catechism class, Mr. Benson, the master "flogs Question [Quigley] across the shoulders, the bottom, the legs. He grabs him by the collar and drags him to the front of the room" (McCourt 1999, 160).

Frank McCourt and his brothers begin to steal food from stores, milk from the steps of rich people's homes, even lemonade from a delivery van behind a tavern when their mother falls ill. When he is old enough, Frank gets a job delivering telegrams, saves up his money, and the memoir ends with his move to America at age 19.

'Tis begins with McCourt's arrival in America and chronicles his next 20 years. McCourt's latest memoir is *Teacher Man* and tells of his experiences of 30 years of teaching in New York City.

Bibliography

Birkerts, Sven. "Then, Again: Memoir and the Work of Time." *Poets & Writers* 33.3 (2005): 21–26.

Borich, Barrie Jean. "What is Creative Nonfiction Writing?" January 14, 2008. http://www. barriejeanborich.net;

Burroughs, Augusten. *Running with Scissors.* New York: St. Martins Press, 2002.

Bush, Barbara. *Barbara Bush: A Memoir.* New York: Scribner, 1994.

Conway, Jill Ker. *When Memory Speaks: Reflections on Autobiography.* New York: Alfred A. Knopf, 1998.

Clark, Mary Higgins. *Kitchen Privileges.* New York: Simon and Schuster, 2002.

Deahl, Rachel. "'Running with Scissors' Lawsuit Settled." *Publishers Weekly.* 30 Aug 2007. www.publishersweekly.com/eNewsletter.

De Luca, Sara. *Dancing the Cows Home.* St. Paul, MN: Minnesota Historical Society Press, 1996.

Didion, Joan. *The Year of Magical Thinking.* New York: Alfred A. Knopf, 2005.

———. *Political Fictions.* New York: Random House, 2001.

———. *The Last Thing He Wanted.* New York: Vintage, 1996.

———. *After Henry.* New York: Random House, 1992.

———. *Miami.* New York: Simon and Schuster, 1987.

———. *Democracy: A Novel.* New York: Simon and Schuster, 1984.

————. *Salvador*. New York: Vintage, 1983.

————. *The White Album*. New York: Simon and Schuster, 1979.

————. *A Book of Common Prayer*. New York: Knopf, 1977.

————. *Play It as It Lays*. New York: Farrar, Straus, and Giroux, 1970.

————. *Slouching Towards Bethlehem*. New York: Farrar, Straus, and Giroux, 1968.

————. *Run River*. New York: Vintage, 1963.

Dillard, Annie. *Pilgrim at Tinker Creek*. New York: Bantam, 1974.

————. *Teaching a Stone to Talk*. New York: HarperPerennial, 1982.

Knapp, Caroline. *Drinking: A Love Story*. New York: Dial Press, 1997.

McCourt, Frank. *Angela's Ashes*. New York: Simon & Schuster, 1998.

————. *Teacher Man*. New York: Scribner, 2005.

Sparks, Nicholas. *Three Weeks with My Brother*. New York: Time Warner, 2004.

Vidal, Gore. *Palimpsest: A Memoir*. New York: Random House, 1995.

————. *Point to Point Navigation—A Memoir 1964 to 2006*. New York: Doubleday, 2006.

Wright, Richard. *Black Boy, The Restored Text*. New York: Perennial Classics, 1993.

Further Reading

Brinkley, Douglas. "Biography." Dec 27, 2007. www.aviv2.com/kien; Bush, Stacy. "Book Reviews." *The Austin Chronicle*. 1 October 1999; Chang, Justin. "Running with Scissors." Oct 13, 2006. http://www.variety.com; Charles, Ron. "Class Act." *The Washington Post*. 13 Nov 2005; Comely, Nancy R., et al. *Fields of Reading*. 8th ed. Boston: Bedford/St. Martin's, 2007; Forrest, Emma. "Dry." *Entertainment Weekly*. 21 May 2002. www.ew.com; Friedman, Vanessa V. "Book Capsule Review: Angela's Ashes." *Entertainment Weekly*. 20 Sept 1996. www.ew.com; Grossman, Lev. "The Color of Grief." *Time*. 3 Oct 2005: 56–57; Halpin, Brendan. *Boston Globe*. 21 Jan 2008. http://www.metacritic.com; Jones, Rodney. "Dangers." *Transparent Gestures*. Boston, MA: Houghton Mifflin, 1989; Kagan, Richard C. "Biography." *Minneapolis Star Tribune*. 27 Dec 2007. http://www.aviv2.com/kien; Kakutani, Michiko. "Teacher Man: A Memoir." *International Herald Tribune*. 18 Nov 2005: 10; Maslin, Janet. "Angela's Ashes Film Review: A New Gloss on Poverty in Ireland." *New York Times*. 24 Dec 1999. http://query.nytimes.com/gst/fullpage.html?res=9B04E0D71539F937A15751C1A96F958260; Minzesheimer, Bob. "Before 'Ashes,' He Was a Teacher." *USA Today* 21 Jan 2008. http://www.usatoday.com/life/books/reviews/2005-11-14-teacher-man_x.htm?POE; Nguyen, Kien. *The Unwanted*. Boston, MA: Little, Brown and Company, 2001; Pelzer, Dave. *A Child Called "It."* Deerfield Beach, FL: Health Communications, Inc., 1993; Perrine, Laurence. *Literature: Structure, Sound and Sense*. San Diego, CA: Harcourt, Brace Jovanovich, 1988; Pinsky, Robert. "'The Year of Magical Thinking': Goodbye to All That." *The New York Times Sunday Book Review*. 9 Oct 2005: 7.1; Saccone, Gregorio D. "Dry: a Memoir by Augustine Burroughs." *The Permanente Journal* 8(1) (2004): 112; Skloot, Floyd. "Frank McCourt Learns as Much as He Teaches is America." *San Francisco Chronicle*. 11 Dec 2005: sec. M: 6; Wyatt, Edward. "Best-Selling Memoir Draws Scrutiny." *The New York Times*. 10 Jan 2006: E1; Yardley, Jonathon. "The Year of Magical Thinking." *The Washington Post*. 2 Oct 2005: sec. WBK: 2; Zousmer, Steve. *You Don't Have to Be Famous*. Cincinnati: Writer's Digest Books, 2007.

DEBBIE K. TRANTOW

B

BEAT POETRY

Definition. Spontaneous, anti-bourgeois, and metaphysical, Beat poetry fuses transcendent themes with idiosyncratic forms. First gaining notoriety in the mid-1950s, the Beats heavily influenced the counter-culture of the 1960s and 1970s before achieving canonical status as a "movement" if not for individual poets. As with most so-called movements and schools of poetry, Beat poetry is less a unified, manifesto-driven faction than a loose grouping of similarly minded experimentalists dissatisfied with both the sociopolitical conformity demanded by the Cold War and the austere formalism of much of the academic poetry of the 1940s and 1950s. Looking back to Walt Whitman as a model of the open, organic form championed by Ralph Waldo Emerson in his essay "The Poet," the Beat poets bridle against traditional metrics and conventions. Via hyper-enjambed lines, fuguelike repetitions, eccentric grammar, and other strategies of excess, Beat Poetry offers a rhetorical counterpart to contemporaneous developments in music and art, such as be-bop and abstract expressionism. Simultaneously delirious and profoundly calm, Beat poetry sounds the depths and scales the heights of the human quest for meaning in a potentially sterile milieu of materialism and ideological paranoia. Intensely spiritual, although never orthodox, Beat poetry's thematic palette ranges widely, from drug use, sexuality, and madness to myth, apocatastasis, and political satire—often within the same poem. Beat poetry's heterodoxy ultimately finds its source in the dissolution of opposites found in Eastern religions such as Zen Buddhism and Hindu as well as in writers such as Whitman, Henry David Thoreau, Henry Miller, William Carlos Williams, Charles Baudelaire, William Blake, and Percy Bysshe Shelley. Existentialism is another key influence. Individually, the Beat poets seek an authentic voice, a new vision that helps reveal the process of their journey toward enlightenment and away from the stagnation of materialism and its institutions.

Although many of the Beat poets received formal academic training, most found the hothouse atmosphere of university poetry both precious and stifling. In reaction to the well-wrought urns of the 1950s' academic poets, the Beats' poems exude raw emotion and employed ragged, free-flowing (anti-) structures. Consequently, performability proves central to the Beats' aesthetic. The Beats consciously strive to rekindle poetry's oral dimension, and their efforts are designed to produce visceral responses from the audience.

Concomitant with Beat poetry's impulsive orality, themes of liberation and mindfulness course through the poems. In the earliest poems, from the late 1940s and 1950s, American patriotism and commodity-driven ideology provoke, simultaneously, a cynicism tinged with gallows humor and an innocence born of spiritual rebirth. This jarring admixture of themes creates a type of electroshock therapy that allows the poets and their audiences to detach from the mind-numbing buzz of jingoism and advertising, as well as from the inconceivable specter of nuclear winter, and empty their minds of the desire that—for the Buddhist—leads only to pain.

The earliest Beat poets included Allen Ginsberg, Jack Kerouac, Gregory Corso, Gary Snyder, Philip Whalen, Diane di Prima, and Lawrence Ferlinghetti. Later writers included LeRoi Jones (Amiri Baraka), Joanne Kyger, Ann Waldman, Michael McClure, Ed Sanders, Ted Joans, Lenore Kandel, Bob Kaufman, and many others. Most critics note a distinction between the East Coast and West Coast Beats, with the former at times overlapping with the New York School and the latter paralleling the San Francisco renaissance. Some writers, such as Ginsberg and Kerouac, were active on both coasts, however, and Beats were also active in Denver, Wichita, Venice Beach, and other locales.

History. Legend holds that Jack Kerouac coined the phrase "beat generation" while holding a narcotic-induced conversation with Allen Ginsberg and John Clellon Holmes in 1948. In the midst of his musings, Kerouac declared that his was a beat generation, which prompted Ginsberg to concur with passion. Holmes would later codify the phrase—without due credit to Kerouac—in a November 16, 1952, article in the *New York Times*. While Kerouac—who, Joyce Johnson recalls, appropriated the term "beat" from Herbert Huncke—initially drew upon the word's slang meanings—exhaustion, lacking resources—he and others quickly saw the term's multifarious possibilities (Charters 2001, 620). Various commentators have associated "beat" with music, religion (beatification), victory/loss, and formal disarray (a mixture). Regardless, from their first informal gatherings in 1943–1944, Kerouac and the earliest Beats saw their aesthetic as both oppositional and energizing, as a "New Vision." Ginsberg later characterized this New Vision as a "return to an appreciation of idiosyncrasy as against state regimentation" leading toward spiritual, sexual, and artistic liberation (Ginsberg 1995, 19).

The area around Columbia University formed the original Beat epicenter, with Ginsberg, Kerouac, and Lucien Carr, among others, attending the school. Other early members of this subterranean world—hardly a "movement" during the 1940s—included William Burroughs, Huncke, Holmes, and Neal Cassady, none of whom attended Columbia. The friends recognized that their dissatisfaction with the status quo led to what Holmes called a "lust for freedom, and the ability to live at a pace that kills . . . led to black markets, be-bop, narcotics, sexual promiscuity, hucksterism, and Jean-Paul Sartre" (Holmes 2001, 224). This effort to, in the words of Jennie Skerl, "erase the boundaries between art and life" (Skerl 2004, 2) resulted in urgent, delirious conversations, passionate sexuality (homosexual, heterosexual, bisexual), all-night parties, and, haltingly at first, literature. In a post-atomic world, the group felt that traditional methodologies, conventional lifestyles, and unexamined patriotism not only lacked spiritual and artistic substance but also were dangerous, deadening. Ginsberg later noted that the group all detected "some kind of spiritual crisis in the West and the possibility of decline instead of infinite American Century Progress—The idea of an apocalyptic historical change" (Gifford 2005, 38).

Troubling setbacks, however, accompanied the embryonic movement, none more life-altering than the 1944 murder of David Kammerer by Carr. Kammerer, a friend of Burroughs, had fought with Carr after the latter had rebuffed his sexual advances. Apparently in self-defense, Carr stabbed Kammerer to death and threw the body in the Hudson. Carr told both Kerouac and Burroughs about the murder, and the men were ultimately held as material witnesses despite Carr's confession. The shock of the ordeal tightened the bond between Burroughs, Kerouac, and Ginsberg. Another traumatic event occurred in 1949 when Ginsberg, who had been allowing Huncke and his confederates to store stolen goods in his apartment, was arrested after a stolen vehicle in which he was a passenger crashed (Raskin 2004, 88). Ginsberg escaped jail, but he was committed to the New York State Psychiatric Institute. This event, along with his possibly apocryphal 1948 vision of William Blake, was pivotal in altering Ginsberg's, and thus the Beats', poetic sensibility. In the hospital, Ginsberg met Carl Solomon, to whom he would later dedicate "Howl," and who would inspire him and validate his unorthodox lifestyle (Raskin 2004, 97). Upon his release from the hospital, Ginsberg briefly attempted to conform to society's expectations, but the experiment was short-lived and Ginsberg much preferred the "subterranean" crowd of Greenwich Village's Pony Stable and San Remo, bohemian bars where he and the other Beats met Gregory Corso, smoked pot, and philosophized (Watson 1995, 121–22).

By the 1952 appearance of Holmes's "This Is the Beat Generation," most of the published "original" Beat writing was in prose, with Holmes and Kerouac having published novels and Burroughs soon to publish *Junky* in 1953. Kerouac's western connections, stemming most famously from his 1948 cross-country trip with Cassady, however, were instrumental both in providing a receptive audience for Ginsberg and Corso and in exposing young West Coast poets such as Gary Snyder and Philip Whalen to a Beat sensibility that dovetails nicely with their own burgeoning poetic of eastern spiritualism. On October 7, 1955, the mythic gathering at the Six Gallery in San Francisco—where Ginsberg moved in 1954—announced the maturity of the Beat poets in stellar fashion, with Ginsberg and several San Francisco Renaissance poets, Philip Lamantia, Michael McClure, Gary Snyder, and Philip Whalen, all reciting their verse. Ginsberg's performance of a draft of "Howl," however, stole the show. The year 1955 also saw the publication of Corso's first volume as well as one by Lawrence Ferlinghetti. Despite Holmes's early publicity, it was not until Ferlinghetti published Ginsberg's *Howl and Other Poems* in 1956 and Kerouac's novel *On the Road* was published to acclaim in 1957 that the Beats reached the national consciousness.

Ginsberg skipped the 1957 obscenity trial prompted by his first book, leaving Ferlinghetti and the ACLU to fight the battle (Raskin 2004, 216–217). On October 3, 1957, almost two years after the Six Gallery reading, Ginsberg's *Howl and Other Poems* was cleared of obscenity charges. Many of the Beat poets would take advantage of this ruling and pursue themes and images deemed taboo only a few years before. The increased publicity, however, spawned what Herb Caen termed the "beatnik" movement, young people attracted more to the nonconformist image of the Beats than to the poetry itself. In the late 1950s and early 1960s, the beatnik fad resulted in stock characters such as Maynard G. Krebs in the television show *The*

Many Loves of Dobie Gillis and beret-wearing, finger-snapping outcasts in *Mad* magazine and on *The Flintstones.* Low-budget films such as *The Beat Generation* (1959) and pulp fiction such as *Beat Girl, Beatnik Wanton,* and *Lust Pad* further contributed to the appropriation of the Beat's milieu (Watson 1995, 260–261). Kerouac, among others, lamented this devolution, particularly its divorce from spirituality and literature. The late 1950s also saw many poets, such as Kenneth Rexroth, Ferlinghetti, and Bob Kaufman, perform their poetry while accompanied by jazz, an innovation that further expanded both the influence of the movement and parodies of its affectations. Nevertheless, the attention did attract talented poets such as Diane di Prima and LeRoi Jones to the fold, and a flurry of poetry volumes appeared, including ones by Kaufman, di Prima, Snyder, Corso, and Ferlinghetti.

The 1960s saw not only some of the Beats' best work—including Ginsberg's *Kaddish and Other Poems* and *Reality Sandwiches,* Snyder's *Myths and Texts* and *Riprap & Cold Mountain Poems,* Jones's *Preface to a Twenty-Volume Suicide Note,* di Prima's *Poems for Freddie,* and Lenore Kandel's *The Love Book,* among many others—but a marked shift in their literary and political influence. Cultural and political events such as Jacobellis v. Ohio (1964), cheap and reliable birth control, the maturation of the Baby Boomers, recreational drugs, feminism, gay rights, and the Vietnam War laid the groundwork for a significant interest in the anti-materialist ethos expounded by the Beat poets. The youth culture in particular looked to poets such as Ginsberg and Ed Sanders for guidance and inspiration in protesting the war and its cultural enablers. Ironically, sales of Beat literature exploded, even as its anti-materialist message failed to inspire many in the academy. Additionally, a "second wave" of Beat poets, such as Ann Waldman and Janine Pommy Vega took heart from the Beat example and expanded its boundaries. Starting in 1969, with the death of Kerouac, however, the Beat movement began to become mythologized.

While its living members continued to write poetry, fans born long after the original Beats began a long process of transforming (or beatifying) the group into a collection of latter-day heroes. In the 1970s and 1980s, numerous popular anthologies, reprints, and testimonials appeared (the academy was more sluggish in praising the Beats), even as new material, such as Snyder's Pulitzer-winning *Turtle Island* and Ginsberg's *Mind Breaths,* appeared. Although some, such as Whalen and Kaufman, withdrew from the public eye, others, such as Ginsberg and Corso, capitalized on their celebrity and lectured and read poetry on a regular basis. Ginsberg in particular reveled in his role as generational spokesman and was quoted frequently by journalists seeking his opinion on important matters of the day. By his death in 1997, most recognized Ginsberg as a giant among contemporary poets. Many of the younger Beats, as well as older ones such as Snyder and Joanne Kyger, now distance themselves from a Beat label they find too constricting. As living, working poets, many feel either trapped, like Snyder, by the legend or believe with Waldman that its influence was merely one of many in their lives. The academy eventually began studying the Beats in earnest in the 1990s and 2000s, and numerous scholarly monographs and articles began to codify the Beat aesthetic and ideology.

Trends and Themes

Open Form. The 1940s and 1950s saw the hegemony of the New Criticism, an approach to literature that emphasized close reading and formalism. As a consequence of this influential movement, much of the poetry produced during this time adhered to strict formal conventions, a phenomenon lamented by the Beat poets, who felt that poems by such luminaries as Cleanth Brooks, early Robert Lowell, and Howard Nemerov lacked emotional significance. In contrast, the Beat poets saw organic, improvisational forms such as those employed by Whitman and Williams, as well as the spontaneous improvisation of Dada and be-bop, as strategies for expanding the range of American poetry. Like Henry Miller, the Beats wanted to destroy the "gold standard" of literature and pursue a form of self-expression that was raw and true. Ginsberg later remarked that "even to entertain the conception in advance of creating a work of art would block your mind from getting at the actual heart-throb of direct expression of the material you started out trying to articulate or voice" (Ginsberg 1974, 106). Ferlinghetti, furthermore, described the core of the Beat aesthetic as an oral one: "The printed page has made poetry so silent. But the poetry that I am talking about here is spoken poetry, poetry conceived of as oral messages" (2001, 169). Open form allows the poetry to be more authentic (of the "street," as Ferlinghetti put it), although the Beats certainly did revise their work, myths to the contrary notwithstanding. In achieving this open, oral form, the Beats took two primary paths, radical enjambment and dislocation, although techniques such as repetition, catalogues, uneven lines, collage, and others were common in Beat poetry. Different recordings of Beat poems, such as Ginsberg's "Howl," indicate the performable aspect of the poetry, with the poets employing different rhythms, cadences, and tones as their moods and relationship to their work alters over time. In poems such as Snyder's "Night Highway Ninety-Nine," McClure's "Peyote Poem," Janine Pommy Vega's "Junk (and the Old Man) Changes," Elise Cowen's "Death I'm Coming," and Jones's "Hymn for Lanie Poo" all exhibit a loose structure that allows the poets to follow their minds without distraction, to free their thoughts from the strictures of convention. This nonlinear construction lets the Beats break free from paradigmatic, and even rational, logic and pursue a more unorthodox (at times transcendent) path. Despite the openness of the form, however, the Beats do not sacrifice complexity of thought, linking their free-flowing lines to themes as varied as atomic annihilation, racism, and Buddhism.

Spirituality. Along with their skepticism of mainstream concepts such as capitalism, formal education, and patriotism, the Beats often found traditional Judeo-Christian religions lacking. Some of the Beats felt that the dogma of such religions robbed them of spiritual purity and of an immediate connection to God. Consequently, many of them, such as Kerouac, Snyder, Kyger, Whalen, and Welch, turned to various strands of eastern religions, among them Buddhism (Theravedan, Zen, and others), Tao, and Hinduism.

Like the transcendentalists before them, the Beats focused on ways to expand their consciousness and break free from the homogenized sociocultural milieu of 1950s America. Among the many lessons that the writers learned was the concept of abandoning desire, which can only lead to suffering (Dukka). They also tried to purify themselves through meditation, although, as Snyder pointed out, many Beats were aided by "systematic experimentation with narcotics" (1992, 306). The goal, Snyder continued, was not to be constantly high, for that "lacks intellect, will, and compassion," all necessary for true illumination. The illuminated individual would be in tune with the natural world and would strive to be compassionate and loving. For the Beats, spirituality and sin was a personal quest. Examples of Beat spirituality may be found in poems such as Ginsberg's

"Thoughts Sitting Breathing," Kerouac's "Sea," Snyder's "Smokey the Bear Sutra," and Waldman's "Pratitya-Samutpada."

Observing America's post-war prosperity as shallow, many Beats held that the superstructures of American capitalism—and of other societies wherein individuals were valued less than the collective—tend to dehumanize and enervate citizens. According to the Beats, technology and progress, although beneficial for improving material wealth and entrenching political and military power, distract many people from reaching their potential. Progress, narrowly defined as technological advancement, leads not to self-knowledge and self-worth—or to an enlightened society—but to accumulation and power. In short, progress shackles most people because it compels them to turn away from their potential in an endless quest for more material goods. If a material need is met, progress creates a new "need" that becomes the focus of attention. A herd mentality ensues, wherein "group think" stifles individual creativity and spirituality. In contrast, the Beats, like Emerson before them, encouraged people to break out of limiting roles—consumer, parent, student, employee, and the like—and search for their true path.

Sexuality. As the censorship travails of "Howl" suggest, a frank treatment of sexuality formed one of the thematic interests of many of the Beat poets and is one reason for their problematic early relationship with the scholarly community. Many Beats felt that just as universities, churches, and businesses had become hollow, enervating institutions that encouraged homogeneity and punished critical thinking, sexuality too had been bound in a straitjacket of anxiety, repression, and hypocrisy. Alternative sexualities, particularly same-sex relationships, nonmarital sex, and so-called fetishes were publicly demonized yet privately practiced, resulting not in healthy, natural enjoyment but in guilt-ridden, closeted behavior. For the Beats, part of self-liberation meant facing one's sexuality and expressing it fully, both physically and rhetorically. Many of the Beats courageously proclaimed their gay and lesbian desires, no small act in an environment where deviation from "normative" sexual behavior could be punished by law or homophobic violence. While the Kinsey reports (*Sexual Behavior in the Human Male* [1948] and *Sexual Behavior in the Human Female* [1953]) and the pioneering sexual research of individuals such as Gershon Legman clearly showed the diversity of American sexual preferences, those tastes were not to be shared publicly if they contradicted the image of the heterosexual nuclear family. Ginsberg's experiences with Carl Solomon, a man institutionalized partly because of his homosexuality, ultimately prompted him to be blunt about his own gay proclivities. Among its other achievements, "Howl" is remarkable for its descriptions of gay sex and for appropriating anti-gay slurs long before the Queer nationalism of the late 1980s and early 1990s. Obscenities, descriptions of intercourse, sexual metaphors—all of these taboo subjects and strategies found their way into Beat poetry, sometimes functioning as the primary theme, as in Kandel's *The Love Book,* sometimes in support of other subjects, as in Ferlinghetti's "Away Above a Harborful." In most cases—although less so in the female Beats—sexuality is employed as a positive, joyous experience that contrasted with the guilt and fear surrounding its official manifestations. Sexuality is posited as a means of breaking away from the bonds of convention and requires neither marriage nor long-term commitment. As with mind-altering drugs such as peyote and LSD, sex is sometimes also seen as a method of reaching beyond one's intellectual limits and tapping into a higher spiritual consciousness. Some Beat women, however, employ sexuality to investigate power and its relation to gender roles.

Context and Issues

Marginalization of Women and Minorities. Despite new collections highlighting the achievements of the female Beats and articles on African American Beat poets, most mainstream readers remain unfamiliar with poets such as Diane di Prima, Anne Waldman, Bob Kaufman, and Ted Joans. To a large degree, this ignorance stems from a lack of inclusion in mainstream undergraduate anthologies, in which students are exposed to various literary movements. In the *Norton Anthology of Literature by Women,* no Beat poets are included, and only Kaufman appears in the *Norton Anthology of African American Literature* (Jones/Baraka is represented by non-Beat works). Such omissions tend to underplay the range of Beat themes, such as abortion (di Prima's "Brass Furnace Going Out"), criticism of the Black Arts Movement (Joans's "A Few Blue Words to the Wise"), metafiction (Waldman's *"avant la letter"*), and the healing power of jazz (Kaufman's "Round about Midnight"). Concomitant with the absence of women and minorities, however, is canonical indifference to the poetry of the Beat poets in general, save for Ginsberg (the most entrenched in the canon), Snyder (a rising figure), Ferlinghetti, Rexroth, and Kerouac. Although figures such as Corso, Whalen, and McClure form part of the Beat myth, they, like Elise Cowen, Janine Pommy Vega, and (early) A.B. Spellman, find little to no representation in key academic anthologies. A key question is whether the continued exclusion of such Beat poets primarily stems from systemic racism/sexism, academic preferences, or popular stereotypes.

War. The Beats grew out of the ashes of World War II, and the Korean War. The Cold War and the Vietnam conflict were key events in shaping the Beat aesthetic in the 1950s, 1960s, and 1970s. Poems such as Ginsberg's "Wichita Vortex Sutra," "Ed Sanders," "Poem from Jail," Rexroth's "Thou Shalt Not Kill," Corso's "Bomb," and di Prima's "Goodbye Nkrumah," for example, all rail against the military-industrial complex and espouse pacifist principles. With America at war once more, many readers are again turning to the alternative political views espoused by the Beat poets. In 1992, Ginsberg, in the aftermath of the first Gulf War, explained the resurgence of interest in the Beat message thusly: "The literature and mythology of the Beat Generation runs counter to the current hypertechnological, homogenized, money-obsessed, security/fear-based, militaristic gross-out. [. . .] All these themes make the original Beat ethos quite user-friendly, compared to the destructiveness of the supposed 'straight' world that can go nuts, killing one hundred fifty thousand people in Iraq for the sake of oil that'll pollute the planet" (Ginsberg 1992, 13–14). The Beats' message of spirituality, love, and peace clearly runs counter to the dictates of blind patriotism, the politics of fear, and go-it-alone foreign policy. A key question with respect to this issue is whether this message is actionable on a national scale or whether it leads to a dangerous quietism in the face of systematic brutalities.

Canonical Rebels. A final issue for considering the Beats in 2007 concerns the effect of their mythos, both academically and popularly. While few younger readers of the Beats will disconnect the poets from their legend to the extent that many beatniks and hippies did in the 1950s and 1960s, many are still more fascinated with the Beats' rebel lifestyle than with their often challenging poetry. Too often, the Beats

BEAT POETRY PREDICTS THE ENVIRONMENTAL MOVEMENT

Even before the popular environmental movement unofficially started with the publication of Rachel Carson's *Silent Spring* (1962), many of the Beat poets showed an affinity for ecological awareness, particularly how it impacted spirituality. With an apparent majority of scientists concurring on the human impact on global warming, Beat poetry's reverence for the natural world and its skeptical view of unrestrained technological progress is again attracting an audience. The Beats' treatment of the environment fuses the personal, the spiritual, and the political in varying degrees, and nature is presented both in its (relatively) untouched state and in its relation to destructive human practices. Poems such as Whalen's "3 Days Ago" and Kyger's "September," Ginsberg's "Sunflower Sutra," and Snyder's "Logging" section of *Myths and Texts* exemplify the quiet contemplation of nature and its ability to spark a heightened spiritual awareness, yet they also interrogate the unintended consequences of human activity on the environment. Snyder especially has welcomed the mantle of spokesperson for the environment, supplementing his poetry with essays on the subject. The Beats' concern with more than "sustainability," with a deeper ecology, holds great appeal for a readership grappling with the consequences of peak oil, global warming, and suburban sprawl. A key question prompted by the Beat poets is whether environmental idealism can gain political traction in a materialist society.

are seen as outrageous rebels rather than as superior poets, with their names carrying a talismanlike quality and their poems—apart from a few frequently anthologized poems by Ginsberg ("Howl," "America," "A Supermarket in California") and Snyder ("Riprap," "Wave," "Axe Handles")—largely unread. Selections from the most common anthologies of American literature, such as those published by Norton, Harper, Bedford, and Heath, do little to demystify the Beats as larger-than-life figures willing to fight the powers-that-be at all costs. Such a limited view becomes problematic, however, in the face of commercials for Gap khakis (silently deleting Joyce Johnson from the original photo), endless repackaging of biographical material, coffee mugs, refrigerator magnets, songs (for instance, 10,000 Maniacs' "Hey Jack Kerouac"), and T-shirts. Such reification clearly departs from the antiestablishment tenor of the poetry, and it bespeaks of a Beat "industry" more than it does for the ability of the literature to stir the souls and minds of the audience. A key question, therefore, is whether the fetishization of the Beat legend will serve to enhance or to harm the Beats' long-term poetic reputation.

Reception. The Beats' initial reception reflected their interest in marginal themes and open forms and was thus largely dismissive. Norman Podhoretz opined in 1958 that the Beats' evinced love of "primitivism and spontaneity is more than a cover for hostility to intelligence; it arises from a pathetic poverty of feeling as well" (Podhoretz 2001, 491). Also in 1958, Herb Caen coined the term beatnik, which described marginalized societal dropouts without the drive for serious literary aspirations. Kerouac responded, but the term stuck, resulting in further marginalization for serious Beat poetry. Lawrence Lipton's 1959 volume *The Holy Barbarians* further entrenched the popular notion of the beatnik. In the early 1960s, however, the Beats did find some admirers, including Thomas Parkinson, editor of an academic volume called *A Casebook on the Beats* in 1961, who noted that the Beats preached not rebellion but "social refusal" and that the poetry's unusual syntax is an "attempt to increase the vocality of the verse" (Parkinson 1995, 450, 460–461). Another early volume on the beatniks was Francis J. Rigney and L. Douglas Smith's. *The Real Bohemia: A Sociological and Psychological Study of the "Beats,"* which saw a range of human behavior rather than just the stereotypical behavior. By the late 1960s, the Beats' popular reception was entrenched, as Baby Boomers strained against institutional conformism. In the early 1970s, the emphasis was on hagiography, as represented by books such as John Tytell's *Naked Angels: The Lives and Literature of the Beat Generation* and Bruce Cook's *The Beat Generation*. With volumes such as Lee Bartlett's *The Beats: Essays in Criticism,* the academy slowly started to catch up with the public in the 1980s, although popular books by far outpaced their academic counterparts. During this period, some of the Beat poets (Ginsberg, Snyder, Ferlinghetti) entered mainstream anthologies and started to receive serious critical attention. Many others, however, including di Prima, Joans, and Waldman lingered on the edge of both the canon and the Beat myth, and even some of the acknowledged figures lacked much sustained criticism. As a result, many critics in the 1990s and beyond began to reevaluate the Beat myth and explore both some of the more marginalized poets and the more "central" figures. Such critics often noted that race and gender were often at play in this marginalization, although such white males as Corso and Welch fared little better in terms of *poetic* evaluation (although they were constantly present in the *biographical* and *cultural* analysis of the Beats). Examples of this trend include Ronna C. Johnson and Nancy M. Grace's *Girls Who Wore Black: Women Writing the Beat Generation,* Brenda Knight's 1996 anthology *Women of the Beat Generation: The Writers, Artists, and Muses at the Heart of a Revolution,* and Richard Peabody's *A Different Beat: Writings by Women of the Beat Generation*. Recent anthologies, articles, and books have somewhat rectified the secondary status of many of the Beat poets, but a clear caste system in the criticism and especially in undergraduate anthologies such as the *Norton Anthology of American Literature* and *Anthology of Modern American Poetry* still exists. Despite lacking the critical attention of contemporaries such as Plath and Brooks, Ginsberg is clearly the most studied of the Beat poets, and his reputation shows no sign of falling since his death in 1997. Most articles, however, focus on Ginsberg's early career, particularly "Howl," and his later work is still awaiting extended debate. The rise of ecocriticism in the 1990s and beyond has led to increased attention for Snyder, but with the possible exceptions of Rexroth, Whalen, and Ferlinghetti, few of the Beats receive substantial *individual* attention. Jones/Baraka, of course, does receive attention, but not primarily for his Beat phase, and Kerouac's poetry is not nearly as studied as his fiction. An occasional article appears on poets such as McClure or Welch, but it hardly constitutes a trend. In sum, much critical work remains to be done on the Beats, particularly on "peripheral" figures and the later poetry. Many collections of esoteric primary material, as well as Beat "encyclopedias" have appeared in the last two decades, but largely, the Beat myth continues to overshadow much of the poetry, and the criticism reflects this.

Selected Authors

Gregory Corso (1930–2001). Although Corso did not take part in the famous Six Gallery reading, he is now regarded as one of the "core" Beat poets. Combining humor with biting social commentary, in poems such as "Marriage" and "Bomb," Corso reveals fundamental paradoxes in the American way of life and respectively challenges both uncritical romanticism and apocalyptic paranoia. Rarely inventive as a stylist, Corso eschews subtlety for attempts to jolt his readers out of their complacency with violent juxtapositions, such as in "Power," where at one point he alternates between love and howitzers, suggesting that power is, at its core, motivated by love. Corso's definitive collection is *Mindfield: New and Selected Poems* (1989).

Diane di Prima (1934–). Along with Waldman, di Prima is among the two most influential female Beats. In collections such as *This Kind of Bird Flies Backward* (1958) and *Seminary Poems* (1991), di Prima feminized Beat poetry by commenting on subjects, such as abortion, female mythology, and pregnancy, ignored or underplayed by her male contemporaries. Poems such as "The Quarrel," "The Practice of Magical Evocation" (a response to Snyder's "Praise for Sick Women"), and "The Killing" intermingle tenderness, humor, and pain in exploring what it means to be a talented female in a world controlled by men. A practicing Buddhist, di Prima also, like many of the Beats, used hallucinogens, at one point living in the notorious Timothy Leary's Millbrook commune. In the 1970s and beyond, di Prima tried her hand at a feminist epic, the *Loba* sequence (16 parts as of 1998), which investigates the experience of women via an archetypal, mythological strategy that plumbs the depths and scales the heights of feminine (un)consciousness. Formerly editing the important Beat periodical *Floating Bear* with Jones, di Prima has also written several plays.

Lawrence Ferlinghetti (1919–). Poet, publisher, cultural spokesman, Ferlinghetti has published over three dozen collections, some of which are *A Coney Island of the Mind* (the title of which alludes to a line from Henry Miller's *Black Spring*), *Tyrannus Nix?*, and *These Are My Rivers: New and Selected Poems, 1955–1993.* Founder of the City Lights bookstore, an influential Beat hangout, Ferlinghetti published many books of Beat poetry, most famously Ginsberg's *Howl and other Poems* in 1956. Ferlinghetti, like Ginsberg, valued the oral elements in poetry, and his style owes much to the improvisational quality of jazz. A ferocious wit, Ferlinghetti employed satire to tackle the most pressing issues of his day, including nuclear annihilation, anti-communist jingoism, and pollution. In poems such as "A Nation of Sheep," "No. 25" (from *Coney Island*), and "Christ Climbed Down," Ferlinghetti indicts the "blather" that arises from an inability to distance one's self from American materialism. The stylistic stamp of e.e. cummings is unmistakable, as is Ferlinghetti's debt to surrealism. Nevertheless, his allusive, boisterous voice is a singular achievement.

Allen Ginsberg (1926–1997). Founding Beat poet and a giant of twentieth-century poetry, Ginsberg was influenced by, among others, Whitman, William Blake, eastern spirituality (especially Buddhism), Henry Miller, Arthur Rimbaud, surrealism, and W.C. Williams. In contrast to the strict formalism that he saw taking root in the 1940s and 1950s, Ginsberg was at his best when employing long enjambed lines packed full of startling images and juxtapositions, as seen in poems ranging from "Howl" and "Wichita Vortex Sutra" to "White Shroud" and "Reverse the Rain of Terror." In writing collections such as *Kaddish and Other Poems, Planet News,* and *Cosmopolitan Greetings: Poems 1986–1992,* he critiqued the repressive and conformist attitudes of the Cold War era and took on an activist's role during the Vietnam War and beyond, proudly exhibiting his open, experimental approach to life and literature. Although his poetry eventually became highly popular, Ginsberg rejected materialism in favor of visionary, ecstatic spiritualism that alternated between the violent and the sublime. Like many Beats, he drew on autobiography, but he placed it in a radically altered context. From his epic performance at the Six Gallery to the end of his life, Ginsberg considered the performable, public aspect of poetry crucial.

Ted Joans (1928–2003). In collections such as *Beat Poems, Funky Jazz Poems,* and *Afrodisia: New Poems,* Joans infused a jazz sensibility with a vigorous sense of social justice. Joans was inspired foremost by the musicality of Langston Hughes, whose work motivated him to pay particular attention to rhythm, and dramatic tension, as in poems like ".38," "It Is Time," and "Think Twice and Be Nice." Joans was renowned for his live performances, which greatly impressed Hughes. Like Jones/Baraka, Joans became disenchanted with the Beat movement, and the political engagement of the Black Arts movement attracted him, resulting in poems such as "Home," "God Blame America," and "To Every Free African."

LeRoi Jones (Amiri Baraka) (1934–). Later renowned for his seminal poetic and theoretical work with the Black Arts movement, Jones was initially an influential Beat poet, supporter, and editor. With di Prima, Jones edited *Floating Bear,* and he established Totem Press, an important alternative publishing venue for several of his Beat contemporaries. He also wrote a blistering retort to Podhoretz's dismissal of the Beat aesthetic. His *Preface to a Twenty Volume Suicide Note . . .* is a key Beat collection that unveils Jones's restless spirit, anticonformism, and unorthodox line. Poems such as "The Bridge" and "In Memory of Radio" underscore his improvisational bent, while "To a Publisher . . . cut-out" and "Notes for a Speech" anticipate Jones's growing social concerns. *Dead Lecturer* shows growing tensions within Jones that would ultimately lead to his new, more polemical, aesthetic, with poems such as "An Agony. As Now" and "Short Speech to My Friends" problematizing the self-absorption (as opposed to transcendent spiritualism) evident in many of the Beats. Disgusted both with Beat poetry's commercialization and its racial indifference, Jones spearheaded the Black Arts movement and became one of its leading writers, arguing not for individual transcendence but for collective action and true street poetry (i.e., poetry comprehensible for nonspecialists and designed to raise racial and class consciousness). Jones changed his name to Amiri Baraka in 1968.

Lenore Kandel (1932–). Aiming for thematic and linguistic authenticity, Kandel's most famous poems, such as "To Fuck with Love," "Hard Core Love," and "Love-Lust Poem," merge raw sexuality, ecstatic self-awareness, and (eastern) metaphysical contemplation, although she did not limit herself to erotica. Subjects such as modern alienation, drug use, circuses, and mental anguish emphasize Kandel's connection to the Beat aesthetic, and her style is influenced by bop and jazz. Kandel never collected her work, which remains accessible only in chapbooks such as *The Love Book* and *A Passing Dragon, A Passing Dragon Seen Again,* and in the small volume *Word Alchemy,* which contained a variety of her lyric poems. Following a devastating motorcycle accident, Kandel vanished from the literary scene in 1967, her small output an everlasting testimony to her potential.

Bob Kaufman (1925–1986). A wide-ranging stylist, Kaufman drew on traditions as diverse as the African griot, Whitman, bop, and surrealism, and he thrived on the live recital of his poetry. He initially eschewed publication in favor of improvisational performances. In works such as *Solitudes Crowded with Loneliness* and *The Golden Sardine,* Kaufman announced his presence as an innovative social critic and jazz appropriator. He also helped found *Beatitude Magazine,* an important Beat periodical. Like Lenore Kandel, Kaufman underwent a self-imposed silence and published virtually nothing in the last part of his life.

Jack Kerouac (1922–1969). Primarily noted for his "spontaneous prose" novels, Kerouac ventured into poetry in works such as *Mexico City Blues, Scattered Poems,* and the final section of *Big Sur*. Although he did write haiku, Kerouac, perhaps predictably, preferred the more epic style visible in the choruses of *Mexico City Blues,* wherein he riffs on metaphysical topics in a sort of cosmic dialectic. Many of the elements of his "spontaneous prose" (for example: "submissive to everything, open, listen"; "Remove literary, grammatical and syntactical inhibition") are echoed in the poetry. Hyperdynamic and formally challenging, the choruses in *Mexico City Blues* engage subjects as diverse as bop, time (and Proust), and alienation. Kerouac's haiku extended from the writer's investigation of Buddhism and were often composed "on the spot" as a jazzy barrage of sound and crystallized metaphysics. Although Kerouac's poetic output pales with that of Ferlinghetti, Jones, Corso, and his other Beat contemporaries, many critics note that his prose is highly poetic and that its rhythms are similar to the open form of the best Beat poetry.

Joanne Kyger (1934–). A poet with an epic sensibility but a lyrical form, Kyger, as H.D. and Adrienne Rich, infuses classical myths with a distinctly feminist view. Challenging the rough-and-ready ethos of many of her male Beat peers, Kyger marries a multifaceted spiritualism with an interrogation of feminine archetypes. Unlike the more transparent autobiographical approach of some of her contemporaries, Kyger employs a "deep" approach to self-examination in collections such as *The Tapestry and the Web, The Wonderful Focus of You,* and *Patzcuaro*. In the former, for example, Kyger reworks *The Odyssey* and subverts Penelope's role as a loyal, if limited, helpmeet by imbuing her with the power to control Odysseus's destiny and in other ways expanding her role. Kyger is also very interested in revealing the importance, humor, and energy inherent in everyday life. Her most recent work has been highly critical of U.S. involvement in Iraq.

Michael McClure (1932–). As both poet and playwright, McClure explores the nexus of the physical and the spiritual, often employing the former as a conduit for the latter. Reveling in the body, seeking synergy with nature, McClure's poetry emphasizes an awareness that leads to unrestrained joy, even amid viciousness and hypocrisy. A prolific poet, McClure, in such books as *Hymns to St. Geryon and Other Poems, Dark Brown, September Blackberries,* and *Simple Eyes,* makes ample use of animal imagery, ecstatic visions, and physical candor. McClure's style ranges widely, but it frequently accentuates the pictorial elements of poetry (capitalization, alternation between long lines and single words, visual symmetry/asymmetry, parentheses, dashes, etc.). Other pervasive features, as seen in such poems as, "Love Lion," "For the Death of 100 Whales," "Rant Block," and "Plum Stones," include mantralike repetition, catalogs, and surprising imagery.

Janine Pommy Vega (1942–). Employing her private pain as a catalyst for transcendence, Pommy Vega investigates how loss can crystallize one's experience of love, self, and spirituality. A teen when she turned her back on middle-class conformity, Pommy Vega became an autodidact, soaking up influences such as Ginsberg, William Carlos Williams, and William Blake, yet she managed to develop a strong individual voice. From early collections such as *Poems to Fernando* and *Journal of a Hermit* to later books such as *Mad Dogs of Trieste: New and Selected Poems, 1975–2000* and *The Green Piano: New Poems,* Pommy Vega documents her ability to withstand both personal (deaths of her husband and parents, abortion, automobile accident, etc.) and political (Cold War, Sarajevo, Iraq, etc.) trauma while expanding her spiritual horizons. Pommy Vega typically uses a plain, direct style that juxtaposes simple, yet often terrifying, images with emblems of survival.

Kenneth Rexroth (1905–1982). A mentor for both many Beat and San Francisco Renaissance poets, Rexroth was himself influenced by Chicago's socialist and avant-garde scene in the 1920s, although he avoided being overly dogmatic. Rexroth's anti-establishment poetics clearly attracted the Beats, though, and although Rexroth later rejected the commercialization of the Beats, he has many similarities with them. Among these are Rexroth's jazzlike rhythms, contemplative themes, and colloquial specificity. In collections such as *The Signature of All Things, In Defense of the Earth,* and *The Love Poems of Marichiko,* Rexroth reveals a growing interest in Asian philosophy and technique, directly presenting his images and revealing a quiet passion reminiscent of some of Snyder's less polemical work. Common Beat themes such as sexuality, anticapitalism, and the environment are present, but Rexroth eschews the explosive rhetoric of a Ginsberg or Sanders, adopting a more restrained poetics that presents sharpened emotions on the verge of release rather than the release itself, a technique evident in poems such as "VII" (from *The Love Poems of Marichiko*), "Fish Peddler and Cobbler," and "Married Blues," although exceptions such as "Thou Shalt Not Kill" appear with fair regularity.

Ed Sanders (1939–). Editor of the important Beat periodical *Fuck You: A Magazine of the Arts* and member of the avant-garde poet-rock band the Fugs ("Swinburne Stomp," "Carpe Diem"), Sanders is a classically trained poet who produces highly unorthodox, colloquial, and confrontational verse. Politically conscious from the start, Sanders has employed derisive, feverish wit in satirizing the destructive powers of war and unrestrained capitalism from Vietnam to Iraq. In such Dionysian books as *Peace Eye, 20,000 A.D., Thirsting for Peace in a Raging Century: Selected Poems, 1961–1985,* and *America: A History in Verse* (this latter an example of what Sanders calls "investigative poetry"), Sanders combines serious themes with irreverent poetics, playful images, and sexual language.

Gary Snyder (1930–). Somewhat younger than the original Beats, Snyder is nevertheless one of the most influential of the movement, winning a Pulitzer Prize in 1974 for *Turtle Island,* a collection that cemented his reputation as an environmental activist. Snyder's early work in *Riprap* and *Myths and Texts* contrast materialist societies with the harder, but ultimately more spiritually rewarding, aboriginal cultures. As with Robinson Jeffers, Snyder could at times appear misanthropic, but like Jeffers, he reserved his most stinging rebukes for those individuals and societies that had lost touch with the land and its spiritual lessons. In poems such as "Ripples on the Surface" and "Straight-Creek—Great Burn," Snyder merges precise environmental detail with human possibilities and losses. Some critics, however, fault Snyder for an overly moralizing, judgmental tone in some of his nature poetry, such as "Mother Earth: Her Whales" or "Smokey the Bear Sutra." Apart from his concern for the environment, Snyder is best known for his spiritual themes. Unlike some of the Beats, Snyder studied Zen Buddhism systematically and strived to avoid a diluted, "Americanized" strain of the lifestyle. His poetry tends to integrate this meditative approach to existence, as in "What Happened Here Before" and "The Blue Sky."

A.B. Spellman (1935–). A student of Sterling A. Brown, who encouraged him to explore the artistic and social possibilities of music, Spellman developed an encyclopedic knowledge of jazz, which helped him to craft an aesthetic that veers between the understated and explosive in his sole book of poetry, *The Beautiful*

Days. In *The Beautiful Days,* Spellman also has made sporadic poetic contributions to various periodicals and anthologies.

Anne Waldman (1945–). Two decades younger than the original Beats, Waldman nevertheless held important roles in later Beat ventures, such as the Jack Kerouac School of Disembodied Poetics. A prolific poet, Waldman's early works revealed an affinity with ur-Beats such as Ginsberg and Corso. In volumes such as *Baby Breakdown* and *Fast Speaking Woman,* Waldman displays a Whitmanesque open line and a fondness for pastiche. In poems such as "All of My Kingdoms" and "Miles Above," Waldman bursts with vibrant energy as she subverts rigid patriarchal institutions and thinking. In recent years, Waldman has turned to the epic, with her multivolume sequence, *Iovis,* which contains both her familiar collage technique and a sweeping, mythic range that interrogates both individual transcendence and collective impediments. Additionally, Waldman, in the anti-academic tradition of the earliest Beats, is a performance artist of the first water and avails herself of a variety of media in her dynamic public events. A practicing Buddhist, Waldman offers feminist spiritual insight lacking in many of her Beat peers.

Lew Welch (1926–1971[?]). A classmate of Gary Snyder and Philip Whalen, Welch was something of a tragic enigma, what Snyder called a "casualty." A talented poet, Welch suffered from both depression and alcoholism, severely limiting his published output. Nevertheless, Welch, influenced by such writers as Robert Service, Gertrude Stein, and William Carlos Williams, transformed his poetic voice from a fairly traditional one to a tight, crisp style that avoided "literary" allusion. In his collection *On Out* and chapbooks such as *Hermit Poems* and *The Song Mt. Tamalpais Sings,* Welch combined an economical vocabulary with a brisk rhythm to explore his troubled life honestly and directly.

Philip Whalen (1923–2002). Although often labeled a Beat, Whalen, as with many of the western Beats, was also a driving force in the San Francisco Renaissance. In collections such as *Like I Say, On Bear's Head,* and *Every Day,* Whalen offers a gentle, playful contrast to some of his more exuberant contemporaries among the Beats. Whalen experimented, like many of the Beats, with open typographical forms, but his subject matter is generally more self-deprecating and quotidian. A Buddhist monk, Whalen's commitment to spiritual matters is unparalleled among the Beats, and his poetry reflects this concern in poems such as "The Dharma Youth League," "Sourdough Mountain Lookout," and "The Expensive Life," although he rarely employs hyperserious rhetoric, preferring to juxtapose metaphysical principles with a variety of earthly pursuits.

Bibliography

Baraka, Amiri. *Preface to a Twenty Volume Suicide Note.* New York: Totem Press, 1961.

Barlett, Lee, ed. *The Beats: Essays in Criticism.* Jefferson: McFarland, 1981.

Burroughs, William S. *Junky.* New York: Ace, 1953.

Carson, Rachel. *Silent Spring.* Boston, MA: Houghton Mifflin, 1962.

Charters, Ann. "Panel Discussion with Women Writers of the Beat Generation." *Beat Down to Your Soul: What Was the Beat Generation?.* Ann Charters, ed. New York: Penguin, 2001, 611–632.

Cook, Bruce. *The Beat Generation.* New York: Scribner, 1971.

Corso, Gregory. *Mindfield: New and Selected Poems.* New York: Thunder's Mouth Press, 1989.

di Prima, Diane. *Freddie Poems.* Point Reyes, CA: Eidolon Editions, 1974.

————. *Seminary Poems*. Point Reyes, CA: Floating Island, 1991.

————. *This Kind of Bird Flies Backwards*. New York: Totem Press, 1958.

Ferlinghetti, Lawrence. "Note on Poetry in San Francisco." *Beat Down to Your Soul: What Was the Beat Generation?*. Ann Charters, ed. New York: Penguin, 2001, 169.

————. *A Coney Island of the Mind*. New York: New Directions, 1968.

————. *These Are My Rivers: New and Selected Poems, 1955–1993*. New York: New Directions, 1993.

————. *Tyrannus Nix?* New York: New Directions, 1969.

Gates, Henry Louis, and McKay, Nellie Y. *The Norton Anthology of African American Literature*. New York: W.W. Norton, 2004.

Gifford, Barry, and Lee. Lawrence. *Jack's Book: An Oral Biography of Jack Kerouac*. New York: Thunder's Mouth Press, 2005.

Gilbert, Sandra M., and Susan Gubar, eds. *The Norton Anthology of Literature by Women*. New York: W.W. Norton, 2007.

Ginsberg, Allen. *Allen Verbatim: Lectures on Poetry, Politics, Consciousness*. Gordon Bell, ed. New York: McGraw-Hill, 1974.

————. *Howl and Other Poems*. San Francisco, CA: City Lights, 1956.

————. *Kaddish and Other Poems*. San Francisco, CA: City Lights, 1961.

————. "Prologue." *Beat Culture and the New America: 1950–1965*. Lisa Phillips, ed. New York: Whitney Museum/Flammarion, 1995, 17–19.

Ginsberg, Allen. *Reality Sandwiches*. San Francisco, CA: City Lights, 1963.

Ginsberg, Allen, and Daurer, Greg. "The *High Times* Interview." *High Times*. February (1992): 13–16. Holmes, John Clellon. "This Is the Beat Generation." *Beat Down to Your Soul: What Was the Beat Generation?*. Ann Charters, ed. New York: Penguin, 2001, 222–228.

Joans, Ted. *Afrodisia: New Poems*. New York: Hill & Wang, 1970.

————. *Jazz Poems: Beat Funky*. New York: Rhino Review, 1959.

Johnston, Allan. "Consumption, Addiction, Vision, Energy: Political Economies and Utopian Visions in the Writings of the Beat Generation." *College Literature* 32.2 (2005): 103–126.

Kandel, Lenore. *The Love Book*. San Francisco, CA: Stolen Paper, 1966.

Kaufman, Bob. *Solitudes Crowded with Loneliness*. New York: New Directions, 1965.

————. *The Golden Sardine*. San Francisco, CA: City Lights, 1967.

Kerouac, Jack. *Big Sur*. New York: Penguin, 1962.

————. *Mexico City Blues*. New York: Grove Press, 1959.

————. *On the Road*. New York: Viking, 1957.

————. *Scattered Poems*. San Francisco, CA: City Lights, 1961.

Knight, Brenda, ed. *Women of the Beat Generation: The Writers, Artists, and Muses at the Heart of a Revolution*. 2nd ed. San Francisco, CA: Conari, 1998.

Kyger, Joanne. *Pátzcuaro*. Bolinas, CA: Blue Millenium, 1999.

————. *The Tapestry and the Web*. San Francisco, CA: City Lights, 1965.

————. *The Wonderful Focus of You*. Calais: Z Press, 1979.

Lipton, Lawrence. *The Holy Barbarians*. New York: Messner, 1959.

McClure, Michael. *Hymns to St. Geryon and Other Poems and Dark Brown*. San Francisco, CA: Grey Fox, 1980.

McClure, Michael. *September Blackberries*. New York: New Directions, 1974.

————. *Simple Eyes*. New York: New Directions, 1994.

Peabody, Richard. *A Different Beat: Writings by Women of the Beat Generation*. London: Serpent's Tail, 1997.

Podhoretz, Norman. "The Know-Nothing Bohemians." In *Beat Down to Your Soul: What Was the Beat Generation?*. Ann Charters, ed. New York: Penguin, 2001, 481–493.

Raskin, Jonah. *American Scream: Allen Ginsberg's Howl and the Making of the Beat Generation*. Berkeley, CA: University of California Press, 2004.

Rigney, Francis J., and Smith, L. Douglas. *The Real Bohemia: A Sociological and Psychological Study of the "Beats."* New York: Basic Books, 1961.

Rexroth, Kenneth. *The Love Poems of Marichiko.* Santa Barbara, CA: Christopher's Books, 1978.

Sanders, Ed. *America: A History in Verse.* Santa Rosa, CA: Black Sparrow, 2000.

Skerl, Jennie. Introduction. In *Reconstructing the Beats.* Jennie Skerl, ed. London: Palgrave Macmillan, 2004, 1–7.

Snyder, Gary. *Myths and Texts.* New York: Totem, 1960.

———. "Note on the Religious Tendencies." In *The Portable Beat Reader.* Ann Charters, ed. New York: Viking, 1992, 305–306.

———. *Riprap & Cold Mountain Poems.* San Francisco, CA: City Lights, 1965.

———. *Turtle Island.* New York: New Directions, 1974.

Spellman, A.B. *The Beautiful Days.* New York: Poets' Press, 1968.

Tytell, John. *Naked Angels: The Lives and Literature of the Beat Generation.* New York: McGraw-Hill, 1976.

van Elteren, Mel. "The Subculture of the Beat: A Sociological Revisit." *Journal of American Culture* 22.3 (1999): 71–99.

Vega, Janine Pommy. *Poems to Fernando.* San Francisco, CA: City Lights, 1968.

———. *Journal of a Hermit.* Cherry Valley, NY: Cherry Valley Editions, 1974.

Waldman, Anne. *Baby Breakdown.* New York: Bobbs-Merrill, 1970.

———. *Fast Speaking Woman.* San Francisco, CA: City Lights, 1975.

———. *Iovis.* Minneapolis, MN: Coffee House Press, 1997.

Watson, Steven. *The Birth of the Beat Generation: Visionaries, Rebels, and Hipsters, 1944–1960.* New York: Pantheon, 1995.

Whalen, Philip. *Every Day.* San Francisco, CA: City Lights, 1965.

———. *Like I Say.* New York: Totem, 1960.

———. *On Bear's Head.* New York: Harcourt, Brace, and World, 1969.

Further Reading

Barlett, Lee, ed. *The Beats: Essays in Criticism.* Jefferson: McFarland, 1981; Charters, Ann. *Beat Down to Your Soul: What Was the Beat Generation?* New York: Penguin, 2001; Johnson, Ronna, and Nancy M. Grace, eds. *Girls who Wore Black: Women Writing the Beat Generation.* New Brunswick: Rutgers University Press, 2002; Knight, Brenda, ed. *Women of the Beat Generation: The Writers, Artists, and Muses at the Heart of a Revolution.* 2nd ed. San Francisco: Conari, 1998; Lee, Robert A., ed., *The Beat Generation Writers.* London: Pluto, 1996; Phillips, Lisa. *Beat Culture and the New America: 1950–1965.* New York: Whitney Museum/Flammarion, 1995; Raskin, Jonah. *American Scream: Allen Ginsberg's Howl and the Making of the Beat Generation.* Berkeley, CA: University of California Press, 2004; Skerl, Jennie, ed. *Reconstructing the Beats.* London: Palgrave Macmillan, 2004; Stephenson, Gregory. *The Daybreak Boys: Essays on the Literature of the Beat Generation.* Carbondale, IL: Southern Illinois University Press, 1990; Tytell, John. *Naked Angels: The Lives and Literature of the Beat Generation.* New York: McGraw-Hill, 1976.

JAMES M. DECKER

BIOGRAPHY

Definition. In everyday usage, the term *biography* is generally understood to refer to an account of an individual's life. Attempts to define the proper aim, form, and scope of such accounts, however, have provided ample fodder for heated debates among biographers, their subjects, their readers, and their critics, the reasons and rationales for writing and reading biographies being diverse enough that there exist multiple standards for evaluating the success of a work. These include whether the biographer sought to be definitive or "of the moment" in his account of the subject's life; whether the account purports to be comprehensive or focused on a specific aspect of the subject's achievements; and whether the biographer sees his primary role to be that of an entertainer, an educator, a reporter, or a historian. Although these roles are not mutually exclusive—and, indeed, the most well-received biographies are often a hybrid of **historical writing** and **literary journalism**—the biographer's perception of his responsibilities affects the style, format, content, and marketing of the published account, including whether it is reviewed and catalogued as history, fiction, or general nonfiction. The term *biography* encompasses scholarly monographs with hundreds of footnotes; glossy coffee-table books consisting primarily of anecdotes and photographs; gossip-spiced chronicles of a celebrity's rise to fame; extended speculation about the subject's inner life, based on clues derived from the subject's artistic output; novelistic portraits with invented scenes and dialogue; and other combinations of textual and visual narrative.

Also referred to as *life writing*, the genre attracted enough academic interest during the twentieth century to merit the establishment of an interdisciplinary Center for Biographical Research (CBR) at the University of Hawaii in 1976. The center and the University of Hawaii Press began publication of a quarterly journal in 1978; other periodicals devoted to the genre include *a/b: Auto/Biography Studies* (first issue 1985), the *Journal of Historical Biography* (first issue 2007), the *Journal of Medical Biography* (first issue 1993), *Life Writing* (first issue 2004), and *Lifewriting Annual: Biographical and Autobiographical Studies* (first issue 2006). Other programs devoted to development, discussion, and promotion of the genre include the Center for the Study of Lives (University of Southern Maine, founded 1988) and the International Auto/Biography Association (founded 1999), the latter a sponsor of biennial conferences. Genealogical and historical organizations that coordinate biographical programs, publications, and resources include the New York Genealogical and Biographical Society (founded 1869). Support groups for professional biographers include the Biography Seminar at New York University (founded 1980) and Women Writing Women's Lives (City University of New York, founded 1990).

There are many issues for scholars of the genre to examine and explore. The range of narrative forms available to biographers raises associated questions about the methods of research and interpretation they elect to pursue; many biographers choose to address this by detailing the parameters and scope of their specific projects in a remarks or acknowledgments section. For example, in his biography of John Wilkes (1726–1797), published by a university press, retired English professor Arthur Cash (b. 1922) signals his awareness of the different types of readers likely to peruse his book:

> I have written this book for a general audience of well-read, intelligent people. I hope scholars will approve of it, but I did not have them in mind as I wrote. I seldom say "it seems" or "the evidence suggests," and I seldom call attention to the quality of the evidence. On the other hand, the notes, which will be of little help to the general reader, are made for the scholar. My view of Wilkes is so different from that usually held by historians, it will certainly be challenged. I want the challengers to have no doubt of the primary evidence I have used, or from what secondary sources I have taken facts. (2006, 395)

In his biography of Andrew Carnegie (1835–1919), published by a commercial press, history professor David Nasaw begins with his evaluations of earlier portrayals of Carnegie, taking pains to note the constraints imposed upon his predecessors and highlighting his access to archives that had been closed or unknown to them. At 878 pages, Nasaw's version of Carnegie's life is clearly intended to serve as a definitive reference work, and he emphasizes his role in judging the evidence presented in older volumes: "My account of Carnegie's life leaves out several of the familiar stories told in the *Autobiography* and retold by his biographers, because I could not independently confirm their validity" (ix). At the same time, Nasaw had previously demonstrated his ability to write popular books with his biography of William Randolph Hearst (1862–1951); consequently, *Andrew Carnegie* was featured in holiday gift catalogs and heavily reviewed in general-interest newspapers and magazines, including two separate assessments in *The New York Times* (Gordon 2006; Hitchens 2006; Parker 2006; Stiles 2006; Yardley 2006). It reached *The New York Times* bestseller list and was a finalist for the 2007 Pulitzer Prize for Biography (the other finalist was Cash's biography of Wilkes).

Its success notwithstanding, several of the book's reviewers expressed dissatisfaction with Nasaw's handling of his resources. *Salon* reviewer T.J. Stiles, himself an award-winning biographer, lauded Nasaw's effort as "the most thorough, accurate and authoritative biography of Carnegie to date . . . I came away convinced that he has read everything Carnegie ever wrote." However, Stiles also opined that Nasaw had fallen short in other areas. In Stiles's view of the genre, he noted:

> Researcher . . . is only one of three roles played by a good biographer. Just as important are the parts of historian and writer—the first to explain the times, the second to craft a purposeful narrative. To put it another way, the researcher provides depth, the historian breadth, the writer life. (2006)

Stiles's conclusion—that Nasaw had concentrated too much on depth—was voiced by another well-regarded biographer, book critic Jonathan Yardley (b. 1939), who declared that:

> *Andrew Carnegie* would be a better book had it been pared down from 800 pages of text to, say, 650, because Nasaw is in love with his research and cannot let go of it even when it becomes redundant, but only readers laboring under constraints of time are likely to complain; this is biography on the grand scale, and on the whole it lives up to its author's ambitions. (2006)

Yardley's prediction of *Andrew Carnegie*'s welcome among other readers suggests a set of universal expectations regarding biographical narratives, but his claim is better treated as a reflection of an individual's personal definition of the genre—one with which other biographers and readers do not necessarily concur. Yardley's belief in an ideal balance of research and exposition informs his reviews of other biographies. For instance, in an appraisal of a study of H.L. Mencken (1880–1956), Yardley simultaneously praises the author's "refusal to get bogged down in quotidian biographical minutiae" and casts it as a weakness, seeing it as the reason several topics were not given the attention he felt they merited (2002). Yardley's preference for "serious inquiry" over the mere "accumulation and recording of facts" colors his use of the term "biography," as does his open disdain for gossip and ideological message mongering. At the same time, Yardley acknowledges that his notions of what constitutes a "biography" are more conservative and idealistic than those espoused by career biographer Nigel Hamilton (b. 1944), who argues that the term "needs to be redefined to encompass the many, many different ways in which real-life depiction is practiced in Western society," including via documentary films and blogs (2007, 2). Although Yardley considers himself "well aware of the limitations" of traditional print biography, he is nonetheless distinctly uncomfortable with Hamilton's eagerness to embrace forms that lean more toward entertainment than enlightenment:

> Where is the line between fact and interpretation? Is biography history or psychological speculation? Is the purpose of biography to celebrate the lives of the famous and notable and thus to provide exemplars for the rest of us, or to reduce them to their mere humanity and thus to comfort us in the knowledge that they too are imperfect? . . . Do we read biography to understand and profit from the lives of others, or do we read it because we want the inside skinny? (2007)

In contrast, biographer and English professor Carl Rollyson applauds Hamilton's efforts to broaden the definition of the genre, agreeing with Hamilton that "biography" has been underrated and underserved as an area of study. Along similar lines, historian Gary Ianziti urges his fellow humanities and social science researchers not to dismiss biographical narratives out of hand when conducting their investigations, observing that the genre has proven itself to be "capable of infinite transformations" (2003, 12), resulting in both books "of high scholarly standard" and others in which the overriding aim is "to provide a good read" (9).

Analyzing the genre from the perspective of its detractors, British biographer Michael Holroyd (b. 1935) cheerfully labels it "the unwanted offspring" of history and literature—a hybrid form that has not yet succeeded in commanding widespread respect or trust (2002, 8–9). Nick Webb (b. 1949), an executive in **science fiction** publishing, declared that "Contemporary biography is the Area 51 of the literary world. There's a lot of circumstantial evidence that it exists, but very few get to visit" (2003, xiii). Joyce Carol Oates's 1988 tirade against "pathography" is often cited in such discussions (see Backscheider, Hamilton, Rollyson), as are the efforts of literary giants such as T.S. Eliot (1888–1965), W.H. Auden (1907–1973), William Makepeace Thackeray (1811–1863), and Matthew Arnold (1822–1888) to discourage would-be biographers (see Holroyd 2002, 29; Edel 1984, 20–21). Vladimir Nabokov tagged biographers as "psycho-plagiarists" (Edel 1984, 20).

The combination of formal resistance and healthy sales points to a disconnect that some observers see between high-minded commentators and the tastes of the public at large. For instance, Laura Claridge (herself a former professor with

THE POPULARITY OF BIOGRAPHY

The suspicion and disdain of such luminaries notwithstanding, the genre's immense popularity among mainstream readers is highly visible in multiple venues. Biographies frequently appear on best-seller charts and year-end "best of" compilations. They are often nominated for major book awards and merit their own category of Pulitzer Prize. They are heavily advertised and regularly reviewed, to the extent that reviews of biographies even attract their own reviews, such as history professor David Greenberg's assessment of the reaction to psychologist C.A. Tripp's thesis on Abraham Lincoln's sexuality (Greenberg 2005). *The New York Times* frequently double-reviews major biographies, printing an evaluation by one of its staff reviewers in a weekday edition and featuring a second assessment in the Sunday *Book Review*.

tenure) credits non-U.S. colleagues with helping her compare "the intimidation of Americans by institutional criticism" against "the greater freedom abroad to stand by one's sensuous reaction to art as a valid criterion for its worth," the latter being more in line with the approach she adopted for her biography of artist Norman Rockwell (2001, xx–xxi). Journalist and editor Tina Brown (b. 1953) breezily admits to perusing Kitty Kelley's "doorstopper" about the Bush family not for insight into "the great issues" but for the gossip:

> The 600 pages of her newest bioporn may get more traction among the public than the snob press would allow . . . most of us know that much of life on and off the world stage is driven by the accidental trivia of vanity, rivalry and buried grudges. (2004)

The hunger for such "trivia" can be witnessed in the longevity of glossy periodicals (and their online incarnations) such as *People* (founded 1974), *Us* (founded 1977), *Entertainment Weekly* (founded 1990), and *Vanity Fair* (1914–1936, relaunched 1983), as well as supermarket-rack tabloids and celebrity-tracking Web sites. The Biography Channel (premiered 1987) runs documentaries around the clock and is considered a cornerstone of the Arts & Entertainment (A&E) cable network; its Web site (www.biography.com; established 1996) contains over 25,000 entries, some in the form of short articles and others as video clips. The proliferation of free online resources such as Wikipedia and "fansites" (Web sites developed in homage to a specific celebrity or group of celebrities, such as the cast of a television show) also attests to the eagerness of the public to collect details about famous people's lives.

However, the market for biographies in printed book form shows no signs of dwindling. Some of the format's longevity can be attributed to individuals who elect to read longer works offline for reasons of physical comfort or situational convenience (such as "beach reading," in which biographies with the portability and pace of light paperback novels are preferred). As sources of information, printed biographies are considered more stable than Web pages, many of which become obsolete or simply vanish when their creators lose interest in maintaining them. Also, prior to its arrival on bookstore shelves, a biography published by a commercial or academic press is typically screened, vetted, and edited by a series of professionally trained staff who have a fiscal stake in the book's success, distinguishing it from the unfiltered and often unattributed content that characterizes many "for the love" nonprofit Web sites. The reputation of a publisher's name may also influence a potential reader's perception of the book's quality; for instance, the Knopf imprint

---

Thus, a growing trend among print publishers is the use of companion Web sites to host expanded versions of the notes and bibliographies for printed biographies. For example, readers of *A Thousand Miles of Dreams* are advised that "a comprehensive bibliography of Chinese and English language materials by and about Ling Shuhua and other further reading suggestions" are available on the publisher's Web site (Welland 2006, 329). Debby Applegate begins her bibliography to *The Most Famous Man in America* by noting that space limitations compelled her to be extremely selective about which sources to list, thus causing her to "peg my citations to the most accurate and accessible versions, referring to digitized copies whenever possible" (495). Applegate established a site, www.themostfamousmaninamerica.com, "to publish much of the information that could not make it into the book."

of Random House has attracted notice for consistently promoting authors who become Pulitzer finalists or winners (Rich 2007).

At the same time, Web sites are easier and cheaper to update than printed volumes and permit the storage of immense quantities of information at relatively little cost.

Likewise, readers of *Brotherhood of the Bomb* are encouraged to visit www.brotherhoodofthebomb.com to download copies of the "much longer and more comprehensive set of endnotes" (Herken 2002, 335).

Additional issues arise when one considers the popularity of **autobiography**. These issues are discussed in a separate entry in this encyclopedia.

History. In surveys and discussions about the history of biography, the author most frequently named from classical times is Plutarch (c. 46–c. 120), although Xenophon (c. 431–355 B.C.E) and Suetonius (c. 71–c. 135) are also considered major figures (Whittemore 1988, 11–12). James Boswell (1740–1795) called Plutarch "the prince of ancient biographers" (23). Plutarch's most influential work has been *Bioi Paralleloi* (Parallel Lives), which includes his study of Alexander the Great (356 B.C.E.–323 B.C.E.). Its strategy of analyzing the characters of famous individuals in pairs—for instance, that of Alexander and Julius Caesar (100 B.C.E–44 B.C.E), Theseus and Romulus (c. 771 B.C.E.–c. 717 B.C.E.), and Demosthenes (384 B.C.E.–322 B.C.E.) and Cicero (106 B.C.E.–43 B.C.E.)—can be seen in countless contemporary works, including Phyllis Rose's study of five Victorian marriages, also titled *Parallel Lives* (1983); other titles include *To Kill a Black Man: The Shocking Parallel in the Lives of Malcolm X and Martin Luther King Jr.* (Lomax 1968); *Hitler and Stalin: Parallel Lives* (Bullock 1992), *Lincoln and Whitman: Parallel Lives in Civil War Washington* (Epstein 2004), and *Jesus and Paul: Parallel Lives* (Murphy-O'Connor 2007). Rose's book, in its turn, has been acknowledged by Katie Roiphe (b. 1968) as one of the inspirations for *Uncommon Arrangements: Seven Portraits of Married Life in London Literary Circles* 1910–1939 (Winner 2007).

The popularity of Plutarch's *Lives* helped preserve it for later generations as it caused many copies of the manuscript to be made, thereby increasing the odds of several of them lasting through the centuries (McCutchen 1998). The *Lives* proved to be immensely popular during the Renaissance era in western Europe; according to Robert Lamberton, "only Aristotle and Plato, among writers of Greek prose, were better represented in the collections of Italian libraries of the fifteenth century," and over 50 Latin translations had been made of sections from *Lives* by 1450 (2001, 190). During this era, editions of the *Lives* also appeared in Italian, Spanish, German, French, and English (McCutchen 1998). Of these, the 1559 French translation by Jacques Amyot (1513–1593) is regarded as especially important because it was the version used by Thomas North (c. 1535–c. 1601) to create the first English translation. North's rendition of Plutarch's *Lives* was in turn actively consulted by William Shakespeare (1564–1616) during the writing of plays such as *Julius Caesar* and *Antony and Cleopatra*. The next major translation of the *Lives* into English was produced by a team of translators led by poet and playwright John Dryden (1631–1700). This translation was updated by poet Arthur Hugh Clough (1819–1861) and republished in 1859. The Dryden-Clough edition is still in active circulation among twenty-first century readers. There is one other "complete" English edition (that is, of the texts pieced together from the various surviving manuscripts; these texts make reference to other sections that have not been found) that was produced by classicist Bernadotte Perrin

(1847–1920), as well as assorted selected *Lives* by other translators. Poet and critic Kenneth Rexroth (1905–1982) favored North's version and asserted that:

> . . . .like the Bible and Shakespeare, *Parallel Lives* is a desert-island book. Classical literature contains a good many greater works of art, and many truer pictures of the ways of men. But Plutarch never palls. He is always engaging, interesting, and above all else, to use a word that will provoke smiles today, elevating. (1968)

Depending on one's definition of the genre, practitioners of "biography" during the Renaissance include Italian architect and painter Giorgio Vasari (1511–1574), best known for *Le vite delle più eccellenti pittori, scultori, ed architettori* [commonly known in English as *Lives of the Artists*] (1550); English antiquarian John Aubrey (1626–1697), whose irreverent style animates his *Brief Lives* (organized and published after his death by assorted editors); Protestant clergyman John Foxe (1516–1587), whose *Actes and Monuments of These Latter and Perillous Dayes* (1563) became known as the *Book of Martyrs;* ironmonger and fisherman Izaak Walton (1593–1683), who wrote about such poets as Herny Wotton (1568–1639), John Donne (1572–1631), and George Herbert (1593–1633); and Thomas Fuller (1608–1661), another clergyman, whose *History of the Worthies of Britain* appeared the year after his death.

Selected Authors. Reed Whittemore observes that "Samuel Johnson (1709–1784) could not have been the first interesting biographical subject who ever lived, but we have so much information about him that it is easy to think the genre began with him" (1988, 101). Johnson's biographer was Scottish lawyer James Boswell (1740–1795), whose name has become synonymous with "a person who records in detail the life of a usually famous contemporary (Merriam-Webster *Collegiate Dictionary,* 11th edition); a famous literary example of such usage is Sherlock Holmes's claim, "I am lost without my Boswell" (Doyle 1891, 12). Johnson was a lexicographer, editor, and writer; his output included *Prefaces, Biographical and Critical, to the Works of the English Poets*, which became known as *Lives of the Poets* (1781) (Lynch n.d.). Boswell was not Johnson's only biographer, or even the first, but his exhaustive efforts to document Johnson's conversation set a new standard for the genre. Whittemore states:

> Never before had so much had material been amassed in the way of actual conversation with a great mind. Never had there been a loyal disciple so industrious in walking about with pen and paper and dutifully collecting his subject's pearls. And, therefore, never before had wholeness in biography been so strenuously reached for. (1988, 129)

Scholar Leon Edel (1907–1997) likewise labels Boswell's *Life of Johnson* "the first great modern biography" (1984, 55). In the eyes of Edel, Harold Nicolson (1886–1968), and other major biographers, Boswell (with significant assistance from Edmond Malone) transformed expectations for biographical writing with his 1,400-page tribute to Johnson and its plethora of "fine everyday details which make Johnson come alive" (Edel 1984, 54–56). According to www.samueljohnson.com, Johnson ranks behind only Shakespeare as the most-quoted English author, and interest in both Johnson and Boswell will likely surge with the 300th anniversary of

Johnson's birth in 2009. Boswell's tactics to steer Johnson's conversation, Johnson's awareness of Boswell's literary ambitions, and other points of debate continue to fascinate contemporary readers, with modern biographies such as Peter Martin's *Life of James Boswell* (2000) striving to assess their achievements anew.

The next landmark biographical work in English literature is widely considered to be *Eminent Victorians* (1918) by (Giles) Lytton Strachey (1880–1932). Strachey was an admirer of Aubrey and a disciple of Freud (Whittemore 1989, 105–106), and his understanding of psychological self-sabotage informs his profiles of Roman Catholic cardinal Henry Edward Manning (1808–1892), nurse Florence Nightingale (1820–1910), educator Thomas Arnold (1795–1842), and general Charles George Gordon (1833–1885), as well as his books *Queen Victoria* (1921) and *Elizabeth and Essex* (1928). Strachey was a member of the Bloomsbury group of writers and artists famed for their eccentricities and defiance of conventional manners, and his antisentimental style is frequently described as "sardonic" and "mocking" (cf. Hamilton 2007, 151–52), even though Strachey also regarded biography as "the most delicate and humane of all the branches of writing" (qd. by Edel 1984, 33). Katie Roiphe, herself known among cultural critics for her rejection of conventional wisdom on feminist issues, cites *Eminent Victorians* as one of the books that led her to consider the study of relationships "as a way of looking at a culture" (Winner 2007). Michael Holroyd says, "We do not imitate Strachey, but it was he who liberated the form for all of us. He was the *enfant terrible*" (2002, 26). Victorian scholar Richard Altick (b. 1915) concludes that Strachey effectively triggered a fad for "book-length debunking of reputations" that resulted in "brightly written, studiously irreverent biographies by the hundreds" (qtd. by Hamilton 2007, 152–153). This post-Strachey period of life writing is sometimes characterized by scholars as the era of "New Biography" (cf. Edel 1984, 31).

Of this era, Paula Backscheider states that "most people would agree with Park Honan's judgment that Richard Ellmann is the best literary biographer to have written in English in the twentieth century" (1999, 12), an opinion reportedly shared by novelist and reviewer Anthony Burgess (1917–1993). Honan is himself regarded as one of the top biographers of Jane Austen (1987), William Shakespeare (1999), and Christopher Marlowe (2005), all of whom perennially attract new efforts to interpret both the facts and the gaps of their lives (Burgess wrote on Shakespeare as well in 1970). Ellmann (1918–1987) specialized in Irish literature and wrote about William Butler Yeats (1865–1939), James Joyce (1882–1941), and other luminaries; his 1989 biography of Oscar Wilde (1854–1900) won the Pulitzer Prize. Ellmann dominates the biographical landscape for anyone wishing to offer new material on these individuals. As one reviewer observed:

> Biographers of James Joyce have a simple choice: tussle with Richard Ellmann or don't try to compete. Ellmann's huge biography, published in 1959 and reissued in a thoroughly revised and expanded 1983 edition, relied not only on the biographer's profound familiarity with primary sources, but interviews, chance encounters, gossip and a whole world of acquaintanceship that no other writer will ever be able to rival. (Lacey 2004)

Another landmark work of biography in the twentieth century was *Portrait of a Marriage: Vita Sackville-West and Harold Nicolson* (1973), which featured three chapters composed by their son, Nigel Nicolson (1917–2004), and two penned by

Sackville-West (1892–1962), using text from a notebook Nigel Nicolson had discovered after her death. In his own memoir, *Long Life,* Nicolson describes canvassing family members and friends to determine whether to pursue publication of his mother's manuscript and the strong reaction to the book (ranging from enthusiastic to "pained") once it saw print (1998). In addition to becoming a best seller, it inspired additional studies of Sackville-West's life and relationships, including Victoria Glendinning's *Vita* (1983), which tied for the Whitbread Biography Award. Nicolson wryly observed that his mother had "posthumously become more central to my life than when she was alive because of the books that I and others have written about her" (1998). In his history of biography, Nigel Hamilton lauds the book for its candid portrayal of nonheterosexual relationships and asserts that it "broke yet another taboo in biographical portraiture," effectively leading the way for biographers to focus more intensely on details previously considered inappropriate for public consumption (2007, 235–39).

Journalist Janet Malcolm's analysis of the fallout from a less successful marriage, that of poets Sylvia Plath (1932–1963) and Ted Hughes (1930–1998), also created a commotion when it appeared (Seligman 2000, 3). Its portrayal of the decades-long antagonism between Plath's survivors and her would-be biographers was viewed by some observers as a "brilliant exposé of the workings of modern biography, as well as an eloquent attack on biography's ghoulish popularity" (Hamilton 2007, 276), whereas others judged Malcolm's defense of Ted Hughes to be suspect and her attitude toward Plath less than charitable (cf. Seligman 2000; Nehring 2004). As English professor Christina Nehring observes, "The history of biographical writing on Plath is vexed; her biographers have had their names made, their health wrecked (Anne Stevenson), and their hearts broken (Emma Tennant) in their endeavors" (2004). Given Plath and Hughes's stature as twentieth-century poets, their outsize personalities, and the unresolvable questions inherent in the tragedy of Plath's suicide and Hughes's destruction of her papers, as well as Malcolm's own tendency to attract controversy, *The Silent Woman* will likely remain essential reading both for individuals fascinated by the Plath-Hughes drama and those interested in contemplating the larger questions of biographical practice and ethics.

Trends and Themes. English professor Paula Backscheider states:

> Until very recently, readers of biographies seemed to have strong preferences, most notably the quest, the marked ambition and achievement of same, the adventures of a hero or dedicated public servant, 'the man of destiny,' and the difficult, misunderstood, often impoverished life of the great literary artist whom we now appreciate more than his contemporaries did. (1999, 103–104)

Elsewhere in her study, Backscheider argues that "each generation asks new things from its writers and new questions about the people who shaped the world we live in" (39). She also observes that:

> biographers, like their readers, are drawn to the culture's favourite stories and kinds of achievement. Many times the choice of a subject is born in a complex desire to answer lingering questions about a particular kind of life story and in the hope of better understanding it—or even sharing in it by recording or celebrating it. (46)

This perhaps articulates the public's abiding interest in books about the Founding Fathers. In spite of the dozens of books already published on the early presidents and other statesmen, new ones continue to sell extremely well and win major prizes. For example, professor Joseph J(ohn) Ellis (b. 1943) won the 2001 Pulitzer Prize in History for *Founding Brothers,* a group biography of John Adams (1735–1826), Aaron Burr (1756–1836), Benjamin Franklin (1706–1790), Alexander Hamilton (1757–1804), Thomas Jefferson (1743–1826), James Madison (1751–1836), and George Washington (1732–1799). After the Pulitzer, Ellis's 1993 biography of Adams was reprinted, and *His Excellency: George Washington* (2004) reached the best-seller lists.

Historian David McCullough (b. 1933), who had won a Pulitzer for his 1992 biography of Harry S. Truman, won a second Pulitzer for *John Adams* (2001). McCullough had originally intended to write a book focusing on both Adams and Jefferson but decided to focus on Adams once his research was under way, realizing that "The problem with Adams is that most Americans know nothing about him"; McCullough said that he himself hadn't truly recognized Adams's heroic qualities until writing the book. In the same interview, McCullough responded to a dissenting reaction to his characterization of Adams's colleagues by stressing that "these men are not perfect. . . . If they were marble gods, what they did wouldn't be so admirable. The more we see the founders as humans the more we can understand them. Imagine starting out to create a country—at the risk of their lives" (Leopold 2001).

The widespread interest in the imperfection of the Founding Fathers—and in the imperfect efforts to interpret aspects of their lives—is especially visible in the case of Benjamin Franklin, about whom over 75 biographies have been registered with the Library of Congress since 2000. This figure includes books for children but does not include the additional dozens of "in his own words" collections in which selections from Franklin's own *Autobiography* and other writings have been repackaged into "new" books. The high volume of activity can be attributed in part to the 300th anniversary of Franklin's birth, which was celebrated in 2006. Interest in Franklin was also heightened by a 2002 PBS documentary that won an Emmy Award, a 2004 History Channel documentary, and an assortment of other television productions centered around the principal actors and events of the American Revolution (including a filmed adaptation of Ellis's *Founding Brothers*).

Franklin also attracts attention because his life was long, complex, and multifaceted, with many elements that can strike a potential author as exaggerated, mythical, or misunderstood by the general public. The urge to investigate such elements has proved irresistible to numerous biographers, including seasoned scholars such as Gordon S. Wood (b. 1933), who had won a history Pulitzer for *The Radicalization of the American Revolution* (1992). In *The Americanization of Benjamin Franklin,* Wood set out:

> to penetrate beneath the many images and representations of Franklin that have accumulated over the past two hundred years and recover the historic Franklin who did not know the kind of massively symbolic folk hero he would become. At the same time [Wood's book] hopes to make clear how and why Franklin acquired these various images and symbols. (Wood 2004, ix)

Put another way, Wood is fascinated not just by the life of Franklin, but by the history of reactions to Franklin's life. He declares that "the criticism that Franklin has aroused over the past two centuries has been as extraordinary as the praise" (4) and later reviews the mythologization of Franklin by Parson Mason Weems (1756–1825) and other admirers (235–246).

Walter Isaacson (b. 1952), another prominent writer, explicitly connects attitudes toward Benjamin Franklin to his biographers' own environments, stating that "each new look at him reflects and refracts the nation's changing values. He has been vilified in romantic periods and lionized in entrepreneurial ones. Each era appraises him anew, and in doing so reveals some assessments of itself" (2003, 3). Isaacson sees such assessments as barometers of the writers' own attitudes toward upward mobility, middle-class utilitarianism, and other socioeconomic movements. Isaacson observes that, while nineteenth-century transcendentalists and early twentieth-century Marxists railed against Franklin's unromantic, bourgeois sensibilities, Franklin was honored as "the most popular subject of American biography" during the decades following the Civil War—an era of industrial revolution—and likewise a figure of admiration following the Great Depression, when Franklin's values again seemed relevant (477–484). He finds current attitudes toward Franklin similarly indicative of early twenty-first–century concerns, citing David Brooks's characterization of Franklin as America's "Founding Yuppie" and dissecting the extent to which the actual details of Franklin's life bear out his reputation (485–493). As the president and CEO of the Aspen Institute, Isaacson heads an institution created as a retreat for executives, intellectuals, professional artists, and other high-powered individuals to consider "the meaning of the good life, leadership, and sound public policy" (2007a). The institute's mission mirrors the questions Isaacson uses to frame his biography of Franklin:

> Whatever view one takes, it is useful to engage anew with Franklin, for in doing so we are grappling with a fundamental issue: How does one live a life that is useful, virtuous, worthy, moral, and spiritually meaningful? For that matter, which of these attributes is most important? These are questions just as vital for a self-satisfied age as they were for a revolutionary one. (2003, 4)

Stacy Schiff (b. 1961) centers her 400-page profile of Franklin (2005) on the last decade of his life, which he spent primarily in France. Schiff's style, notable for its blend of factual detail and memorable characterizations, has helped her earn her status as an elite biographer; her study of *Véra (Mrs. Vladimir Nabokov)* was named the 2000 Pulitzer Prize winner in biography, and an earlier book on Antoine Saint-Exupéry (1900–1944) was a finalist for the 1995 prize. Schiff's preoccupation with the play of personalities is evident from the start of *A Great Improvisation*, which she begins with a detailed cast of characters: John Adams (1735–1826) is introduced as "brilliant Massachusetts writer, orator, lawyer, statesman; austere, thin-skinned, fretful. . . . Trailed through Paris a reputation for vanity and gracelessness" (xi). Schiff concludes her capsule resumé for statesman Arthur Lee (1740–1792) with a series of pithy observations: "Like Franklin, a youngest son of a vast family. Unlike Franklin, a man of bilious temperament. Never married, as no woman could be found who met his standards" (xvi). Another individual, Paul Wentworth (d. 1793), is summed up with "Audacious, artful master spy. With 20 aliases, assorted disguises, and a host of invisible inks, eluded even the peerless Paris police. Highly cultivated; in Beaumarchais's nervous opinion, 'one of the cleverest men in England'" (xvii).

Schiff's account of Franklin's adventures in France likewise feature significant attention paid to character-defining details. For instance, in discussing playwright Pierre-Augustin Caron de Beaumarchais's correspondence with the French minister of foreign affairs, she notes that "Beaumarchais signed his name only when he feared that distress, or fatigue, had disfigured his handwriting. It never did. And his inimitable style was signature enough" (69). Schiff's epilogue casts Franklin's diplomatic achievements as a triumph of his personal traits:

> He was indeed a man of frightening versatility, more difficult to embrace for his very breadth. He was a natural American in only one respect: He proved that there is no such thing. He was willing at all times to put practice before theory, especially in France, when his country's fate hung in the balance. To the end he favored modest experience over grandiose hypotheses. The latter were all too pleasing "till some experiment comes and unluckily destroys them," he observed, proof that he was not a Frenchman after all. He was no less the revolutionary for being a congenial and cool-headed late bloomer. (412)

Schiff's supplementary materials similarly display her flair for mixing lively assessment with scholarly organization. Her chronology of Franklin's life includes entries such as, "1716: Serves as his father's assistant; dislikes the business" (413) and "1789: Bastille falls on July 14. Franklin submits first three parts of *Autobiography* to French friends. Subsists on diet of laudanum" (417). In the "Notes" section, Schiff offers candid assessments of the sources she consulted with judgments such as "All of Benjamin Franklin's letters combined do not pack the descriptive punch of a single Abigail Adams missive" (424), "*The Letters of Richard Henry Lee* (ed. Ballagh) and *Letters of William Lee* (ed. Ford) make for spellbinding reading; the diary of Arthur Lee less so" (439), and "Andrew Stockley's *Britain and France at the Birth of America* (2001) makes for a useful corrective to years of lopsided French and American accounts" (447).

Other recent biographers have found it profitable to concentrate on Franklin's scientific endeavors. Historian Joyce E. Chaplin felt that, prior to her own book, most biographies of Franklin had failed to "make sense of the connections between the public life and the life in science" (2006, 5). Chaplin voices grave concerns about present-day scientific illiteracy, presenting Franklin as a model she clearly wishes twenty-first–century policy makers would strive to emulate (357–359). Science writer Tom Tucker, for his part, sees Franklin's penchant for hoaxes as a trait "not fully explored by scholars until the mid-twentieth century and ever since then has remained curiously beyond mainstream notice" (2003, xvii). Convinced that Franklin never flew the famous kite, Tucker is as invested as his historian counterparts in separating Franklin's purported achievements from his actual accomplishments (which, in Tucker's view, include manipulating the myth of his experiments with electricity into diplomatic leverage).

The desire to educate the general public about an individual's true personality, as opposed to the persona developed by that individual or that perpetuated by his or her contemporaries, can also be witnessed in the biographies produced of living political figures such as Senator Hillary Rodham Clinton (b. 1947). Clinton's campaign for the U.S. presidency, her complex marriage, the rumors of corruption dogging both her career and that of her husband (former president Bill Clinton, b. 1946), and her status as a role model for other women (cf. Broder 1997) are among the controversial elements of her life that make her a highly marketable subject, such that the on-sale dates of two recent biographies on her (Gerth and Natta 2007, and Bernstein 2007) caused high-profile jockeying for sales advantage by the books' publishers. The strong credentials of the books' authors (all three of them having won Pulitzer Prizes for investigative reporting) also fueled interest in their content. The authors were taken to task by some of their reviewers for excessive bias, insufficient insight, or both (cf. Dallek 2007 and Kakutani 2007), but this has become inevitable with virtually any noteworthy book published on Clinton; journalist Christopher Andersen's *American Evita* (2004) drew similar heat during its stint on the best-seller lists.

Another woman whose marital woes were widely publicized during her lifetime was Diana, Princess of Wales (1961–1997). The tenth anniversary of her death prompted a renewal of magazine and television attention to her story, including reviews of Tina Brown's *The Diana Chronicles*, which drew particular attention not only because of the timing but because of Brown's own status as a glamorous media executive (cf. Maslin 2007; Kimmelman 2007; and Weber 2007). However, interest in Diana's life and death had remained substantial through the decade since her passing, sustained by high-profile motion pictures such as *The Queen* (2006), by the combination of romance and tragedy shaping the trajectory of her life, and by the charisma that had elicited near-worship from thousands of admirers during her lifetime. As of 2007, the Library of Congress listed over 40 separate subject headings for "Diana, Princess of Wales"; recent titles include *The Way We Were* (Burrell 2006) and *A Royal Duty* (Burrell 2003), books by a former servant; and *Diana* (2006) by Sarah Bradford, an aristocrat and historian whose earlier book on Queen Elizabeth II (1996) had caused a sensation in her native Britain; the front cover on one of the paperback editions of *Diana* proclaims, "*Finally, the complete story.*"

The members of the Kennedy family, often described as the U.S. equivalent to royalty, have also continued to interest biographers and their readers. Bradford titled her book on Jacqueline Kennedy Onassis (1929–1994) *America's Queen* (2000); Andersen, too, has written about both the British royal family (*The Day Diana Died*, 1998; *Diana's Boys*, 2001; and *After Diana*, 2007) and the Kennedys (*The Day John Died*, 2001; *Sweet Caroline*, 2003); and writer Jay Mulvaney compared the two in *Diana and Jackie* (2002). Newer books about the Kennedys include *Brothers: The Hidden History of the Kennedy Years* (Talbot 2007), *The Kennedy Mystique* (Goodman 2006), *The Private Passion of Jackie Kennedy Onassis* (Moon 2005), *Grace and Power: The Private World of the Kennedy White House* (Smith 2004), and *Mrs. Kennedy: The Missing History of the Kennedy Years* (Leaming 2001). As the titles suggest, the Kennedys continue to be alluring subjects in part because the general public perceives an ongoing disconnect between the images they projected and the realities of their lives, and in part because a number of readers are specialists or collectors for whom the minutiae of the Kennedys' lives are as fascinating as their major accomplishments (*The Private Passion*, for instance, is actually about Onassis's love of horses). Nigel Hamilton sees the focus on "fragments" of people's lives (including entire books on the aftermaths of their deaths) as part of a trend that has been building since the 1960s (2007, 215–16).

The urge to reassess a famous person's life against his or her reputation—particularly if any of the evidence hints at conditions formerly considered shameful, such as mental illness or homosexuality—can be witnessed in books such as *Lincoln's Melancholy* (Shenk 2005), which examines Abraham Lincoln's (1814–1882) battles with depression, and *The Intimate World of Abraham Lincoln* (Tripp 2005), which argued that Lincoln's deepest attachments were to men. Although Tripp's book was generally deemed weak and unconvincing, its publication prompted reviewers to produce thoughtful commentary on trends in historical scholarship, the provability (or lack thereof) of hidden traits, and the relevance of sexuality-based theses (cf. Capozzola 2005; Greenberg 2005; O'Hehir 2005; Stansell 2005; and Shenk 2005, 34–37). *Lincoln's Melancholy,* which was named a "best book" of its year by the *New York Times,* the *Washington Post,* and the *Atlanta Journal-Constitution,* impressed its readers in part because the author had taken pains to document trends in interpretations of Lincoln's inner life, noting shifts in critical perception over the twentieth century and how they affected the types of evidence historians were willing to evaluate (Shenk 2005, 4–8, 221–43). Shenk observes that "works on Lincoln in recent years bear the mark of increased appreciation for the firsthand observations of his life. At the same time, we've seen an increase in narrowly focused studies, some of which pluck out bits and pieces from the Lincoln record to assemble a cartoon portrait of modern fantasies" (242–43). Writing several years after *Lincoln's Melancholy,* essayist Adam Gopnik (b. 1956) echoes a similar theme, having followed a reading list of "the recent Lincoln literature" provided to him by an acquaintance:

> There's a lot to read. In books published in the past two years alone, you can read about Lincoln's "sword" (his writing) and about his "sanctuary" (the Soldiers' Home just outside Washington, where he spent summers throughout the war). You can read a book about Lincoln's alleged love affair with a young officer, and one about Lincoln's relations, tetchy but finally triumphant, with Frederick Douglass. There is no part of Lincoln, from manhood to death, that is not open and inscribed. You can learn that some of Lincoln's intimates believed his melancholy was rooted in extreme constipation ("He had no natural evacuation of bowels," a friend explained) and also what formula was used to embalm him, a gruesome but far from trivial point. (2007)

Efforts to debunk popular myths and opinions of Lincoln also appear to be on the rise, leading to titles such as *Lincoln Legends: Myths, Hoaxes, and Confabulations Associated with Our Greatest President* (Steers 2007) and *Lincoln Unmasked: What You're Not Supposed To Know About Dishonest Abe* (DiLorenzo 2006).

The awareness that interpretations shift with time plays a role in the development of series such as "The American Presidents," which debuted in 2002, featuring each chief executive of the United States in a new book about his life and career. According to its Web site (www.americanpresidentsseries.com), each book is designed to be "compact enough for the busy reader, lucid enough for the student and authoritative enough for the scholar"; as such, the books are uniform in size and each less than 200 pages long. The stature of the editor-in-chief, historian Arthur M. Schlesinger Jr. (1917–2007), helped attract prominent contributors such as convicted Watergate counsel John Dean (b. 1938) on Warren G. Harding (1865–1923), former *Harper's* editor Lewis H. Lapham (b. 1935) on William Howard Taft (1857–1930), and retired senator Gary Hart (b. 1936) on James Monroe (1758–1831), which in turn sparked interest in readers who might have otherwise bypassed the volumes on these men.

Biographies on active politicians are inherently nondefinitive, given their subjects' ongoing activities, and inevitably subject to accusations of bias, no matter how neutral a stance the author may strive to maintain. They range from glossy photo-heavy narratives on Barack Obama (Dougherty 2007) to behind-the-scenes accounts such as *Ambling into History* (Bruni 2002), presented by a reporter who covered George W. Bush's 2000 presidential campaign. Because one of the unique features of the

Bush presidencies is the father-son connection between George H.W. Bush (b. 1924) and George W. Bush (b. 1946), many of the books produced during George W.'s terms in office have focused on the family and its hold on power, with titles such as *American Dynasty* (Phillips 2004); *Secrecy and Privilege: Rise of the Bush Dynasty from Watergate to Iraq* (Parry 2004); *The Bushes: Portrait of a Dynasty* (Schweizer and Schweizer 2004); and *The Family: The Real Story of the Bush Dynasty* (Kelley 2004). Books about individual members of the family tend to refer to "dynasty" as well, including *Barbara Bush: Matriarch of a Dynasty* (Kilian 2002); *First Son: George W. Bush and the Bush Family Dynasty* (Minutaglio 1999); and *W: Revenge of the Bush Dynasty* (Mitchell 2003).

In general, traditional biographies for adults—even those concentrating on a specific trait or era of the subject's life—currently tend to average between 300 and 500 pages. Among nontraditional formats, **graphic novels** have appeared on the lives of Danish physicist Niels Bohr (Ottaviani and Purvis 2004), American activist Malcolm X (Helfer and DuBurke 2006), and French Canadian revolutionary Louis Riel (Brown 2006), with "graphic biographies" of Ronald Reagan, Nelson Mandela, and Fidel Castro formally scheduled for publication in the near future as well.

Context and Issues. In the introduction to her biography of Rockwell, Laura Claridge asserts that:

> . . . most readers nowadays hold truth to be a complicated achievement, and few among us believe anyone's telling of a life to be the final word, the only way of its telling. Because those of us in the twenty-first century are close to Rockwell's times—seeing them, quite rightly, as the context from which our own lives emerge—we mine such lives as a means to understand the families that spawned us and the selves we've become. (2001, xx)

Although many other writers have voiced perspectives similar to Claridge's, the degree to which biographers present themselves as experts on the lives of other individuals remains one of the most contentious aspects of the genre. A biographer's assumption of such authority—particularly if the subject did not or could not authorize or condone his or her decision—may be considered flattering or judged presumptuous. The biographer's determination to ascertain and confirm the details of another individual's life may be seen as a worthy quest to obtain and present the truth, but even when biographers enjoy "authorized" status, conflicts may arise when their interpretations of events fail to match the recollections of the subjects or their heirs. As Webb wryly notes, "There are many people over whose feelings the author can clodhop, and they will all have a different view of the person from the one offered. Some of those views will appear not to refer to the same person at all" (2003, xiii-xiv). Backscheider asserts that:

> . . . good biography must be collaboration—even with a dead subject, there must be empathy and a real or developed understanding of the social, emotional, and historical world. But good biography is always at his its heart somewhat adversarial. The biographer must ferret out the hidden, the buried, the most shameful secrets. (1999, 45)

Some biographies are produced when a writer feels compelled to investigate discrepancies or gaps in their family histories. In her prologue to *A Thousand Miles of Dreams* (2006), Sasha Su-Ling Welland (b. 1969) outlines some of the cultural, linguistic, and philosophical issues she wrestled with in attempting to reconcile her grandmother and great-aunt's conflicting accounts of their lives: "What I often mis-interpreted as dishonest hiding behind [the Chinese] language is a cultivated ability to move between formal and informal registers. . . . Suppressing my American desire for exposé and working toward an understanding of these equally meaningful lev-els of language, I moved beyond the quest for a single immutable truth" (12). An anthropology and women's studies professor, Welland presents her interpretation of the lives of Amy Shuhao Ling Chen (1904–2006) and Ling Shuhua (1900–1990) both as an academic study, with formal bibliographic citations, and as a memoir, interweaving the details of Shuhao and Shuhua's lives with her own adventures in China, delineating her interactions with her grandmother and questioning her motives in reading her great-aunt's short stories, asking "Can I learn to approach them as literature rather than clues to a family I understand too little?" (174).

In a similar vein, Jennet Conant's interest in the lives of atomic physicists was fueled by her "peculiar legacy" (xviii) and her family's reluctance to discuss her grandfather's involvement with the Manhattan Project, a mystery compounded by the myths surrounding a great-uncle's suicide during the bomb's development. As Nigel Nicolson had with *Portrait of a Marriage,* Conant wrestled with her aware-ness that her airing of long-held secrets would be regarded in some circles as unseemly and even disloyal:

> I . . . struggled with the problem of prying into what many of my grandfather's friends and colleagues might regard as a dark corner of his illustrious career. James Conant was a very private, proud, and tidy man and placed a premium on appearances. He would have loathed seeing his family's mess tipped onto the page. There were also gap-ing holes in the story. My grandmother was acutely aware that graduate students would one day paw her private papers, and she set about methodically destroying any-thing incriminatingly personal in the record, ripping pages out of diaries and burning most of her mother's and brother's letters. (2002, xvii)

Biographies written by members or friends of the subject's family command inter-est in part because such individuals frequently do have access to sources not avail-able to the general public. However, their direct participation in their subjects' lives also means that these writers' versions of events must be treated with additional caution. Screenwriter Gavin Lambert (1924–2005), a friend of Natalie Wood (1938–1981), characterized her sister Lana's 1984 memoir (Wood 1984) as "remarkably untruthful" (2004, 326) and credits the existence of his own account to Wood's surviving spouse, Robert Wagner, whom Lambert quotes as saying, "When you tell the truth about Natalie as you see it, I shall be at peace" (355). The multiple biographies about Wood highlight the issue of competing agendas among family members: Lambert wrote his account with the blessing and cooperation of Natalie Wood's widower and daughters, whereas Suzanne Finstad (b. 1955) con-sulted Lana Wood for *Natasha* (2001), later stating that Wood had provided her with "insight and intimate information she had not revealed in her own memoirs" (Finstad 2001a). Although the *San Francisco Chronicle* named Finstad's account the best film book of its year, Lambert cites it sparingly in his notes.

Other biographers may view their projects as complementary rather than com-peting, such as Nick Webb and M.J. Simpson, whose biographies of science fiction author Douglas Adams (1952–2001) both appeared within a few years of Adams's untimely death. Webb was a friend of Adams and his family as well as a professional colleague; as the official biographer, he had access to Adams's papers, and his aim was to produce a book that was "good company—like the man himself" (2003, xiv). His style is wry and informal, with phrasings such as "Two minor digressions from this period . . ." (in order to relate anecdotes about Adams's personal generosity to the author and another friend, 268–270) and pronouncements such as, "Of course it would be lovely for any chap if the woman in his life gave him unconditional support and admiration for every notion, no matter how daft, but in the long term she would not be doing him a favour at all" in describing the ruthless intelligence of Adams's wife (227). In a similar vein, Webb calls Adams's family tree "something I will not attempt to describe. What with infant mortality, marriage between distant cousins, and age disparities it looks as if someone quite disturbed had tried to draw the Tube map from memory" (23).

Simpson, a journalist specializing in science fiction criticism, completed a book of similar length that focused on Adams's career, supporting his detailed examination of Adams's history with almost 30 pages of references (2003). Although Webb was the biographer formally commissioned by Adams's heirs, Simpson had been one of the most prominent fans of *The Hitchhiker's Guide to the Galaxy*, to the extent that he was entrusted with updating and expanding *Don't Panic,* a much-revered guide to the series often regarded as an Adams biography in its own right (Gaiman 2002). Simpson's pocket volume on *The Hitchhiker's Guide* (2001) was praised in Webb's acknowledgments as "very useful" and "essential reading" (xi). Thus, the majority of Adams's friends and colleagues were happy to assist his project as well as Webb's. In the words of one reviewer:

> Ultimately, I find myself unwilling to recommend either book at the exclusion of another. As with most people, Douglas Adams is too complex for a single interpretation. While Webb and Simpson don't offer very different views, there are facets covered in one work that aren't covered in the other. Read both in close succession (preferably right after *The Salmon of Doubt,* which could be called Douglas' own fragmented autobiography) and you'll get the idea. (Sauvé 2005)

In Adams's case, his biographers all also agree that he was not fully trustworthy where specifics of his life were concerned. Webb noted Adams's tendency to offer biographical revelations that had evolved into "suspiciously polished artifacts" (xiv). Gaiman elaborates upon the same theme:

> The other thing that fascinates me now [in addition to "accidental" elements of the Hitchhiker series], especially looking at some of the biographies that are coming out now, is how much of Douglas' story has been invented post–1987 when I did the first draft of the book. There are major *Hitchhiker's Guide to the Galaxy* antidotes [sic] that cannot be found in *Don't Panic* because Douglas hadn't made them up yet. (Huddleston 2003)

Simpson, whose efforts to debunk Adams's invented anecdotes garnered both praise and scorn, included a lament in his introduction to the American edition of *Hitchhiker.* Speaking of Adams's underproductive collaboration with comedian Graham Chapman, Simpson writes that "trying to determine the accuracy of conflicting stories told by two notoriously inaccurate raconteurs after more than two decades is a thankless and ultimately pointless task" (xix). Simpson also used the introduction to include information about Adams's life that had surfaced since the publication of the first British edition, rather than attempting to "shoehorn" the new material into the original text (xvii).

The drama of conflicting, irreconcilable stories and personality clashes helps drive the sales of biographies on nuclear physicists. Some of the major storylines in the saga of twentieth-century atomic energy research include a secret meeting between Niels Bohr (1885–1962) and Werner Heisenberg (1901–1976) in 1941 that came to be seen as the end of their friendship; a series of arguments between Bohr and Albert Einstein (1879–1955) regarding Bohr's interpretation of quantum mechanics; and the 1953 government hearing on J. Robert Oppenheimer (1904–1967). The Bohr-Heisenberg meeting inspired Michael Frayn's play *Copenhagen* (1998), which won the 2000 Tony Award for best play and was later adapted for television with renowned actors Stephen Rea, Daniel Craig, and Francesca Annis. The play, in turn, generated so much interest that Bohr's family decided to release unpublished documents related to the meeting in 2002, 10 years ahead of schedule, the better "to accommodate the present interest and to avoid undue speculation about the contents" (NBA 2002). The Oppenheimer hearing, which resulted in Oppenheimer's security clearance being revoked, created permanent rifts in the scientific community between his defenders and his detractors (cf. Conant 2002, 291–92; Herken 2002, 316).

At the turn of the millennium, some of the participants and witnesses to these conflicts were still alive and available to discuss their perception of these events. At the same time, most of the central figures had passed away. As individuals become incapacitated or die, researchers lose direct access to those individuals as sources of oral history; on the other side of the coin, out of consideration for the other participants in their activities, some individuals or their heirs stipulate that their archives remain sealed for a given period after their deaths. Thus, the total range of source material for books on the atomic era will remain in flux for several decades to come, triggering fresh interpretations of familiar stories as letters, notes, and other materials become known and available to biographers. In *Einstein,* which reached the top of the *New York Times* best-seller list in 2007, Walter Isaacson notes that he received "early and complete access to the wealth of new Einstein papers that became available in 2006" (2007, xv). In *Oppenheimer: Portrait of an Enigma,* Jeremy Bernstein described the incidents and concerns that had caused 40 years to elapse before he felt ready to write about the man:

> Things are both easier and more difficult—for the same reason. Nearly all the actors in this drama are dead. There are still a few of Oppenheimer's California students left, and a few of the people who were at Los Alamos with him, but nearly every week I read a new obituary. This means that I am no longer constrained by their presence, but it also means that I can no longer get their advice. (xi)

Science historian Abraham Pais (1918–2000) died before finishing his own book on Oppenheimer. Robert P. Crease, who completed the manuscript, was charged with adding only enough material to make the biography publishable, thus restricting him from "addressing topics that Pais himself clearly intended to discuss" or that would otherwise have been expected in a biography of Oppenheimer (Pais 2006, xvii–xviii). In contrast, *American Prometheus* (Bird and Sherwin 2005) was widely lauded upon its publication as the most ambitious book on Oppenheimer to date and received the 2006 Pulitzer Prize in biography.

The attitudes of subjects and their families toward biographical subjects vary widely, ranging from cheerful cooperation to active hostility. In his biography of

Bohr, Pais noted that Bohr's sons declined to review his manuscript, "essentially because they felt that mine should be an independent view and assessment" (1991, vi). Andrew Wilson says that his subject, novelist Patricia Highsmith, "was adamant a biography should not be written while she was alive—indeed, she blocked several attempts—but secretly quite proud that one might be written when she was no longer around to witness the result" (2003, 9). When the children of businessman Joseph P. Kennedy (1888–1969) asked Nasaw to write his biography, Nasaw initially refused the opportunity, accepting it only after the family made it clear that they would not demand final approval of Nasaw's manuscript (Mehegan 2006). Regarding her biography of Aristotle Onassis, Bradford indicated that she had notified Onassis's children of the project but that they were under strict orders from their mother not to authorize or collaborate with any biographers; at the same time, she believed her track record as a reputable biographer helped her obtain interviews with other individuals who seldom granted them (CNN 2000).

Some biographers, such as Hamilton, Rollyson, and Kitty Kelley, revel in their unauthorized status, believing that it frees them to tell unflattering truths that an authorized biographer would be pressured to suppress. Their methods are both deplored and admired by their colleagues; Backscheider, for instance, notes that Hamilton's obsessive collection of nontraditional evidence allowed him to craft an unprecedentedly detailed portrait of John F. Kennedy's early years, but that Hamilton's style was self-centric enough "to trigger the testing and doubting of evidence" (1999, 75–76); the same can be said of reactions to Rollyson and Kelley's works (cf. Brown 2004). A *New Republic* editor concluded, "The real shame here isn't that Kitty Kelley resorts to shoddy journalistic methods to uncover some basic truths. It's that so few others have used scrupulous journalistic methods to find them" (Crowley 2004).

Reception. The 2007 Pulitzer Prize winner, *The Most Famous Man in America*, attracted praise both for its vivid portrayal of a nineteenth-century sex scandal and the writer's ability to highlight its relevance to modern concerns:

> One cannot view Beecher's career without thinking of the many charismatic men who were driven to heady heights by their unquenchable longing for approbation and who risked their legacies by letting this longing shade into lust—men of indisputable stature such as Martin Luther King, Jr., John F. Kennedy, and Bill Clinton. (Applegate 2006, 471)

Major prizes such as the Pulitzer automatically result in publicity for a book, raising its profile and often its sales. According to a Knopf representative, sales of *American Prometheus* doubled after it was named the 2006 Pulitzer winner (Rich 2007).

Columbia University administers both the Pulitzer Prizes (via its Graduate School of Journalism) and the Bancroft Prizes (via its trustees). The Bancroft Prizes reward outstanding work in the fields of American history and diplomacy; recent Bancroft winners include works on Jonathan Edwards (Marsden 2003) and William Randolph Hearst (Nasaw 2000). The Lambda Literary Foundation, which supports gay, lesbian, bisexual, and transgender literature, administers an annual biography prize; recent winners include *February House: The Story of W.H. Auden, Carson McCullers, Jane and Paul Bowles, Benjamin Britten, and Gypsy Rose Lee, Under One Roof in Wartime America* (Tippins 2005); *Warrior Poet: A Biography of Audre Lorde* (De Veaux 2004); *Ridiculous! The Theatrical Life and Times of Charles Ludlam* (Kaufman 2002); and *The Scarlet Professor: Newton Arvin—A Literary Life Shattered by Scandal* (Werth 2001).

PULITZER PRIZES IN BIOGRAPHY OR AUTOBIOGRAPHY

The most recent Pulitzer prizes in biography or autobiography have included:

2007	*The Most Famous Man in America: The Biography of Henry Ward Beecher* by Debby Applegate (Doubleday)
2006	*American Prometheus: The Triumph and Tragedy of J. Robert Oppenheimer* by Kai Bird and Martin J. Sherwin (Alfred A. Knopf)
2005	*de Kooning: An American Master* by Mark Stevens and Annalyn Swan (Alfred A. Knopf)
2004	*Khrushchev: The Man and His Era* by William Taubman (W.W. Norton)
2003	*Master of the Senate* by Robert A. Caro (Alfred A. Knopf)
2002	*John Adams* by David McCullough (Simon & Schuster)
2001	*W.E.B. Du Bois: The Fight for Equality and the American Century, 1919–1963* by David Levering Lewis (Henry Holt and Company)
2000	*Vera (Mrs. Vladimir Nabokov)* by Stacy Schiff (Random House)

Source: Pulitzer Prize Web site, http://www.pulitzer.org/.

Milestones such as deaths can also revive interest in a biography (cf. Bosman 2007), as can "biopics" (movies based on the lives of real people). Some motion-picture directors buy the rights to popular biographies to use as their primary sources; films produced from specific books include *Marie Antoinette* (based on Fraser 2001), *A Beautiful Mind* (based on Nasar 1998), and *The Life and Death of Peter Sellers* (based on Lewis 1997).

Many of the authors named above (Bradford, Isaacson, and Nasaw among them) have developed a substantial following among readers of nonfiction. Other established authors in the genre include Robert Caro (b. 1935), Robert Dallek (b. 1934), Victoria Glendinning (b. 1937), David Levering Lewis (b. 1936), Diane Middlebrook (b. 1939), Arnold Rampersad (b. 1941), and Claire Tomalin (b. 1933).

In her essay on the art and appeal of biography, Selma G. Lanes observes that the genre exerts a special hold on its readers because it is "a socially and intellectually acceptable form of voyeurism. It can be instructive, even spiritually or morally uplifting for us with regard to our own lives in flux" (Lanes 2004, 28). The first decade of the twenty-first century saw many rules and customs in transition as the United States sought to cope with the events of September 11, 2001; with advances in technology; and with emotionally charged debates among both policy makers and the general public about issues such as gay marriage and the war in Iraq. As society adjusts to new realities, the expectations of mainstream readers regarding biographers' choices of approach, method, and style will likewise shift. Biographers will continue to offer stories about the Kennedys, the Windsors, and other charismatic celebrities, as well as strive to do justice to new subjects, but their interpretations will inevitably reflect the concerns of the era in which they themselves are living, rather than that of the subject or those of earlier biographers.

Bibliography

Andersen, Christopher. *The Day Diana Died*. New York: Morrow, 1998.
———. *The Day John Died*. New York: Morrow, 2000.
———. *Diana's Boys: William and Harry and the Mother They Loved*. New York: Morrow, 2001.

———. *Sweet Caroline: Last Child of Camelot.* New York: Morrow, 2003.

———. *American Evita: Hillary Clinton's Path to Power.* New York: Morrow, 2004.

———. *After Diana: William, Harry, Charles, and the Royal House of Windsor.* New York: Hyperion, 2007.

Applegate, Debby. *The Most Famous Man in America: The Biography of Henry Ward Beecher.* New York: Doubleday, 2006. http://www.themostfamousmaninamerica.com.

Backscheider, Paula R. *Reflections on Biography.* New York: Oxford, 1999.

Bernstein, Carl. *A Woman in Charge: The Life of Hillary Rodham Clinton.* New York: Knopf, 2007.

Bernstein, Jeremy. *Oppenheimer: Portrait of an Enigma.* Chicago: Ivan R. Dee, 2004.

Bird, Kai, and Sherwin, Martin J. *American Prometheus: The Triumph and Tragedy of J. Robert Oppenheimer.* New York: Knopf, 2005. www.americanprometheus.org.

Bosman, Julie. "Death Propels Anna Nicole Smith Biography from the Backlist to the Front Burner." *New York Times* 15 Feb. 2007. http://www.nytimes.com/2007/02/15/books/15anna.html.

Boswell, James. *Life of Johnson.* 3rd ed. R.W. Chapman, ed. Introduction by Pat Rogers. Oxford: Oxford University Press, 1799.

Bradford, Sarah. *Elizabeth: A Biography of Britain's Queen.* New York: Farrar, Straus, & Giroux, 1996.

———. *America's Queen: The Life of Jacqueline Kennedy Onassis.* New York: Viking, 2000.

———. *Diana.* New York: Viking, 2006.

Broder, Jonathan. "Diana's Big Sister." *Salon* 3 Sept. 1997. http://www.salon.com/sept97/news/news970903.html.

Brown, Chester. *Louis Riel: A Comic-Strip Biography.* Montreal: Drawn and Quarterly, 2003.

Brown, Tina. "Kitty Kelley, Derided and Delicious." *Washington Post* 16 September 2004. http://www.washingtonpost.com/wp-dyn/articles/A24853-2004Sep15.html.

———. *The Diana Chronicles.* New York: Doubleday, 2007.

Bruni, Frank. *Ambling Into History: The Unlikely Odyssey of George W. Bush.* New York: HarperCollins, 2002.

Bullock, Alan. *Hitler and Stalin: Parallel Lives.* New York: Random House, 1992.

Burrell, Paul. *A Royal Duty.* New York: Putnam, 2003.

———. *The Way We Were: Remembering Diana.* New York: Morrow, 2006.

Capozzola, Christopher. "The Gay Lincoln Controversy." *Boston Globe* 16 Jan. 2005. http://www.boston.com/news/globe/ideas/articles/2005/01/16/the_gay_lincoln_controversy.

Cash, Arthur H. *John Wilkes: The Scandalous Father of Civil Liberty.* New Haven, CT: Yale University Press, 2006.

Cassidy, David. "Werner Heisenberg and the Uncertainty Principle." Online exhibit based on book of the same name. College Park, MD: Center of the History for Physics, 2002. http://www.aip.org/history/heisenberg.

Chaplin, Joyce E. *The First Scientific American: Benjamin Franklin and the Pursuit of Genius.* New York: Basic Books, 2006.

Claridge, Laura. *Norman Rockwell: A Life.* New York: Random House, 2001.

Conant, Jennet. *Tuxedo Park: A Wall Street Tycoon and the Secret Palace of Science That Changed the Course of World War II.* New York: Simon & Schuster, 2002.

CNN. "Sarah Bradford Chats about Her Jackie Kennedy Onassis Biography, *America's Queen.*" Transcript. CNN.com 26 Oct. 2000.

———. "Interview with Two Writers About New JFK Jr. Book." Transcript, interview of Jay Mulvaney and Susan Tift regarding Klein 2003. CNN.com 1 July 2003. http://transcripts.cnn.com/TRANSCRIPTS/0307/01/se.08.html.

Crowley, Michael. "Kitty Kelley: Colonoscopist to the Stars." *Slate* 15 Sept. 2004. http://www.slate.com/id/2106746.

Dallek, Robert. "Shining a Halogen Light on a Senator's Dark Corners." *New York Times* 5 June 2007.

De Veaux, Alexis. *Warrior Poet: A Biography of Audre Lorde.* New York: Norton, 2004.

DiLorenzo, Thomas J. *Unmasked: What You're Not Supposed to Know about Dishonest Abe.* New York: Crown Forum, 2006.

Dougherty, Steve. *Hopes and Dreams: The Story of Barack Obama.* New York: Black Dog & Leventhal, 2007.

Doyle, Arthur Conan. "A Scandal in Bohemia." In *The New Annotated Sherlock Holmes.* Leslie S. Klinger, ed. New York: Norton, 1891 [2005].

Edel, Leon. *Writing Lives: Principia Biographica.* New York: Norton, 1984.

Ellis, Joseph. *Founding Brothers: The Revolutionary Generation.* New York: Knopf, 2000.

———. *Passionate Sage: The Character and Legacy of John Adams.* New York: Norton, 2001 [1993].

———. *His Excellency: George Washington.* New York: Knopf, 2004.

Epstein, Daniel Mark. *Lincoln and Whitman: Parallel Lives in Civil War Washington.* New York: Ballantine, 2004.

Finstad, Suzanne. *Natasha: The Biography of Natalie Wood.* New York: Harmony, 2001.

———. "Live Online" discussion of *Natasha.* Washingtonpost.com 26 July 2001.

Fraser, Antonia. *Marie Antoinette: The Journey.* New York: Talese, 2001.

Gaiman, Neil. *Don't Panic: Douglas Adams and The Hitchhiker's Guide to the Galaxy.* London: Titan, 2002.

Gerth, Jeff, and Van Natta, Don, Jr. *Her Way: The Hopes and Ambitions of Hillary Rodham Clinton.* New York: Little, Brown, 2007.

Goodman, Jon. *The Kennedy Mystique: Creating Camelot.* Washington, DC: National Geographic, 2006.

Gopnik, Adam. "Angels and Ages: Lincoln's Language and Its Legacy." *New Yorker* 27 May 2007.

Gordon, John Steele. "The Sunny Steel Baron and His Bootstraps Fortune." *New York Times* 30 Oct. 2006. http://www.nytimes.com/2006/10/30/books/30gord.html.

Greenberg, David. "The Gay Emancipator? What's Wrong with *The Intimate World of Abraham Lincoln?*" *Slate* 14Jan. 2005. http://www.slate.com/id/2112313.

Hamilton, Nigel. *Biography: A Brief History.* Cambridge, MA: Harvard University Press, 2007.

Helfer, Andrew, and Randy DuBurke. *Malcolm X: A Graphic Biography.* New York: Hill and Wang, 2006.

Herken, Gregg. *Brotherhood of the Bomb: The Tangled Lives and Loyalties of Robert Oppenheimer, Ernest Lawrence, and Edward Teller.* New York: Henry Holt, 2002. Additional material at http://www.brotherhoodofthebomb.com.

Hitchens, Christopher. "Rich Man's Burden." *Atlantic Monthly* December (2006) Republished at Powell's Books "Review-a-Day" Web site (19 December 2006). http://www.powells.com/review/2006_12_19.html.

Holroyd, Michael. *Works on Paper: The Craft of Biography and Autobiography.* Washington, DC: Counterpoint, 2002.

Huddleston, Kathie. "Neil Gaiman Hitchhikes Through Douglas Adams' Hilarious Galaxy." *Science Fiction Weekly* 1 Dec. 2003. http://www.scifi.com/sfw/issue345/interview.html.

Ianziti, Gary. "Re-Thinking Biography." Paper presented to the Social Change in the 21st Century Conference, Centre for Social Change Research, Queensland University of Technology, 21 November 2003. http://eprints.qut.edu.au/archive/00000131/01/Gary_Ianziti.pdf.

International Auto/Biography Association (IABA), 2007. http://www.iaba.org.cn.

Isaacson, Walter. *Benjamin Franklin: An American Life.* New York: Simon & Schuster, 2003.

———. *Einstein: His Life and Universe.* New York: Simon & Schuster, 2007.

——— 2007a. "Letter from Walter Isaacson." http://www.aspeninstitute.org. [Accessed May 17, 2007.]

James, Caryn. "The Importance of Being Biased." *New York Times* 27 Mar. 1994. http://query.nytimes.com/gst/fullpage.html?res=9E00E7DC1E3DF934A15750C0A96 2958260.

Kakutani, Michiko. "Today's Managing Partner in Team Clinton & Clinton." *New York Times* 5 June 2007. http://www.nytimes.com/2007/06/05/books/review/05kaku.html.

Kaufman, David. *Ridiculous! The Theatrical Life and Times of Charles Ludlam.* New York: Applause, 2002.

Kelley, Kitty. *The Family: The Real Story of the Bush Dynasty.* New York: Doubleday, 2004.

Kilian, Pamela. *Barbara Bush: Matriarch of a Dynasty.* New York: Dunne, 2002.

Kimmelman, Michael. "The Former Queen of Buzz Conjures a Golden Heyday." *New York Times* 11 June 2007. http://www.nytimes.com/2007/06/11/books/11tina.html.

Lacey, Josh. "Only an Irish Clown." *The Guardian* 12 June 2004. http://books.guardian.co.uk/review/story/0,,1236066,00.html.

Lambert, Gavin. *Natalie Wood: A Life.* New York: Knopf, 2004.

Lamberton, Robert. *Plutarch.* New Haven, CT: Yale University Press, 2001.

Lanes, Selma G. *Through the Looking Glass: Further Adventures and Misadventures in the Realm of Children's Literature.* Boston: Godine, 2004.

Leaming, Barbara. *Mrs. Kennedy: The Missing History of the Kennedy Years.* New York: Free Press, 2001.

Leopold, Todd. "David McCullough Brings 'John Adams' to Life." CNN.com 7 June 7 2001. http://archives.cnn.com/2001/SHOWBIZ/books/06/07/david.mccullough/index.html.

Lewis, Roger. *The Life and Death of Peter Sellers.* New York: Applause, 1997.

Lomax, Louis E. *To Kill a Black Man: The Shocking Parallel in the Lives of Malcolm X and Martin Luther King Jr.* Los Angeles: Holloway House, 1968.

Lynch, Jack. n.d. "A Guide to Samuel Johnson." http://andromeda.rutgers.edu/~jlynch/Johnson/Guide/index.html. [Accessed July 1, 2007.]

Malcolm, Janet. *The Silent Woman: Sylvia Plath and Ted Hughes.* New York: Knopf, 1994.

Marsden, George M. *Jonathan Edwards: A Life.* New Haven, CT: Yale University Press, 2003.

Maslin, Janet. "The Diana Chronicles." *New York Times* 8 June 2007. http://www.nytimes.com/2007/06/08/books/08book.html.

McCullough, David. *Truman.* New York: Simon & Schuster, 1992.

———. *John Adams.* New York: Simon & Schuster, 2001.

McCutchen, Wilmot H. "Plutarch." Postscript to *15 Ancient Greek Heroes from Plutarch's Lives*, 1998. http://www.e-classics.com/index.html.

Mehegan, David. "Author Enjoys Full Access for Book on Kennedy Patriarch." *Boston Globe* 5 Aug. 2006. http://www.boston.com/ae/books/articles/2006/08/05/author_enjoys_full_access_for_book_on_kennedy_patriarch/.

Minutaglio, Bill. *First Son: George W. Bush and the Bush Family Dynasty.* New York: Times, 1999.

Mitchell, Elizabeth. *W: Revenge of the Bush Dynasty* Rev. ed. New York: Berkeley, 2003.

Moon, Vicky. *The Private Passion of Jackie Kennedy Onassis: Portrait of a Rider.* New York: Regan, 2005.

Mulvaney, Jay. *Diana and Jackie: Maidens, Mothers, Myths.* New York: Griffin, 2002.

Murphy-O'Connor, Jerome. *Jesus and Paul: Parallel Lives.* Collegeville, MN: Liturgical Press, 2007.

Nasar, Sylvia. *A Beautiful Mind: The Life of Mathematical Genius and Nobel Laureate John Nash.* New York: Touchstone, 1998.

Nasaw, David. *The Chief: The Life of William Randolph Hearst.* Boston: Houghton Mifflin, 2000.

———. *Andrew Carnegie.* New York: Penguin, 2006.

Nehring, Christina. "Domesticated Goddess." *Atlantic Monthly* April 2004. http://www.theatlantic.com/doc/200404/nehring.

Nicolson, Nigel. *Long Life: Memoirs*. New York: Putnam, 1998.

Niels Bohr Archive (NBA). "Release of Documents Relating to 1941 Bohr-Heisenberg Meeting." Niels Bohr Archive (6 Feb. 2002). http://www.nba.nbi.dk/release.html.

Oates, Joyce Carol. "Adventures in Abandonment." *New York Times* 28 Aug. 28 1988. http://query.nytimes.com/gst/fullpage.html?res=940DE4D81539F93BA1575BC0A96 E948260.

O'Hehir, Andrew. "The Sexual Life of Abraham Lincoln." *Salon* 12 Jan. 2005. http://dir.salon.com/story/books/review/2005/01/12/lincoln/index.html.

Ottaviani, Jim, and Leland Purvis. *Suspended in Language: Niels Bohr's Life, Discoveries, and the Century He Shaped*. Ann Arbor, MI: G.T. Labs, 2004.

Pais, Abraham. *Niels Bohr's Times, In Physics, Philosophy, and Polity*. Oxford: Clarendon, 1991.

———. *J. Robert Oppenheimer: A Life*. With supplemental material by Robert P. Crease. New York: Oxford, 2006.

Parker, Richard. "Pittsburgh Pirates." *New York Times* 5 Nov. 2006. http://www.nytimes. com/2006/11/05/books/review/Parker.t.html.

Parry, Robert. *Secrecy and Privilege: Rise of the Bush Dynasty from Watergate to Iraq*. Arlington, VA: Media Consortium, 2004.

Phillips, Kevin. *American Dynasty: Aristocracy, Fortune, and the Politics of Deceit in the House of Bush*. New York: Viking, 2004.

Rexroth, Kenneth. "Plutarch, *Parallel Lives*." In *Classics Revisited*. New York: New Directions, 1968.

Rich, Motoko. "3 Books from Knopf Take Prizes in Pulitzers." *New York Times* 18 Apr. 18 2007. http://www.nytimes.com/2007/04/18/books/18puli.html?fta=y.

———. 2007a. "Rival Books on Hillary Clinton Play Leapfrog on Debut Dates." *New York Times* 22 May 2007. http://www.nytimes.com/2007/05/22/books/22book.html.

Rollyson, Carl. *A Higher Form of Cannibalism? Adventures in the Art and Politics of Biography*. Chicago: Ivan R. Dee, 2005.

———. "Biography: The Highest Form of Cannibalism?" *New York Sun* 14 March 14 2007. http://www2.nysun.com/arts/biography-the-highest-form-of-cannibalism/.

Rose, Phyllis. *Parallel Lives: Five Victorian Marriages*. New York: Knopf, 1983.

Sauvé, Christian. Sept. 2005. www.christian-sauve.com.

Schiff, Stacy. *A Great Improvisation: Franklin, France, and the Birth of America*. New York: Holt, 2005.

Schweizer, Peter, and Rochelle Schweizer. *The Bushes: Portrait of a Dynasty*. New York: Doubleday, 2004.

Scott, Janny. "For Unauthorized Biographers, the World Is Very Hostile." *New York Times* 6 Oct. 1996. http://www.nytimes.com/books/98/11/22/specials/welty-unauthorized.html.

Seligman, Craig. "Brilliant Careers: Janet Malcolm." *Salon* 29 Feb. 2000. http://archive. salon.com/people/bc/2000/02/29/malcolm/index.html.

Shenk, Joshua Wolf. *Lincoln's Melancholy: How Depression Challenged a President and Fueled His Greatness*. Boston: Houghton Mifflin, 2005. www.lincolnsmelancholy.com.

Simpson, M.J. *Hitchhiker: A Biography of Douglas Adams*. 1st American ed. Boston: Justin, Charles & Company, 2003.

Smith, Sally Bedell. *Grace and Power: The Private World of the Kennedy White House*. New York: Random House, 2004.

Stansell, Christine. "What Stuff!" *New Republic* (9 Jan. 2005 online; 17 January 2005 print). Republished at Powell's Books "Review-a-Day" Web site 13 Jan. 13 2005.

Steers, Edward, Jr. *Lincoln Legends: Myths, Hoaxes, and Confabulations Associated With Our Greatest President*. Lexington, KY: University Press of Kentucky, 2007.

Stiles, T.J. "Man of Steel—and Ink." *Salon* 25 Oct. 2006. http://www.salon.com/books/ review/2006/10/25/nasaw/index.html.

Talbot, David. *Brothers: The Hidden History of the Kennedy Years*. New York: Free Press, 2007.

Tippins, Sherrill. *February House: The Story of W.H. Auden, Carson McCullers, Jane and Paul Bowles, Benjamin Britten, and Gypsy Rose Lee, Under One Roof In Wartime America.* Boston: Houghton Mifflin, 2006.

Tripp, C.A. *The Intimate World of Abraham Lincoln.* Lewis Gannett, ed. New York: Free Press, 2005.

Tucker, Tom. *Bolt of Fate: Benjamin Franklin and His Electric Kite Hoax.* New York: Public Affairs, 2003.

Webb, Nick. *Wish You Were Here: The Official Biography of Douglas Adams.* New York: Ballantine, 2003.

Weber, Caroline. "Tabloid Princess." *New York Times* 10 June 2007. http://www.nytimes. com/2007/06/10/books/review/Weber-t.html?n=Top/Reference/Times%20Topics/ People/D/Diana,%20Princess%20Of%20Wales.

Welland, Sasha Su-Ling. *A Thousand Miles of Dreams: The Journeys of Two Chinese Sisters.* Lanham, MD: Rowman & Littlefield, 2006.

Werth, Barry. *The Scarlet Professor: Newton Arvin—A Literary Life Shattered by Scandal.* New York: Talese, 2001.

Whittemore, Reed. *Pure Lives: The Early Biographers.* Baltimore: Johns Hopkins, 1988.

———. *Whole Lives: Shapers of Modern Biography.* Baltimore: Johns Hopkins, 1989.

Wilson, Andrew. *Beautiful Shadow: A Life of Patricia Highsmith.* New York: Bloomsbury, 2003.

Winner, Lauren. "Creative Marriage, British Style: PW Talks With Katie Roiphe." *Publisher's Weekly* 23 April 2007. http://www.publishersweekly.com/article/CA6434983.html.

Wood, Gordon S. *The Americanization of Benjamin Franklin.* New York: Penguin, 2004.

Wood, Lana. *Natalie: A Memoir by Her Sister.* New York: Putnam, 1984.

Yardley, Jonathan. "The Sage of Baltimore." *Atlantic Monthly* Dec. 2002. Republished at Powell's Books "Review-a-Day" Web site (17 Dec. 2002). http://www.powells.com/ review/2002_12_17.html.

———. "How an Ambitious Scottish Immigrant Rose from Hardscrabble Roots to the Pinnacle of Industry." *Washington Post* 15 Oct. 2006. http://www.washingtonpost.com/wpdyn/ content/article/2006/10/12/AR2006101201097.html.

———. "Why Are We So Fascinated by the Lives of Others?" *Washington Post* 25 Mar. 2007. http://www.washingtonpost.com/wp-dyn/content/article/2007/03/22/ AR2007032201670.html.

Further Reading

Backscheider, Paula R. *Reflections on Biography.* New York: Oxford, 1999, www.biography.com; Hamilton, Nigel. *Biography.* Cambridge, MA: Harvard, 2007; Holroyd, Michael. *Works On Paper.* Washington, DC: Counterpoint, 2002; Rollyson, Carl. *A Higher Form of Cannibalism?* Chicago: Ivan R. Dee, 2005; Shenk, Joshua Wolf. "Afterword: 'What Everybody Knows.'" In *Lincoln's Melancholy,* 221–243. Boston: Houghton Mifflin, 2003; Whittemore, Reed. *Whole Lives: Shapers of Modern Biography.* Baltimore: Johns Hopkins, 1988; Zarnowski, Myra. *History Makers: A Questioning Approach to Reading and Writing Biographies.* Portsmouth, NH: Heinemann, 2003.

PEGGY LIN DUTHIE

C

CHICK LIT

Definition. Much of the fiction written by American women in the twenty-first century can be termed "popular," owing to its sustained engagement with an expansive but clearly defined readership. Since the 1990s, popular women's fiction has been dominated by "chick lit," a term that has come to signify a particular brand of commercial fiction. In her article "Who's Laughing Now? A Short History of Chick Lit and the Perversion of a Genre," novelist Cris Mazza credits herself with inventing the taxonomy in her capacity as co-editor of an anthology of new women's writing. The stories in *Chick-Lit: Postfeminist Fiction* sought "not to embrace an old frivolous or coquettish image of women but to take responsibility for our part in the damaging, lingering stereotype" (Mazza 2000, 18). Mazza coined the term hoping that critics would recognize its "ironic intention"; as she observes, the ironic inflection of the term evaporated with the inception of the "second incarnation" of chick lit (2000, 18). It is this second incarnation that became a publishing phenomenon in the 1990s and continues to thrive in the twenty-first century.

Arguably, tone is the defining characteristic of the genre. The signature tone of chick lit is humorous, irreverent, and journalistic. Many writers of chick lit novels began their careers as columnists and use their social commentaries as source material for their fictional worlds. *Bridget Jones's Diary* (1996) evolved from British writer Helen Fielding's newspaper columns for the *Independent* and later the *Daily Telegraph*. Candace Bushnell's column "Sex and the City" provided the material for her first novel and the hugely influential HBO television series (1998–2004).

From its inception, chick lit secured the readership of the younger demographic through its engagement with contemporary issues and popular culture. Over the past decade, chick lit has sprouted a variety of subgenres. Although commentators on the genre regularly announce its decline, it continues to expand and attract a wider range of women readers.

"IT'S ABOUT YOU!"

Today's chick lit is written by, about, and for women. When asked to explain the popularity of the genre, readers emphasize the importance of identification. The epigram of the Web site "chicklitbooks.com" reflects this appetite for the familiar: "It's hip. It's smart. It's fun. It's about you!" (Ferriss and Young 2005, 1). For many readers, chick lit provides an antidote to the unrealistic images of women's lives presented by the media. As women's choices seem to proliferate, the media continues to fixate on issues of female identity and to debate women's place and function in contemporary society. Many chick lit novels privilege multiple viewpoints, enabling readers to experience vicariously the narratives of women who chose differently from them.

History. Chick lit entered the public's consciousness as a generic term after the publication of Fielding's *Bridget Jones's Diary* in 1996. In her introduction to *The Feminist Bestseller,* Imelda Whelehan observes that Fielding's novel "facilitated a shift in the way contemporary young women's lives were discussed and described" and "spoke to a new generation of women about the complexities of their lives" (Whelehan 2005, 4).

Writers of the genre trace its roots as far back as the nineteenth century, claiming parentage in Jane Austen, Charlotte Brontë, and Edith Wharton. Reviewers register these affinities while recognizing the relative frivolity of chick lit: the *Sunday Telegraph's* image of Bushnell as "Jane Austen with a martini" graces the covers or opening pages of her novels. Bushnell has identified herself as a postmodern Edith Wharton. Regarding the heroine of *Trading Up* (2003), her third novel, Bushnell states: "If anything, Janey. . . is like Lily Bart from *The House of Mirth*" ("Lipstick Jungle"). In "Hypotext in the City: *The House of Mirth* at the Millennium," Pamela Knights examines Wharton's presence in contemporary American women's fiction; her illuminating essay includes an analysis of Bushnell's engagement with Wharton's narratives. In "Mothers of Chick Lit?" Juliette Wells compares Wharton's representation of New York society in *The House of Mirth* with postmodern depictions.

THE CHICK-LIT BRAND

Bridget Jones's Diary sparked a publishing boom in Great Britain and the United States. A multitude of novels chronicling the daily struggles of single women followed in its wake. Chick lit became an instantly recognizable brand, which, a decade later, continues to sell itself. The packaging of chick lit novels testifies to its status as a distinct genre: readers scan the pastel covers for the familiar motifs of chick lit as much as they seek out individual authors: shoes, lipsticks, cocktails, and handbags are prevalent.

Publishing houses have created imprints to cater solely to this burgeoning market. "Strapless," an imprint of Kensington Publishers, and "Red Dress Ink," a division of Harlequin Publishing, dedicate themselves entirely to the production of chick lit. "Red Dress Ink" identifies itself in this way: "a women's fiction program that depicts young, single, mostly city-dwelling women coping with the pressures that accompany a career, the dating scene, and all the other aspects of modern life in America" (Ferriss 2005, 194). Web sites dedicated to chick lit assert its credentials as a distinct genre: they offer definitions, forums, bibliographies, and dictionaries of chick lit slang, as well as advertising the novels themselves.

Plum Sykes, a British-born chick lit writer who lives in and writes about Manhattan, also claims parallels with Wharton: "Honestly, if Edith Wharton published *The Custom of the Country* now, it would be considered chick lit" (Solomons 2004). *Bridget Jones's Diary* shared some of the plot of Jane Austen's *Pride and Prejudice*, including the lead male character named Darcy, who initially shuns and insults the female lead character. To further cement the connection, Colin Firth, the actor who played Mr. Darcy in the acclaimed 1995 BBC television production of *Pride and Prejudice*, also played the Mark Darcy character in the 2001 movie of *Bridget Jones' Diary*.

Publishers have attempted to capitalize on these broad, thematic parallels by re-marketing nineteenth-century literary classics. In 2006, Bloomsbury and Headline published editions of Brontë's *Jane Eyre* (1847) and the novels of Jane Austen with pastel covers sporting silhouettes of the young heroine. Reviewers have identified young adults as the primary market for these editions; the *Guardian* includes the repackaged Bloomsbury classics in its recommendations for teenage readers ("Teenage Picks"). However, Bloomsbury clearly issued these new editions with the readers of chick lit in mind. American popular fiction writers such as Meg Cabot have been chosen to write brief prefaces to the novels, entitled "Why You Should Read . . ."

Literary critics continue to dispute these lines of descent. Many acknowledge the parity in basic subject matter but argue that the similarity ends there. In "Mothers of Chick Lit?" Juliette Wells illuminates the stylistic differences between nineteenth-century literary texts and today's popular women's fiction. She compares Fielding's description of the hero in *Bridget Jones: The Edge of Reason* with Charlotte Brontë's rendering of Rochester in *Jane Eyre,* emphasizing the richness of Brontë's prose:

> While Helen Fielding supplies us only with a succinct declarative statement about Mark Darcy's looks, Charlotte Brontë captures in words the features of Mr. Rochester's face, relates them to the qualities of his personality, convincingly explains why Jane should be so drawn to a man who would not usually be considered handsome, and tantalizes our interpretive skills by insistently using language of mastery and enslavement. Fielding's sentence, immediately comprehensible, passes by almost without our noticing it; Brontë's sentences invite us to savor and ponder her choice of words. (Wells 2005, 65)

Twentieth-century touchstones open up the most fertile line of enquiry into the history of the genre. Modern paradigms for today's chick lit include Rona Jaffe's *The Best of Everything* (1958), Helen Gurley Brown's *Sex and the Single Girl* (1962), Mary McCarthy's *The Group* (1963), Jacqueline Susann's *Valley of the Dolls* (1966), and, more recently, Nora Ephron's *Heartburn* (1983). Indeed chicklit Web sites have begun to identify such novels as models for the genre (Skurnik 2006). Written on the brink of second-wave feminism, these mid-century novels broke new ground with their candid representations of female sexuality and the issues that informed women's everyday lives. In *The Best of Everything*, Jaffe explores taboos such as abortion, infidelity, and sexual harassment. The novel's epigram comes from an advertisement in the *New York Times:* "You Deserve the Best of Everything," in many ways the mantra of today's chick lit. *The Best of Everything* was reissued in 2005 in recognition of its contemporary relevance. Speaking with Renée Montagne in 2005, Jaffe registers parallels with *Sex and the City* (1996). She recalls writing the novel to engage with the covert narratives of women living in the "hypocritical" and "secretive" atmosphere of the fifties. She credits her novel's enduring success to its identifiable narratives: "people saw themselves reflected in it . . . they realized that . . . they weren't alone and it made them feel great." In her foreword to the 2005 edition of the novel, Jaffe asserts, "The honesty of *The Best of Everything* paved the way for other authors" (Jaffe 2005, ix).

The heroines in *The Best of Everything* have come to the city seeking the best career, the best man, and the best apartment. The novel opens with the image of the hundreds of women who navigate the city every morning:

> You see them every morning at a quarter to nine, rushing out of the maw of the sway tunnel, filing out of Grand Central Station, crossing Lexington and Park and Madison and Fifth avenues, the hundreds and hundreds of girls . . . Some of them are wearing chic black suits (maybe last year's but who can tell?) and kid gloves and are carrying lunches in their violet-sprigged Bonwit Teller bags. None of them has enough money. (Jaffe 2005, 1)

This opening paragraph launches the predominant themes and images of today's chick lit: the frenzy of the city, the career girl working to support herself, the preoccupation with acquisition and aesthetics. Jaffe's representation of New York anticipates chick lit's preoccupation with urban spaces. She presents the city as an arena attuned to the demands of the single woman. The heroines' emotional trajectories are mirrored by the city's seasonal changes, and their demands are catered to by New York's social calendar: "Some girls know that there is a fifth season in New York, the season of the Summer Bachelor" (Jaffe 2005, 243).

Jaffe's primary heroine, 20-year-old Caroline Bender, serves as a model for the chick lit heroine. Having lost her fiancé, she seeks work at a publishing firm, a popular line of work for the postmodern heroine. Caroline's initiation into a treacherous work environment foreshadows novels such as Lauren Weisberger's *The Devil Wears Prada* (2003) and *The Nanny Diaries* (2002) by Emma McLaughlin and Nicola Krause. On her first day at the office, Caroline realizes that "the working world was more complicated than she had ever dreamed" (Jaffe 2005, 14).

Although chick lit writers distinguish their narratives from romance novels, the undeserving suitor masquerading as the hero remains a staple of their fiction. Caroline's fiancé reappears, but it takes her most of the novel to understand that he is not worthy of her. The satellite heroines pursue narrative lines that have retained their place as subsidiary stories in today's chick lit: the narrative of the divorced, single mother and the struggling, doomed actress.

Brown's *Sex and the Single Girl* undoubtedly paved the way for writers of chick lit, not only by foregrounding the single woman's narrative but also by contesting generic boundaries. Brown's text is a generic hybrid: part autobiography, part journalism, part survival guide. Formally and thematically, *Sex and the Single Girl* anticipates Bushnell's *Sex and the City*, another taboo-defying text that resists generic categorization. In 2003, Barricade Books reissued Brown's novel with a prefatory title, announcing it as the prototype for Bushnell's text; the cover of the latest edition reads, *Before There Was Sex and the City, There Was Sex and the Single Girl*. Brown's defiant tone and journalistic technique set the standard for contemporary chick lit writers: the rallying cries of independence, the cataloguing of masculine types, and emphatic rejection of the "singleton" stigma echo throughout today's chick lit. Chapter titles such as "Where to Meet Them," "Money Money Money" and "The Apartment" would not look out of place in a twenty-first-century chick lit novel. Brown's opening characterization of the single girl as sassy, tough, and desirable prefigures the heroines of today's chick lit:

> the single woman, far from being a creature to be pitied and patronized, is emerging as the newest glamour girl of our times. She is engaging because she lives by her wits. She supports herself. She has had to sharpen her personality and mental resources to a glitter in order to survive in a competitive world and the sharpening looks good. Economically she is a dream . . . Why else is she attractive? Because she isn't married, that's why! She is free to be The Girl in a man's life or at least his vision of The Girl, whether he is married or single himself. (Brown 2003, 6)

Another notable model for contemporary American chick lit is Mary McCarthy's *The Group* (1963). Bushnell observes that *The Group* tells "the same story" as her latest novel, *Lipstick Jungle* (2005), and Susann's *Valley of the Dolls*: "It has lousy men, crappy apartments, birth control, lesbian friends" ("Lipstick Jungle"). *The Group* follows the lives of eight Vassar graduates; each chapter presents a different center of consciousness. Again, McCarthy's novel engages frankly with the taboo subjects of the day: lesbian relationships, contraception, the breast/bottle debate. Although the controversy surrounding some of these subjects has diminished, the reflections of McCarthy's heroines remain relevant. One heroine, Polly, discovers that she can feel "quite happy and self-sufficient" without a man and wonders whether "it might be almost a deprivation to get married" (McCarthy 1966, 245). Polly later marries but believes that her married classmates secretly covet the lives of resolutely single women, such as Helena: "It was felt that they at least had 'done something'" (McCarthy 1996, 284). As the single girl determined to establish herself in the male-dominated publishing world, Libby MacAusland is clearly another paradigm for the twenty-first–century chick lit heroine.

The term *gossip* surfaces frequently in association with popular women's fiction: in her introduction to *Valley of the Dolls* Julie Burchill describes the text as "three decades of gossip columns distilled into one fat novel" (Burchill 2005, x); Michiko Kakutani (1989) of the *New York Times* characterizes McCarthy's *The Group* as "a chatty gossip sheet" (Bushnell's novels have been categorized as 'Gossip Lit'; Mark Goldblatt (2003) describes Weisberger's *The Devil Wears Prada* as "the most gossipy novel in recent years." However, McCarthy's text differs from chick lit in several ways. Literary critics stress the disposability of chick lit, but *The Group* continues to resonate with a wide readership. Unlike many chick lit writers, McCarthy does not segregate women's preoccupations from broader social issues. The third-person narrator of *The Group* casts a satirical eye over America's privileged classes. The novel opens on the familiar image of single women assembling in New York, but the appreciation of the city's plurality is captured with a tinge of irony that is rare in today's chick lit:

> They were in the throes of discovering New York, imagine it, when some of them had actually lived there all their lives, in tiresome Georgian houses full of waste space in the Eighties or Park Avenue apartment buildings, and they delighted in such out-of-the-way corners as this . . . (McCarthy 1966, 5)

Where today's chick lit heroines wrangle over designer labels, McCarthy's Vassar graduates argue over political affiliations and worry about the effects of privilege: "Great wealth was a frightful handicap; it insulated you from living" (McCarthy 1966, 26). The influence of the feminist movement on the group is clear. The women insist that they are a "different breed . . . from the languid buds of the previous decade" and that they will work in the fall, "at a volunteer job if need be" (McCarthy 1966, 12). One heroine, Priss, regrets relinquishing her "job and social ideals" for her husband and suspects that he would be "far happier himself if she were where she longed to be—in Washington, as a humble cog in the New Deal, which he hated—and he could boast of 'my Bolshevik wife'" (McCarthy 1966, 325).

Susann's *Valley of the Dolls* is often cited as the best-selling novel of all time. In the television series *Sex and the City*, a reformed New York party girl who has moved to the suburbs insists on the redundancy of Susann's narratives: "Life isn't a Jacqueline Susann novel, 'four friends looking for life and love in the big city'" ("The Baby Shower"). At the end of the episode, the suburban housewife returns to New York in a desperate attempt to recuperate this narrative. This nod to Susann testifies to the novel's relevance for the single heroines of American chick lit. Spanning three decades, *Valley of the Dolls* charts the lives of three friends striving to climb the ladder of the entertainment industry. Like Jaffe, Susann opens her novel with the most sympathetic character, Anne Welles, securing her position as primary heroine. The novel begins in 1945 with a moment that has become a staple of the chick lit plot: the arrival of the heroine in New York: "The temperature hit ninety degrees the day she arrived. New York was steaming—an angry concrete animal caught unawares in an unseasonable hot spell. But she didn't mind the heat or the littered midway called Times Square. She thought New York was the most exciting city in the world" (Susann 2003, 1). For chick lit heroines, the city, usually New York, is a site for reinvention, adventure, and enterprise: "There was an acceptance at face value in New York, as if everyone had just been born, with no past heritage to acknowledge or hide" (Susann 2003, 6).

Valley of the Dolls is undoubtedly darker than contemporary chick lit. The "dolls" of the title signify the red or black pills that the heroines come to rely on as relationships begin to founder. In this world, even female friendship—often the only anchor for the chick lit heroine—is tainted by betrayal. Like Jaffe and McCarthy, Susann admits the reader into uncharted territory, tackling taboos such as birth control, breast cancer, sexual experimentation, and prenuptial agreements. The novel also dramatizes the alienation experienced by women who seem to "have it all"—a theme that Bushnell in particular would explore toward the end of the century.

In *Heartburn*, Ephron gives voice to the woman scorned. Wells speculates that this narrative is "too wrenching" for chick lit but notes that this subject takes center stage in British writer Elizabeth Buchan's *Revenge of the Middle-Aged Woman* (2002) (Wells 2005, 68). One is more likely to encounter this narrative in "hen lit," a subgenre for more mature readers. However, Ephron's heroine ends up pursuing the narrative line of the single women of chick lit. It is well documented that the novel is a thinly veiled account of the breakdown of Ephron's marriage. Heroine Rachel Samstat, a Jewish American food writer, is seven months pregnant with her second child when she discovers that her husband has been having an affair. She leaves Washington and heads for New York where she will claim her identity as a single woman. Through Rachel, Ephron presents the single woman's narrative as one of mobilization: "Things happen to you when you're single. You meet new men, you travel alone, you learn new tricks, you read Trollope, you try sushi, you buy nightgowns, you shave your legs. Then you get married and the hair grows in" (Ephron 1983, 14). Rachel's evaluation recalls Brown's account of the single life and reads like a commentary on the lives of today's chick lit heroines. On the plane to New York, she recognizes: "part of me was secretly relieved to be done with swatches and couches . . . and that part of me was thinking: Okay, Rachel Samstat, finally something is happening to you" (Ephron 1983, 16). Upon arriving, her "heart does a little dance" at the sight of "people on the street rushing around looking for action, love, and the world's greatest chocolate chip cookie" (Ephron 1983, 35).

Contemporary chick lit writer Jennifer Weiner recalls reading Ephron's novels and "being completed taken" by her "frank, funny, wry voice" ("Snarkspot"). Through Rachel's voice, Ephron addresses the questions that continue to dominate women's fiction today. She wonders why women view marriage as their ultimate destination and unveils the secret longings of the married woman: "It seemed to me that the desire to get married—which, I regret to say, I believe is fundamental and primal in women—is followed almost immediately by an equally fundamental and primal urge, which is to be single again" (Ephron 1983, 84). Such speculation is echoed by one of the heroines in the television series *Sex and the City*: "Married people just want to be single again" ("The Chicken Dance").

Rachel narrates with the signature irreverence of the chick lit heroine, satirizing the hypocrisy of men and Washington's social scene. Some of her humor is directed at herself. Intertextual references acknowledge the hold of fictional narratives over women. Rachel scoffs at the myths that shape women's aspirations—the "Lillian Hellman fantasy" that "the big man and the *big* woman march into the sunset together and live happily ever after" (Ephron 1983, 134, Ephron's italics)—but concedes that she has capitulated to a particular stereotype, exemplified by a heroine in an earlier popular novel: "I felt like a character in a trashy novel; I even knew which trashy novel I felt like a character in, which made it worse: *The Best of Everything*" (Ephron 1983, 153). The metatextual dimension of *Heartburn* foreshadows twenty-first century chick lit; as the conventions of the genre become ever more familiar, chick lit has become increasingly self-referential. In her metatextual commentary Rachel anticipates one of the conventions of contemporary chick lit—the need for the happy ending. Halfway through the novel, she assures the reader that her story will end happily because she "insist[s] on happy endings" (Ephron 1983, 99). A happy ending for Rachel constitutes self-assertion rather than union with a new man; she throws a key lime pie at her husband's face before leaving him for good.

Popular women's fiction has undergone significant changes over the past 50 years. Mid-century incarnations confronted the possibility of death, illness, suicide, and depression. In *The Best of Everything*, Gregg, the would-be actress, dies after trying to escape a man she mistakes for a rapist. *The Group* opens where many chick lit novels leave off and refuses to reward all its heroines with a happy ending. At the beginning of the novel, "pairs and trios of young women" arrive at the wedding of one of their classmates, the beautiful Kay (McCarthy 1966, 5). It takes Kay's death, a probable suicide, to reunite "the group" in the final chapters. *Valley of the Dolls* registers the dearth of plotlines for women in the fifties and sixties: marriage, motherhood, and beauty are finite. By the end of the novel, the women's ideals are in tatters. Jennifer, the beautiful "actress," seeks self-definition beyond her body but kills herself after a mastectomy; Neely is locked into the narrative of the self-destructive movie star; Anne wins the man she loves but capitulates to the lure of the "dolls" when he is unfaithful. At the end of the novel she looks forward only to a time when there would be "nothing left—no hurt, no love" (Susann 2003, 467).

Trends and Themes. In its formative years, chick lit centered on the preoccupations of the single, young female. The genre has since expanded to incorporate many aspects of women's lives, such as marriage, motherhood, careers, and self-image. Not all chick lit trades on the identification factor by presenting readers with the world of their everyday lives. The comedy of manners, a different but equally popular strain of chick lit, transports readers into the glamorous worlds captured on the covers of women's magazines. By satirizing the modeling or entertainment industries, these novels offer escapism while reassuring the reader that the image belies the reality. In some of the most popular chick lit novels, the two worlds collide—hapless, neurotic, single women are let loose among the princesses of the social elite. In *Bergdorf Blondes* (2004), Plum Sykes places the dowdy English girl in the company of New York's platinum blondes: young women who "work" only to sustain the impression that their lives "are fabulous beyond belief" (Sykes 2005, 1). In *Everyone Worth Knowing* (2005), Weisberger drops an English 20-something into the heady world of Manhattan's hot spots.

For many chick lit heroines, financial status is the most significant identity category. As the beneficiaries of feminism, these professional, independent, urban heroines flaunt their credentials as consumers. Consumerism is frequently presented as a bonding experience that connects the most estranged chick lit heroines. The sisters in Weiner's *In Her Shoes* (2004) have only one thing in common: their love of footwear. Chick lit novels abound with references to brand names, signaling the predominance of the "must have" mentality. Even heroines on limited salaries equate acquisition with success. Moments of personal triumph are usually accompanied by material gain of some kind. In *The Nanny Diaries*, Mrs. X gives Nan a pair of old Prada shoes. For Nan, this offering represents a victory over Manhattan's most conspicuous consumers: "PRADA! P-R-A-D-A. As in Madonna. As in *Vogue*. As in, watch me walk off in style, you khaki-wearing, pager-carrying, golf-playing, *Wall Street* Journal toting . . . arrogant jerk-offs!" (Krause and McLaughlin 2002, 67).

HBO's adaptation of *Sex and the City* continues to exert its influence on chick lit in many ways, but its celebration of consumerism has had perhaps the most enduring effect. Every week viewers tuned in to find out what designer labels the heroines were brandishing. At times, shopping is presented as a means of overcoming boredom, loneliness, or sexual frustration. In one episode, Carrie, the primary heroine, reports: "With no man in sight I decided to rescue my ankles from a life of boredom by purchasing too many pairs of Jimmy Choo shoes" ("Where There's Smoke," 1998).

Much popular women's fiction celebrates female community and presents friendship groups as a form of surrogate family. Most heroines are single at the beginning of the chick lit novel and rely on urban networks for support. Emulating Jaffe, Susann, and McCarthy, contemporary women writers often privilege plural perspectives and voices to reflect the relational sensibility of their heroines. The titles of chick lit often announce friendship or community as their dominant theme: Rebecca Wells's *Divine Secrets of the Ya-Ya Sisterhood* (1996) and Alisa Valdes-Rodriguez's *The Dirty Girls' Social Club* (2003). The forms of some chick lit novels reflect this theme. *The Dirty Girls' Social Club* is a sequence of stories, each focusing on an individual heroine. Elissa Schappell's acclaimed novel *Use Me* (2000) is composed of linked but self-contained stories, two of them narrated by the primary heroine's best friend. Bushnell's *Four Blondes* (2000) is a sequence of stories and novellas. The heroines do not know each other, but their stories of alienation are linked by strong thematic resonances.

Many heroines of contemporary women's fiction work in the same fields as their creators: publishing, journalism, or advertising. Novels, such as *Sex and the City, The Nanny Diaries,* and *The Devil Wears Prada* have been read as coded autobiographies. Chick lit heroines often favor "confessional form[s]" such as diary entries, e-mails, and newspaper columns: spaces where they are licensed to address taboo subjects and express self-doubt (Whelehan 2005, 5).

One of the most prevalent conventions of contemporary chick lit is the happy ending. Where Susann and McCarthy spurned neat, upbeat resolutions, contemporary writers rarely leave readers worrying about the futures of their heroines; marriage usually beckons. Exceptions include *The Devil Wears Prada,* in which the heroine begins the novel with the apparently perfect boyfriend and ends it single. She is rewarded, however, with a burgeoning career in writing.

Sensing perhaps the saturation of the market for tales of the singleton in the city, some writers have begun to test the boundaries of the genre. One of the fastest-growing subgenres is "mystery lit," a hybrid that interweaves the paradigmatic narratives of chick lit and crime novels. Janet Evanovich's immensely popular Stephanie Plum stories cross generic and formal boundaries: the detective heroine appears in novels, novellas, and short stories. Helen Fielding's latest novel, *Olivia Joules and the Overactive Imagination* (2003), has a spy for its heroine. In these generic hybrids, narratives begin to overlap. As they delve into the secret histories of their neighbors, the sleuthing heroines start to question their own choices. The appeal of this trend is reflected in the popularity of the television series *Desperate Housewives,* which first aired in the United States in 2004 on ABC. Created by Marc Cherry, the series is a dark comedy about the lives of suburban housewives. The themes of the series resonate strongly with chick lit; the characters are immediately recognizable types: the mother who has foregone her career to raise her hyperactive children; the bored ex-model who is having an affair; the single mother seeking love; and the control freak obsessed with the art of housekeeping. Generic suburban narratives are offset by the murder mystery that brings the housewives together. When fellow housewife Mary Alice commits suicide, the women unite to solve the mystery of her death. A tale of abduction, murder, and blackmail unfolds. Multiple murders follow in the second season.

"Ethnic lit" is a particularly popular subgenre that addresses the standard themes of chick lit alongside broader social issues. Race and class ideology shape the lives of these heroines as much as gender politics. The success of Terry McMillan's novel, *Waiting to Exhale* (1992), alerted publishers to a gap in the market. Until this point, most chicklit depicted and targeted white, middle-class women. McMillan's novel centers on four African-American women who support each other through relationship difficulties. Like most ensembles in popular women's fiction, the characters follow different trajectories—the single mother, the mistress, and the betrayed wife all feature—but are empowered by their connections with each other. As Lisa A. Guerroro notes, romance and career trajectories in *Waiting to Exhale* are circumscribed by race and gender ideology; each of McMillan's heroines must counter the potency of the "Ideal of White Womanhood" in their daily lives (McMillan 1993, 177). The only forum for self-actualization is friendship.

In 2001, Latina journalist Alisa Valdes-Rodriguez earned an advance of $475,000 for her first novel, *The Dirty Girls' Social Club*. Following the publication of the novel, *Time* magazine hailed Valdes-Rodriguez as "the Godmother of chica lit." Reviews noted strong affinities with McMillan's novel and praised Valdes-Rodriguez for fusing light fiction with political commentary. The novel follows the experiences of six Boston University graduates who assemble twice a year to catch up on each other's lives. Friendship is the one constant in the lives of the *sucias* (Spanish for "dirty girls"). One heroine describes the *sucias* as her "anchor in this city for a decade" (Valdes-Rodriguez 2001, 109). Lauren serves as the primary narrator and draws on the narratives of the "dirty girls" in her newspaper column, *My Life*. Lauren fulfills all the criteria of the identifiable chick lit heroine: she is a neurotic, irreverent journalist who uses her column to confess her flaws, and she falls in love with the wrong men and eats only when she is happy.

Through her representation of six women of varied ethnic backgrounds, Valdes-Rodriguez challenges the homogenization of Latinas in America. In her spirited commentary, Lauren confronts these issues head-on:

> Here's how my job interview went: *You're a Latina? How . . . neat. You must speak Spanish, then?* . . . With a name like Lauren Fernández, they figured Spanish was part of the package. But that's the American disease as I see it: rampant, illogical stereotyping. We would not be America without it. I admit I did not tell them I was half white trash, born and raised in New Orleans. (Valdes-Rodriguez 2004, 10)

Valdes-Rodriguez strains the boundaries of chick lit and delivers—through Lauren—a metacommentary on the limitations of the chick lit heroine. When Lauren proposes writing about racial tensions, her boss instructs her to tone down the aggression and aim for "you go, girl, sassy" (2004, 180). He designates her column as the "'syncopated counterbalance to all the dreary stuff in the rest of the paper'" (180).

By the end of the novel, secrets have been shared—stories of domestic abuse and hidden sexuality are released—and the group affirms its bonds. *The Dirty Girls' Social Club* concludes with the wedding of one heroine and looks forward to the wedding of another. Other *sucia* have abandoned unhealthy relationships and discovered the values of solitude. Valdes-Rodriguez has since written two more novels and founded a festival entitled the "Chica Lit Club Fiesta."

Some of the most popular chick lit novels of the twenty-first century focus on career paths, treating romance as a subsidiary plot. Young, single heroines striving for financial independence take assistant positions in the hope of working their way into publishing or supporting themselves through postgraduate courses. Chauvinistic co-workers and tyrannical women bosses are a common feature of "work lit," also known as "office lit" and "assistant lit." These novels often blur the line between fiction and autobiography; two of the most successful incarnations of this subgenre evolved from the experiences of the authors. Co-written by two former Manhattan nannies, *The Nanny Diaries* is a comedy of manners. Nan, a 20-something student from a liberal, middle-class family, supports herself by looking after the dysfunctional children of Manhattan's social elite. The prologue of the novel reads like a nanny's survival guide; it is peppered with "Nanny Facts" and warnings about Manhattan's affluent mommy figures:

She is always tiny. Her hair is always straight and thin; she always seems to be inhaling and never exhaling. She is always wearing expensive khaki pants, Chanel ballet flats, a French striped T-shirt, and a white cardigan. Possibly some discreet pearls. In seven years and umpteen interviews the I'm-mom-casual-in-my-khakis-but-intimidating-in-my-$400-shoes outfits never changes. (Krause and McLaughlin 2002, 2)

When Nan meets Mrs. X, an apparently typical Park Avenue mommy, she becomes nanny to her son, Grayer. How Mrs. X fills her time remains a mystery, yet she expects Nan to adhere to her tight schedule of pedicures and "charity work"; she asks her to run personal errands for her without specific instructions and airs her dissatisfaction with Nan through condescending, "exquisitely passive aggressive" notes (Mendelsohn 2002): "It has come to our attention that after you left in such a hurry last night there was a puddle of urine found beneath the small garbage can in Grayer's bathroom . . . Such a glaring oversight gives me pause as to the consistency of your performance" (Krause and McLaughlin 2002, 221).

The novel satirizes the twenty-first century cult of childhood and unveils the child's function as status symbol: Mr. and Mrs. X approach child rearing as a kind of competitive sport. Nan is quizzed by a development consultant on Grayer's progress and upbraided for neglecting to read him the *Wall Street Journal* and serve "'bilingual meals'" (Krause and McLaughlin 2002, 178). Mrs. X abdicates responsibility for her son by adopting the latest jargon of parenthood: when Grayer is rejected by a prospective school, she wonders if Nan has "'set him up for a potentially deleterious self-esteem adjustment'" (176). The novel also makes a serious political point. One of the "Nanny Facts" registers the race and class prejudice of Manhattan's parents: "in every one of my interviews, references are never checked. I am white. I speak French. My parents are college educated. I have no visible piercings and have been to Lincoln Center in the last two months. I'm hired" (4).

In *The Nanny Diaries*, Krause and McLaughlin venture into new territory, but the staples of chick lit are present: Nan intimates her frustration to the reader through capitalized inner monologue, a technique also deployed by Bushnell. When her roommate's boyfriend moves in, Nan begins the familiar, fruitless quest for an affordable studio apartment; then a romance develops with a man who lives in the same building as the X family. Krause and McLaughlin observe the stylistic conventions of chick lit. Chapter titles resemble column headings: "Holiday Cheer at $10 an Hour" and "Night of the Banking Dead." *The Nanny Diaries* reached number one in the *New York Times* best-seller list and was declared a "national phenomenon" by *Newsweek*.

The success of Weisberger's *The Devil Wears Prada* verifies the appeal of voyeuristic "revenge" narratives. Reviewers of the novel immediately commented on affinities with *The Nanny Diaries*. *The Devil Wears Prada* dramatizes a year in the life of Andrea Sachs, a college graduate who moves to New York, having spent 23 years "embodying small-town America" (Weisberger 2003, 10). She lands a job as junior assistant to Miranda Priestly, the "Devil in Prada," and the most powerful woman in the fashion world. Assured that she will be able to fast-track her way into journalism if she survives the year, Andrea endures months of humiliation before finally standing up to Miranda. In the process, she loses her *"supportive and adorable"* boyfriend, Alex (127, Weisberger's italics). Like *The Best of Everything*, *The Devil Wears Prada* deals with the difficult transition from college to the workplace. At the beginning of the novel, Andrea reflects that all of her friends are in entry-level jobs that provide no outlet for creativity or self-expression: "Each swore she'd actually gotten dumber in the short amount of time since graduation, and there was no escape in sight" (18). In work lit novels, the workplace demands the same compromises as romantic relationships. Women can lose their identities to jobs just as easily as they can to men.

Readers have expressed frustration that heroines such as Nan and Andrea fail to challenge the older, wealthier woman; Weisberger and Krause and McLaughlin save self-assertion for the final pages. Having been dismissed unceremoniously by Mr. and Mrs. X, Nan records her excoriating verdict of their parenting on the Nanny-cam. Weisberger bucks one chick lit trend by leaving the romantic destiny of her heroine open. Andrea's knight in shining armor arrives in the form of a female mentor; an editor serves as *deus ex machina*. Andrea acknowledges the triteness of her ending: "It was storybook-like, nauseating, really, how well we'd instantly hit it off" (Weisberger 2003, 388). In the final pages, Andrea claims the voice of the chick lit writer who capitalizes on her experience to expose the realities of the entertainment and fashion industries. She writes "tongue-in-cheek pieces on fashion shows" and "snarky stuff on being a celebrity assistant" (388).

Context and Issues. Chick lit's status as literature remains the subject of much debate. Many women writers object to the term and draw a firm line between chick lit and more literary incarnations of women's fiction. The most savage indictments come from acclaimed women writers such as Doris Lessing and Beryl Bainbridge. In an interview for the *Guardian*, Bainbridge describes chick lit as "a froth sort of thing" and adds: "As people spend so little time reading, it's a pity they perhaps can't read something a bit deeper, a bit more profound, something with a bit of bite to it" (Bainbridge 2001). Some commentators voice reservations about the connotations of the term "chick lit." Curtis Sittenfield of The *New York Times* writes: "To suggest that another woman's ostensibly literary novel is chick lit feels catty . . . doesn't the term basically bring down all of us?" ("Sophie's," 2005). Other commentators express concern that chick lit has closed down other narratives for women. Stacey D'Erasmo laments the paucity of plots reflected in contemporary popular women's fiction: "the marital quest of the fashionable, sexually well-traveled, 30-something woman has become so popular as to seem like the dominant narrative of life on earth right now" (Howard 1999). In an article for *Book Magazine*, Anna Weinberg parodied the genre by compiling a "Make Your Own Chick Lit" recipe, listing the formulae of the successful chick lit novel (Harzewski 2005, 34). Some writers welcome associations with chick lit. Valdes-Rodriguez views the genre as a vehicle for delivering her "message": "I like being called a beach read. I don't want to preach to the choir. I can sit here and say Latinos come in all shades for the rest of my life and no one would care. I'm trying to create a human being in a fun, fashion-y way and get the message across" (Acosta 2006).

In 2005, Suzanne Ferriss and Mallory Young edited a lively collection of essays entitled *Chick Lit: The New Woman's Fiction,* outlining the themes and preoccupations of the genre as well as its limitations. The essays focus specifically on chick lit's cultural significance. Imelda Whelehan examines chick lit's embattled relationship with feminism in detail in *The Feminist Bestseller*. She observes that "feminism lurks in the background" of much chick lit "like a guilty conscience" (Whelehan 2005, 176). Whelehan acknowledges that the genre engages women readers for whom feminism has lost its currency: "Chick lit is built on a tacit acknowledgement that feminism has failed to speak to 'ordinary' women" (214). As Whelehan notes, overt feminists feature primarily as objects of parody in chick lit. Feminism is misunderstood by some of Bushnell's heroines. *Trading Up* openly asks whether the tenets of feminism have a place in twenty-first century New York. Dodo Blanchette, a dowdy lifestyle reporter, exemplifies the contradictions of contemporary feminism: "[she] called herself a neofeminist; she believed in women helping other women . . . She had tons of girlfriends, and her favorite expression was 'Women rule!' . . . Like many young women of her generation, she had no qualms about using sex to get ahead'" (Bushnell 2004, 187).

From its inception, chick lit has provided rich source material for film and television adaptations: *Sex and the Single Girl, The Group, Valley of the Dolls, The Best of Everything,* and *Heartburn* have all been made into films. Contemporary filmmakers continue to capitalize on the genre's identifiable narratives. Fielding's *Bridget Jones* novels, McMillan's *Waiting to Exhale,* Weiner's *In Her Shoes,* and Wells's *Divine Secrets of the Ya-Ya Sisterhood* have been made into highly successful romantic comedies. Weiner's *Little Earthquakes* (2004) has been optioned by Universal Pictures, and HBO has bought the rights to the Weiner novel *Good in Bed* (2002). Francis Ford Coppola purchased the rights to Melissa Bank's best seller, *The Girls' Guide to Hunting and Fishing* (1999) shortly after its publication. *The Devil Wears Prada* was released as a film starring Meryl Streep in 2006; the film bowed to convention more than the novel by granting its heroine both a fulfilling new job and reconciliation with her boyfriend.

The most influential adaptation of contemporary chick lit is HBO's television series *Sex and the City.* The critical volume of essays, *Reading Sex and the City* (2004), attends primarily to the television series. Bushnell's text features the dominant motifs of chick lit, such as the cocktail, the handbag, and the shoe, but it was the television series that planted these images firmly in the public's consciousness. In many ways, HBO's adaptation approximates chick lit more than its source material. In the frenetic world of Bushnell's novel, relationships are fleeting, and plot lines are fragmented. The television series centers consistently on a surrogate family of four single New York women. Although some viewers praised the series for its candid depiction of female sexuality, others saw only pathos in the lives of the characters. In "Sex, Sadness, and the City," Wendy Shalit writes: "Despite the hype, *Sex and the City* is not about girls who just want to have fun . . . in fact it is a lament for all the things of inestimable value that the sexual revolution has wrecked." She criticized the series for its skewed message about female liberation, claiming that it "confus[ed] sexual sameness with equality and imagin[ed] that competing with men in debauchery was part of [the heroines'] social emancipation" (Shalit 1999). Reviewers repeatedly observed that the heroines deride wives but bemoan the dearth of available men in the city: "The new single-girl pathos seems more like a plea to be unliberated, and fast. These characters really do just want to get married; they just don't want to look quite so naïve about it" (D'Erasmo 1999). Occasionally, the characters themselves comment on these contradictions. Miranda Hobbes, played by Cynthia Nixon, often articulates the feminist viewpoint. In "Take Me Out to the Ball Game," she complains that the friends' dialogue centers persistently on men: "How does it happen that four smart women have nothing to talk about, other than boyfriends?"

By the end of the series, the women are pursuing the familiar narratives of chick lit. In "Sex and the City: A Farewell," executive producer Michael Patrick King claims that the series is "about defining different ways to be." However, the series ends by securing each woman in a long-term relationship. Fairy-tale plotlines that the women dismissed as "urban relationship myth[s]" in previous episodes come to fruition. The commitment-phobic male, Mr. Big, tracks Carrie down and tells her that she is "the one" ("The Man" and "An American Girl"). In the end, the heroine is not only reunited with Mr. Big but with New York, which, in an earlier episode, she speculates "may be her one great love" ("Anchors Away"). Miranda morphs into a different archetype. She marries the father of her baby and is removed from Manhattan, no longer a suitable setting for her life. Living in Brooklyn and caring for her mother-in-law as well as working as a lawyer, she resembles the heroines of "mommy lit," struggling to juggle multiple roles. The final line of the television series shifts the emphasis firmly back to self-fulfillment: Carrie's voice-over assures the viewer that "the most exciting, challenging and significant relationship of all is the one you have with yourself" ("An American Girl"). However, like the contemporary chick lit novel, the series refuses to contemplate the narrative of the mature singleton; rather it acknowledges the paucity of plots for women who will remain alone. In one of the final episodes, Carrie tells her friends: "Ladies, if you are single in New York, after a certain point there is nowhere to go but down" ("Splat!").

Selected Authors

Candace Bushnell (1959–). With the publication of her first work of fiction, *Sex and the City*, Bushnell established herself as a spokesperson for "a particular type of single woman—smart, attractive, successful, and . . . never married" (Bushnell 2004, 25). All four of Bushnell's texts navigate New York's social scene and comment explicitly on sexual politics and urban subjectivity. Read together, they form a kind of linked sequence, as characters and plotlines cross textual boundaries.

Although classified and marketed as a novel, Bushnell's *Sex in the City* is, like *Sex and the Single Girl,* a generic hybrid. It is composed of columns written by Bushnell in the 1990s for the *New York Observer*. The text reads more like a collection of essays than a novel. Bushnell initially envisaged *Sex and the City* as fiction, but her publisher "wanted it to be journalism." They eventually reached a "quiet, happy understanding" that her first text would be "fiction written as journalism" (Bushnell 2003). The columns are narrated by two 30-something women: an anonymous first-person commentator, whom Bushnell later acknowledged as herself, and her alter ego, Carrie, who writes a column.

Bushnell's fiction regularly appears in chick lit bibliographies, but this categorization is in some ways misleading. The aggressive pace and fractured structure of Bushnell's fiction distinguishes it from much chick lit. Most significantly, Bushnell feels no obligation to make her characters sympathetic. Simon Hattenstone of the *Guardian* refers to the cast of characters in *Four Blondes* as "a gallery of vile creatures" (Hattenstone 2001). In Bushnell's fictional world, characters and narratives are dispensed with once they have served their purpose; genuine enduring relationships are elusive. The on/off relationship between Carrie and Mr. Big constitutes one of the few sustained narrative lines in *Sex and the City*. Also missing in Bushnell's fictional world is the optimistic tenor of much chick lit. The tone of *Sex and the City* is often mordant, and the mood is resolutely unromantic. Moreover, Bushnell's first novel focuses on men as much as women. As Mandy Merck notes in "Sexuality and the City," the novel's first chapter features four straight men, a gay male couple and eventually "my friend Carrie" (Merck 48; Bushnell *Sex* 7).

In *Sex and the City*, Bushnell casts an unflinching eye over the mating rituals of New York. She immediately broadcasts the redundancy of the romantic narratives associated with the city's past:

> Welcome to the Age of Un-Innocence. The glittering lights of Manhattan that served as backdrops for Edith Wharton's bodice-heaving trysts are still glowing—but the stage is empty. No one has breakfast at Tiffany's, and no one has affairs to remember—instead, we have breakfast at seven A.M. and affairs we try to forget as quickly as possible. (Bushnell 2004, 2)

Some of the city's women capitalize on this shift by adopting male habits; they congratulate each other on their one-night stands, their ability to control their emotions, and their objectification of men. Very few of the men in the novel are named; the narrators categorize them into subspecies: "Toxic Bachelor," "Modelizer," "Mr. Big," "Mr. Groovy," "Mr. Marvelous."

Despite their protests to the contrary, the single women in the novel are pursuing the destiny of New York's iconic romantic heroines. As well as boasting about their sexual enterprises, they share strategies for snaring a man: "The thing you have to realize is that, in terms of socialization for men, getting them ready for marriage, New York is a terrible place . . . Single men don't tend to hang around with couples. They're not used to that idea of coziness and family. So you have to get them there mentally" (Bushnell 2004, 154).

Bushnell revised the ending of her first novel to champion the single woman. In its original incarnation, *Sex and the City* closed with the reassurance that "Carrie and Mr. Big are still together" (Bushnell 1996, 228). When the novel was reissued in 2004, Bushnell changed the ending. The final line of the latest version violates the conventions of chick lit by inverting gender roles and affirming the possibility of happiness for the woman without a mate: "Mr. Big is happily married. Carrie is happily single" (Bushnell 2004, 245).

Described by Bushnell as "four novellas," *Four Blondes* was also marketed as a novel. The four heroines do not cross over into each other's narratives, but some characters do recur. Significantly, it is the male power players who move between stories: Tanner Hart, the movie star, and Comstock Dibble, the movie producer, feature in two of the stories. Bushnell distinguishes between the heroines of this text and the women in *Sex and the City:* the blondes "are not looking for men, they're looking for some kind of meaning, and their place in the world" (Hattenstone 2001). For Bushnell's blondes, the quest for meaning gathers pace when they reach 30. The narrator of the first story, "Nice 'N Easy," is Janey Wilcox, "a sort of lukewarm celebrity" who trawls the upper echelons of New York, seeking men to spend the summer with (Bushnell 2001, 3). Now in her thirties, she struggles to maintain the persona of the "It girl": "Something happens when you get into your thirties. People catch on to your shit. Especially men. It's important to look like you're doing something, even if you're not" (35). Janey objects to the assumptions that frame beautiful women, yet her beauty ultimately redeems her. She lands a lucrative modeling contract and finds a way of telling her story. In a commercial she tells the camera: "'I don't know where I'm going . . . But I know I'm going somewhere'" (94), a line that resonates with female viewers.

In the second story Bushnell lifts the veil from the world of the "Smug Marrieds" who torment singletons such as Fielding's Bridget Jones. Having "hit all her landmarks in style" by the age of 34, Winnie wakes up every morning feeling depressed (109). She berates herself for investing in the myth that propels women towards marriage: "What was all that crap about men that she grew up with? That one day, one of these (pitiful) specimens was going to fall in love with her . . . and make her whole" (Bushnell 2001, 155). However, men provide short-term answers for Bushnell's blondes. An affair with a movie star revitalizes Winnie.

The longest and darkest story in *Four Blondes* concerns Cecelia Luxenstein, a society princess suffocating under the pressure of living the dream. Like Winnie and Janey, she is trying to calculate her next move but, having achieved the life that women are supposed to covet, she is obliged to disguise her misery: "I'm the one who's miserable, but you can't tell people that, can you? Especially if you're a woman. Because marriage is supposed to make you happy, not make you feel like a rat trapped in a very glamorous cage with twenty-thousand-dollar silk draperies" (Bushnell 2001, 191). For Cecelia, as for Janey and Winnie, the thirties usher in uncertainty and dread. She mourns the loss of the vitality that characterized her twenties: "I was all instinct then. Raw, aggressive instinct, and I lived my life like an alien thing was driving me. But now that thing is gone" (208).

Four Blondes concludes with "Single Process," a story that revisits the premise of *Sex and the City*. The journalist narrator travels to London to discover what men and women really want. When she encounters what appears to be the perfect family, the wife shatters her illusions, revealing her "black fantasy" in which her husband dies and she is "still young" and "free" (Bushnell 2001, 305). Reflecting on the wife's confession, the narrator acknowledges her investment in the Cinderella story: "I wanted the big, great, inspiring story about an unmarried career woman who goes to London . . . and meets the man of her dreams and marries him. She gets the big ring and the big house and the adorable children, and she lives happily ever after" (306). The journalist's wish becomes a self-fulfilling prophecy. In true chick lit style, Bushnell's heroine meets a promising man on the way back to New York.

Bushnell refers to *Trading Up* as "technically my first novel" ("Writer's Craft," 2003). In this more unified narrative, Janey Wilcox takes center stage as a MAW, a twenty-first–century acronym that stands for "Model/Actress/Whatever." She hovers precariously on the fringes of the entertainment industry, "convinced that she has great reserves of untapped talents" (Bushnell 2004, 7). *Trading Up* delivers Bushnell's most ruthless dissection of New York society. The narrator constantly reminds us of the city's hidden agenda: "The surface of New York's social interactions was as smooth and shiny as a sheet of ice, but underneath were water moccasins and snapping turtles" (Bushnell 2004, 37). The hypocrisy of urban discourses is epitomized by the city's most powerful media conglomerate Splatch Verner: "On the surface, 'the company' appeared to take care of its employers . . . it was politically correct, spouting its commitment to multiculturalism . . . but below the surface it was business as usual, run by men who tacitly agreed that their work was the closest thing to going to war without going to war" (74). Gender boundaries remain fixed in Bushnell's twenty-first–century New York. An old lover's insinuations serve as a "niggling reminder" to Janey of "everything that was wrong with New York: A man could sleep with as many women as he liked, but when it came to sex, there were still quite a few people in society who clung to the old-fashioned notion that a woman shouldn't have too many partners" (Bushnell 2004, 14). Janey spends much of the novel trying to mask her sexual history. When Bushnell takes a lengthy detour into her heroine's past, we learn why: Janey once worked as a sex slave on a rich man's yacht.

In *Trading Up*, sex is treated repeatedly as a form of currency or consumption. Comstock Dibble expresses sexual aggression by demanding payment for a screenplay that Janey never completed for him. Janey's sister Patty views the "'traditional marriage'" as "a woman's obviously cynical exchange of sex, housework and child-raising for a roof over her head" (Bushnell 2004, 135); a man at a party identifies the fantasy of "the girl in the ad" as "the driving force behind the consumer-oriented male" (256).

Bushnell engages explicitly with Wharton's narratives in this novel. Janey proposes a cinematic adaptation of *Custom of the Country,* clearly perceiving affinities between Undine Spragg's strategies and her own. She meets Selden Rose, a successful movie producer, who pursues her as a candidate for his second wife. As Knights observes, Rose casts himself as the heroine's rescuer, thereby emulating his namesake, Lawrence Selden in Wharton's *The House of Mirth*: "He had fervently believed that if he could get her away from this world, the real Janey Wilcox would blossom" (Bushnell, 91). Bushnell's narrative commentary exposes his romantic spin as the replication of a hackneyed narrative: "Many of his counterparts . . . had recently taken second wives, trading in their first wives . . . for more exciting women who were ten or fifteen years younger" (Bushnell 2004, 74–75). Marriage to Selden does little to quell Janey's ambition. By the end of the novel, details of her transaction with Dibble emerge and the media brand her a "Model?/Actress?/Whore?" When Selden is issued an ultimatum by his boss—his job or his wife—he fulfills his role as rescuer and chooses Janey. The city is less forgiving. Janey receives an invitation to the post-Oscar party and leaves Selden. She is unaware that by accepting the invitation she is participating in one of the "in-jokes" of show business; every year the hosts invite the "Bimbo of the Year." Again Bushnell pondered several destinies for her heroine. The first draft of the novel left Janey "crazy on the plane" to Los Angeles ("Writer's Craft," 2003). Bushnell's publisher suggested that she reward Janey for her trials, and Bushnell agreed to give her the last laugh in true chick lit style; Janey meets Dibble on the plane and hands him her screenplay. As the novel ends, she is on the brink of Hollywood fame. By turning her story into gold, she forges her own revenge narrative, managing to "beat everyone and all these men at their own game" ("Writer's Craft," 2003).

Bushnell has referred to her next novel, *Lipstick Jungle,* as "my *Valley of the Dolls*" ("Lipstick Jungle"). The narrative observes a familiar structure, following the lives of three highly successful New York women: Wendy Healy, a movie producer, who is married to a metrosexual househusband; Victory Ford, a fashion designer, who has yet to find a relationship that can equal her career; and Nico O'Neilly, a married magazine editor who has an affair with an underwear model to escape feelings of "desperate emptiness" (Bushnell 1996, 28). *Lipstick Jungle* registers how female narratives have expanded since the era of Susann's dolls. All three heroines are financially independent; Nico is the main breadwinner, and Wendy supports her husband. Like Susann, Bushnell deals with taboos affecting contemporary women. Wendy, who at times yearns to be "a single, self-actualized person on her own," suffers physical abuse at the hands of her six-year-old son (Bushnell 1996, 107). Victory reflects on the lies that society feeds women: "Still being single and in your forties was a state of being the world couldn't really comprehend . . . But if you were wildly successful, you could make your own rules for how you wanted to live your life . . . Why did the world never tell women about this kind of happiness?" (367–368).

Lipstick Jungle delivers Bushnell's most positive outlook on women's urban narratives so far. The novel presents New York as an empowering site for the single woman. Bushnell populates the urban landscape with feminine tropes that align the power of female sexuality with the glamour of the city: "As the helicopter swooped low, past the tall buildings that resembled a forest of lipsticks, Nico felt a frisson of something close to sexual excitement . . . New York City was . . . certainly one of the few places in the world where women like her could not only survive but rule" (Bushnell 1996, 34). Like Susann, Brown, and Jaffe, Bushnell dramatizes both sides of urban life, illuminating its hazards well as its possibilities. Her heroines marvel at the roles that the city offers them but raise objections about the stereotypes and prejudices that threaten to contain them. The greatest fear of the women is that they will be consumed by the city's demands. With imagery redolent of Susann's novel, they remind themselves of the cautionary tale of Sarah-Catherine, "the quintessential example of a particular kind of girl who came to New York, thrived for a while, and then was eaten alive" (Bushnell 1996, 112). In *Valley of the Dolls*, Susann represents the city as "an angry concrete animal" (1996, 1).

In *Lipstick Jungle*, Bushnell ties up some of the narrative threads from *Trading Up*. Readers have surmised that she left Janey on the brink of stardom to set up a sequel. The next installment of Janey's life has yet to materialize, but in *Lipstick Jungle* Bushnell pursues Selden Rose's story. Shortly after divorcing Shane, Wendy marries Selden; he finally provides a happy ending for a woman who can match his talent but does not need to be rescued from herself. By leaving Shane and marrying Selden, Wendy subverts gender stereotypes: "Wendy was like one of those successful men who gets divorced and finds new happiness right away, while the woman is left steaming at home" (Bushnell 1996, 418). Victory finds a man who comes to terms with her success, and Nico recovers her enthusiasm for life and ends the affair. The novel ends with the women marveling at all they have achieved.

Melissa Bank (1960–). Commentators on American chick lit often trace the genre back to Bank's best-selling debut novel, *The Girls' Guide to Hunting and Fishing*. However, critics continue to debate Bank's status as the godmother of American chick lit, some arguing that the label does not reflect the subtlety of her writing. The 2005 publication of her second novel, *The Wonder Spot*, did little to settle the debate. The conventions of chick lit characterize both novels. Jane Rosenal and Sophie Applebaum are single, slightly neurotic, and witty; they move from the suburbs of Philadelphia to the city where they take jobs in publishing and advertising. When Sophie arrives in New York, she is buoyed by the sense of possibility. As she walks through the city she "feel[s] like there were a thousand ways my life could go" (Bank 1999, 85). The reality is less exhilarating. Urban life for Bank's heroines is fragmented and restless. Dingy apartments and unsuitable boyfriends come and go, and expectation gives way to estrangement. At one point, Sophie seems to articulate questions about the limitations of the generic chick lit heroine and her place in the world: "I realize that I don't know anything about the history of New York or the history of the United States or the history of anywhere, modern or ancient; I have no grasp of geography; I don't even really know what physics is. All this contributes to my overall lack of substance" (Bank 2005, 199).

Marketed as a novel, *The Girls' Guide* is a collection of linked stories covering 20 years of the heroine's life. This more open, pliable form enables Bank to explore key moments that shape Jane's identity rather than limiting herself to the single, end-determined trajectory of much chick lit. In one story, "You Could Be Anyone," Bank shifts tense and narrative perspective. The narrator shares Jane's tone but does not identify herself explicitly. The shift to the present tense and detached second-person narration enables Jane to distance herself from her most harrowing narrative: breast cancer and the breakdown of her relationship. The self in this story remains strictly provisional. Through her form, Bank addresses but contains some of the more serious issues that chick lit shuns. *The Wonder Spot* is more unified in its consistent use of Sophie's perspective, but each "chapter" could stand alone as a short story. The title story appeared in *Speaking with the Angel,* an anthology edited by Nick Hornby.

In *The Girls' Guide,* Bank also uses her flexible form to explore tangential narratives. The narrator of one story, "The Best Possible Light," is Nina, Jane's neighbor and a mother of three adults. Jane is referred to only once in the story, and Nina herself does not feature in Jane's stories. Affinities between these two heroines are immediately apparent. Like Jane, Nina is painfully aware of who she is supposed to be. Through Nina, Bank enters the territory of "hen lit," exploring identities that are projected upon mature women. On hearing that her son is to father his fiancée's baby as well as his ex-wife's, Nina narrates: "Then, everyone turns to me, as though I'm going to deliver some kind of pronouncement. I get these voices in my head of what The Mother is supposed to say—maybe something about how it will all work out" (Bank 1999, 121).

The presence and influence of parents also distinguishes Bank's fiction from much chick lit, in which surrogate families dominate. The most defining event in Jane's young adulthood is the death of her father. Through this loss, Bank reveals how the patriarchal gaze shaped her heroine's narrative: "Something changed then. I saw my life in scale: it was just my life. It was not momentous, and only now did I recognize that it had once seemed so to me; that was while my father was watching" (Bank 1999, 189). This epiphany opens up Jane's destiny; her father's mantra, *"Don't take the easy way out, Janie,"* gradually loses currency in her narrative (192). Bank returns to this theme in *The Wonder Spot.* When Sophie loses her father, she takes her first risk, leaving her job to travel to Los Angeles with her boyfriend. Like Jane, she struggles to tune out the patriarchal voice: "It was the idea of my father that I couldn't shake. I knew what he would have thought of Demetri—not that he would've said so. He would've said, *What are you going to do in Los Angeles?*" (Bank 2005, 166).

Jane's commentary provides much of the humor in *The Girls' Guide.* Throughout the novel, Bank engages with and subverts the jargon of popular psychology, which is both a shaping discourse and object of parody in much chick lit. Bank prefaces each of her stories with sound-bites from self-help books, often overturning them in the stories themselves. Jane expresses suspicion toward these discourses: "I think, 'Self-help? If I could help myself, I wouldn't be here'" (Bank 1999, 240). Ellen Fein and Sherrie Schneider's best-selling guide to snaring a husband, *The Rules* (1995) not only prefaces the title story but infiltrates the narrative itself; the authors become speaking subjects in Jane's imagination, goading her on as she embarks on a new relationship. To her horror, Jane finds that the advice initially works, but she is so exhausted by adhering to the rules that she eventually gives up. Jane is irked by one rule in particular, *"Don't be funny,"* and protests: "Funny is the best thing I am" (Banks 1999, 214; Bank's emphasis, 255). Her objection to this rule is a rallying-cry for the witty heroines of chick lit.

Both Sophie and Jane eventually find love in relationships that promise to be empowering. Despite Bank's allegiance to the conventions of chick lit, critics disagree about her place on the continuum of popular women's fiction. Some identify her as one of the innovators of the genre. *Booklist*'s Kristine Huntley describes *The Girls' Guide* as a "standout in a genre that was finding its footing at the time." Elisabeth Egan protests at the way that Bank is "unceremoniously lumped together with fellow literary It girl Helen Fielding" and notes that Jane Rosenal, the heroine of *The Girls' Guide,* "share[s] none of the flibbertigibbet qualities so celebrated in her British counterpart." Egan praises Bank for moving beyond the unitary plotline of the quest for Mr. Right: "It's as though she suspects her audience is tired of all the Bridget Jones clones trooping through the best-seller list."

Reviews of *The Wonder Spot* were more restrained. Sittenfield reluctantly classifies the novel as standard chick lit, arguing that Bank's subject matter is by no means "lightweight" but that she writes about it in a "lightweight way." Catherine Shoard writes: "There really is no plot here other than the no-show of Mr. Right, and, for all its literary noodlings, *The Wonder Spot* is chick lit." Joanne Briscoe of the *Guardian* states that "There is not much further [Bank] can go in this particular direction" but adds that "within the limits she sets herself, she achieves something close to perfection."

Jennifer Weiner (1970–). Jennifer Weiner began her writing career as a journalist commenting on, among other matters, Generation X culture. Her first novel, *Good in Bed,* became an international best seller. Weiner associates herself with chick lit and identifies tone as the genre's essential characteristic: "I think the only must-have is the book's voice—funny, woeful, smart, sarcastic, wounded but still strong." She defines the chick lit heroine thusly: "A smart-yet-wounded female heroine, who's young(ish), accomplished but insecure, dealing with (pick one) body image woes, misery, a dysfunctional family, or a tyrannical boss, trying to find her way in life" ("Roundtable," 2004). Weiner's fiction abides by these rules. Cannie Shapiro, the heroine of *Good in Bed,* fits this model and, like most chick lit heroines, dwells on her shortcomings. Like Ephron's Rachel Samstat, she recognizes herself as an incarnation of a fictional stereotype: "So here I am. Twenty-eight years old, with 30 looming on the horizon. Drunk. Fat. Alone. Unloved. And, worst of all, a cliché, Ally McBeal and Bridget Jones put together" (Weiner 2002, 19). Like Weiner, Cannie is a journalist whose job is to be "the eyes and ears on 20-something Philadelphia" (Weiner 2002, 60). Her ex-boyfriend also writes a column, "Good in Bed," in which he shares the trials of "Loving a Larger Woman" (Weiner 2002, 14).

Wish fulfillment drives Weiner's narratives. In particular, she has been praised by reviewers and readers for rewarding plus-size heroines with happy endings. In the course of *Good in Bed,* Cannie tries to lose weight, win her boyfriend back, and sell her screenplay: her own fairy tale about a film star who falls in love with a journalist. She achieves the one goal that is not informed by social pressures. She ends the novel happily married to a new man and financially independent after selling her screenplay.

In Her Shoes (2004) explores women's identities and choices by following the divergent narratives of two sisters, Maggie and Rose. Rose, Weiner's signature heroine, is overweight—frumpy but smart. Maggie is beautiful but unable to hold down a job or establish any roots. After their mother's death, their father marries a woman who is obsessed with controlling Rose's weight. Weiner interweaves the sisters' narratives with the story of an elderly woman, Ella, who has become estranged from her granddaughters, who turn out to be Rose and Maggie. The friction between the sisters reaches its height when Maggie sleeps with Rose's boyfriend. The separation of the sisters prompts a re-examination of their lives. For Rose, this involves giving up her job as an attorney and becoming a dog-sitter. Maggie finds a letter from Ella and tracks down her grandmother. By the end of the novel, the sisters are reunited, and Rose marries the man whom readers have recognized as Mr. Right from the start.

In her next two novels, Weiner ventures into the territory of chick lit subgenres. *Little Earthquakes* is "mommy lit": it presents three female friends who support each other through the challenges of new motherhood. Becky, instantly recognizable as the sympathetic, overweight nurturer of the group, has an interfering mother-in-law; the beautiful Ayinde discovers that her husband has been unfaithful; Lia is recovering from a miscarriage; Ephron's influence on Weiner emerges in *Little Earthquakes;* Becky, a chef, shares her menu ideas with the reader, just as Rachel Samstat shares her recipes.

Goodnight Nobody (2005) is mystery lit. When an apparently perfect wife and mother is found dead, neighbor Kate Klein turns detective. Kate has substituted the signature narrative of chick lit for the domestic narrative of hen lit. A former New York gossip columnist, she is now a Connecticut wife and mother. As the mystery unravels, Kate begins to seek satisfaction beyond these roles. When her ex-lover becomes her accomplice, her marriage begins to fall apart and Kate must re-evaluate her life.

Although Weiner identifies herself as a writer of chick lit, she is eager to test the limits of the genre. On her blog, she expresses light-hearted relief that the cover of her collection of short stories, *The Guy Not Taken* (2006), bears "the minimum daily allowance of pink."

Rebecca Wells (1952–). Rebecca Wells's Ya-Ya novels achieved best-seller status by word of mouth; sales of *Divine Secrets of the Ya-Ya Sisterhood* soared after a recommendation from Oprah's Book Club. Although they are a staple of chick lit glossaries, the Ya-Ya novels straddle the boundary between the literary and the popular. Dan Webster describes *Divine Secrets of the Ya-Ya Sisterhood* as "a literary icon of pop culture" and places Wells in the esteemed company of Anne Tyler and Fannie Flagg. Spanning 60 years in their entirety, the Ya-Ya novels appeal to a broad age range. So far, the series consists of three novels: *Little Altars Everywhere* (1992), *Divine Secrets of the Ya-Ya Sisterhood* and *Ya-Yas in Bloom* (2005). The Ya-Yas are four lifelong friends who grew up together in the South in the 1930s and 1940s. The novels trace the development of their friendship alongside the present-day relationship between Ya-Ya Vivi Walker and her daughter Sidda. As the series progresses, the Ya-Yas take up a more central position: *Little Altars Everywhere* is composed of the first-person narratives of the Walkers and their servants; *Divine Secrets* juxtaposes Sidda's present with the Ya-Yas' past; and *Ya-Yas in Bloom* transports us back to the genesis of the Ya-Ya sisterhood.

Set primarily in Louisiana, Wells's novels depart from some of the norms of chick lit. Moving through the stories of the past and present, Wells explores the political and religious ideologies that inform the heroines' lives. Elizabeth Boyd identifies the southern belle narrative as a burgeoning "subgenre" of contemporary popular women's fiction and attributes this resurgence to Wells's Ya-Ya novels. Where some texts satirize southern manners, others endorse "the old feminine ways" as a means of regaining power (Boyd 2005, 160). Wells's novels both celebrate and lightly satirize the figure of the southern belle while illuminating the conventions that contain her. Underpinning the Ya-Ya sisterhood is a strong oral tradition. The friends delight in recounting their pasts and retelling their stories. Fragments of narratives are released across the three novels, and stories overlap and expand as new details are revealed.

Wells's primary themes will be familiar to chick lit aficionados: female community, gender politics, and postmodern alienation. Like Valdes-Rodriguez, Wells champions female friendship as the only outlet for self-definition and expression:

> Four children—a husband—a house, dripping goddamn boiling water over the chicory coffee every morning of the world. Everything gets sucked out of me, every ounce of my high school goldenness, every single iota of my college education—gone. The only thing left is the Ya-Yas. (2000, 84)

Like most chick lit heroines, the Ya-Yas rely on humor as their most effective survival strategy: "Of all the secrets of the Ya-Ya Sisterhood the most divine was humor" (Wells 2000, 422). The Sisterhood becomes a means of debunking gender roles and contesting romantic paradigms. Sidda recalls vividly how the husbands of the Ya-Yas registered the primacy of the Sisterhood: "Every year the Ya-Yas threw themselves a party to celebrate another anniversary of their friendship. And the husbands actually brought gifts! Sidda remembered more about Ya-Ya anniversaries than she did about Vivi and Shep's" (Wells 1996, 90).

Vivi Walker's narrative addresses the preoccupations of hen lit and dramatizes the dilemma of the older woman: what does the heroine do when her children have left home? The present-day Vivi struggles to make sense of her children's departure: "It was all so fast and furious—having them, raising them, watching them go. I thought when Baylor left: *Alright now, this is when my life can begin!* But it never did begin and I can't tell you why" (Wells 2000, 289, Wells's italics). In *Little Altars Everywhere*, Vivi's narrative opens with a lament for her girl self. She hankers after the choices that are available to women in the 1990s: "Maybe if I'd been born later, I wouldn't have gotten married. I'd have enjoyed what I wanted, then moved on . . . But I was born before you could do what you wanted" (Wells 2000, 280).

Wells tempers cries for sexual liberation and independence with nostalgia for the communal sensibility of the rural South. Through Sidda's narrative, she questions the value of urban narratives and queries the authenticity of the celebrated support networks that feature so heavily in chick lit. She asks whether communities such as the Ya-Ya sisterhood are sustainable in postmodern urban America. *Divine Secrets* opens with the voice of a 40-year-old Sidda who seems to have it all. She lives in Manhattan and has a highly successful career and a loving fiancé. Nevertheless, she wrestles with the malaise common to Bushnell's heroine: "Sidda had the life she'd always dreamed of; she was a hot director, engaged to marry a man she adored. But all she wanted to do was lie in bed, eat Kraft Macaroni and Cheese, and hide from the alligators" (Wells 1996, 7). As a young girl, Sidda resists becoming a "full-fledged Junior Ya-Ya" (Wells 1996, 297); as an adult she yearns for the intimacy of the Sisterhood: "The four of their scents were *in key*. Their very bodies harmonized together. Surely this made it easier for them to forget things and forgive each other, not to have to constantly 'work' on this, the way we do now. This has never happened to me with a group of women" (Wells 1996, 62, Wells's italics). Whelehan notes how Fielding engaged women readers who, like Bridget Jones, were "lamenting an excess of freedom and stumbling under the burden of choice and autonomy" (Whelehan 2005, 5). Sidda's narrative reads like such a lament. She longs for the "improvisational laziness" of the Ya-Yas and seeks release from urban introspection: "She felt ashamed of her insularity. She longed for rambunctiousness, for the communal craziness in which she'd been raised. She felt sick at the thought of her constant questioning, her constant self-examination" (Wells 1996, 207).

All of the Ya-Ya novels end on a note of celebration as connections between women are reaffirmed. By *Ya-Yas in Bloom*, Vivi is an active 68-year-old: "My life is so full. I might be a card-carrying member of AARP, but I am not retired. Or retiring, for that matter! Hah! I am busy, busy, busy. Workout at the club every single weekday. *Bourrée* with the Ya Yas. Cruises with Shep. *And* spending time in that garden of his" (Wells 2005, 2, Wells's italics); Vivi asserts her identity in the conversational tone of chick lit: triumphant exclamations, italics, and repetition exemplify the discourse of the chick lit heroine. Through her voice, Wells opens up the chick lit narrative of reinvention and self-acceptance to women of all ages. Wells is currently working on a novel entitled *Splitting Hairs* about a new heroine, a Louisiana beautician. She plans to return to the Ya-Yas in her next novel.

Bibliography

Acosta, Marta. "Celebrity Dish and 'Chica Lit': Alisa Valdes-Rodriguez writes of music, stars, fashion, love affairs and la vida loca." May 7 2006. <http://www.sfgate.com>.

Akass, Kim, and Janet McCabe, eds. *Reading Sex and the City*. New York: Macmillan, 2004.

"Alisa Valdes-Rodriguez: The Godmother of Chica Lit." Aug. 13 2005. <http://www.time.com>.

"An American Girl in Paris—Part Deux." *Sex and the City*. DVD. Directed by Tim Van Patten. HBO: 2004.

"Anchors Away." *Sex and the City*. VHS. Directed by Charles McDougall. HBO: 2003.

Bank, Melissa. *The Girls' Guide to Hunting and Fishing*. New York: Penguin, 1999.

———. *The Wonder Spot*. London: Viking-Penguin, 2005.

"Beryl Bainbridge denounces chick-lit as froth." Aug. 23 2001. <http://books.guardian.co.uk/bookerprize2001>.

Boyd, Elizabeth B. "Ya Yas, Grits, and Sweet Potato Queens: Contemporary Southern Belles and the Prescriptions that Guide Them." In *Chick Lit: The New Women's Fiction*. Suzanne Ferriss and Mallory Young, eds. New York: Routledge, 2005, 159–172.

Briscoe, Joanne. "Carrot Pennies and Cashmere Twinsets." July 2 2005. <http://books.guardian.co.uk/reviews>.

Brown, Helen Gurley. *Before There Was Sex and the City There was Sex and the Single Girl*. New York: Barricade Books, 2003.

———. *Sex and the Single Girl*. New York: Random House, 1962.

Burchill, Julie. "Valley of the Dolls." In *Valley of the Dolls* by Jacqueline Susann. London: Virago, Sykes, Plum, 2005, ix–xii.

Bushnell, Candace. "Candace Bushnell on the Writer's Craft." 2003. Interview by Bill Thompson. <http://www.eyeonbooks.com>.

———. *Four Blondes*. London: Abacus, 2001.

———. "Jungle Fever: Candace Bushnell's Women Grow Up." Interview by Alex Richmond. Sept 21–28 2000. <http://www.citypaper.net>.

———. *Lipstick Jungle*. London: Abacus, 2005.

———. *Sex and the City*. London: Abacus, 1996.

———. *Sex and the City*. London: Abacus, 2004.

———. *Trading Up*. London: Abacus, 2004.

"Chick Lit Author Roundtable." 2004. <http://www.authorsontheweb.com/features/>.

"Chick Lit Books: Hip, Smart Fiction for Women." 2008. <http://www.chicklitbooks.com>.

D'Erasmo, Stacey. Review of *Sex and the City* by Bushnell. *New York Times Magazine*. qtd. in Howard, Gerald. *Salon*. Sept. 28 1999. <www.salon.com/books/feature>.

Desperate Housewives. Created by Marc Cherry. ABC 2004.

Egan, Elisabeth. "Melissa Bank Scores with No. 2." Review of *The Wonder Spot* by Bank. May 29 2005. <http://www.suntimes.com>.

Ephron, Nora. *Heartburn*. New York: Knopf, 1983.

Ferriss, Suzanne, and Mallory Young. *Chick Lit: The New Woman's Fiction*. New York: Routledge, 2005.

Fielding, Helen. *Bridget Jones's Diary: A Novel*. London: Pan-Macmillan, 1997.

———. *Olivia Joules and the Overactive Imagination*. London: Picador, 2003.

Goldblatt, Mark. "The Devil and the Gray Lady." Review of *The Devil Wears Prada* by Weisberger. June 10 2003. <http://www.nationalreview.com>.

Guerrero, Lisa A. "'Sistahs Are Doin' It for Themselves': Chick Lit in Black and White." In *Chick Lit: The New Women's Fiction* by Suzanne Ferriss and Mallory Young. New York: Routledge, 2005, 87–101.

Harzewski, Stephanie. "Tradition and Displacement in the New Novel of Manners." In *Chick Lit: The New Women's Fiction* by Suzanne Ferriss and Mallory Young. New York: Routledge, 2005, 29–46.

Hattenstone, Simon. "All About Sex." Review of *Four Blondes* by Bushnell. Feb. 5 2001. <http://books.guardian.co.uk/departments/generalfiction>.

Heffernan, Virginia. "Cosmopolitan Girl." Review of *Trading Up* by Bushnell. July 13 2003. <http://query.nytimes.com>.

Howard, Gerald. "How Dawn Powell Can Save Your Life." *Salon*. Sept. 28 1999. <www.salon.com/books/feature>.

Huntley, Kristine. Review of *The Wonder Spot* by Bank. March 15 2005. <http://www.metacritic.com>.

Jaffe, Rona. "Foreword." In *The Best of Everything* New York: Penguin, 2005, vii–ix.

———. *The Best of Everything*. New York: Penguin, 2005.

"Jaffe's 'Best of Everything' Stands the Test of Time." Interview by Renée Montagne. *Morning Edition* 27 July 2005.

Kakutani, Michiko. "Mary McCarthy, 77, Is Dead; Novelist, Memoirist and Critic." Oct. 26 1989. <http://nytimes.com/books/00/03/26/specials>.

Knights, Pamela. "'Hypertexts' and the City: *The House of Mirth* at the Millennium." In *Edith Wharton's The House of Mirth*. Janet Beer, Pamela Knights, and Elizabeth Nolan, eds. New York: Taylor and Francis, 2007, 127–142.

Krause, Nicola, and Emma McLaughlin. *The Nanny Diaries*. New York: St Martin's Press, 2002.

Mabry, A. Rochelle. "About a Girl: Female Subjectivity and Sexuality in Contemporary 'Chick' Culture." In *Chick Lit: The New Woman's Fiction* by Suzanne Ferriss and Mallory Young. New York: Routledge, 191–206.

Mazza, Cris. "Who's Laughing Now? A Short History of Chick Lit and the Perversion of a Genre." In *Chick Lit: The New Woman's Fiction* by Suzanne Ferriss and Mallory Young. New York: Routledge, 17–28.

———. Review of *The Group* by McCarthy. <http:www.nytimes.com>.

Mazza, Cris, and Jeffrey DeShell, eds. *Chick-Lit: Postfeminist Fiction*. New York: Fiction Collective, 2000.

McCarthy, Mary. *The Group*. Harmondsworth: Penguin, 1966.

McMillan, Terry. *Waiting to Exhale*. New York: Pocket Books, 1993.

Mendelsohn, Daniel. "Nanny Cam." March 4 2002. <http://newyorkmetro.com>.

Memmott, Carol. "Chick Lit, for Better or Worse, is Here to Stay." June 20 2006. <http://www.usatoday.com>.

Merck, Mandy. "Sexuality in the City." In *Reading Sex and the City*. Kim Akass and Janet McCabe, eds. New York: Macmillan, 2004, 48–64.

Schappell, Elissa. *Use Me*. New York: Perennial-Collins, 2000.

"Sex and the City: A Farewell." Directed by Rachel McDonald Salazar. HBO: 2004.

Shalit, Wendy. "Sex, Sadness and the City." Autumn 1999. <http://www.city-journal.org>.

Shoard, Catherine. "Still Mad About the Boys." Review of *The Wonder Spot* by Bank. Oct. 7 2005. <http://www.dailytelegraph.co.uk>.

Sittenfield, Curtis. "Sophie's Choices." Review of *The Wonder Spot* by Bank. June 5 2005. <http://query.nytimes.com>.

Skurnik, Lizzie. "'Good Girl Chick Lit.'" July 7 2006. <http://washparkprophet.blogspot.com.>

Solomons, Deborah. "Hazards of New Fortunes." May 30 2004. <http:www.nytimes.com>.

"Splat!" *Sex and the City*. DVD. Directed by Julian Farino. HBO: 2004.

Susann, Jacqueline. *Valley of the Dolls*. London: Virago, 1966, 2003.

Sykes, Plum. *Bergdorf Blondes*. London: Penguin, 2005.

"Take Me Out to the Ball Game." *Sex and the City*. VHS. Directed by Allen Coulter: HBO: 1998.

"Teenage Picks." The *Guardian* 3 Oct. 2006. http://books.guardian.co.uk/childrenslibrary.

"The Baby Shower." *Sex and the City*. VHS. Directed by Susan Seidelman. HBO: 1998.

"The Chicken Dance." *Sex and the City*. VHS. Directed by Victoria Hochberg. HBO, 1998.

"The Man, the Myth, the Viagra." *Sex and the City*. VHS. Directed by Victoria Hochberg. HBO, 1998.

Valdes-Rodriguez, Alisa. *The Dirty Girls' Social Club*. Arrow: London, 2004.

Webster, Dan. "Rebecca Wells." March 3 2003. <http://www.spokesmanreview.com>.

Weinberg, Anna. "She's Come Undone." *Book Magazine* July-Aug. 2003: 47–49.

Weiner, Jennifer. *Good in Bed*. London: Simon and Schuster, 2002.

———. *Goodnight Nobody*. London: Simon and Schuster, 2005.

———. *In her Shoes*. London: Simon and Schuster, 2004.

———. *Little Earthquakes*. London: Simon and Schuster, 2004.

Weiner, Jennifer. "Snarkspot." 18 and 23 July 2006. <http://www.pkblogs.com/jenniferweiner.>

———. *The Guy Not Taken*. London: Simon and Schuster, 2006.

Weisberger, Lauren. *The Devil Wears Prada*. London: HarperCollins Publishers, 2003.

———. *Everyone Worth Knowing*. New York: Downtown Press, 2006.

Wells, Juliette. "Mothers of Chick Lit? Women Writers, Readers, and Literary History." In *Chick Lit: The New Women's Fiction* by Suzanne Ferriss and Mallory Young. New York: Routledge, 47–70.

Wells, Rebecca. *Divine Secrets of the Ya-Ya Sisterhood*. London: Pan Macmillan, 1996.

———. *Little Altars Everywhere*. London: Macmillan, 2000.

———. *Ya-Yas in Bloom*. London: HarperCollins, 2005.

Whelehan, Imelda. *The Feminist Bestseller: From Sex and the Single Girl to Sex and the City*. Basingstoke: Macmillan, 2005.

"Where There's Smoke." *Sex and the City*. VHS. Directed by Michael Patrick King. HBO: 1998.

Further Reading

Akass, Kim, and Janet McCabe, eds. *Reading Sex and the City*. New York: Macmillan, 2004; Benson, Heidi. "10 Years After 'Bridget Jones,' Chick Lit Grows Up, Gets Serious and Stops Wearing Pink." http://www.sfgate.com; Dellecese, Cheryl. "Love, Life, and Literature." *Smith Alumnae Quarterly* 2005 http://saqonline.smith.edu; Boyd, Elizabeth B. "Ya Yas, Grits, and Sweet Potato Queens: Contemporary Southern Belles and the Prescriptions That Guide Them." In *Chick Lit: The New Woman's Fiction* by Suzanne Ferriss and Mallory Young. New York: Routledge; Whelehan, Imelda. *The Feminist Bestseller: From Sex and the Single Girl to Sex and the City*. Basingstoke: Macmillan, 2005.

RACHEL LISTER

CHILDREN'S LITERATURE

Definition. In "Publishers and Publishing," an essay in *The Oxford Encyclopedia of Children's Literature,* university professor Daniel Hade asserts that "the production of children's books is an enterprise conducted by adults for children in order to make a profit" (Zipes 2006, 3, 298). Although the circulation of children's books in the twenty-first century involves countless nonprofit entities such as schools, libraries, and literacy organizations, Hade's cynicism-tinged statement does highlight the modern reality of children's book publishing as a multi-billion-dollar business. Sales of hardcover and softcover books for children totaled over $4.7 billion in 2005, accounting for nearly 20 percent of total industry sales (and nearly 45 percent if one factors in textbooks) (AAP 2006, viii). The *2007 Children's Writer's and Illustrator's Market,* a 440-page directory, details the submission requirements of "more than 800 places to get published."

It has become customary for bookstores and libraries to have separate, sizable children's departments, featuring junior-scale furnishings, playful decorations, a story-time series, and even child-configured computer terminals, all designed to attract children, their parents, and their teachers. Periodicals such as *Publisher's Weekly* and *The New York Times Book Review* often produce several special issues per year to highlight new and forthcoming books for children. There are graduate-level programs specializing in the study of children's literature at The Ohio State University, Illinois State University, the University of Georgia, and other accredited institutions; and formal academic journals such as *The Lion and the Unicorn* circulate studies on themes such as "The First World War and Popular Culture" (2007) and "Asian American Children's Literature" (2006).

However, despite all this activity, defining what constitutes "children's literature" is a problematic exercise, and one inevitably resistant to consensus—so much so that the very difficulty of defining the genre inhabits a recurring lament among critics and theorists specializing in the field (see, for instance, Sutton and Paravanno 2004 and Jones 2006). One factor is the considerable overlap between mature and juvenile audiences, particularly in the realms of science fiction, fantasies, and mysteries. For instance, the works of J.R.R. Tolkien (1892–1973) and J.K. Rowling (b. 1965), initially marketed to children, command such devotion among their adult fans that there are entire societies and conferences devoted to analyses of their novels. Mark Haddon's *The Curious Incident of the Dog in the Night-Time* (2003) and Philip Pullman's *The Amber Spyglass* (2001), categorized as children's books, each were named Whitbread Book of the Year—an award that encompasses the entirety of British publishing for all ages. Similarly, the tales of authors such as Arthur Conan Doyle (1859–1930), Agatha Christie (1890–1976), Bram Stoker (1847–1912), and Orson Scott Card (b. 1951) have demonstrated sustained cross-generational appeal even though they were originally written for adults. The bibliographies of authors such as Gregory Maguire (b. 1954), Ursula K. Le Guin (b. 1929), Sharyn McCrumb (b. 1948), and Madeleine L'Engle (b. 1918) testify to their successes in creating works for audiences spanning a variety of ages, and the more enduring efforts of classic raconteurs such as Mark Twain (1835–1910) and Charles Dickens (1812–1870) are frequently cross-shelved in both the children's and general inventories of libraries and bookshops.

History. Individuals interested in learning about the history and scope of children's literature in depth have an abundance of resources at their disposal. When it first appeared in 1953, *A Critical History of Children's Literature* (Meigs et al.

1969) was a landmark publication in the field, but it has since been superseded by more up-to-date surveys such as *The Norton Anthology of Children's Literature: The Traditions in English* (Zipes et al. 2005). *The Oxford Encyclopedia of Children's Literature* (Zipes 2006) devotes four volumes to significant authors, illustrators, characters, themes, and genres. *The Children's Literature Review: Excerpts from Reviews, Criticism, & Commentary on Books for Children and Young People* (1976–present) is a hardcover reference journal, featuring an average of 20 selections per year. *Something about the Author: Facts and Pictures About Authors and Illustrators of Books for Young People* is another series published by the same company (Thomson Gale) that compiles biographical sketches of individuals who have written or illustrated at least one book-length work for children.

Major periodicals specializing in reviews of children's books include *The Horn Book Magazine* (founded 1924), *Bulletin of the Center for Children's Books* (founded 1947), and *School Library Journal* (founded 1954). All three publications supplement their printed issues with well-developed, frequently updated Web sites that offer archives, news, and other resources. All three magazines also sponsor annual prizes, of which the *Boston Globe-Horn Book* Award is the most prominent. *The Horn Book* also issues a comprehensive semi-annual guide that strives to assess almost all the hardcover children's books newly published during the prior season (totaling over 2,000 titles per *Guide*).

A number of reference works are marketed not only to institutions but to the general public as well, and have proven popular enough to merit revised and updated editions. These include *The Essential Guide to Children's Books and Their Creators* (Silvey 2002, 2nd ed.,), *The New York Times Parent's Guide to the Best Books for Children* (Lipson 2000, 3rd ed.), *Valerie and Walter's Best Books for Children* (Lewis and Mayes 2004, 2nd ed.), *Children Tell Stories* (Hamilton and Weiss 2005, 2nd ed.), and *The Read-Aloud Handbook* (Trelease 2006, 6th ed.). Such books frequently contain themed chapters, indices, and hundreds of annotated recommendations, enabling individuals interested in a specific topic or genre to pursue it in depth and more efficiently than a keyword or subject header search (via print or online) might otherwise allow. The first edition of Kathleen Odean's *Great Books for Girls* (1997) received exceptional reviews, leading to a revised edition in 2002 and three additional works in the series: *Great Books for Boys* (1998), *Great Books about Things Kids Love* (2002), and *Great Books for Babies and Toddlers* (2003). Other reference guides bear the names of retail organizations with a following among consumers keen on supporting independent booksellers. These include *Book Sense Best Children's Books* (2005) and *Under the Chinaberry Tree* (Ruethling and Pitcher 2003).

The use of the term *booktalk*, now commonplace among reading professionals and enthusiasts, gained significant traction after the publication of Aidan Chambers's *Booktalk* (1985). Defined by education consultant Ellen A. Thompson as "an energetic discussion about a book or books, done with a whole class, small groups, or an individual child," *booktalks* are short "pitches" designed to hook prospective readers into reading the books themselves (Thompson n.d.). Booktalks differ from traditional reports and reviews in their scope and intent because they are geared to be teasers rather than summaries or assessments of the books in question; library media specialist Nancy Keane likens the aim of a booktalk to that of a trailer for a movie (Keane n.d.). A leading proponent of this approach, Keane maintains an online database of over 5,000 "ready to use" booktalks and has published print compilations of them as well, including *Booktalking across the Curriculum* (2002). (Her "ready-to-use" thematic bibliographies, such as *The Big Book of Children's Reading Lists* [2006], are also well regarded.) Other influential advocates of booktalking include Lucy Schall (*Booktalks and More,* 2003), Rosanne J. Blass (*Booktalks, Bookwalks, and Read-Alouds,* 2002), Ruth Cox Clark (*Tantalizing Tidbits for Middle Schoolers,* 2005), and Kathleen A. Baxter (co-writer of a series called *Gotcha!* with Marcia Agnes Kochel and Michael Dahl).

Although some booktalks are generated merely as assigned projects—one online tip sheet styled itself as a guide to "Book Talks: You Can't Live With Them and You Can't Pass Without Them"—their ability to foster interest in deserving books has proved effective, such that many authors, institutions, and publishers now incorporate them into publicity campaigns as a matter of course (Coiro 2000; Young 2003). In addition to in-person presentations, enterprising educators have also utilized digital technology, including podcasts and Web videos to engage students in the production and dissemination of booktalks.

Trends and Themes

Categorizing Children's Books. Subcategories commonly employed to describe children's books defy easy standardization. For instance, a library or retailer may elect to organize the books in its collection based on age-related reading levels, labeling each item as "preschool" (approximately ages 0–4), "beginner" or "easy" (approximately ages 4–8), "intermediate" or "middle" (approximately ages 8–12), and young adult (approximately ages 12–18). To optimize the use of limited space, books sorted into the first two categories may be combined into a larger section or redivided based on the books' physical formats (for instance, creating one section for picture books and a separate one for the slender paperbacks known as "chapter books"). Another age-based scheme is the one used by the Borders bookstore chain, which defines the stages as "read to me" (all ages), "baby" (0–4 years), "read together" (3–6 years), "learn to read" (3–7 years), "read to myself" (7–9 years), "independent reader" (8–12 years), and "young adult" (13 years and older).

Grade-based rubrics for catalogs, reviews, and reading lists are also popular. Bookmuse.com divides its recommendations into "grades K–2," "grades 3–5," "grades 6–8," and "young adult" (and its themed categories include a section for "reluctant readers"). The children's literature journal *The Horn Book* uses the terms "preschool," "primary," "intermediate," and "high school," coding some books to more than one level.

The Association for Library Service to Children (ALSC), a division of the American Library Association (ALA), compiles annual "Children's Notable Lists" in which the categories "loosely" correspond to the following groups:

> Younger readers—preschool–grade 2 (age 7), including easy-to-read books
> Middle readers—Grades 3–5, ages 8–10
> Older readers—Grades 6–8, ages 11–14
> All ages—Has appeal and interest for children in all of the above age ranges (ALSC 2007)

The Children's Book Council guidelines for "Choosing a Children's Book" are organized in the following sequence: "Babies and Toddlers," "Nursery School and Kindergarten," "Early School Years (Ages 5–8)," and "Older Children (Ages 9–12 and older)" (CBC 2006).

The placement of a book into a specific category may be dictated not only by the reading ability of its intended readers, but also by its subject matter, particularly in relation to the perceived maturity (or lack thereof) of the age group in question. This sometimes becomes a matter of debate, formal complaints, and even lawsuits when adults seek to protect children from topics or narratives they consider too difficult or out-of-bounds. In recent years, books frequently condemned for "being unsuited to age group" have included *It's Perfectly Normal* (Harris and Emberley 1994); *And Tango Makes Three* (Richardson and Parnell 2005); *What My Mother Doesn't Know* (Sones 2001); and Dav Pilkey's Captain Underpants series (1997–present). The ALA's Office of Intellectual Freedom tallied over 1,750 formal complaints in this category between 1990 and 2005, and estimates that the actual number of incidents probably totaled four or five times that figure (ALA 2006). Similarly, book retailers reportedly field comments such as "I have a fifth grader who reads at an eighth-grade level, but I don't want him/her to be exposed to 'young adult content'" on a regular basis (Powells 2007), and some stores display "mature content" cautions on the shelves intended for older children. In short, some adults view the age or grade classification of a book as much a warning as a recommendation. Although they may not necessarily object to the book's availability to the general public, they may protest its inclusion in a school's library or on a classroom syllabus, particularly if they consider the topic sensitive enough to require direct parental supervision (such as a child's introduction to sexual education).

That said, children's books are often targeted by individuals who feel certain topics, styles, or attitudes are wholly inappropriate for the genre, or indeed for any book in current circulation. Would-be censors may be politically, culturally, and religiously conservative *or* liberal: some books have drawn fire for "offensive language" and "anti-family content" and others for "racism," "sexism," "insensitivity," and "anti-ethnic" content (ALA 2006). At this writing, the most frequently challenged books during the first decade of the twenty-first century include Rowling's Harry Potter series (1997–2007), Maya Angelou's *I Know Why the Caged Bird Sings* (1969), Judy Blume's *Forever* (1975), Robert Cormier's *The Chocolate War* (1974), Chris Crutcher's *Whale Talk* (2001), Jane Leslie Conly's *Crazy Lady* (1993), Phyllis Reynolds Naylor's Alice series (1985–present), John Steinbeck's *Of Mice and Men* (1937), Alvin Schwartz's Scary Stories series (1981–1991), and Mark Twain's *The Adventures of Huckleberry Finn* (1885) (ALA 2006). In addition to the reasons cited above, children's books have also been deemed objectionable due to their perceived mishandling of sexuality, violence, or religion. (Attempts to ban the Harry Potter novels have often focused on the books' setting at a boarding school for wizards; some adults consider Rowling's world a glorification of witchcraft to an unacceptable degree.) Many of the above-mentioned books are over a quarter-century old, and some of them were best sellers and award nominees as well (for example, *Harry Potter and the Prisoner of Azkaban* captured Stoker and Whitbread awards, and *Crazy Lady* was a Newbery Honor Book) . In spite of repeated efforts to remove them, many of these books have attained the status of literary classics, well regarded not only among professional educators but by the public at large. Since 1981, a coalition of prominent book-related associations (including the ALA, the American Booksellers Association, the American Society of Journalists and Authors, and the Association of American Publishers) have co-sponsored an annual "Banned Books Week" in hopes of increasing general awareness of (and, by extension, resistance to) campaigns to restrict access to books tagged as controversial.

A positive aspect of age- and grade-based recommendations is their function as benchmarks for individuals working with children, provided they are regarded as prescriptive rather than restrictive. Given the diversity of children's interests and abilities within any specific age- or grade-based range, there are invariably both "reluctant readers" and "gifted" students for whom the average will respectively prove to be either overly ambitious or insufficiently engaging. However, given the staggering number of children's books in print (as well as many out-of-catalog titles still in active circulation via libraries and secondhand vendors), the task of matching a child to the books most appropriate to his or her abilities, interests, and needs has perhaps never been so daunting or overwhelming, and the recommendations in guidebooks such as E.D. Hirsch Jr.'s Core Knowledge series (*What Your First Grader Needs to Know; What Your Second Grader Needs to Know,* etc. [revised editions 1998]) at least provide a starting point for parents and tutors seeking a frame of reference.

This chapter is intended to serve as an introduction to children's literature popular in recent years and will focus primarily on works created for readers under 13, as well as the plethora of resources available to individuals interested in the genre. There is a separate entry in this encyclopedia delineating current trends in **Young Adult Literature,** as well as surveys of contemporary **Fantasy Literature, Graphic Novels, Science Fiction, Speculative Fiction,** and other genres with strong followings among both juvenile and adult readers. This chapter will profile mainly authors and illustrators from the United States, but it should be remembered and recognized that there are many creators of children's books from other countries—such as Britain's Pauline Baynes (b. 1922), Eva Ibbotson (b. 1925), Michael Morpurgo (b. 1943), Jacqueline Wilson (b. 1945), David Almond (b. 1951), Debi Gliori (b. 1959), and Christian Birmingham (b. 1970), to name but a few—who have enjoyed critical and commercial success in North America as well as on their native continents. Another caveat is that this entry can introduce only a few of the individuals and works currently prominent in children's literature, no matter what criteria one ultimately uses to define it; because the boundaries of the genre are themselves blurry and subject to constant reassessment, virtually any survey of its leading practitioners is likely to encounter dissenting opinions about which authors and illustrators merit such attention.

Contexts and Issues. Although reading stories aloud to children has existed as an informal parenting strategy for generations, it was not widely endorsed as a teaching method until the final decades of the twentieth century, and at times it has even been disparaged as a poor use of classroom time. The shift toward viewing regular reading aloud as an essential component of raising and educating children began to gather momentum in the early 1980s, with journalist Jim Trelease at the vanguard. As an elementary school volunteer, Trelease had noticed a correlation between children whose teachers read aloud to them and children who enjoyed reading on their own, as well as the enthusiastic response of students to his booktalks. After consulting academic publications on the subject, Trelease concluded that there was both a need to publicize this correlation to the general public and, at the time, a need to remedy the dearth of guides to suitable books (Trelease 2006, xxi).

First published in 1979, and updated approximately every five years since then, Trelease's *The Read-Aloud Handbook* has sold over two million copies and is now considered a classic reference for parents and educators. Since its initial publication, a number of read-aloud programs have been established, many of them devoted to recruiting community volunteers to read to schoolchildren and supplying free books. One such program, BookPALS (Performing Artists for Literacy in Schools), also sponsors "Storyline Online" and "Storyline Phone Lines," through which it offers video and audio recordings of professional actors reading picture books (www.bookpals.net). Another initiative, Reach Out and Read, was founded in 1989 and encourages pediatricians to act as read-aloud advocates. It distributes over 4.6 million books a year through its 3,200-plus programs (www.reachoutandread.com). Corporations, such as Motheread, address "child development and family empowerment issues" by offering classes on both storytelling and self-esteem, not only among traditional families but among those with special challenges such as that of a parent in prison (www.motheread.org).

Another prominent read-aloud advocate is Esmé Raji Codell, a "readiologist" also known as "Madame Esmé." In addition to writing *How to Get Your Child to Love Reading: For Ravenous and Reluctant Readers Alike* (2003), Codell established a private children's library in Chicago and maintains an influential Web site (www.planetesme.com). Former school librarian Judy Freeman now performs as a "children's literature troubadour" and has published a series on *Books Kids Will Sit Still For* (1990–2006), as well as compiling detailed annual guides to the 100 children's books she rates as the best of the previous year's publications. Australian author Mem Fox, popular in the United States for picture books such as *Where Is the Green Sheep?* (2004), *A Particular Cow* (2006), and *The Magic Hat* (2002), is also well known for her passionate advocacy of reading aloud, both via her lectures and her book *Reading Magic* (2001).

The increase of interest in read-aloud curricula in recent years has spawned additional resources for teachers (and, by extension, librarians and parents) in the form of curriculum guides such as Judy Bradbury's Children's Book Corner series. The Association of Booksellers for Children established the E.B. White Read Aloud Award in 2004. Its winners have included Deborah Wiles's *Each Little Bird that Sings* (2005); Chris Van Dusen's *If I Built a Car* (2005); Judy Sierra and Marc Brown's *Wild About Books* (2004); Judy Schachner's *Skippyjon Jones* (2003), which has since become a series; James Howe's *Houndsley and Catina* (2006), also now a series; and Watty Key's *Alabama Moon* (2006).

Multimedia Promotions and Spin-Offs. The public television shows *Reading Rainbow* (premiered 1983) and *Between the Lions* (premiered 2000) have done much to enhance the visibility of good picture books both on the air and online, as have the Web sites of major literacy organizations such as Reading is Fundamental (www.rif.org). Some children's publishers make a point of featuring interactive games, quizzes, contests, polls, forums, and other bonuses on their Web pages to attract repeat visits from grade-school readers, a tactic also employed by creators such as Beverly Cleary (b. 1916), Eric Carle (b. 1929), R.L. Stine (b. 1943), Jan Brett (b. 1949), and Kevin Henkes (b. 1960) on their official sites. Characters with such sites include Holly Hobbie's eponymous heroine; Marc Brown's Arthur; Stan, Jan, and Mike Berenstain's Berenstain Bears; Eric Hill's Spot; and Beatrix Potter's Peter Rabbit (ALA 2006a).

The use of celebrity power to promote reading is evident in the poster campaigns of both the American Library Association and the Association of American Publishers. The ALA's "READ" series has included images of heartthrobs Orlando Bloom (with Tolkien's *The Lord of the Rings*) and Ewan McGregor (with *Beatrix Potter: The Complete Tales*), as well as stars of children's films such as Alan Rickman (with J.D. Salinger's *Catcher in the Rye*) and Dakota Fanning (with E.B. White's *Charlotte's Web*). The AAP's "Get Caught Reading" campaign has included popular characters from *Star Wars, Avenue Q, Batman,* and *Naruto,* as well as singer-actress Queen Latifah, baseball player Johnny Damon, and various members of the U.S. Congress.

The premiere of a film adaptation also characteristically increases sales of a book. The release of a movie from a major studio may be coordinated with a reprinting of the book with a "tie-in" cover; if the subject matter or characters are sufficiently franchisable, there may also be action figures, calendars, production diaries, and other collectibles that help heighten the book's profile. For instance, the tie-ins to the 2007 movie version of *Harry Potter and the Order of the Phoenix* included a flip book, a deluxe coloring book, two poster books, a sticker book, and a set of slot-together "building cards" with which one could create a model of Hogwarts (Childrens Bookshelf 2007). The 2005 adaptation of C.S. Lewis's *The Lion, the Witch, and the Wardrobe* (1950) triggered 25 tie-in books and put a boxed edition of *The Chronicles of Narnia* onto the *New York Times* best-sellers list; a similar surge was seen in sales of J.R.R. Tolkien's work from 2001 to 2003 when the *Lord of the Rings* films premiered (La Monica 2005; Mehegan 2005).

Other successful film adaptations during the first decade of the twenty-first century include *Shrek* (2001; based on the 1990 picture book by William Steig); *Bridge to Terabithia* (2007; based on the 1997 novel by Katherine Paterson); *The Night at the Museum* (2006; based on the 1993 picture book by Milan Trenc); *The Polar Express* (2005; based on the 1985 picture book by Chris Van Allsburg); *Nanny McPhee* (2006; based on Christianna Brand's *Nurse Matilda* novels from the 1960s); *Holes* (2003; based on the 1998 novel by Louis Sachar); *Meet the Robinsons* (2007; based on William Joyce's *A Day with Wilbur Robinson,* 1990) and *Lemony Snicket's A Series of Unfortunate Events* (2004; based on the first three books in that series). With advances in computer-generated imagery (CGI) technology making special visual effects more feasible, live-action remakes of book-based animation classics were also a noticeable trend. These included *Charlotte's Web* (2006; based on the 1953 novel by E.B. White); *How the Grinch Stole Christmas* (2000; based on the 1957 picture book by Dr. Seuss); and *The Cat in the Hat* (2003; based on another 1957 picture book by Dr. Seuss) (Box Office Mojo 2007). Some classics are repeat favorites for radio, television, film, and theatrical adaptations; these include Mary O'Hara's *My Friend Flicka* (1941), Laura Ingalls Wilder's *Little House on the Prairie* series (1932–1943), *Anne Frank: The Diary of a Young Girl* (1952), Roald Dahl's *Charlie and the Chocolate Factory* (1964), Lewis Carroll's *Alice's Adventures in Wonderland* (1865), Carolyn Keene's Nancy Drew series (1930–present), and Frances Hodgson Burnett's *A Little Princess* (1905). "Junior novelizations" of blockbuster movies such as *Pirates of the Caribbean* are common, as are simplified versions of books for older children. For example, the "movie storybook" version of *Charlotte's Web* (for ages five to seven) reached the *New York Times* best-seller list for picture books during the winter of 2007.

Toys and clothing inspired by popular children's books have become a staple both of upscale retail bookshops and mail-order catalogs. For instance, *How Do Dinosaurs Say Goodnight?* (Yolen 2000) (and its more than half-dozen sequels) have been the inspiration for a pajama set and a plush toy as well as a rag book (one printed on fabric instead of paper, for children too young to handle standard picture books with care); the *Ella the Elegant Elephant* (D'Amico and D'Amico 2004) series has received similar treatment. Other picture books deemed both appealing and enduring enough to be marketed with toys based on their characters include Michael Bond's *Paddington Bear* (1958); Don Freeman's *Corduroy,* another bear (1968); Holly Hobbie's Opal the pig (1997–present); David Shannon's *No, David!,* a troublemaking toddler (1998); Dan Vaccarino's *Good Night, Mr. Night* (1997); and Simms Taback's *There Was An Old Lady Who Swallowed a Fly* (1998).

Bestsellers and classics are also frequently candidates for multiple formats, in which the book may be produced not only as a hardcover and a softcover, but abridged, re-illustrated, and sold in a format more accessible to younger readers. Laura Joffe Numeroff's *If You Give a Mouse a Cookie* (1985) and its sequels have been packaged in many combinations, including book-and-doll, mini-book-and-cassette-tape, and printed as a 17 × 15-inch "big book" (a format in which enlarged illustrations help the reader-performer overcome the visibility issues otherwise inherent in group story times). *The Best Mouse Cookie* (1999) is a board-book variation of the story (in which the "pages" are sturdy slabs of cardboard, the better to withstand the direct attention of infants and toddlers), and *Mouse Cookies and More: A Treasury* (2006) offers recipes, songs, and other activities to supplement the series. Other spin-offs from established classics include *Mary Poppins in the Kitchen* (Travers 1975 [2006]) and *Green Eggs and Ham Cookbook* (Brennan 2006).

Another category of spin-off is the expansion, reformulation, and repackaging of a familiar series into multiple versions or threads. One type of expansion can be seen in the dozens of products related to A.A. Milne's "Winnie the Pooh," some bearing images drawn by the original illustrator, Ernest Shepard (1879–1976), whereas others are licensed derivations of the many Disney animated movies. Another type consists of series that are updated and reformulated to reflect changing cultural norms or to revive their appeal to contemporary audiences. The "Nancy Drew" and "Hardy Boys" mystery brands now consist of more than 100 volumes, some belonging to the original series established by the Stratemeyer Syndicate, and others to later generation "Files," "Notebooks," "Clue Crew" stories, graphic novels, and other permutations (Fisher 2007).

The publishing history of Wilder's Little House series offers examples of all the spin-off types mentioned above. The first eight books of the series (from *Little House in the Big Woods* to *These Happy Golden Years*) were published between 1932 and 1943 and were originally illustrated by Helen Sewell and Mildred Boyle. (A ninth manuscript, *The First Four Years,* was posthumously published in 1971.) In 1953, the series was reissued as a uniform set with illustrations by Garth Williams. This edition became established as the "classic" version of the series to the majority of its readers, many of whom were unreservedly vocal in expressing their dismay when the publisher revealed plans to increase interest in the series among contemporary children by replacing the Williams drawings with staged photographs (Marell-Mitchell 2006).

Prior to the 1990s, individuals interested in reading beyond the original series were generally limited to a selection of Wilder's travel writings, several biographies, and Barbara M. Walker's *The Little House Cookbook* (1979), the last also illustrated by Williams. During the 1990s, with the blessing and cooperation of the Wilder literary estate, the expansion of the Little House franchise kicked into full gear. Four spin-off series were created, each centered on the childhood of a female relative of Laura Ingalls: the books on Wilder's great-grandmother and grandmother began to appear in 1999 and were initially written by Melissa Wiley; the series on

Rose Wilder Lane (Wilder's daughter) was published between 1993 and 1999 with the byline of Roger Lea Macbride, Lane's heir; and the series on Caroline Quiner Ingalls (Wilder's mother) featured seven books (1996–2005), four by Maria D. Wilkes and three by Celia Wilkins. Additional volumes in the Martha and Charlotte series are anticipated, but the publisher's decision to replace the existing books with significantly shorter versions prompted Wiley to resign from the project (Wiley 2007).

During the height of the franchise's popularity (from approximately 1997 to 2000), dozens of excerpts from the core novels were formatted anew as picture books and chapter books, rendering them accessible to children younger than Wilder's original audience. Additional selections were combined to produce gift anthologies such as *Little House Sisters* (1997). During this period, activity books such as *My Little House Sewing Book* (1997) also proliferated. Although the pace of spin-off publications has slowed down, interest in the Little House series remains intense enough to inspire countless events, tours, clubs, and other educational efforts in Wilder's honor, and the museums associated with sites she immortalized in her novels average over 20,000 visitors each year (Laura Ingalls Wilder Memorial Society 2007). William Anderson and Leslie A. Kelly's *The Little House Guidebook* (rev. ed. 2002) has provided both historical background and extensive sightseeing tips for would-be tourists.

L.M. Montgomery's *Anne of Green Gables* series (1908–1939) commands a large-scale following comparable to that of the Little House sequence, bringing over 130,000 pilgrims each year to the Green Gables homestead on Prince Edward Island, Canada. Venerated as a Canadian icon, the character of Anne is wildly popular in Japan as well as in the United States, where numerous film, television, and stage adaptations have met with commercial success, and the *Anne of Green Gables* Licensing Authority had granted almost a hundred licenses as of spring 2007; detailed plans to commemorate the 2008 centenary of the first book were already in full development by mid-2006, including the commissioning of an estate-authorized "prequel" and a gift book based on Montgomery's scrapbooks (Gordon 2006; Hunter 2006).

As a career writer, Montgomery was far more prolific than Wilder, and the *Anne* series continues the heroine's story into middle age, with Anne's role becoming increasingly peripheral as the narrative focus shifts to her children and their friends. Given these factors, and the entry of the earlier books into the public domain, the publication history of *Anne of Green Gables* (outside of the 100th-anniversary publications) more closely resembles that of another classic, Louisa May Alcott's *Little Women* (1868): rather than generating spin-offs and sequels, publishers have generally elected either to reissue the writers' lesser-known works or to produce new editions of the opening book in each series, competing with existing editions on the basis of price, illustrations, or supplemental material. For instance, the 2001 Aladdin edition of *Anne of Green Gables* includes a foreword by highly regarded novelist Katherine Paterson (b. 1932).

Little Women remains another perennial favorite for dramatizations. Recent versions include a 2005 Broadway musical, which toured nationally for a year, and a critically acclaimed opera by Mark Adamo (b. 1962) that was broadcast on "Great Performances" in 2001 and has since been added to the repertory of over 20 companies (Schirmer 2007). The book's continuing influence on American literature was also evident when the 2006 Pulitzer Prize for fiction was awarded to Geraldine Brooks's *March*, a novel featuring the father of Alcott's "little women" as its central character. As with other writers of her stature, there is a society dedicated to preserving her Massachusetts home as a museum, and running educational programming based on events and activities depicted in *Little Women*, such as "Plumfield Fun Week" and "Meg's Wedding" (Louisa May Alcott Memorial Association 2007).

Literary Tourism. The popularity of a children's character, book, or franchise can both inspire and perpetuate interest in locales associated with either the story or its production. During the first decade of the twentieth century, a number of new books offered assistance to travelers interested in planning their vacations with childhood favorites in mind. These included *Storied City: A Children's Book Walking-Tour Guide to New York City* (Marcus 2003), *Storybook Travels: From Eloise's New York to Harry Potter's London* (Bates and La Tempa 2002), and *Once Upon a Time in Great Britain* (Wentz 2002). The interest in this subgenre was perhaps heralded by the 1999 republication of *How the Heather Looks: A Joyous Journey to the British Sources of Children's Books* by legendary editor and reviewer Joan Bodger (1921–2002). Previously out of print for over 30 years, Bodger's travelogue had attained the status of "an underground classic" among aficionados of children's literature (Donnelly 2000) and reportedly enjoyed the status of "the book most often stolen by retiring children's librarians" (Bodger 1999, 299). The reception of its return to print was mixed, however; although Bodger's sunny narration was celebrated by some critics with encomiums such as "timeless" (Thomas 2000) and "smart" (Donnelly 2000) by some contemporary reviewers, others felt that the book exhibited an "absent-minded elitism" (Cohoon 2001) that modern readers might find "an exclusionary drag" (Wilson 2000).

Travel accounts of a more recent vintage can be found on LiteraryTraveler.com, a well regarded Web site featuring professional essays on literature-inspired travel. The site regularly posts articles on pilgrimages inspired by popular children's books (including Faith Ringgold's *Tar Beach* and J.D. Salinger's *Catcher in the Rye*) and the reports in the March 2007 children's literature issue explored locations associated with iconic characters and authors such as William Blake (1757–1827), Ludwig Bemelmans (1898–1962), Roald Dahl (1916–1990), Astrid Lindgren (1907–2002), Robert McCloskey (1914–2003), and P(amela) L(yndon) Travers (1899–1996).

Detailed online travelogues have become a common practice on personal Web sites as well; the affordability of digital photography and the flexibility of online storage permit online authors to illustrate their chronicles more lavishly than would generally be feasible in a printed equivalent, as well as to share their experiences with like-minded enthusiasts. For instance, Susan Cooper's "The Dark Is Rising" sequence (1965–1977) has inspired a number of its devotees to seek out Wales for themselves (see Given 2002 and Green 2007 for examples). Mark Scott's account of his visit, featuring photographs taken by another fan of the series, cites Jean Valencia's description of her trip as the nudge he needed to finish assembling his own recollections (Scott n.d.; Valencia 1997).

The American Girl collection of books, dolls, and accessories has become one of the most recognizable franchises in upscale children's "edutainment," so much so that a *New York Times* review recently began with the observation, "*Anne of Green Gables* [an off-Broadway musical adaptation] appears to be going for the American Girl demographic" (Midgette 2007). The demographic in question has made the "American Girl Place" entertainment complexes in New York, Chicago, and Los Angeles popular destinations for mother-daughter vacations. Billed as "More than just a store—it's an experience!," each Place consists of multiple shops (including a girl-centric bookstore), a theatre, and a cafe. Originally centered on heroines representing historical periods in America's past, the brand has evolved to include contemporary characters (such as their "2007 Girl of the Year," a 10-year-old service-dog trainer named Nicki. In tandem with Nicki's story (Creel 2007), the company released a nonfiction treasury called *Girls and Their Dogs* (American Girl 2006). It has also attracted praise for its "Smart Girl's Guides" (such as *The Smart Girl's Guide to Friendship Troubles* (Criswell 2003), written by a certified social worker) and other advice tomes such as *The Big Book of Help* (Holyoke 2004).

Reception. In their introduction to a *Horn Book* issue on "the line between books for children and books for adults," the magazine's editors quoted John Rowe Townsend's 1971 declaration that "the only practical definition of a children's book today—absurd as it sounds—is 'a book which appears on the children's list of a publisher'" (Sutton and Paravanno 2004). Although this is indeed an absurd line to draw, it underscores the inherent inconclusiveness of attempts to confine the genre to any one set of age- or topic-delimited boundaries. In discussing the books that children fix upon as their favorites, critic Selma G. Lanes observed that "the meeting of a book and a child's individual need is a fragile and fortuitous happening" that may seem random or peculiar, although adults can foster suitable connections by ensuring the child's access to a wide variety of books (1972, 201–202). Because adults handle the bulk of children's literature purchases—be it for their dependents or for themselves—the popularity and shelf-life of such books is ultimately determined as much by their ability to capture and retain the attention of mature as well as juvenile readers. When asked about controversy and contentiousness in children's literature, historian Leonard S. Marcus mused about how the events of *Harry Potter and the Goblet of Fire* "seemed to comment on some of the things that were happening in the world" during the period he was reading it aloud to his son, which coincided with the horrors of September 11, 2001. Marcus concluded that, although such connections are seldom specifically anticipated or intended, "children's books have a way of resonating with real experience in unexpected ways. And the children's books we remember make sense in precisely that way" (Serlin and Selznick 2002).

Selected Authors

The Harry Potter Phenomenon. When the seventh and final book of J.K. Rowling's Harry Potter series became available for pre-order, it captured the top spot on several online retailers' best-seller lists within hours and remained there for weeks. The last four books in the series each broke records for first printings, with a run of 12 million copies set for *Harry Potter and the Deathly Hallows* (2007). The opening volume, *Harry Potter and the Philosopher's Stone* (1997; U.S. title *Harry Potter and the Sorcerer's Stone*), appears to be established as a classic, with approximately 0.5 million copies in annual sales a decade after its initial publication (Rich and Bosman 2007), as well as over 60 authorized editions in translation. The movie versions of the books were produced and marketed with the author's active cooperation and have been box-office blockbusters as well (Pandya 2007).

The popularity of Rowling's storytelling has been attributed to a number of elements, including her inventive sense of humor, her playful allusions to classical myths and fairy tales, her realistic portrayal of human relationships, and her ability to sustain a suspenseful, mystery-laden plot across the seven years depicted in the seven-book saga. Her cast of characters includes unreliable or unhelpful adults, devious and daring children, and a host of unpredictable magical creatures (some amusing, others malevolent). As reviewers such as Alison Lurie and Stephen King have observed, some readers are drawn to the series because they can readily identify with its orphan hero and his Cinderella-style emergence into the wizarding world:

> From the point of view of an imaginative child, the world is full of Muggles [the series' term for non-wizards]: people who don't understand you, make stupid rules, and want nothing to do with the unexpected or the unseen. Harry's story also embodies the common childhood fantasy that the dreary adults and siblings you live with are not your real family; that you have more exciting parents, and are somehow special and gifted. (Lurie 2003, 117)

Other readers are enthralled by the books' richly detailed settings, which range from the medieval castle housing Harry's boarding school to the contemporary sports stadium conjured for the Quidditch World Cup. Others find themselves entranced by the complexity of the series' heroes and villains: Rowling is unafraid to invest her protagonists and their allies with significant flaws and blind spots, which contribute to numerous misperceptions, misunderstandings, and miscalculations. These, in turn, help fuel the narrative drive of the series: as university professor Barbara Carman Garner stated, "The most pressing question in the *Potter* books is, 'Who can be trusted?'" (Zipes 2006, 3: 369). With each volume in the series, the question becomes increasingly urgent—and its possible answers correspondingly difficult to discern, with the true loyalties of certain key characters the subject of passionate debate among their fans.

The Harry Potter series is not without its faults or its detractors. For some readers, the laws governing the Harry Potter universe are inconsistent and poorly constructed. Some critics find Rowling's "good" characters unlikable, arguing that they are no better than bullies and elitists, and others feel that the books endorse lying and other undesirable behaviors. Some readers relish the ethnic diversity of Rowling's cast and the strong personalities of her female characters, but others regard her handling of these elements as superficial. And, as with any other popular author, some readers consider Rowling to be overrated or discover that her prose is simply not to their taste (in a poll of "books Brits are most likely to own but are unable to finish," *Harry Potter and the Goblet of Fire* was the fiction runner-up [Jury 2007]).

On the other hand, the books also have been praised by children's literature specialists not only for their literary merit, but for their ability to engage "reluctant readers." Jim Trelease calls Harry Potter "the best thing to happen to children's books since the invention of the paperback" (250); in a chapter titled "Lessons from Oprah, Harry, and the Internet," Trelease analyzes Rowling's popularity both in comparison to other children's best-sellers and in the context of other claims on children's leisure time. He cites the length of books as a positive factor, asserting that "consuming that many words, students are getting prodigiously better at reading—many for the first time—and *enjoying* it. . . . Harry Potter has children willing to read books that are eight times longer than *Goosebumps* and twice as long as *Heidi*" (Trelease 2006, 142–143).

Unfortunate Events and Fractured Fairy Tales. By the time the last book in *A Series of Unfortunate Events* appeared on October 13, 2006, Lemony Snicket's saga of the much persecuted Baudelaire children had appeared on the weekly *New York Times* "Children's Best-Sellers" list over a hundred times. In addition to the 13 novels that form the core of the series, there have also been authorized side entertainments such as a CD of songs (originally composed for the audiobook editions of the novels), several blank books, an *Unauthorized Autobiography* (2002), and *The Beatrice Letters,* a collection of simulated correspondence in the style of Nick Bantock's *Griffin and Sabine* (1991). Snicket is the pseudonym of Daniel Handler (b. 1970), who poses as the author's representative during promotional events and interviews.

Laden with literary allusions and melodramatic disclaimers, the series was acclaimed for its combination of shameless erudition, twisted humor, and outrageous plots. One reference guide describes the first book as "an Edward Gorey drawing come to life, or a parody of every dreadful Victorian orphan novel you've never read . . . one of the funniest books for children ever written" (Lewis and Mayes 2003, 336). As with many traditional fairy tales, the stories offer their readers the vicarious pleasure of identifying with the brave, talented, and wildly unlucky Baudelaire orphans as they contend with villainous adults and other menaces. At the same time, the arch narration and baroque plot contrivances help sustain an atmosphere of unreality that serves as a cushion, distancing readers from the protagonists' travails.

In his assessment of the full series, reviewer Henry Alford (b. 1962) admired Handler's "interesting and offbeat" efforts to educate his readers:

> In between all the exotic ethnic food references and the gallows humor and the teaching of words like "denouement" and "vaporetto," the books seem at times like a covert mission to turn their readers into slightly dark-hued sophisticates. To be sure, there'll be a payoff for those gothically inclined young readers who, as adults, see the sick joke at the heart of characters named Klaus and Sunny. Or consider the series' early lessons in postmodernism—the author loves to tell us to put the book we're reading down, and in *The Carnivorous Carnival,* he repeatedly gives us the definition of déjà vu; in *The Penultimate Peril,* he tells us we don't need to read the next three chapters in any particular order. The reader who receives such training is amply prepared for the rocky narrative landscapes of Borges and Eco. (2006)

In a sense, Handler's droll manipulations can be considered heirs of the narrative strategies deployed in *The Stinky Cheese Man and Other Fairly Stupid Tales* (1992), a picture book that cemented the reputations of writer Jon Scieszka (b. 1954) and illustrator Lane Smith (b. 1959) as masters of satirical, multilayered storytelling. The team had already caused a sensation with their first collaboration, *The True Story of the Three Little Pigs* (1989), which presented its version of events from the perspective of an "Alexander T. Wolf" protesting his innocence. For *The Stinky Cheese Man,* Scieszka, Smith, and designer Molly Leach combined their talents to produce a bold, attitude-packed book in which their text, art, and layout choices all amplify the stories' seemingly freewheeling plots and characterizations. In an essay examining the power of good design, Scieszka observed that "some people have described our books as 'wacky' and 'zany' and 'anything goes.' . . . In order to create the humor and illusion of wacky/zany/anything goes, there has to be a reason for *everything* that goes" (Scieszka 1998).

Thirteen years after the book's publication, *The Norton Anthology of Children's Literature* asserted, "As an 'advanced' multireferential text, *The Stinky Cheese Man* has not (yet) been bettered. It assumes intertextual skills, its collage medium is deliberately ironic, and its characters try to break the bounds of the book" (Zipes et al. 2005, C32). *Stinky Cheese Man*'s runaway success (so to speak) has been credited with paving the way for other creators to pursue unconventional and experimental approaches to storytelling (Britton 2002), having proved that "dark," "weird," and "sophisticated" work for children can be commercially viable; Scieszka himself notes that *The Three Pigs* was "rejected everywhere" until an editor at Viking elected to gamble on it (Scieszka 2006).

In addition to promoting a climate in which personas such as Lemony Snicket could flourish, Scieszka and Smith's collaborations also raised the profile of the "fractured fairy-tale" genre. Lewis and Mayes observe that "now, a season doesn't go by without an abundance of fairy-tale retellings that are fractured, skewed, or otherwise toyed with" and make a point of highlighting several dozen of their own favorites (225–226). David Wiesner's version of *The Three Pigs* (2001) earned the Caldecott Medal for its virtuosic depictions of the pigs' escape from the traditional storyline into several others (collecting a fiddling cat and a besieged dragon along the way), with the visual action merrily sliding from one style of picture-book illustration into the next. At one point, the pigs fold a "page" of the original story into a paper airplane, and they are later shown tilting and arranging the remaining pages to re-enter and conclude the story.

A subcategory of the "fractured fairy-tale" genre consists of myths reinterpreted through a feminism-informed lens. For readers troubled by the passivity of traditional damsels in distress (or repelled outright by celebrations of womanly victimhood)—and also for readers who simply enjoy sassy parodies—these often-humorous variations offer alternate scenarios where princesses aren't always yearning for rescue, much less automatically grateful to their would-be rescuers. Such re-imaginings include *Falling for Rapunzel* (Wilcox 2003), in which the heroine cheerfully misinterprets the prince's increasingly frustrated commands for access to her tower; *The Princess and the Pizza* (Auch and Auch 2002), in which the impoverished heroine enters a cooking contest in order to win the hand of "Prince Drupert"; and Gerald Morris's The Squire's Tale series (1998–present), in which an assortment of young protagonists struggle to make sense of the disconnect they witness between the idealism of Arthurian chivalry and the less admirable behaviors of the knights and courtiers they encounter during their adventures.

Although Morris's straightforward prose is stylistically worlds removed from Lemony Snicket's eccentric excesses, it could be argued that the two authors share an irony-tinged awareness of the distance and self-delusion that so often exists between cherished principles and actual practice—an awareness lurking beneath both Morris's sly glimmers of humor and Snicket's outlandish posturings, as well as Scieszka's skewerings of "happy ever after" transformations. Morris's compassionate but realistic acknowledgment of his heroes' flaws echoes Snicket's refusal to spare the Baudelaire children from uncomfortable and regrettable decisions. After one such error results in tragedy, Snicket sadly reflects, "It is very difficult to make one's way in this world without being wicked at one point or another, when the world's way is so wicked to begin with" (Handler 2005, 316). The moral ambiguity inherent in such a declaration is not far removed from the ancient, maddening complexities and unresolved conundrums that have driven other twenty-first-century authors to construct radically altered versions of familiar stories, to craft new narratives that liberate stock characters from unsatisfactory fates, or to challenge a story's postulates by presenting its events from the perspective of an antagonist or a secondary character.

Other Trends among Recent Best Sellers. The success of "Harry Potter" has been both blamed and credited for the plethora of new books in the 2000s featuring magic, dragons, and other fantastical elements, but humorous escapism has also long acted as a key ingredient in explicitly educational series such as Joanna Cole's The Magic School Bus (1986–present) and Mary Pope Osborne's Magic Tree House (1992–present). Both retailers and educators unabashedly use "If you like Harry Potter, you'll like . . ." stratagems to interest children toward other fantasy sequences such as tales of "Septimus Heap" (2005–present, by Angie Sage) and "The Spiderwick Chronicles" (2003–present, by Tony DiTerlizzi and Holly Black). The latter has also elicited comparisons to Lemony Snicket's series in both design and tone, prompted by such devices as leaves artistically obscuring back-cover blurbs and pseudo-cautionary mottoes such as "Go away/close the book/put it down/do not look."

Another recurring element among top-selling titles is the perennial irresistibility of bunnies. They may appear as sentient toys, such as in *The Remarkable Journey of Edward Tulane* (DiCamillo 2006), or as anthropomorphic representations of children, such as in *Not a Box* (Portis 2007) and in dozens of titles by Rosemary Wells (b. 1943). Their popularity echoes that of enduring classics such as Margery Williams's *The Velveteen Rabbit* (1922) and Margaret Wise Brown's *Goodnight Moon* (1947).

A notable trend in intermediate-level literary fiction has been the popularity of books featuring a type of self-reliant, unconventional pre-teen girl—enough to attract a measure of backlash against the frequency of such characters (cf. Sutton 2007a). One reviewer admitted groaning upon realizing she had received "another book with a plucky, young, motherless heroine—if she gets a dog and names it after a supermarket, I'm out of here [an allusion to Kate DiCamillo's *Because of Winn-Dixie*]" (Smith 2007). The current parade of feisty female orphans, however, including Maud Flynn in *A Drowned Maiden's Hair* (Schlitz 2006) and Karen Cushman's *Rodzina* (2003), appeal to readers eager for antidotes against portrayals of passive, prettiness-defined heroines—a contingent substantial enough to merit compilations such as The Anti Princess Reading List (Mommy Track'd 2007). In the beginning reader realm, series featuring imperfect yet likable leads such as Junie B. Jones (1992–present, by Barbara Park) and Judy Moody (2000–present, by Megan McDonald) have proved popular. Picture-book characters in the 2000s praised for their confidence and style include Olivia the pig (in the Ian Falconer series, 2000–present) and Fancy Nancy (2005–present, by Jane O'Connor and Robin Preiss Glasser), both of whom have been compared to Kay Thompson's classic *Eloise* (1955).

Another intriguing trend has been the attention given to novels in which the illustrations are integral to the narrative rather than merely decorative. These include Lynne Rae Perkins's *Criss Cross* (2005), Brian Selznick's *The Invention of Hugo Cabret: A Novel in Words and Pictures* (2007), and Gene Luen Yang's *American Born Chinese* (2006), the last a graphic novel shortlisted for several prizes traditionally granted to conventional chapter books. The success of these titles may well inspire more writer-artists to investigate this variation of storytelling.

Awards. The Newbery and Caldecott Medals, administered by the American Library Association, are regarded as two of the top prizes in the field of children's literature. The Newbery Medal program was initiated in 1921 by Frederic G. Melcher, a prominent bookseller and *Publisher's Weekly* editor. During the years that followed, it became apparent that a second, separate award for picture books would be welcome; as a result, the Caldecott Medal was established in 1937. For each award, a winner and several runners-up are named; the runners-up are known as "honor" books, a designation used by several other children's award programs as well.

A title that wins the Newbery or Caldecott Medal is ensured a permanent listing in many reference books and library brochures. The prizes are well publicized and customarily increase both the immediate and long-term sales of the award winners. A number of schools, libraries, and retailers have adopted the practice of holding "Mock Newbery" and "Mock Caldecott" elections each winter, in which the participants read and vote upon books perceived as contenders for each award. Such exercises help stimulate discussion and sales of new titles since books are generally eligible only within their first year of publication.

The official criteria of the awards mandate that they are to be granted only on the basis of excellence, rather than "for didactic intent or for popularity" (ALSC 2007). Although many authors on the winners and honors lists become established classroom and household favorites, others never catch hold among the general public, and still others fall out of favor (and subsequently lapse out of print) as fashions in storytelling and scholarship change.

As with any major prize, the decisions of the Newbery and Caldecott award committees have not lacked critics. In 2007, the selection of Susan Patron's *The Higher Power of Lucky* became front-page news on *The New York Times* (as well as the subject of an editorial in support of the book) after *Publisher's Weekly* reported significant debate about the winner among children's literature professionals (Bosman 2007; Maughan 2007a and 2007b). The controversy centered on the author's use of the word "scrotum" and whether it rendered the book age-inappropriate for its intended audience. In the judgment of some librarians, the book was too problematic to add to their collections, whereas other participants in the debates criticized decisions against purchasing the title as tantamount to censorship.

In discussing the contretemps, some longtime observers of the field noted that vocal dissent was to be expected with any awards process. *Horn Book* editor Roger Sutton commented, "In my going-on-30 years in this field I can't think of a Newbery choice that wasn't reviled and/or ridiculed by a significant number of librarians" (Sutton 2007b). Maurice Sendak's *Where the Wild Things Are,* which received the 1964 Caldecott Medal, was pronounced to be too frightening for its intended audience in such venues as *Ladies Home Journal* by experts such as child psychologist Bruno Bettelheim (1903–1990) (March 1969; excerpted in CLR 1976). The strong reaction both for and against Sendak's story has become legendary in the lore of children's literature, and its status as a landmark picture book has been the subject of extended analyses (CLR 2002). *Smoky Night,* a story set during the 1992 Los Angeles race riots, won the 1995 Caldecott Medal; its author, Eve Bunting, recalled "a lot of disgruntled talk after the Caldecott. One of the judges said she got so much flack she had to take to her bed" (Bunting 2006).

On the other side of the coin, questions regarding whether the award shortlists lack diversity are also raised on a regular basis (cf. Parravano and Adams 1996;

Sutton 2007a). That said, the authors of Newbery winners since 2000 include an African American (Christopher Paul Curtis (1954–) and two Asian Americans (Linda Sue Park (1960–) and Cynthia Kadohata (1956–)), and recent Caldecott honors titles have included books about Harriet Tubman (Weatherford 2006), Rosa Parks (Giovanni 2005), and Martin Luther King Jr. (Rappaport 2002). Jacqueline Woodson was a Caldecott finalist for *Coming On Home Soon* (2004) and a Newbery finalist for *Show Way* (2005), both works inspired by African American history, as were Marilyn Nelson's *Carver* (2001) and Russell Freedman's *The Voice that Challenged A Nation* (2004).

The ALA sponsors a number of other prizes, including the Belpré Medal (for Latino authors and illustrators) and the Coretta Scott King Award (for African American authors and illustrators). The *Boston Globe-Horn Book (BG-HG)* Awards, established in 1967, are also influential among children's literature professionals. There is often overlap among the *BG-HB* finalists and those of the Newbery and Caldecott committees: *The Hello, Goodbye Window* (Juster 2005) was the 2006 Caldecott medalist and a *BG-HB* honors book; *The Man Who Walked Between the Towers* (Gerstein 2003) won both the Caldecott medal and the *BG-HB* picture-book prize; *An American Plague* (Murphy 2003) was a *BG-HB* winner in nonfiction and Newbery honors book. Illustrators appearing multiple times on major awards lists include David Wiesner (b. 1956), Chris Raschka (b. 1959), and Mo Willems (b. 1968); favorite authors among the committees include Susan Cooper (b. 1935), Sharon Creech (b. 1945), Marilyn Nelson (b. 1946), Cynthia Rylant (b. 1954), Lynne Rae Perkins (b. 1956), Kate DiCamillo (b. 1964), and M(atthew) T(obin) Anderson (b. 1968).

Nonfiction. Although the awards programs generally highlight outstanding stand-alone volumes, nonfiction children's books are often generated in series that are specifically "reinforced" or "library bound"—a colorful, durable, jacketless hard-cover format that holds up well to repeat shelvings. There are series devoted to virtually every area of interest, including crafts, holidays, science, social studies, arts, animals, and sports. Enslow Publishers' Fun Holiday Crafts Kids Can Do! series includes games and activities in honor of Earth Day and Kwanzaa as well as Christmas and Halloween. Scholastic's second Cornerstones of Freedom series includes a profile of Air Force One, the U.S. commander-in-chief's airplane, that offers anecdotes about individual presidents' styles (such as the meals they enjoyed eating) as well as a historical and logistical overview of "the Flying White House" and photographs conveying how its occupants conduct business en route (January 2004). In history series such as Heinemann's Picture the Past, there is a marked effort to convey details that will help the student visualize the reality of distant cultures; for instance, in *Life in a Roman Fort* (Shuster 2005) informs its readers that "sponges and sticks were used as toilet paper, and then washed and reused" (19) and features a recipe for "army porridge" (29). Series for older children such as Lerner's Military Hardware in Action feature more advanced vocabulary and data, such as the beam, propulsion, and displacement details for assorted U.S. vessels in Mark Dartford's *Warships* (2003). Collections developed in reaction to recent events include Scholastic's Natural Disasters set, which covers emergency responses to hurricanes, tsunamis, and other calamities.

Many of these nonfiction series are deliberately formulaic in tone and design, relying on well-chosen stock photographs, simple line illustrations, colored back-grounds, and frequent use of sidebars to maintain the reader's interest. Such books often incorporate the use of boldface type to emphasize key terms to the student; there is also customarily a glossary in the back, as well as several books or Web sites listed for those interested in further reading, and sometimes additional appendices such as timelines or places to visit. Four notably well-designed series that stand out from the crowd are the Eyewitness guides produced by Dorling Kindersley, the biographies produced by National Geographic, and the Encyclopedia Prehistorica volumes produced by Candlewick.

One of the more engaging series to appear in recent years has been Franklin Watts's You Wouldn't Want to Be . . . narratives, which have included *You Wouldn't Want to be a Pirate's Prisoner! Horrible Things You'd Rather Not Know* (2002), *You Wouldn't Want to Be a Civil War Soldier! A War You'd Rather Not Fight* (2004), *You Wouldn't Want to Be at the Boston Tea Party! Wharf Water Tea You'd Rather Not Drink* (2006), and the like. As their titles indicate, these books feature second-person storytelling in which the student is treated to playful but deromanticized perspectives of life in the specified role, with cartoon-style yet historically grounded depictions of the scenarios such individuals would have encountered. The You Wouldn't Want to Be . . . volumes include the anecdotal sidebars and elementary glossaries of more traditional series, but in attitude, they reflect the trend in larger society of viewing history through a more realistic lens, even at the popular culture level (as witnessed in PBS-based reality television shows such as "Frontier House" and "Texas Ranch House"). Efforts to distinguish myth from actual practice can also be seen in books such as *Piratepedia,* where the writers note that there has only been one verifiable case of "walking the plank" (Niehaus and Hecker 2006, 122).

Poetry. The design of poetry books for children has evolved into a lively and sophisticated art, one in which the use of multiple fonts and colors help accent the texts and concepts presented. The strategy of getting children interested in poetry by encouraging them to write their own is on display in engaging picture guidebooks such as *A Kick in the Head* (Janescko 2005) and Jennifer Fandel's Understanding Poetry series, which examine a broad range of forms and techniques in tandem with hip, humorous illustrations. *A Kick in the Head* delineates the format of more esoteric forms (such as blues poems and pantoums) as well as those of more familiar poetic structures (such as haiku and sonnets), and represents a second collaboration by veteran anthologist Paul Janescko and popular illustrator Chris Raschka (the first being *A Poke in the I,* a collection of concrete poems). In *Puns, Allusions, and Other Word Secrets,* intermediate-level readers are asked to consider concepts such as "wrenched rhyme" and "dramatic monologues" in poems by John Ciardi, Audre Lorde, and others, as well as to participate in activities such as writing a poem about a single day from three different points of view (Fandel 2006, 44). Robin Hirsch's *FEG: Stupid (Ridiculous) Poems for Intelligent Children* (2002) also revels in wordplay, comedy, and loopy footnotes; for the poem "But Not Now a Wonton Tub," Hirsch comments, "This . . . may well be the lamest, most pathetic palindrome ever composed. Actually, the poem was written (or rather made up spontaneously) in the car to try and justify the pitiful palindrome that comes at the end. Surely, you can do better" (23).

Among living practitioners, the most prominent representative of children's poetry is currently Jack Prelutsky (b. 1960), who was designated Children's Poet Laureate in September 2006 by the Poetry Foundation (itself founded in 2003 as a result of a $100 million donation to *Poetry* magazine). Other major poets and poetry editors for children active in the 2000s include Lee Bennett Hopkins, with anthologies such as *Got Geography!* (2006) and *Oh, No! Where Are My Pants? and Other Disasters* (2003); Douglas Florian, author of *Handsprings* (2006) and *A Pig is Big* (2000); Susan Katz, whose books include *Looking for Jaguar* (2005), *A Revolutionary Field Trip* (2004), and *Mrs. Brown on Exhibit* (2002); J. Patrick Lewis, with *Please Bury Me in the Library* (2005) and *Once Upon a Tomb* (2006), as well as *Wing Nuts: Screwy Haiku,* a collection co-written with Janeczko (2006); Georgia Heard, who selected the poems for *This Place I Know* (2002), an anthology created in response to September 11, 2001; and Janet S. Wong, whose collections include *Twist* (2007) and *Knock on Wood* (2003), as well as a creative writing book (*You Have To Write,* 2002) and assorted picture books.

Among deceased poets, individuals whose works continue to captivate new generations of readers include Shel Silverstein (the 20th anniversary edition of *A Light in the Attic* appeared in 2001, and the 30th anniversary edition of *Where the Sidewalk Ends* in 2004), Dr. Seuss (*Oh the Places You'll Go!* routinely returns to the *New York Times* best-seller list during graduation season), and Robert Louis Stevenson, whose *Child's Garden of Verses* has been reprinted since 1885 in dozens of editions, of which the most popular include versions illustrated by Tasha Tudor (1981/1999) and Thomas Kinkade (1999). The Poetry for Young People picture-book series, initiated in the mid-1990s, continues to grow, adding annotated volumes on topics such as "Animal Poems" (Hollander 2004) and "The Seasons" (Serio 2005), as well as ones on individual poets such as Langston Hughes (2006) and William Blake (2007).

Bibliography

Association of American Publishers (AAP). *2005 Industry Statistics.* New York: AAP, 2006.

ALA (American Library Association). "Challenged and Banned Books." 2006. http://www.ala.org/ala/oif/bannedbooksweek/challengedbanned/challengedbanned.htm.

———. "Great Web Sites for Kids." 2006a. http://www.ala.org/ala/alsc/greatwebsites/greatwebsitesfavorite.htm.

Association for Library Service to Children (ALSC). "ALA—Awards and Scholarships." 2007. http://www.ala.org/ala/alsc/awardsscholarships/awardsscholarships.htm.

Alford, Henry. "Children's Books" [review of Lemony Snicket's *The End* and *The Beatrice Letters*]. *New York Times,* Oct. 22 2006. http://www.nytimes.com/2006/10/22/books/review/Alford.t.html?_r=2&ref=review&oref=slogin&oref=slogin.

American Girl. *Girls and Their Dogs.* Middleton, WI: Pleasant Company Publications, 2007.

Anderson, William. *The Little House Guidebook.* Rev. ed. Photographs by Leslie A. Kelly. New York: Harper, 2002.

Auch, Mary Jane, and Auch, Herm. *The Princess and the Pizza.* New York: Holiday House, 2002.

Bates, Colleen Dunn, and Susan La Tempa. *Storybook Travels: From Eloise's New York to Harry Potter's London, Visits to 30 of the Best-Loved Landmarks in Children's Literature.* New York: Three Rivers, 2002.

Blake, William. *Poetry for Young People: William Blake.* John Maynard, ed. Illustrated by Alessandra Cimatoribus. New York: Sterling, 2007.

Blass, Rosanne J. *Booktalks, Bookwalks, and Read-Alouds: Promoting the Best New Children's Literature Across the Elementary Currriculum.* Westport, CT: Libraries Unlimited, 2002.

Bodger, Joan. *How the Heather Looks: A Joyous Journey to the British Sources of Children's Books.* Toronto: McClelland and Stewart, 1999 [Originally published 1965].

Book Sense. *Book Sense Best Children's Books: 240 Favorites for All Ages Recommended by Independent Booksellers.* New York: Newmarket, 2005.

Bosman, Julie. "With One Word, Children's Book Sets Off Uproar." *New York Times,* 18 Feb. 2007. http://www.nytimes.com/2007/02/18/books/18newb.html.

Box Office Mojo. 2007. http://www.boxofficemojo.com.

Bradbury, Judy. *Children's Book Corner: A READ-ALOUD Resource with Tips, Techniques, and Plans for Teachers, Librarians, and Parents (Grades 1 and 2).* Westport, CT: Libraries Unlimited, 2004.

Brennan, Georgeanne. *Green Eggs and Ham Cookbook: Recipes Inspired by Dr. Seuss!* New York: Random House, 2006.

Britton, Jason. "A New Day for Design: Five Art Directors Discuss the Evolving Field of Children's Book Design." *Publisher's Weekly,* 28 Oct. 2002: 28–32.

Borders. *Borders Monthly* 10, 26 Dec.–29 Jan. 2007.

Bunting, Eve. Interview by DownHomeBooks.com. May 2006. http://www.downhomebooks.com/bunting.htm.

Children's Book Council (CBC). "Choosing a Children's Book." 2006. http://www.cbcbooks.org/readinglists/choosing.html.

Children's Literature Review (CLR). "Maurice Sendak." *Children's Literature Review* 1 (1976): 166–173.

———. "Maurice Sendak." *Children's Literature Review* 74 (2002): 12–185.

Codell, Esmé Raji. *How to Get Your Child to Love Reading: For Ravenous and Reluctant Readers Alike.* Chapel Hill, NC: Algonquin, 2003.

Coiro, Julie. "Motivating Middle and High School Readers with Booktalks." *Suite 101,* Oct. 1, 2000. http://www.suite101.com/article.cfm/reading/49394.

Cohoon, Lorinda B. Review of Joan Bodger, *How the Heather Looks: A Joyous Journey to the British Sources of Children's Books.* H-Albion, H-Net Reviews. March 2001. http://www.h-net.org/reviews/showrev.cgi?path=11635985222013.

Creel, Ann Howard. *Nicki.* Illustrated by Doron Ben-Ami. American Girls Today series. Middleton, WI: American Girl, 2007.

Criswell, Patti Kelley. *A Smart Girl's Guide to Friendship Troubles: Dealing With Fights, Being Left Out and the Whole Popularity Thing.* Illustrated by Angela Martini. American Girl Library series. Middleton, WI: American Girl, 2003.

D'Amico, Carmela, and Steven D'Amico. *Ella the Elegant Elephant.* New York: Arthur A. Levine, 2004.

Dartford, Mark. *Warships.* Military Hardware in Action series. Minneapolis, MN: Lerner, 2003.

Donnelly, Daria. "Hey! Harry Potter Has Cousins!" *Commonweal* 7 Apr. 2000. http://findarticles.com/p/articles/mi_m1252/is_7_127/ai_61764170.

Driscoll, Michael, ed. *A Child's Introduction to Poetry: Listen While You Learn About the Magic Words that Have Moved Mountains, Won Battles, and Made Us Laugh and Cry.* Illustrated by Meredith Hamilton. New York: Black Dog and Leventhal, 2003.

Fandel, Jennifer. *Puns, Allusions, and Other Word Secrets.* Mankato, MN: Creative Education, 2006.

Fisher, Jennifer. "The Nancy Drew Sleuth Unofficial Website." 2007. http://www.nancydrewsleuth.com.

Fox, Mem. *Reading Aloud: Why Reading Aloud to Our Children Will Change Their Lives Forever.* New York: Harcourt, 2001.

Freedman, Russell. *The Voice that Challenged a Nation: Marian Anderson and the Struggle for Equal Rights.* New York: Clarion, 2004.

Freeman, Judy. *Books Kids Will Sit Still For: The Complete Read-Aloud Guide.* 2nd ed. New York: Bowker, 1990.

———. *Books Kids Will Sit Still For 3: A Read-Aloud Guide.* Westport, CT: Libraries Unlimited, 2006.

————. *More Books Kids Will Sit Still For: A Read-Aloud Guide*. New Providence, NJ: Bowker, 1995.

Giovanni, Nikki. *Rosa*. Illustrated by Brian Collier. New York: Henry Holt, 2005.

Given, David. "Susan Cooper's Wales: A Literary Pilgrimage" [online travelogue]. 2002. http://www.cowlark.com/susan-cooper.html.

Gordon, Shelley M. "Anne 2008" press release, July 24 2006. http://www.gov.pe.ca/visitorsguide/index.php3?number=1016050.

Green, Michele Erica. "Our Trip to England, March–April 2007." 2007. http://www.littlereview.com/england2/englnd07.htm.

Guignon, Anne. "Reading Aloud: Are Students *Ever* Too Old?" *Education World* 5 Nov. 2001. http://www.education-world.com/a_curr/curr081.shtml.

Hamilton, Martha, and Mitch Weiss. *Children Tell Stories: Teaching and Using Storytelling in the Classroom*. Katonah, NY: Richard C. Owen, 2005.

Handler, Daniel. *The Penultimate Peril*. New York: HarperCollins, 2005.

Harris, Robie H., and Michael Emberley. *It's Perfectly Normal: Changing Bodies, Growing Up, Sex, and Sexual Health*. Boston: Candlewick, 2004.

Hollander, John, ed. *Poetry for Young People: Animal Poems*. Illustrated by Simona Mulazzani. New York: Sterling, 2004.

Holyoke, Nancy. *The Big Book of Help! Both of the Absolutely Indispensable Guides to Life for Girls*. [Combines *Help!* and *More Help!*, two earlier volumes.] Illustrated by Scott Nash. Middleton, WI: American Girl, 2004.

Hughes, Langston. *Poetry for Young People: Langston Hughes*. David Roessel and Arnold Rampersad, eds. Illustrated by Benny Andrews. New York: Sterling, 2006.

Hunter, Yvonne. "Penguin Group (Canada) to Become the Official Book Publisher of L.M. Montgomery 100th Anniversary Editions" press release, October 26 2006. http://www.newswire.ca/en/releases/archive/October2006/26/c5272.html.

Janeczko, Paul B., ed. *A Poke in the I: A Collection of Concrete Poems*. Illustrated by Chris Raschka. Cambridge, MA: Candlewick, 2001.

————. *A Kick in the Head: An Everyday Guide to Poetic Forms*. Illustrated by Chris Raschka. Cambridge, MA: Candlewick, 2005.

January, Brendan. *Air Force One*. Cornerstones of Freedom, Second Series. New York: Children's Press, 2004.

Jones, Katharine. "Getting Rid of Children's Literature." *Lion and the Unicorn* 30.3 (2006): 287–315.

Jury, Louise. "Unfinished Masterpieces: Beckham Joins Joyce on List of Books We Never Complete." *The Independent* 12 March 2007. http://www.independent.co.uk/arts-entertainment/books/news/unfinished-masterp.htmls-beckham-joins-joyce-on-list-of-books-we-never-complete-439913.html.

Keane, Nancy. *Booktalking Across the Curriculum: The Middle Years*. Westport, CT: Libraries Unlimited, 2002.

————. *The Big Book of Children's Reading Lists: 100 Great, Ready-to-Use Book Lists for Educators, Librarians, Parents, and Children*. Westport, CT: Libraries Unlimited, 2006.

————. n.d. "Booktalks Quick and Simple." http://nancykeane.com/booktalks/faq.htm.

King, Stephen. "Wild About Harry." *New York Times* 23 July 2000. http://www.nytimes.com/books/00/07/23/reviews/000723.23kinglt.html.

La Monica, Paul R. "The Fox, the Witch, and the Wardrobe: Disney Has a Lot Riding on the Success of *The Chronicles of Narnia* but So Does News Corp." *CNNMoney.com*, Dec. 9 2005.

Lanes, Selma. *Down the Rabbit Hole: Adventures and Misadventures in the Realm of Children's Literature*. New York: Atheneum, 1972.

Laura Ingalls Wilder Memorial Society. 2007. http://www.discoverlaura.org.

Lefebvre, Benjamin. "The Little House Archive." 2006. http://roomofbensown.net/lhotp.

Lewis, Valerie V., and Walter M. Mayes. *Valerie & Walter's Best Books for Children: A Lively, Opinionated Guide*. New York: HarperCollins, 2004.

Leonard, John Leonard. "Nobody Expects the Inquisition." *New York Times* 13 July 2003. http://query.nytimes.com/gst/fullpage.html?res=9c04e1de113af930a25754c0a9659c 8b63.

Lipson, Eden Ross. *The New York Times Parent's Guide to the Best Books for Children*. New York: Three Rivers Press, 2000.

Louisa May Alcott Memorial Association. "Orchard House—Home of the Alcotts." 2007. http://www.louisamayalcott.org.

Lurie, Alison. *Boys and Girls Forever: Children's Classics from Cinderella to Harry Potter*. New York: Penguin, 2003.

Marcus, Leonard M. *Storied City: A Children's Book Walking-Tour Guide to New York City*. New York: Dutton, 2003.

Maughan, Shannon. "Listservs Buzz Over Newbery Winner." *Publisher's Weekly,* 15 Feb. 2007a. http://www.publishersweekly.com/article/CA6416737.html.

———. "Controversy Over Newbery Winner: A Followup." *Publisher's Weekly,* 22 Feb. 2007b. http://www.publishersweekly.com/article/CA6418417.html.

Mehegan, David. "'Narnia' Books Getting a Boost from Film." *Boston Globe* 5 Oct. 2005. http://brothersjuddblog.com/archives/2005/10/supersized_subc.html.

Meigs, Cornelia, Anne Thaxter Eaton, Elizabeth Nesbitt, and Ruth Hill Viguers. *A Critical History of Children's Literature: A Survey of Children's Books in English*. Rev. ed. New York: Macmillan, 1969.

Midgette, Anne. "An Orphan's Tale Retold, Refined and Repackaged." *New York Times* 10 Apr. 2007. http://theater2.nytimes.com/2007/04/10/theater/reviews/10gabl.html.

Mitchell-Marell, Gabrielle. "Little House Under Renovation." *Publisher's Weekly* 4 Dec. 2006. http://www.publishersweekly.com/article/CA6396630.html.

Mommy Track'd. "The Anti Princess Reading List." *Mommy Track'd—The Working Mother's Guide to Managed Chaos*. 2007. http://mommytrackd.com/readingroom. php?id=5.

Murphy, Jim. *An American Plague: The True and Terrifying Story of the Yellow Fever Epidemic of 1793*. New York: Clarion, 2003.

Niehaus, Alisa, and Alan Hecker. *Piratepedia*. New York: Dorling Kindersley, 2006.

New York Times. "One Troublesome Word." *New York Times* 21 Feb. 2007. http://www.nytimes.com/2007/02/21/opinion/21wed4.html.

Pandya, Gitesh. "All Time Domestic Blockbusters." *Box Office Guru*. http://www.boxofficeguru. com/blockbusters.htm. [Accessed April 2, 2007]

Parks Canada. "Attendance 2001–2002 to 2005–2006." Sept. 15 2006. http://www.pc.gc.ca/ docs/pc/attend/table2_e.asp.

Parravano, Martha V., and Lauren Adams. "A Wider Vision for the Newbery." *Horn Book* (January/February 1996). http://www.hbook.com/magazine/editorials/jan96.asp.

Portis, Antoinette. *Not a Box*. New York: Harper, 2006.

Powell's. Powellsbooks.kids newsletter, January 19 2007. http://www.powells.com/ kidsnews.html. "Children's Bookshelf." *Publisher's Weekly* electronic newsletter, 12 Apr. 2007.

Rappaport, Doreen. *Martin's Big Words: The Life of Dr. Martin Luther King, Jr.* Illustrated by Bryan Collier. New York: Hyperion, 2001.

Rich, Motoko, and Julie Bosman. "'Bye Harry,' Sob Booksellers, Investors . . . Oh, and Kids." *New York Times* 2 Feb. 2007. http://gawker.com/news/new-york-times/bye-harry-sob-booksellers-investors----oh-and-motoko-rich-and-julie-bosman-233471.php?mail2=true.

Richardson, Justin, and Peter Parnell. *And Tango Makes Three*. Illustrated by Henry Cole. New York: Simon and Schuster, 2005.

Ruethling, Ann, and Patti Pitcher. *Under the Chinaberry Tree: Books and Inspirations for Mindful Parenting*. New York: Broadway Books, 2003.

Scieszka, Jon. "Design Matters." Designed by Molly Leach. *Horn Book* (Mar./Apr. 1998). http://www.hbook.com/publications/magazine/articles/mar98_scieszka_leach.asp.

———. Interviews. Reading Rockets. 2006. http://www.readingrockets.org/books/interviews/scieszka/transcript.

Schirmer Inc. "Mark Adamo." Jan. 2007. http://www.schirmer.com.

Schlitz, Laura Amy. *A Drowned Maiden's Hair: A Melodrama.* Cambridge, MA: Candlewick, 2006.

Scott, Mark. n.d. "Susan Cooper's Wales." http://www.thelostland.com/scwales.htm.

Serio, John N. *Poetry for Young People: The Seasons.* Illustrated by Robert Crockett. New York: Sterling, 2005.

Serlin, David, and Brian Selznick. "Where the Wild Things Were: An Interview with Leonard S. Marcus." *Cabinet* 9 Winter 2002–2003. http://www.cabinetmagazine.org/issues/9/wherewild.php.

Shuter, Jane. *Life in a Roman Fort.* Picture the Past series. Chicago: Heinemann, 2005.

Silvey, Anita, ed. *The Essential Guide to Children's Books and Their Creators.* Boston, MA: Houghton Mifflin, 2002.

School Library Journal (SLJ), Staff of. "One Hundred Books that Shaped the Century." *School Library Journal* 1 Jan. 2000. http://www.schoollibraryjournal.com/article/CA153035.html.

Smith, Julia Null. "Review of Picture Books." *Austin American-Statesman* Apr. 1 2007. http://www.statesman.com/life/content/life/stories/books/04/01/1kidsbooks.html.

Sones, Sonia. *What My Mother Doesn't Know.* New York: Simon and Schuster, 2001.

Sutton, Roger. "I Just Want To Say This One Thing About the Newbery." *Read Roger* Web log Jan. 24 2007a. http://www.hbook.com/blog/2007/01/i-just-want-to-say-this-one-thing.html.

———. "Second Verse, Same as the First." *Read Roger* Web log Mar. 6 2007b. http://www.hbook.com/blog/2007/03/second-verse-same-as-first.html.

Sutton, Roger, and Martha V. Parravano. "Guess How Much I Love You, Catcher in the Rye?" *Horn Book* May/June 2004.

Thomas, Mary. Review of Joan Bodger's *How the Heather Looked. CM: Canadian Review of Materials,* Sept. 22 2000. http://www.umanitoba.ca/cm////vol7/no2/heather.html.

Thompson, Ellen A. n.d. "Rah-rah reading!" http://www.scholastic.com/librarians/ab/articles/rahrah.htm [Accessed Apr. 15, 2007.]

Travers, P.L. *Mary Poppins in the Kitchen: A Cookery Book with a Story.* Illustrations by Mary Shepard. Orlando, FL: Harcourt, 1975 (reissued 2006).

Trelease, Jim. *The Read-Aloud Handbook.* 6th ed. New York: Penguin, 2006.

Valencia, Jane. "An American Harper in Wales." 1997. http://www.eldalamberon.com/jane.html.

Vandergrift, Kay. "Vandergrift's Children's Literature Page." 2007. http://www.scils.rutgers.edu/~kvander/ChildrenLit/reading.html.

Weatherford, Carole. *Moses: When Harriet Tubman Led Her People to Freedom.* New York: Hyperion, 2006.

Wentz, Melanie. *Once Upon a Time in Great Britain: A Travel Guide to the Sights and Settings of Your Favorite Children's Stories.* New York: St. Martin's Griffin, 2002.

Wilcox, Leah. *Falling for Rapunzel.* Illustrated by Lydia Monks. New York: Putnam, 2003.

Wiley, Melissa. "Here in the Bonny Glen: Little House." 2007. http://melissawiley.typepad.com/bonnyglen/little_house/index.html.

Wilson, Martin. "Off the Bookshelf" column (review of *How the Heather Looks*). *Austin Chronicle* 5 Nov. 1999. http://www.austinchronicle.com/gyrobase/Issue/review?oid=74524.

Yolen, Jane. *How Do Dinosaurs Say Goodnight?* Illustrated by Mark Teague. New York: Blue Sky Press, 2000.

Young, Terrence E., Jr. "Booktalking." American Library Association. 2003. http://www.ala.org/ala/aasl/aaslpubsandjournals/kqweb/kqreviews/networth/v32n1.htm.

Zipes, Jack, ed. in chief. *The Oxford Encyclopedia of Children's Literature*. New York: Oxford University Press, 2006.

Zipes, Jack, Lissa Paul, Lynne Vallone, Peter Hunt, and Gillian Avery. *The Norton Anthology of Children's Literature: The Traditions in English*. New York: Norton, 2005.

Further Reading

Griswold, Jerry. *Feeling Like a Kid: Childhood and Children's Literature*. Baltimore, MD: Johns Hopkins, 2006; Lanes, Selma G. *Through the Looking Glass: Further Adventures and Misadventures in the Realm of Children's Literature*. Boston: David R. Godine, 2004; Smith, Cynthia Leitich. *Children's and Young Adult Literature Resources*. http://www.cynthialeitichsmith.com/lit_resources/cyalr_index.html; Trelease, Jim. *The Read-Aloud Handbook*. 6th ed. New York: Penguin, 2006; Zipes, Jack D. *Sticks and Stones: The Troublesome Success of Children's Literature from Slovenly Peter to Harry Potter*. New York: Routledge, 2001.

PEGGY LIN DUTHIE

CHRISTIAN FICTION

Definition. Christian Fiction is a term used to designate works of fiction specifically intended for or marketed to Christian readers. Unlike most literary genres, Christian Fiction is delineated primarily in marketing terms. While particular authors are associated with and prominent in the production of Christian Fiction, the primary factors in whether or not a work is designated as such are more often its publisher and consumer identification. Rather than thinking of Christian Fiction as a unique genre, it may be helpful to think of it as a compilation of subsets of other genres. Some of the most popular genres within Christian Fiction include: **Historical Fiction, Romance Novels, Fantasy Literature,** Supernatural Fiction, and **Children's Literature.** Christian Fiction addresses itself predominantly to Protestant readers. A broad definition of the term can be used to allow the inclusion of Roman Catholic authors and commercially successful or historically significant works that deal with religious themes or characters. As the term is currently most widely used, however, Christian Fiction generally refers to works specifically tailored to meet the specifications and guidelines of its publishers in order to create a fictional work that is deemed appropriate for the target audience.

Because the definition of Christian Fiction depends upon extrinsic factors as well as intrinsic qualities to distinguish it from mainstream works by Christian authors, the categorizing of works within the genre can appear somewhat arbitrary. This qualification is especially true of works old enough to be in the public domain. John Bunyan's *The Pilgrim's Progress* has all the intrinsic features of Christian Fiction but is readily available in over a dozen editions, many by commercial publishers not

---

IS THERE A WIDER AUDIENCE FOR CHRISTIAN FICTION?

The narrow focus of a marketing-derived definition, combined with the exclusion of works of academic or historical interest from the category, may appear to make Christian Fiction a deprecatory label. For an author to eschew it is generally not thought of as a rejection of his or her identity as a Christian but rather a desire to address a wider audience. John Grisham, Graham Greene, and Madeleine L'Engle are examples of writers who have been open about their religious affiliations, but whose literary success and reputation extend beyond Christian audiences and hence are not widely thought of as authors of Christian Fiction.

marketing directly to Christian audiences. Edmund Spenser's *The Faerie Queen,* like Bunyan's work, is widely anthologized. Despite these works' obvious Christian themes and historical influence, they do not lend themselves to the designation of Christian Fiction since interest in them extends beyond exclusively Christian readers.

History. If Christian Fiction is thought of as a marketing term, then its history is that of a series of canonical authors and more that of its publishers. The major publishers of Christian Fiction are Zondervan, Tyndale House, Thomas Nelson/Westbow Press, Bethany House Publishers, and Harvest House Publishers. Christian Fiction is usually a product line or division within a company and not an exclusive focus. Alternately, it may be the central focus of the subsidiary of a larger company that has a diverse range of publishing or media related products.

Defining Christian Fiction by market also means that authors who achieve success both within and outside of Christian reading circles will be difficult to classify. The two most prominent examples of this difficulty are C.S. (Clive Staples) Lewis and George MacDonald. Lewis's renown for writing Christian apologetics combined with the explicitly Christian themes of his allegorical and fantasy fiction helped make his works fixtures at Christian bookstores even before Christian Fiction was thought of as a separate genre. Lewis would be a notable figure for his literary criticism (*A Preface to Paradise Lost, Studies in Words,* and *An Experiment in Criticism, English Literature in the Sixteenth Century: Excluding Drama*) and apologetics (*Mere Christianity, Miracles,* and *The Great Divorce*) even if he had not written fiction. It could be argued that Lewis wrote for a Christian audience, but that this audience was viewed as a subset of the general reading audience and not totally divorced from it.

George MacDonald was a Scottish minister and author of fiction in the nineteenth century. Although he was widely known and read during his lifetime, many of MacDonald's works fell out of print during the twentieth century. C.S. Lewis edited an influential anthology of excerpts from MacDonald's works and famously credited MacDonald's fantasy work, *Phantastes,* for influencing his own thought. G.K. (Gilbert Keith) Chesterton similarly praised MacDonald's *The Princess and the Goblin.* In addition to his fantasy works and compilations of sermons, MacDonald also wrote novels revolving around the lives of Christian characters beginning with *David Elginbrod* (1862). These works, sometimes referred to as the Scottish Novels, helped the genre of Christian Fiction to take shape when they were reissued in edited and abridged form by Michael Phillips beginning in the 1980s.

It must be conceded that Phillips has been successful in reviving interest in MacDonald's novels, which can be found increasingly in unedited, reissued form in addition to the edited forms more widely sold in Christian Fiction venues. Whether this renewed interest has come at the cost of marginalizing MacDonald as a literary figure is an open question. One of Phillips's biographical sketches states that his purpose in editing MacDonald's fiction was to attract a publisher and "to make MacDonald's stories and spiritual wisdom attractive and compelling to a new and less literarily patient reading audience" (Macdonaldphillips.com Web site 2006, Online). This quote implies a tailoring of the material to the tastes and requirements of the market audience, which is a primary feature of Christian Fiction, but it also helps clarify the distinction between MacDonald's work and Phillips's use of it. Ultimately, it could be argued that it is Phillips (as an editor and author) who is producing Christian Fiction and not MacDonald, even if variants of MacDonald's work are currently more widely read than the originals.

The literary work from the past that most closely resembles the description, effect, and cultural work of the Christian Fiction of today may be Charles M. Sheldon's *In His Steps*. Sheldon's novel, originally published in 1896, is best known for popularizing the slogan "What would Jesus do?" It was published serially by a weekly religious magazine, *The Advance,* and proved immensely popular among Christian readers (Neighbors 1998, Online). The novel focuses on the Reverend Henry Maxwell and his parishioners, who experience spiritual growth and insight as they respond to a stranger's call to help the poor and powerless by vowing to act in their respective professions as they believe Jesus would have acted were he in their place.

Like George MacDonald, Sheldon was also a Christian minister, but he wrote while still heading a congregation. Perhaps for that reason, *In His Steps* is generally more positive in its depiction of institutional religion, an attitude that is more typical of Christian Fiction since it is directed toward a religiously orthodox and socially conservative audience. In addition to its generally positive portrayal of institutional religion, *In His Steps* shares several other stylistic features with later Christian Fiction. The style is plain in order to attract the broadest possible audience. Chuck Neighbors points out that Sheldon developed *In His Steps* as one of a series of sermon stories designed to increase church attendance. The context in and purpose for which the narrative was created required an episodic and thematic repetitiveness, features that make it easy to pick up or put down at any point within the narrative, but which can lead to criticisms that it lacks narrative or moral complexity. This style is not without historical antecedents or parallels, but it differs widely from the movement toward psychological depth, ambiguity, and narrative complexity privileged throughout most of the twentieth century.

The late 1970s and the 1980s began to see the emergence of Christian Fiction as a genre with Christian publishers marketing contemporary authors producing new works and not simply disseminating classic literature deemed appropriate for Christian audiences. Paul C. Gutjahr has argued persuasively that the growth of Christian Fiction in general, and the Christian Novel in particular, can be tied to the emergence of the Internet company, Amazon.com, which provided a means of word-of-mouth advertising (in the form of customer reviews), distribution, and marketing previously lacking for product lines geared toward a niche audience (Gutjahr 2002, 218). The Internet provided an alternate means of distribution for products not carried by more traditional or conservative independent Christian booksellers. Two writers whose success at this time helped define the nature and future direction of Christian Fiction were Janette Oke and Frank Peretti.

Trends and Themes. *The Left Behind* series, conceived by Tim LaHaye and written primarily by Jerry B. Jenkins, had an unquestionable influence in the development and direction of Christian Fiction as a literary genre. Published by Tyndale House, a publishing company of Christian books and other media, its popularity coincided with (and could reasonably said to have helped prompt) a greater interest in publishing companies to produce works of fiction directly targeted at Christian readers.

The seminal novel in the franchise, initially published in 1995, was entitled *Left Behind: A Novel of the Earth's Last Days*. Set during and immediately after the rapture (instantaneous ascent into heaven of true Christians), the novel is roughly structured around the responses to world events of four characters that are left behind on earth after the rapture: Rayford Steele, a pilot; Chloe Steele, Rayford's daughter; Buck Williams, a journalist; and Bruce Barnes, an assistant pastor.

Although garnering mixed reviews, *Left Behind* achieved a commercial success that is indisputable. It prompted twelve sequels and another three prequels as well as a series of books for adolescents that mirror the events in the novel but center around youthful protagonists. At least three of the novels have been made into motion pictures, although these have been primarily disseminated through church showings and direct to video sales rather than theatrical runs. The series was also the subject of at least one computer video game, *Left Behind: Eternal Forces,* in which players assume the role of characters in the novel and attempt to evangelize and recruit onlookers to fight the propaganda and attacks of the Global Community Peackeepers. The first two novels, *Left Behind* and *Tribulation Force* have also been reproduced as graphic novels, each in five volumes.

Critical responses to *Left Behind* have been sparse. While some Christian readers and critics have used the series popularity to promote or question theological interpretations of its source material, most secular reviews have tended to engage in cultural criticism, opting to conjecture about the causes and meaning of the work's popularity rather than engaging in any sort of formal analysis. Some of the more notable critical responses are mentioned in the "Context and Issues" section below.

One of the most significant effects of the *Left Behind* franchise may have been that its success instigated a broader and more sustained effort within Christian and secular publishing to service the market of Christian readers. Before the success of *Left Behind,* the prevalent attitude appears to have been that for a Christian artist (writer, musician, or performer) to be successful, he or she would have to produce a "cross-over" work—one that appealed to audiences outside of the target demographic of his or her genre. *Left Behind* demonstrated in the publishing industry what Mel Gibson's *The Passion of the Christ* would illustrate a decade later in the film industry: niche marketing could, in some circumstances, result in commercial profits that could be comparable to those generated by mass market works of fiction or film. Since the publication and success of *Left Behind* in the mid-1990s, no other single work or series of Christian Fiction has emerged to rival its popularity and impact. What has emerged is an awareness of the Christian consumer as a marketing force. Niche marketing as a trend is not unique to Christian publishing. However, it has had an especially marked effect in changing the face of that industry as indicated by the growing diversity of product lines within Christian Fiction and the increasing participation in major publishing corporations in servicing the Christian market, either through the creation of subsidiaries, or through business partnerships with traditional Christian publishers.

Founded in 1931 as a bookselling company, Zondervan is one of the oldest and most widely recognized publishers of Christian books, in large part because of its partnership with the International Bible Society in producing the New International Version of the Bible in the 1970s and its chain of bookstores bearing its name (Zondervan Web site 2006, Online). Gutjahr has classified Zondervan as the publishing house "most committed to producing Christian novels in the mid-twentieth century" but points out that its success in doing so was hindered by independent Christian bookstore owners (Gutjahr 2002, 213–214). Its visibility has risen more recently due to the success of Rick Warren's *The Purpose Driven Life* in 2002. Although Zondervan is prominent among Christian publishers, its production of Christian Fiction has not been as extensive as its production of other types of Christian publications. Authors of Christian Fiction who have published with Zondervan include Karen Kingsbury and Cindy Kenney.

Karen Kingsbury's biography identifies her as an inspirational novelist, and she has trademarked the label Life-Changing Fiction to describe her work. This definition is used to characterize the desired effect of the fiction on the audience as opposed to the intrinsic qualities of it. These desired effects include "improved marriages, spiritual awakening and new-found hope" (Karen Kingsbury: Life Changing Fiction Web site 2006, Online). Kingsbury has had at least one novel, *Deadly Pretender*, adapted into a made for television film, *Every Woman's Dream*. Her work also includes two titles, *One Tuesday Morning* and *Beyond Tuesday Morning* in the "911 Series," which focuses on fictional characters responding to the terrorist attacks on the World Trade Center in New York on September 11, 2001.

Cindy Kenney has written over twenty children's books featuring the characters from VeggieTales. These characters were developed in a line of home videos by Big Idea, Inc., in which simply animated vegetables reenact Biblical stories or other stories designed to reinforce moral lessons. Kenney is identified as a senior managing editor for Big Idea, which owns the VeggieTales name. The VeggieTales books, which bear her name as author, are published by Zonderkidz, the children's group of Zondervan, and carry the series label Big Idea Books.

Established in 1962, Tyndale House Publishers was founded by Kenneth N. Taylor. Primarily known for publishing *The Living Bible*, a paraphrase of the Christian Bible in contemporary English, Tyndale House also published works from prominent Christian authors of non-fiction, including Josh McDowell and James Dobson. In addition to the *Left Behind* franchise, Tyndale also publishes works by Karen Kingsbury, Frank Peretti, Catherine Palmer, Francine Rivers, Dee Henderson, and Brock and Bodie Thoene.

Brock and Bodie Thoene have written over forty novels in various series of Historical Fiction. Much of their work centers on the nation of Israel, much with a pro-Zionist flavor. Bodie Thoene is the primary writer of the team, with Brock providing historical research necessary for the genre (Bodie and Brock Thoene Official Web site 2007, Online).

Francine Rivers wrote Romance Novels before becoming a "born-again" Christian, at which time she began writing works with Christian themes (Francine Rivers Web site 2007, Online). Her best known title is probably *The Last Sin Eater*, which was adapted into a feature film by FoxFaith in 2007.

Thomas Nelson is one of the oldest and longest established Christian publishers. Named after its founder, Thomas Nelson's original mission was to provide Christian works and literary classics to the general public. Thomas Nelson was acquired by Sam Moore and the National Book Company in the 1960s (Thomas Nelson Web site, Online). Spurred by sales of the New King James Version of the Christian Bible, Thomas Nelson was also an active participant in the renaissance of Christian Fiction, publishing works by Frank Peretti, Stephen R. Lawhead, and Ted Dekker.

Stephen R. Lawhead has written novels in the genre of mythic history as well as imaginative fiction. He was an editor and staff writer for *Campus Life* magazine before writing *The Dragon King Trilogy* and *The Pendragon Cycle*. The latter consisted of five novels set against the backdrop of Arthurian Romance: *Taliesen, Merlin, Arthur, Pendragon,* and *Grail* (Stephen R. Lawhead Web site 2007, Online). He has also published a novel, *Hood,* using the Robin Hood legend as inspiration.

Ted Dekker is part of the second wave of Christian Fiction authors, writing full-time since 1997. Dekker writes Horror Fiction and, as mentioned above, collaborated with Frank Peretti to write *House*. His best known title is probably *Thr3e*, which was made into a feature film in 2006.

Context and Issues. The genre and its authors have not escaped criticism. It is perhaps not a coincidence that Christian Fiction's rise paralleled the success of political and religious conservatism in the United States symbolized by the popularity and political success of Ronald Reagan. Because the targeted readers of Christian Fiction are part of an evangelical tradition that is in general suspicious of the purported demoralizing power of art and hostile to the ideologies and philosophies informing most of the prominent literary movements of the twentieth century, it may not be surprising that work directed toward them is often accused of lacking rhetorical sophistication, imagination, ambiguity, or complexity.

Jay R. Howard has described Peretti's work as part of what Donald Heinz called the New Christian Right's attempt to create a "counter-mythology" against that of "secular humanism" (Howard 1993, 195). Kenneth R. Morefield has gone so far as to label LaHaye's and Jenkins's *Left Behind* franchise "evangelical pornography." Implicit in both critiques is the observation that the moral belief system informing the producers and consumers of Christian Fiction support an "oversimplified picture of social reality" (Howard 1993, 195) that distorts or caricaturizes antagonists to Christian characters and, by implication, the readers who share their beliefs.

A less dramatic but still substantial criticism of Christian Fiction is that by promoting the production of fiction tailored to the beliefs of a particular audience, it obscures the value of moral or spiritual insight into the human condition that may be embedded or found in traditional genre works directed toward a general audience. Scott Derrickson argues that the production of great art consistent with any ideological perspective is to some degree dependant upon familiarity with the historical movements and masterpieces of its medium. He also states that "nothing is more easily resisted than subcultural religious language" (Derrickson 2002, 23). The creation of a separate genre in which Christian themes can be unilaterally addressed and advocated without serious resistance from readers or opposition from other works can potentially create a marginalized ghetto that retards not only Christian interaction with secular art, but secular culture's interaction with Christian ideas. Compartmentalizing art from different ideological or theological perspectives could be argued to mitigate whatever latent power art has to engender dialogue which might retard the increasing polarization over religious and social issues currently so prevalent in the United States.

Reception. The commercial success of Mel Gibson's *The Passion of the Christ* in 2004 was large enough to make studios and publishing companies take note of the economic potential in marketing to evangelical Christians. Twentieth-Century Fox has since launched FoxFaith, a distribution label for "morally driven" films with "overt Christian Content." As is typical in the industry in general, the publishing of Christian Fiction is increasingly one part of a company's diverse product line that spans several media forms. There have been theatrical, television, and direct-to-video adaptations of works by LaHaye, Dekker, and Oke within the last decade, and Walden Media has begun producing film adaptations of C.S. Lewis's *Narnia* series. While Fox created its own distribution line to target the Christian audience, it is likely that there will continue to be cooperative efforts between larger studios with production resources and smaller, faith-based companies that hold the rights to titles of possible interest to the Christian market. Zondervan, for example, became a subsidiary of HarperCollins in 1988.

The increased attention paid to Christian consumers of media entertainment has generally been looked upon favorably by those consumers. There have, however, been some cultural critics who have raised questions about the rising commercialization of Christian art and media entertainment. E.J. Park has suggested that "commercialized forms make a mockery of serious things without even intending to do so, because they exist to serve the logic of commercialism" (Park 2006, 70). He further reminds Christian readers that form matters and, echoing Marshall McLuhan, that the medium as well as the content carries with it messages, some of which may ironically or deliberately undermine that of the content.

M. Leary has further commented that commercial concerns have not only affected Christian art but the criticism surrounding and evaluating it as well. Leary claims that there is a "theoretical vacuum" in which "Christian film criticism" operates. According to Leary, unless critics of Christian media "respond to this vacuum with a set of focal points, identity markers, and theologically-based critical strategies," (Leary 2007, Online) then critical inquiry into Christian film and fiction will continue to be dominated by the marketers, rather than by consumers or critics. The blurred line between marketing and criticism is neither new nor unique to fiction or film directed toward Christians. Because Christian Fiction has garnered very little academic interest or inquiry, the bulk of criticism of individual titles has been in commercial venues that are, perhaps, more susceptible to the influence of the marketing efforts of studios and publishers.

Selected Authors. If there is a single title or work that marks the beginning of Christian Fiction in its current form, it is probably Janette Oke's *Love Comes Softly*. Published in 1979 by Bethany House, *Love Comes Softly* eventually sold over eight million copies and spawned a made-for-television film adaptation. Oke would eventually pen seven additional novels in the series, which eventually grew to comprise over seventy novels. *Love Comes Softly* is an historical romance, combining the genres of Historical Fiction and Romance Novel as is common in Christian Fiction.

The protagonist of the novel is Marty Clarige, a pregnant 19-year-old who suddenly finds herself a widow while traveling West during the 1800s and, in desperation, accepts a marriage of convenience.

The predominance of the Romance Novel within the genre of Christian Fiction, both in its emergent and current form, is testament to the preponderance of women readers in the Christian Fiction market (Fisher 2000, 6). While it may initially seem odd that the Romance Novel would be such a popular genre within Christian Fiction, Oke's success demonstrated that there was a market for work that conformed to the conventions of the Romance Novel but which did not endorse nor portray sexual encounters that would be inconsistent with conservative religious or social values. It is not uncommon for publishers of Christian Fiction to provide publishing guidelines that specifically address the depiction of human sexuality in such a way that helps clearly delineate examples of Christian Fiction from other Romance Novels or from Historical Fiction. Tyndale House Publishers, for example, instructs prospective authors that:

> "While many Christian stories have characters that are romantically attracted to each other, they must at the same time uphold the principles of Biblical sexual purity. Along with physical attraction, healthy Christian dating relationships should also involve spiritual, intellectual and emotional attractions." (Tyndale House Publishers 2006, Online)

Tyndale was not Oke's publisher, nor is Christian Romance one of its major product lines, but its publishing standards are not unique. As with secular Romance Novels, there can be variations between publishers and series in what sorts of content is permitted. The foundation of such restrictions upon current, orthodox interpretations of Biblical guidelines for sexual relationships is, of course, the major demarcating line between Romance Novels that are Christian Fiction and those that are not.

Frank Peretti published his first novel, *This Present Darkness* in 1986. It deals with the denizens of a small town, Ashton, whose conflicts are paralleled by a battle between angelic and demonic forces. It was followed by a sequel, *Piercing the Darkness,* in 1989. The two novels have sold over 3.5 million copies (Frank Peretti Web site 2006, Online), helping expand the parameters of Christian Fiction beyond the Romance Novel and demonstrating that new works could be commercially successful. Peretti's other works include *Tilly* (1988), a prose retelling of a radio drama that deals with the issue of abortion, *Prophet* (1992), a thriller set in the world of media journalism, *The Oath* (1995), a murder mystery/horror story, and *The Visitation* (1999), about a self-proclaimed messiah who appears in a small town in Washington. He has also written youth fiction, including an eight book series called *The Cooper Kids Adventure Series* and an additional two book series called *The Veritas Project,* about a family of investigators that alternately evokes *The X-Files* and The Hardy Boys. More recently, he has teamed with Ted Dekker to produce *House* (2006), a supernatural thriller.

Peretti's role in expanding the borders of Christian Fiction cannot be understated. While maintaining themes and techniques similar to earlier, didactic fiction such as Sheldon's *In His Steps,* Peretti's work skirted the fringes of genres previously rejected by Christian readers: Horror, **Suspense Novels,** and Political Thrillers. While his early work might be called derivative—*This Present Darkness* sometimes reads like C.S. Lewis's *The Screwtape Letters* in narrative form—Peretti's ability to put a Christian spin on hot button issues or popular genres helped create diversity within Christian Fiction that a slavish adherence to formula or historical tastes would not. Rather than simply repeat the success of *This Present Darkness* with further allegorical works about spiritual warfare, Peretti's subsequent work used different genres to explore contemporary issues from an evangelical Christian perspective. He describes that progression this way:

> In *This Present Darkness,* it was spiritual warfare and intercessory prayer. In *Piercing the Darkness,* it had to do with the encroachment of neo-paganism into the educational and legal system. And in *Prophet,* it dealt with the Truth and really living by the Truth. In *The Oath,* it was sin depicted as this monster waiting to devour us that we just kind of ignore. In *The Visitation,* it was the false Christ that so many of us are serving. We have our own idea of what Jesus ought to be like. And in *Monster*—whoooh!—there's a whole lot of different messages. My first idea was evolution. One of evolution's best-kept secrets is that mutations don't work. They're not beneficial. I believe that if I can just create a story that somehow addresses that one leg of evolution, I can get people thinking. I can't make a big scientific argument. I can just tell the story. One of the best ways to really combat the fortress of Darwinism is to allow people to wonder about it, to acquaint them with the controversy so that they know there is one. (Frank Peretti Web site 2006, Online)

Peretti's influence on the formation of Christian Fiction is undeniable. Peretti created a template for the integration of overtly Christian content into genre work that has been utilized by subsequent authors of Christian Fiction such as Ted Dekker and Terri Blackstock. Peretti also illustrated that Christian Fiction could perform the cultural work of reinforcing the theological, cultural, and political positions of its audience by embodying the perceived consequences of those positions in narrative form. Unlike its antecedents, Peretti's Christian Fiction—most notably *Piercing the Darkness* and *The Prophet*—did not limit itself to depicting the individual lives of Christians and their immediate environment but also depicted those individuals and their subculture interacting with the largely secular cultural and political world from with which they are enmeshed. This latter trait was picked up on and extended by Tim LaHaye and Jerry B. Jenkins in their *Left Behind* franchise, and Peretti's literary (if not theological) influence on the series is evident. In fact, LaHaye reportedly approached Peretti about writing *Left Behind* before settling on Jenkins as his partner (Gutjahr 2002, 216).

With the emergence of a Christian market of readers and a group of authors following in Peretti's wake who were willing to tailor their fiction to it, Christian Fiction became a staple of Christian publishers and not merely an afterthought.

Bibliography

Dekker, Ted. *Thr3e.* Nashville, TN: Word Publications, 2003.

Kingsbury, Karen. *Beyond Tuesday Morning.* Grand Rapids, MI: Zondervan, 2004.

———. *Deadly Pretender.* New York: Dell, 1994.

———. *One Tuesday Morning.* Grand Rapids, MI: Zondervan, 2003.

LaHaye, Tim, and Jerry B. Jenkins. *Left Behind: A Novel of the Earth's Last Days.* Wheaton, IL: Tyndale House, 1995.

Lawhead, Stephen R. *Arthur.* Westchester, IL: Crossway Books, 1989.

———. *Grail.* New York: Avon, 1996.

———. *Hood.* Nashville, TN: WestBow, 2006.
———. *Merlin.* Westchester, IL: Crossway Books, 1988.
———. *Pendragon.* New York: W. Morrow, 1994.
———. *Taliesen.* Westchester, IL: Crossway Books, 1987.
Oke, Janette. *Love Comes Softly.* Minneapolis, MN: Bethany Fellowship, 1979.
Peretti, Frank. *The Oath.* Dallas, TX: Word Publications, 1995.
———. *This Present Darkness.* Westchester, IL: Crossway Books, 1986.
———. *Piercing the Darkness.* Westchester, IL: Crossway Books, 1989.
———. *Prophet.* Wheaton, IL: Crossway Books, 1992.
———. *Tilly.* Westchester, IL: Crossway Books, 1988.
———. *The Visitation.* Nashville, TN: Word Publications, 1999.
Rivers, Francine. *The Last Sin Eater.* Wheaton, IL: Tyndale House, 1998.

Further Reading

About Fox Faith [Online, 2007]. FoxFaith Web site. <http://www.foxfaith.com/>; About the Author [Online, 2006]. Frank Peretti Web site. <http://frankperetti.com/biography-119>; About the Author [Online, 2007]. Stephen R. Lawhead Web site. <http://www.stephenlawhead. com/author/>; About the Authors [Online, 2007]. Bodie and Brock Thoene Official Web site <http://www.thoenebooks.com/about.asp>; Become an Author. [Online, 2006]. Tyndale House Publishers Web site. <http://www.tyndale.com/authors/details.asp?id=10>; Biography. [Online, 2007]. Francine Rivers Web site. <http://www.francinerivers.com/about.asp>; Carpenter, Humphrey. *The Inklings: C.S. Lewis, J.R.R. Tolkien, Charles Williams, and Their Friends.* London: Allen & Unwin, 1978; Christopher, Joe R., and Joan K. Ostling. *C.S. Lewis: An Annotated Checklist of Writings about Him and His Works.* Kent, OH: Kent State University Press, 1973; Derrickson, Scott. "Behind the Lens: A Christian Filmmaker in Hollywood" *The Christian Century* 30 Jan. 2002: 20–24; Duriez, Colin. The *C.S. Lewis Encyclopedia : A Complete Guide to His Life, Thought, and Writings.* Wheaton, IL: Crossway Books, 2000; Fisher, Allan. "Evangelical-Christian Publishing: Where It's Been and Where It's Going." *Publishing Resource Quarterly* 14.3 (Fall 1998): 3–11; Frequently Asked Questions. [Online, December 2006]. Frank Peretti Web site. <http://www.frankperetti.com/ frequentlyaskedquestions.htm>; Full Biography [Online, December 2006]. Karen Kingsbury: Life Changing Fiction Web site <http://www.karenkingsbury.com/aboutKaren/biography/>; Gutjahr, Paul C. "No Longer Left Behind: Amazon.com, Reader-Response, and the Changing Fortunes of the Christian Novel in America." *Book History* 5 (2002): 209–236; Hein, Rolland. *George MacDonald: Victorian Mythmaker.* Nashville: StarSong, 1993; Howard, Jay R. "Vilifying the Enemy: The Christian Right and the Novels of Frank Peretti." *Journal of Popular Culture* 28.3 (1994): 193–206; Leary, M. How Should We Then Review? [Online, 2007]. The Matthew's House Project Web site. <http://www.thematthewshouseproject.com/ criticism/columns/mleary/jan07.htm>; MacDonald, Greville. *George MacDonald and His Wife.* 1924. With an Introduction by G.K. Chesteron. Whitehorn, CA: Johannesesn, 1998; Miller, Timothy. *Following In His Steps: A Biography of Charles M. Sheldon.* Knoxville: University of Tennessee Press, 1988; Morefield, Kenneth R. *Left Behind* as Evangelical Pornography. [Online, 2007]. The Matthew's House Project Web site. <http://web.mac.com/ zkincaid/iWeb/MHP/culture/68059FA6-2AAC-4601-A2D8-FD17B780E6CF.html>; More-field, Kenneth R. "Why Christian Fiction?: Expressing Universal Truth in a Relative World." PhD dissertation, Northern Illinois University, 1998; Neighbors, Chuck. The Story of *In His Steps.* [Online, December 2006]. <http://www.mastersimage.com/articles/ihs.htm>; Our History [Online, December 2006]. Zondervan Web site <http://www.zondervan.com/Cultures/ en-US/Company/History.htm?QueryStringSite=Zondervan>; Park, E. J. "A Tale of Two Kitties." *Christianity Today* 50.2 (2006): 68–70; Raeper, William, ed. *The Gold Thread: Essays on George MacDonald.* Edinburgh: Edinburgh University Press, 1990; The Future: Who is Michael Phillips? [Online, December 2006]. Macdonaldphillips.com Web site. <http://www.

macdonaldphillips.com/future.html>; Thomas Nelson History [Online, July 2007]. Thomas Nelson Web site. <http://www.thomasnelson.com/consumer/dept.asp?dept_id=1118916& TopLevel_id=100000>.

KENNETH R. MOREFIELD (LAURA K. SCHUBERT
CONTRIBUTED RESEARCH FOR THIS ENTRY.)

COMEDIC THEATRE

Definition. The word *comedy* is derived from *komos*, a Greek term denoting acts of celebration, revelry, or merrymaking. In theatre, the word *comedy* is often tied to Aristotle's description of the genre that exists in opposition to his seminal definition of tragedy. In *The Poetics*, Aristotle is credited with saying that

> Comedy [is] an imitation of men worse than the average; worse, however, not as regards any and every sort of fault, but only as regards one particular kind, the Ridiculous, which is a species of the Ugly. The Ridiculous may be defined as a mistake or deformity not productive of pain or harm to others [. . .]. (Aristotle 2000, 48–49)

Traditional definitions of comedy, with roots in Aristotle and neoclassicism, have set up expectations of the genre that include amusing plots, as well as light and funny characters whose adverse situations ultimately result in happy, morally acceptable conclusions.

However, the notion of combining elements of comedy and tragedy in theatre has long been broached by playwrights and theorists, further complicating definitions of each genre. The mixing of elements of comedy and tragedy has become especially prominent in the twentieth century, giving rise to multiple subgenres of comedy including tragicomedy, tragifarce, and satirical drama. Leonard Pronko suggests that, "In a universe without absolutes tragedy is impossible. [. . .] pure comedy is no longer possible either [. . .]," and that the rise of relativism has blurred, if not erased, clear delineations such as those put forth by Aristotle (Pronko 1962, 205). Further tensions lie in debates about high and low, official and unofficial elements of comedy in theatre. Moreover, comedy has historically played a significant role in the expression of difficult or taboo issues, or even politically dangerous points of view. Despite the blurring of various genres and definitions, comedy in theatre continues to embrace elements of humor, silliness, light-heartedness, and entertainment.

Comedy as dramatic literature remains difficult to separate from theatrical performance. As such, the definition of comedic theatre has grown to include many popular forms of entertainment, such as stand-up comedy, musical comedy, musical revue, burlesque, farce, vaudeville, puppet shows, and other forms of amusement.

History. American theatre history often credits the Greeks, specifically Aristophanes (*The Birds, The Frogs, The Clouds*), with legitimizing comedy on the stage. The history of comedy spans many centuries and countries, offering a rich but often undocumented tradition of humor and merriment on the stage. Historians recognize the presence of comedy throughout the development of European theatre: Greek comedy, Roman comedy, farces from the Middle Ages, various Renaissance comedy including *commedia dell'arte, commedia erudita* (intellectual/educated comedy), and romantic comedy, as well as English Restoration comedy, sentimental comedy, comedy of tears, and comedy of manners—among others.

The complicated history of comedic forms across Europe contributed to a diverse tradition of comedy in the American theatre, reflecting specific cultural and socio-political circumstances of the country. Moving away from specifically

British sensibilities, playwright Anna Cora Mowatt has been credited with creating a distinctly American comedic theatre. Her play, *Fashion, or, Life in New York* (1845), is a satirical comedy commenting on high-society manners of nineteenth century New York City. Around the same time, vaudeville and burlesque shared the stage with comedy of manners, demonstrating the co-existence of high and low society in the city centers, as well as diversity in the realm of the comedic American theatre.

The late nineteenth and early twentieth century gave birth to a number of performances focusing on specific ethnic experiences by Jewish comedians, including the famous George Burns and Fanny Brice, and black minstrel performers, such as Bert Williams, who employed elements of song and dance, physical comedy, and vaudevillian techniques on stage. Importantly, during the Harlem Renaissance (1920s), black comedy flourished in theatres, popular cabarets, and newly published literature by and about blacks. This era also gave way to great musicals—written by and starring black artists—most importantly the legendary *Shuffle Along* (1921), which became a major Broadway hit.

Also in the 1920s, The Marx Brothers became hugely popular with their improvisational comedy, which included vaudeville acts, musical revues, and musical comedy. *Animal Crackers* (1928–1929), one of their most successful musical comedies, was developed in collaboration with George S. Kaufman. Kaufman, who often depicted eccentric characters and poked fun at high society manners and values, pushed the boundaries of situational comedy by adding elements of farce to well-structured commercial comedic plays. He successfully collaborated with Moss Hart on plays such as *You Can't Take It with You* (Pulitzer Prize in 1937) and *The Man Who Came to Dinner* (1940), both of which continue to be produced on American regional, community, and school stages.

The late 1920s and 1930s were further marked by a proliferation of comedy of manners, written by notable playwrights such as Phillip Barry (*Paris Bound* [1927] and *The Philadelphia Story* [1939]) and S.N. Behrman (*Biography* [1932], *Rain from Heaven* [1934], and *End of Summer* [1936]). Behrman, one of Broadway's most recognized writers of "high comedy," questioned the role of comedy in a violent and unjust world in his play *No Time for Comedy* (1939). Robert E. Sherwood used humor to address the stupidity of war in his plays *The Road to Rome* (1927) and *Idiot's Delight* (1936), commenting on the horrors of war and satirizing its political players. In general, playwrights of this period employed light-hearted comedy to frame social issues of the day.

With the start of the Great Depression, the 1920s and 1930s also saw a rise in the popularity of musical theatre. Musical theatre writers began to incorporate dramatic stories into light comic forms such as farce and burlesque, moving away from showgirl musicals, such as the Ziegfeld Follies, and toward musical theatre that integrated music, dance, character, and setting to advance an actual plot. *Showboat* (1928), written by Jerome Kern and Oscar Hammerstein II, set the stage for musical comedies, such as *Anything Goes* (1934), *Guys and Dolls* (1950), and *Hello, Dolly!* (1964), which depicted everyday American characters and continued to bridge the gap between story and music. Overall the 1940s saw little in the way of new comedic plays. Historian Oscar Brockett refers to the period between 1940 and 1970 as the "golden age of musical comedy" (Brockett 2003, 504). In addition, Mel Watkins suggests that the Harlem Renaissance gave rise to sophisticated black humor that was "pointedly critical of American racism [and that] by the late 1940s, some of this material was creeping into the stage humor of pioneer comics like Redd Foxx and Moms Mabley" (Watkins 2002, 112).

With the rise of realism on the American stage (in plays by Arthur Miller, Tennessee Williams, and Lillian Hellman—to name a few), the mid-twentieth century comedic theatre began to focus on psychological realism and complex characters. The sense of comedy

> no longer [resulted] from misunderstanding and mistaken identity, as in the majority of comic plays and farces; rather, it [emerged from] characters' mismatched personalities [and their] differing life attitudes. (Listengarten 2004, 460)

Additionally, a significant cross-pollination existed at this time between comic writers for the stage, television, and film—a trend that continues to permeate writing in the twenty first century—and further complicated the nature of comedy on stage. Neil Simon's romantic comedy *Barefoot in the Park* (1963), as well as his plays *The Odd Couple* (1965) and *The Sunshine Boys* (1972), frequently include "sharp one-liners" typical of comedy sketches for television and film. Despite comedy's increasing interest in psychologically defined characters, popular commercial theatre at this time remained removed from the rather serious public reaction to the country's political upheavals, namely the Vietnam War and the civil rights movement.

T.S. Hischak points out that "Broadway had come to depend on Neil Simon for reliable and satisfying comedies" (Hischak 2001, 9), but in the 1970s and 1980s comedic theatre of other forms gained attention at Off Broadway, Off-Off Broadway, and regional theatres. John Guare's *The House of Blue Leaves* (1971), a successful dark farce; Tina Howe's *The Art of Dining* (1979) and A.R. Gurney's *The Dining Room* (1982), comedies of contemporary manners; Beth Henley's dark comedy *Crimes of the Heart* (1978); and Charles Ludlum's *The Mystery of Irma Vep* (1984), an Edwardian style spoof, all employ elements of comedy to raise questions about relationships and social norms of the time period.

In many ways, comedy in the late twentieth century became a platform for exploring (sometimes philosophically) issues of identity as they relate to gender, race, sexual orientation, religion, and class. Furthermore, comedy on the stage often challenged the status quo as writers and performers began to confront traditional American values and represent marginalized topics and minority voices on the stage. In addition to the development of many important stand-up comics and monologists (such as Richard Pryor, Lily Tomlin, Whoopi Goldberg, and Spalding Gray), this time period saw the commercial success of playwrights such as Wendy Wasserstein (*Isn't it Romantic* 1981), Herb Gardner (*I'm Not Rappaport* 1985), Christopher Durang (*Sister Mary Ignatius Explains It All for You* 1979) and Jane Wagner (*The Search for Signs of Intelligent Life in the Universe* 1985), all of whom used comedy to draw attention to, if not subvert, prescribed societal roles and values. This period also produced a number of quirky, farcical comedies such as *Reckless* (1983) by Craig Lucas and *All in the Timing* (1994) by David Ives, among others, pushing the genre of comedy into the realm of fantasy and absurdity.

If the 1970s and 1980s foregrounded issues of self-identity on stage, comic theatre in the 1990s is marked by intellectual humor, popularization of culturally specific comedy, as well as political satire. Playwrights such as Steve Martin (*Picasso at the Lapin Agile* 1993) and Theresa Rebeck (*Spiked Heels* 1992) employ humor to reflect on post-modern sensibilities and notions of relativism, which continue to permeate intellectual debates in the twenty first century. Moving between stage and screen, commercially successful comedians such as Latino artists John Leguizamo and George Lopez, Asian American performer Margaret Cho, black stand-up comedians Whoopi Goldberg and David Chappelle, as well as lesbian performer Ellen DeGeneres achieved broad popular appeal with their culturally specific humor. Furthermore, the use of comic elements within serious and often political plays is reflected in the work of Suzan Lori-Parks, Jose Rivera, and Russell Lee, who, like many playwrights of this time, employ dark irony and cynicism to disrupt the audience's complacency, while enabling the audience to process uncomfortable realities. At the same time, physical comedy based in uncomplicated plots and improvised situations continued to co-exist with darker, more serious forms of comedy; artists such as Bill Irwin (*Fool Moon* 1993, developed in collaboration with David Shiner) adapted the comic styles of Charlie Chaplin and Buster Keaton for contemporary audiences. In the same way, commercially popular, light-hearted comedies continued to entertain Broadway and regional theatre audiences.

Trends and Themes. Trends in theatre emerge out of societal contexts and issues. The twenty-first century reflects many of the same issues confronted by artists in the late twentieth century, but is further marked by increased globalization, international conflict, and national and personal isolation. Stand-up comedy and solo performance, which once relied on exploding audience expectations and identity constructs, have come to focus on developing complicity between the artists and audience around issues of race, gender, sexuality, and politics.

An explosion of comedy on the American stage that addresses issues of identity (cultural and otherwise) reflects "the political potential of comedy as an activist theatrical discourse" (Glen 2005, 426). For instance, playwright Richard Greenberg uses comedy to address race, sexuality, and national identity politics in his award-winning play *Take Me Out* (2003). The Nibras Theatre Collective, and other Arab American theatre troupes, formed a yearly New York Arab American Comedy Festival in 2003 "to negotiate stereotypes and joke about 'their' habits, fears, accents, misunderstandings, and the challenges of living between two cultures" (Basiouncy 2006, 331). Similarly, performance groups such as the Chicano troupe Culture Clash employ biting satire and intellectual humor, coupled with song, dance, and pop culture references, to resist stereotypes and cultural assumptions (Glen 2005: 413). Other writers and performers from marginalized groups employ self-deprecating jokes about cultural and social practices and familial relationships to both satirize stereotypes and celebrate cultural idiosyncrasies.

COMEDIC THEATRE ON BROADWAY

On Broadway, musical comedy remains the most popular genre. *Urinetown* (2001) ventures into the territory of satire, making fun of local and national political systems, while also rejecting conventions of musical theatre through self-parody. Other commercially successful musicals, such as *The Producers* (2001), *Avenue Q* (2003), *The 25th Annual Putnam County Spelling Bee* (2005), and *Monty Python's Spamalot* (2005), further illustrate recent trends in musical theatre, including the use of satire and spoof to poke fun at theatrical convention, political-correctness, the sanctity of childhood, and cultural myths and narratives.

Several themes and through-lines define the scope of contemporary American comedic theatre. As artists explore their role in an increasingly unstable political and cultural landscape, comedy highlights Americans' anxiety about fulfilling social roles and expectations. With the rise in minority rights, contemporary comedy draws on new complexities in relationships, acknowledging expanded and multi-faceted notions of what constitutes family and romantic love in the twenty first century. Contemporary comedic theatre pokes fun at idealized dating and courting rituals, as well as social expectations of various human relationships and gender roles.

Contexts and Issues. Contemporary comedy is shaped by often serious philo-sophical and political currents. Post-modern thinking, or the questioning of univer-sal or accepted norms, permeated the twentieth century and pushed theatre artists to question the stability of meaning in life and on stage, addressing notions of "real" and "constructed" identity. The destabilization of authority and the destruction of hierarchies have blurred traditional boundaries of class and culture, as well as distinctions between high and low art.

With globalization, or increased access to shared knowledge, culture, and markets, the American theatre has become a place for exploring questions of identity and responsibility—not just to one's self, but to the world at large. Playwrights and per-formers use the stage to comment on moral and political relativism, as well as con-cepts of identity as they relate to the politics of religion, gender, class, sexuality, and nationalism.

Although globalization and postmodern thinking already permeated the psyche of the American theatre, the terrorist attacks of 9/11, followed by the Iraq War (2003–) and an increase in America's political polarization, heightened the theatre's attention to the relativity of truth and the constructed nature of identity.

Furthermore, the increased popularity of television and film pushed American theatre to acknowledge broader audience expectations while seeking a distinct identity from media-based, popular entertainment. Although aspects of multi-media have found their way into contemporary American theatre, both stylistically and thematically, theatre often addresses issues and experiments with styles that generate less mass appeal.

The similarities and tensions among these different mediums are negotiated by many commercially successful comedic writers and performers who currently work across television, film, and theatre.

Comedy remains an important tool for artists in the twenty first century to explore contemporary contexts. Issues of isolation and alienation, societal polarization, and fear of lost identity, as well as the relativity of moral values, are some of the serious topics that permeate various comedic plays. Artists' seeming obsession with the insta-bility of meaning has resulted in a body of plays and performances that address questions of power in representation, as well as issues of self-reflection, identity, and diversity. At the same time, artists use comedy to parody social anxieties, as well as offer a humorous perspective on life.

Reception. While diverse artists and audiences have found a voice in various arenas of contemporary comedy, critics continue to criticize the genre for its mass appeal and frequent lack of sophistication.

With the advance of technology and the rise of popular culture, theatre developed a symbiotic relationship with television and film. Many of today's popular comedi-ans got their start on television shows such as *Saturday Night Live,* and comedic

CRITICS AND COMEDIC THEATRE

Critics continue to have a complicated relationship to comedy. As early as fourth century B.C.E., comedy was viewed as trivial, and thus second class, in relation to more serious approaches to drama. However, at the same time, comedy is celebrated for its ability to broach dangerous or controversial topics such as political corruption, war, and hypocrisy, as well as its ability to make audiences laugh at life's irony and personal folly. Even well-structured and commercially popular comedies have been criticized for appealing to audiences' baser nature, as well as lacking depth.

writers regularly move between stage and screen. Writers often adapt their stage scripts for the screen (*Prelude to a Kiss* 1992 and *Freak* 1998), while some develop original works for television, film, and theatre. Moreover, comic writers for theatre have found success in publishing novels, stories, and essays, adding additional layers to the interdisciplinary nature of drama.

In opposition to the mass appeal of comedy in television and film, several contemporary writers employ theatre as a somewhat elitist venue to experiment with innovative styles and explore complex social and philosophical concepts. Simultaneously, the increasing cost of theatre tickets further contributes to the elitist stature of the art form, an interesting paradox to comedy's longstanding tradition of speaking to the masses and satirizing those in power.

Selected Authors. Christopher Durang is a prolific playwright, and occasional actor and screenwriter, known most for his daring and often dark comedies that seriously address issues of religion, sexuality, child abuse, and family dysfunction. While his full-length plays have enjoyed successful runs on Broadway, Off-Broadway, and prominent regional stages, they continue to attract professional, community, and school-based venues nationally. Durang also has written over 1,000 one-act plays and satirical sketches that parody and satirize everything from sex and politics to well-known plays and artists. Critics have referred to Durang's comedies as autobiographical and angry, as well as absurdist and biting.

In 1978, *A History of the American Film,* a playful parody of Hollywood movies, was produced on Broadway, earning the young Durang a Tony nomination for Best Book of a Musical. One of Durang's most popular plays, *Sister Mary Ignatius Explains It All For You* (1981), which satirizes the traditional practice and dogma of Catholic school teachers from the mid-twentieth century, ran for two and a half years Off-Broadway. Durang's success continued throughout the 1980s with several new plays, including *Beyond Therapy* (1982), *Baby with the Bath Water* (1983), and *The Marriage of Bette and Boo* (1985)—the latter being an admittedly autobiographical play about his parents' troubled marriage. More recently, Durang has attracted audiences with *Betty's Summer Vacation* (1999), which Durang labels as a play about the "tabloid-ization" of American culture; *Mr. Bob Cratchit's Wild Christmas Binge* (2002), a playful parody of Charles Dickens's *A Christmas Carol;* and *Miss Witherspoon* (2005), a contemplative farce that delves into notions of an afterlife, which was listed on *Time Magazine*'s "Ten Best Plays of 2005."

While not all of Durang's plays have gained critical acclaim, Durang's body of work is celebrated for being wickedly funny and, above all, truthful. Many of Durang's plays are timely, referencing pop culture and addressing social issue of the day, making several of his pieces feel outdated only a decade after their original productions. His comedies, however, remain honest reflections on life's challenges and absurdities, and never fail to make audiences both laugh and cringe. Durang's new musical, *Adrift in Macao,* opened in Philadelphia in 2006.

Whoopi Goldberg (formerly Caryn E. Johnson) is a well-known American comedian, film actor, and singer who is often referred to as both "a clown and social critic." She received her first major recognition as a stand-up comedian in 1983 for *The Spook Show,* in which she performed four different characters. A year later, under the direction of Mike Nichols, the show was transformed into the famous Broadway production titled *Whoopi Goldberg* (1984); twenty years later, the show was successfully remounted at the Lyceum Theatre on Broadway as *Whoopi* (2004). For her numerous theatre, film, and television credits in the genre of comedy, Goldberg received the prestigious Mark Twain Prize for American Humor (2001), as well as an invitation to host the Academy Awards.

Goldberg is a master of improvisation and belongs to the type of stand-up comedians who sharpen their craft on feet before writing their stories down on paper. She is also a master of total transformation; in her show *Whoopi,* she leads her audience through the lives of six distinct characters, capturing their diverse personalities, experiences, worldviews, and accents and ultimately presenting a multifaceted picture of life.

Goldberg's comic sensibility allows for the fusion of farcical incongruity, satirical tone, and compassion. Mel Gussow writes in his *New York Times* theatre review that

> As she tells her tales of misfits and outcasts, and even as she offers wry satiric comments, she is consistently disarming. Bantering mischievously with the audience, she warms up a Broadway theater, winning us as her confederates. (Gussow 1984)

As her work expresses strong commitment to issues of gender, poverty, and race, Goldberg simultaneously emphasizes the universal nature of the concerns she explores and refuses to be pigeonholed as "female comedian" or "African American" (Lavin 2004, 104). While embracing the voices of diversity in contemporary American comedy, she is extremely attuned to the humanistic qualities of her characters. Suzanne Lavin notes: "[Goldberg's] characters are bound together, not by race or gender, but by the vulnerability of human beings as they try to negotiate the tough obstacles of life" (Lavin 2004, 110).

Lisa Kron's playwriting and acting career was fomented in the 1980s by the East Village performance art climate. Coming to New York City from a small Michigan town, she immersed herself in East Village performance venues such as Dixon Place, P.S. 122, WOW Café, and La MAMA, where the spirit of experimentation encouraged artists to push aesthetic and socio-political boundaries through their unorthodox artistic explorations. Making her career as a writer and solo performer in shows such as *101 Humiliating Stories* (1993) and *2.5 Minute Ride* (1996), Kron also became a co-founder of the award-winning theatre company "The Five Lesbian Brothers." Her most recent play, *Well* (2004), had a successful run at the Public Theatre in New York City and made a Broadway debut in 2006. In all three performance pieces, Kron uses elements of autobiography to explore both the emotional implications of remembering and the limitations of memory in performance. In *101 Humiliating Stories,* Kron presents her personal account of a series of mortifying episodes from various stages in her life, ranging from embarrassing junior high school incidents to public declarations—perhaps imaginary—of her homosexuality. In *2.5 Ride,* Kron chronicles her personal journey to the Holocaust Museum in Auschwitz with her aging father whose parents perished in the Holocaust. In this piece, she collides horrifying moments with humor to experiment with audience reaction; she notes, "[. . .] you might not know for a second whether you are at Auschwitz or at an amusement park. The show does not tell you when to laugh and when to be solemn. The response is up to you" (Kron 2001, xiv).

In *Well,* Kron steps away from a purely solo performance aesthetic, but remains faithful to her stylistic principle in which comedy is often born out of a sense of discomfort or awkwardness. The action in *Well* revolves around her complicated relationship with her mother, as well as the playwright's own complex attitude toward issues of health and illness. This play moves beyond traditional storytelling and toward an exploration of the process of both "dramatizing" and "performing" memory on stage.

Critics have noted Kron's theatrical talent for creating a balance between heartwrenching emotional moments and "high-flying comedy." Critics have also referred to Kron as one of the best American stand-up memoirists, continuing the legacy of the late Spalding Gray.

John Leguizamo is an actor/performer and writer, most known for starring in films such as *Romeo and Juliet* (1996), *Moulin Rouge* (2001), and *Land of the Dead* (2005). However, despite his popular roles on the big screen, Leguizamo is also noted for his dynamic personality and hilarious sense of humor on the American stage. In a series of one-man shows, Leguizamo takes on multiple characters and voices, mimicking people from his past (and present) and employing humor to reflect on his difficult childhood, relationships, and multi-ethnic stereotyping.

Leguizamo, who writes and performs his own material, hit Off-Broadway in 1991 with his witty show, *Mambo Mouth,* in which he portrayed seven different Latino characters. Two years later, he returned to the stage with *Spic-O-Rama* (1993), in which he humorously satirized stereotypes of Latinos in the United States. Leguizamo then debuted on Broadway in 1998 with *Freak,* his somewhat autobiographical one-man show in which he used comedy to comment on family dysfunction. Later, Leguizamo toured *John Leguizamo Live!* (2001), which later became *Sexaholix: A Love Story* (2002), incorporating physical and vocal comedy, dancing, and sentimental stories of family and love to win his audiences over. Importantly, Leguizamo also created and starred in the 1995 Latino-oriented variety television show called *House of Buggin'* which gained positive reviews but only lasted for one season.

"Leguizamo was rightly identified as the first Latino performance artist/stand up monologist with cross-over star potential" (Winer-Bernheimer 1998, 1). Each of Leguizamo's stage shows was eventually filmed for television, and his performances appealed to audiences from various ethnic and socio-economic backgrounds. Leguizamo has earned Obie, Emmy, and CableACE awards, and was nominated for a Golden Globe Award for his achievements as a comedian. While Leguizamo continues to garner praise as a colorful and energetic writer and performer, many critics have hopes that his comedy will become more mature, edgy, and complicated. Leguizamo's memoir, *Pimps, Hos, Playa Hatas and All the Rest of My Hollywood Friends: A Life,* was released in 2006.

David Lindsay-Abaire's farcical comedy *Fuddy Meers* (1998), which began as a playwriting project during his studies at Julliard, brought the playwright instant public and critical acclaim. Following its completion, the play was workshopped at the Julliard School and then received a staged reading at the Eugene O'Neill Theater Center in 1998. After its successful opening at the Manhattan Theatre Club's Stage II, the play was transferred to the Minetta Lane Theatre in 2000. "I love dark and disturbing inappropriate humor. [. . .] I'm trying to write outrageous farce with an underlying sadness, a real weight that peeks through the silliness," writes Lindsay-Abaire (Lindsay-Abaire 2000, 35). In his stylistic approach, marked by the infusion of dark farce and absurdity with light lyrical comedy, he is similar to his peer Craig Lucas. Other artists who influenced his style and technique include Georges Feydeau, Eugene Ionesco, George S. Kaufman and Moss Hart, The Marx Brothers, Abbott and Costello, as well as the more contemporary Christopher Durang, one of Lindsay-Abaire's Julliard playwriting professors.

The inspiration for the plot of *Fuddy Meers* came from a television news report on a book about neurological disorders; in particular, Lindsay-Abaire was drawn to the story's description of amnesia in which a patient's memory was erased during sleep. In *Fuddy Meers*, Claire suffers from this form of amnesia, and her inability to remember her past thrusts her into a kaleidoscope of silly, absurdist, and violent events. She is kidnapped by a limping, lisping, half-deaf man in a ski mask, a nod to Lucas's masked character in *Reckless*, who tries to convince Claire that her husband is about to murder her. In the remainder of the play, Claire faces a series of absurd revelations and grotesquely violent situations revolving around her dysfunctional and abusive family. The tragifarcical world of this play is dangerous and unpredictable, but aspects of "joyous lunacy" prevail in the end producing a thoroughly entertaining effect for the audience. Critics have referred to this play as a "wild ride comedy," an "absurdist-nightmare farce," and a "dark, sweet and engaging comedy."

Lindsay-Abaire's less successful, whimsical comedies include *A Devil Inside* (1997) and *Wonder of the World* (2001). His later play *Rabbit Hole* (2006) departs from his earlier comedic work in its lyrical and heartbreaking exploration of parental grief over a child's tragic death. The play's heartfelt and grave scenes, however, are frequently interspersed with lighter moments of laughter and humor, helping the characters to cope with their loss and ultimately leading the family through a healing process.

Craig Lucas's career in theatre encompasses play and screen writing as well as theatre and film directing. His comedies, *Reckless* (1983) and *Prelude to a Kiss* (1988)—which brought him popular and critical recognition, are riddled with suspense and the threat of violence—perhaps reflecting some of Lucas's personal experiences. After writing romantic comedies in the 1980s and early 1990s, he ventured into the realm of tragedy in plays such as *The Dying Gaul* (1998) and *Singing Forest* (2004). His screenwriting includes adaptations of several of his own plays.

Lucas is a master of constructing plots in which a chain of coincidences results in comic absurdity. Rachel Fitsimmons in *Reckless* runs away from her house on Christmas Eve in a desperate attempt to save her life after her alienated husband announces that he has taken "a contract out on [her] life" (Lucas 1989, 8). Her extraordinary journey is laden with peculiar encounters and incredible circumstances adding elements of both fantasy and eccentricity to a story about a woman who ultimately finds herself in search of identity and purpose in life. The whirlwind of events in the play fuses comedy with tragedy as the main character ends up in a homeless shelter and others die of champagne poisoning and a self-imposed hunger strike. The play's development seems rather random but the arbitrary events in *Reckless* give away the playwright's intention to emphasize the problematic relationship between the irrational and the logical, between chance and predictability.

In *Prelude to a Kiss,* Lucas foregrounds elements of fantasy in the structure and style of romantic comedy, resulting in a blend of fantasy and romance. A young woman is suddenly drawn to a strange old man who unexpectedly appears at her wedding party; they kiss and exchange souls. As a result of the soul exchange, she is forced to experience both the physical and psychological challenges of old age, which prompts her to re-evaluate her own humanity. Critics have praised Lucas's plays for raising important issues of identity, sexual or otherwise, and exploring connections (or lack thereof) between chance and logic. The surreal and the realistic are infused together as the playwright interweaves disparate plot lines while embarking his characters on "identity" trips full of comic and serious encounters.

Recently, Lucas received attention for writing the book to the light-hearted musical drama, *Light in the Piazza,* which was produced at the Lincoln Center Theatre in 2005 and won six Tony Awards. Critics emphasized the distinct humanistic quality of this musical; Michael Feingold, a theatre critic for *The Village Voice,* posits:

> It's not a self-reflexive spoof of anything, not a carpentered-up trip through anyone's catalog of songs, not a technological barrage of noise and effects. [. . .] It is a story about human beings told through music—a phenomenon so rare nowadays that it deserves praise just for existing. (Feingold 2005)

Steve Martin has been called "the leading man of American Comedy" and is a well-known film actor, stand-up comedian, and writer of screenplays, novels, stories, editorials, and plays. He started writing jokes for the *Smothers Brothers Comedy Hour* during his college years and later performed with *Saturday Night Live* before spending decades as an actor and screenwriter for films such as *Roxanne, My Blue Heaven,* and *The Pink Panther.*

In the 1990s, Martin took a hiatus from his career in film and began writing comedic plays. In his first play, *Picasso at the Lapin Agile* (1996), Martin details a fictional meeting between a young Albert Einstein and Pablo Picasso at a bar in Paris, combining low comedy with philosophical musing on notions of relativity and aesthetics. In 2001, Theatre Communications Group (TCG) listed *Picasso at the Lapin Agile* in its top ten most produced plays of the year, and productions continue to receive critical acclaim over a decade after the play's premiere in 1993. Martin's play *The Underpants* (2002), an adaptation of Carl Sternheim's classic 1910 farce, was an Off-Broadway success and demonstrates Martin's penchant for physical humor and "literary slapstick." "The play, written as a wicked satire on the middle class, has become in Mr. Martin's hands an ambitious amalgam of comic book and social commentary, made out of sex jokes, slamming doors and sophisticated repartee" (Weber 2002). Martin's other comedic plays include *Wasp, Zig-Zag Woman,* and *Patter for the Floating Lady* (each published in a 1996 collection of his work), as well as the yet unpublished *Guillotine.*

Martin's comedies often rely on witty dialogue and elements of farce, parody, and self-referential humor, while his stand-up routines include self-deprecating jokes and "schoolboy" humor. While Martin is certainly a celebrated icon of American pop culture, he has occasionally been criticized for tedious jokes or over-the-top, silly gags. However, Martin's comic genius earned him the Mark Twain Prize for American Humor in 2005, as well as invitations to host the Academy Awards and serve as editor for the Modern Library's Wit and Humor Series.

Theresa Rebeck, whose writing has been produced extensively on prominent American stages, as well as television, film, and radio, has earned the title of "brainy, matter of fact woman of theatre" (Hart 2005, 46). With an early background in acting and writing, and a Ph.D. in Victorian Literature, Rebeck writes smart and emotionally compelling plays. However, "much to her own surprise, she is frequently cited as a 'funny' playwright," says Sarah Hart of *American Theatre* magazine, who agrees that, "[Rebeck's] plays *are* funny—but not one-liner funny" (Hart 2005). In fact, Rebeck's writing has been called everything from sickly funny to dark and absurd—and often in a review of a single play. Rebeck is also considered a master of satire, and many of her plays offer sharp commentary on society, culture, politics, and human relationships.

Rebeck's plays move away from comedy in the purest sense of the word, and borrow elements of style and form from Chekhovian and Shakespearian drama, as well as Victorian melodrama and Greek tragedy, to name a few. Her play *The Scene* (2006), which details the affair of an out-of-work New York actor who is married to a successful news producer, played to sold-out houses and has been called a shrewd comedy "which updates a film-noir, femme-fatale story for today's Manhattan" (Isherwood 2007). Rebeck's one-woman show *Bad Dates* (2003) is a fantastical comedy that chronicles the sometimes scary humor of a single mother re-entering the dating scene, while her play *Spiked Heels* (1992) is a contemporary comedy of manners that draws on elements from George Bernard Shaw's *Pygmalion* to explore sexual harassment, as well as the nature of power, perception, and gender roles. Rebeck's other comedies include *View of the Dome* (1996), *Loose Knit* (1994), and *The Family of Mann* (1994).

While Rebeck's comedies sometimes have been criticized as trivial and seemingly unfinished, her plays are repeatedly produced and celebrated for their poignant commentaries on various aspects of society. Rebeck also has earned multiple awards for her work on *NYPD Blue,* won the National Theatre Conference Award (for *The Family of Mann*), and earned the William Inge New Voices Playwriting Award. Her play *Omnium Gatherum* (co-written with Alexandra Gersten-Vassilaros 2003) was a finalist for the Pulitzer Prize.

Wendy Wasserstein, who died in 2006 at the age of 55, was an award-winning writer whose comedies are rooted in the tradition of American Jewish culture. She employed humor to celebrate life under most calamitous circumstances. Her body of work includes many commercially successful plays, film and television scripts, as well as other genres of literature. In Wasserstein's early play *Isn't It Romantic* (1981) the main character Janie Bloomberg—a young idealistic writer, somewhat overweight, somewhat confused about her identity—embarks on a painful journey of self-discovery leading her to defy the conventional social norms imposed by her domineering mother. Wasserstein's ability to diffuse feelings of sadness and disillusionment in her plays with humorous situations and her characters' self-deprecating humor has frequently been noted by critics. C.W.E. Bigsby writes that *Isn't It Romantic* "in some ways elaborates a familiar vaudeville and Jewish routine, and much of its humor derives precisely from the familiarity of the central character [who] is vulnerable, unclear what she wants, but aware that she is, indeed, a comic figure" (Bigsby 1999, 340).

In *The Sisters Rosensweig* (1993) Wasserstein similarly aims at creating a delicate balance "between the bright colors of humor and the serious issues of identity [and] self-loathing" (Wasserstein 1993). The action in the play revolves Sara Goode's fifty-fourth birthday celebration, during which an unexpected guest tries to compel Sara to return to her Jewish roots which she relinquished years earlier. Through humorous repartees and painful discussions, Sara ultimately finds emotional solace in familial relationships and recognizes the significance of her past. Despite the abundance of poignant personal discoveries in the play, its spirit is far from being melodramatic or melancholy. Wasserstein's characters laugh at their own inability to confront their loneliness and disillusionment; they mock their own idiosyncrasies and, sometimes, narrow-mindedness, as they struggle to both re-assert themselves in society and stay true to their ideals and beliefs.

In Wasserstein's last play, *Third* (2005), the sense of humor is less prevalent than in her earlier plays, but the characters' resilience and their need to celebrate life and human connection remain as strong. In *Third*, Wasserstein continues to focus on strong, independent female characters in their search for emotional fulfillment. In this play, Laurie Jameson, a prominent Shakespeare scholar at a small, liberal college, mistakenly accuses her student of plagiarism. Fiercely passionate about her political views, Wasserstein's main character is eventually forced to confront her own ethical value system. What makes Wasserstein's heroines unique is their ability to both grasp the extent of alienation from their family and/or community and recognize the necessity for change, which manifests in either acknowledging their identity or transforming their path. Their sincere appreciation for humor is what helps Wasserstein's characters persevere.

Critics have consistently praised Wasserstein's gift for comedy, often citing the commercial success of her plays. The popular appeal of Wasserstein's comedies should not overshadow the important issues the playwright raises regarding her female characters' plight for independence and professional satisfaction that often comes with the sacrifice of their familial and communal contentment.

Bibliography

Aristotle. The Poetics. Trans. Ingram Bywater. In *Theatre/Theory/Theatre: The Major Critical Texts from Aristotle and Zeami to Soyinka and Havel.* Daniel Gerould, ed. New York: Applause, 2000.

Basiouncy, Dalia. "New York Arab America Comedy Festival." *Theatre Journal* 58.2 (2000): 327–331.

Bermel, Albert. *Comic Agony: Mixed Impressions in the Modern Theatre.* Evanston, IL: Northwestern University Press, 1993.

Bigsby, C.W.E. *Contemporary American Playwrights.* Cambridge: Cambridge University Press, 1999.

———. *Modern American Drama, 1945–2000.* Cambridge: Cambridge University Press, 2000.

Bogosian, Eric. *The Essential Bogosian.* New York: TCG, 1994.

Buckley, Michael. "A Chat with Theresa Rebeck; Remembering Uta Hagen." *Playbill,* 18 January 2004. http://www.playbill.com/news/article/83844.html.

Brandt, George. "Twentieth-Century Comedy." In *Comic Drama: The European Heritage.* W.D. Howarth, ed. London: Methuen, 1978.

Brantley, Ben. "Life: Does it Get Any Better after Death." *New York Times,* 30 Nov. 2005. http://theater2.nytimes.com/2005/11/30/theater/reviews/30with.html.

———. "Lisa Kron's 'Well' opens on Broadway, With Mom Keeping Watch." *New York Times,* 31 March 2005. http://theater2.nytimes.com/2006/03/31/theater/reviews/31well.html.

Brockett, Oscar G., and Franklin J. Hildy, eds. *The History of the Theatre.* 9th ed. Boston: Allyn and Bacon, 2003.

Carr, C. *On Edge: Performance at the End of the Twentieth Century.* Hanover, NH: Wesleyan University Press, 1993.

Charney, Maurice. *Comedy High and Low.* New York: Oxford University Press, 1978.

Cohen, S.B., ed. *From Hester Street to Hollywood: The Jewish-American Stage and Screen.* Bloomington, IN: Indiana University Press, 1983.

Durang, Christopher. *Mrs. Bob Cratchit's Wild Christmas Binge.* New York: Dramatists Play Service, 2005.

Elliott, Robert C. *The Power of Satire: Magic, Ritual, Art.* Princeton, NJ: Princeton University Press, 1960.

Feinberg, Leonard. *The Satirist: His Temperament, Motivation, and Influence.* Ames, IA: Iowa State University Press, 1963.

Feingold, Michael. "Passione All'Americana." *The Village Voice,* 19 April 2005. http://www.villagevoice.com/theater/0516,feingold1,63169,11.html.

Foley, F. Kathleen. "Intimate, Wryly Agile 'Picasso.'" *Los Angeles Times,* 28 Feb. 2002.

Gelven, Michael. *Truth and the Comedic Art.* Albany, NY: State University of New York press, 2000.

Gilbert, Joanne R. *Performing Marginality: Humor, Gender, and Cultural Critique.* Detroit, MI: Wayne State University Press, 2004.

Glen, Antonia Nakano. "Casting Themselves: Culture Clash and the Comedy of Resistance." *Contemporary Theatre Review* 15.4 (2005): 413–426.

Guthke, Karl S. *Modern Tragicomedy: An Investigation into the Nature of the Genre.* New York: Random House, 1966.

Goldberg, Whoopi. *Book.* New York: Rob Weisbach Books, 1997.

Greene, Victor R. "Ethnic Comedy in American Culture." *American Quarterly* 51.1 (1997): 144–159.

Gussow, Mel. "Whoopi as Actress, Clown and Social Critic." *New York Times,* 28 Oct. 1984. http://theater2.nytimes.com/mem/theater/treview.html?_r=1&res=9A0DE1D E1539F93BA15753C1A962948260&oref=slogin.

Hart, Sarah. "A Date with Theresa Rebeck." *American Theatre,* October 22.9 (2005): 26–28, 146. http://www.tcg.org/publications/at/Oct05/rebeck.cfm.

Hirst, David. *Tragicomedy.* London: Methuen, 1984.

Hischak, T.S. *American Theatre: A Chronicle of Comedy and Drama, 1969–2000.* Oxford: Oxford University Press, 2001.

Hoy, Cyrus. *Hyacinth Room: An Investigation into the Nature of Comedy, Tragedy, and Tragicomedy.* New York: Knopf, 1964.

Hutcheon, Linda. *A Theory of Parody: The Teachings of Twentieth-Century Forms.* New York: Methuen, 1985.

Isherwood, Charles. "The Tuna Fish Can Incident and Other Injustices of Life." *New York Times,* 16 June 2005. http://theater2.nytimes.com/2005/06/16/theater/reviews/ 16laug.html.

———."All About Ego, Showbiz and a Little Black Dress." *New York Times,* 16 Jan. 2007. http://theater2.nytimes.com/2007/01/12/theater/reviews/12scen.html?fta=y.

Jenkins, Ron. *Acrobats of the Soul: Comedy and Virtuosity in Contemporary American Theatre.* New York: TCG, 1988.

Kron, Lisa. *2.5 Minute Ride and 101 Humiliating Stories.* New York: TCG, 2001.

———.*Well.* New York: TCG, 2006.

Lang, Candace. *Irony/Humor: Critical Paradigms.* Baltimore: Johns Hopkins University Press, 1988.

Lavine, Suzanne. *Women and Comedy in Solo Performance.* New York: Routledge, 2004.

Lindsay-Abaire, David. *Fuddy Meers.* New York: Dramatists Play Service, 2000.

———."Lost in the Funhouse: An Interview with Lindsay-Abaire." By Celia Wren. *American Theatre* 17.6 (2000): 35.

Listengarten, Julia. "From Eccentricity to Endurance: Jewish Comedy and the Art of Affirmation." In *A Companion to Twentieth-Century American Literature*. D. Krasner, ed. London: Blackwell Publishing, 2004, 456–472.

Lucas, Craig. *Reckless*. New York: Dramatists Play Service, 1989.

———. *Prelude to a Kiss*. New York: Broadway Play Publishing, 1990.

Littleton, Daryl J. *Black Comedians on Black Comedy: How African Americans Taught Us to Laugh*. New York: Applause, 2006.

Martin, Steve. *Picasso at the Lapin Agile and Other Plays*. New York: Grove, 1996.

Olson, Kirby. *Comedy after Postmodernism: Rereading Comedy from Edward Lear to Charles Willeford*. Lubbock, TX: Texas Tech University Press, 2001.

Olsen, Lance. *Circus of the Mind in Motion: Postmodernism and the Comic Vision*. Detroit, MI: Wayne State University Press, 1990.

Segal, Eric. *The Death of Comedy*. Cambridge: Harvard University Press, 2001.

Shershow, Scott Cutler. *Laughing Matters: The Paradox of Comedy*. Amherst, MA: University of Massachusetts Press, 1986.

Simon, Neil. *Proposals*. New York: Samuel French, 1998.

Sorell, Walter. *Facets of Comedy*. New York: Grosset and Dunlap, 1972.

Styan, J.L. *The Dark Comedy: The Development of Modern Comic Tragedy*. 2nd ed. London: Cambridge University Press, 1968.

Sutton, Dana F. *The Catharsis of Comedy*. Boston, MA: Rowman and Littlefield, 1994.

Wasserstein, Wendy. *The Sisters Rosensweig*. San Diego, CA: Harcourt Brace, 1993.

———. *Isn't It Romantic*. New York: Dramatists Play Service, 1998.

———. "Third." *American Theatre* 23.4 (2006): 72–87.

Watkins, Mel. *On the Real Side*. New York: Simon and Schuster, 1999.

———, ed. *African American Humor: The Best Black Comedy from Slavery to Today*. Chicago: Lawrence Hill Books, 2002.

Weber, Bruce. "Knickers in a Twist, or Panties with a Mind of Their Own." *New York Times*, 5 April 2002.

Winer, Linda. "Celebrity Culture Caught with its Pants Down." *Knight Ridder Tribune Business News*, 12 Jan. 2007.

Winer-Bernheimer, Linda. "Funny, but Little to Freak Out About." *Los Angeles Times*, 14 Feb. 1998.

Further Reading

Bakhtin, Mikhail. *Rabelais and His World*. Trans. Helene Iswolsky. Bloomington, IN: Indiana University Press, 1984; Bogosian, Eric. [online January 2007] Official Web site of Eric Bogosian. www.ericbogosian.com; Bottoms, S.J. *Playing Underground: A Critical History of the 1960s Off-Off-Broadway Movement*. Ann Arbor, MI: University of Michigan Press, 2004; Curry, R.R., ed. *Perspectives on Woody Allen*. New York: G.K. Hall, 1996; Durang, Christopher. [online January 2007]. "Christopher Durang: Playwright and Actor." www.christopherdurang.com; Hutcheon, Linda. *A Poetics of Postmodernism: History, Theory, Fiction*. New York: Routledge, 1988; Kolin, Philip C., and Colby H. Kullman, eds. *Speaking on Stage: Interviews with Contemporary American Playwrights*. Tuscaloosa, AL: University of Alabama Press, 1996; La Farge, Benjamin. "Comedy's Intention." *Philosophy and Literature* 28 (2004): 118–136; Limon, John. *Stand-up Comedy in Theory; or, Abjection in America*. Durham, NC: Duke University Press, 2000; Martin, Steve. [online January 2007]. Official Web site of Steve Martin. www.stevemartin.com; Nelson, T.G.A. *Comedy: The Theory of Comedy in Literature, Drama, and Cinema*. Oxford: Oxford University Press, 1990; Schechter, Joel. *Durov's Pig: Clowns, Politics, and Theatre*. New York: TCG, 1985; Ulea, Vera. *A Concept of Dramatic Genre and the Comedy of a New Type: Chess, Literature, and Film*. Carbondale, IL: Southern Illinois University Press, 2002.

JULIA LISTENGARTEN AND MEGAN ALRUTZ

COMIC BOOKS

Definition. Comic books contain narrative, sequential series of images, usually accompanied by text in a thin magazine-like format, and typically include traditional literary components such as plot, subplots, characters, setting, dialogue, and symbolism. While some comic books contain complete single narratives in one issue, most are serialized across multiple issues over time and develop multiple storylines and arcs across the entire series. The sequential images and text within comic books are usually written to be read horizontally, but occasionally may be read vertically, or in other alternative ways. Multiple *"panels"* on a comic book page that contain illustrations and characters' thoughts or speech are scripted within *"balloons,"* while narrative or explanatory text typically appears in boxes on the edges or outside of the panel frame. Comic book images emphasize the text and dialogue, allowing for quick and frank communication, though exploring the relationship between the images and text is necessary for fleshing out the story and understanding and interpreting what goes on in the *"gutters"* between the *panels*. Most comic books are created by teams of writers and artists rather than by individuals. Often writers pitch ideas to editors or vice versa and next seek out collaborators while considering desired talent, finances, and scheduling. Heavy consultation between writers and artists is typically required, with inkers and pencillers brought in later in the process to add color and text to the work.

Comic books are a versatile genre used for educational, commercial, and most commonly entertainment purposes. Teachers may use them for developing student's reading skills or may have students write and illustrate their own comic books as a composition or narrative writing exercise. Commercial uses of comic books seem to be less prominent, but may be produced for promotional materials such as giveaways, product information guides or instructions, and newsletters. However, most comic books created, purchased, and read in the United States are those written and published for leisure and entertainment purposes. There are many different audiences and readers of mainstream entertainment comic books, though most typically attract adolescent and adult male readers, many titles are available for children as well as other audiences depending on the purpose of the comic book and nature of its contents. Comic book fans and readers tend to maintain active online communities to share criticism and analysis of titles and actively participate in the growing comic book convention circuit.

Comic books relate to other forms of literature such as comic strips, **graphic novels**, **manga**, and **zines**. Argued to be the predecessor of the comic book, comic strips are frequently collected and published in comic book or book format after initial publication and distribution in newspaper or online environments. *Graphic novels,* an emerging literary form over the last thirty years, are related to comics in a couple ways. First, their methods and modes of narrative storytelling images are similar, and second, many titles commonly referred to as *"graphic novels"* are actually known in the industry as "trade paperbacks." Trade paperbacks are comic book issues of the same title collected into hard- or softbound volumes usually containing six issues or a complete story arc. *Graphic novels*, on the other hand, are works usually defined as not previously published in serialized comic book form, are often lengthier than comic books, and tend to appeal to a wider variety of audiences. *Manga*, the Japanese term for comics and cartoons, refers to comic books from Japan or those of similar aesthetic. *Manga* in the United States typically sells in the same formats as comic books or *graphic novels*, but also may come in pocket-sized books. It is recognized for its distinct artistic style, which includes exaggerated and youthful facial features and often communicates and depicts ideas rather than actual physical realities. *Manga* has recently grown in popularity in the United States, especially among children and pre-teens. Lastly, often self-published *zines* have a relationship to comic books. A *zine* (an abbreviation of *magazine*) is a non-commercial publication containing text and images, usually offering some sort of narrative or storyline. They may be originally created by hand or computer and are usually reproduced for distribution by photocopying or printing multiple copies of the original. *Zines* often address political, personal, social, or sexual content outside of the mainstream and more traditional media, and can be found in underground social circles and more recently on the shelves of independent book and comic book sellers and libraries.

History

The Silver Age. Superhero comics survived under the Code's strict guidelines because they often depicted worlds where good and evil were clearly distinct and justice prevailed. However, some publishers had to re-launch superheroes in compliance with the Code. This phenomenon started the trend of re-imagining superheroes for new audiences and resulted in more heroes earning their own titles. Marvel's director at the time, Stan Lee, also contributed to the success of the superhero comic book movement. Working in the industry since the age of seventeen, Lee collaborated with artists Jack Kirby and Steve Dick to create a new breed of superheroes that struggled with their human flaws. Lee's superheroes were not perfect or godlike, but behaved more like people who happened to be superheroes and exemplified undesirable yet endearing human characteristics like confusion, insecurity, and alienation. Others were re-developed with a science fiction influence, like the Green Lantern, while superhero teams like the Justice League of America and The Avengers also emerged.

Readership and fan interest in comic books continued to grow throughout the early 1960s. By now, many creators in the industry had grown up with comic books and had received formal training to enter the profession. The Academy of Comic Book Arts and Sciences was formed and sponsored and distributed annual fan awards, or "Alleys," going to the best comic books of the year. Sales were good, prices were raised, and superhero popularity continued, but did drop off later in the decade due to low sales. Many consider this drop in sales and readership the end of the Silver Age of American comic books, though publishers continued to experiment with new distributors, pricing models, means of circumventing the Code, and new genres, all in an attempt to maintain or entice new readers.

The Bronze Age. Underground comics emerged during the late 1960s and grew throughout the early 1970s, transitioning into the Bronze Age of American comic books. Based primarily in San Francisco, but with artists and publishers in New York and other cities, underground comics were produced by individuals and addressed social issues or concerns of the counterculture, such as experimentation, drug-altered states of mind, rejection of sexual taboos, and ridicule of "the establishment."

Mainstream comic books continued to change in attempt to maintain and attract readership. Popular creators were shuffled around, non-superhero comic books re-emerged, and the Code was loosened, to name a few changes. At about forty years

UNDERGROUND COMICS

Underground comics commonly contained profanity, nudity, and drug use or sex perversion and bent the rigid social mores typically found in public expression of the time. They attracted liberal youth and college students and were often sold in shops with other counterculture expressions like drug paraphernalia or underground art.

Robert Crumb was a prominent figure in underground comics, with additional contributors S. Clay Wilson, Art Spiegelman, Trina Robbins, and many others. As the women's liberation movement also emerged, underground comics offered a prime vehicle for feminist art and expression, and introduced women to the comic book industry. The Wimmen's Comix Collective was formed in 1972 and published several long-running anthologies and comics featuring women artists. Mainstream comic book publishers even tried to break into the underground scene by establishing their own "mainstream underground" titles. However, by the mid-1970s, distribution networks for underground comics began to break down as many shops selling them became outlawed.

strong, major players in the industry began to retire while some switched publishers, like Jack Kirby's move from Marvel to DC Comics. Non-superhero titles exploded in popularity, while many others strived to address relevant social issues like drug abuse, feminism, or civil rights. In 1971, the Comics Code Authority loosened its rules in order to allow for better reflections of modern society within comic books. Stories about drug addiction were now permissible if they were presented in a vile and unjustifiable manner. In response to the changes in the Code and the emerging interest in depicting current social and political issues, a number of ambitious new titles appeared during this time and attempted to advance comic books as a genuine literary and art form. While many of those titles failed with mainstream audiences, their core fan bases supported and drove the future of some titles with their interest in comic art and narrative constructs.

As small bookshops and newsstands became less interested in stocking comic books due to their low profit margin, entrepreneurial specialty comic book shops, publishing companies, and distribution companies emerged throughout the late 1970s and early 1980s. New models of creation and distribution offered more control for comic book creators and publishers began granting more freedom on projects, ownership of their characters, and profit shares. Publishers began targeting their most loyal readers rather than continually trying to entice mainstream or new readers. Marvel and DC Comics' duel for top sales fostered the creation of numerous new characters and titles, and social issues of the counter-culture revolution surfaced in new titles featuring female and African American superheroes.

The Modern Age. The 1978 feature film release of *Superman* and the subsequent licensing of superhero and comic book characters for toys and other merchandise set the stage for growth and revitalization of the industry, bringing comic books and superheroes into mainstream media and retail for the Modern Age. *Star Trek, Raiders of the Lost Ark,* and *Alien,* are a few examples of 1980s comic book movies that came to be the highest grossing genre in Hollywood (Jones 2004, 326). The resulting increase in revenues to the comic book publishers caused concern for creators and artists who did not maintain ownership of their characters or receive cuts of profits they generated. Newer publishers on the scene offered creators unprecedented ownership and profit-sharing plans, forcing DC Comics and Marvel to offer royalties or other incentives to keep their talent. Jack Kirby, creator of Superman, was involved in a dispute with Marvel over their failure to return his original artwork or grant him proper credit or rights to his co-creations, like the Hulk, X-Men, Fantastic Four, and many others. The issue was resolved after fans actively came to his support, while other artists embraced their new freedom to create and tell stories of a range and complexity they had not dared before.

The Modern Age of comics also presented characters with a more hard-edged, self-examining style. Artist and writer Frank Miller's re-inventive work on the *Daredevil* series explored the darker side of the hero by examining the psychological motivations behind his actions. In *Batman: The Dark Knight Returns,* Miller revised Batman into a bitter, over the hill vigilante fighting against a fascist Superman in a Gotham City gone to hell, ultimately motivating Warner Brothers to make the Batman movie a reality (Jones 2004, 330). Miller's work redirected the superhero genre and helped set the stage for future creators through his development of superheroes with human emotions, conflicts, and problems. Newspaper editorials and fundamentalist religious groups publicly criticized the increase of darker themes and content. DC Comics responded in 1986 by launching its own rating system in attempt to alert parents and readers to age-appropriate titles.

The revision of superheroes and storylines to reflect a darker, more grim and gritty reality also generated popular anti-heroes such as the Punisher, Wolverine, Spawn, and independent publishers like Dark Horse Comics. Independent and small press comic books were growing, and while limited by distribution channels, they helped to revitalize and strengthen the entire comic book industry by establishing a collector's market spawning independent titles and specialty comic book shops. By the late 1980s collectors would buy almost any new title to get in on the comic book collector market, even as publishers produced more titles of questionable quality. DC Comics and Marvel maintained control of the mainstream market, yet to compete and boost readership and collectibility they created storylines stirring up their respective superhero universes. DC Comics' *Crisis on Infinite Earths,* aimed to simplify and reorganize their universe of worlds and characters, revitalizing their whole line of superheroes. A year later Marvel launched its *New Universe* series, marking the beginning of Marvel's second cosmological and mythological universe, but the series never took off and was phased out.

During the late 1980s and early 1990s, superheroes again dominated the comic book and mass market world. Marvel celebrated its 50th anniversary as well as the success of the 1989 feature film *Batman,* which broke every box office record to date (Jones 2004, 331) and increased the influx of comic book movie franchises into American popular culture. A number of independent comic book publishers arose, like Image Comics, and DC Comics' Vertigo imprint, offering alternatives to superheroes, like Neil R. Gaiman's *Sandman,* Miller's *Sin City,* and Todd McFarlane's *Spawn,* the latter two of which were eventually adapted into feature films. The 1990s appeared to be a time of growth, but things changed in the mid-1990s with the fall of the collector market and Marvel's declaration of bankruptcy. Even the new *Batman and Robin* feature film was a critical and financial flop. Marvel eventually worked its way out of financial trouble, but publishers had to continue offering gimmicks to attract readers back to the genre.

Trends and Themes. The American comic book industry today is comprised of many successful writers and artists like Geoff Johns, Jim Lee, Alex Ross, and particularly Brian Michael Bendis, along with a growing number of women creators like Jessica Abel, Devin Grayson, and Gail Simone. Yet, some of today's most influential writers are native to England and Scotland, such as Warren Ellis and Mark Millar. Bendis, Ellis, and Millar are known particularly for their carefully developed characters and storylines, dynamic dialogue, attention to and commentary on political and global issues, and for vastly redefining and re-envisioning American superheroes.

Context and Issues

The Golden Age. The modern American comic book emerged in the 1930s when two sales employees at Eastern Color Printing Company, Max C. Gaines and Harry I. Wildenberg, decided to package regular newspaper comic strips into a tabloid-sized magazine, called *Funnies on Parade,* to pass on to distributors for use as advertising premiums or giveaways. A successful model, imitations of the comic book format grew and became widely recognized in 1935 when new and original content was commissioned. Many comic books during this time grew from detective story and science fiction roots; it wasn't until 1938 that the industry was put on the map with its first "star" in Superman.

Created by teenagers Joe Shuster and Jerry Siegel, Superman became the United States' first hero since Davy Crockett and Paul Bunyon, and offered readers fantastic realities unworkable in other visual entertainment media of the time. The success of Superman and other heroes like Batman and the Green Lantern resulted in hundreds of costumed imitators throughout the next several years as comic books flourished, sales climbed, and readership reached its prime.

The emergence of World War II and decreasing health and economic standards cultivated readers' desires for happy stories and humor, adventure, magic, fantasy, detective, war, romance, crime, and Wild West genres were developed for comic books. Teenage romance characters such as Archie and adventure stories about Sheena, Queen of the Jungle, helped meet this need, while "kiddie" comic books from Disney and Looney Toons offered humor to children and adults with fun characters like Donald Duck, Porky Pig, and Elmer Fudd. By 1945 comic books reflected women's more visible role in society of joining the workforce while men were away at war. Female heroines emerged with Pocket Comics' Black Cat, the first major costumed action heroine in comic books, and later with Wonder Woman. Aside from superheroines, characters like Patsy Walker, Millie the Model, and Nellie the Nurse offered stereotypically portrayed American career women in the workplace with humor and innocent romance, setting the stage for the romance comic boom that hit in 1947 as publishers looked for ways to expand readership and audiences due to the slump in superhero sales and circulation. Educational and animal comic books also became popular as comic book reading became a habit of most children and teenagers. Humor comics further fueled the boom as the industry continued to grow at a fast pace.

Cowboy comics briefly emerged as the next hot trend, but were quickly eclipsed by criminal stories depicting sex, violence, and lurid tales of murder and mayhem to re-entice adult readers. The crime comic book boom morphed into horror comics, which continued to depict murder and gore; although stories were carefully crafted to include social, moral, and philosophical messages. However, vociferous parents and critics focused only on the violent, gothic plots and sensually drawn women, which plummeted the general public's opinion of comic books. People feared that the messages these comic books communicated to children and teens were undermining or replacing parents, teachers, and religious leaders as moral authorities.

This attitude created the climate for a fallout of comic book success and invited the censorship of the Comics Code Authority. In 1954, psychiatrist Fredric Wertham published *Seduction of the Innocent*, positing a petition against comic books. Wertham spun his contention that comic books were stimulus for destructive and criminal behavior, even though none of his research demonstrated such conclusions. Critics of Wertham felt his logic discredited the ability of children and teenagers to distinguish fantasy from reality, and omitted evidence that comic books help children learn to read. In fact, many organizations were dedicated to producing educational comic books with subjects ranging from religious messages, prevention of sexually transmitted diseases, or messages against smoking, drinking, and drugs. Regardless, Wertham's speculations stirred up a storm and led the comic book industry to self-censor to protect itself from overzealous censors or lawsuits. The industry adopted the Comics Code Authority in October 1954, to monitor editorial and advertising content in comic books. A seal of approval displayed on comic book covers alerted news dealers and parents to the suitability of what was being sold to children, and many news dealers refused to sell comic books not displaying the seal.

Wertham and the Code are often credited for the downfall of the Golden Age of American comic books. Critics of the Code felt it placed comic books on a childlike level through the prohibition of plot devices like crime, triumph of evil, violence, illicit sexual relations, and narcotics or drug addiction. Comic book writers and artists also were not able to deal with real world social or political issues with any sort of honesty or truthfulness. Formerly popular crime and horror comic books nearly vanished after being relegated to relying more on suspense in the stories rather than detailed gore, resulting in the emergence of mystery stories and the revival of superheroes.

Reception. The turn of the millennium saw a rise in independent and literary comic books and graphic novels, with the continuing influence of comic books in other areas of popular culture. Fantagraphics's independent publications garnered increased attention, like Chris Ware's *Jimmy Corrigan, the Smartest Kid on Earth*, serialized in the *Acme Library*, and Gilbert and Jamie Hernandez's revival of their *Love and Rockets* series. Mainstream comics continued to stimulate American film and television and more movies and shows based on comic books were developed. Film adaptations of the X-Men, Spider-Man, and other superheroes and comics became prominent in the market while television shows such as the *Smallville* and the *Justice League Unlimited* cartoon were successful.

Selected Authors

Brian Michael Bendis (b. 1967). Following art school, well-known comic book writer and occasional artist Brian Michael Bendis emerged in the comic book world in the 1990s with independent, creator-owned series and later began working with Image Comics where he developed *Torso*, about the hunt for the Cleveland Torso Murderer. Well known for his dialogue style and story arc pace, Bendis's transition from crime and noir stories to superhero noir stories began in 2000 when Marvel asked him to revitalize Spider-Man for their Ultimate line.

Bendis embraced the opportunity and was largely successful revamping the popular superhero and appeased even hardcore fans. In *Ultimate Spider-Man* Bendis brought Peter Parker into the new century and created a story about a kid who gets powers during modern times as opposed to the Peter Parker of 1962. Instead of getting bit by a radioactive spider as in the original, Bendis's Parker gets bitten by Osborn Industries' genetically engineered spider that has been subject to drug tests. Rather than working at the *Daily Bugle* print newspaper office, the new Parker is employed at the *eBugle*, an online newspaper. Parker's Aunt May and Uncle Ben are younger than in previous iterations, and his love interest, Mary Jane, has more intellectual interests than her 1960s predecessor.

Bendis's Spider-Man remains a human being underneath the costume and has more problems than powers. Spider-Man is strong, but he can also be hurt physically and emotionally, just like anyone else, and Parker has everyday problems like the rest of us: getting laundry done, money worries, and deadlines at work. Bendis's leisurely pace allows readers to better know Spider-Man and his supporting cast, rendering more depth of character, a major point of praise for Bendis's reworking of this title. *Ultimate Spider-Man* was generally well received by old and new fans alike. A best seller its first month in publication and later a successful feature film, some fans still had their criticisms, but most were pleased Bendis did not mess with the essentials of Stan Lee and Steve Ditko's original character. In fact, many argue Bendis improved upon the original by creating a more enriched Spider-Man mythos through his fleshed out characters and dialogue.

Bendis's *Alias* was another groundbreaking title he contributed to the American comic book scene. In 2001, *Alias* was the debut title in Marvel's new "MAX Comics," a mature-themed line aimed at adult readers, often depicting scenes of sex and violence. Bendis was prepared to tone down the sex and violence when he pitched *Alias* to Marvel, but instead they decided to bypass the irrelevant Comics Code Authority and released their own rating system, one demonstration of Bendis's influence on today's comic book industry.

Blending crime and superhero genres, *Alias* focuses on Jessica Jones, a former superheroine turned private investigator. Through Jessica Jones and the MAX Comics line, Bendis was able to explore typically taboo aspects of superheroes' lives, such as their moral principles, decisions, and "humanity." Jones, a self-declared failed superheroine, is self-destructive and has quite an inferiority complex due to her lack of acceptance within the superhero loop. When a routine missing persons case not only reveals, but video records the secret identity of Captain Marvel, Jones finds herself in a dilemma calling into question Jones's principles and the power dynamics of her former and current relationship to the superhero world. Not only is she faced with "outing" one of the most well-known heroes, but also with the decision to render him powerless by exposing his true identity. In essence, Jessica realizes absolute power can inflict powerlessness and loss of will on others, and wrestles over which side of this power dynamic she belongs on. Readers experience her struggle through her self-destructive behavior including excessive drinking, foul-mouthed blow-ups, and promiscuity. Moral and ethical decisions are not typically fleshed out for comic book characters, especially superheroes, but Bendis shows readers explicitly how Jessica battles her dilemma and her self-worth through her reckless actions, ultimately rendering her more human and relatable.

Alias illustrates Bendis's knack for natural, engaging dialogue, and for altering the Marvel universe to influence the comic book industry one character at a time. Within the first two months on the stands, *Alias* sold out despite its graphic scenes of violent or sexual nature inappropriate for younger audiences.

Warren Ellis (b. 1968). British writer Warren Ellis has played a prominent role in today's American comic books as a prolific creator displaying breadth and diversity of subjects, genres, and forms. He is known for his approachable and consistent Internet presence through various comics and culture message boards, forums, and blogs he hosts online, creating a strong connection with his fans. A writer of comic books since 1994 when he began working for Marvel, Ellis has been key in redefining and ushering the superhero into the twenty-first century. Ellis's work often displays grim worldviews and frequently explores various futures rather than pasts while also addressing current issues around popular culture, technology, gender roles, global politics, and human rights. In 1999, Ellis and artist Bryan Hitch collaborated on one of his most highlighted titles, *The Authority,* featuring a team of superheroes striving to change the world for the better, rather than merely maintain the status quo. Critics and readers alike responded positively to Ellis's treatment of the superhero in *The Authority.* Ellis avoided stereotypical superpowers and personalities by developing human characters that happen to have superpowers and display a sense of humor regarding their overblown celebrity status, demonstrating their ability to deconstruct their roles within society and explicitly recognize and comment on the importance of world peace and human rights over their own notoriety.

Rather than traditional powers like flying or superhuman strength, Ellis's Authority heroes display more advanced and unique powers. Jack Hawksmoor, "King of the Cities," demonstrates superhuman agility and strength and has the capability to "read" and control urban environments through telepathy, allowing him to link into and control any city through such means as the animation and possession of architecture and infrastructure. Meanwhile, Angie Spica distilled numerous intelligent technological devices into nine pints of liquid machinery to replace her blood and became "The Engineer" with nanotechnology flowing through her body offering infinite mechanical abilities, such as tapping into technological infrastructures or creating weapons.

The Authority was also groundbreaking through its positive portrayal of a homosexual couple on the team. Apollo and Midnighter, at first glance, seem to be stereotypical muscle-ridden, masculine heroes yet are romantic partners in a caring, monogamous relationship. While homosexual characters are not new to comic books, positive and prominent portrayals of homosexual characters are. Ellis's readers see the tender, intimate side of their relationship several times without being distracted from the main plot. He illustrates a healthy rather than dysfunctional homosexual relationship between essential characters when typically homosexual comic book characters are portrayed in poor light or end up killed off.

Apollo and Midnighter's groundbreaking relationship in *The Authority* generally garnered positive responses from readers. There was some controversy regarding a panel illustrating a kiss between the two men and Ellis was asked to alter it to show Apollo kissing Midnighter on the cheek instead. Readers responded indignantly to DC Comics editors questioning why a series regularly depicting murder, genocide, and events of mass destruction should warrant censoring an innocuous kiss between a homosexual couple. Aside from pushing the boundaries of the superhero and gender roles, *The Authority* also speaks volumes to current world issues such as global politics and human rights. At the turn of the millennium, the team encounters global political and economic superpowers such as the Europe and Japan, as well as terrorist-prone and vulnerable cities such as London, Los Angeles, and New

York. Fighting to protect inhabitants of planet Earth the team fights colonization by other planets and protects human rights by punishing those committing genocide and political corruption in their nations.

Ellis's more recent collaboration with artist Ben Templesmith on *Fell* is another series widely recognized for its dense storytelling and experimentation with comic book forms and models of production. In *Fell*, Detective Richard Fell has been transferred "from over the bridge" to Snowtown, a resident described "feral city" that is run-down, decayed, and plagued with poverty and crime. An illustration of Ellis's grim worldview, Snowtown offers an anonymous depiction of a mixture of many existing urban contexts and problems, and Templesmith's gloomy colors and gritty illustrations enhance that feeling.

Detective Fell goes about his work trying to make sense of this city whose desperate citizens have given up on it yet spray paint the city's tag everywhere as a form of protective magic, in hopes the city won't destroy what has already been labeled its own. Fell goes about solving unique and bizarre crimes in each issue, but citizens question his practices. Crime is such a prevalent part of daily life in Snowtown, they don't understand Fell's motivations for solving crimes that will just occur again the very next day, or hour, for that matter. It seems as if Fell wants to change Snowtown for the better, rather than maintaining the status quo, sentiments Ellis's characters in *The Authority* also exhibit.

Aside from the dense and meaningful stories, Ellis's experimentation with the form of *Fell* is perhaps its greatest contribution to modern American comic books. Creator owned, *Fell* was conceived by Ellis and designed to be accessible to readers financially and contextually. At $1.99 per issue (well under the price of today's comics costing between $2.50 and $3.99) readers could enter a comic shop with pocket change and leave with a self-contained story in one issue rather than longer story arcs requiring the purchase of multiple issues. Undertaking a comic sticking to this price point meant both Ellis and artist Templesmith remained uncompensated until issues were printed and actually sold.

Ellis's low cost model required compressed stories with shorter page counts, but was supplemented with "back material" including unfinished artwork, author notes expanding on the story, and reader responses. Still in production, *Fell* has been positively received by readers and critics alike for both its form and content, and has garnered several comic book award nominations. Readers have shown gratitude to Ellis and Image Comics for developing a low cost pricing model and appreciate Ellis's full use of the shorter page count through carefully developed dense and full storylines in each issue.

Mark Millar (b. 1969). Scottish comic book writer Mark Millar began writing comics as a college student. Initially his work was submitted to and published by British comic book presses, like the popular *Saviour,* which Trident Comics published in the early 1990s. DC Comics brought Millar into the mainstream American comics scene where he immediately established a high-profile by taking over Warren Ellis's *The Authority* in 2000. However, scheduling, artist, and censorship problems with editors and competing lucrative offers from publishers caused Millar to move to Marvel in 2001 where he began working on their *Ultimate* line of comics.

Marvel's *Ultimate* line aimed to increase readership by revamping popular Marvel Universe characters to make them accessible and attractive to new readers. Millar played a seminal role in re-writing the Marvel character histories through his work on *Ultimate X-Men, Ultimate Fantastic Four,* and most notably *The Ultimates.* In the Ultimate Marvel Universe, The Ultimates (known as The Avengers in previous Marvel Universes) are a team of superheroes banded together to fend off supervillains and other superhuman threats. Millar's task was not to merely provide a face-lift to these Marvel Universe characters, but to start from scratch and rebuild them anew.

The Ultimates included core members from The Avengers, like Captain America, Iron Man, Thor, Wasp, Giant Man, and The Hulk, with a handful of others. The Ultimates team is funded by the United States military through S.H.I.E.L.D. (Strategic Hazard Intervention, Espionage and Logistics Directorate), a counterterrorism intelligence unit directed by Nick Fury, former U.S. Army hero and spy. Fury, with the backing of the U.S. government, hopes to reinvigorate the super-soldier program that originally spawned Captain America and recruits The Ultimates to fight against increasingly threatening global meta-human and mutant activity.

Emergent themes in Millar's *The Ultimates* series reflect current global and domestic issues such as homeland security, colonization and genocide, and the United States' motives and involvement with the Middle East. Early on The Ultimates face protecting homeland security and the challenge of controlling their own member, The Hulk, as he rampages New York City going after his ex-girlfriend's date in a jealous rage, killing over eight hundred civilians. Millar carefully develops his characters before moving on to his next story arc where The Ultimates protect the Earth from colonization and possible extinction, reflecting current genocide crimes and the imperialistic global climate. Millar wanted his superheroes to be working and fighting relevant and meaningful battles rather than chasing down supervillains, and this is apparent in the sequel, *The Ultimates 2,* where the team begins to face potential involvement in United States foreign relations in the Middle East. Pressured by the White House to work with European Union supersoldiers, members of The Ultimates begin to question their role in helping the United States push for increasing global power and control of oil resources. Climatically the group faces off against the Liberators, a superhero force comprised of recruits from enemy nations in the series like Iran, North Korea, China, Russia, and Syria, reflecting the recent threat of attacks on American land. Battling the Liberator's invasion on United States soil, The Ultimates organize a counter-offensive and successfully defeat the invaders one-by-one.

Throughout the larger obstacles facing The Ultimates Millar weaves in subplots and themes allowing for character development such as: Janet (the Wasp) and Hank Pym's (Giant Man) marital issues; Bruce Banner's (The Hulk) internal struggles over his abilities as a research scientist trying to reformulate the super soldier serum; and Steve Rogers's (Captain America) adjustments to living in the modern world after being resurrected from a World War II incident in 1945. The rich subplots also reveal tensions within the group. Some members distrust Bruce Banner because of his volatility and perceived lack of mental stability, while Hank Pym is jealous of the attention Steve Rogers has been paying his wife, Janet. Other tensions relate to the goals and mission of their team. Thor, in particular, feels they should not be used as a tool for the U.S. to establish its power with preemptive strikes, and is quite vocal about his opinions, causing some to question his loyalty to the group. Meanwhile, their celebrity status causes other tensions. Some team members share snide remarks regarding Tony Stark's (Iron Man) numerous television news talk show appearances and romantic trysts with leading ladies of Hollywood, or demonstrate jealousy about Captain America's potential movie deal.

Readers familiar with the Marvel Universe were likely skeptical Millar could successfully re-write decades old mythology without alienating fans and characters or destroying the continuity of the existing Marvel Universe, but responses to *The Ultimates* were mostly favorable, especially among reviewers and critics. Some hardcore fans blasted Millar and his work on various comic book message boards and blogs, but the soaring sales figures spoke to the success of Millar's undertaking.

Millar's exploration of American domestic issues continued in his much anticipated seven-part *Civil War* series published by Marvel Comics in 2006 and 2007. Considered a "Marvel Comics Event," the storyline included superheroes fighting against one another in an ideological battle that could forever change the Marvel Universe. The basis of the conflict regarded the Superhuman Registration Act, a law passed by the U.S. government that required all superhumans to register their powers and identities with the government or be persecuted by S.H.I.E.L.D. (the government-funded superhuman counterterrorism and intelligence unit). The law registered superhumans, and non-government enforcers like civilian supporters. Reaction to the policy among superheroes was mixed, creating a divide between former allies with the pro-registration camp, led by Iron Man, and the anti-registration camp, led by Captain America.

Millar uses this conflict as a basis to explore many current domestic issues facing the United States, such as the immigration reform debate, the politically and ideologically divided climate of the nation, and the erosion of civil liberties. The Superhuman Registration Act and the superhuman's reactions to it reflect some of the debates surrounding the United States' immigration reform issue. Some heroes feel they shouldn't have to register with the government since they already positively contribute to society by capturing supervillains or protecting the public. On the other hand, the pro-registration camp recognizes the value of standardized training for superhumans and feels the registration process would allow for more legitimacy and respect from the American public.

Millar's political allegory continues with the divided superhero community replicating the currently divided political ideologies of the American public under the current administration. The philosophical war the superheroes are experiencing brings up issues of government oversight and involvement in the private lives of its citizens, including the erosion of civil liberties. The anti-registration camp feels that being forced to work for the government produces governmental lackeys and, ultimately, that it undermines their freedom to perform their work as they choose. They also feel that their civil liberties are threatened because if they register and reveal their true identities, then their privacy and safety are at risk. Regardless of whether or not they register they will be subject to heavy surveillance by registration enforcers or by S.H.I.E.L.D.

Millar's *Civil War* was highly anticipated and sales soared, though reader response remained mixed, as is normal with a major comic book event such as this. Millar's undertaking changed the Marvel Universe in a big way and readers will continue to learn to what extent the future Marvel storylines involving *Civil War* characters develop from the outcome of the war. Even *Civil War's* numerous "crossovers" or "tie-ins" (stories that combine two or more otherwise separated characters, stories, settings or universes that meet and interact with each other) demonstrated the multitude to which this conflict altered and influenced the mythology of the Marvel Universe. While crossovers and tie-ins are normal in the comic book industry, Millar's *Civil War* spawned over one hundred comic book issues under over twenty titles, demonstrating the impact of *Civil War* on the Marvel

Universe and comic book industry. Numerous new titles were also developed from the plotlines in *Civil War,* which illustrate and unfold the results of the war in the entire Marvel Universe.

Women in Today's Comic Book Industry. Some criticize the comic book industry for remaining a "boys club" due to the prominent number of males in the field, yet female editors, writers, and artists are becoming more common and gaining more recognition for their work in the medium. American writer Devin Grayson's (b. 1971) *Batman: Gothic Knights* emerged in 2000, making her the first woman to have a regular ongoing writing assignment on the Batman title and garnered distinction and recognition among the industry and from fans. Grayson's Batman marked a new direction in that she brought a concern for relationships to the character, something her male contemporaries did not display as well in their stories. Nominated in 1999 and 2000 for the Comics Buyer's Guide Award for Favorite Writer, Grayson is still an active comic book writer today. In 2005 she wrapped up a five year run on *Nightwing,* wrote the creator owned *Matador* for DC Comics' Wildstorm imprint, and in 2006 published *DC Universe: Inheritance,* a novel about fathers and sons, starring Batman, Nightwing, Green Arrow, Arsenal, Aquaman, and Tempest.

Jessica Abel (b. 1969) is another American comic book writer and artist gaining recognition whose work leans more toward the independent or alternative genre of comic books. Abel self-published her embellished hand-bound comic book *Artbabe* in the early 1990s, which was eventually picked up by Fantagraphics for publication. Abel delved into longer comic books in 2000 when she started *La Perdida,* originally a five part series later reissued as a single volume in 2005. Receiving positive critical response, *La Perdida* featured a Mexican American woman, Carla, venturing into Mexico City in search of her identity after being raised only by her white American mother. Abel's work often includes the experiences of Generation X characters and demonstrates careful attention to communicating her characters' gestures and facial expressions. Recently Abel has worked on *Carmina,* a prose novel for teens, *Life Sucks,* a new graphic novel, and a textbook about making comics.

Gail Simone is yet another prominent woman writer in today's comic book industry. Simone first entered mainstream comics with her work on *Deadpool* (later relaunched as *Agent X*) in 2002, but had previously been noticed by comic book fans through her *Women in Refrigerators* website cataloging the many instances in which female comic book characters were victimized in plot devices for male protagonists. Simone took over DC Comics' *Birds of Prey,* featuring an all-female cast of characters. Her work on this title has garnered credit for her balance of suspenseful action, thoughtful character development, and humor. Simone has also contributed to DC Comics' 2006 "Infinite Crisis" event through the *Villains United* series, in which she revitalized the Catwoman character. She remains active in the online comic book community through her "You'll All Be Sorry" weekly column on the Comic Book Resources website, and through *Bloodstains on the Looking Glass,* her blog. She continues to write and recently has worked on a series for *Gen 13* as well as *Welcome to Tranquility,* a creator owned project for Wildstorm.

Bibliography

Abel, Jessica. *Artbabe* [Issues 1–5]. Self-published, 1992–1996.

———. *Artbabe* [Vol. 2] [Issues 1–4]. Seattle, WA: Fantagraphics, 1997–1999.

———. *La Perdida.* New York: Pantheon Books, 2006.

———. *Carmina*. New York: HarperCollins, forthcoming in 2007.

———. *Life Sucks*. New York: First Second, 2008.

Bendis, Brian Michael. *Torso*. Orange, CA: Image Comics, 2001.

———. *Ultimate Spider-Man: Power and Responsibility* [Vol. 1]. New York: Marvel Comics, 2001.

———. *Ultimate Spider-Man: Learning Curve* [Vol. 2]. New York: Marvel Comics, 2001.

———. *Alias*. New York: Marvel Comics, 2002.

Benton, Mike. *The Comic Book in America: An Illustrated History*. Dallas, TX: Taylor Publications, 1989.

Burton, Tim. *Batman*. Warner Home Video, 1989.

Donner, Richard. *Superman*. Warner Home Video, 1978.

Ellis, Warren. *The Authority: Relentless* [Vol. 1]. LaJolla, CA: Wildstorm/DC Comics, 2000a.

———. *The Authority: Under New Management* [Vol. 2]. LaJolla, CA: Wildstorm/DC Comics, 2000b.

———. *Fell* [Issues 1, 2, 4, 5]. Orange, CA: Image Comics, 2006.

Gaiman, Neil. *The Sandman* [Issues 1–75]. New York: Vertigo, 1989–1996.

Grayson, Devin. *Batman: Gothic Knights* [Issues 1–32]. New York: DC Comics, 2000–2002.

———. *Nightwing* [Issues 53, 71–100, 108–117]. New York: DC Comics, 2000–2005.

———. *Matador* [Issues 1–6]. LaJolla, CA: Wildstorm/DC Comics, 2005.

———. *DC Universe: Inheritance*. New York: Warner Books, 2006.

Jones, Gerard. *Men of Tomorrow: Geeks, Gangsters, and the Birth of the Comic Book*. New York: Basic Books, 2004.

Justice League Unlimited. 2001–2007. Created by Gardner Fox. Warner Brothers Entertainment.

Lucas, George. *Raiders of the Lost Ark*. Paramount Home Video, 1981.

McFarlane, Todd. *Spawn* [Issues 1–73]. Orange, CA: Image Comics, 1992–1998.

Millar, Mark. *Saviour* [Issues 1–5]. Leicester, UK: Trident Comics, 1990.

———. *Ultimate X-Men* [Issues 1–12, 15–33]. New York: Marvel Comics, 2000–2003.

———. *The Ultimates: Superhuman* [Vol. 1]. New York: Marvel Comics, 2002.

———. *Ultimate Fantastic Four* [Issues 1–6]. New York: Marvel Comics, 2003–2004.

———. *The Ultimates: Homeland Security* [Vol. 2]. New York: Marvel Comics, 2004.

———. *The Ultimates 2: Gods and Monsters* [Vol. 1]. New York: Marvel Comics, 2005.

———. *Civil War* [Issues 1–3, 5, 6]. New York: Marvel Comics, 2006–2007.

Miller, Frank. *Batman: The Dark Knight Returns* [Issues 1–4]. New York: DC Comics, 1986.

———. *Daredevil* [Issues 168–191]. New York: Marvel Comics, 1981–1983.

———. *Sin City* [Issues 1–13]. Dark Horse Comics, 1991–1992. Milwaukie, OR.

Schumacher, Joel. *Batman and Robin*. Warner Home Video, 1997.

Scott, Ridley. *Alien*. Twentieth Century Fox Home Entertainment, 1984.

Simone, Gail. *Deadpool* [Issues 65–69]. New York: Marvel Comics, 2002.

———. *Agent X* [Issues 1–15]. New York: Marvel Comics, 2002–2003.

———. *Birds of Prey* [Issues 56–102]. New York: DC Comics, 2003–2007.

———. *Villains United* [Issues 1–6]. New York: DC Comics, 2005.

———. *Gen 13* [Vol. 4] [Issues 1–4]. LaJolla, CA: Wildstorm/DC Comics, 2006–2007.

———. *Welcome to Tranquility* [Issues 1–6]. LaJolla, CA: Wildstorm/DC Comics, 2006–2007.

———. *Bloodstains on the Looking Glass* [Online January 2007]. http://happystains.blogspot.com/.

———. *You'll All Be Sorry* [Weekly Column] [Online January 2007]. www.comicbookresources.com/columns.

———. *Women in Refrigerators* [Online January 2007]. http://www.unheardtaunts.com/wir/.

Smallville. 2001–2007. Created by Alfred Gough and Miles Millar. Warner Brothers Entertainment.

Ware, Chris. *Acme Novelty Library*. New York: Pantheon, 2005.

Wertham, Fredric. *Seduction of the Innocent*. New York: Rinehart, 1954.

Wise, Robert. *Star Trek*. Paramount Home Video, 1980.

Further Reading

Benton, Mike. *The Comic Book in America: An Illustrated History.* Dallas, TX: Taylor Publications, 1989; Klock, Geoff. *How to Read Superhero Comics and Why.* New York: Continuum, 2002; McCloud, Scott. *Reinventing Comics: How Imagination and Technology are Revolutionizing an Art Form.* New York: Perennial, 2000; McCloud, Scott. *Understanding Comics.* New York: HarperPerennial, 1994; and Wright, Bradford. *Comic Book Nation: The Transformation of Youth Culture in America.* Baltimore, MD: Johns Hopkins University Press, 2001.

LESLIE BUSSERT

COMING OF AGE FICTION

Stories of adolescents confronting the travails of growing up constitute one of the most readily identifiable genres in American fiction. Oddly enough, the preponderance of such works has resulted in critical inattention, with few scholars willing to take on the formidable project of taxonomizing a hurly-burly form whose twenty-first-century exemplars can range from winsome explorations of savant idealism (Jonathan Safran Foer's *Extremely Loud and Incredibly Close,* 2005) to prurient exposés of teenage decadence (Nick McDonnell's *Twelve,* 2002). The relative paucity of scholarship is unfortunate, for how authors deploy the genre's conventions can reveal a great deal about how the cultural identity of the American teenager is construed at any given historical moment—a concern usually left to sociologists, who more likely look to film and popular music rather than literature as proof texts. Although works such as John Updike's *Rabbit, Run* (1960) helped shaped perceptions of the Silent Generation, and, to a far less canonical extent, cult classics like Richard Fariña's *Been Down So Long it Looks Like Up to Me* (1966) and Douglas Coupland's *Generation X* (1991) influenced enduring images of hipsters and slackers, the social function of coming-of-age fiction is frequently subsumed within more familiar academic concerns such as gender, race, and class. For contemporary fiction, this means that a stellar novel such as Tobias Wolff's *Old School* (2003) garners attention more for what its prep-school setting says about Fitzgeraldesque aspiration and elitism than how its pre-Kennedy assassination milieu reflects the predominance of baby-boomer nostalgia. Debut efforts by J.T. LeRoy (*Sarah,* 2000), Nell Freudenberger (*Lucky Girls,* 2004), and Curtis Sittenfeld (*Prep,* 2005), meanwhile, are alternately praised as wunderkind achievements or dismissed as publishing hype. As a result, what their protagonists' maladjustment says about the current state of the American family and its effect on such central teenage temptations as sex, drug abuse, and consumerism remains unexamined. To appreciate fully how coming-of-age fiction at least reinforces, if not directly enables, the construction of generational identity, authors and readers alike must acknowledge how the genre's central themes and traits are constantly rearticulated within ongoing "moral panics"—those cultural debates in which

> the official or press reaction to a deviant social or cultural phenomenon [associated with young people] is 'out of proportion' to the actual threat . . . It implies that public concern is in excess of what is appropriate if concern were directly proportional to objective harm. (Springhall 1999, 7)

Definition. At its most basic, coming-of-age fiction involves young people confronting one or more moral crises associated with maturation. Although these crises typically revolve around major initiation rituals—loss of virginity, high-school

THE CATCHER IN THE RYE

The quintessential example of the resistance to growing up, of course, is J.D. Salinger's *The Catcher in the Rye* (1951), in which Holden Caulfield clings furiously to childhood innocence in a desperate effort to elude the contagion of "phoniness" that he believes infects adults. Despite the rebellion and insouciance that the genre promotes, its exemplary narratives rarely challenge the underlying ideologies of adulthood. Nowhere, for example, does *The Catcher in the Rye* question whether the "traditional" nuclear family is a historical quirk rather than a universal ideal—it merely expresses sorrow over parents being too distracted by material pursuits to give that ideal more than lip service.

or college graduation, entry into the work world, even marriage and/or unplanned parenthood—the protagonists' attitude toward initiation is usually influenced by his or her regard for the moral example set by parents and mentors, which in turn determines the degree to which characters are willing to assume the responsibilities of productive adulthood. From the 1920s to the 1980s, coming-of-age stories expressed reservation about the moral compromises that these responsibilities entail and questioned the meaningfulness of the rewards society dispenses for fulfilling them. The genre thus has a long, canonical history of valorizing youth as the ethical apogee of the life cycle, with any capitulation to elders' standards deemed a falling away from the idealism and intuitive certainty that young people are said to embody.

History. By and large, contemporary novels reiterate this ideal. As such, what Leslie Feidler first asserted in 1958 remains true today: fictional adolescents are often a "projection of our [adult] moral plight . . . of *our* guiltiness in failing to protect and cultivate children's original purity with enough love and security" (24). This projection is never more apparent than when a fictional text such as Tom Wolfe's salacious campus parody *I Am Charlotte Simmons* (2004) is cited as anecdotal evidence of youth's disaffection in nonfiction studies such as Jean M. Twenge's *Generation Me: Why Today's Young Americans Are More Confident, Assertive, Entitled—and More Miserable Than Ever Before* (2006). That is, fictional teens are often taken as prima facie evidence of what *real* adolescents are experiencing, with little critical investigation into who writes such narratives and who their intended audience might be.

One reason that most critics shy away from cataloguing the genre's formal traits is that, in practice, just about every element of the above definition requires qualification. For starters, there is no consensus on the age boundaries that constitute "young people." Works such as Leif Enger's *Peace Like a River* (2001) take their cues from Harper Lee's *To Kill a Mockingbird* (1961) and employ Scout Finch-style characters on the cusp of puberty. Others—Marshall Boswell's *Alternative Atlanta*, Dave King's *The Ha-Ha* (both 2005)—recall Beat Generation classics by centering upon aimless thirty- and even forty-year-old protagonists suffering from extended adolescences. Nor does the genre display any consensus about the success of maturation. Some efforts follow the *David Copperfield* model by concluding with heroes and heroines completing the *bildung* process (Lauren Grodstein's *Reproduction is the Flaw of Love*, 2004; Kim Wong Keltner's *The Dim Sum of All Things*, 2005). Others are more akin to F. Scott Fitzgerald's *This Side of Paradise* by resisting the equation of growing up and narrative closure (Dan Pope's *In the Cherry Tree*, 2003).

Attitudes toward popular culture and its potential effect on identity formation differ as well. In some cases (Debra Weinstein's *Apprentice to the Flower Poet Z.,* 2004, Gordon Korman's *Born to Rock,* 2006), art is a genuine medium of self-making; in others, it represents the soullessness of consumerism (Brad Whittington's *Welcome to Fred,* 2003). In the end, one cannot even say that the genre appeals to a specific reader. Coming-of-age narratives aimed at teenage readers tend to be tagged "young-adult fiction" (Lauren Myracle's *TTYL,* 2004, and *TTFN,* 2005). Those aimed at a generational segment are generally marketed to a "hip" collegiate audience (Marisha Pessl's *Special Topics in Calamity Physics,* 2006), while others fall into that unfortunately named "**chick-lit**" category (Ann Brashare's *Sisterhood of the Traveling Pants* series, 2001–). Still others achieve recognition as "serious" literature (Mark Haddon's *The Curious Case of the Dog in the Night-Time,* 2003). In select cases—Alice Sebold's *The Lovely Bones* (2002), Ian Caldwell and Dustin Thomason's *The Rule of the Four* (2004)—the maturation drama may even seem secondary in comparison to more prominent generic elements drawn from supernatural, horror, or mystery/suspense.

Additionally, coming of age need not even dramatize the concerns of the present generation. In many cases, the form appears in historical novels as a means of dramatizing social changes in a past decade, as when Mark Childress in *One Mississippi* (2006) explores racism and homophobia in the mid-1970s South or Don DeGrazia in *American Skin* (2000) treats the same topics in the late 1980s Chicago hardcore punk scene. Nor can one speak of a definitively "American" experience. By far, the most pronounced trend in the genre in recent years is the preoccupation with multiculturalism, with authors such as Edwidge Danticant, Jhumpa Lahiri, Chris Abini, and Jeffrey Eugenides exploring issues of double consciousness, assimilation, and nationalism through the maturation plot's standard conventions and motifs.

Despite the variety of works that can be labeled coming-of-age fiction, the genre draws its conventions from several recognizable narrative forms that imbue it with mythic depth and relevance. Foremost among these is the quest plot found in classic Greek epics such as the *Odyssey* and later medieval romances, whether the *Romance of the Rose* or *Sir Gawain and the Green Knight.* Because quest narratives are structured as a series of temptations that test a young warrior's moral virtue, the plot functions as an allegory of the journey of life, with young people striving to maintain the purity of their convictions in a fallen world rife with sin. Holden Caulfield's fantasy of protecting children from falling off the cliff of rye while they play is his version of the knightly charge, with the fall a symbol of the Biblical fall into knowledge that would cost the children their prelapsarian innocence. In contemporary versions, Foer's *Extremely Loud and Incredibly Close* most overtly evokes this motif. After his father is killed in the September 11, 2001, terrorist attacks, the book's precocious narrator, Oskar Schell, sets out through New York City to discover the meaning of a secret key belonging to his lost parent. Other exemplars of this tradition subvert and even parody its pretension to chivalric nobility: Tristan Egolf's *Skirt and the Fiddle* (2002) reads like a slapstick inversion of *Pilgrim's Progress,* with its violin-prodigy hero, Charlie Evans, attempting to maintain his love for Louise Gascoygne as he navigates farcical scenarios instigated by his best friend, the anarchist Tinsel Greetz.

A related genre from which coming-of-age fiction has long borrowed is the picaresque. Emerging from sixteenth-century Spain with the anonymously published *Lazarillo de Tormes* and in eighteenth-century England with Henry Fielding's

Joseph Andrews and *Tom Jones* (not to mention Daniel Defoe's *Moll Flanders*) the picaresque chronicles the adventures of a roguish hero whose journey is more of an episodic ramble than a moral quest. In the American tradition, the most influential picaresque novel has been Mark Twain's *The Adventures of Huckleberry Finn* (1884). With the popularity of Jack Kerouac's *On the Road* (1957), the American picaresque became known as the "road novel" by employing the thrill of interstate travel as a metaphor for adrenaline-rush exploration of illicit sex, drugs, and music. Like many a contemporary picaresque, Dave Eggers's *You Shall Know Our Velocity!* (2002) wears its Beat Generation affinities on its sleeve, but with a twist: instead of emulating the scheming and petty thievery of Sal Paradise and Dean Moriarty, Eggers's Will and Hand jaunt the globe attempting to give away an undeserved inheritance. In a similar vein, David Schickler's *Sweet and Vicious* (2004) updates another popular variation of the picaresque, the "on-the-lam" novel, with a pair of star-crossed lovers, Henry and Grace, running both from mobsters and their own haunted pasts. It is perhaps indicative of the increasingly global and multi-ethnic mindset of contemporary writers that twenty-first-century road novels rarely stay within American borders. In addition to Eggers's *Velocity,* several modern picaresque roam to international as opposed to domestic settings.

Even more than the quest narrative and the picaresque, coming-of-age fiction emerges from the *bildungsroman* tradition said to begin with Goethe's *Wilhelm Meister's Apprenticeship* (1794–1796). The earliest Romantic versions of the "novel of development" resisted the entry into adulthood by equating innocence with childhood. By the Victorian era, however, this resistance gave way to an emphasis on social adjustment, with characters like Dickens's eponymous David Copperfield and Pip in *Great Expectations* (1861) assimilating painful lessons in love, money, and social standing to become respectable (and productive) young men.

This Side of Paradise (1920), Fitzgerald's first novel (and his most popular during his lifetime), significantly broke with the Dickens model in one important aspect: rather than depict Amory Blaine shouldering the burden of maturity, *Paradise* ends with him still stranded in uncertainty: "I know myself, but that is all—" reads the book's final line. The lack of resolution was why Fitzgerald's publisher, Charles Scribner's Sons, twice rejected the novel before finally recognizing its virtues lay in style rather than plot resolution.

From the 1950s through the 1970s, it became something of a political statement for *bildungsroman* to follow Fitzgerald's example and resisting narrative closure as a means of protesting the supposed conformity demanded by adulthood. Thus the famous final scene of Charles Webb's *The Graduate* (1963), in which Benjamin Braddock, after rescuing his girlfriend, Elaine, from an undesirable wedding ceremony, poses a question with generational implications: "Where does this bus go?"

BILDUNGSROMAN

In 1921, the *bildungsroman* was such a conventional form that F. Scott Fitzgerald could complain that "the most overworked art-form at present in America is this 'history of the young man ... [which] consists chiefly in dumping all your youthful adventures into the reader's lap with a profound air of importance, keeping carefully within the formulas of Wells and James Joyce" (1921, 43).

(237). Interestingly, in the 1980s and 1990s, it became more common in works such as David Leavitt's *The Lost Language of the Cranes* (1986) and Julia Alvarez's *How the Garcia Girls Lost Their Accents* (1991) for *bildungsroman* to reject adolescent indirection with emphatic recognitions of the need to grow up. Especially for writers born after 1960, this trend reflects the Generation X insistence that the baby-boomer unwillingness to relinquish youth forced the subsequent generation to assume responsibility for maintaining familial and communal ties at an early age. It is too soon to measure how Generation X's children will regard the *bildung* process, but a cursory glance suggests that contemporary novels lean more toward the Victorian model. Some (Sandra Cisnero's *Caramelo*, 2002; Claire Massud's *The Emperor's Children*, 2006) outright insist on maturation as necessary for emotional well-being. Others seem to reject it by challenging conventional definitions of what it means to be "grown up" (Ann Packer's *The Dive from Clausen's Pier*; Joyce Carol Oates's *I'll Take You There*, both 2002). Even so, such works do so less out of a Salinger-like nostalgia for childhood innocence than a desire to retain the right to define one's own milestones of maturity.

Trends and Themes. In my study of twentieth-century coming-of-age narratives, *Alienated-Adolescent Fiction* (2001), I suggest that five general themes can be traced through the genre. They provide a functional paradigm by which to measure the changes in post-2000 works.

Five Themes in Coming-of-Age Narratives

1) Alienated-youth fiction portrays rebellion as youth's response to adults' view of them as a social problem. Stereotyped as a potential threat to cultural stability, adolescents realize that the sole power they possess is their ability to fluster and frighten their elders. By defying convention, youth act out their status as "different" in order to insist that they exist beyond the norms of adult comprehension . . .

2) Although alienated-youth fiction celebrates teenage rebellion, it does not suggest that withdrawal will cure youth's discontent. Instead, teen readers are urged to recognize that they can begin to overcome the spiritual emptiness of modern America only by addressing these problems rather than running away from them. These works thus teach youth that they can transform the conditions through engagement, not detachment . . .

3) Alienated-adolescent fiction presents the view that one key to the growth of self-understanding is the development of a unique voice. Through personalized forms of expression, young people are able to articulate and thus comprehend their disaffection . . .

4) As they depict the process of adolescent self-development, authors encourage teens to open themselves to new experiences, to experiment, and to make identifications across cultural boundaries. In particular, popular culture provides a resource through which young people can fashion their sense of who they are—and who they would like to be . . .

5) Alienated-adolescent fiction does not speak exclusively to young people. It also addresses adults, seeking to energize their concerns for teenagers by reminding them of their responsibility to provide youth a meaningful future . . . (99–105)

While contemporary coming-of-age fiction has not abandoned these themes, it deploys them in proportions that are markedly different from such genre classics as *Catcher* or Sylvia Plath's *The Bell Jar* (1963), resulting in a curiously distinct impression of its regard for maturation. Whereas earlier works dramatized the adolescent dread of growing up, contemporary versions depict youth as having, out of necessity, to assume the gauntlet of adult responsibility, largely because of the failure and ineptitude of elders. As noted above, the pendulum seems to have swung more to the adult side of the youth continuum. These novels are ultimately less interested in the agency of youth as social protest than with young people's obligation to the repair of institutions like home and the family that, in their decayed state, are said to subject teenagers to duress and uncertainty.

1. Youth as a Social Problem. The most striking trend among contemporary depictions of these themes is the relative lack of emphasis on the first topic. In previous decades, youth was a social threat that young people were only too happy to act upon as a means of defining themselves against adult foils. Nowhere was this most evident than in what I call the "youth-at-risk" narrative, a subgenre that extends from pulpy juvenile-delinquent tales of the late-1940s and 1950s (Irving Shulman's *The Amboy Dukes,* Evan Hunter's *The Blackboard Jungle*) to the 1980s' two most notorious descent-into-decadence novels, Jay McInerney's *Bright Lights, Big City* (1984) and Bret Easton Ellis's *Less Than Zero* (1985) (*Alienated Youth Fiction* 88–91). Perhaps because these latter two works are now as widely ridiculed as they ever were read, imitations have dwindled since the peak of the Generation X debates in the mid-1990s. Before then, publishers routinely hyped potential blockbusters such as Donna Tartt's *The Secret History* (1992) as literary extensions of *Zero,* but now such comparisons are likely to invite derision.

Consider the fate of Nick McDonnell's *Twelve,* one of only a handful of works since 2000 to openly embrace the "youth-at-risk" tradition. Nearly every reviewer felt compelled to remark upon the similarities between *Twelve* and *Less Than Zero,* in part because, like Ellis, McDonnell published his debut at an exceedingly young age (eighteen, as opposed to Ellis's twenty) but also because, in light of the *Zero* template, the downward spiral of its main character, White Mike, seems exceedingly predictable. If not for the era-specific brand names, whole passages could be mistaken for Ellis's disaffected prose:

> Claude walks down Mulberry Street in his dark green North Face parka. In his pockets he is carrying: One clear plastic prism filled with weed, one Coach wallet containing $965 . . . one Citibank ATM card, one American Express Platinum card . . . and one Nokia cell phone . . . (McDonnell 2006, 77)

Although *Twelve* sold a striking 300,000 copies, reviews were mixed at best, with many commentators dismissing McDonnell as an example of publishing nepotism. (His father was at the time the managing editor of *Sports Illustrated* and his godfather brokered a book deal with good friend Morgan Entrenkin, head of *Atlantic Monthly*/Grove Press [Quart 171]). Significantly, McDonnell's second novel, *The Third Brother* (2005), tones down the chic detachment in favor of a conventional narrative grounded in the far more somber context of September 11, 2001.

Despite the rarity of narratives like *Twelve,* at least one prominent "moral panic" has emerged throughout the past decade to distinguish contemporary coming-of-age fictions from past treatments. On April 20, 1999, two students at Littleton, Colorado's Columbine High School, Eric Harris and Dylan Klebold, massacred twelve fellow teenagers and a teacher with assault rifles, in the process wounding two dozen others before committing suicide. The incident was the deadliest school shooting in American history, but it was by no means the only one of its era. At least five incidents had occurred by 1999 (Kentucky, Tennessee, Arkansas, and Mississippi) inspiring heated debates over issues as diverse as gun control, high school bullying, and violent rock music. As the bloodiest of them, "Columbine" quickly became a cultural touchstone inspiring numerous literary adaptations that have appeared with only a little less frequency than the lamentable (and seemingly endless) real-life copycat incidents. A short list of coming-of-age novels based on Harris and Klebold's killing spree includes Todd Strasser's *Give a Boy a Gun* (2000), Mark A. Rempel's *Point Blank* (2002), Douglas Coupland's *Hey, Nostradamus!* (2003), Lionel Shriver's *We Need to Talk about Kevin* (2003), Francine Prose's *After* (2004), Jim Shepard's *Project X* (2005), Kali VanBaale's *The Space Between* (2006), Jodi Picoult's *Nineteen Minutes* (2007), and C.G. Watson's *Quad* (2007).

Typically, the main dramatic concern of these novels is the survivors' struggle to determine who or what is responsible for such explosions of teen violence. There is no shortage of blame to go around: bullying, high-school cliques, parental neglect, and the supposed emptiness of American life all come under indictment. What is most dramatically interesting is how these books structure the postlapsarian plot of the conventional coming-of-age narrative into redemptive quests for adult solutions to these social ills. Typically, these works involve a dramatic admission of culpability on the part of either fellow students or parents that, without absolving the actual murderers of criminal responsibility, nevertheless insists that society at large is to blame, and not the killers' individual pathology. In some cases, the culpability is even literal. In Picoult's best-selling *Nineteen Minutes,* Josie Cormier shocks a packed courtroom during the trial of a teen assailant when she admits that she, not the killer, had shot her boyfriend Matt Royston during a locker-room siege. However unpremeditated, her firing upon Matt is an empathic act of identification with the ostracized gunman, Peter:

> [Josie] realized that in that one moment, when she hadn't been thinking, she knew exactly what he'd felt as he moved through the school with his backpack and guns. Every kid in this school played a role: jock, brain, beauty, freak. All Peter had done was what they all secretly dreamed of: be someone, even for just nineteen minutes, who nobody else was allowed to judge. (Picoult 2007, 440–441)

Although certainly not justifying Peter's murder spree, Josie's actions are meant to explain how adolescents can snap under the psychological pressures of growing up and resort to such heinous crimes.

In other cases, the redemptive gesture is less a confession than a Christ-like sacrifice on the part of survivors to redeem adults who have allowed these adolescent pressures to build. In Coupland's *Hey, Nostradamus,* Jason manages to disarm and kill a gunman in a 1988 attack in his high school, only to have the fellow senior whom he secretly married the weekend before, Cheryl, die in his arms. The following fifteen years covered in the novel find Jason suffering not only survivor's guilt, but enduring community suspicion that he was involved in the massacre. At a climactic moment, Jason's father, a religious fanatic named Reg, even denounces him as a murderer. Unable to bear the burden of suspicion, Jason simply vanishes into the woods, insisting that "[r]edemption exists, but only for others. I believe, and yet I lack faith. I tried building a private world free of hypocrisy, but all I ended up with was a sour little bubble as insular and exclusive as my father's" (Coupland 1991, 135). Jason's disappearance remains unsolved at the narrative's end, but it proves a catalyst for shaking Reg out of the intolerance that allowed him to suspect his own son of homicide.

A secondary theme among school-shooting novels is teenagers' response to adult efforts to police their youth culture to prevent future murder sprees. Prose's *After* takes this topic to dystopian extremes. Just as post-Columbine commentators blamed Harris and Klebold's homicidal rage on video games and Goth-rock music, so, too, school authorities in *After* ban kids from reading *The Catcher in the Rye* and establish a detention facility called Camp Turnaround, from which no teens ever return. Marketed to a young-adult audience (as were *Point Blank* and *Project X*), *After* panders a little too blatantly to teen paranoia over the equation between parental oversight and totalitarianism. At the same time, novelists can be too arch in insisting that moral panics are inspired as much by adult prurience as concern for adolescents. DBC Pierre's *Vernon God Little,* a surprise 2003 Booker Prize winner, satirizes parental anxieties over youth's indiscretions as part of a larger American fascination with crime, celebrity, and spectacle. When the eponymous hero is accused of being a conspirator in a school rampage committed by his friend Jesus Navarro, he takes to the road to escape to Mexico, but his pursuit by the police becomes the subject of a reality television show. This plot point owes a great deal to Oliver Stone's 1994 film *Natural Born Killers* and suggests how its real interest is not adolescence but American media culture. Indeed, Pierre (real name: Peter Warren Findley) is so intent on ridiculing the phenomenon of moral panics that the empathic power of the Columbine story completely evaporates, and the characters prove little more than caricatures.

If a conclusion can be drawn from post-2000 coming-of-age novels' treatment of the "at risk" theme, it is that few authors are willing to depict teenage delinquency as a genuine crisis. Instead, authors insist that moral panics elevate maladjustment to epidemic status so adults can seize upon scapegoats for adolescent problems. Whereas *The Blackboard Jungle* and even *Less Than Zero* emphatically insist that youth have fallen prey to amorality, contemporary works portray youth as victims of adult prejudice, arguing that elders fixate on teenagers to excuse themselves from confronting social ills of their own making. As such, there is a paucity of true "bad boys" in contemporary narratives—even the mass murderers are merely misunderstood.

2. Ethical Engagement. Because contemporary coming-of-age novels seem less inclined to threaten adults with rebellion and anarchy, it should not be surprising that they likewise deemphasize withdrawal and insist instead on the imperative of moral agency. One sure sign of this commitment is fictional youth's essential traditionalism. Whereas mid-century novels reveled in sexual experimentation and pharmacological derring-do, recent *bildungsroman* yearn for a return to the security of conventional mores, which it is youth's duty to preserve and reinvigorate. This surprising conservatism is perhaps most overt in narratives about children of the 1960s, who must decide whether the legacy of that vaunted decade is personal liberation or solipsism. In a majority of such works, the answer is decidedly the latter.

An example of this trend is Goldberry Long's *Juniper Tree Burning* (2001), which tells the story of a child of hippies who so resents her unconventional upbringing that she rebels by embracing upper-class suburban life. So thoroughly does Juniper reject her parents' alternative lifestyle that she changes her name to the anonymous sounding "Jennifer Davis." Even when Jennifer abandons her perfect husband to take to the road and retrace the final days of her dead brother Sunny Boy Blue, she is not questing for bohemian gnosis but resenting the instability of her nomadic childhood, which has left her feeling unworthy of love:

> If I've ever wanted anything, it's a membership in the real world of family and kids and bedtime stories, the reliable progression of the small rituals like cornflakes for breakfast and after school piano lessons . I couldn't imagine a man who was capable of loving me . . . or, for that matter, a man I could love back. (Long 2001, 79–80)

Although Juniper/Jennifer's journey involves accepting and forgiving those responsible for her past, it also requires a commitment to avoiding the divorce, drug abuse, and poverty that marked her and Sunny Boy's childhood. Only by doing so will she spare her own daughter the confusion and self-loathing that has impeded her maturation.

Another obvious subgenre in which the ethical engagement theme is prominently configured as entry into adulthood is that unfortunately labeled niche known as "lad lit," the male counterpart to "chick lit." "Lad lit" novels include: Thomas Beller's *The Sleepover Artist* (2001), Mark Barrowcliffe's *Girlfriend 44* (2001), Steve Almond's *My Life in Heavy Metal* (2004), Kyle Smith's *Love Monkey* (2004), and Scott Mebus's *Booty Nomad* (2006). These novels follow a common arc in which—regardless of their individual, often madcap plot premises—the struggle to outgrow promiscuity parallels a quest for paternal acceptance, usually culminating in an afterward in which the formerly directionless hero finds happiness at least in monogamy, if not in matrimony. The best of such works is Boswell's *Alternative Atlanta,* in which graduate-school dropout Gerald Brinkman pines for the married love of his life, Nora, while struggling to reconcile with his eccentric, distracted father, Paul. Only when Gerald learns a secret that explains his and Paul's alienation can he assure himself he can avoid a similar pattern of irresponsibility, and he can save Nora from her unhappy relationship. The novel ends with a flash forward that demonstrates Gerald's commitment to adulthood: not only are he and Nora married, but he has given up his unremunerative career as a local music critic to finish his doctoral degree. In this way, such books insist that young men must resolve their conflicts with their fathers before they themselves can become men.

Yet ethical commitment is not always marked by as climactic an entry into adulthood as marriage and parenthood. At other times, protagonists may come of age by making small stands for their intuitive sense of right instead of giant leaps for maturity. In *Peace Like a River,* eleven-year-old Reuben Land must choose between breaking the law and betraying his brother, Davy, who is hiding from the law after being charged with murder. Rueben's ultimate unwillingness to turn Davy in reflects his growing awareness that, because adult laws are prone to corruption, individual conscience must guide one's decisions in life. In Jack Riggs's *When the Finch Rises* (2003), Raybert Williams resolves not to perpetuate the brutality of the adult world after his best friend Palmer Conroy chastises him for gratuitously killing a bird with his new BB-gun. Palmer's anger teaches Raybert the necessity of breaking the cycle of violence into which the two friends have been raised. In other cases, the choices are more whimsical. In Jim Lynch's *The Highest Tide* (2005), thirteen-year-old Miles O'Malley's obsession with ecologist Rachel Carson leads him to discover a rare sea creature. The sudden attention he receives corrupts the purity of his conservationism until he decides to reject his celebrity and rejoice in the humility of scientific pursuit. As these examples suggest, these moral gestures can be self-consciously modest. Not unlike James Joyce's classic epiphany story "Araby," however; contemporary works suggest that the crucibles of initiation come from the most everyday of experiences. Consequently, these books argue, moral development requires a consistent conscientiousness on the part of young people, for the danger of committing harm in the world may lie in the mundane rather than the melodramatic.

A subgenre in which this smaller sort of ethical commitment is especially apparent is the Southern coming-of-age novel, the majority of which are cast in the kiln of *To Kill a Mockingbird*. Much as Scout Finch recognizes the responsibility she inherits by virtue of her father Atticus's heroic defense of the falsely accused African American Tom Robinson, so, too, modern-day Southerners find themselves taking decidedly unpopular stances for racial equality, often at great personal risk. Thus, in Sue Monk Kidd's *The Secret Life of Bees* (2001), fourteen-year-old Lily Owen escapes the racism of her rural South Carolina hometown with her African American nanny, Rosaleen, after Rosaleen insults a group of white men. In Michael Morris's *Slow Way Home* (2003), Brandon Willard helps rebuild the pauper's hospital founded by his spiritual mentor, Sister Delores, when it is burned to the ground after the nun commits to aiding impoverished blacks as well as whites. And in Childress's *One Mississippi,* Daniel Musgrove must aid the first-ever African American prom queen at Minor High School, Arnita Beecham, to regain her identity after a bout of amnesia from a car accident leaves her with no memory of her race.

Other Southern works insist these heirs of Scout must recognize their own racism. In "Segregation," one of the short stories that constitute George Singleton's composite novel, *Why Dogs Chase Cars* (2004), Mendal Dawes undergoes a public excoriation at the hands of a black friend who lets him know in the middle of a segregated South Carolina movie theatre that he is not as racially aware as he would like to believe:

> Shirley Ebo went into her high-whining voice and said things about how white people thought they knew everything, how white people didn't know what really went on in the world, how white people were the poison of the earth. She yelled, "Mendal sits down there now, but he wants to be up here with me." (Singleton 2004, 126)

A further development in the genre is the employment of African American protagonists whose ethical commitment requires overcoming the self-hatred that racism can imbue in blacks. Such is the storyline of Christopher Wilson's *Cotton* (2005), in which the titular hero outgrows his bitterness at 1960s racism by identifying with other persecuted minorities, specifically gay women. As Cotton declares upon summarizing what his friendship with Fay teaches him, "I want to live among ugly and beautiful, young and old, black and white, man and woman, with beast, fish, and fowl" (Wilson 2005, 299).

However diverse the types of ethical engagement, their aim in these novels is similar: they allow fictional teens to enter adulthood assured of their moral purpose. If one criticism can be made of this trend, it is that these books' insistence on resolving the maturation drama suggests contemporary novelists are not truly confronting the temptations that *discourage* young people from growing up. That is, in an increasing youth-oriented American culture—some would say an increasingly *juvenile* culture—the majority of these books accept adulthood as a goal instead of recognizing the countervailing pressures in popular culture to remain all that youth connotes: carefree, selfish, and irresponsible. As such, their endings can sometimes feel like a narrative obligation rather than authentic growth. Whereas the coming-of-age novel once equated growing up with growing old, today's versions are apt to accept that maturity is achieved through a single initiation rite rather than through an ongoing *process* of trial and error.

3. *Cultivating Voices.* An important vehicle for realizing maturity in the genre is the development of an individual voice that will allow young people to articulate their values. This is the area in which contemporary coming-of-age novels are most progressive. Fictional teens not only avail themselves of the verbal ingenuity that is the legacy of Salinger, Kerouac, and other canonical spokesmen for alienated youth; they also employ dialogic strategies, innovative points of view, unconventional mixtures of typography, and even emulations of new technologies to create self-actualizing languages. While there is no shortage of Holden-esque irony, most novelists recognize that hipster glibness and au courant slang by themselves are ineffectual means of avoiding conformity. Nor, with the exception of McDonnell's *Twelve,* is there much interest in emulating the zombie-like detachment of *Less Than Zero.* Because contemporary teens seek engagement, they must couple these devices of resistance with more positive techniques that allow for the creation of empathy and community.

One consistent technique handed down from canonical works from *Huckleberry Finn* to Kaye Gibbons' *Ellen Foster* (1984) is the use of a voice that conveys the saintly outsiderness of the main character. Several recent *bildungsroman* project a savant aura meant to demonstrate the essential purity of their child-heroes—even Gibbons retains the disarmingly folksy style that account for much of *Foster*'s popularity in her recent sequel, *The Life All Around Me by Ellen Foster* (2005). The novel opens with a letter to the president of Harvard in which a petitioning Ellen explains why her application for admission (at fifteen) cannot be completed in its entirety:

> A person who graduated from there is supposed to grade me on how close I come to being Harvard material, and I need to let you know that I went to town to meet the man we have, but when I got to his nursing home I found him unaware. He'd had another stroke the day before . . . (Gibbons 1984, 2–3)

Instead of Southern whimsy, Foer in *Everything Is Illuminated* employs frequent malapropisms as his teenaged narrator, Alexander Perchov, attempts to translate his Ukrainian observations into broken English: "All of my many friends dub me Alex, because that is a more flaccid-to-utter version of my legal name. Mother dubs me Alex-stop-spleening me! because I am always spleening her" (Foer 2002, 1). Still other authors seize upon various cognitive disorders in order to project a peculiarity of perspective. Much of the interest in *The Curious Incident of the Dog in the Night-Time* arose from Mark Haddon's use of an autistic point of view: "My name is Christopher John Francis Boone. I know all the countries of the world and their capital cities and every prime number up to 7,057" (Haddon 2003, 2). While these devices can grow gimmicky and even grating, they allow authors to suggest the nonconformity of their character's innate innocence.

Curiously, the technique least conducive to realizing maturity is the most traditional: humor. As a satire of moral panics, Pierre's *Vernon God Little* utilizes a number of comedic tools to convey the absurdity of social attitudes toward youth: there are outlandish similes ("Mr. Abdini is fat the way anvils are fat" [Pierre 2003,

49]), deflating honorifics that undermine adult authority ("ole Silas," "ole Mr. Deutschman"), and generous helpings of obscenity (Vernon's favorite word is "fucken"). While Pierre deftly sustains this voice throughout the narrative, the lack of variation disallows any hint of growth, and Vernon ends the book as much as he begins it: as a smart aleck. Perhaps the most obvious sign of the character's lack of mature reflection is the homosexual slur with which he metes justice to two characters who turn out to be the real accomplices in the school shooting for which Vernon is nearly executed: "Now they'll have all the boys they could wish for, up there in prison. Somehow you sense they might be doing a little more receiving than giving, though" (275).

More effective are narrative voices in which such derision attacks prejudice instead of perpetuating it. The tone of Rebcecca Godfrey's *The Torn Skirt* (2002), for example, never impedes empathy for Sara Shaw's descent into drug abuse and crime because its mordancy has a discernable purpose. Sara is rebelling against the bureaucratic clichés that define young women's behavior without any effort to understand it. As Sara scoffs upon reading a juvenile-hall report on her delinquency: "'Impressionable' and 'troubled.' They should have called me a harlot and a slut, a poseur and a tease, a nubile and naïve, a slattern and a sleaze, a vandalist, an anarchist, a dirty dilettante with a fatal and fervent disease" (Godfrey 2002, 176). Here alliteration allows Sara to parody the moral presumptions plied to young women to police their sexual maturation; the exaggeration is her way of appropriating and emptying such terminology by implying the prurience motivating it. *The Torn Skirt* demonstrates how young women must rebel against such stereotypes, lest the "bad" girl remain a mere stimulant for scandal instead of a true liberator of sexual prejudice.

Yet even this type of humor is essentially reactionary, for by *responding* to adult anxieties, it remains inexorably yoked to them. To free teenagers from elders' discourse, authors often employ a plethora of metatextual methods that, more than simply denounce adults' narrative authority to judge teen behaviors, outright fracture it through narrative framing. On the surface, for example, Joe Meno in *Hairstyles of the Damned* (2004) seems to accomplish little but express contempt for adult values when hero Brian Oswald begins a mock history report with a burst of invective: "American History can suck it. The U.S.A. can suck it. The Thirteen Colonies can suck it. George Washington can suck it . . ." (Meno 2004, 21). Yet in telling the story of Brian's unconventional romance with fellow punk-music lover Gretchen, Meno mixes in several forms meant to reproduce the non-linear modes in which teens speak to each other, including lists, lyrics excerpted from their favorite music, and even Internet icons. A particularly clever device is the sporadic use of typefaces that approximate handwriting. Shifting out of standard Roman type for a passage or chapter in scripts like Bradley-Hand or SM_scriptism has become common in adolescent narratives since 2000—Picoult also does it in *Nineteen Minutes,* as does Watt Key in his *Huckleberry Finn*-style picaresque *Alabama Moon* (2006). The effect is to lend authenticity to the narrative voice, for print styles emulating chirography suggest that readers have gained immediate access to a teenage protagonist's mind.

One could even argue that this design trend represents an innovation analogous to the use of (supposedly) unedited diary passages in *Go Ask Alice* (1971), the young-adult classic "discovered" by drug-counselor Beatrice Sparks after one of her teen patients overdosed in the late 1960s. It elides any hint of adult mediation in the text, and encourages us to "hear" that voice as we see it "written" in a young person's own hand. The recent rise of e-mail- and text-message epistolary novels like Myracle's *TTYL* and *TTFN* likewise accomplish something similar by seeming to recreate not only young people's language, but the media through which they communicate.

Yet the title of Myracle's third entry after *TTYL* and *TTFN* in her "Internet Girls" series—*l8r, g8r* (2007)—suggests the limits of these metatextual efforts. It is one thing for an adult author to borrow Internet-speak for such post-2000 "tween" phrases as *talk to you later* and *ta-ta for now*. To translate into this code an old-fashioned saying like *later, gator* that is more reminiscent of Bill Haley and the Comets than Paris Hilton reveals just how difficult it is to create an "authentic" adolescent voice without revealing one's adult subjectivity. Arguably, such techniques are most effective when they are part of a variety of strategies that help give voice to adolescence by paradoxically calling attention to how rarely teenagers are able to break out of adult frames and speak directly in narrative. The most celebrated coming-of-age novel of recent years, Junot Díaz's *The Brief Wonderous Life of Oscar Wao* (2007), makes these frames manifest in such a way to remind us that the *paysage moralisée* is a social experience that affects not only individual teenagers but siblings, friends, and family. By using multiple perspectives (including Oscar's mother, Beli, his sister, Lola, and his best friend), chapter cue cards, footnotes, and a mélange of styles, Díaz depicts "voice" (and, by extension, identity) as more than mere attitude and slang. Rather, in *Oscar Wao* it is a *process* of discovery that involves a synthesis of influences. As one reviewer noted,

> The tale of Oscar's coming-of-age is in some ways the book's thinnest layer, a young-adult melodrama draped over a multigenerational immigrant family chronicle that dabbles in tropical magic realism, punk-rock feminism, hip-hop machismo, post-postmodern pyrotechnics and enough polymorphous multiculturalism to fill up an Introduction to Cultural Studies syllabus. (Scott 7:9)

One might simply revise this to say that elevating the maturation process beyond melodrama requires representing (and understanding) it through a myriad of "polymorphous" voices.

4. Popular Culture and Identity Formation. Another interesting difference between contemporary and classic maturation narratives is how uncontroversial the place of popular culture has become in the genre. Classic texts like *The Catcher in the Rye* evince a strain of modernist elitism by denouncing movies, television, and popular music as agents of conformity that youth must resist to avoid the soulless consumerism of post-WWII America. (Even the celebrated be-bop fixation of the Beat Generation was less about embracing popular art forms than about mining the last few subcultural veins of authenticity that the "culture industry" had yet to obliterate). By the 1980s, it was common for reviewers of Bobbie Anne Mason's *In Country* (1985) or Jay McInerney's *Story of My Life* (1988) to decry the constant namedropping of mass-culture artifacts. By and large, post-2000 coming-of-age novels reveal little anxiety about the moral consequences of characters looking to comic books or hip-hop for models of self-making. The marketplace is here to stay, these works insist, and, as a result, few resort to the old "Frankfurt School" argument of cultural studies by portraying teenagers as victims of false needs instilled by corporate interests. Rather, these novels are apt to support the more recent stance of theorists who argue that teenagers are not passive receptacles but active creators who *produce* the meanings of the goods they buy.

Wolff's *Old School* is one of the few recent works seemingly preoccupied with whether popular culture possesses sufficient aesthetic value to inspire adolescent development. When Ayn Rand visits an elite New England prep school in the early 1960s, she shocks the unnamed narrator by recommending Mickey Spillane over Ernest Hemingway. "What you find in Hemingway is what is wrong with the so-called literature of this country," she declares. "Weak premises. Weak, defeated people"—as opposed to Spillane, whose Mike Hammer "doesn't torture himself in the current fashion with the decadent niceties. Mike knows evil from good and destroys it without hesitation or regret" (Wolff 2003, 85). While Wolff parodies Rand's will-to-power positivism, his main point is to illustrate the dangers of consuming *any* cultural commodity, high or low, without sufficient awareness of the solipsism it may encourage. Desperate to win a creative-writing contest whose prize is a tête-à-tête with Hemingway, the protagonist plagiarizes a short story and is promptly expelled from his prestigious institution. Interestingly, he comes to recognize his dishonesty in passing someone else's experience off as his own *in both the story* and *in his life,* for the ambition that drove him to err had nothing to do with craft or work—it was to become as famous as Hemingway. Only by recognizing the juvenility of this fantasy can the narrator appreciate that the truest reward of art is self-awareness. As such, *Old School* is less concerned with what literature is "legitimate"—Spillane or Hemingway—than in limning its value in cautioning against vanity. As Wolff's hero decides,

> Even as I lived my life I was seeing it on the back of a book. And yet in all those years [of adolescence] I actually wrote very little, maybe because I was afraid of not being good enough to justify this improvised existence, and because the improvising became an end in itself and left scant room for disciplined invention. (Wolff 2003, 156)

Childress's *One Mississippi* dramatizes an ancillary danger: what happens when adults appropriate those cultural models that are youth's province. After his family moves from Indiana to the Deep South, Daniel Musgrove discovers that music is one of the few resources for overcoming regional differences and making with friendships with new classmates. Whether Billy Paul's "Me and Mrs. Jones" or Cher's "Gypsies, Tramps, and Thieves," the hits of 1973 serve as networks of identification by which he can appreciate the diversity of his peers' tastes and personal investments in art. When the local Baptist youth minister decides to make religion more accessible by producing an original rock opera, Daniel and his friends feel their favorite medium has been stolen. Entitled *Christ!* and featuring such numbers as "Joseph, You've Got to Believe Me" (sung by Mary, of course), the musical is an obvious take-off on *Jesus Christ Superstar, Godspell,* and other early 1970s ersatz efforts to recast youth music as all-ages entertainment. As Daniel realizes, the power of rock music to foster communal ties among adolescents is dampened when adults seize upon it to instill doctrinal lessons.

Whereas *One Mississippi* satirizes pop culture, Jonathan Lethem's *The Fortress of Solitude* (2003) treats its power to create connections with a seriousness that borders on reverential. In addition to their dramatic function, references are textural, recreating the sprawl of 1970s culture, highlighting the moment when comic books and AM radio first became media for mainstreaming racial diversity after the hard-fought

Civil Rights battles of the 1960s. In effect, pop culture for Lethem is an image of integration: as white child Dylan Ebdus develops a fondness for soul music and African American Mingus Rude revels in Superman comic books, their friendship has the potential to transcend racial difference. That promise is foiled, however, by a series of sociocultural events that lock the friends into stereotypical opportunities and pitfalls. While Dylan is sent to a prestigious college to become an artist, Mingus ends up in and out of addiction and prison. In the end, the two friends have little substantive connection but the memories of their mutual fascinations of their childhood (including the magic ring that they believe allowed them to fly). As many reviewers noted, the title of the book refers to the Arctic ice castle that is both Superman's base of operations and hideaway. As such, it reflects the extremes of pop culture's influence on young people: its power, on the one hand, to encourage the imaginative flights of fancy that can change the world, but also the escapist lure that can tempt them to retreat into fantasy.

5. The Ideal Adult Addressee. Critics are apt to think of coming-of-age novels as speaking to a generational cohort. The books seem to either look back in time to assess the cultural changes that shaped the author and audience's mutual childhood (as in the case of *The Fortress of Solitude* and *One Mississippi*), or, in the case of young-adult fiction, they examine the current-day conditions influencing the peer group presently in the throes of maturation (as in *Twelve* and *TTYL*). Often overlooked, however, is the presence of an implied adult audience who bears responsibility for fictional teens' struggles—the audience who most likely has the power to rectify those dilemmas. As Charles Acland writes, the narratological design of adolescent fiction is usually staged as a "plea for that guiding hand that demonstrates the method of integration back into the realm of the normal youth, which in turn signifies the easy flow toward the adult" (Acland 1995, 121). Appealing to the lending of that "guiding hand" thus becomes the purpose of the story, and modeling its function is the job of implied addressee. That audience may be the non-specific, unnamed "you" that Holden addresses throughout *Catcher,* or it may be a more fully dramatized mentor figure like Dr. Nolan in Plath's *The Bell Jar.* Regardless of the degree to which the addressee is physically present, the aim is to "interpellate" real-life readers by urging them to recognize the failings of these fictional authority figures in their own responses to teen problems and to spark a recommitment to solving them.

This function is overt in school-shooting novels that are narrated from the perspective of the killers' parents, as opposed to the teenage victims. In both Shriver's *We Need to Talk About Kevin* and VanBaale's *The Space Between,* it becomes the job of mothers in particular to break the silence of grief and guilt to acknowledge the family issues that led to their children's devastating violence. In *The Space Between,* Judith Elliott admits her negligence in a court deposition when she and husband Peter are sued by families of the teens that their son murders: "There were moments Peter or I sensed something was wrong [with Lucas], knew something was wrong and didn't act on it. Yes, we squandered . . . we squandered opportunities to do more, to help him" (VanBaale 2006, 268). More than an acceptance of guilt, the confession forces the plaintiffs to recognize *their own* similarly squandered opportunities to shepherd their children's maturation because, like the Elliotts, they were distracted by careers and pastimes, and the lawsuit is dropped. The plot twist is meant to urge to adult readers to not blame such incidents on aberrant parenting, but to recognize the Elliotts' failures in themselves. Only then, such novels argue, will future tragedies be averted.

Because contemporary *bildungsroman* tend toward the Dickensian model of maturation by resolving their protagonists' initiation process, the message to the implied reader is apt to be one of reconciliation instead of remonstrance. Much of Jennifer Davis's self-destruction in *Juniper Tree Burning* is fueled by her resentment of her unconventional mother, Faith. As she outgrows the selfishness that drives her to abandon her husband, however, Jennifer comes to recognize the bond she and Faith share as women, and the direct address becomes a gesture of forgiveness for the daughter's own abandonment: "Faith. You made Sunny Boy Blue. You made me. Don't that count for anything at all? . . . Oh, Mama. We are the same, you and me. We aren't opposites at all" (Long 2001, 441–442). In both cases, growing up requires what may be the most mature of gestures: forgiveness. Sebold's *The Lovely Bones* takes this idea even further as the impossible reconciliation (because the narrator has been murdered) leads to the blessing of letting go. As Susie Salmon watches helplessly from the afterlife, her parents and sister succumb to grief and bitterness over her unsolved case. Susie finally resolves to free them of their burden, first by bringing love to her sister and second by avenging her own death and protecting other young women. The novel's final words bespeak the self-sacrifice of allowing her family closure by fading into their past: "I wish you all a long and happy life" (Sebold 2002, 328).

In still other cases, the interpellation is achieved through metatextual devices that dramatize the need for adult concern. Both Gibbons's *The Life All Around Me by Ellen Foster* and Curtis Sittenfeld's *The Man of My Dreams* (2006) include epistolary chapters that serve as direct addresses to the ideal reader. Strasser's *Give a Boy a Gun* includes footnotes that excerpt real-life accounts of Columbine and other school shootings to lend urgency to his insistence (explicitly stated in his dedication) that "gun use and gun availability is horribly, insanely, out of control" (Strasser 2000, i). The last words of Martone's *Slow Way Home* belong not to Brandon Willard, but to a statistic in the author's acknowledgments meant to dramatize the seriousness of the parental neglect that leads Brandon's grandparents to abduct and raise him: "It is estimated that 2.5 million grandparents are raising grandchildren in the United States. Most are doing so with little or no financial support. I thank them for taking responsibility for the future and offer my humble gratitude" (Morris, 280). The key words here, of course, are "taking responsibility for the future": coming-of-age novels dramatize the duty adults have in ensuring that youth are given the security and tools requisite for growing up. If there is a major difference between past and present in how this point is made, it is that contemporary authors have little compunction about stating it directly and explicitly.

Context and Issues. Unfortunately, the coming-of-age novel seems to play a decreasing role in the cultural construction of the post-2000 teenager. As recently as the 1990s, as the example of Coupland's *Generation X* demonstrates, novels had the power to shape sociological perceptions as much as *Catcher* and *On the Road* did in the 1950s and 1960s. (Indeed, *Generation X* was so influential in this regard that few people even remember it was a novel and not a nonfiction study). Despite the unprecedented popularity of J.K. Rowling's *Harry Potter* series (1996–2007), fiction is wholly overshadowed by music, television, movies, and video games as commentators search for proof texts for understanding the mindset of the emerging generation.

That said, one concern that does consistently bring *bildungsroman* to the forefront of moral-panic debates is the subject matter of young-adult novels. As American culture grows more explicit, the appropriateness of books marketed directly to a twelve-to-eighteen-year-old demographic and tackling such issues as sex, drugs, and violence becomes a matter of controversy. In such discussions, the issues addressed can range from the putative harmfulness of exposing youth to such topics to their realism, with commentators questioning the degree to which adult prurience motivates the inquiry into just how wild youth have gone. Thus, in a 2004 *Harper's* article, Frances FitzGerald asks why the subgenre of young-adult fiction known as the "problem novel"—a coming-of-age story in which the protagonist must confront a pressing social issue, whether unplanned pregnancy, incest, self-mutilation— "constitute[s] the largest category of books published for teens" when teens themselves show a marked preference for fantasies like *Harry Potter* or "junior chick-lit series about girls with snarky attitudes and great clothes" (i.e. Ceicily von Zeigesar's *Gossip Girl* books, 2001–). The answer, FitzGerald argues, rests in the *adult* belief that literature should serve a "therapeutic" function by "realistically depict[ing] the problems adolescents face these days . . . from drug addiction to child abuse"—a desire that creates an "increasing grimness" in youth fiction as authors and publishers scramble to tackle ever darker concerns. However noble the desire of these adults to offer teens tools for navigating young-adult dilemmas, the problem novel presupposes that "what [adults] call 'edgy Action' or 'gritty realism' reflects the lives of *most* young people," overlooking the fact that many children do *not* suffer these ills and read not for "healing" but "out of sheer curiosity" (Fitzgerald 2004, 68; emphasis added).

For Caitlin Flanagan in *The Atlantic Monthly,* the adult fixation with the adolescent loss of innocence is never more unrealistic than when these books address sexual mores. Young-adult novels such as Paul Ruditis's *The Rainbow Party* (2005)—which claims to expose the phenomenon of the teen "train party," at which girls line up to fellate a series of male partners—so exaggerate parental fears as to degenerate into ludicrousness:

> [T]he current oral-sex hysteria [that both the 'train-party' panic and Ruditis's narrative appeal to] presupposes not only that a limitless number of young American girls have taken on the sexual practices of porn queens but also that American boys are capable of having an infinite number of sexual experiences in rapid succession. It requires believing that a boy could be serviced at the school-bus train party—receiving oral sex from ten or fifteen girls, one after another—and then zip his fly and head off to homeroom . . . (Ruditis 2005, 169)

Such moral panics, Flanagan argues, risk perpetuating rather than redressing the sexualization of adolescence. By insisting that teen indulgence in such baroque, dehumanizing practices is widespread enough to constitute a crisis, portraits like *The Rainbow Party* drown out serious discussion of what is "normal" and healthy erotic initiation and discourage dialogue between adults and youth.

As the supposed "train party" crisis suggests, gender is another central concern in which contemporary novels play a role. This is especially apparent in the debates surrounding *bildungsroman* marketed as "chick lit." While not every book in this genre focuses on the coming-of-age experience, several do. Their protagonists' quest for romantic fulfillment is often indicative of the desire to enter adulthood through marriage. The question involving these female-centered initiation plots is whether they stereotype women as dependent upon male affection. As supporters defend the genre for foregrounding women's experience and creating more economic opportunities for women writers, detractors question whether the emphasis on dating and fashion limits women's right to tackle "serious" subject matter.

The mixed reviews accorded Melissa Bank's *The Wonder Spot* (2005) are indicative of the disagreement that plagues cultural attitudes toward female maturation. Joanna Briscoe praises the story of Sophie Applebaum's coming of age for bringing depth and poignancy to the overly familiar elements of chick-lit:

> The chick-lit phenomenon has done a great disservice to Melissa Bank. While still packaged in a format suggesting an urban odyssey of man-hunts and screw-ups for its wacky-little-me heroine, her books are infinitely finer than [books inspired by Helen Fielding's *Bridget Jones's Diary,* 1996]. There is such depth to her shallows, such art to her artlessness, that her work resembles chick lit purely in its surface details. (Bank 2005, 27)

Yet in the *New York Times,* Curtis Sittenfeld concludes the exact opposite:

> To suggest that another woman's ostensibly literary novel is chick lit feels catty, not unlike calling another woman a slut—doesn't the term basically bring down all of us? And yet, with *The Wonder Spot,* it's hard to resist. A chronicle of the search for personal equilibrium and Mr. Right, Melissa Bank's novel is highly readable, sometimes funny and entirely unchallenging; you're not one iota smarter after finishing it. I'm as resistant as anyone else to the assumption that because a book's author is female and because that book's protagonist is a woman who actually cares about her own romantic future, the book must fall into the chick-lit genre. So it's not that I find Bank's topic lightweight; it's that Bank writes about it in a lightweight way. (2005, 7:9)

These opposing views suggests a deep divide about what extremes constitute "deep" and "lightweight" treatments of female experience—a divide that is itself reflective of the wholly understandable vulnerability and defensiveness women feel toward representations of "growing up female."

Yet another cultural concern arising from the coming-of-age novel involves the publishing industry's role in discovering and promoting young practitioners of the genre. Since F. Scott Fitzgerald, the marketplace has hungered for wunderkinds who may or may not possess the talent to live up to the attention that the cultural fixation with adolescence attracts. Since 2000, at least two major scandals have rocked the publishing industry by demonstrating the duplicitous ends to which some writers will go to feed the demand for phenoms. After winning raves for *Sarah*—a supposedly autobiographical novel of teenage prostitution— J.T. LeRoy was hailed as the first voice of Generation Y. Yet rumors immediately began to circulate that the twenty-year old street orphan was the invention of an older author previously unable to break into the fiction market. The rumors were finally proven true in 2005–2006 when independent investigations by *New York Magazine* and *the New York Times* exposed LeRoy as forty-year-old Laura Albert, a Brooklyn-born, San Francisco-based freelance writer who hired her boyfriend's half-sister, Savannah Koop, to play the part of J.T. in public appearances. While Albert defended the hoax by claiming J.T. was an alter ego, her unmasking led many critics to disparage the verisimilitude of *Sarah* and subsequent LeRoy books—the exact same verisimilitude, coincidentally, that many of those same critics had previously applauded. The controversy also raised doubts about the viability of Albert's career. As of late 2007, the third LeRoy novel, *Labour,* remains unpublished, two full years after it was originally scheduled to appear.

The second controversy to impugn coming-of-age authors' veracity involves Kaavya Viswanathan, who at the precious age of eighteen won a $500,000 advance from Little, Brown for a young-adult novel entitled *How Opal Mehta Got Kissed, Got Wild and Got a Life.* Shortly after the book's publication in 2006, *The Harvard Crimson* accused Viswanathan of plagiarizing passages from two *bildungsroman* by Megan McCaffrey, *Sloppy Firsts* (2001) and *Second Helpings* (2004). Subsequent investigations revealed additional phrases and sentences lifted from Meg Cabbott's *The Princess Diaries* (2000) and Sophie Kinsella's *Can You Keep a Secret?* (2003). Viswanathan initially denied the charges, but she and her publishers were shortly forced to issue an apology to McCaffrey—though to little avail. When the controversy did not subside, Little, Brown recalled *Opal* and cancelled the young student's contract for a second novel. While Viswanathan was rightly excoriated for plagiarizing, the book industry was itself condemned for being so eager to capitalize on the teenage market that it failed to properly ensure the book's originality. The uproar not only raised questions about the maturity and professionalism of publishing wunderkinds but the commodification of adolescence as well. As it turned out, the co-owner of *Opal*'s copyright with Viswanathan was a well-known "book-packaging company," Alloy Entertainment, whose editorial teams often "craft proposals for publishers and create plotlines and characters before handing them over to a writer (or a string of writers)" (Rich and Smith 2006, 24). While no Alloy employee was accused of complicity in Viswanathan's plagiarism, the company was harshly criticized for its "assembly-line" production to literature for young people. Aside from its ethical implications, the scandal was perhaps the most vivid reminder of the past decade that coming-of-age novels are products produced by adults for young people. As such, their "plotlines and characters" speak as much to what adults presume about teens as about how youth themselves experience adolescence.

Reception. While the cultural debates over coming-of-age novels focus on the genre's *extratextual* effect on young readers and writers, the critical reception is apt to address *intratextual* issues of voice, form, and storyline. Despite differing in orientation, aesthetic assessments and sociological analyses share a common concern with the realism of maturation narratives. In particular, book reviewers ask whether the *Bildungsroman* has become such a publishing staple that its narrative conventions have degenerated into formula, leading authors to merely imitate the *Catcher in the Rye* model instead of reflecting the true experience of teens today.

The question is understandable given how frequently readers are encouraged to regard contemporary novels as "updates" of Holden Caulfield's story. Thus, a blurb on the back cover of *Vernon God Little* describes its eponymous hero as "Holden Caulfield on Ritalin," while a reviewer of Katherine Taylor's *Rules for Saying Goodbye* deems its heroine, Katherine, a "female Holden for our day" (Eyre 2007, D:8). Robin MacKenzie, the hero of K. M. Soehnlein's *The World of Normal Boys* (2001) is a "gay Holden Caulfield," while Tangy Mae Quinn in Delores Phillips's *The Darkest Child* (2004) is "Holden Caulfield reborn as African American and female." The comparisons have grown so commonplace that they even take place *within* the novel. As blogger Megan Walton noted of Randall DeVallance's *Dive* (2005):

Arthur Trezeguet, the first-person narrator, is intended to be a modern-day Holden Caulfield. This is not to say he actually reminds anyone of Holden Caulfield, but it is glaringly obvious that this was precisely what the author had in mind. If you missed the various clues connecting Arthur Trezeguet to the original angsty, sensitive, Holden, Arthur is kind enough to help you: "My English teacher told me I reminded her of Holden Caulfield . . . I've always liked Holden Caulfield. He's sort of like a brother to me." (Walton 2005)

Such invocations of Holden almost dare reviewers to deride the aim of these contemporary novels as cashing in on Salinger's enduring popularity. Reviewing Benjamin Kunkel's *Indecision* (2005), *New York Times* critic Michiko Kakutani affected her own mock-Holden voice to dramatize what she interpreted as Kunkel's lack of originality:

If you really want to hear what I think about this guy Dwight Wilmerding [the protagonist of *Indecision*], the first thing I should tell you is that he kind of reminds me of me . . . In *Indecision,* Dwight—or this ghostwriter he got, Benjamin Kunkel—goes into a lot more of all that David Copperfield kind of stuff than I ever would, and he's a helluva lot older than I was when I went through my madman phase, but still, you've gotta admit we're coming from the same sort of place. (Kakutani 2005, E:1)

Kakutani concludes her assessment by seizing upon one of Holden's favorite words to suggest that Kunkel wholeheartedly imitates *Catcher* in order to reap the rewards of reaching the target audience associated with the book:

[The conclusion] reads more like something [Holden's] brother [D. B.] might have written for the movies than a real-life experience . . . Old Dwight's book really knocked me out, and if there's one thing I hate, it's Hollywood. But then Dwight—who doesn't have as big a thing about phonies as I do—might not mind selling his story to some producer. He might not even mind being played by [young Hollywood actors like] Jake Gyllenhaal or Josh Hartnett or Topher Grace. (Kakutani 2005, E:1)

The implication is that a genre that was once the refuge of those who refused to conform has become a hot product for those hoping to hawk a commodity.

Such criticism is part of a larger trend among reviewers that ask whether post-2000 coming-of-age novelists draw from a too-common vernacular of adolescent touchstones that adds little to the canon. If reviews are any indication, commentators are growing impatient with adolescent angst, romantic uncertainty, and parental disaffection. In an otherwise positive review in the *New York Times*, Mark Sarvas describes Larry Doyle's *I Love You, Beth Cooper* (2006) as "less a novel than a novelization of a movie not yet made, a bibliography of teenage-loser angst" (Sarvas 2007, 7:19). The review suggests that Doyle channels not only Holden Caulfield, but stereotypical cinematic antecedents like those who populate such John Hughes films as *The Breakfast Club* (1985). When another reviewer describes Curtis Sittenfeld's *Prep* as "George Eliot writ[ing] *Sweet Valley High*" (the popular 1980s YA series), one senses critics questioning whether adolescent narrative have not become so commonplace as to lose any specifically "literary" value (Eyre 2005, 26). Another Sittenfeld reviewer enforces the point by comparing the novel to a popular teen TV show: "*Prep* seems to be about rich-girl teenage drama, and who needs that when we have *The O.C.?*" (Steuver, C:1). That attitude is especially apparent in the drubbing given Wolfe's campus farce *I Am Charlotte Simmons.* The thought of a zeitgeist-defining observer as influential as the author of *The Right Stuff* and *The*

Bonfire of the Vanities turning his microscope on the frat parties, keg tapping, and sex escapes of American co-eds drove reviewers to distraction. "Like an epidemiologist tracing contamination downstream, Wolfe has shifted his laboratory of elegant rot from the adult world into that of its children," wrote the *Boston Globe* (Elder 2004, D:6).

> When Wolfe detailed how bond traders and speculators work [in *Bonfire*], he caricatured power, always worth doing. Here he is attempting to caricature college life with a ponderous if sharp-clawed intensity quite beyond its subject's weight. Also skewing it. Few of us, after all, trade bonds or run real estate empires; many of us, and our children, have been to college and know that Wolfe presents, at best, a dumbed-down part as a dumbed-down whole. (Elder 2004, D:6)

In other words, Wolfe's depiction of adolescence resembled the image of teenagers perpetuated in exploitative teen films and reality TV shows more than "real" adolescents, reinforcing the idea that youth as a topic no longer bears the "weight" of seriousness accorded it during the heyday of *The Catcher in the Rye*.

Other reviewers look to internal traits instead of the marketplace to measure the relative realism of literary adolescence. In a *Commentary* essay, Sam Munson complains that Jhumpa Lahiri's *The Namesake* (Munson 2003, 68–72) and Jonathan Lethem's *The Fortress of Solitude* fall prey to the "shapelessness to which every novel dealing with childhood and its sequels seems prone" (69). Because maturation dictates stages of character development, authors are apt to lose dramatic potency as they follow a protagonist from milestone to milestone, thereby causing the singularity of the epiphanic moment to flatten into a dispassionate humdrumness over the course of a plot. *The Namesake,* Munson claims, is thus "linear to the point of monotony," with Gogul Ganguli, the American-born son of Bengali immigrants, going "through the same set of motions with the same uneasy indifference throughout: unsure of himself in primary school, unsure of himself at Yale, unsure of himself as he studies for his licensing exam as an architect" (Munson 2003, 70). Similarly, the hero of *The Fortress of Solitude* to Munson is "made of exceptionally thin stuff" because of the sameness of his reactions to events:

> About his inner life we learn very little other than that he feels uncomfortable in Brooklyn as a child, in Vermont as a college student, and in Berkeley as an adult. Since he also serves as his author's chosen lens on reality, it is perhaps no wonder that the world around him tends to assume a similar characterlessness. (72)

As a result, "[l]ike Gogol in *The Namesake,* Dylan remains without shape . . . [as] does the world he inhabits" (Munson 2003, 72). What Munson suggests is that the obligation of following a character across an age span enervates a plot's rising action until the form becomes *too* verisimilitudinous: like adolescence itself, these books degenerate into muddles.

Selected Authors. A four-decade-old observation by W. Tasker Witham in *The Adolescent in the American Novel, 1920–1960* (1964) remains relevant today: "Even a cursory glance at the fiction about adolescence . . . reveals two very obvious facts[:] First, the majority of novels emphasizing the adolescence of the protagonist are first novels, and secondly, most of them are largely autobiographical" (Witham 1964, 17). These "facts" suggest why so few authors work within the genre for the entirety of their career. To cite but one representative example, Sue Monk Kidd followed *The Secret Life of Bees* with *The Mermaid's Chair* (2005), the story of a *middle-aged* protagonist. That minority of writers who do repeatedly examine adolescence are often harshly criticized for not "outgrowing" their interest in the coming-of-age process and tackling more epic (i.e. adult) issues. Such authors may even be labeled "minor" writers for merely reiterating the conventions and formulae of the *bildungsroman* instead of forging more original artistic visions. Judgments on wunderkind writers who fail to follow up the breakthrough books *at all*— whether due to premature death, writer's block, or exasperation with the publishing industry—are often treated especially harsh. These authors are said to repeat the pattern of Salinger, Plath, and Harper Lee as opposed to, say, Joyce Carol Oates or Philip Roth: if at all, they are remembered for a single work as opposed to an *oeuvre*.

The first new millennium writer heralded for a *bildungsroman* was Tristan Egolf (b. 1972), whose *Lord of the Barnyard: Killing the Fatted Cat and Arming the Aware in the Corn Belt* was celebrated in 1999–2000 as a hipster take on breadbasket America reminiscent of Richard Brautigan's *Trout Fishing in America* (1967). As a *New York Times* reviewer noted, Egolf had the sort of a "mediagenic" back story guaranteed to garner interest in a debut novel:

> The twenty-seven-year-old American author, something of an autodidact, collected over fifty rejection slips from publishers [in America] before being befriended by the daughter of the French novelist Patrick Modiano. She found him busking on the streets of Paris and introduced his manuscript to her father. And, sure enough, *Lord* . . . is exactly the sort of fauvist extravaganza Europeans welcome as quintessentially American: brash, vigorous, violent and crude. (Miller 1999, 10)

Nearly every review of the novel mentions Egolf's history as an aspiring punk rocker with an aversion to the creative-writing programs minting most young writers today; having dropped out of Temple University after only three semesters and spending several subsequent years vagabonding through Europe, Egolf struck the press as a decidedly unique if undisciplined talent. As the *Times* concluded,

> *Lord of the Barnyard* is the book a shrewder novelist would have stashed in a drawer, chalking it up to various lessons learned and letting a second, more polished work serve as his debut. The question is: Can Egolf learn to write dialogue, to fully imagine characters and to get over his adolescent misanthropy without refining the fire right out of his work? (Miller 1999, 7:10)

The question, unfortunately, would prove moot. Although Egolf's second novel, *Skirt and Fiddle,* is indeed "more polished" than *Lord,* it received far less attention and sold poorly. Shortly afterward, Egolf began suffering from depression and personal problems that culminated in his May 7, 2005, suicide at the age of thirty-three. Speculation began almost immediately as to whether this tragic end would transform the fading star into a romantic cult figure. As a rather tasteless *Toronto Star* headline read, "Death Be Not a Career Killer": "The awful truth is that creating a much-praised, little-read work like Egolf's *Lord of the Barnyard* is only half the job when you're striving for artistic immortality," the paper insisted. "You need mystique, and the best route to it is to die young" (Fraser 2005, H15). Sadly, the observation has proved at least partially true. Egolf remains an admired figure among collegiate-aged audiences, albeit more for his tragic biography than for the artistry of *Lord.* His other works, however, garner modest interest. When posthumously published in

2006, his final completed novel, *Kornwolf*, generated fewer reviews and sales than *Skirt and Fiddle*.

The same year that *Skirt and Fiddle* appeared, an even younger author burst upon the scene with a *bildungsroman* that achieved broad commercial (as opposed to Egolf's cult) success. Born in 1977, Jonathan Safran Foer was barely twenty-five when *Everything is Illuminated* was hailed as *the* novel of 2002 by a range of tastemakers, including his former Princeton professor Joyce Carol Oates. Based on a 1999 journey to the Ukraine to uncover Foer's family past, the picaresque proved a captivating mixture of postmodern ambition and faux-naif voice. Contrasting a self-consciously "literary" narrative by a fictionalized character named "Jonathan Safran Foer" with a broken-English version of the same trip by an American-obsessed translator named Alex, *Everything Is Illuminated* struck many as nothing less than a twenty-first century *Tristram Shandy*, with Foer even borrowing the Sternian trick of inserting unconventional graphic devices into the text. (Thus, on one page, the phrase "We are writing" is repeated more than two hundred times). For most reviewers, the book's audacity alone suggested a writer of major significance. *The* [London] *Times* both summarized and repeated the praise when it stated,

> You will have to ignore everything you read about this novel. For you will read that *Everything Is Illuminated* is a work of genius, that its author, at twenty-four, has staked his claim for literary greatness, that it's a new kind of novel, that after it things will never be the same again. You won't believe it and you'll decide not to read the book on principle. And that would be a disaster, because it's all true. ("Luminous Talent," 2005)

Inevitably, such unabashed hyperbole invited a backlash against Foer's second, 9/11-inspired novel, *Extremely Loud and Incredibly Close*, which appeared three years later in 2005. To his credit, Foer avoided the dreaded sophomore slump by integrating this picaresque into the context of American fears of terrorism, thereby avoiding the appearance of repeating himself. Nevertheless, a greater number of critics took issue with his multimedia devices. Especially controversial was the book's conclusion, in which hero Oskar Schell claims to discover photographs of his father falling from the Twin Towers: "I found the pictures of the falling body. I ripped the pages out of the book. I reversed the order, so the last one was first, and the first was last. When I flipped through them, it looked like the man was floating up through the sky" (Foer 2005, 325). The final fifteen pages recreate the illusion of Oskar's "flip book" by reprinting in reverse sequence photographs by eyewitness Lyle Owerko of an actual 9/11 victim hurtling through space. This child-oriented form, coupled with Oskar's insistence that such imaginative tricks allow Americans to remember how, if events had been otherwise, "[w]e would have been safe" come September 12, 2001, offended critics who found it overly sentimental and escapist (2005, 351). *New York Press* commentator Harry Siegel was especially vocal in his objections, claiming that Foer's fondness for "saintly" child narrators was solipsistic and that the ultimate message of this "Oprah-etic paean to innocence" amounted to nothing more than the sort of life lesson found in any feel-good self-help tome: "Most of all, we learn the search, not the treasure, is the thing, which readers may recognize from the pages of Robert Fulghum's classic of inspirational mush *All I Really Need to Know I Learned in Kindergarten*" (Siegel, "Extremely Cloying"). However vituperative, Siegel's critique reflects a burgeoning belief among critics that Foer must move beyond precocious child protagonists to maintain his reputation.

Another rare author to follow a widely praised coming-of-age novel with a second *bildungsroman* is Curtis Sittenfeld, whose *The Man of My Dreams* (2006) followed eighteen months after her best-selling *Prep*. Although not as technically inventive as *Everything Is Illuminated*, *Prep* was touted for breathing contemporary life into the boarding-school genre that had seemingly gone out of fashion since the days of *Catcher* and *A Separate Peace*. Like those books, it criticizes the temptation of its heroine, Lee Fiora, toward snobbery and East-Coast elitism while also providing a female perspective on the typical maturation experiences (especially sex). Exactly what accounted for the book's unexpected sales (140,000 hardbacks and nearly three times as many paperbacks) remains a mystery that the publishing industry continues to ponder. Some credited it to "creative marketing and publicity":

> A team of four publicists made belts that matched the cover for giveaways, and sent splashy gift bags (holding pink and green flip-flops, the belt, notebooks, lip gloss) with the galleys to magazines. The pitch letter included photocopies of the publicists' own high school yearbook photos . . . (Boss 2007)

Yet that explanation fails to take into account Sittenfeld's talent, which created "coveted crossover market appeal: in addition to young women, [*Prep*] was read by adolescents, more mature readers and males"—at least, "according to anecdotal evidence" (Boss 2007, 3:1).

In the end, *Prep*'s popularity suggests the enduring appeal of the coming-of-age novel and how readers discover fresh pleasure in its established conventions. Yet that appeal seems most intense with first-time novelists, especially *young* first timers. Audiences are far more fickle when writers like Sittenfeld are perceived as going to the well of adolescence once too often. At about two-thirds the length of *Prep*'s four-hundred-plus pages, *The Man of My Dreams* is more economical in its storytelling, suggesting that Sittenfeld has matured in terms of tempo and dramatic buildup. (*Prep*'s slow pace was one of its few recurring criticisms). Yet the persistent focus on the minutiae of teen dating rituals led some reviewers to accuse the author of "navel-gazing":

> Sharp glimpses of dull phenomena . . . were [*Prep*'s] hallmark. And Ms. Sittenfeld's embrace of the unremarkable is even clingier the second time around. In *The Man of My Dreams* her drab heroine is made special mainly by endless reserves of myopia and self-pity. An amazing number of episodes involve pizza, despite the limited range of pizza as a literary device. (Maslin 2006, E:9)

The story of Hannah Gavener's dependency on older men—prompted by her father's inattentiveness—also troubled critics. Many found the heroine "defined almost entirely in terms of her relationships," a perception

> due in part to [Hannah's] own myopia, but also to the structure of the narrative: Hannah doesn't have hobbies, interests or real friends—nothing outside her interactions with men. The only other thing that motivates her is paying off her student loans, and even that's to stick it to dear old dad. When, at the book's end, she ostensibly finds fulfillment teaching autistic children, it feels forced. Her emotional world is too constrained. Such a limited worldview makes for a limited character; to show how much

she's grown, she tells a story about one of her students, but she seems equally pleased that she's no longer embarrassed to talk to people 'with food in [her] teeth.' Even in a world where small victories matter, it is difficult to call this a real triumph. (Thomas 2006, R:9)

Again, what is striking is that *Prep* likewise ended with a "small victory," yet few commentators found fault with it. The tendency for writers to be criticized for using techniques and devices employed in previous novels suggests that it may be harder to write a successful *bildungsroman* the *second* time out, as opposed to the first.

Conclusion. As this essay suggests, the coming-of-age novel faces little danger of extinction. Its prominence among fictional genres is matched only by its resiliency as it adapts to the needs and ideals of succeeding generations. If the prevailing trends of the twenty-first century hold true, we can expect continued emphasis on completing the *Bildung* cycle and less Holden-esque resistance to growing up. This suggests that authors are still reassessing the legacy of the 1960s and the fixation with youth that characterized the baby-boom generation. We can also expect more heterogeneous amalgamations of styles as authors ground the traditional maturation plot in other literary forms.

If there is one failing to the novel's development over the past decade, it is that, for all the experimentation of *Everything Is Illuminated* and *The Brief Wondrous Life of Oscar Wao,* authors have avoided any metafictional exploration of the genre's history and social function. That is, coming-of-age novels accept at face value the importance of initiation rites without tackling in any extensive way the manner in which those rites allow American culture to both police and sensationalize youth. Indeed, "youth" as a social value appears to be falling out of fashion in these books. From Fitzgerald to Salinger and Kerouac, the genre depicted the *paysage moralisée* as a *felix culpa*—a fall out of moral surety into compromise and hypocrisy. Today's authors are more likely to look to adulthood as a reward for surviving the perils of adolescence. It would be tempting to regard this tendency as itself mature if it were not for the aura of nostalgia in these books. Longing for family and community, many fictional teenagers pine for a past in which meanings and mores were stable—a past that never existed, in other words. While the genre deserves kudos for outgrowing the fatalism of *Less Than Zero,* books like *Jupiter Tree Burning* would do well to demonstrate a more self-reflexive awareness of how its regard for adulthood risks appropriation in the ongoing culture wars over "traditional" values.

Bibliography

Almond, Steve. *My Life in Heavy Metal.* New York: Grove, 2004.
Bank, Melissa. *The Wonder Spot.* New York: Viking, 2005.
Barrowcliffe, Mark. *Girlfriend 44.* New York: St. Martin's, 2001.
Beller, Thomas. *The Sleepover Artist.* New York: Norton, 2001.
Boswell, Marshall. *Alternative Atlanta.* New York: Delacorte, 2005.
Brashare, Ann. *Sisterhood of the Traveling Pants.* New York: Delacorte, 2001.
Caldwell, Ian and Thomason, Dustin. *The Rule of the Four.* New York: Dial, 2004.
Childress, Mark. *One Mississippi.* Boston: Little, Brown, 2006.
Cisneros, Sandra. *Caramelo.* New York: Knopf, 2002.
Coupland, Douglas. *Generation X: Tales for an Accelerated Culture.* New York: St. Martin's, 1991.

———. *Hey, Nostradamus!* New York: Bloomsbury, 2003.

Díaz, Junot. *The Brief Wondrous Life of Oscar Wao.* New York: Riverhead, 2007.

DeGrazia, Don. *American Skin.* New York: Tandem, 2000.

Eggers, Dave. *You Shall Know Our Velocity!* San Francisco: McSweeney's, 2002.

Egolf, Tristan. *Lord of the Barnyard: Killing the Fatted Calf and Arming the Aware in the Corn Belt.* New York: Grove, 2000.

———. *Kornwolf.* New York: Grove, 2006.

———. *Skirt and Fiddle.* New York: Grove, 2002.

Enger, Leif. *Peace Like a River.* Boston: Atlantic Monthly Press, 2001.

Fitzgerald, F. Scott. *This Side of Paradise.* New York: Scribners, 1920.

Foer, Jonathan Safran. *Everything Is Illuminated.* New York: Houghton Mifflin, 2002.

———. *Extremely Loud and Incredibly Close.* New York: Houghton Mifflin, 2005.

Gibbons, Kaye. *The Life All Around Me by Ellen Foster.* New York: Harcourt, 2005.

Godfrey, Rebecca. *The Torn Skirt.* New York: Harper Perennial, 2002.

Grodstein, Lauren. *Reproduction is the Flaw of Love.* New York: Free Press, 2004.

Haddon, Mark. *The Curious Case of the Dog in the Night-Time.* New York: Doubleday, 2003.

Keltner, Kim Wong. *The Dim Sum of All Things.* New York: Avon, 2005.

Key, Watt. *Alabama Moon.* New York: Farrar, Straus, & Giroux, 2006.

Kidd, Sue Monk. *The Secret Life of Bees.* New York: Viking, 2002.

King, Dave. *The Ha-Ha.* Boston: Little, Brown, 2005.

Korman, Gordon. *Born to Rock.* New York: Hyperion, 2006.

Lahiri, Jhumpa. *The Namesake.* New York: Houghton Mifflin, 2003.

Lethem, Jonathan. *The Fortress of Solitude.* New York: Doubleday, 2003.

Long, Goldberry. *Jupiter Tree Burning.* New York: Simon and Schuster, 2001.

Lynch, Jim. *The Highest Tide.* New York: Bloomsbury, 2005.

Massud, Claire. *The Emperor's Children.* New York: Knopf, 2006.

McDonnell, Nick. *The Last Brother.* New York: Grove, 2006.

———. *Twelve.* New York: Grove, 2002.

Mebus, Scott. *Booty Nomad.* New York: Miramax, 2004.

Meno, Joe. *Hairstyles of the Damned.* Chicago: Akashic Books, 2004.

Miller, Laura. "Down on the Farm." The *New York Times* March 28, 1999: sec. 7:10.

Morris, Michael. *Slow Way Home.* San Francisco: HarperSan Francisco, 2003.

Munson, Sam. "Born in the U.S.A." *Commentary* 116 (November 2003): 68–72.

Myracle, Lauren. *L8r, g8r.* New York: Abrams, 2007.

———. *TTFN.* New York: Abrams, 2005.

———. *TTYL.* New York: Abrams, 2004.

Oates, Joyce Carol. *I'll Take You There.* New York: Ecco, 2002.

Packer, Ann. *The Dive from Clausen's Pier.* New York: Knopf, 2002.

Pessl, Marisha. *Special Topics in Calamity Physics.* New York: Viking, 2006.

Phillips, Delores. *The Darkest Child.* New York: Soho, 2004.

Pierre, DBC. *Vernon God Little.* New York: Canongate, 2003.

Picoult, Jodi. *Nineteen Minutes.* New York: Atria, 2007.

Pope, Dan. *In the Cherry Tree.* New York: Picador, 2003.

Prose, Francine. *After.* New York: Joanna Colter, 2003.

Quart, Alissa. *Branded: The Buying and Selling of Teenagers.* New York: Perseus, 2003.

Rempel, Mark A. *Point Blank.* New York: Thomas Nelson, 2002.

Riggs, Jack. *When the Finch Rises.* New York: Ballantine, 2003.

Ruditis, Paul. *The Rainbow Party.* New York: Simon Pulse, 2005.

Salinger, J.D. *The Catcher in the Rye.* Boston: Little, Brown, 1951.

Schickler, David. *Sweet and Vicious.* New York: Dial Press, 2004.

Sebold, Alice. *The Lovely Bones.* New York: Picador, 2002.

Shepard, Jim. *Project X.* New York: Vintage, 2005.

Shriver, Lionel. *We Need to Talk about Kevin*. New York: Counterpoint, 2003.

Singleton, George. *Why Dogs Chase Cars*. New York: Algonquin, 2004.

Sittenfeld, Curtis. *The Man of My Dreams*. New York: Random House, 2006.

———. *Prep*. New York: Random House, 2005.

———. "Sophie's Choices." The *New York Times* July 5, 2005: sec. 7:9.

Smith, Kyle. *Love Monkey*. New York: Morrow, 2004.

Soehnlein, K. M. *The World of Normal Boys*. New York: Kensington, 2001.

Strasser, Todd. *Give a Boy a Gun*. New York: Simon Pulse, 2000.

VanBaale, Kali. *The Space Between*. Montgomery, AL: River City Publishing, 2006.

Watson, C. G. *Quad*. New York: Razorbill, 2007.

Webb, Charles. *The Graduate*. New York: NAL, 1963.

Weinstein, Debra. *Apprentice to the Flower Poet Z*. New York: Random House, 2004.

Whittington, Brad. *Welcome to Fred*. Nashville, TN: B&H Publishing Group, 2003.

Wilson, Christopher. *Cotton*. New York: Harcourt, 2005.

Wolfe, Tom. *I Am Charlotte Simmons*. New York: Farrar, Straus, & Giroux, 2004.

Wolff, Tobias. *Old School*. New York: Knopf, 2003.

Further Reading

Acland, Charles. *Youth, Murder, Spectacle: The Politics of "Youth in Crisis."* Boulder, Co: Westview, 1995; Boss, Shira. "The Greatest Mystery: Making a Best Seller." The *New York Times* May 13, 2007: sec. 3:1; Briscoe, Joanna. "Carrot pennies and cashmere twinsets: Melissa Bank's stories may look like chick lit, but they have surprising depths, says Joanna Briscoe: *The Wonder Spot* by Melissa Bank." *The Guardian* July 2, 2005: 27; Curnutt, Kirk. *Alienated-Youth Fiction*. Farmington Hills, MI: Gale, 2001; Elder, Richard. "College Try: Tom Wolfe's Overwrought Attempt at Skewering University Life Is Nasty, Brutish, and Long." *The Boston Globe* November 7, 2004: sec. D:6; Eyre, Hermione. "I Didn't Know George Eliot Wrote *Sweet Valley High* . . ." *The Independent* October 2, 2005: 26; —. "A Female Holden for Our Age: The Like-Named Narrator of Katherine Taylor's Debut Novel is, Like Her East Coast Boarding School Girlfriends, Haunted by the Need to Suffer. So Suffer They Do, in Blue-chip Misery and Nothing Good Can Come of That." *The Toronto Star* July 27, 2007: sec. D:8; Fiedler, Leslie A. "Boys Will Be Boys!" *New Leader* 41 (28 April 1951): 24–26; FitzGerald, Frances. "The Influence of Anxiety: What's the Problem with Young Adult Novels?" *Harper's* 309 (September 2004): 62–69; Fitzgerald, F. Scott. "Public Letter to Thomas Boyd." 1921. *F. Scott Fitzgerald on Authorship*. Ed. Matthew J. Bruccoli with Judith S. Baughman. Columbia: University of South Carolina Press, 1996. 43–44; Flanagan, Caitlin. "Are You There, God? It's Me, Monica: How Nice Girls Got So Casual about Oral Sex." *The Atlantic Monthly* 297 (January/February 2006): 167–182; Fraser, Garnet. "Death Be Not a Career Killer." *The Toronto Star* May 21, 2005: sec. H:15; Kakutani, Michiko. "Who's Afraid Of Holden Caulfield?" The *New York Times* August 23, 2005: sec. E:1; "Luminous Talent in the Spotlight." *The* [London] *Times* July 7, 2005. http://entertainment.timesonline.co.uk/tol/arts_and_entertainment/books/books_group/article541500.ece; Maslin, Janet. "The Myopic Navel-Gazer Can't See Her Way to Love." The *New York Times* May 18, 2006: sec. E:9; Rich, Motoko and Dinitia Smith. "Teen-lit Packages: Forget the Writer in the Garret." The *International Herald Tribune* April 28, 2006: 24; Sarvas, Mark. "Beauty and the Geek." The *New York Times* July 1, 2007: sec. 7:19; Scott, A.O. "Dreaming in Spanglish." *New York Times Book Review* September 30, 2007: sec. 7:9; Siegel, Harry. "Extremely Cloying & Incredibly False: Why the author of *Everything Is Illuminated* is a fraud and a hack." *New York Press* (undated). http://www.nypress.com/18/15/news&columns/harrysiegel.cfm; Springhall, John. *Youth, Popular Culture and Moral Panics: Penny Gaffs to Gangsta Rap, 1830–1996*. London: Palgrave Macmillan, 1999; Steuver, Hank. "Move Over, Holden: Curtis Sittenfeld Writes About Boarding School Life as if She's Been There." *The Washington Post* February 23, 2005: sec. C:1; Thomas, Louisa. "Love's Labors." The *Los Angeles Times* May

14, 2006: sec. R:9; Twenge, Jean M. *Generation Me: Why Today's Young Americans Are More Confident, Assertive, Entitled—and More Miserable Than Ever Before.* New York: Free Press, 2006; Walton, Megan. "*Dive* by Randall DeVallance." *Bookslut* (May 2005). http://www.bookslut.com/fiction/2005_05_005389.php; Witham, W. Tasker. *The Adolescent in the American Novel, 1920-1960.* New York: Ungar, 1964.

KIRK CURNUTT

CONTEMPORARY MAINSTREAM AMERICAN FICTION

Definition. As with most attempts at a normative definition, any prescriptive characterization of "contemporary mainstream American fiction" necessarily remains both partial and subjective. All four of the words in the category lead to judgment calls and, thus, controversy. "Contemporary," for instance, is highly relative, with some critics defining the term as roughly equivalent to post-World War Two, while others push the date back to the 1960s or 1970s. In the former instance, the war functions as the boundary between "high modernism" and "postmodernism." In such a view, new theories regarding the nature, or possibility, of Truth started to proliferate in literature and thus mark a new phase in prose fiction. The middle date pushes back the "start" of postmodernism, while the latter pursues a more strictly chronological path. Narrower perspectives are certainly possible, and many younger readers would challenge the notion that a 37-year-old book, written decades before their birth, could possibly be contemporary. Roughly, then, the debate over what constitutes "contemporary" regards whether the category should highlight simple chronology or underscore what James M. Mellard calls, after Thomas Kuhn, a paradigm shift in which nascent, "naïve" literary experiments "explode" into the dominant mode before approaching "entropy" and becoming largely supplanted by a new hegemonic discourse (Mellard 1980, 11, 39). Mellard adds, however, that any novel could be "identified as naïve or critical, or sophisticated depending on its relationship to other items in a hypostatized series," a remark that problematizes the application of the label "contemporary" based on chronology alone (6). The paradigm approach thus employs a "big picture" approach that seeks to identify the general moment—usually a malleable one based on the publication of a significant text (which one, though?) or a clustering of writers pursuing similar thematic and aesthetic aims—when a new spirit infused the fiction of an era. One problem with such a view, however, is that the "landmark" texts are often poorly received by the public and critics of the day, with the older mode still dominating both the marketplace and the critical investigation. Another dilemma with the paradigm approach is that it can offer undue weight to the exceptional text and ignore modest inroads made by less experimental writers. Thus, the stylistic excursions of a William Faulkner or T.S. Eliot overshadow the tentative—but possibly more influential in terms of readying a wide audience for more radical strategies—steps of a James Branch Cabell or a Vachel Lindsay. Further, critics on the cusp of a paradigm shift will likely misidentify or overemphasize certain traits and ignore or underplay others. The chronological approach, of course, offers its own limitations, not the least of which is an ever-receding past. Does one limit "contemporary" to five years? Ten? Twenty? The period under question will necessarily appear arbitrary and subject to revision. A strictly age-based definition might also over stress a writer's connection to the present and diminish his or her response to previous generations of fiction. A compromise position might merge a manageable segment of time with an awareness of how this period fits into past and emerging trends. Given the scope of this entry, the period from 2000–2006 will suffice, but with an effort to contextualize recent fiction with a more paradigmatic view.

The idea of "mainstream" is no less ineffable than that of "contemporary." A simple equation of "mainstream" with "popular," for instance, breaks down when one contemplates that much so-called "genre fiction," such as romance novels or science fiction, frequently outsells fiction deemed by many critics to be mainstream. Another possible explanation of mainstream, that it appeals to a broad audience (with respect to education, class, race, etc.), might hold more promise. Yet, it too fails under scrutiny in that the primary category contains a variety of sub-categories, such as **historical fiction** or *bildungsroman*, which do not necessarily attract a wide swath of the reading public, whereas some genre fiction, such as mysteries or "**chick lit**" do. Mainstream might denote confluence with the cultural zeitgeist, yet American culture, with its highly fragmented niche markets—reflected in the plethora of television networks, music genres, Web sites, sneakers, pain relievers, toilet bowl cleaners, and other entertainment formats and consumer products that are ubiquitous in the United States—hardly embraces a monolithic approach to entertainment. One might view mainstream as a transparent catch-all category for any book that fails to fit squarely into any of the major genres (**romance, science fiction, fantasy, mystery,** or horror), but this seems fruitless as well, depending on it does on a negative definition (i.e., mainstream is not genre fiction). An ideological approach to the question might suggest that "mainstream" functions as a reflection of a particular socio-political outlook—capitalism—even when it appears to be in opposition to the hegemonic discourse. In this view, even the most vicious of a mainstream writer's attacks leave most questions unasked—and thus reinforce the ideological base. It seems apparent, though, that "mainstream" denotes readier access for an audience, that a familiarity with conventions (as with genre fiction) or an ability to decode intricate linguistic or formal experiments (as with avant-garde fiction) is not expected. While mainstream fiction might draw from multiple generic codes, it reorganizes them sufficiently enough that the non-specialist reader can negotiate them with ease. Simultaneously, mainstream fiction does not overly stress the experimental nature of its language or structure. Its goal is not to privilege esoteric skills, but to encourage readers to engage the material. Mainstream fiction thus represents a bridge between the niches of convention (genre fiction, which establishes parameters for characterization, theme, etc.) and anti-convention (avant-garde fiction, which self-consciously extols the idiosyncratic). It lacks both the transparency of the genre—where even "surprise" endings are coded—and the opacity of the radically experimental—where disorientation is *de rigueur.*

"American" might initially appear the easiest term to define, yet it, too, poses some challenges. First, one might apply the broad label "American" to writers of both South and North America—which in turn would open the canon to works written in English, French, Spanish, Portuguese, and a host of indigenous languages. Nevertheless, one might also claim that the *word* "American" is sufficiently associated around the globe with the United States that debate is moot. Nevertheless, even with a narrowly nationalistic use of the *word*, interpretive problems arise. Chief among these regards whether residency, citizenship, and birth are co-equal in determining whether one is an "American" writer. T.S. Eliot, born and educated in the United States yet residing in England, appears in anthologies of both American and English writers. W.H. Auden, born and educated in England, yet residing in the United States, appears for the most part only in anthologies of English writers. Both were naturalized citizens of their adopted countries. What, moreover, is one to do with novelists such as Vladimir Nabokov or Anaïs Nin, both of whom were born outside of the United States yet wrote significant bodies of work within their adopted countries. Are they treated differently than Saul Bellow, who was born in Canada, yet immigrated to the United States as a young child? Self-identification offers one possibility: which country does a writer claim? The problem, though, is that many writers resist precisely such limiting notions of identity. Some writers indeed revel in their multi-nationalistic status. For the purposes of this entry, "American" will connote a writer with strong self-identified geographic and thematic connections to the United States, but not necessarily citizenship.

Fiction itself is a problematic category, particularly when juxtaposed with another prose rubric, autobiography. As recent controversies connected with James Frey and JT LeRoy (Laura Albert) demonstrate, the public often demands a "purity" of autobiography that it would not require of fiction, a category that theoretically has more license to rely on "complete" imagination. As James Olney, a prominent theorist of autobiography, observes, however, the notion of autobiography as revealing verifiable Truth requires an archeological metaphor in which "memory is something fixed and static" (Olney 1998, 19). This contrasts with a more flexible metaphor, weaving, in which the writing process "will bring forth ever different memorial configurations and even a newly shaped self" (20). The latter metaphor, the one that Olney champions, clearly holds more in common with fiction, that supposed bastion of the imagination, than it does with unadulterated transcriptions of autobiographical experience. Given the propensity for memory to filter, distort, and omit, autobiography shares definite traits with the fabulist nature of fiction. The boundary blurring travels both ways, however, as fiction frequently draws upon historical models—as in Russell Banks's *Cloudsplitter,* for instance—or the author's own experiences (as with Tim O'Brien's *Going after Cacciato*). The "accuracy" and frequency of such factual information varies widely, however, with some authors seeking to replicate their models in painstaking detail and others using them more as catalysts than as templates. Still other writers consciously undercut their factual paradigms, employing what Linda Hutcheon calls "historiographic metafiction," a process wherein "theoretical self-awareness of history and fiction as human constructs . . . is made the grounds for its rethinking and reworking of the forms and contents of the past" (Hutcheon 1988, 5). Yet another group of writers seeks to reject photographic mimesis in order to "disturb us by dislodging us from our settled sense of reality" by proffering "[a] new version of the real" (Hume 1984, 56). Thus, in both autobiography and fiction, writers contemplate the interpenetration of empirical fact and imaginative construct. Fiction is generally given a wider berth in altering verifiable events; although the more an audience is invested in the actual incident the more likely the outcry if a writer takes liberties with "the facts." Time tends to decrease that investment and increase credulity. For the purposes of this definition, one might distinguish between fiction and nonfiction by focusing on the communal stress placed on authorial self-expression as opposed to fact. The outrage over Frey and LeRoy stemmed not so much from the text itself as from the perceived misrepresentation of the narrative, a misrepresentation that disgruntled readers by "preparing" them for a narrative experience ostensibly grounded in "reality," but that in practice presented "facts" that were patently untrue. While Frey may create "facts" that correspond to some internal essence or psychological truth, the readers reject it as false, fictional. With nonfiction, most audiences expect facts to subordinate authorial creativity. A history book may be well-written—and even reveal an idiosyncratic vision—yet its utility will be called into question should its facts fail to correspond to documented "reality." With fiction, however, more allowance is made for writers to manipulate "reality," even to the point that in non-mimetic fiction physical laws may be defied or created. Fiction thus becomes a category of prose wherein an interpretive community recognizes that a narrative's mimetic coherence and accuracy is coincidental to the author's personal creative impulses.

History. Many novelists and critics of the 1960s and 1970s agreed with Henry Miller's 1954 assessment of "literature as a dead duck." More specifically, fiction was seen by many, including novelist John Barth, as "exhausted" and unlikely to transcend the towering achievements of modernists such as Faulkner and Fitzgerald. Barth in particular lamented that "A good many current novelists write turn-of-the-century-type novels, only in more or less mid-twentieth-century language and about contemporary people and topics" (Barth 1984, 66). Many, like Raymond Federman, who resisted such characterizations—or at least foresaw continued possibilities in the novel form—tended to laud the merits of what he called surfiction, in which "the primary purpose of fiction [is] to unmask its own fictionality, to expose the metaphor of its own fraudulence" (Federman 1981, 8). Patricia Waugh later referred to this principle as "metafiction," and noted the paradox of both aiming for the "construction of a fictional illusion" and the desire for "laying bare . . . that illusion" (Waugh 1984, 6). While such techniques initially belonged to the province of the avant-garde—writers such as Alain Robbe-Grillet, Ronald Sukenick, and Helmut Heissenbüttel—it quickly infiltrated the "mainstream" and manifested itself in broadly popular novels by the likes of E.L. Doctorow, John Fowles, Richard Brautigan, and many others. The postmodern concern with exposing "metanarratives" sustained a great number of mainstream novelists of the 1970s, although the phenomenon tended to be wedded with more traditional subject matter than the avant-garde leaned toward. Historical epics, genre fictions, and other archetypal narratives—treated with a high level of playful irony and self-consciousness—abounded and prompted some, bored by what they perceived as jaded decadence rather than experimentalism—to reiterate that the novel had lost its cachet.

However, Jago Morrison aptly contends that "it seems extraordinary how misguided this 'death of the novel' thesis turned out to be" and argues that "contemporary fiction was to undergo a renaissance over the next twenty years, reestablishing itself as the preeminent literary form by the turn of the twenty-first century" (Morrison 2003, 4). Morrison further avers that the thesis itself stemmed from provincial reading habits and narrow critical concerns, limitations that were exploded by a diverse group of novelists who explored both rich thematic terrain and stylistic innovation (6). Indeed, a common criticism of the postmodern critique of "grand narratives" charged that the strategy occurred just as marginalized groups were wading into the flow of power, that all of a sudden the myth-making, paradigm-enforcing possibilities of narrative were presented as illusory after all. Rosemary Hennessey sums up dissatisfaction with such (non)arguments with her claim that most feminisms "raise the possibility that emancipatory movement requires normative grounds and closure" (Hennessey 1993, 3). Precisely at the moment when a significant segment mainstream fiction (albeit largely white and male) was contemplating the death of the author and the arch fictionality of its enterprise, a juggernaut of writers committed to the social power of the novel burst onto the scene. Some, like Toni Morrison, Rolando Hinojosa, and Edmund White, employed technically complex structures (many drawing from

African and indigenous sources rather than from the avant-garde), but numerous writers, such as (early) Alice Walker, Victor Villaseñor, and Ernest J. Gaines, eagerly adopted realistic conventions and eschewed strategies designed to place screens between the readers and the content. Such writers attempted to combine the ability to entertain with efforts at social justice, and they often targeted audiences put off by the sometimes perplexing self-consciousness and thematic intricacies of writers such as Thomas Pynchon, Kathy Acker, or William Burroughs. In a world clouded by racial, sexual, and economic disparity, many writers and readers equated the postmodern turn with self-indulgence or even irresponsibility.

Mainstream fiction of the 1970s and 1980s also rejected the stylistic pyrotechnics of postmodernism by building on the "New Journalism" of writers such as Truman Capote, Norman Mailer, and Tom Wolfe. These writers and followers, such as Joyce Carol Oates and Joan Didion, examined "real" events through a fictionalized lens, sometimes even injecting themselves into the narrative. Other writers, including Bret Easton Ellis, Jay McInerney, and Tama Janowitz, avoiding self-consciousness and often judgment, examined the hollowness of modern materialist culture. Such novelists often used a "numb" style that depicted gross excess, violence, and betrayal as through a camera lens. Another class of socially realistic writers avoided the spare style of the "brat pack" writers and hearkened back to the full—and critical—style of Emile Zola or Theodore Dreiser. John Updike, John Irving, and others portrayed the malaise of the suburbs in an unapologetically detailed, exuberant way that mixed humor, sex, and middle-class ethos. Another trend, however, involved the mixture of fantasy and realism that had infused Latin American fiction since the appearance of Gabriel García Márquez's *One Hundred Years of Solitude*. Known as magic (or magical) realism, this concept influenced a number of American writers, including Tim O'Brien, Toni Morrison, Ana Castillo, and Paul Auster. Some mainstream writers, like Kurt Vonnegut, employed an amalgamation of science fiction and recognizable settings to critique modern America.

In addition to the themes of lack of community and the maximalist approach to presenting American life in the novel, environmentalism also emerged, often linked with feminism and general cultural critique, in novels by writers such as Jane Smiley, Barbara Kingsolver, and Annie Proulx. Personal identity continued to constitute a major fictional theme, particularly with respect to race, where the intersections between history and the present were explored in books by writers such as Morrison, Meena Alexander, Julia Alvarez, and Louise Erdrich. Another trend was the rise of the graphic novel, which, building on the success of Art Spiegelman and Alan

BOWLING ALONE AND MAXIMALISM IN AMERICAN LIFE

In the 1990s, a fin de siècle mood dominated American fiction, with authors such as Jeffrey Eugenides, Rick Moody, and Richard Russo looking back on the dissolution of American communal spirit and the rise of the "bowling alone" phenomenon noted in 2000 by sociologist Robert D. Putnam. The apocalyptic mood extended to novels set in the distant past as well, as writers such as Bobbie Ann Mason, Russell Banks, and T. Coraghessan Boyle considered the ways in which historical events reflect archetypal behavioral patterns still relevant for a millennial audience. David Foster Wallace, Jonathan Franzen, and Eugenides typified a movement toward "maximalism" that merged an avalanche of details with comic, digressive observations of American life (although the old hand at this form, Pynchon, continued to explore it).

Moore in the mid-1980s, started to enter mainstream consciousness, as seen in the commercial viability of works by such artists as Daniel Clowes, Seth (Gregory Gallant), and Dave McKean. Anxiety about modern culture, particularly its speed and apparent vacuity, continued to manifest itself in many novels, such as those by Nicolson Baker, Richard Ford, and Bobbie Ann Mason. The events of 9/11 shattered the contemplative—even narcissistic—disposition of 1990s fiction and introduced stark political realities to the novels of the new century.

Trends and Themes

Commodification. Drawing on a theme that has been present in American literature at least since the late nineteenth century, numerous writers have presented characters caught in the whirlwind of materialism. However, whereas in earlier generations such designer labels, scrupulously detailed products (both real and imagined), and crass consumerism generally found themselves linked with a critical view of the United States, the current generation of writers does not necessarily draw such an unequivocal position. While some writers, of course, still equate materialism with moral bankruptcy; others view the capitalist landscape as an inevitable force of sorts, a neutral background that in and of itself does not determine moral worth. Writers such as Wallace and Boyle perhaps implicitly fault their characters (and by extension their country) for shallowness, but just as frequently "positive" characters use the same electronic gimcracks and shop at the same homogeneous malls as the "negative" ones. The difference is often not even one of quantity, but rather is more related to self-definition and whether the character can behave in an ethical way toward others. Detailed descriptions of consumption—often with sociological precision—offer more of a meta-narrative in which *all* characters, good and bad, operate. In contrast with these generic portraits are more negative ones proffered by writers such as Franzen and Mason. In such instances, the "neutrality" of conspicuous consumption is subverted; as such self-indulgence is often juxtaposed with characters (frequently in other countries) who cannot fathom such excess—and the indifference to it. Materialism in such venues acts as a soothing drug that allows individuals to ignore suffering on a global scale and concentrate instead on petty struggles.

Diversity. No longer relegated solely to "ethnic" sections, multicultural fiction is decidedly mainstream, yet, both old hands (such as Alice Walker) and new (like Jhumpa Lahiri) demonstrate that race and ethnicity continue to unsettle the American landscape. Reexaminations of historical struggles and events, such as Jim Crow and the Harlem Renaissance, continue to attract novelists as audiences seek enlightenment on topics that serve as mere footnotes in "mainstream" history books. Such treatments seek to give a voice to subalterns marginalized by history. Historical research—often using alternative sources—is supplemented with imaginative renderings of characters, as the stories of these lost, faceless individuals are often viewed as equally important with the recoverable facts. Such books frequently investigate the economic and cultural forces at play in overt and institutionalized racism, and others present past events as allegories of the contemporary scene. Observers of current racial and ethnic topics often focus on the psychological effects of living in a culture that purports to be "colorblind" yet that in actuality is obsessed with difference. Glass ceilings, affirmative action, culture clashes, and everyday indignities are popular topics, as is the very notion of identity. While legal protection and "fair" rules ostensibly exist, historical inequalities and contemporary inequities (such as sentencing laws that disproportionally impact minorities) dispute the idea of a level playing field. Border cultures also constitute an emerging theme, as does the generation tension within members of the same race/ethnicity. Discrimination against immigrants (and perceived immigrants) is another popular theme.

Environmentalism. With the ominous specters of global warming, peak oil, and suburban sprawl present in the headlines, environmental issues are appearing with an increased frequency in American fiction. Commitment to such issues, however, varies widely, with some authors, such as Barbara Kingsolver, exploring them as the primary theme, while others, like Mary Gaitskill, place them in the background as an ever-encroaching, but apparently unstoppable, threat that causes characters anxiety. For those who place the environment at the center of the narrative, a dominant concern is the impact of unchecked consumerism—ever spurred on by corporate profit-lust—on physical spaces. In such an equation, the individual functions both as potential environmental warrior/healer and as the source of the destruction. In the former case, characters might either aggressively pursue those entities that threaten ecological sustainability or simply follow a non-materialist path. In the latter formulation, authors chart individual complicity with irresponsible industries, as characters mindlessly consume products that they do not "need" and that have adverse ripple effects on the environment. In both scenarios, authors seek to rebut the notion that humans are "above" the environment, that their exceptionalism allows them to act with impunity. Rather, our relationship with the environment affects us in tangible physical and psychological ways. Those authors who are more causal in their allusions to the environment will generally focus on another source for their plotline; yet make significant references to the environment. An urban character, for example, might, in the course of pursuing a relationship, notice an ominous haze overhead or chance upon a conversation about global warming. Rarely, then, is the environment presented merely as a lush setting detached from its connection to humanity; instead, it is viewed as a reciprocal space that must be protected from human avarice.

Gender Roles. The social construction of gender is a frequently explored topic in contemporary fiction. Despite, or perhaps because of, living in a "post-feminist" world, the issue of gender-based power continues to attract novelists. Many allied topics are explored by both male and female writers, including the social construction of gender (Eugenides), class differences (Sandra Cisneros), environment (Kingsolver), race (Morrison), and age (Anne Tyler). The unvarnished criticisms of faceless patriarchal targets are far less likely to occur than in decades past. Male characters are generally more nuanced—even sympathetic to some degree—and the female protagonists are sometimes less sure of how to proceed, partly because they possess similar impulses. The battle, then, frequently is an internal one in which the protagonist must come to terms with herself before she can challenge the institutionalized sexism and gender prejudice (frequently within the family) that complicate her life. Feminism is thus personalized and functions on the micro-level. True change, many novelists imply, occurs with a groundswell of personal behavior rather than with an *a priori* ideology. Individual women—sometimes aware of theoretical feminism, sometimes not—can more effectively impact their local environment, and thus the world, via their commitment to a specific cause such as reproductive rights, globalization, or pornography. Through superior moral conviction, such characters can puncture seemingly airtight "logical" arguments and expose them as sophist rationalizations. The feminine in this view is seen as a particular way of thinking, one that places ethical considerations above callous self-interest.

Maximalism. A trend that started in the 1990s (and is best represented by Wallace's 1996 *Infinite Jest*), Maximalism employs multiple, interlaced narratives, an ironic tone, and a style characterized by hyperallusivity and the detritus of modern life. Frequently focused on young, materially successful characters, fiction using this style juxtaposes a crush of detail with an almost allegorical narrative in which individual characters are generally far less realized than the environments(s) in which they operate. The prose equivalent of hypertext, Maximalist novels generally operate with a frenziedly digressive principle, although interlaced plotlines occasionally merge at the novel's conclusion. Typically, employing urban settings, Maximalist fiction masquerades as a form of hyperrealism—no phenomenon of modern life is too big or small to be noticed and commented on at length—yet an element of postmodern fantasy pulses at its core. The world is recognizable, yet it often appears as though it is as distorted in a parallel dimension. Common events and objects warrant musings rendered in microscopic detail that is extraordinarily self-conscious. A kind of postmodern picaresque, invented, most argue, by Thomas Pynchon, Maximalist fiction scoffs at the minimalist restraint of Raymond Carver or Amy Hempel and revels in presenting mini-essays on every conceivable subject as it follows its legion of characters (perhaps more properly deemed caricatures) and plot twists. Such fiction frequently, but not always, refrains from explicit judgments about the culture it presents, a propensity that has prompted some commentators to label Maximalist fiction amoral. Nevertheless, the weight of its excesses rarely prevents Maximalist fiction from indeed presenting a critical picture of modern life—yet no viable solution seems forthcoming either.

Technology. While novelists of the 1980s and 1990s grappled with the presence of the personal computer and the Internet, twentieth-century writers represent an even wider array of technologies, from cell phones and PDAs to video games and iPods. As in science fiction and cyberpunk (see entries in this volume), in "mainstream" fiction writers often depict technology as a negative presence designed not to aid characters but to stunt them. Slaves to the machines, such characters are frequently at a loss as to how to negotiate life and detach themselves from their electronic leashes. The pace of life as directed by (generally cryptic) machines has exceeded the ability to process the various stimuli, resulting in a psychological numbness and loss of control. The smallness of the human experience contrast with the apparently limitless (although soulless) possibilities of progress, and characters often feel powerless and incomplete. Writers, such as Walter Kirn, will often barrage readers with a multiplicity of details that bury characters and their emotions under fragments of half-digested technologies. Further, they will even discourage an intimate bond between reader and character by using so many characters that they appear little more than interchangeable parts, far less important than their contemporary milieu. The technological screen dominates, and humanity struggles to compete, as more and more "necessities" flood the market daily and encroach on both self-contemplation and interpersonal relationships. At the same time, the characters will frequently be reluctant to function without their technological crutches and often need a life-altering journey to a less technology-oriented environment, be it rural America or a third-world nation. Any salvation will be a personal one, played in a minor key, for the corporate powers behind the "desire" for more and more technology and speed appear faceless and inevitable.

Terrorism. While terrorism was a staple in genre fiction prior to 9/11, the terrorist attacks in New York, Pennsylvania, and Washington, D.C., brought the topic a new urgency. The loss of control so evident in much contemporary fiction dovetails effectively with the fear and paranoia sparked by the 9/11 attacks and the wider "War on Terror" that indelibly marked the early twenty-first century. As with most themes, terrorism draws a number of fictive responses, ranging from confusion to indignation, and the topic itself serves both as a principal theme and a backdrop (sometimes merely *there,* sometimes functioning as a life-altering moment). While some novelists attempt to explore the conditions that breed terrorism, most American novelists, perhaps recognizing the limits of their understanding or the dearth of published insight into the terrorist psyche, focus on the effects of the terror, both the tangible destruction and death and the emotional and cultural shock left in its wake. Several authors have contrasted the "end of history" complacency endemic to the 1990s with the horrified astonishment that followed 9/11, while other writers explore America's narcissistic materialism and its relation to global poverty as apparently inexplicable ideology clashes with scenes of western excess. Dragging their self-absorbed characters into a dialogue with history, such authors reveal that America has a long way to go. Undoubtedly, the best 9/11 novel will be written many years hence. Writers who have recently dealt directly or indirectly with terrorism include Jonathan Safran Foer, John Updike, Claire Messud, Jay McInerney, William Gibson, and Tom Robbins. See the **Terrorism Fiction** entry for further information.

Violence. Coupled with the emergence of terrorism as a mainstream theme was the heightened presence of extreme violence in unlikely fictional spaces. Idyllic suburbs, cozy rural towns, nondescript tourist spots—these become the scenes for unimagined and life-altering brutality. Such violence decenters the reader, just as media depictions of spree killers, child abductions, and rapes disorient those who think themselves far removed from the tumult of the third world or the inner city. Violence renders quotidian concerns meaningless, and it places the survivors in precarious psychological states. Some novelists, such as Cormac McCarthy, explore violence's potential to shape masculine identity, while others, such as Alice Sebold, investigate its ability to destroy the self. Violence also frequently functions as a metaphor of American life, with its emphasis on gross self-interest. Power relationships are often at the heart of fictional investigations of violence, among them gender, class, and race. Frequently, the violence occurs not at the hands of a random, fatal stranger but from a neighbor, a relative, or a friend. This subcurrent is perhaps even more difficult to understand than arbitrary violence, for it suggests that even within the confines of one's home, where one is presumably protected, physical safety is in peril. Alcohol and drug abuse swirl around this type of violence, as do family history and patriarchal institutions. Survival is a corollary theme, with some characters managing by countering violence with more violence and others groping their way toward wholeness (while also experiencing difference, loss, anger, and anguish).

Contexts and Issues

E-books. Facing enormous competition from social networking sites (e.g., Facebook and MySpace), video games, YouTube, and other technology-based entertainment, contemporary fiction writers must, like television producers, present their materials in a variety of easily accessible formats.

A number of dedicated e-readers have recently appeared on the market, bringing with them the possibility of an expanded market share, specifically the "millennial generation." By recasting print novels into downloadable "content," e-readers such as amazon.com's Kindle, Jinke's HanLin, and Sony's PRS-500 can store hundreds of titles in a device as small as a paperback. Some devices also include wifi, which allows readers to download new books on the fly. Vendors such as ebooks.com offer a wide variety of titles, including contemporary fiction. The new generation of e-readers corrects previous problems such as excessive power use, blurry screens, and eyestrain. It remains to be seen whether such devices (or the podcasts discussed below) will have an effect on content. One might speculate, however, that interactive features could easily be embedded, as could formerly cost-prohibitive visuals. Such features might, for example, enhance Maximalist fiction by offering further information on the narrative's plethora of details, or it might serve to reproduce documents pertaining to historical novels. Alternative endings, hyperlinked "cut-ups," and other non-linear strategies could certainly be manipulated by willing authors. Novelist Walter Kirn even envisions a novel with feedback that functions as "a sort of floating workshop around the as-yet-unfinished book" (Kirn 2006). One easily sees writers such as David Foster Wallace and Jeffrey Eugenides being attracted to such possibilities.

Film. Adaptations, certainly not a new trend, continue to abound in the twenty-first century. Always a risky proposition, adaptations of well-known novels frequently spark heated reactions, often framed in terms of "betrayal." Some recent adaptations of contemporary American novels include *The Bee Season, The Namesake,* and *No Country for Old Men.* Filmmakers have, surprisingly, largely left Maximalist fiction alone—although Franzen's *The Corrections* is in preproduction. With their general focus on surfaces, interlaced narratives, and the young, such novels would appear ready-made for adaptation. Far more than the complex, interior-driven novels that are often selected (for example, *The Human Stain*), novels such as *Drop City* and *Extremely Loud and Incredibly Close* would require less narrative innovation, as much of their verbal "clutter" could be captured silently. Frequently, the strongest adaptations are of lesser-known novels, where the spectator's feelings of "faithlessness" are not usually at issue. Graphic novels offer a natural bridge between text and screen, and it is hardly coincidental that as graphic novels enter the mainstream significant number of adaptations have appeared (For example, *V for Vendetta, Sin City,* and *The 300*). Reverse adaptations also continue a dominant trend, although typically these will be linked to genre fiction, such as science fiction and action books, than with mainstream fiction. See the **Film Adaptation** entry for further information.

The Oprah Effect. While her experiences with Jonathan Franzen and James Frey prompted her to focus much of her attention on "classic" fiction, Oprah Winfrey's impact on novel sales has been phenomenal. Started in 1996, "Oprah's Book Club" has selected fiction—most of it American—which Winfrey felt epitomized spiritual self-improvement. Accordingly, the books on the list range from Pearl S. Buck's *The Good Earth* to Cormac McCarthy's *The Road.* Selection for the club has netted hundreds of thousands of sales, but it has also developed a reading community, as Oprah posts reading guides and other materials on her site. Beyond the well-publicized boost from the lower echelons of sales to the top of the bestseller lists, economist Richard Butler determined that a selection by Oprah netted a long-term sales benefit, both in terms of time spent in the top 150 and in paperback sales,

BLOGS, PUBLISHING, AND MARKETING ON THE WEB

Despite increased competition from non-traditional media, especially the Internet; the public continues to buy print-based fiction. Recent data indicates that traditional publishers bring out more novels than ever before, a staggering 160,000 in 2005, although most sell in relatively paltry numbers (Turner 2006). In fact, some evidence suggests that the Internet may spur sales, especially of lesser-known quantities by allowing writers to network, post excerpts, blog, and the like. The Brautigan Library, founded in honor of Richard Brautigan and dedicated to "publishing" the works of those rejected by mainstream publishers, may be in storage (and no longer accepting submissions), but the Internet enables amateurs and professionals alike to share or sell their work with the public. Self-published fiction is by no means a new idea, but never before have self-published authors had the instantaneous ability to reach such a broad audience. Many "corporate" sites, such as amazon.com and books.google.com, allow readers to sample pages from books published on both large and small presses, and the former's review section offers wary buyers the comfort of sampling the experiences of people who have already read the books. These reviews often have much in common with the more "underground" phenomena of blogs and fanboy sites, such as those found on blogcritics.com, goodreads.com, or myspace.com. Enterprising authors may share their progress with similar-minded "friends" who can double as consumers in tailor-made niche markets. In this regard, music is far more advanced, as witnessed by the stunning success of Colbie Calliat. Further, a recent experiment by the band Radiohead, in which the group allowed consumers to purchase their music without a record company serving as middleman, will no doubt inspire "name" writers to follow suit. Stephen King and others have offered Internet-only content, and excising publishers from the loop seems a natural next move. Many enterprising amateur authors also offer podcasts of their work, although as of yet no fiction writer counterpart of Calliat has yet appeared. Several guidebooks have appeared, however, which suggest that it is only a matter of time before a traditional publisher lifts someone out of the ranks of the amateur and into the elite.

when compared with other bestselling books (Walch 2004). Although Franzen bristled about being included with authors he felt less serious than he, and Oprah took Frey to task for "lying" in his memoirs, publishers—and many authors—continue to covet Oprah's endorsement. Although some suggest that consumers spurred by Oprah buy, but do not finish, her selections, the Club's net effect on reading has been remarkable.

Reception. Predictably, reception of the contemporary novel ranges widely—even wildly—with praise and damnation attending individuals, authors, novels, and genres. Critics of contemporary American fiction include Anis Shavini, who laments the stranglehold of MFA programs on the publishing scene, a phenomenon that Shavini sees as limiting the thematic palette to a narrow range of "bland, uniform, and unappetizing" subjects far removed from "the ordinary fabric of life" (Shavini 2004, 681). Shavini observes that this trend results in self-indulgence and dime store therapy. Another critic of contemporary American fiction, James Wood, further avers that such self-indulgence leads to bloated, unwieldy novels that sacrifice aesthetics for hip irony, that merely offer "props of the imagination, meaning's toys" rather than the human source of vitality and meaning (Wood 2004, 169). Both observations hint that the innovations of the mid-1990s are beginning to calcify—as most experiments inevitably do. External forms, no matter how initially dynamic, eventually atrophy into clichés ripe for parody and counter-revolution. As in any era, rhetorical flash must be coupled with substance, and forms must be fluid enough to capture recognizable human emotion and behavior. Both Shavini and Wood represent those critics who feel that the contemporary American novel needs a thorough irrigation so that it may regain an emotional *authenticity* that they feel is lacking because of excessive attention to setting.

Other critics, however, deny such generalizations and argue that the future of American fiction "is in splendid shape" (Williamson, 2002, 674), in that while a certain degree of "assembly line" prose inevitably appears, numerous writers have "rebelled against their teachers" in order to pursue personal voices and themes (667). Jeffrey F.L. Partridge further adds that the spacious "broad highway" of American literature offers a helpful counter-narrative to the monolithic literature of the past (Partridge 2001, 459). Walter Kirn suggest that form, too, will continue to evolve as novelists grapple with emergent technologies such as instant messaging, social networking, and text messaging. Modes that he feels function paradoxically as they reveal rich communal connections yet simultaneously function in isolation: too much happens each day, it happens all at once, and yet, in some ways, nothing happens at all. "A day that's spent processing electronic signals like a sort of lonely arctic radar station (my day, your day, a lot of ours) is hard to dramatize" (Kirn 2006). He views novelists as up to the inherent challenges, and suggests that a balance between the type of reference-heavy background that troubles Wood and the humanity that Shivini seeks will materialize as the transition from older technologies to the newer portable technologies fades and the technologies themselves start to matter less than the stories they help to convey. These more sanguine critics recognize the pitfalls of being trapped within the surfaces of life, yet they also observe that every generation of writers has its growing pains. Indeed, one might, with Raymond Williams, note that contemporary literature always contains residual, dominant, and emergent forms (Williams 1977, 122). Thus, forms and themes that share more in common with the nineteenth-century novel (residual) mingle with mainstream concepts (dominant) and experiments that may or may not become dominant (emergent). Optimists such as Kirn feel that the more turgid, emotionless trends in fiction will die off as novelists adapt and seek the forms that best capture the individual and communal themes that still compel their readership.

Selected Authors. In a field as crowded as the contemporary mainstream novel, an enormous amount of subjectivity comes into play when choosing which authors to discuss. In the following section, the focus is on those writers deemed "significant" by critical consensus, as determined by reviews, critical articles, and the like. In addition, some lesser-known writers have been included as examples of specific trends. One may find information about other writers considered "mainstream" in other entries in this volume, including **African American Literature, Coming of Age Fiction, Historical Fiction, Magical Realism, Native American Literature, Regional Fiction, Urban Fiction,** and many other categories.

Julia Alvarez: Alvarez released two novels, including *In the Name of Salome* and *Saving the World. In the Name of Salome* follows Camilla as she tries to recapture the essence of her mother, a famous poet who died when her daughter was three. The novel examines the themes of exile, poetry, female relationships, political activism, and Latin American history, but it avoids the fantastic elements of magical realism. Alvarez employs a dual narrative structure, with the mother's history told in chronological order and the daughter's in reverse chronological order, a strategy that results in highlighting the connectedness between the two. Her novel *Saving the World* juxtaposes the stories of two women separated by time yet connected in spirit and idealism. Drawing on historical analogues—as is typical with Alvarez—the book parallels a real quest to eradicate small pox with a modern effort to eliminate AIDS. Class and gender issues are foregrounded, and the book employs a style that alternates between the present and the past.

Russell Banks: Banks explores the recent past in his novel *The Darling,* a book set in Liberia, Ghana, and the United States and focused on the intersections of (privileged) idealism and race. Hannah, the novel's white American protagonist, fully invests herself into improving conditions in Liberia, yet when the country descends into brutal violence, she departs (ironically attempting to save some chimpanzees from slaughter—even as humans are dying en masse) and thus confirms her outsider status, just as when she earlier flees from her connection with the Weather Underground. Banks's prose is straightforward and earnest, sometimes to the point of being turgid. Martin Scorcese plans to film *The Darling.*

Saul Bellow: Bellow rounded out his prodigious, Nobel Prize-winning career with *Ravelstein* (2000), a pseudo-memoir of his experiences with Allan Bloom. Bellow's Ravelstein, a quasi-closeted homosexual, blends philosophical genius with conspicuous consumerism. Ravelstein and Chick (the Bellow character) hold riveting conversations on topics sublime and silly. Among its various themes, the ineffable quality of friendship, and the inability of language to convey it, is perhaps the most important. Bellow employs an episodic style that mimics a relaxed, digressive conversation, and his prose is direct and humorous.

T.C. Boyle: The energetic Boyle published four novels between 2000 and 2006: *A Friend of the Earth, Drop City, The Inner Circle,* and *Talk Talk.* In the first book, Boyle presents a distressing view of the future, wherein environmental activism has clearly failed to stop the will of materialist excess. Most species have vanished, the climate is in tumult, and *A Friend of the Earth* satirizes the self-absorption and self-righteousness of the environmental movement (circa the early 1990s) even as it underscores the accuracy of its jeremiads. Boyle alternates between the 1990s and his dystopian future, developing his theme in characteristic detail, yet never ignoring the human element. *Drop City* explores many of the same themes—particularly that of shallow idealism—although its focus is on a hippie commune, a place where smarmy platitudes mask a reality of selfish practice. Boyle comically contrasts this group hypocrisy with a truly self-reliant character, Sess, whose life at times is brutal. In *The Inner Circle,* Boyle's satiric target is Alfred Kinsey ("Prok"), the infamous sex researcher. Boyle weaves the fictional memoir of one of Kinsey's researchers in examining the subculture of the Kinsey Institute and its effects on human behavior. As in the previous works, this novel contrasts well-intended but naïve idealism with the more morally ambiguous reality (as, for example, when narrator John Milk must, for the cause, sleep with both Kinsey and his wife). Boyle's plot is fairly thin: however, and Milk's innocence at times strains credulity. Boyle takes on a more contemporary theme in *Talk Talk,* a book that examines the effect of identity theft on a deaf teacher. Dana and her boyfriend vow to track the thief, and issues of self-esteem, violence, and obsession pervade the narrative. Lacking Boyle's trademark satiric humor, the novel's thriller characteristics are somewhat undercut by Boyle's style, which at times piles on details that detract from the action.

Michael Chabon: Chabon, whose earlier novels had worked on a small but elegant scale, transformed his fiction mightily with the epic *The Amazing Adventures of Kavalier and Clay,* which won the Pulitzer Prize in 2001. In his earlier fiction, Chabon earned a well-deserved reputation for lyricism and social realism. Retaining these qualities, Chabon expanded his canvas to the past and added fantasy elements as well. Exploring the early years of the comic industry, Chabon covers a breathtaking number of themes, including Jewish identity, cultural assimilation, capitalism, fidelity, homosexuality, censorship, and escapism. Emotionally mature, the book runs the gamut from the petty to the sublime and adroitly contrasts the experiences of the two protagonists, Sammy Clay and Josef Kavalier as they develop their character, "The Escapist." While a large novel, *The Amazing Adventures of Kavalier and Clay* does not belong in the same Maximalist category as Wallace or Pynchon, as the human element always outweighs the conflict between surfaces and shadows that make up much of those writers' works. Chabon has been working on a screen adaptation of the novel. Along with Jonathan Franzen and other contemporary American writers, Chabon appeared on *The Simpsons* in 2006.

Don DeLillo: DeLillo proffered two works between 2000 and 2006, *The Body Artist* and *Cosmopolis.* The first book, a novella in sharp contrast to the Maximalist *Underworld,* examines a much smaller milieu than is typically DeLillo's wont. A fragment of a marriage is followed by a poignant study of loss, as Lauren Hartke comes to grips with the suicide of her husband and ultimately develops an act of performance art after "discovering" a strange man sleeping in her house. DeLillo allows both major actions to occur "off stage," informing the reader with new accounts that relate the information. DeLillo's style is claustrophobic and dark, concerned with the elasticity of time and mental survival. One senses that with another small novel, *Cosmopolis,* DeLillo is exploring new terrain; that he has exhausted the sweeping narratives that he presented in the 1990s. Here, DeLillo examines a single day in America before the tech bubble burst and before 9/11 altered the cultural and political landscape. Observing a myriad of cultural and historical details, DeLillo traces a billionaire as he makes his way, with postmodern self-consciousness—through New York before his apparent murder at the hands of a former, now homeless, employee. Spiritual emptiness, technological amorality, and cold ambition—these themes permeate the narrative. DeLillo here returns to his characteristic prose style, a hyperaware, sophisticated medley of lyricism and sub rosa tragedy.

E.L. Doctorow: Doctorow offered two novels, *City of God* (2000) and *The March* (2005) in addition to two collections of stories and a book of nonfiction. Using his trademark staccato style, *City of God* whirls through the fictional and real world of Everett, a novelist with a penchant for history and liquor. The book also contains a plot wherein an Episcopalian priest befriends two rabbis and ultimately converts. The characters ponder the nature of God and course through timeless and time-bound philosophical and historical debates. Doctorow interweaves high and low culture and decenters his readers through radical shifts in perspective and tone. In *The March,* Doctorow leaves the twentieth century for the nineteenth and recreates Sherman's march to the sea during the Civil War. Doctorow, however, sets his sights on the internal lives of his characters—both Union and Confederate, free and slave—rather than on well-known external events. In the process, Doctorow captures both the war milieu and the roots of many of the racial and political problems of the twentieth and twenty-first centuries. Doctorow ranges comfortably between high and low dialects, and maintains a brisk pace.

David Eggers: Eggers released two novels between 2000 and 2006, *You Shall Know Our Velocity* and *What Is the What: The Autobiography of Valentino Achak Deng*. *You Shall Know Our Velocity* follows a pair of men who travel across the globe in an effort to give away the remains of $80,000. The quest theme is in full force here, although the characters are only dimly aware of what they are seeking, and the journey itself proves rather mundane. Class issues—and American imperialism—form one of the book's thematic pillars, and the power and arbitrariness that attend the charity seem to make the characters even guiltier than the money itself. Eggers's prose is alternatively comic and plodding. He handles a much darker theme in *What Is the What,* a book that shares the life story of Valentino Achak Deng, who, after escaping the brutality of the Sudan, is ironically mugged in his Atlanta apartment. Based on a real incident (Deng is really the man's name), the novel blurs the line between reality and fiction. An interesting twist is Eggers's device of having Deng tell his story to a series of different listeners—none of whom care (even those who theoretically should) overly much about what he is saying, all of it horrific. A fictional memoir, Eggers avoids the pitfalls of Frey in that he may reconstruct conversations, invent narrative bridges, and the like with impunity yet remain emotionally faithful to Deng's tribulations.

Bret Easton Ellis: Ellis's *Lunar Park* (2005) merges a fictionalized memoir (using, à la Henry Miller, a character bearing the author's real name) with an exploration of post-9/11 terrorism and paranoia, as well as with a series of bizarre events (stalking, abduction, and hauntings). While Ellis draws heavily from his own past as a shock-author, he gives himself a fictional wife and son, and he completely fabricates the book's latter stages. In perhaps an attempt at a metaphorical exorcism (or self-absolution), the book contemplates the price of celebrity and self-indulgence for both the writer and world. Ellis the character seems trapped in the imagination of Ellis the writer—or is it the other way around? Ellis's prose is as cuttingly ironic as ever.

Louise Erdrich: A busy Erdrich penned four novels between 2000 and 2006: *The Last Report on the Miracles at Little No Horse* (2001), *The Master Butchers Singing Club* (2003), *Four Souls* (2004), and *The Painted Drum* (2005). *The Last Report* chronicles the life of a nun who passes as a priest after being banished from her convent. Set on an Ojibwe reservation, the novel investigates a diversity of topics, such as the power of faith, forbidden sexuality, deception, and sainthood. Narratologically complex, the novel combines a number of realistic and fantastic modes, and it merges both native and Catholic traditions. In *The Master Butchers Singing Club,* Erdrich depicts a German immigrant who settles in North Dakota following World War I. The title character's voice brings solace to the troubled souls of the idiosyncratic town, and acts as an anchor amidst the sprawling, violent plot. Erdrich's prose is both dense and lyrical. *Four Souls,* a much smaller novel, returns to characters familiar to readers of *Tracks,* most notably Fleur Pillager. Erdrich employs three narrators to tell of Fleur's vengeance on John James Mauser, who took her land. The clash of native and capitalist cultures is foregrounded here, and the futility of revenge is a central theme. Tragi-comedy is the dominant mode, particularly when Fleur heals Mauser so that her vengeance will be more honorable. *The Painted Drum* relates the story of an Ojibwe artifact "liberated" from a New England farm. Using a combination of realism and myth, Erdich deftly and powerfully develops three interrelated stories that explain the genesis of the drum and its impact on the lives of those who have encountered it. The power of living tradition is on full display in this novel, as the drum is transformed from an art object back into a vital spiritual force.

Jeffrey Eugenides: Eugenides won the Pulitzer Prize for his Maximalist opus *Middlesex* (2002), as novel that interweaves a contemporary tale of hermaphroditism with a historic one of Greek immigration. Raised as a girl, Calliope Stephanides undergoes sexual reassignment therapy, but bolts before surgery—and changes to a male identity, Cal. In the historical narrative, themes of incest, recreated identity, and assimilation appear, paralleling the experience of Cal/Calliope. Awash in contemporary and historical detail, the complex narrative offers both a *bildungsroman* and a family epic. Written in the vibrant, hyperaware prose style Eugenides developed in *The Virgin Suicides, Middlesex* is expansively lyrical and briskly paced.

Richard Ford: Ford supplemented two story collections with one novel, *The Lay of the Land* (2006). *The Lay of the Land* returns to Ford's most famous character, Frank Bascombe, as he contemplates life in post-election 2000. The presumed dead husband of Frank's second wife has reappeared, sparking a separation, and Frank's first wife, now a widow, intimates that she wants to reunite. Adding to Frank's troubles is prostate cancer, for which he is undergoing treatments, and the emotional turbulence caused by two sons, one living and one dead. Frank's Thanksgiving weekend is one of contemplation and, finally, violence. Like Updike in his *Rabbit* series, to which the Bascombe books are often compared, Ford combines his protagonist's self-examination with a survey of the contemporary scene, and his oft-comic prose is packed with detail.

Jonathan Franzen: Franzen's Maximalist novel *The Corrections* (2001) examines the impact of materialist excess in the wake of the Clinton 1990s. Pondering themes such as globalism (and the impact of an insatiable United States on the world scene), disposable culture, image-driven mores, and corporate ravenousness, the novel also traces the very modern problems of the Lambert family, whose members suffer from a variety of physical and mental dysfunction. Franzen reveals how capitalism has infiltrated every aspect of American life, suggesting that many of the problems faced by the Lamberts are both directly and indirectly a result of an environment dedicated to shallow materialism, a place where "corrections" are superficial and practically designed to miss the mark. With a sharp, singular prose style, Franzen moves from overwrought earnestness to lampoon with ease. Franzen famously disparaged his inclusion in Oprah's Book Club, a move lamented by his publishers and that prompted Winfrey to concentrate more on "classic" books. A film version of the National Book Award-winning novel is planned, although pre-production has been plagued with problems.

Mary Gaitskill: Gaitskill's *Veronica* (2005), which garnered a nomination for the National Book Award, offers a dark, yet at times poignant, examination of protagonist Alison's rise as a model and long, sordid decline into a sick, middle-aged maid. The eponymous character serves less as a focal point than as a means of redemption for Alison, who recalls Veronica's battles with AIDS and uses memories of her relationship to gain strength in her own struggle with hepatitis. Gaitskill employs the sometimes disorienting strategy of moving from Alison's memories of the past to her "real-time" present, often without many narrative cues. Such a method, however, reinforces the impact of the past on Alison's present situation. Gaitskill also uses a discordant lyricism in describing deeply disturbing sexual violence and other sordid materials, which highlight both Alison's strange attraction to the seamy glamour and morally repugnant people of the modeling world and her precarious position there. Intriguingly, as she recalls the past, Alison moves from the concrete hostility of the present to the lush environs of nature, where, in a subtly ecofeminist moment, she experiences something like redemption.

Gail Godwin: Godwin brought out two novels, *Evenings at Five* (2003) and *Queen of the Underworld* (2006), books that show her range. In the first small "novel," Godwin recreates her own life with composer Robert Starer, who died in 2001. A testament to a loving relationship, the book examines the transformation from pleasant everyday life to tragic illness, death, and the mourning process. Godwin, while painting a touching portrait, does not engage in hagiography, and she shows Rudy's grating side as well as his sweet one. In *The Queen of the Underworld*, Godwin is far removed from such an intimate setting, locating this narrative in the Cuban-Miami milieu of 1959. The book follows a young journalist as she absorbs a new culture and learns her trade. Full of eccentric grotesques, such as Madam Ginevra Brown, the novel is written in quirky, richly detailed prose.

Rolando Hinojosa: Hinojosa released a single novel, *We Happy Few* (2006), during this entry's chronological parameters. *We Happy Few* represents Hinojosa's attempt at an academic novel, a setting seemingly far removed from the "Klail City" environs of his earlier efforts—yet some of his recurrent characters do appear in the novel. "Belken State" is in turmoil as its ailing president must be replaced, a process that finds Hinojosa shifting perspectives feverishly as he accounts for the various factions and interests in the petty world of academe. Added to the mix is the murder of a regent's transvestite nephew. Hinojosa continues his adaptation of the traditional *estampa* form, and the book's quick shifts perfectly echo its multicultural subject matter.

John Irving: Irving added two titles to his impressive list of novels, *The Fourth Hand* (2001) and *Until I Find You* (2005). *The Fourth Hand* further reveals Irving's mastery of bizarre, off-kilter humor, as it relates the tale of a stunningly handsome reporter who, after losing his hand to a lion while taping a story, receives a hand transplant from a man whose widow wants "visiting rights." Wallingford, the reporter, sleeps with the widow and fathers her child. Wallingford, a rake with dubious morals, attempts to transform his life, with uneven results. Unlike many of Irving's novels, this one is fairly confined to a limited cast, and the prose, while at times charming, is perhaps too earnest for the subject matter. *Until I Find You* relates the life of Jack Burns, an actor who has survived an unconventional education in an all-girls' school, where he served as a sexual toy for the older students. The sexual abuse is presented matter-of-factly, and an older Jack eventually "misses" some of his abusers. Literally and figuratively questing for his missing father, Jack eventually finds him—predictably a far different man than that of Jack's boyish romanticizations. The novel contains a host of eccentric characters, although the plot is largely secondary. The prose is abundantly detailed, perhaps repetitively so with respect to Jack's sexual experiences.

Gish Jen: Jen penned a single novel, *The Love Wife* (2004), during the 2000–2006 period. Jen leaves behind the Changs of her first two novels and portrays a complex American family, the Wongs, who consist of a second-generation Chinese father, a Caucasian mother, two adopted Asian daughters, and a biological son who physically favors his mother. Added to the mix is Lan, Carnegie's relative from China, who exploits existing tensions between Janie (pejoratively labeled Blondie by her mother-in-law) and her daughters. Issues of assimilation, teen angst, racial insecurity, and family pervade this humorous, but ultimately not comic, novel.

Relying heavily on dialogue, Jen shifts perspectives frequently, a phenomenon that grants her characters substantial depth.

Barbara Kingsolver: Kingsolver, recently focused more on nonfiction, released *Prodigal Summer* in 2000. An ecofeminist novel set in Appalachia; *Prodigal Summer* develops a trio of narrative threads all connected by their characters love for the earth in spite of skepticism from their neighbors. Kingsolver emphasizes the variety and balance required for healthy ecosystems—human relationships included. Presenting an array of scientific information along with her plot, Kingsolver pointedly contrasts her three female characters' concern for the environment with the ridicule of a community that seems ignorant of the ecological and economic havoc wreaked by unthinking environmental exploitation. She avoids unvarnished didacticism, however, and her characters are human rather than ideological cut-outs. The natural environment is, however, oddly pastoral at times, a realm lacking the brutal quality of nature. Kingsolver's prose is lush, sometimes breathlessly so.

Jhumpa Lahiri: Lahiri followed up her Pulitzer Prize-winning story collection with a novel, *The Namesake* (2003). The book depicts the Gangulis, a Bengali family whose immigrant parents inevitably clash with the American values of their children. Identity, especially that of Gogol, the Gangulis's son, forms the novel's thematic core, and Lahiri deftly portrays the marginalized world of the children of immigrants: not of the old world, yet not quite confident or accepted in their own. Lahiri's prose is vibrant and detailed. A film of *The Namesake* appeared in 2007.

Bobbie Ann Mason: In addition to two story collections, Mason produced one novel, *An Atomic Romance* (2005). Sixty years after Hiroshima, Mason's novel explores the familiar terrain of nuclear danger through the eyes of Reed Futrell, a nuclear plant worker who has been unsettled by his girlfriend's insistence that he undergo tests to determine whether his job is harming him. The relationship forms the book's core, although environmental and genetic risks filter through the narrative, with Reed trying to get Julia to reconnect and Julia leaving for a trip to Chicago. Julia, politically engaged and skeptical, contrasts well with the trusting, unconcerned Reed, and the pair form a microcosm of American attitudes toward nuclear power. Mason's prose is digressive, yet it is suited to the characters, particularly Reed.

Cormac McCarthy: McCarthy released two novels, *No Country for Old Men* (2005), and the Pulitzer Prize-winning *The Road* (2006). Using a spare style that deviates from much of his previous fiction, *No Country for Old Men* takes place in the same border environs of his famous trilogy. An extremely violent book, McCarthy's Anton Chigurh is a psychopath of the first rank, a ruthless killer who spouts philosophy. Llewelyn Moss, a welder, stumbles across a blown drug deal and absconds several million dollars. He is pursued by Chigurh and protected by Sheriff Tom Bell. McCarthy employs a dual narrative style, interlacing a third-person perspective with Bell's musings, and his somber prose serves the epic battle of good versus evil well. *No Country for Old Men* appeared as a film in 2007. In *The Road*, McCarthy further explores the impact of violence, but on a much wider scale: postapocalyptic desolation. A father and son (born shortly before the unnamed catastrophe that has wiped out most of the population) attempt to maintain a moral code as they scavenge for food and try to avoid the less ethically scrupulous survivors who resort to cannibalism. The father is dying, however, and wonders whether he should kill his young son, whose moral compass is a very real drawback in an anarchic world. As with his previous novel, *The Road* adopts a stately, economical prose style that is rich with stark figurative language.

Toni Morrison: Morrison added to her Nobel Prize-winning résumé with one novel, *Love* (2003). In the short yet dense *Love,* Morrison explores not only the title emotion but an array of others as well, including Love's opposite, Hate. Ranging decades before and after the death of the late Bill Cosey, an African American entrepreneur, Morrison investigates the relationships that surrounded him. As is typical with her late fiction, Morrison challenges her readers both thematically and linguistically, and *Love* tackles the American dream, institutionalized racism, the unpredictability of human emotions, and gender roles, among others topics, in an intricate, metaphor-rich prose style. As with *Beloved, Love* contains an intriguing spectral character, in this case the dynamic L., a cook whose commentary cuts through the book's layers of deception and obfuscation.

Joyce Carol Oates: Oates, ultra-prolific and talented as ever, produced *eleven* novels (four under various pen names), three novellas, and four short story collections (not to mention her work in drama and nonfiction!) in the first seven years of the twenty-first century. Of these, the most significant are *Blonde* (2000; short-listed for the National Book Award and Pulitzer Prize) and *The Falls* (2004; Prix Femina Etranger winner). *Blonde* is an epic novel that explores the life of Marilyn Monroe. Oates's meticulous research depicts the familiar outline of the actress's life (and Oates comments that despite the novel's heft she constrains herself to viewing only representative incidents from Monroe's experience), but the book's true strength is in its imagined recreation of Monroe's interior life, replete with dreams, vulnerabilities, and myths. Oates also appropriates and alludes to numerous fairy tales, which juxtapose poignantly with the real-life tragedy. Written in a full, realistic prose style, *Blonde* attempts to portray the psyche behind the label. *The Falls* follows protagonist Ariah as she witnesses her husband fling himself over Niagara Falls on their honeymoon and then attempts to rebuild her life—including a marriage to a lawyer who becomes entangled in the Love Canal case and ultimately alienated from his family before his suspicious demise. Oates then jumps ahead sixteen years to depict the couple's children as they unravel their parents' history. Obsession, secrets, greed, environmental devastation, and redemption lie at the novel's core, and Oates masterfully employs an intense prose style that never loses focus.

Tim O'Brien: O'Brien's *July* interlaces a depiction of a thirty-first reunion with flashbacks cataloguing the impact of the Vietnam War on the participants. Physical and emotional scars abound, and O'Brien's use of nonlinear form allows him to blur the line between past and present. Indeed, for most of the characters, the past is not past at all, but rather is a constant presence. Both pro- and anti-war classmates are tracked by O'Brien's prose, and he underscores that the wounds of the intergenerational conflict have not healed. The lives behind the ideologies, however, have decayed markedly, via cancer, drug use, divorce, and other life crises. O'Brien employs gallows humor, but the ethical core of the novel prevents it from descending into bitterness. Another O'Brien trait, magical realism, is present in several fantasy scenes.

Cynthia Ozick: Ozick produced one novel, *Heir to the Glimmering World* (2004) in addition to her *Collected Stories* (2006). *Heir to the Glimmering World* unfolds the story of the Mitwissers, a Jewish family fleeing from the ever-encroaching anti-Semitism of Hitler's pre-war Germany. In New York City, Mitwisser, an intellectually circumscribed academic sponsored by an eccentric millionaire, hires the orphaned

Rose Meadows as his assistant/nanny. Rose becomes fascinated with the esoteric world of research, and Ozick creates a plausible environment. Thematically, the book deals with an obscure Jewish sect, class conflict, faith, and identity. Ozick's prose is economical yet descriptive, although her characterization falters with some of the lesser characters.

Annie Proulx: Proulx, in addition to two story collections, released one novel, *That Old Ace in the Hole* (2002). In the book, Proulx catalogues a series of bizarrely named characters, but she chiefly follows Bob Dollar, an agent for the "Global Pork Rind Corporation" who is surveying potential locations for new hog farms. Proulx's characters, especially Ace Crouch, generally oppose the farms and long for the ecological purity of the past—and they extol the past nearly to the point of driving Dollar to despair. More eco-comic than Kingsolver, Proulx nonetheless tackles the very real problem of introducing alien species into an ecosystem, not to mention the faceless greed of corporate agribusiness. Proulx's prose is comically unique, occasionally to the point of absurdity with respect to similes, and it employs a picaresque format, with individual stories taking the narrative in numerous directions (her use of idiosyncratic names further connects the book to the picaresque tradition).

Thomas Pynchon: After a nine-year silence, Pynchon offered the epic *Against the Day* in 2006, a prime example of Hutcheon's historiographic metafiction. Set during the progressive era, the novel offers both the extraordinary attention to detail and the Gnosticism that Pynchon is famous for. Deceptive in its surfaces—drawn from sources such as boy's adventure novels, westerns, spy novels, and detective fiction—the book weaves a tangle of themes that will dominate the twentieth century, from labor disputes and technology-driven warfare to esoteric scientific debates and religious chicanery. As with all of Pynchon's Maximalist novels—he did, of course, invent the genre—characterization is at a minimum, with the dozens of "major" characters and hundreds of minor ones cumulatively representing History rather than individual psychologies. Real historical events, such as the Ludlow Massacre, merge with cryptic fictional plots that suggest how the optimism of the fin de siècle era transformed into jaded pessimism where every utopian vision masks totalitarian longings. Comic irony abounds, yet it is a dark humor born of tragic possibility. Stylistically, the novel takes its cue from a variety of genres (such as those mentioned above), but it interlaces its narratives so that no single style dominates. Rather, the book presents a bricolage wherein individual moments are the equivalent of geologic layers, and readers must, with Joseph Frank, read spatially.

Philip Roth: Roth maintained his steady pace with four novels, *The Human Stain* (2000), *The Dying Animal* (2001), *The Plot against America* (2004), and *Everyman* (2006), of which the first and third are the strongest. In *The Human Stain*, Roth continues the story of Nathan Zuckerman, although he is more of a narrator here than a protagonist per se. As in Bellow's *Ravelstein*, Zuckerman must write an apologia that he has been putting off—in this case a defense of his a friend who retired after being accused of making racially insensitive remarks. The twist, however, is that Coleman Silk has only been "passing" as a Jew and is, in fact, of African ancestry. Roth uses this intriguing scenario to expose academic and political hypocrisy, as well as to explore the social construction of race, and he does so with a richly brocaded prose style. An adaptation of the novel appeared in 2003. *The Plot against America* portrays an America in which aviator (and Iron Cross-winning anti-Semite) Charles Lindbergh defeated FDR in the presidential election of 1940. A staunch isolationist,

Lindbergh not only out-Chamberlains Chamberlain, but also endorses voluntary work camps for American Jews as part of the Office of American Absorption. As with some of his other texts, Roth uses his own family as characters, and he draws heavily on his childhood experiences in depicting America's not-so-latent anti-Semitism during the Depression and World War II. Roth's style—realistic, nuanced, and idiomatic—clashes at times with the awkward dubiousness of some of his alternative history, especially towards the latter parts of the narrative.

Richard Russo: Russo recently published both a collection of stories and a Pulitzer Prize-winning novel, *Empire Falls* (2001). Set in a fading mill town, *Empire Falls* tracks Miles Roby, manager of the Empire Grill, as he contemplates his wasted potential and lackluster life. Nevertheless, Russo utilizes the humorous insights that have marked his earlier works to steer the book clear of self-pity or melodrama. The book drifts back in time, tracing not only Roby's life, but also that of his family and that of his employer, the Whitings. A 2005 HBO adaptation won a Golden Globe for best miniseries.

Alice Sebold: Sebold followed up her debut memoir with *The Lovely Bones* (2002), a novel that depicts a rape/murder victim watching her family and friends from beyond the grave. Susie Salmon's survivors respond to the horror in a variety of ways, some self-destructive, some inspirational, and Susie, ensconced in a tailor-made heaven, uses each response to bolster her own understanding—and hope. In using a supernatural narrator, Sebold merges omniscience with intimacy without appearing gimmicky, and the novel's prose is subtly detailed. *The Lovely Bones* is scheduled to appear as a film in 2009.

Jane Smiley: Between 2000 and 2006, Smiley produced two novels, *Horse Heaven* (2000) and *Good Faith* (2003). In previous novels, such as *1000 Acres* and *Moo,* Smiley revealed a tendency to invest everyday actions with, respectively, tragic and comic importance. In *Horse Heaven,* she experiments with anthropomorphism in examining the simultaneously rarified and mundane world of horseracing. Approaching magical realism far more than any of her previous books, the novel parallels the jaded lives of its human protagonists with the magical lives of its horses, creatures that Smiley portrays as having rich mental lives. Several characters, most significantly Rosalind Maybrick, undergo redemptive transformations, and some significant class contrasts are apparent (particularly between the owner-class and those who serve them and the horses). Stylistically, the novel interlaces a variety of settings and perspectives, and the tone is generally comic. The second novel, *Good Faith,* offers a far less appealing cast of characters, and it setting is far seamier, despite its physical charms. Examining the dubious ethics behind the real estate boom (and accompanying Savings and Loan scandal) of the early 1980s, Smiley's novel offers both the detail that its author is known for and an ironic critique of oily hypocrisy. The American dream's underbelly is clearly present here, but Smiley allows the small-town charm of her characters to present such ambition (and its concomitant petty Machiavellianism) to distract the readers from fully hating them. Smiley adds her characteristic didacticism (explaining financial intricacies not with the irony of a Wallace or Boyle, but with earnestness) to a first-person perspective and a compelling style.

Amy Tan: Tan contributed two novels, *The Bonesetter's Daughter* (2001) and *Saving Fish from Drowning* (2005), between 2000 and 2006. In *The Bonesetter's Daughter,* Tan juxtaposes the story of Ruth Young and that of her mother, LuLing. Obviously, Tan's main focus is on mother-daughter relationships, but she also examines assimilation, secrecy, and Alzheimer's. LuLing's story also differentiates between bonesetters (healers) and bonesellers (charlatans), and it shows a China very much transitional in its attitudes toward women. Tan employs first-person narration for LuLing and third-person narration for Ruth, a strategy that contrasts the dramatic (LuLing) with the mundane (Ruth). Tan's style, sensitive to the nuances of language, is detailed and warm.

Anne Tyler: Tyler added three novels to her oeuvre, *Back When We Were Grownups* (2001), *The Amateur Marriage* (2004), and *Digging to America* (2006). The first, which in 2004 was adapted into a television movie, represents Rebecca Davitch, a 53-year-old widow who decides to recapture her potential self. Written in Tyler's typically plain prose, the book shows a mid-life crisis in full flower, but it focuses on family dynamics as few authors are able. *The Amateur Marriage* investigates the birth and death of a thirty-year marriage, in the process exploring how divorce can both liberate and paralyze. Tyler selects episodes from the marriage to demonstrate the whole, and her powers of observation are on display. In *Digging to America,* Tyler compares two couples, one white-bread, one Iranian American, who adopt Korean daughters and meet annually for an "arrival party." Thus, the question of multicultural American identity rises to the fore, and Tyler also examines how 9/11 alters perceptions of Muslim Americans. Weaving humorous anecdotes with serious insights, Tyler extends her range in this narrative.

John Updike: The ever-prolific Updike produced four novels (*Gertrude and Claudius, Seek My Face, Villages,* and *Terrorist*) as well as a short story collection (*Licks of Love*) that contains *Rabbit Remembered,* a novella. In *Gertrude and Claudius,* a short (for Updike) novel, Updike refashions Shakespeare's *Hamlet,* presenting Gertrude's relationship with Claudius in a much more positive light. As in his earlier retelling of *The Scarlet Letter,* Updike reads against the grain of his source text, in this instance portraying Hamlet as a shallow narcissist. Replete with historical details, the novel portrays a sympathetic Gertrude whose husband is unaffectionate and scheming. In all, he presents a feminist revision common of the classic play. Updike's next novel, *Seek My Face* presents an interview between an older female artist and a budding journalist. Updike employs flashbacks as Hope, the artist, recalls her Pollock-like first husband and Warhol-like second husband. Gradually, Hope and Kathryn, the journalist, bond, and Hope muses over the gender dynamics of the art scene, a milieu well captured by Updike, who writes quite frequently on art. In *Villages,* Updike returns to the theme that made him famous, New England ennui and its attendant sexual trysts. Framed by three villages inhabited by main character Owen Mackenzie, *Villages* traces a sexual history from virginal petting through connubial boredom and countless affairs—and back again to monogamy as AIDS appears on the horizon. Updike's hyperrealism is on display, particularly in his sexual scenes, though these seldom reach the ecstatic heights of *Couples. Terrorist* is Updike's response to 9/11, and it follows the radicalization of a young American Muslim, who, scorning his mother's religious indifference, romanticizes the Egyptian father who abandoned him when he was a toddler. Ahmad is ultimately recruited to drive a bomb into the Lincoln Tunnel, but after prematurely ejaculating (with his pants on) because of the efforts of a prostitute who coincidentally happens to be a classmate whom he was secretly attracted to, it is unclear whether he will go through with it. Updike, however, portrays Ahmad's diction and mannerisms in a stilted fashion that is hardly explained by his diligent study of the Koran. The centerpiece of *Licks of Love,* the novella *Rabbit Remembered,* depicts how Rabbit Angstrom's family recalls the dead patriarch. Annabelle Byer, Rabbit's illegitimate daughter, appears suddenly at Thanksgiving, with predictably fiery results, and the gathering demonstrates that life goes on without Harry—yet is unquestionably influenced by him. Rabbit's wife, Janice, has married Harry's nemesis Ronnie, who rails with gusto against Bill Clinton, and Nelson has transformed his life dramatically—so much so that he accepts Annabelle without hesitation. Stylistically, the book dovetails with the *Rabbit* tetralogy, and the book is larded with cultural references and social details.

Alice Walker: Walker published *The Way Forward Is with a Broken Heart* (2001), a collection of fictionalized memoirs, and *Now Is the Time to Open Your Heart* (2005), a novel, in addition to her forays in poetry and nonfiction. In the first book, Walker gathers a series of stories—some of which parallel significant events in her life, while others are primarily fictional—that examine her archetypal subjects: race, sexuality, and love. Walker frequently employs humor, even when the subject might suggest a more somber note, and she offers love as a redemptive act. In *Now Is the Time to Open Your Heart*, Walker follows a burned-out writer, Kate, known for her spirituality as she attempts to regain her passion and spiritual center. Haunted by a dream of a dry river, she lights out for the Colorado and Amazon Rivers in search of insight. At the same time, her lover, Yolo, undertakes his own quest. With some help from a local herb/drug, Kate regains her thirst for life. Walker's prose varies from sharp mimesis to cloudy mysticism.

David Foster Wallace: Wallace released *Oblivion,* his third collection of short stories, in 2004. While readers wait for a follow-up to his Maximalist opus *Infinite Jest,* Wallace's stories offer a prelude of what is to come. Breezily ironic and focused on both modern shallowness and contemporary anxiety, stories such as "Mr. Squishy" and "Good Old Neon" eschew rigid plots in favor of alinear prose wherein large blocks of text bombard readers with details. Wallace probes such themes as the soulless cynicism of focus groups, the spiritual emptiness of material success, and the mindless cult of youth. One of Wallace's primary strengths is his ability to echo other voices preternaturally, and this collection delivers, whether in the form of a now-grown sufferer of ADD/ADHD, a self-doubting yuppie, or a

---

NATIONAL BOOK AWARDS

The National Book Awards are perhaps the most prestigious American book awards, currently awarding prizes in four categories: fiction, nonfiction, poetry, and young people's literature. Here are the most recent fiction winners.

2007	*Tree of Smoke* by Denis Johnson. Farrar, Straus & Giroux.
2006	*The Echo Maker* by Richard Powers. Farrar, Straus & Giroux.
2005	*Europe Central* by William T. Vollmann. Viking.
2004	*The News from Paraguay* by Lily Tuck. HarperCollins.
2003	*The Great Fire* by Shirley Hazzard. Farrar, Straus & Giroux.
2002	*Three Junes* by Julia Glass. Pantheon.
2001	*The Corrections* by Jonathan Franzen. Farrar, Straus & Giroux
2000	*In America* by Susan Sontag. Farrar, Straus & Giroux

Source: National Book Foundation Web site. http://www.nationalbook.org/.

fading journalist. Unlike Pynchon or Smith, Wallace is content to focus on a smaller circle of characters, yet he obsesses on minutia that portend larger cultural significance, as though by highlighting their very triviality he creeps closer to American Essence.

Bibliography

Alvarez, Julia. *In the Name of Salome*. Chapel Hill, NC: Algonquin Books, 2000.

———. *Saving the World*. Chapel Hill, NC: Algonquin Books, 2006.

Banks, Russell. *The Darling*. New York: HarperCollins, 2004.

Barth, John. *The Friday Book*. New York: Perigee, 1984.

Bellow, Saul. *Ravelstein*. New York: Viking, 2000.

Boyle, T.C. *Drop City*. New York: Viking, 2003.

———. *A Friend of the Earth*. New York: Viking, 2000.

———. *The Inner Circle*. New York: Viking, 2004.

———. *Talk Talk*. New York: Viking, 2006.

Chabon, Michael. *The Amazing Adventures of Kavalier and Clay*. New York: Random House, 2000.

DeLillo, Don. *Cosmopolis*. New York: Scribner, 2003.

Doctorow, E.L. *City of God*. New York: Random House, 2000.

———. *The March*. New York: Random House, 2005.

Eggers, Dave. *What is the What*. San Francisco: McSweeney's, 2006.

———. *You Shall Know Our Velocity*. San Francisco: McSweeney's, 2002.

Ellis, Bret Easton. *Lunar Park*. New York: Knopf, 2005.

Erdrich, Louise. *The Last Report on the Miracles of No Horse*. New York: HarperCollins, 2004.

———. *The Master Butchers Singing Club*. New York: HarperCollins, 2003.

———. *The Painted Drum*. New York: HarperCollins, 2005.

Eugenides, Jeffery. *Middlesex*. New York: Farrar, Straus, and Giroux, 2002.

Ford, Richard. *The Lay of the Land*. New York: Alfred A. Knopf, 2006.

Franzen, Jonathan. *The Corrections*. New York: Farrar, Straus, and Giroux, 2001.

Hume, Kathryn. *Fantasy and Mimesis: Responses to Reality in Western Literature*. New York: Methuen, 1984.

Federman, Raymond, ed. *Surfiction: Fiction Today and Tomorrow*. 2nd ed. Chicago: Swallow, 1981.

Gaitskill, Mary. *Veronica*. New York: Pantheon, 2005.

Godwin, Gail. *The Queen of the Underworld*. New York: Random House, 2006.

Hennessey, Rosemary. *Materialist Feminism and the Politics of Discourse*. New York: Routledge, 1993.

Hinojosa, Rolando. *We Happy Few*. Houston, TX: Arte Publico Press, 2006.

Hutcheon, Linda. *The Poetics of Postmodernism: History, Theory, Fiction*. New York: Routledge, 1988.

Irving, John. *Until I Find You*. New York: Random House, 2005.

Jen, Gish. *The Love Wife*. New York: Knopf, 2004.

Kingsolver, Barbara. *Prodigal Summer*. New York: HarperCollins, 2000.

Kirn, Walter, and Gary Shteyngart. "The Novel 2.0." *Slate*. 10 Oct. 2006. http://www.slate.com/id/2151004/entry/2151016/.

Lahiri, Jhumpa. *The Namesake*. Boston: Houghton Mifflin, 2003.

Mason, Betty Ann. *An Atomic Romance*. New York: Random House, 2005.

McCarthy, Cormac. *No Country for Old Men*. New York: Knopf, 2005.

———. *The Road*. New York: Alfred A. Knopf, 2006.

Mellard, James M. *The Exploded Form: The Modernist Novel in America*. Urbana: University of Illinois Press, 1980.

Morrison, Jago. *Contemporary Fiction*. New York: Taylor and Francis, 2003.

Morrison, Toni. *Love*. New York: Knopf, 2003.

Oates, Joyce Carol. *Blonde*. New York: Ecco, 2000.

———. *The Falls*. New York: Ecco, 2004.

O' Brien, Tim. *July, July*. Boston: Houghton Mifflin, 2002.

Olney, James. *Memory and Narrative: The Weave of Life-Writing*. Chicago: University of Chicago Press, 1998.

Ozick, Cynthia. *Heir to the Glimmering World*. Boston: Houghton Mifflin, 2004.

Partridge, Jeffery F. L. "'Extreme Specialization' and the Broad Highway: Approaching Contemporary American Fiction." *Studies in the Novel* 33 (2001): 459–472.

Proulx, Annie. *That Old Ace in the Hole*. New York: Scribner, 2002.

Putnam, Robert D. *Bowling Alone: The Collapse and Revival of American Community*. New York: Simon and Schuster, 2000.

Pynchon, Thomas. *Against the Day*. New York: Penguin, 2006.

Roth, Phillip. *The Human Stain*. Boston: Houghton Mifflin, 2000.

———. *The Plot against America*. Boston: Houghton Mifflin, 2004.

Russo, Richard. *Empire Falls*. New York: Alfred A. Knopf, 2001.

Sebold, Alice. *The Lovely Bones*. Boston: Little, Brown, 2002.

Shivani, Anis. "The Shrinking of American Fiction." *The Antioch Review* 62 (2004): 680–690.

Smiley, Jane. *Good Faith*. New York: Alfred A. Knopf, 2003.

———. *Horse Heaven*. New York: Knopf, 2000.

Tan, Amy. *The Bonesetter's Daughter*. New York: G.P. Putnam's, 2001.

Turner, Barry. "Another Turn of the Screw." 17 Aug. 2006. *Times Online* http://www.timesonline.co.uk/article/0,,923-2315786,00.html.

Tyler, Anne. *The Amateur Marriage*. New York: Alfred A. Knopf, 2004.

———. *Digging to America*. New York: Alfred A. Knopf, 2006.

Updike, John. *Gertrude and Claudius*. New York: Alfred A. Knopf, 2000.

———. *Seek My Face*. New York: Knopf, 2002.

Walch, Tad. "Y Study Shows Oprah's Influence." *Deseret Morning News* 19 Dec. 2004. http://deseretnews.com/dn/view/0,1249,595113603,00.html.

Wallace, David Foster. *Oblivion*. New York: Little, Brown, 2004.

Waugh, Patricia. *Metafiction: The Theory and Practice of Self-Conscious Fiction*. New York: Routledge, 1984.

Williams, Raymond. *Marxism and Literature*. New York: Oxford University Press, 1977.

Williamson, Eric Miles. "The Future of American Fiction." *Southern Review* 38 (2002): 666–674.

Wood, James. *The Irresponsible Self: On Laughter and the Novel*. New York: Picador, 2005.

Further Reading

Annesley, James. *Blank Fictions: Consumerism, Culture, and the Contemporary American Novel*. London: Pluto, 1998; Bell, Bernard W. *The Contemporary African American Novel: Its Folk Roots and Modern Literary Branches*. Amherst: University of Massachusetts Press, 2004; Dandridge, Rita B. *Black Women's Activism: Reading African American Women's Historical Romances*. New York: Peter Lang, 2004; Fitzpatrick, Kathleen. *The Anxiety of Obsolescence: The American Novel in the Age of Television*. Nashville: Vanderbilt University Press, 2006; Jacobs, Naomi. *The Character of Truth: Historical Figures in Contemporary Fiction*. Carbondale: Southern Illinois University Press, 1990; Millard, Kenneth. *Coming of Age in Contemporary American Fiction*. Edinburgh: Edinburgh University Press, 2007; Myers, B.R. *A Reader's Manifesto: An Attack on the Growing Pretentiousness in American Literary Prose*. New York: Melville House, 2002; Nicol, Bran. *Postmodernism and the*

Contemporary Novel: A Reader. Edinburgh: Edinburgh University Press, 2003; Peck, Dale. *Hatchet Jobs: Writings on Contemporary Fiction.* New York: New Press, 2005; Smiley, Jane. *Thirteen Ways of Looking at a Novel.* New York, Knopf, 2005.

JAMES M. DECKER

CYBERPUNK

Definition. Cyberpunk is a subgenre of **science fiction** and is characterized by two key features: the fictional portrayal of a computer-generated, alternate virtual world and the flaunting of a "punk" attitude toward society, technology, and the human body. This punk attitude is exhibited by the adolescent cyber-cowboys, eager to trade in life in the postapocalyptic urban zones for an adventure on the digital frontier envisaged behind the computer screen. Summarized by Bruce Sterling (1954–), the chief propagator of the genre, as a coinciding of "the realm of high tech, and the modern pop underground," cyberpunk combines two aspects treated as mutually exclusive by most science fiction writers before the rise of cyberpunk in the early 1980s (Sterling 1986, xi).

Cyberpunk's characteristic style derives from the juxtaposition of dystopian urban space and utopian computer-generated space, thus contributing a new pattern to the pool of science fiction motifs. Though already proclaimed dead in 1988, shortly after it began, related forms continue to thrive in other narrative media, notably television, cinema, and computer and role-playing games. To qualify as cyberpunk, these works share at least some, if not all, of the following family resemblances in terms of style, physical setting, social milieu, and fictional characters, which will be elaborated upon based on Gibson's *Neuromancer.*

History. Cyberpunk emerged in the early 1980s and was already proclaimed dead toward the end of the decade. It has perhaps left a greater mark on "contemporary culture at large" than on science fiction literature (Landon 1992, 120). Though author and editor Gardner Dozois (1947–) does not claim to have coined the term himself and he reports that it was already in use at science fiction workshops and conventions when he employed it for the first time, he is generally credited with publicizing the name "cyberpunk" (Dozois 1984). Among that new generation of 1980s science fiction writers sharing a common aesthetic he includes Sterling, Gibson, Lewis Shiner (1950–), Cadigan, and Greg Bear (1951–). Yet, Shiner and Bear had only a marginal connection to the genre and quickly distanced themselves from it.

NAMING *CYBERPUNK*

Several authors have coined their own name for these virtual reality environments and have chosen to develop different characteristics further. William Gibson (1948–), the main representative of the cyberpunk genre, is generally credited with having created the term *cyberspace* in his short story "Burning Chrome" (1986e), which prefigures the so-called Sprawl trilogy (1984–1988), consisting of the quintessential cyberpunk novel, *Neuromancer* (1984), *Count Zero* (1986b), and *Mona Lisa Overdrive* (1988). Cyberspace is described by Gibson as "non-space of the mind" and "consensual hallucination" (Gibson 1984, 51), in other words as an abstraction of data or a specific space-time, which provides the "central metaphor" for cyberpunk fiction (Suvin 1989, 44). The matrix, the net, the grid, or the Metaverse are other labels used by key writers associated with the genre to be discussed in greater detail below.

Michael Swanwick (1950–) attempts to provide a first chronology of cyberpunk rekindling Dozois's polarization between humanists and cyberpunks in the process, a contrast that provoked many lively debates (Swanwick 1986, 50). He mentions Kim Stanley Robinson (1952–) as one representative of the humanists, who he regards as focusing more on character and the development of philosophical issues, concerns he perceives missing in cyberpunk fiction. Swanwick also excludes Bear, Rudy Rucker (1946–), and Lucius Shepard (1947–) from the inner circle of cyberpunk writers. This illustrates that cyberpunk did not understand itself as a school, movement, or even a coherent group of writers although marketing efforts were made to that effect. Gibson himself stated along with others that he perceived the label as the beginning of the end, as innovation degenerating into trite formula (Tatsumi 1987a, 14–15). The humanists, represented by John Kessel (1950–), further warned against the inherent danger of mannerism as well as criticizing cyberpunk's flat characters, plot contrivances, and romantic imagery.

Coincidentally a short story by Bruce Bethke (1955–) entitled "Cyberpunk" (1983) precedes Dozois's use of the term in print, yet it is generally not included among the body of cyberpunk fiction collected in any of the genre-defining anthologies, *Mirrorshades* (1986), *Burning Chrome* (1986a), or *Storming the Reality Studio* (1991). Bethke's story about teenage hackers who break into computer systems using their parent's phone lines shares one element of cyberpunk fiction, the illegal invasion of data stored on a computer. The hackers manipulate school records, bank accounts, and flight-traffic control systems, but the story does not provide a coherent vision of the space inside the computer. The teen breaking and entering is less profit-oriented than motivated by rebellion and a general mistrust of authority. "True Names" (1981), a novella by Vernor Vinge (1944–), is another precursor of cyberpunk and anticipates its networked computer systems. It presents a world where computer hackers fight artificial intelligences for control over the world, never revealing their actual names by which they could be traced in the real world.

The term *cyberspace* first appeared in Gibson's 1981 short story "Burning Chrome" as the name for a retrofitted computer model with which Bobby accesses the matrix. Apparent Sensory Perception, a device to access another person's feelings was first featured in "Fragments of a Hologram Rose," first published in 1977, from which evolved simstim (short for "simulated stimuli") in "Burning Chrome." The latter also featured ICE, an acronym for intrusion countermeasure electronics, aggressive killer viruses protecting valuable information that the cyber cowboy has to defeat by risking his own life.

Sterling often referred to "the Movement" as "a loose generational nexus of ambitious young writers" among whom he included Gibson, Rucker, Shiner, John Shirley (1953–), and himself, but not Cadigan, despite the fact that one of her short stories, "Rock On," also appeared in the *Mirrorshades* anthology (Sterling 1986, xi). Sterling's prefaces to the story collections *Mirrorshades* and *Burning Chrome* serve as the genre's artistic manifestos and together with his columns in the fanzine *Cheap Truth* he undoubtedly was cyberpunk's most ardent promoter. He announced the revolution by underlining the novelty in cyberpunk, which he saw as resulting from a combination of so-called "hard" and "soft" science fiction elements or a merging of an interest in avant-garde technology with other concerns previously associated with the New Wave, above all its focus on "inner space," alternate realities, often induced by hallucinogenic drugs and rock 'n roll (Sterling 1986, xv).

The punk aesthetic is as much related to a rebellious attitude toward the genre's elders as to a general interest in punk and rock music. According to Sterling, the punk heritage provided "shock value" and cyberpunk shared with punk a defiance of "cultural and aesthetic norms" (McCaffery 1991, 288). The deliberately crude, unrefined lyrics and the use of noise as sound functioned as a critique of the music industry. Cyberpunk displays a similar irreverence toward technology characterized by retrofitting and recycling used parts, thus defying their original design and intended use. When extended to prosthetics and implants, it results in a blurring of boundaries between natural and artificial as much as a subversion of good taste (Porush 1992, 256).

Sterling added another important notion, which firmly established cyberpunk in the publishing landscape. By coining the term *slipstream* as a parody of *mainstream* he appealed to the creative tension between high-brow and low-brow, Literature and subculture and located the writers as a pop-culture avant-garde beyond what are sometimes perceived as the confining walls of the "SF ghetto" (Sterling 1989).

The majority of the definitive cyberpunk short stories collected in *Mirrorshades* and *Burning Chrome* first appeared in *Omni* magazine, a publication combining short science fiction and science reporting. Other glossy life-style magazines, many of which are associated with California Bay Area alternative culture, like *Mondo 2000, Whole Earth Review, boing-boing,* and *Wired,* helped smooth the transition toward a digital subculture in its own right. They featured music and fiction reviews as well as articles on new electronic gadgets such as the first head-mounted virtual reality displays for private use. Many of these also pioneered online content and communities including contributions from writers associated with the cyberpunk field. The Internet was as much a part of cyberpunk's fictional content as it was a part of the proliferation of the genre to a community of readers and fans beyond the traditional readership of science fiction. A photocopied fanzine like *Cheap Truth* to which some cyberpunk authors contributed using pseudonyms was now easily accessible online. Sterling's "Catscan" columns from *Science Fiction Eye* magazine, instrumental in staging many cyberpunk debates, are still archived on the WELL (Whole Earth 'Lectronic Link). Internet newsgroups, listserv mailers, and personal Web sites opened up new channels of dissemination to spread the hype.

Cyberpunk in the mainstream media was often conflated with the meaning of hacker, highlighting the criminal aspects of stealing data (Elmer-Dewitt 1991, 43). Yet two years later *Time* magazine called it a "new subculture" and "the defining counterculture of the computer age" (Elmer-Dewitt 1993, 49). Hafner and Markoff's *Cyberpunk: Outlaws and Hackers on the Computer Frontier* (1991) and Sterling's *The Hacker Crackdown* (1992) tell of the efforts of law enforcement to control illicit data piracy but also of organizations like the Electronic Frontier Foundation and their defense of freedom of information and the preservation of civil liberties. Criminal and libertarian discourse were thus closely intertwined, especially when hackers were described as "deviant social class," "enemies of the state," or "juvenile technodelinquents" but also celebrated as "popular folk heroes" and underdogs fighting against large corporations (Ross 1991b, 112, 116).

From the vantage point of literary criticism, cyberpunk is frequently seen as related to other postmodern writing, for example Thomas Pynchon's *Crying of Lot 49* (1965) or Don DeLillo's *White Noise* (1984); a case in point is the anthology *Storming the Reality Studio* (McCaffery 1991). In the introduction McCaffery classifies cyberpunk as "postmodern science fiction" while also distinguishing it from "mainstream postmodernism" (McCaffrey 1991, 1, 10). A conference held in June 1989, whose proceedings are collected in *Fiction 2000* (Slusser and Shippey 1992), also generated more academic interest and established cyberpunk in the general field of contemporary literature.

Trends and Themes

Style. At its best, "cyberpunk is truly characterized only by its style" or "aesthetic cohesion" (Rabkin 1992, 275; Suvin 1991, 351). Though when reduced to mere formula or subcultural fashion, cyberpunk quickly exhausted its novelty value. *Neuromancer*'s narrative is rich in "surface detail" (Hollinger 1990, 37) and dominated by a dense, descriptive style with alternating story lines converging toward the resolution of the plot, the merging of two artificial intelligences, Neuromancer and Wintermute. Showing rather than telling helps create a fast-paced action-adventure story packed with dialogue reminiscent of the hard-boiled detective style in its use of metaphors interspersed with snippets of street lingo. The descriptions are saturated with Japanese and European brand names symbolizing technological progress. Concrete, rust and chrome, as well as neon-lit corporate logos prevail in the sprawling cities littered with the ruins of modernity, such as the decaying geodesic domes of an older version of the future imagined by another generation of writers. The joint "iconographies of science fiction and *film noir*" literally encapsulate a critique of modernity and a trashing of the earlier pulp tradition of **science fiction** to be elaborated on in the contexts and issues section (Bukatman 1993, 142; McHale 1992). The reflective sunglasses or mirrorshades, which almost gave the genre its label, are the genre's most recognizable accessory. The reflective chrome surfaces hide the wearer's eyes and disguise his or her emotions. Enhanced with electronics, they can also serve as miniaturized screens. This emphasis on reflective surfaces is often interpreted as symptomatic of postmodernity to which a lack of depth, affect, and historicity are ascribed (Jameson 1991; Sponsler 1992).

Setting and Milieu. The framing narrative, set in the dark, urban *noir* atmosphere of Chiba City, Japan, is contrasted with Case, the protagonist's adventures in the luminous geometries of cyberspace, thus "urban space and cyberspace become reciprocal metaphors" (Bukatman 1993, 145). Cyberspace, as well as the large conurbations from Boston to Atlanta, is dominated by multi-national enterprises beyond the confines of a nation state, too powerful to be controlled by mere government or law. Black market trade in human organs, drugs, computers, and information thrives in the back alleys where everyone and everything is for sale. References to Japanese culture like the larger-than-life corporations or *zaibatsus* and lethal *shuriken* weapons provide an exotic flavor to a technologically advanced yet also traditional society (Sato 2004).

Drugs enhance and alter consciousness as do computers, which when networked form seemingly infinite seas of data and give rise to a potentially unlimited parallel universe in which to hunt for data. In cyberspace, everything is translated into digital bits and bytes before it can be exchanged or stolen: money, information, knowledge, human memories, and even entire personalities. From this digital Petri dish new life-forms such as artificial intelligences emerge like impossible-to-control digital genies out of a bottle.

Fictional Characters. Case, the main character in *Neuromancer*, is the archetypical cowboy, hacker, and data pirate. Like all cyberpunk protagonists with the notable exception of those created by Pat Cadigan (1953–), he is a young Caucasian male, enhanced with sockets that allow him to plug into the computer and access cyberspace directly. He is a mercenary fighting neither for higher moral ground nor political ideals but only for profit, the thrill of simulated speed in cyberspace, or simply his survival. Only the fittest survive according to strictly Darwinian laws; those that make it are the most adept at manipulating computers and dodging killer virus programs.

Woman warriors like Case's sidekick Molly are often subsidiary fictional characters but not necessarily less charismatic. Whether as love object or sex symbol, surgically-enhanced warrior with retractable knife-blade implants or superior fighting machine, they often watch out for the young cyberpunks, a theme elaborated in Japanese cyberpunk **manga and anime** (Sato 2004).

As a rule, the fictional characters often serve the mundane function of advancing the plot. They are not fully rounded characters and subordinate to the detailed portrayal of the fictional universe. However, there are many colorful new creatures emerging from the interstices of the cyber-world: ghosts, holograms or other hybrid creatures, which transcend the boundaries between natural and artificial life, human and machine.

Context and Issues. With their emphasis on technology and concomitant social and cultural changes, cyberpunk and science fiction have been regarded as "quintessentially postmodern" (Sponsler 1992, 627; Bukatman 1992). However, on the whole, cyberpunk's attitude toward technology can be characterized as ambivalent. Dystopian elements "[r]ather than a gleaming, utopian vision of progress" are portrayed, yet the subversive potential invested in the cyber cowboy and the anarchic hope invested in the subcultural fringe such as the Panther Moderns, a group of media terrorists in *Neuromancer,* are also symptomatic of a "nostalgia for human control" (Bukatman 1993, 140, 141). Utopian hope resides in the spaces "for new social interaction" (Bukatman 1993, 145), in the hope that the underdogs can topple the omnipresent corporations by subverting the system from within. Nonetheless, "cyberpunk is fundamentally ambivalent about the breakdown of the distinctions between human and machine, between personal consciousness and machine consciousness" and various contributors to the genre attribute different values to the new technologies (Csicsery-Ronay 1991, 191).

Whereas Gibson's vision of cyberspace results in the elated speed rush and contempt of the flesh or meat in favor of the "bodiless exultation" in cyberspace (Gibson 1984, 6), feminist critics have found this kind of disembodiment problematic. They perceive the penetration of cyberspace ultimately as an invasion of the female, the matrix as womb, if only metaphorically (Springer 1991, 306; Nixon 1992, 226; Stockton 1995, 591; Hicks 1996, 64). Before elaborating feminist departures and critiques, a closer look should be paid to Cadigan's adaptation of the same themes to very different ends.

Cadigan is one of the few writers associated with the genre to explore the psychological dimensions of cyberspace and the "human-machine interface [. . .] as potentially liberating" (Wolmark 1994, 121). All three of Cadigan's Mindplayer novels, *Mindplayers* (1987), *Synners* (1991), and *Fools* (1992), share the same universe while exploring notions of franchised personalities that can be copied, merged, exchanged, erased, or stolen. Though Cadigan does not give virtual space, which is accessed by connecting to a computer system through the human optical nerve, a specific name, this mind-to-mind contact opens up many avenues for exploration.

In *Mindplayers* the main character, Deadpan Allie, gives up a life of illegal mindplay to train as a licensed Pathosfinder and becomes an expert at observing and interpreting people's mental projections in virtual space, which are all expressions of subconscious dreams and desires. She learns to remain emotionally detached in order to help others dream lucidly and to help them visualize their problems on their mind's screen. Jerry Wirerammer, her friend and former partner in illegal mindplay, chooses a different career path. He engages in illegal bootlegging to exploit the opportunities of copying and cloning memories—a concrete example for the "plurality and fragmentation of the self" referred to by postmodern theorists (McHale 1992, 160). As Allie gains more control over mindplay and learns to maintain a sense of self, Jerry loses control and his identity becomes diluted to such an extent that the original one is entirely lost. The novel thus highlights the different uses of altered states of consciousness, inherently neither good nor bad. Mind-to-mind contact always has a profound effect on everyone; memories leave traces and change people.

Synners, Cadigan's most cyberpunk novel, hinges on the phrase "change for the machines," which turns into a "philosophical comment about the nature of the technologized human" (Balsamo 1996, 134). Originally meant as a request for change to buy soda from a machine, it becomes one of the main paradigms of the novel involving an entertainment industry conspiracy to promote brain implants for marketing music videos. Visual Mark is the original "synner" who synthesizes images to accompany rock music and who uploads his visual projections via his implanted sockets directly to the net. Since she is quite aware of the fact that there is no turning back, his girlfriend Gina tries to stop him before he escapes through a trap door into digital space. Once in the net, Visual Mark's body merely sustains his mind so that when he suffers a stroke, it triggers the collapse of the entire computer network. Part of him can survive in a new synthesis with the virus program Art Fish but his human body dies. Transcendence comes at a price and immortality is only partial at best. Finally, the net is reconstructed from a self-sufficient, isolated computer operated by Sam, who uses an insulin pump to draw energy from her own body to operate it. The latter illustrates one aspect of cyborg history (short for cybernetic organism) and its roots in medical technology. Contact lenses, implants to improve hearing, artificial organs, or prosthetic legs can all be seen as representing examples of hybrid man-machine existence (Haraway 1991). The cyborg as an image of the posthuman determines its "iconic status for postmodern culture" (Christie 1991, 195), and it has enriched the critical discourses of feminism and cyberfeminism alike (Braidotti 1993; Plant 1997). Cyberfeminism takes Donna Haraway's seminal essay "Manifesto for Cyborgs" originally published in 1985 as its point of departure. For Haraway, the cyborg functions as a visionary image that dislocates the boundary between human and machine. When placed in this context, Cadigan may be seen as belonging to a lineage of feminist science fiction writers from Joanna Russ (1937–) to Marge Piercy (1936–), especially Piercy's *He, She, and It* (also published as *Body of Glass*) (1991), which shares some of the themes of cyberpunk fiction. Though cyberpunk as such, especially the male contributors to the genre, can at best be read as "covert feminist science fiction" (Gordon 197), science fiction as a publishing genre offered new ways for women writing science fiction to break into "the boys club" (Nixon 1992; Ross 1991a). Notoriously difficult to classify, Kathy Acker (1947–1997) in *Empire of the Senseless* (1988) even borrows entire phrases from *Neuromancer* subverting them toward her feminist agenda with a punk edge.

Cadigan's *Fools,* which concludes the Mindplayer trilogy, is the most complex and difficult to read book. It uses a theatre metaphor to orchestrate at least three main female personae: an actress, a police officer, and a memory junkie that has gone and bought one famous personality too many. Actor and role are inextricably linked as the actress takes on new roles as if they were costumes, as the police officer goes into deep under cover impersonating other personae, and as the memory junkie downloads new memories. It is impossible to determine which persona is the original identity, because all three women narrate in the first person singular and all three appear equally real. The plot structure is driven by the reader's desire to locate the original identity, yet this desire for closure is ultimately frustrated. Despite the potential for role playing, this detail is not used to explore gender swapping, a phenomenon often observed in actual Internet chat rooms and online communities (Turkle 1997).

Another dominant trend in reading cyberpunk, apart from its concern with the posthuman, focuses on its relation to postmodernity as reflecting a "world shaped by transnational corporate hegemony" (Rosenthal 1991, 81). It is interpreted as "the supreme literary expression if not of postmodernism, then of late capitalism itself" (Jameson 1991, 417n) and as mirroring post-industrialist society (Olsen 1992, 142). The emphasis on consumer culture, on surface detail, and on the apparent depthlessness of the screen is read as symptomatic of virtual culture at the close of the millennium. Cyberspace is viewed as "extension (and implosion) of the urban topography" (Buktman 1989, 48). The notion of implosion or a "collapsed future" as opposed to adventures in outer space or the distant future (Csicsery-Ronay 1992a, 29), as well as the concepts of simulation and hyperreality (Porush 1992, 246) are adopted from Jean Baudrillard (1929–). Baudrillard is an influential poststructuralist French critic, who regards the logic of capitalism as based on a symbolic exchange as a result of which reality ultimately becomes indistinguishable from simulation.

Whereas postmodern*ity* refers to a new era beyond modernity, postmodern*ism* highlights literary techniques such as bricolage or what Gibson calls "cultural mongrelization" (McCaffery 1991, 266), as well as intertextuality and a self-referential foregrounding of its own rules of construction. Thus cyberpunk's self-conscious use of images and icons associated with the pulp history of science fiction, for example cyberpunk's "architecture of broken dreams" epitomized in Gibson's short story "The Gernsback Continuum" (1986d, 5), expresses its irreverence toward its own heritage. Cluttered with consumer items, trash and garbage, cyberpunk undermines notions of progress and revels in the "destruction of the icons and monuments of modernity" (Heuser 2003, 43).

Stephenson's *Snow Crash* (1992) is situated on the borderline to a new generation of cyberpunk writers or "postcyberpunks" (Person 1998), a term that lacks clear definition. Stephenson was neither affiliated with the other cyberpunk writers nor included in the genre-defining anthologies. Yet, according to the formal characteristics outlined at the beginning, he fits the cyberpunk category while also stretching its limits toward the mainstream and postmodern fiction. The main character, Hiro Protagonist, an allegorical hero-as-protagonist, helps to prevent the world's infection with the vicious snow crash virus, which turns people into submissive and babbling followers of media mogul and religious missionary Bob L. Rife. Though he works in a dead-end job as a pizza delivery boy, Hiro is one of the founding fathers of the Metaverse and belongs to the hacker elite. He can write code and define the rules of his appearance and existence in the Metaverse. People entering the Metaverse design their own avatars or incarnations with which they interact in the virtual world, sometimes from scratch and sometimes from ready-made parts. This explains why Hiro is able to win a sword fight in the Metaverse, after all he defined and wrote the very rules of the game: "[I]f you need a tool, you just sit down and write it" (329), he explains, thus foregrounding the writing process, a typical feature of postmodern fiction. Stephenson goes even further and rewrites the history of mankind from the vantage point of information theory, according to which the Infocalypse of Babel accounts for the diversity of languages on earth. Genetic code, ancient myth, biblical stories, and even ideas are all broken down into informational 'memes.' In the process he offers the reader "the possibility of reflecting on [fictional] world making itself" (McHale 1992, 157). The Metaverse constitutes a comic book reality with different rules for dying and the disposal of bodies, a universe where "magic is possible" because it "is a fictional structure made out of code" that can incorporate other fictional worlds (Stephenson 1992, 197). This opens the door to further metafictional possibilities, for example the inclusion of other genres or plot scenarios not commonly associated with science fiction, such as fantasy or history. The holodeck in *Star Trek: The Next Generation* universe functions in a similar way, allowing for the incorporation of a spaghetti western ("A Fistful of Datas") or Shakespeare's *Henry V* ("The Defector").

Reception. Authors departing from a cyberpunk sensibility often show a continuing fascination with the hard-boiled but in more clearly pronounced form. Additionally, the experimentation with different forms of virtual worlds is still an important theme for science fiction written in the late twentieth and early twenty-first century. British science fiction writers such as Kim Newman (1959–) and his *The Night Mayor* (1989), Jeff Noon (1957–), most notably his *Vurt* (1993), and Richard Morgan (1965–) with his *Altered Carbon* (2001) and its sequels are frequently mentioned as having developed cyberpunk further in that direction. Furthermore, the fascination with artificial intelligence and virtual reality can also be found in mainstream contemporary American writers such as Richard Powers (1957–), for example his *Galatea 2.2* (1995) and *Plowing the Dark* (2000).

Despite its short life-span as a subgenre of North American science fiction, cyberpunk made waves beyond its science fiction boundaries into mainstream literature, other media, and an emerging cyberculture. Its defining style, characteristic cluster of motifs and icons, as well as its aesthetic sensibility were imbued with new life as they were translated and adapted for computer games, **graphic novels**, movies, and role-playing games. Cyberpunk made a lasting impression on science fiction worldwide, as the large body of Japanese cyberpunk-inspired fiction demonstrates. Japanese **manga**, **anime** films, and TV-series are closely related to cyberpunk's setting and milieu, for example *Akira* and *Tetsuo, the Iron Man* (both 1988), or the more recent *Ghost in the Shell* (1995).

Finally, there is a continuing legacy of cyberpunk role-playing games, including the original *Cyberpunk 2020* rule book as well as four editions of *Shadowrun,* whose first rule book was published in 1989. The latter represents an interesting new hybrid form combining the high-tech elements of cyberpunk science fiction with the detailed dragons, goblins, and ogres usually only populating **fantasy literature**. The role-playing game is still being widely played and it has inspired numerous novels based on the same universe.

Selected Authors. Facetious critics have called cyberpunk a one-man genre consisting solely of Gibson. Though this is extreme, it illustrates the lack of consent about a coherent cyberpunk canon. Indeed, most critical attention has focused on Gibson and Cadigan. Other fiction within the force field of cyberpunk, as well as media adaptations derived from it, continues to show a keen interest in the combination of virtual reality with a low-life criminal underworld, most notable in the more pronounced expression of hard-boiled conventions (see, e.g. Kim Newman's 1989 *Night Mayor*). By the late nineties, the core cyberpunk writers, including Shirley and Sterling, had moved into other genres and directions but a fascination with the exploration of virtual reality continues, especially in movies inspired by the genre. For want of a better term, the label *postcyberpunk* implies an opening up of genre conventions, a focus on ordinary life as a generation of young writers has grown up and become more mature. Perhaps they even accomplished the "fusion of the cyberpunk/humanist schism of the 1980s" (Person 1998, 12).

Other authors are more or less closely associated with cyberpunk, either because they appeared on the same convention panels, or because their short stories were published in the same anthologies. The question of who truly belongs to the group and on which grounds remains unresolved, a choice which inevitably also depends on one's definition of the genre. On the basis of formal criteria it makes more sense to look at which works best reflect the characteristic features mentioned at the beginning of this entry. Before the development of cyberpunk themes in other media are illustrated, the most important authors, other than Gibson and Cadigan, fitting the cyberpunk description are discussed in the following paragraphs.

Sterling's key role as promoter of the genre is supported by his translation of new scientific ideas and new forms of social organization into fiction. His juxtaposition of shapers and mechanists in the novel *Schismatrix* (1985b) and the short story collection *Crystal Express* (1989) creates a universe with two warring factions: one characterized by a belief in technological modification, prosthetics, and artificial organs; the other defined by a belief in genetic modification as extending and enhancing life. First published in 1981 his earlier novel, *The Artificial Kid* (1985a) starring the media combat artist that lends the book its name, in some ways anticipates cyberpunk. The Artificial Kid films, records, and then sells his edited adventures to the public as he explores the ecology of the planet Reverie. This interest in ecology with the added emphasis on global warming is taken up again in Sterling's *Heavy Weather* (1994). His latest novel, *The Zenith Angle* (2004), is closer to a cyberthriller than science fiction and resumes his interest in computer security in a post-9/11 world.

NOTABLE CYBERPUNK AUTHORS

Pat Cadigan
William Gibson
Rudy Rucker
John Shirley
Neal Stephenson
Bruce Sterling
Walter Jon Williams

The cyberthriller theme is another strong tendency that can be seen as related to, if not derived from, cyberpunk (see, e.g. movies like *Strange Days* (1995) or *The Net* (1998)). Especially *Strange Days* explores identity issues and questions of real and fake memories. When memories can be downloaded, manipulated, and exchanged, characters often end up confused about what is real and what is imaginary. A theme for which Philip K. Dick was famous and which characterizes the movie *Blade Runner* (1982) based on Dick's 1968 novel *Do Androids Dream of Electric Sheep?* The movie precedes cyberpunk, but shares its *future noir* sensibility (Bruno 1990). Its elliptic, witty dialogue is also favored by the hard-boiled detective style, as are the dark and rainy city scenes portrayed through steam rising from the gutters contrasted with the glow of neon signs.

Shirley, an author often associated with the inner circle of cyberpunk writers and a musician in several punk bands, represents the most obvious connection to the genre's punk roots. Shirley's near-future setting in *City Come A-Walkin'* (1980) illustrates his influence on the genre because it anticipates many of the cyberpunk icons such as the infinite reflection of the city in the silver mirrorshades of the protagonist. Shirley's short story "Freezone" (1985) encapsulates the universe elaborated in his A Song Called Youth trilogy consisting of *Eclipse* (1987), *Eclipse Penumbra* (1988), and *Eclipse Corona* (1989). The short story is dominated by the contrast between Rick Rickenharp's nostalgia for old-school, authentic rock and the artificial, electronic "minimono style."

Rudy Rucker also declared himself a cyberpunk and was invited to the 1985 cyberpunk panel in Texas, though his novels in the Ware-series, *Software* (1982), *Wetware* (1988), *Freeware* (1997), and *Realware* (2000), only marginally touch on cyberpunk motifs. More deeply informed by scientific thought and by Rucker's real-life interest in mathematics and cellular automata, the series evolves from an emerging society of robots with artificial intelligence. Rucker also tried to coin his own label, transrealism, which he regards as "breaking down consensus reality" to explore strange new life-forms in other dimensions (Rucker 1991, 437).

Walter Jon Williams (1953–) contributed the novel *Hardwired* (1986) to the nexus of cyberpunk works, a novel that bears some semblance to the cyberpunk sensibility. The main character, a modern-day cowboy who plugs into the electronic interface of his car, delivers contraband across the American continent while being randomly bombarded by a hostile satellite surveillance system. Another marginally related writer, Jack Womack (1956–), uses a satirical approach to urban life and centers his Ambient series, *Ambient* (1987), *Terraplane* (1988), *Heathern* (1990), *Random Acts of Senseless Violence* (1993), *Elvissey* (1993), and *Going, Going, Gone* (2000), around a pseudo-fascist corporate media-state, a near-future dystopia of capitalism derailed. Due to the lack of a cohesive vision of virtual reality, neither Williams nor Womack is at the core of the cyberpunk genre. The same can be said for Marc Laidlaw (see, e.g. his 1999 *Dad's Nuke*) and Lewis Shiner (see, e.g. his 1984 *Frontera*). Both have occasionally been included in some anthologies and some panels, but on the level of content they do not share the dominant themes that define cyberpunk.

The punk aspect of cyberpunk is also alluded to by the somewhat ironic label of "steampunk," used to describe cyberpunk stories involving a technological focus but set in the past, such as Gibson and Sterling's collaboration on *The Difference Engine* (1991) or DiFilippo's *Steampunk Trilogy* (1995). *The Difference Engine* is an alternative history set in Victorian England and deals with a steam-powered computer invented by Charles Babbage. "Biopunk" entails a focus on "bioengineering" and "reconfigured humans" and represents another undercurrent emerging from within cyberpunk, although it is a label that has never been widely adopted (Mc Hale 1992, 161). Greg Bear's *Blood Music* (1985), in which an out-of-control lab experiment results in organic matter greedily feeding on humans by sucking them down the drains, can be considered as a precursor to this branch of development.

Both Gibson and Cadigan continued to explore other virtual worlds following their Sprawl and Mindplayer trilogies. Gibson's Bridge trilogy, named after one of the trilogy's locales, the San Franciso-Oakland Bay bridge, includes *Virtual Light* (1993), *Idoru* (1996), and *All Tomorrow's Parties* (1999). After both San Francisco and Japan have been destroyed by earthquakes, the bridge offers refuge to a multi-cultural community living under the radar of the pervasive surveillance devices of corporate society. Virtual reality is no longer a space reserved for the elite but an "ecology of celebrity" (Gibson 1993, 2) filled with other popular media phenomena like the virtual idol or *idoru* that becomes an artificial intelligence in *All Tomorrow's Parties*. The trilogy is as much concerned with media stardom as with the secret and mythological rebuilding of post-quake Japan. Cadigan continues to explore virtual reality combined with a detective fiction element in *Tea From an Empty Cup* (1998) and *Dervish is Digital* (2000). The plot revolves around detective Dore Konstantin, who is trying to find out how a murder that was committed in virtual reality could have resulted in the actual death of the person in real life. By putting on a hotsuit, Konstantin can enter virtual space as a different person, depending on how the suit was programmed. In the

---

CYBERPUNK IN MOVIES, TV, AND ONLINE

Adaptations of cyberpunk fiction cover a wide range of different media but most are based on Gibson's work. *Neuromancer* was adapted as a graphic novel and a computer adventure game. The short story "Burning Chrome" was even adapted for the stage. A movie version of "Johnny Mnemonic," based on a script by Gibson, was released in 1995, and *New Rose Hotel*, also inspired by an early Gibson short story, was released straight to video in 1998. Yet in many ways the *Matrix* trilogy (1999–2003) is considered the visually most successful translation of cyberpunk into film. This is due to its convincing portrayal of the virtual space inside the computer enhanced by the "bullet time" super slow-motion effect created especially for the movie.

Gibson also wrote *Agrippa* (1992), an experimental, highly ephemeral, autobiographical poem on computer disk, programmed to erase itself after one reading. But a lot more closely related to cyberpunk in style and theme are two episodes for *The X-Files*, "Kill Switch" (1998) and "First Person Shooter" (2000), which Gibson wrote together with Tom Maddox. In "Kill Switch" special agents Mulder and Scully chase the murderer of a Silicon Valley pioneer killed by a sentient artificial intelligence, which suddenly learned to steer weapons and satellite surveillance systems. In "First Person Shooter" the two FBI agents enter a virtual reality gaming laboratory in which a virtual character has run amok and suddenly started killing people. Especially the female special agent, Scully, makes fun of the exaggerated "voluptuous vixen" and virtual killer, who was scanned into the system by one of the game designers. As the game designer confesses this, she calls the virtual character her "goddess"—clearly an allusion to Haraway's empowering image of the cyborg. Whereas Scully finds the appearance of the aberrant virtual character, Jade Blue Afterglow, reprehensible, Mulder simply considers entertainment.

second volume, Dervish, who is a deadly jester able to hide in the pixels of the digital universe and able to materialize anywhere he likes, breaks all the rules of the cyberworld: he destroys virtual property, illegally trades weapons, steals online time, and stalks his ex-wife. The challenge for detective Konstantin is to find out where Dervish's body is located in the outside world before she can have him arrested for his crimes.

Bibliography

Acker, Kathy. *Empire of the Senseless.* New York: Grove Weidenfeld, 1988.

Balsamo, Anne. "Feminism for the Incurably Informed." In *Technologies of the Gendered Body.* Durham, NC: Duke University Press, 1996, 218–246.

Barr, Marleen S. *Future Females, the Next Generation.* Lanham, MD: Rowman and Littlefield, 2000.

Benedikt, Michael, ed. *Cyberspace.* Cambridge, MA: MIT, 2000.

Bethke, Bruce. "Cyberpunk." *Amazing Science Fiction Stories* 57.4 (1983): 94–105.

Bladerunner: The Director's Cut. DVD. Directed by Ridley Scott. Warner, 1982.

Braidotti, Rosi. "Cyberfeminism with a Difference." In *Feminisms.* Sandra Kemp and Judith Squires, eds. Oxford: Oxford University Press, 1997.

Bruno, Giuliana. "Ramble City." In *Alien Zone.* Annette Kuhn, ed. London: Verso, 1990.

Bukatman, Scott. "The Cybernetic (City) State." *Journal of the Fantastic in the Arts* 2 (1989): 43–63.

———. "Amidst these Fields of Data." *Critique* 33.3 (1992):199–219.

———. *Terminal Identity.* Durham, NC: Duke University Press, 1993.

Cadigan, Pat. *Mindplayers.* New York: Bantam Spectra, 1987.

———. *Synners.* New York: Bantam Spectra, 1991.

———. *Fools.* New York: Bantam Spectra, 1992.

———. *Tea from an Empty Cup.* London: HarperCollins, 1992.

———. *Dervish is Digital.* New York: Tor, 2000.

Christie, John R.R. "A Tragedy for Cyborgs." *Configurations* 1.1 (1991): 171–196.

Csicsery-Ronay, Istvan, Jr. "Cybcrpunk and Neuromanticism." In *Storming the Reality Studio.* Larry McCaffery, ed. Durham, NC: Duke University Press, 1991.

———. "Futuristic Flu, or, the Revenge of the Future." In *Fiction 2000.* George Slusser and Tom Shippey, eds. Athens, GA: University of Georgia Press, 1992a.

———. "The Sentimental Futurist." *Critique* 23.3 (Spring 1992b): 221–240.

Dozois, Gardner. "Science Fiction in the Eighties." *Washington Post,* Dec. 30, 1984.

Elmer-Dewitt, Philipp. "Cyberpunks and the Constitution." *Time,* April 8 1991: 43.

———. "Cyberpunk." *Time,* March 1, 1993: 48–50.

Gibson, William. *Neuromancer.* New York: Ace, 1984.

———. *Burning Chrome.* New York: Ace, 1986a.

———. *Count Zero.* New York: Ace, 1986b.

———. "Johnny Mnemonic." In *Burning Chrome.* New York: Ace, 1986c.

———. "The Gernsback Continuum." In *Burning Chrome.* New York: Ace, 1986d.

———. "Burning Chrome." In *Burning Chrome.* New York: Ace, 1986e.

———. *Mona Lisa Overdrive.* New York: Bantam Spectra, 1988.

———. *Virtual Light.* New York: Bantam Spectra, 1993.

———. *Idoru.* New York: Putnam, 1996.

———. *All Tomorrow's Parties.* New York: Putnam, 1999.

———. *Pattern Recognition.* New York: Putnam, 2003.

Gibson, William and Dennis Ashbaugh. The Agrippa Files. [cited January 20, 2007]. Available from http://agrippa.english.ucsb.edu/UC Santa Barbara's Transcription Project. Keving Begos, Jr. Publisher.

Gibson, William and Bruce Sterling. *The Difference Engine.* New York: Bantam, 1991.

Gibson, William, and Tom Maddox. "Kill Switch." *The X-Files,* 1998, 45 mins. Fox, 15.
———. "First Person Shooter." *The X-Files,* February 27 2000, 45 mins. Fox, DVD.
Gordon, Joan. "Ying and Yang Duke it Out." In *Sorming the Reality Studio.* Larry McCaffery, ed. Durham, NC: Duke University Press, 1991.
Hafner, Katie, and John Markoff. *Cyberpunk.* New York: Simon and Schuster, 1991.
Haraway, Donna. "Manifesto for Cyborgs: Science, Technology, and Socialist Feminism." In *Simians, Cyborgs, and Women: The Reinvention of Nature.* New York: Routledge, 1991, 149–181. Originally published in *Socialist Review* 80 (1985): 65–108.
Heuser, Sabine. *Virtual Geographies: Cyberpunk at the Intersection of the Postmodern and Science Fiction.* Amsterdam: Rodopi, 2003.
Hicks, Heather. "Whatever It Is That She's Since Become." *Contemporary Literature* 37.1 (1996): 62–93.
Hollinger, Veronica. "Cybernetic Deconstructions: Cyberpunk and Postmodernism." *Mosaic* 23.2 (1990): 29–44.
Jameson, Fredric. *Postmodernism, or, the Cultural Logic of Late Capitalism.* Durham, NC: Duke University Press, 1991.
Johnny Mnemonic. DVD. Directed by Robert Longo. Sony, 1995.
Kemp, Sandra, and Judith Squires, eds. *Feminisms.* Oxford: Oxford University Press, 1997.
Kessel, John. "The Humanist Manifesto." *Science Fiction Eye* 1.1 (1987): 52–56.
Kuhn, Annette, ed. *Alien Zone: Cultural Theory and Contemporary Science Fiction Cinema.* London: Verso, 1992.
Landon, Brooks. *The Aesthetics of Ambivalence.* Westport, CT: Greenwood Press, 1992.
McCaffery, Larry, ed. *Storming the Reality Studio: A Casebook of Cyberpunk and Postmodernism.* Durham, NC: Duke University Press, 1991.
McHale, Brian. "Elements of a Poetics of Cyberpunk." *Critique* 23.3 (1992): 140–175.
Nixon, Nicola. "Cyberpunk: Preparing the Ground for Revolution or Keeping the Boys Satisfied?" *Science-Fiction Studies* 19.2 (1992): 219–235.
Olsen, Lance. "Cyberpunk and the crisis of postmodernity." In *Fiction 2000.* George Slusser and Tom Shippey, eds. Athens, GA: University of Georgia Press, 1992.
Penley, Constance, and Andrew Ross, eds. *Technoculture.* Minneapolis, MN: University of Minnesota Press, 1991.
Person, Lawrence. "Notes Toward a Postcyberpunk Manifesto." *Nova Express* 4.4 (1998): 11–12.
Plant, Sadie. "Beyond the Screens: Film, Cyberpunk and Cyberfeminism." In *Feminisms.* Sandra Kemp and Judith Squires, eds. Oxford: Oxford University Press, 1997.
Porush, David. "Frothing the Synaptic Bath: What Puts the Punk in Cyberpunk." In *Fiction 2000.* George Slusser and Tom Shippey, eds. Athens, GA: Georgia University Press, 1992.
Rabkin, Eric S. "Undecidability and Oxymoronism." In *Fiction 2000.* George Slusser and Tom Shippey, eds. Athens, GA: University of Georgia Press, 1992.
Rosenthal, Pam. "Jacked In: Fordism, Cyberpunk, Marxism." *Socialist Review* 21.1 (1991): 79–105.
Ross, Andrew. "Cyberpunk in Boystown." In *Strange Weather: Culture, Science and Technology in the Age of Limits.* London: Verso, 1991a.
———. "Hacking Away at the Counterculture." In *Technoculture.* Constance Penley and Andrew Ross, eds. Minneapolis, MN: University of Minnesota Press, 1991b.
Rucker, Rudy (von Bitter). *Software.* New York: Ace, 1982.
———. *Transreal!* Englewood, CO: WCS Books, 1991.
Sato, Kumiko. "How Information Technology has (not) Changed Feminism and Japanism: Cyberpunk in the Japanese Context." *Comparative Literature Studies* 41 (3), 2004, 335–355.
Shiner, Lewis. *Frontera.* New York: Baen, 1984.
Shirley, John. *City Come A-walkin'.* New York: Dell, 1980.

———. "Freezone." In *Mirrorshades*. Bruce Sterling, ed. New York: Ace, 1986.

———. *Eclipse*. New York: Warner, 1987.

———. *Eclipse Penumbra*. New York: Warner, 1988.

———. *Heatseeker*. Los Angeles: Scream Press, 1989a.

———. "Beyond Cyberpunk: The New Science Fiction Underground." *Science Fiction Eye* 1.5 (1989b): 30–43.

———. *Eclipse Corona*. New York: Warner, 1990.

Slusser, George, and Tom Shippey, eds. *Fiction 2000: Cyberpunk and the Future of Narrative*. Athens, GA: University of Georgia Press, 1992.

Spinrad, Norman. "The Neuromantic Cyberpunks." In *Science Fiction in the Real World*. Carbondale, IL: Southern Illinois University Press, 1990.

Sponsler, Claire. "Cyberpunk and the Dilemmas of Postmodern Narrative." *Contemporary Literature* 33.4 (1992): 625–644.

Springer, Claudia. "The Pleasure of the Interface." *Screen* 32.3 (1991): 303–323.

Stephenson, Neal. *Snow Crash*. New York: Bantam Spectra, 1992.

Sterling, Bruce. *The Artificial Kid*. Harmondsworth: Penguin ROC, 1985a.

———. *Schismatrix*. New York: Viking, 1985b.

———. ed. 1986. *Mirrorshades*. New York: Ace.

———. *Crystal express*. New York: Ace, 1989.

———. "Catscan: Slipstream." *Science Fiction Eye* 1.5 (1989): 77–80.

———. *The Hacker Crackdown*. New York: Bantam, 1993.

Stockton, Sharon. "The Self Regained." *Contemporary Literature* 35.4 (1995): 588–612.

Suvin, Darko. "On Gibson and Cyberpunk SF." In *Storming the Reality Studio*. Larry McCaffery, ed. Durham, NC: North Carolina University Press, 1991, 349–365. Originally published in *Foundation* 46 (Autumn 1989): 40–51.

Swanwick, Michael. "A User's Guide to the Postmoderns." *Isaac Asimov's Science Fiction Magazine* 10.8 (1986): 22–53.

Tatsumi, Takayuki. "An Interview with William Gibson." *Science Fiction Eye* 1.1 (1987a): 6–17.

———. "The Japanese Reflection of Mirrorshades." *Science Fiction Eye* 1.1 (1987b): 27–42.

Turkle, Sherry. *Life on the Screen: Identity in the Age of the Internet*. New York: Simon and Schuster, 1997.

Vinge, Vernor. *True Names*. New York: Baen, 1987.

Wachowski, Any and Larry. *Matrix*. DVD. Warner: 1999.

Williams, Walter Jon. *Hardwired*. New York: Tor, 1986.

Wolmark, Jenny. *Aliens and Others: Science Fiction, Feminism, and Postmodernism*. Iowa City, IA: University of Iowa Press, 1994.

Further Reading

Butler, Andrew M. *Cyberpunk*. Harpenden, England: Pocket Essentials, 2000; Cavallaro, Dani. *Cyberpunk and Cyberculture*. London: Athlone Press, 2000; Gillis, Stacy. *The Matrix Trilogy: Cyberpunk Reloaded*. London: Wallflower, 2005; Heuser, Sabine. *Virtual Geographies: Cyberpunk at the Intersection of the Postmodern and Science Fiction*. Amsterdam: Rodopi, 2003; McCaffery, Larry, ed. *Storming the Reality Studio: A Casebook of Cyberpunk and Postmodernism*. Durham, NC: Duke University Press, 1991; Tatsumi, Takayuki. *Full Metal Apache: Transactions between Cyberpunk Japan and Avant-Pop America*. Durham, NC: Duke University Press, 2006.

SABINE HEUSER

D

DRAMATIC THEATRE

Definition. Dramatic writing differs from other narrative forms, such as fiction, in ways that will be outlined below. We will make a distinction in this chapter between dramatic, meaning serious, and comedic writing. This will focus on serious dramatic literature.

Gary Vena and Andrea Nouryeh in the preface to their book *Drama and Performance: An Anthology* (1996, vii) suggest the dramatic script is a "work of literary art whose structure differs considerably from other genres and must be evaluated accordingly." When we think of dramatic writing, we understand it is different from other literary genres in that the action is done by each of the characters themselves, without a narrative or omniscient voice telling the readers about what these characters are doing. The characters, literally, speak for themselves. Jeffrey H. Huberman, James Ludwig and Brant L. Pope, in their *The Theatrical Imagination* (1997, 46), call this "The Action Factor," meaning: "Drama is the imitation of human actions." What is vital to action is conflict. Robert Cohen in his *Theatre: Brief Version* (2003, 6) writes this about action: "Action is not merely movement, of course: it is argument, struggle, persuasion, threats, seduction, sound, music, dance, speech, and passion. It comprises all forms of human energy, including language, spatial dynamics, light, color . . . It is *live* action, ordinarily unmediated by videotape or cinematic celluloid." The story, if there is one, is unfolded by each character as it is done.

For a work to be considered dramatic literature it must have characters who act. The dramatist creates a world through the characters' language and other devices of the genre that will be discussed below.

Context and Issues. From the beginning of Western theatre in ancient Greece, successful playwrights knew what they wrote needed to be acted out in order for the work to fully come to life. Vena and Nouryeh (1996, viii) continue: "So while other literary works reach their potential as words of art in the act of reading, either silently or aloud, dramas seem incomplete without the spectacle of production."

Robert Edmund Jones, the twentieth-century director/set designer, in his *The Dramatic Imagination* (1990, 36), wrote: "The loveliest and most poignant of all stage pictures are those that are seen in the mind's eye." Dramatists must write for readers to be able to see and create in their mind's eye. Vena and Nouryeh (1996, viii–ix) suggest that dramatic literature demands more from the reader's imaginations than most other forms of literature. They say:

> We must see and understand what is explicitly said and done, as well as be alterted [sic] to what is implied and left unspoken. We need to be able to determine where the action is taking place, which characters are present even if they are not speaking, and what is happening from moment to moment . . . In essence, our role as readers is two-sided: that of spectator and director, capable of visualizing the play as if we were witnessing it or creating it on stage.

We get clues from the playwrights. The first clue is the dramatist personae, or cast list. The second is the stage directions that tell us time and place, perhaps some details about the characters, and perhaps what they are doing. Playwrights are able to tell us a lot about the characters through the language they use to write their stage directions. Take this example from master playwright Tennessee Williams (1911–1983), who in an early scene in his *A Streetcar Named Desire* (1951, 14–15) goes far in creating stage directions that allow the reader to experience Blanche's emotional life:

> She continues to laugh. Blanche comes around the corner, carrying a valise. She looks at a slip of paper, then at the building, then again at the slip and again at the building. Her expression is one of shocked disbelief. Her appearance is incongruous to this setting. She is daintily dressed in a white suit with a fluffy bodice, necklace and earrings of pearl, white gloves and hat, looking as if she were arriving to a summer tea or cocktail party in the garden district. She is about five years older than Stella. Her delicate beauty must

avoid a strong light. There is something about her uncertain manner, as well as her white clothes, that suggests a moth.

Also through Williams's stage directions, his readers can get a feel for the mood of the play, as shown in this excerpt, also from *Streetcar:*

Lurid reflections appear on the wall around Blanche. The shadows are of a grotesque and menacing form. She catches her breath, crosses to the phone and jiggles the hook. Stanley goes into the bathroom and closes the door. (128)

Other playwrights utilize a more straight-forward approach to writing stage directions. For example, in Claire Boothe Luce's (1903–1987) 1936 play, *The Women,* we can see the use of stage directions to paint a simple picture of each character:

As curtain rises, JANE, a pretty and quite correct little Irish-American maid, is arranging the tea-table. Four women are playing bridge in a smoking-car cloud of smoke. They are: NANCY, who is sharp, but not acid, sleek but not smart, a worldly and yet virginal 35 . . . (5)

For post-modernism there hardly needs to be an interest in narrative, and so this style of writing allows for a lot of freedom in form. Even stage directions may be different, as we can see from this example of the structuralist play *Double Gothic* (1978) by Michael Kirby (1931–1997):

Scene	Character	Line	Seconds of darkness
A–1	HEROINE A	"My suitcase!"	11
B–1	HEROINE B	"There's a star."	12
(Now the people are handing something to someone else).			
A–5	ANTAGONIST A/HELPER A	"Put them on."	13

Drama and Performance: An Anthology, p. 1067.

One of the main qualifying characteristics of dramatic literature is that the story is revealed within an element of time. Playwrights may employ real time, when the time elapses as it would in a segment of real life. Fifteen minutes is fifteen minutes, for example. But more usual is what Vena and Nouryeh (1996, ix) call "psychological time," which "depict[s] the crucial or pivotal moments from the characters' lives to represent their journeys toward selfhood." There are a variety of ways that playwrights structure their works. There are linear forms that move from beginning, middle and end, to plays that jump around in time. For example, Diana Son's (born 1965) 1998 *Stop/Kiss* jumps backward and then forward in order to tell a story that is poignant, joyous and quite disturbingly sad.

Exposition is used in dramatic literature. Exposition, according to Vena and Nouryeh (1996, x): "Establishes the background or circumstances in which we encounter our characters." A prologue may be utilized in a form of a monologue, or long speech. Also, a prologue can be a short, separate scene outside the body of the play, which may be utilized to tell expository information like who the characters are and other details of the world of the play. During the English

Renaissance, playwrights such as William Shakespeare (1564–1616) utilized the prologue quite often. In contemporary American dramatic literature it is rarely used. Exposition may be told in the beginning scenes of the play by characters in natural conversation.

The denouement is the resolution where a restoration of order may occur, but it does not always have to. Very often in dramas the work may just end. Order is not restored, nothing is resolved, and the play simply ends. In contemporary drama there is no necessity for the work to finish with a clear resolution for it to be considered a play of quality. Distinctions of greatness can disregard this convention of tying up the loose ends. The last character's speech can end and so with it, the work. Greatness is defined by other conventions such as: language, structure, depth of character, and timelessness of the themes.

The dramatic playwright utilizes monologues (longer portions of speech that one character says to another character) and dialogue (speech spoken by people in conversation either in pairs or small or large groups). Soliloquies were often used in the Renaissance by playwrights such as William Shakespeare; however, they are more infrequent in modern and contemporary drama. A soliloquy differs from a monologue in that the speaker is alone on stage. In contemporary times, a speech is considered a "speech" or "monologue" and we no longer call a lone bit of text a soliloquy. Nouryeh and Vena (1996, xi) say this about text in dramatic literature:

> Language in the form of dialogue nourishes the playwright's craft. The spoken lines illuminate the characters' motives and behaviors. Vocabulary, dialectical patterns, and colloquialisms easily establish social status. Rhythms of speech determined by the interplay of articulation and pause reveal personality and convey the rational thoughts and irrational emotions of the speakers . . . Whether verse or prose, words control character development and themes.

The story, characterization, plot and conflict are all revealed by how the character speaks, just as much as what they actually say. Different playwrights may be known for how they handle speech, for instance: Tennessee Williams for his poetic realism and David Mamet (born 1947) for his terse gritty realism (not to mention numerous uses of foul language).

The overwhelming difference for readers of dramatic literature is that they are being asked to imagine a world that exists in a specific time and place on the stage. The greatest of playwrights are aware that their words are only as powerful as what they spark to the reader's imagination and collect in their mind's eye. Therefore, it is very important that the voice of the character be specific to each character and that the playwright truthfully depicts the range of human experience.

What makes a work dramatic versus comedic is that the play is a more serious work, in tone, than a comedic work. Comedies, simply put, are funny. Within the realm of the dramatic are plays that are darkly humorous or absurd, where readers may laugh out loud or chuckle silently to themselves. However, for our purposes, even if the reader chuckles during a reading, in order for it to be a drama (versus comedy): it must be sad, disturbing or tragic, with an overall sense of seriousness. According to Vena and Nouryeh (1999, 1199) a comedy is: "In the classical drama, a literary format that pays homage to the hero's triumph over calamity; rooted in ritual much like tragedy, except that renewal and rebirth are celebrated." So, though the two genres of drama and comedy both stem from ancient Greek tragedy, they are, since modern times, different in tone, situation, and outcome.

Trends and Themes

Early Roots/Classical Dramatic Literature. Dramatic literature certainly has its roots in ancient ritual and storytelling, but the beginnings of Western dramatic literature are firmly rooted in the plays of the ancient Greeks who wrote as early as 5th century B.C. Thirty-three plays from the dramatic writers Aeschylus (525–456 B.C.), Sophocles (496–406 B.C.) and Euripides (480–406 B.C.) are still in existence. Nearly a century after these great dramatic writers, Aristotle (384–322 B.C.), the ancient philosopher, wrote his *Poetics* (350 B.C.), which analyzed and defined the notions of literature, especially drama, and more specifically tragedy. The *Poetics* established criteria for critics, actors, writers, and historians throughout the ages to be able to uniformly judge dramatic literature. Playwrights do not have to adhere to Aristotelian demands, but most playwrights, throughout the ages, were and are, aware of Aristotelian criteria.

This chapter focuses specifically on American dramatic literature written between 2000–2005; therefore it is important to concentrate on the history of American dramatic literature. Though there is an established connection between the ancient tradition that has a profound effect on European theatre history, we will start our discussion of American dramatic literary history in 19th century America. To fully understand American drama one would need to fully study classical, Western, and Eastern forms of theatre throughout a wide variety of periods and styles since they have all had a unique impact on the total variety of American dramatic literature.

Dramatic Literature in Early North America. The earliest theatre in America was melodrama. Melodrama is best explained as plays with heightened emotion and complete polar opposite notions of good and evil. The hero always wins. The American melodrama is highlighted by two types: the frontier melodrama and the temperance melodrama and within this form, there are comedies and dramas. We will focus on the dramas.

Early examples of the frontier type are: David Belasco's (1853–1931) *The Girl I Left Behind Me* in 1893 and Frank Murdoch's (1843–1872) more famous *Davy Crockett* (1872), which made villains of Native Americans and glorified frontier life. W.H. Smith (dates unknown) wrote the temperance melodrama: *The Drunkard; or, the Fallen Saved* (1844), which depicted overly tragic visions of the effects of alcohol on otherwise noble persons. Playwrights like Augustin Daly (1838–1899) who wrote the melodrama *Under the Gaslight* (c. 1869), which is still widely performed today, were interested in the Little Theatre Movement, bringing their plays to frontier and expanding cities, instead of waiting for audiences to come to them. This affected the plays being written during this time period. Plays of social and literary merit that allowed for a greater integrity in acting than the plays that had gone before them were of interest to these diverse and wider audiences. It was a precursor to the more sophisticated and complex realistic plays to occur in the later nineteenth century and into the twentieth and twenty-first. Another important early melodrama was written by the African American abolitionist writer William Wells Brown (1814–1884), whose *The Escape; or, A Leap For Freedom* (1858) was left unproduced until 1971 at Emerson College in Boston. The play shows the horrors of American slavery and has an unlikely hero who escapes enslavement. The Melodrama, like many of the American dramatic forms, came out of Europe, from France.

Twentieth Century. We see that American dramatic literature is born from European artistic movements. American writers adopted these and other styles including: Melodrama from France and Germany; Realism and Naturalism from Russia, Norway and Sweden; anti-Realism from Germany, the United Kingdom, Russia and other European countries; Expressionism from Germany; and Absurdist forms from Ireland, France, Romania, and other European countries. It could be argued that there is not a wholly American dramatic style until we come to the 1960s with the Black Arts Movement, which will be discussed at greater length below.

Reception. In the early twentieth century, prior to the birth of Realism in America, plays were much like the previous century's melodramas, but with more and more sensational topics explored. It wasn't until Eugene O'Neill (1888–1953) that America got its earliest playwright of international repute. In 1915 the Provincetown Players was founded in Massachusetts by O'Neill. Inspired by the European realistic playwrights: Anton Chekhov (1860–1904, Russian), Henrik Ibsen (1828–1906, Norwegian) and August Strindberg (1849–1912, Swedish), O'Neill went on to receive a 1936 Nobel Prize. He won Pulitzer Prizes for four of his plays: *Beyond the Horizon* (1920); *Anna Christie* (1922); *Strange Interlude* (1928); and *Long Day's Journey Into Night* (1957). A list of O'Neill's other plays include: the Expressionistic *The Hairy Ape*, the classical tragedy-inspired *Mourning Becomes Electra, A Moon For the Misbegotten, Long Day's Journey Into Night, The Iceman Cometh, All God's Chillun Got Wings,* and *Desire Under the Elms.* Because of O'Neill's influence other playwrights began experiments with writing styles inspired by Europeans. A few of these early American playwrights include: Maxwell Anderson, (1888–1959) poet-dramatist who with his *What Price Glory?* (1926) was sharply critical of the First World War and also experimented with plays in verse, inspired by earlier Western periods and playwrights; Susan Glaspell (1876–1948) whose feminist *Trifles* (1916) is still important today; and, Elmer Rice's *The Adding Machine* (1923), which experimented with early silent film conventions making its way into dramatic literature and focused on the central character's inner psychology.

In the 1930s playwrights wrote about the working classes following the Depression. These plays were very much interested in social issues and in making change through the power of dramatic writing and their subsequent performances. These playwrights include Clifford Odets (1906–1963), who largely wrote for The Group Theatre (1931–1940) and was interested in Naturalistic and Realistic acting styles and was influenced by the Russian Konstantin Stanislavsky (1863–1938) and his Moscow Art Theatre (founded in 1897). Cheryl Crawford (1902–1986), one of the Group's founders and producers, said during a videotaped interview that the Group was made up of New York actors wanting to do plays in their own unique voice. Odets provided them their dramatic voice with his plays: *Awake and Sing!, Waiting for Lefty* and *Golden Boy.* In *Waiting for Lefty* the audience raised their arms and shouted, along with the characters on stage, "Strike! Strike!" The play took New York by storm, showing the importance of having a theatre interested in the plights of the masses. Other writers of this period were: Lillian Hellman (1905–1984) who wrote the highly acclaimed: *The Children's Hour, Toys in the Attic* and *The Little Foxes,* and Langston Hughes (1902–1967) whose play *Don't You Want to Be Free?* was an Expressionistic voice of African Americans post-Depression who wanted to be able to bond with other workers and experience true societal freedoms. Hughes was an important Harlem Renaissance artist who wrote in a variety of literary genres. Of note: all these playwrights and others in the 1930s were examined under the House Un-American Activities Committee, challenged as Communists. For some, this was the end of their career.

In the following period, 1945–1960, we see American Realism become most important as the dramatists look at life in American cities and in American homes. Arthur Miller (1915–2005) Pulitzer Prize winner for *Death of a Salesman* (1949) and author of many more plays through the subsequent decades, including: *All My Sons, The Crucible, A View From the Bridge;* Tennessee Williams (1911–1983) who wrote: *Summer in Smoke, A Streetcar Named Desire* (Pulitzer Prize in 1948), *Night of the Iguana,* and numerous other dramatic works that were also made into films that dealt largely with gritty stories of men stuck in hiding and abandoned desperate women who loved them. He wrote of the Old South from its gentility into its more modern grit as well as poetically looked at people suffering for their desires disallowed by American society, such as homosexuality and women's longing for love and sensual pleasure. He wrote for Lee Strasberg (1901–1982), the artistic director of The Actors Studio (founded in 1947), which grew out of the collapse of The Group Theatre. The Studio was made up of a courageous and plucky group of actors, playwrights and directors (such as Elia Kazan, 1909–2003) who wanted an American theatre that showed all of the American torment of human experience, as Stanislavsky's Moscow Art Theatre with writers such as Anton Chekhov, did for Russian life. Other writers of this juicy period include: William Inge (1913–1973), *The Dark at the Top of the Stairs, Picnic* and *Bus Stop,* and Lorraine Hansberry (1894–1965) for her groundbreaking *A Raisin in the Sun,* which allowed readers and audiences a glimpse into the personal and home life of an African American chauffeur. Glynne Wickham in his *A History of the Theatre* (1985, 236) suggests that this period is when the United States had become the "undisputed pace-setter of change and innovation in all areas of dramatic art."

The 1960s brought a theatre of dissent; a theatre that experimented with notions of what constituted drama, and largely, what is a play. Notable at this time for dramatic literary contributions, were the playwrights involved in the Black Arts Movement. Amiri Baraka (born 1934), formerly LeRoi Jones, was a recent Poet Laureate of New Jersey, and wrote important American plays such as: *Dutchman, The Toilet,* and *The Slave.* Sonia Sanchez (born 1934) wrote the lyrical and poignant *Sister Son/ji.* Adrienne Kennedy (born 1931) became known for her *Funnyhouse of a Negro.* Ed Bullins (born 1935) wrote *In the Wine Time, The Corner* and *Clara's Ole Man,* to name just a few titles from his extensive list of plays.

In the 1970s and 1980s the Off-Broadway theatre emerged, which allowed for more intimate and less commercial plays. Issues that weren't fully explored on Broadway and larger commercial venues were able to be explored, such as: complex and sometimes taboo relationships in the plays of Sam Shepard (born 1943) who wrote *True West* and *Lie of the Mind;* and Mamet who wrote the testosterone-fueled *Glengarry Glenn Ross* and *Speed-the-Plow;* feminist Wendy Wasserstein (1950–2006) winner of the Pulitzer Prize for Drama for her play *The Heidi Chronicles;* AIDS and gay themes by writer Larry Kramer (born 1935) who wrote *The Normal Heart,* which was a finalist for the Pulitzer Prize; and African American playwright August Wilson (1945–2005) whose strong influence on the American drama will be discussed further below.

The 1990s was a time to explore the richness of what the preceding generations of American dramatists had uncovered in themes as well as in the styles of writing. In the twenty-first century we can look forward to new and young writers experimenting still further with structure and themes. Since 9/11, themes of violence and war and hate, have been explored by these playwrights in ways earlier generations did not dare try. Below we will examine some of these fresh writers, as well as the previous generations' writers who are still forging ahead.

Selected Authors

Edward Albee (1928–). Albee won three Pulitzer Prizes for: *A Delicate Balance* (1967), *Seascape* (1975) and *Three Tall Women* (1994). He also authored the highly acclaimed *Who's Afraid of Virginia Woolf?,* which starred Elizabeth Taylor and Richard Burton in the film version of 1966. Though he is arguably one of America's best writers, his work has received favorable and not so favorable critiques over the years. In an interview with David Richards (1994) for *The New York Times* following Albee's third Pulitzer Prize, the playwright said:

> But there is not always a great relationship between popularity and excellence. If you know that, you can never be owned by public opinion or critical response. You just have to make the assumption you're doing good work and go on doing it. Of course, there are the little dolls you stick pins in privately. (http://query.nytimes.com/gst/fullpage. html?res=9C01E0DD173DF930A25757C0A962958260)

In 2004 and 2005 Overlook Press published *The Collected Plays of Edward Albee, Volume 1 (1958-65)* and *Volume 2 (1966-77).* According to the author's note in the preface (6), "The plays contained within these anthologies include some changes the author has made over the years. Although he may revisit these texts again one day, he considers them to be, at this point, the definitive versions for both reading and performance."

David Auburn (1969–). Auburn is the author of the 2001 Pulitzer Prize winning *Proof,* which is also the recipient of the Joseph Kesselring Prize, the Drama Desk Award, and the 2001 Tony Award for Best Play. It was made into a film in 2005 and starred Anthony Hopkins and Gwyneth Paltrow. The play is a sort of ghost play about whether or not a twenty-something daughter has inherited her mathematician father's genius or insanity. Structurally the play should be noted for its non-linear use of time. It is not told in real time, though it has a realistic, slice of life feel to it, as though readers experience something that could happen in real life. Because of this experiment with time structure Cohen (2003) calls the play post-modern.

Nilo Cruz (1960–). Cruz is the Cuban American dramatist of *Anna in the Tropics,* which won the 2003 Pulitzer Prize for Drama. It is a poetic play about a cigar manufacturing family in 1929 Tampa. At that time the owners would hire a lector to read to the cigar rollers. When the machines came in, that was the end of that tradition. Ben Brantley (2003) writes in a *New York Times* review:

> *Anna in the Tropics* reaches for the artistic heavens—specifically, that corner of eternity occupied by the plays of Anton Chekhov, where yearning is an existential condition . . . Although Mr. Cruz's tone is definitely Chekhovian in its sense of a gentle, pre-modern world on the brink of extinction, the Anna of the play's title refers to a creation by another Russian writer: Leo Tolstoy's Anna Karenina . . . The resulting confrontations and collisions are rendered in some of the most densely lyrical language from an

American playwright since Maxwell Anderson. (http://theater2.nytimes.com/mem/
theater/treview.html?html_title=&tols_title=ANNA%20IN%20THE%20
TROPICS%20(PLAY)&pdate=20031117&byline=By%20BEN%20BRANTLEY&id=
1077011429146)

Anna in the Tropics also won the notable American Theater Critics/Steinberg New
Play Award at the Humana Festival of New American Plays in Louisville, Kentucky.

Other plays by Cruz include: *Betty and Gauguin, Dancing on Her Knees, A Park
in Our House, Hortensia and the Museum of Dreams, A Bicycle Country, Night
Train to Bolina, Two Sisters and a Piano, Beauty of the Father,* and *Lorca in a
Green Dress.* He has translated two plays by Federico García Lorca (1898–1936,
Spanish): *Doña Rosita* and *The House of Bernarda Alba.*

Tom Donaghy (1964–). In his plays people talk, but they do not listen. Perhaps the most
successful of these plays is *Northeast Local.* All his plays have some sort of disengage-
ment with characters not communicating—especially when dealing with their homosexuality. The theme of parents not wanting to acknowledge a gay son is something
that floats throughout his plays. Brantley (2000) in a *New York Times* review says:

> Looking for sourness and disenchantment within the cute and eccentric is a specialty
> of Mr. Donaghy . . . Like many playwrights of his generation, including Nicky Silver
> [date of birth unknown] and David Greenspan [born 1956], he portrays fractured fam-
> ilies that are not so much dysfunctional as beyond functioning at all. You can't go home
> again in these fretful comedies because home, in its mythic sense, has ceased to exist.
> (http://theater2.nytimes.com/mem/theater/treview.html?html_title=&tols_title=
> BEGINNING%20OF%20AUGUST,%20THE%20(BOOK)&pdate=20001012&
> byline=By%20BEN%20BRANTLEY&id=1077011429268)

Though Brantley calls them comedies, they are more absurd dramas, so that is
why we place them in dramatic literature.

Donaghy's plays include: the one-act *The Dadshuttle,* which was made into a
short film that the playwright directed; *Northeast Local* with compelling characters
and a more accessible story; and *Minutes From the Blue Route. The Beginning of
August and Other Plays* was published in 2000 by Grove Press.

Eve Ensler (1953–). Ensler wrote *The Vagina Monologues* in 1996, which has
impacted dramatic literature as well as women's history. Ensler interviewed hundreds of women and talked with them about how they felt about their bodies,
specifically their vaginas. This resulted in a dramatic work that is as fearless and
daring as it is joyous, celebrating, entertaining, comedic and dramatic, and it has
opened the possibility for people of all ages and genders to dialogue about this once-
previous taboo subject. In her 2004 *The Good Body,* published by Villard, a division of Random House, the writing was created in the same way but this time the
focus is on the writer's and other women's thoughts and obsessions about their
bellies.

San Francisco's American Conservatory Theatre (founded in 1965) Web site states
that the playwright:

> Through her honest, insightful, and sometimes naughty portrayal of genuine experiences
> and real-life obsessions . . . strips the complicated issue of body politics down to its inti-
> mate essence, once again destroying pre-conceived notions about what women really
> think. This is new theater at its finest: *The Good Body* will move, inspire, entertain—and
> just might make you blush a bit in the process.

Horton Foote (1916–). Horton Foote has received two Academy Awards and one Pulitzer Prize in 1995 for *The Young Man From Atlanta.* As Williams wrote solely about the South, Foote has focused on life in a fictional Texas town. His plays have been produced on Broadway, Off-Broadway, Off-Off-Broadway, and at many regional theatres. His titles include: *The Carpetbagger's Children, Last of the Thortons, The Chase, The Trip to Bountiful, Lily Dale, The Widow Claire, The Death of Papa, Dividing the Estate, Talking Pictures, The Roads to Home,* and many one-act plays.

Brantley (2000), in his *New York Times* review of *Last of the Thorntons,* writes:

> In the plays of Horton Foote, the road to home is ultimately a road to nowhere. His chronicles of lives in the fictional hamlet of Harrison, Tex., [sic] are pervaded with a sense of rootlessness that hardly accords with the American ideal of small-town solid-ity. (http://theater2.nytimes.com/mem/theater/treview.html?html_title=&tols_title=LAST%20OF%20THE%20THORNTONS,%20THE%20(PLAY)&pdate=20001204&byline=By%20BEN%20BRANTLEY&id=1077011432574)

He continues: "*The Last of the Thorntons* . . . is, in its way, as unrelenting an assessment of the human condition as *Waiting for Godot* [Samuel Beckett, Irish, 1948–1949]." And Michael Feingold (2001) writing for *The Village Voice* says:

> In his plays, the flat landscape seems to breed flat recitals of data that pass for dialogue, flat assertions that pass for conflict, flat terminations that pass for dramatic resolution. Yet in this stagy aridity, Foote can grow a wavery ambiguity resembling the empty husk of drama, like the silage fed to cattle in the arid air outside his Texas interiors. The nutritive grain the husk might have contained has inexplicably vanished; to ask where and how only deepens the mystery. Like objects viewed from a great distance on an open plain, Foote's plays are never what they appear to be, but impossible to define as anything else. (http://www.villagevoice.com/theater/0051,sightlines,20993,11.html)

Brantley (2002) in a *New York Times* review says about *The Carpetbagger's Children:* "Few dramatists today can replicate this kind of storytelling with the gentle mas-tery that Mr. Foote provides" (http://theater2.nytimes.com/mem/theater/treview.html?html_title=&tols_title=CARPETBAGGER'S%20CHILDREN,%20THE%20(PLAY)&pdate=20020326&byline=By%20BEN%20BRANTLEY&id=1077011432326).

Charles Watson (2003, 1) writes in his biography about Foote:

> He is not a social protester like Arthur Miller, a constant experimenter with dramatic techniques like Eugene O'Neill, nor a psychological investigator like Tennessee Williams. Rather it is his sensitivity to the troubled men and women who live in Southeast Texas that gives his work unity.

His work is regarded as in the same vein as Anton Chekhov's.

Pamela Gien (c. 1957–). Gien's play *The Syringa Tree* received an Obie for Best Play in 2001. It adds to the rich literary tradition of one-person shows. This play was adapted into a film directed by Larry Moss (dates unknown), the Los Angeles and New York City acting coach and teacher who authored the acting book *The Intent to Live* (2004). Ms. Gien grew up in a suburb of Johannesburg. From her seemingly personal piece, largely concerned with apartheid's racism and violence, she creates a dozen or more roles spanning 20 years' time. The main character is the little girl, ostensibly, herself. Bruce Weber (2000) in a *New York Times* review called Gien a "gifted writer [who] has an unyielding spine as a storyteller" (http://query.nytimes.com/gst/fullpage.html?res=9E01E2DE133BF932A1575AC0A9669C8B63).

Richard Greenberg (1958–). Greenberg is the 2003 Tony Award winner for Best Play for *Take Me Out.* His other twenty-four plays include: *The Author's Voice, The American Plan, Eastern Standard, Three Days of Rain, The Dazzle,* and *The Violet Hour.* He, like Tony Kushner (born 1956) and the creator of the musical *Rent,* Jonathan Larson (1960–1996), is among the early group of dramatists writing about people living with HIV. Greenberg talks about being a gay playwright and suggests that he does not want to only write in any one theme or genre so that he is only known as a "gay playwright." He states in an interview with Jim Provenzano (date of interview unknown): "All you ever do is write about what you don't know, or who you aren't. That's the whole point, to go outside the lines of yourself." Brantley (2006) in *The New York Times,* says of Greenberg's work that: "existential enigmas and conundrums of faith . . . always pepper this playwright's work" (http://theater2.nytimes.com/2006/04/20/theater/reviews/20rain.html?pagewanted=print).

In addition to gay themes the playwright also deals with the question of time, how memories of the past influence the present and vice versa.

Three Days of Rain depicts life for three riddled New Yorkers who struggle to find their identity. It explores how adult children wrestle with confusions with their parent's struggles. Chicago's Steppenwolf Theatre (founded in 1974) describes this play as one that:

> Evaluates the emotional desolation, the lack of answers and the negativity of the 1990s, and then spins backward to reveal the premises of a happier decade that progressively broke down into the defeated present.

On a different theme is *The Violet Hour,* a wonderfully biting play about literary figures, the future, and how to be on the artistic and commercial cutting edge. Faber and Faber, Inc. published the work in 2004. Charles Isherwood (2003, 3) of *Variety* puns that it is: "A chamber piece that muses on the elusive intersections between the past, the present and the future . . . Greenberg has concocted an ingenious time-travel story with a novel twist."

John Guare (1938–). Guare's first major success was in 1968 with the one-act *Muzeeka,* which won an Obie Award. In 1971, he met great acclaim with *House of Blue Leaves,* a semi-autobiographical play that won him an Obie and the New York Drama Critics Circle Award for the Best American Play of 1970–71. He also received four Tony Awards during its 1986 revival. Guare also authored *Six Degrees of Separation* (1990), which won the New York Drama Critics Circle Award, the Dramatists Guild Hull-Warriner Award and an Olivier Best Play Award. The playscript was made into a movie in 1993 starring Will Smith and Stockard Channing. In 2002 Guare wrote a play about Ulysses S. Grant called *A Few Stout Individuals.* Also in 2002, he wrote the book to the successful Broadway musical, *Sweet Smell of Success,* based on the 1957 film of the same name. In 2003 Guare won The PEN/Laura Pels Foundation Awards for Drama. Brantley (2002) comments about *A Few Stout Individuals* in a *New York Times* review:

> The evening's dominant subject is the nature and purpose of memory. This in turn is weighed from the points of view of both Western and Eastern civilizations, of history and

art, of mortality and immortality. The scope of reference matches the play's ambitions, with allusions to everything from Pompeii to Edmund Wilson, all tossed into one crazy salad. Mr. Guare also returns happily to two of his favorite subjects: the circus of celebrity and the circus known as New York City. (http://query.nytimes.com/gst/fullpage. html?res=9D0CE2DB1739F930A25756C0A9649C8B63&partner=rssnyt&emc=rss)

Cohen (2003, 104) claims that Guare is "an eternal experimenter . . . always provocative, always challenging norms."

Stephen Adly Guirgis (c. 1972–). Guirgis's plays are heavily character-driven and usually deal with religion, death and/or persecution. They include: *The Last Days Of Judas Iscariot,* set in a modern-day courtroom, which sets forth the question as to whether or not Judas could find redemption; *Our Lady of 121st Street,* which explores what happens when a dead alcoholic nun's body turns up missing at her own funeral and probes the flaws of each of the complex and struggling characters; *Jesus Hopped The A Train,* about two prisoners in Riker's Island; and *In Arabia We'd All Be Kings.* All four plays are published in an anthology by Faber and Faber in 2003. Guirgis is a member of New Dramatists, MCC Theater Playwrights' Coalition, New River Dramatists, The Actors Studio Playwright/Directors Unit, as well as LABrynth Theatre, for which Philip Seymour Hoffman is a member; he has directed several of Guirgis' plays. Brantley (2005) in a *New York Times* review says that Guirgis writes with: "a fierce and questing mind that refuses to settle for glib answers, a gift for identifying with life's losers and an unforced eloquence that finds the poetry in lowdown street talk" (http://theater2.nytimes.com/mem/theater/treview.html?res=9B06E0DB133DF930A35750C0A9639C8B63).

A.R. Gurney (1930–). Gurney writes comedies and dramas that deal with academic life and critiques White Anglo-Protestant viewpoints. He also retells Biblical stories and ancient Greek dramas. His plays: *The Dining Room, The Golden Age, What I Did Last Summer, The Cocktail Hour, Love Letters,* and *Another Antigone* make Gurney one of America's most successful playwrights. In 2001 and 2003, respectively, he wrote two new plays: *Buffalo Gal* and *O Jerusalem.* His awards include: the Drama Desk, the Rockefeller Foundation, the Lucille Lortel Foundation, and the American Academy of Arts and Letters. His collected play volumes are published with Smith and Kraus, Inc.

Tony Kushner (1956–). Kushner, a gay Jewish socialist, perhaps best known for *Angels in America: A Gay Fantasia on National Themes* (1991) for which he won the Pulitzer Prize, had two important publications in 2000 by TCG, Inc. The first was *Homebody/Kabul* and the second was *Death & Taxes: Hydriotaphia & Other Plays. Angels* was made into both a television miniseries in 2003 starring Al Pacino (born 1940) and Meryl Streep (born 1949) and other celebrated actors, as well as an opera by Peter Eötvös (born 1944, Hungarian), which debuted in 2006. Andrea Bernstein (1995) in a *Mother Jones* article, says Kushner is most concerned with "the moral responsibilities of people in politically repressive times" (http://www.motherjones.com/arts/qa/1995/07/bernstein.html).

In that same article Kushner himself says:

You have to have hope. It's irresponsible to give false hope, which I think a lot of playwrights are guilty of. But I also think it's irresponsible to simply be a nihilist, which quite a lot of playwrights, especially playwrights younger than me, have become guilty of. I don't believe you would bother to write a play if you really had no hope.

Neil LaBute (1963–). When people read a LaBute play, they may be surprised to learn that he attended Brigham Young University and was a member of The Church of Jesus Christ of Latter-day Saints, since the themes of his plays address human darkness without preaching this as evil. Brantley (2001), in a *New York Times* review, said: "This is a writer, after all, who has built his reputation on presuming to know, like the Shadow, exactly what evil lurks in the hearts of men" (http://query.nytimes.com/gst/fullpage.html?res=9806E3DD163FF932A25753C1A9679C8B63).

LaBute has achieved acclaim from critics for these dark portraits. In 2000 he wrote *Bash: Latter-Day Plays,* a trio of short plays that expose good Latter-day Saints doing bad things. This play resulted in his disfellowship (which is not as harsh as excommunication) from the LDS Church. He has since formally left the church.

LaBute's 2002 response to 9/11, *The Mercy Seat,* focuses on the main character, an employee of the World Trade Center, who was away when the planes hit because he was with his mistress. This character then considers using the tragedy as a way to leave his family. *The Shape of Things* (2001) was made into a film in 2003 and deals with such timeless questions as what art is, and brings with it a hip and contemporary psychopathic twist. It also deals with emotional intimacy and what people are willing to do for love. He is a vibrant playwright who offers shocking and surprising scripts that reach out to a contemporary audience. His other plays include: *Fat Pig, Autobahn: A Short Play Cycle,* and *This is How it Goes: A Play.* He is the author of several screenplays including: *Nurse Betty, In the Company of Men* and *Your Friends and Neighbors.*

Warren Leight (c. 1957–). Warren Leight is a serio-comic writer whose autobiographical *Side Man* won the 1999 Tony Award for Best Play and his 2001 *Glimmer, Glimmer and Shine,* which is not a sequel to the Tony winner, also dealt with the world of jazz musicians and the difficulties presented for families involved with that life. Evan Yionoulis, the director of the two above-mentioned productions, wrote the Foreword in the Grove Press (2001, vii) publication of the latter-mentioned play, in which he said:

> I was attracted to the play's exploration of how the choices of one generation impact the next and how the avoidance of excess doesn't always lead to balance. It's a piece about a broken family whose members are forced to confront one another again and for the first time. There is wonderful comic energy but also a great deal of heart.

Leight also authored musicals and is the Vice-President of the Writers Guild of America, East Council; and a member of the Dramatists Guild Council. Critics have likened Leight to O'Neill and the comic playwright Neil Simon (born 1927).

Tracey Letts (1965–). Actor as well as playwright, Letts is a member of the esteemed Steppenwolf Theatre Company and is the author of *Bug,* which is set in a run-down Okie motel where Agnes, a divorced waitress with a penchant for cocaine, befriends Peter, a soft-spoken Gulf War veteran. They shack up while she hides from her violent ex-husband who is recently released from prison. They soon realize that the motel has a bug infestation problem, which they come to believe is part of a conspiracy against Peter and part of the side-effects of experiments conducted while he was at a veteran's hospital. The play is funny, but also shocking, violent, and even repulsive. Brantley (2004) writes in *The New York Times* that the play is: "obscenely exciting." *Bug* enjoyed critical acclaim during its Off-Broadway run. *Man From Nebraska* was a Pulitzer Prize finalist in 2004 and Letts's early work

Killer Joe is about homicidal trailer trash. Letts's most recent play, *August: Osage County* has been called by many critics one of the best American plays in recent memory, is a black comedy about a highly disturbing family. It opened on Broadway in late 2007.

Romulus Linney (1930–). Linney is a highly regarded dramatist who has created many adaptations for the stage. In addition to writing novels and short stories, Linney has won two Obie awards, (one for sustained excellence in playwriting), two National Critics Awards, three DramaLogue Awards, and numerous fellowships, including grants from the Guggenheim and Rockefeller Foundations. He has written: *Lark, Klonksy and Schwartz, The Sorrows of Frederick, Holy Ghosts, Childe Byron, Heathen Valley,* and most recently, an adaptation of Ernest L. Gaines's novel *A Lesson Before Dying,* for which Linney said to interviewer Mary Flinn (2002) that he was a "very faithful adaptor." *Lesson* was published in 2001 by Dramatists Play Service, Inc. In 2000, Smith and Krauss published *Nine Adaptations for the American Stage,* which include: *Gint, Lesson* and *Lark.*

Linney is a member of the American Academy of Arts and Science, the American Academy of Arts and Letters and many other institutions for dramatists. He is the father of the popular actress Laura Linney.

Kenneth Lonergan (1962–). Lonergan, author of 2002's *Lobby Hero,* is probably better known to commercial audiences for his 2000 screenplay *You Can Count On Me.* Contemporary legend has it that Lonergan began writing the script for the film during a writer's circle at New York's Ensemble Studio Theatre (founded in 1969). This fact encourages young writers to also write in a workshop environment. *Lobby Hero* can be considered a comedy; however, the genre it sits in is more comfortably seriocomic, since Lonergan explores more serious themes of loneliness and missed connections with a clear dramatic weight. Other plays include: *Waverly Gallery* (nominated for a Pulitzer), a touching serio-comedy that seems quite personal, about a 50-year old adult child dealing with her ailing mother and her son whose relationship with his grandmother is very dear to him. Brantley (2001) in a *New York Times* review says this about Lonergan:

> Mr. Lonergan knows that the road to ruin is paved with intentions that are neither good nor bad but overwhelmingly mixed. His characters—whether addled by drugs (as in *Youth*), Alzheimer's (*Waverly*) or everyday indecision—are a combustible brew of impulses that they can't begin to sort out. (http://query.nytimes.com/gst/fullpage.html?res=9F04EFD8113AF937A25750C0A9679C8B63&partner=rssnyt&emc=rss)

David Mamet (1947–). Mamet was an actor and director before he reached success in 1976 with three Off-Off Broadway plays: *The Duck Variations, Sexual Perversity in Chicago,* and *American Buffalo,* which was made into a film in 1996. His works are known for their clever, clipped, and sometimes vulgar speech and for his interest in high-octane masculinity. The way he writes has become signature and many playwrights try to copy his terse style. Other plays include: *Glengarry Glen Ross* (1984 Pulitzer Prize winner), about the underbelly of corporate greed, which was made into a film in 1992 starring Alec Baldwin, Al Pacino, and an all-star cast; *Speed-the-Plow,* about the ugliness of the entertainment business; and *Oleana* (film version in 1994) about what constitutes sexual harassment between a college professor soon to be tenured and a young female student. Comedic writer David Ives (born 1950) both spoofs and honors Mamet with his work *Speed-the-Play.* More recent plays include: *Faustus,* his adaptation of the Jacobean play, which appeared at San Francisco's Magic Theatre (founded in 1967) and was published by Vintage Books, and *Boston Marriage* in 2002, which was also made into a film. Mamet has taught at the Yale Drama School and New York University. His awards are numerous and they include: Obie Awards in 1976 and1983; New York Drama Critics Circle Awards in 1977 and 1984; and the Tony Award in 1987. Mamet, with actor William H. Macy (born 1950), created the Atlantic Theater Company (founded in 1983) and the Atlantic Theatre's actor training program where they believe that the story of the play and the intent of its playwright are essential to the creative process. He has also written books on acting, directing, writing, as well as the film and theatre businesses, which include: *True and False: Heresy and Common Sense for the Actor* (1999), *Writing in Restaurants* (1987) and *Three Uses of the Knife* (2002).

   Donald Margulies (1954–). Margulies is a writer who is interested in Jewish themes. In 1992, Margulies achieved notoriety with *Sight Unseen,* about a painter who leaves a London exhibition of his artwork to visit his former lover. He explores themes of: Anti-Semitism, art, and lost love. *Sight Unseen* won an Obie for Best New American Play. Some of his other plays include: *Found a Peanut, The Loman Family Picnic, Pitching to the Star, Luna Park, What's Wrong With This Picture?, The Model Apartment,* and *The God of Vengeance* (Theatre Communications Group, Inc., 2004), an adaptation of the 1906 Yiddish melodrama written by Shalom Asch about a father who, though renting to a brothel on the first floor of his tenement building, desires that his daughter lives the American Jewish dream, marrying well to a rabbi. His daughter, however, is more preoccupied with her relationship with one of the prostitutes. The 2000 Pulitzer Prize winner *Dinner With Friends* exposes the vulnerability of contemporary middle-class marriages. It was made into a film in 2001, directed by Norman Jewison. Margulies was nominated for a Pulitzer for *Collected Stories* (1996), which played on Broadway with the legendary Uta Hagen as the Jewish writer toward the end of her career betrayed by her young disciple, and was made into a PBS Teleplay. He was elected to the Dramatists Guild Council in 1993 and received grants from: the New York Foundation for the Arts, the National Endowment for the Arts and the John Simon Guggenheim Foundation.

   Terrence McNally (1939–). Early in his career, McNally was a protégé of the noted playwright *Edward Albee.* Later in his career, McNally became successful with *Frankie and Johnny at the Claire de Lune* (1987), starring Kathy Bates (born 1948) Off-Broadway and later starred Al Pacino and Michelle Pfeiffer in the 1991 film version. The Broadway revival starred Edie Falco (born 1963) of the famed TV show *The Sopranos* and Stanley Tucci (born 1960). McNally is a groundbreaking writer in his fierce works that speak against homophobia. Plays of this category include: *Lips Together, Teeth Apart;* the collaboration with Kander and Ebb on the musical *Kiss of the Spider Woman,* for which he wrote the book; *Love! Valour! Compassion!;* and *The Lisbon Traviata* and *Master Class,* both about diva opera soprano Maria Callas. *Master Class* won the 1996 Tony Award for Best Play and the Pulitzer Prize. In 1997, McNally's *Corpus Christi* was the focus of many church and religious right uprisings that tried to ban the play and several of its productions. The play reclaims the story of Jesus, creating a world where his disciples are homosexuals. The premiere performance at the Manhattan Theatre Club was cancelled due to death threats against board members, but Tony Kushner and other playwrights threatened to remove their plays if *Corpus Christi* was not produced. The board allowed the production to proceed. About 2,000 protesters picketed the opening, but the play continued and still continues to be produced.

In addition to four Tony Awards, McNally also received two Guggenheim Fellowships, a Rockefeller Grant, the Lucille Lortel Award, the Hull-Warriner Award, and a citation from the American Academy of Arts and Letters. He has been a member of the Dramatists Guild Council since 1970 and has served as vice-president since 1981. Recent plays include: *The Stendhal Syndrome: Full Frontal Nudity and Prelude & Liebestod* (2004) where McNally explores art, lust and longing and *Dedication or the Stuff of Dreams* (2005), which suffered from terrible critical reviews in its New York production.

Arthur Miller (1915–2005). Perhaps he could be considered the quintessential American playwright. His long body of work and recent death mark an era in dramatic literature made rich because of his contribution. Many of his plays are now considered American classics and they include: *The Crucible, A View from the Bridge, After the Fall, All My Sons,* and *Death of a Salesman* (1949 Pulitzer Prize in Drama winner). *Resurrection Blues* and *Finishing the Picture* are his last works, written in 2002 and 2004, respectively. Robert Cohen (2003, 99–100) says about Miller: "No other playwright in the current theatre has so aggressively called society to task for its failures nor so passionately told the audience to pay attention to the world around them."

Milly S. Barranger in *Theatre: A Way of Seeing* (2002, 90) calls Miller a "moralist and social dramatist." Barranger continues: "His plays deal with the individual's responsibility in the face of society's emphasis on such false values as material success and personal happiness at any price."

Anne Nelson (dates unknown). Nelson, who never wrote a play before *The Guys,* was a former war correspondent who covered El Salvador in the early 1980s and currently is Adjunct Associate Professor of International and Public Affairs at Columbia University. *The Guys* is autobiographical, and it is about her dealings with a downtown New York fire chief following 9/11, who, following the disaster, she assisted in writing the all too numerous eulogies. The play enjoyed a successful run at the Flea Theatre, an Off-Off Broadway theatre in downtown New York City, where Sigourney Weaver and Bill Murray created the roles, and performed to local audiences, including groups of firefighters. It was published in 2002 by Random House. The result is a moving dramatic work that articulates the emotions and longings many people have faced since September 11.

Lynn Nottage (1964–). Nottage has enjoyed recognition as an up and coming African American female playwright. Nottage's collection of plays: *Crumbs From The Table of Joy: And Other Plays* was published by TCG, Inc. in 2004, and includes *Crumbs from the Table of Joy, POOF!, Por'knockers; Mud, River, Stone;* and *Las Meninas.* Jason Zinoman in a *New York Times* article (2004) calls Nottage: "An equal-opportunity satirist, Ms. Nottage sends up characters of several races" (http://query.nytimes.com/gst/fullpage.html?res=9C01E2DC1630F930A25755C0A 9629C8B63).

In 1999/2000 Nottage received a NEA/TCG grant for a residency at Philadelphia's Freedom Theatre (founded in 1966) it is the oldest African American theatre. She was awarded: Playwriting Fellowships from Manhattan Theatre Club, New Dramatists and the New York Foundation for the Arts, where she is a member of their Artists Advisory Board. In addition, she received a Guggenheim Fellowship in 2005. In 2003 *Intimate Apparel,* inspired by Nottage's own grandmother, tells the story of an African American seamstress's romantic troubles and entanglements and the world of the women around her who use her undergarments. The play was a contender for the Pulitzer Prize.

Dael Orlandersmith (1959–). Orlandersmith is an actress, poet and playwright who is best known for her Obie Award winning *Beauty's Daughter* (1995) and the 2002 Pulitzer Prize Finalist in Drama, *Yellowman,* which, according to Annie Nakao in *The San Francisco Chronicle* (2004) is: "a lyrical and brutal examination of the complexities of internalized prejudice and its centuries-old roots in slavery." In a September 1996 taping of the radio show "This American Life," Orlandersmith performs *When You Talk About Music* in which she portrays a thirty-one-year-old male who meets a black woman at a mutual friend's wedding and finds how much he misses musical expression. Other plays include: *The Gimmick,* which deals with art and race; *Monster,* about a violent family history that passes from one generation to another, with the narrator, a young women, using stories, poetry and a variety of characters to introduce and juxtapose situations. Her collection, *Beauty's Daughter, Monster, The Gimmick: Three Plays* is published by Vintage Books (2000).

Suzan-Lori Parks (1964–). Parks has enjoyed great critical acclaim as a young African American female. While attending Mount Holyoke College, Parks was a student of James Baldwin (1924–1987). He suggested she write plays; thankfully, she listened. Parks credits Mount Holyoke later in life for her success. She said in a newspaper interview that she was inspired by Pulitzer Prize-winning playwright Wendy Wasserstein. In 2001, *The Red Letter Plays* were published by TCG books with: *In the Blood* and *Fucking A. Topdog/Underdog* was the winner of the 2002 Pulitzer Prize for Drama. Since 2000, she authored: *365 Plays/365 Days,* for which she wrote a play a day for an entire year. Robert Cohen (2003, 114) writes:

> Writing about the black experience in America—slavery, lynchings, poverty, discrimination, minstrelsy, and racism are common themes—she rejects both realism and easy polemics, preferring a savagely comic irony and freshly minted language to diatribes or bald recountings.

Adam Rapp (1968–). Rapp was the recipient of the Herbert & Patricia Brodkin Scholarship, two Lincoln Center le Compte du Nouy Awards, a fellowship to the Camargo Foundation in Cassis, France, the 1999 Princess Grace Award for Playwrighting, a 2000 Suite Residency with Mabou Mines, a 2000 Roger L. Stevens Award from the Kennedy Center Fund for New American Plays, and the 2001 Helen Merrill Award for Emerging Playwrights. Rapp's prolific list of plays include these titles written between 2000–2005: *Animals and Plants, Bingo with the Indians, Blackbird, Dreams of the Salthorse, Faster, Finer Noble Gases, Gompers, Mistral, Nocturne* and *Stone Cold Dead Serious.*

Bruce Weber in a *New York Times* review (2003) says of Rapp:

> He writes with an urgent, galloping imagination, as if his fingers on the keyboard can't keep up with his racing brain. An eager experimenter, he needs a governor, or the self-editing impulse that generally comes with age—or at least a strict dramaturge . . . His overall subject is coming of age in the contemporary American heartland, an enterprise he views as fearful and portrays with pained sympathy. Generally set in Illinois (Mr. Rapp grew up in Joliet), but with a clear sense that the American landscape is full of places that are hopelessly distant from opportunity, his plays are full of horribly lost teenagers who are entirely unequipped for the assumption of citizenship. Casually

vulgar, poorly educated, television-savvy, arrogant and grabby, they seem to know nothing of substance that any current adult might recognize as useful, aside from bits of technological expertise. (http://query.nytimes.com/gst/fullpage.html?res= 9C0DE5DF173AF93BA25757C0A9659C8B63)

John Patrick Shanley (1950–). Shanley grew up in the Bronx. In his personal biography that appears in the *Playbill* for his 2005 Pulitzer Prize winning *Doubt, a parable,* he writes:

John Patrick Shanley is from the Bronx. He was thrown out of St. Helena's kindergarten. He was banned from St. Anthony's hot lunch program for life. He was expelled from Cardinal Spellman High School. He was placed on academic probation by New York University and instructed to appear before a tribunal if he wished to return. When asked why he had been treated in this way by all these institutions, he burst into tears and said he had no idea. Then he went in the United States Marine Corps. He did fine. He's still doing okay.

Shanley's list of plays include: (plays from the 1980s) *Welcome to the Moon, Danny and the Deep Blue Sea, Savage In Limbo, The Dreamer Examines His Pillow, Italian American Reconciliation, Women of Manhattan, All For Charity;* (plays from the 1990s) *The Big Funk, Beggars in the House of Plenty, What Is This Everything?, Kissing Christine, Missing Marisa, Four Dogs and a Bone, The Wild Goose, Psychopathia Sexualis;* and (plays from 2000) *Where's My Money?, Cellini, Dirty Story, Doubt, a parable, Sailor's Song,* and *Defiance.*

Brantley writes in a *New York Times* review (2005):

Doubt is an unusually quiet work for Mr. Shanley, a writer who made his name with rowdy portraits of bruising love affairs. But gentleness becomes this dramatist. Even as *Doubt* holds your conscious attention as an intelligently measured debate play, it sends off stealth charges that go deeper emotionally. (http://query.nytimes.com/gst/ fullpage.html?res=9801E4D8123CF932A35757C0A9639C8B63&sec=&spon=& pagewanted=all)

Sam Shepard (1943–). Shepard has made a great impact on New York's off-off-Broadway theatre scene and he has a long list of plays written in the 1970s and 1980s. He is also a film actor and director, and has appeared on the cover of *Newsweek* after marrying actress Jessica Lange, when they met on the set of their film *Frances.* In 1976 Shepard moved to San Francisco where he was the playwright in residence at the Magic Theatre, where much of his work received world premieres. The most notable of these works include: *Buried Child* (1979 Pulitzer Prize winner), *Curse of the Starving Class, True West* and *A Lie of the Mind* in 1985. In 1986 *Fool for Love* was made into a film by Robert Altman. Also, he went from Off-Off Broadway, to the larger spotlight of Broadway with his play *A Lie of the Mind.* Robert Cohen (2003, 105) says of Shepard's plays, that they are:

basically prose poems; the language is musical, and the subject matter, which is generally contemporary and American, suggests modern myth more than everyday reality. His plays, which invariably involve sex and violence, create arresting . . . images and tantalize the audience with moments of extreme surface realism that ultimately open into something more abstract.

In 2002 Vintage Books published: *The Late Henry Moss, Eyes for Consuela, When the World Was Green: Three Plays,* and *When the World Was Green* with Joseph Chaiken (his profound mentor and collaborator). *The God of Hell* was published in 2005 by Vintage Books.

Anna Deavere Smith (1950–). Smith does not shy away from controversy. She is celebrated for her one-woman dramatic works inspired by American current events. She writes these works from interviews with people directly or indirectly involved. As she performs them she takes on the gestures, voice, and emotional and psychological characteristics of as many as 40 men and women who make up her plays. She was awarded the prestigious MacArthur Fellowship (known as the "genius grant") in 1996. Her non-fiction dramas include: the 1991 *Fires in the Mirror,* about the Crown Heights Riots, which followed a young African American child's accidental death at the hands of a rabbi; the 1992 *Twilight: Los Angeles,* which dealt with the Los Angeles riots following the Rodney King verdict. In 2003 Anchor Books published her new works: *House Arrest and Piano: Two Plays.* Barranger (2002, 328) claims that Smith: "As a creator and performer . . . sets out to use the words of the voiceless and the powerful in society, creating a sophisticated and poetic dialogue about race relations in contemporary America."

Paula Vogel (1951–). Paula Vogel is a feminist author who won the 1998 Pulitzer Prize in Drama as well as the Obie, the Lortel Best Play Award, the Best Off-Broadway Play from the Outer Critics Circle, the Best Play from the Drama Desk, and the Best Play from the New York Drama Critics Circle. The awards are for *How I Learned to Drive,* which is about a pedophile and the complex relationship he has with his teenage and then college-age relative by marriage. Uncle Peck, the pedophile, is not a wholly unlikable character, and that allows for a highly nuanced work. Barranger (2002, 81) says of Vogel: "Unlike most writers on political issues, she is not interested in persuading audiences to adopt political or moral positions but rather to understand that there are no easy answers."

Other plays are: *Hot 'N' Throbbing,* with a new publication dated 2000, published by Dramatists Play Service, Inc.; *Swan Song of Sir Henry, Meg, Apple-Brown Betty, Desdemona, A Play about a Handkerchief, Bertha in Blue, The Oldest Profession, And Baby Makes Seven, The Mineola Twins,* and *The Long Christmas Ride Home. Baltimore Waltz* is another of her well-known plays, which is an autobiographical account of her brother who died of AIDS. Alvin Klein in his *New York Times* review (1993) says of the play: "it is a piece of original design, fresh imagination and extraordinary empathy that touches the heart" (http://query.nytimes.com/gst/fullpage.html?res=9F0CEED71239F935A25756C0A965958260).

August Wilson (1945–2005). In his life he wrote a decalogy of ten full-length plays. The plays are rich with deeply felt monologues that capture a variety of African American voices throughout a century. Each play represents a decade in twentieth century African American history. This cycle of plays include: *Gem of the Ocean* (2003) about the 1900s; *Joe Turner's Come and Gone* (1984) about the 1910s; *Ma Rainey's Black Bottom* (1982) about the 1920s; *The Piano Lesson* (1986, Pulitzer Prize winner) about the 1930s, which was made into a movie in 1995; *Seven Guitars* (1995) about the 1940s; *Fences* (1985, Pulitzer Prize winner) about the 1950s; *Two Trains Running* (1990) about the 1950s; *Jitney* (1982) about the 1970s, first published in the United States by The Overlook Press in 2003; *King Hedley II* (2001) about the 1980s; and *Radio Golf* (2005) about the 1990s. His list of awards is long, they include: seven New York Drama Critics Circle Awards for Best Play, six Tony

Award nominations for Best Play, two Drama Desk Awards for Outstanding New Play, the Tony Award for Best Play (*Fences*), the Literary Lion Award from the New York Public Library, the American Theatre Critics' Association Award (*Two Trains Running*), the National Humanities Medal (1999), and The Freedom of Speech Award at the U.S. Comedy Arts Festival (2004). Cohen (2003, 106) says of Wilson: "He glories, though not always uncritically, in black life, and is not at all interested in synthesizing races or glossing over cultural differences. A poet still, Wilson blends drama with profound observation and glorious, though disturbing, humanity."

Oscar Hijuelos, author of *The Mambo Kings Play Songs of Love* and the forthcoming *Twain and Stanley Enter Paradise* was a friend of Wilson. He retells this story in a 2005 *New York Times* article about a time they spent together:

> He loved discussing literature: Ralph Ellison, Gabriel García Márquez, James M. Cain, Jorge Luis Borges and Tennessee Williams were but a few of the writers we talked about over the years. We tried to maintain a scholarly tone about such things, especially when our wives were around, but when it was just the two of us, our upbringings kicked in and our language was riddled with scatological turns of phrase. August's sentences blossomed with such language, especially when we came to the history of slavery and the black man in this country. (http://www.nytimes.com/2005/10/09/opinion/09hijuelos.html)

Lanford Wilson (1937–). Wilson is a prolific writer whose plays include: (from the 1960s) *Balm in Gilead, The Rimers of Eldrich*, and *The Gingham Dog*; (from the 1970s) *Lemon Sky, Serenading Louie, Hot L Baltimore, The Mound Builders, Fifth of July*; (the 1980s) *Talley's Folly* (Pulitzer Prize winner of 1980), *A Tale Told*, later revised and renamed *Talley & Son, Angels Fall, Burn This*; (the 1990s) *Redwood Curtain, Sympathetic Magic*; and the 2000 *Book of Days*, published by Grove Press. Cohen (2003, 103) calls Wilson's work: "gentle, poetic, natural, and wise; increasingly his works focus on the larger social and philosophical contexts of contemporary life." He was a founding member with notable director Marshall W. Mason (born 1940) of the famed Circle Repertory Company (1969–1996) in New York City, where many of his plays had their debut.

Doug Wright (dates unknown). Wright is the recipient of a Pulitzer Prize and Tony Award for Best Play for *I am My Own Wife* in 2004. The play was created through exercises, research and interviews about the German transvestite Charlotte von Mahlsdorf, a survivor of both Nazism and Communism in East Germany. In a *New York Times* (2003) review Bruce Weber writes: "it is terrific enough to raise the highest expectations" (http://query.nytimes.com/gst/fullpage.html?res=9D0CE6D71031F93BA15756C0A9659C8B63).

In 2005 Faber and Faber, Inc. publish *Quills and Other Plays: Interrogating the Nude* about Marcel Duchamp and Man Ray and a very interesting exploration about art, novelty, and government; *Watbanaland,* which has political overtones of hunger, poverty, and American marriage; *Quills* about the Marquis de Sade, which is humorous but also darkly grotesque and poignant. The publication offers a colorful introduction entitled *Willful Misbehavior,* which provides an anecdote about a time in the writer's young life where he decided he like the "forbidden" in art. His plays certainly explore the forbidden. Wright has said about his own work:

> No human appetite is too base, no idea so holy, no institution so revered that it should be spared art's scrutiny. At its best, art can function in a society as its collective

conscience. And such a conscience is useless unless it can operate unchecked. Propaganda provides answers; art should stimulate questions. Dali, Duchamp and de Sade did more than churn out pages of prose or canvas after canvas. They each took center stage in their own time as agitators, while—at the same time—revolutionizing their respective crafts. I hope to follow their example. (http://www.mindspring.com/~horizonco/plays/quills/author.htm)

Mary Zimmerman (dates unknown). Zimmerman is a stage director and playwright most celebrated for her contemporary myths. She is a member of Chicago's Lookingglass Theatre Company (founded in 1989) and an artistic associate of The Goodman Theatre (founded in 1925). Much of her work is created while she works with her company of actors and designers; the company members will read source material together, while Zimmerman is responsible for weaving the dramatic text from their findings and collaborative engagement. Her play *Metamorphoses,* based on David R. Slavit's translation of *The Metamorphoses of Ovid,* was published in 2002 by Northwestern University Press. Deborah Garwood (2003, 71) in "Myth as Public Dream: The Metamorphosis of Mary Zimmerman's *Metamorphoses*" in *PAJ: Performing Art Journal,* states:

At the most accessible level, [*Metamorphoses*] provides abundant opportunities for the playwright to theatricalize myth as a hybrid of antiquity and twentieth-century culture. King Midas resembles a 1920s American industrialist millionaire. Erysichthon, though dressed in a toga, comes across as a greedy mogul unconcerned about the environment who pays dearly for incurring Ceres' wrath. The tale of Orpheus and Eurydice, as told by Ovid and by Rilke's poem, creates a poetic bridge between myth and modernism, artistic process and its inviolate root in the unconscious.

RECENT PULITZER PRIZES IN DRAMA

1990	*The Piano Lesson* by August Wilson
1991	*Lost in Yonkers* by Neil Simon
1992	*The Kentucky Cycle* by Robert Schenkkan
1993	*Angels in America: Millennium Approaches* by Tony Kushner
1994	*Three Tall Women* by Edward Albee
1995	*The Young Man From Atlanta* by Horton Foote
1996	*Rent* by the late Jonathan Larson
1997	(No Award)
1998	*How I Learned to Drive* by Paula Vogel
1999	*Wit* by Margaret Edson
2000	*Dinner With Friends* by Donald Margulies
2001	*Proof* by David Auburn
2002	*Topdog/Underdog* by Suzan-Lori Parks
2003	*Anna in the Tropics* by Nilo Cruz
2004	*I Am My Own Wife* by Doug Wright
2005	*Doubt, a parable* by John Patrick Shanley
2006	(No Award)
2007	*Rabbit Hole* by David Lindsay-Abaire

Source: Pulitzer Prize Web site. http://www.pulitzer.org/

Zimmerman received numerous awards, including the prestigious MacArthur Fellowship in 1998. Other works include: *Journey to the West, The Secret In The Wings, The Odyssey, The Arabian Nights, The Notebooks of Leonardo da Vinci* and *Eleven Rooms of Proust*. She is the director and co-librettist of the 2002 opera *Galileo Galilei* with music by Philip Glass (born 1937) commissioned by the Goodman Theatre.

Bibliography

Albee, Edward. *The Collected plays of Edward Albee*. Woodstock, New York: Overlook Press, 2004.

Auburn, David. *Proof: A Play*. New York: Faber & Faber, 2001.

Barranger, Milly S. *Theatre: A Way of Seeing*. Belmont, California: Wadsworth/Thomson Learning, 2002.

Cohen, Robert. *Theatre, Brief Version*. 6th ed. Boston: McGraw-Hill Custom Pub, 2003.

Cruz, Nilo. *Anna in the Tropics*. New York: Theatre Communications Group, 2003.

Donaghy, Tom. *The Beginning of August and Other Plays*. New York: Grove Press, 2000.

Ensler, Eve. *The Good Body*. New York: Villard, 2004.

———. *The Vagina Monologues*. New York: Villard, 2001.

Foote, Horton. *The Carpetbagger's Children*. New York: Dramatists Play Service, 2002.

———. *The Last of the Thorntons*. Woodstock, NY: Overlook, 2000.

Greenberg, Richard. *Three Days of Rain*. New York: Dramatists Play Service, 1999.

———. *The Violet Hour*. New York: Faber & Faber, 2004.

Guare, John. *A Few Stout Individuals*. New York: Grove Press, 2003.

———. *Six Degrees of Separation*. New York: Random House, 1990.

Guirgis, Stephen Adly. *Our Lady of 121st Street; Jesus Hopped the A Train; In Arabia We'd All Be Kings*. New York: Faber & Faber, 2003.

Gurney, A.R. *Collected Plays*, Volumes I and III. Lyme, NH: Smith and Kraus, 1997; 2000.

Kushner, Tony. *Angels in America: A Gay Fantasia on National Themes*. New York: Theatre Communications Group, 1993.

LaBute, Neil. *Bash: Latterday Plays*. Woodstock, NY: Overlook, 2003.

———. *The Mercy Seat*. New York: Faber & Faber, 2003.

———. *The Shape of Things*. New York: Faber & Faber, 2001.

Leight, Warren. *Glimmer, Glimmer, and Shine*. New York: Grove Press, 2001.

Letts, Tracy. *Bug*. New York: Dramatists Play Service, 2005.

Linney, Romulus. *Nine Adaptations for the American Stage*. Hanover, NH: Smith and Kraus, 2000.

———. *Six Plays*. New York: Theatre Communications Group, 1993.

Lonergan, Kenneth. *Lobby Hero*. New York: Grove Press, 2001.

———. *The Waverly Gallery*. New York: Grove Press, 2000.

Mamet, David. *Glenngary Glen Ross*. New York: Grove Press, 1984.

———. *Oleana*. New York: Vintage, 1993.

Margulies, Donald. *Sight Unseen and Other Plays*. New York: Theatre Communications Group, 1995.

McNally, Terrence. *Corpus Christi*. New York: Grove Press, 1998.

———. *Frankie and Johnny in the Clair de Lune*. Garden City, NY: Fireside Theatre, 1987.

Miller, Arthur. *Collected Plays*. New York: Viking, 1981.

Nelson, Anne. *The Guys*. New York: Random House, 2002.

Nottage, Lynn. *Crumbs From the Table of Joy and Other Plays*. New York: Theatre Communications Group, 2004.

Orlandersmith, Dael. *Beauty's Daughter, Monster, The Gimmick: Three Plays*. New York: Vintage, 2004.

Parks, Suzan-Lori. *The Red Letter Plays*. New York: Theatre Communications Group, 2001.

Shanley, John Patrick. *Doubt: A Parable.* New York: Theatre Communications Group, 2005.

Shepard, Sam. *Fool for Love and Other Plays.* New York: Bantam, 1984.

———. *A Lie of the Mind.* New York: New American Library, 1987.

———. *Seven Plays.* New York: Bantam, 1981.

Smith, Anna Deavere. *Fires in the Mirror.* New York: Anchor, 1993.

———. *House Arrest and Piano: Two Plays.* New York: Anchor, 2004.

———. *Twilight: Los Angeles.* New York: Anchor, 1994.

Son, Diana. *Stop/Kiss.* Woodstock, NY: Overlook, 1999.

Vena, Gary, and Andrea Nouryeh, eds. *Drama and Performance: An Anthology.* New York: HarperCollins College Publishers, 1996.

Vogel, Paula. *How I Learned to Drive.* New York: Dramatists Play Service, 1997.

Watson, C. S. *Horton Foote: A Literary Biography.* The Jack and Doris Smothers series in Texas history, life, and culture, no. 9. Austin: University of Texas Press, 2003.

Wickham, Glynne. *A History of the Theatre.* 2nd ed. Oxford: Phaidon, 1992.

Wilson, August. *Century Cycle.* New York: Theatre Communications Group, 2007.

Wilson, Lanford. *Collected Plays: 1965–1970.* Lyme, NH: Smith and Kraus, 1996.

Wright, Doug. *I Am My Own Wife.* New York: Dramatists Play Service, 2005.

———. *Quills and Other Plays.* New York: Faber & Faber, 2005.

Zimmerman, Mary. *Metamorphosis: A Play.* Evanston, IL: Northwestern University Press, 2002.

Further Reading

American Conservatory Theatre's website: http://act-sf.org/goodbody/; Bernstein, Andrea. "Tony Kushner: ARTS:The award-winning author of Angels in America advises you to trust neither art nor artists." *Mother Jones:* July/August 1995; Brantley, Ben. "A Fractious Family's Decline, With Vintage Mustiness." *The New York Times:* March 26, 2002; Brantley, Ben. "As a Nun Stands Firm, The Ground Shifts Below." *The New York Times:* April 1, 2005; Brantley, Ben. "Bewildered Ringmaster In a Celebrity Circus." *The New York Times:* May 13, 2002; Brantley, Ben. "Enough Said About *Three Days of Rain.* Let's Talk Julia Roberts!" *The New York Times:* April 20, 2006; Brantley, Ben. "Judas Gets His Day in Court, but Satan Is on the Witness List." *The New York Times:* March 3, 2005; Brantley, Ben. "Lonely People Aren't Nice; Just Ask One." *The New York Times:* October 12, 2000; Brantley, Ben. "Motel Tale: Down and Out (and Itchy and Scratchy) in Oklahoma." *The New York Times:* March 1, 2004; Brantley, Ben. "The Poetry of Yearning, The Artistry of Seduction." *The New York Times:* November 17, 2003; Brantley, Ben. "The Road to Ruin? Through the Lobby, Sir." *The New York Times:* March 14, 2001; Brantley, Ben. "They Meet in a Gallery, God Looking On." *The New York Times:* October 11, 2001; Brantley, Ben. "Wry Smiles Temper the Anguish of Old Age." *The New York Times:* December 4, 2000; Garwood, Deborah. "Myth as Public Dream: The Metamorphosis of Mary Zimmerman's *Metamorphoses.*" *PAJ: A Journal of Performance and Art,* 25.1 (2003) 69–78; Feingold, Michael. "Sightlines: Francine Russo on Circus Oz; Michael Feingold on *The Last of the Thorntons.*" *The Village Voice:* December 27–January 2, 2001; Flinn, Mary. "Interview with Mary Flinn and Romulus Linney" [Online, Spring 2002, vol. 1, no. 1]. Blackbird: an online journal of literature and the arts. http://www.blackbird.vcu.edu/v1n1/features/linney_r_81502/linney_r_text.htm; From the Playwright http://www.mindspring.com/~horizonco/plays/quills/author.htm; Hijuelos, Oscar. "A Last Round With August Wilson." *The New York Times:* October 9, 2005; Isherwood, Charles. "Future tense in delicate *Violet.*" *Variety:* November, 2003; Klein, Alvin. "At Yale Rep, *The Baltimore Waltz.*" *The New York Times:* May 16, 1993; Nakao, Annie. "Play explores corrosive prejudice within black community." *The San Francisco Chronicle:* January 28, 2004; "OUTfield: An Interview with Playwright Richard Greenberg," Jim Provenzano on-line at Temenos: http://www.temenos.net/articles/04-09-04.shtml; Ozols, Jennifer Barrett. "Eve Ensler Redefines the Meaning of *Good Body.*" *Newsweek:* November 12, 2004; Richards, David. "Critical Winds Shift for Albee, A Master of the Steady Course." The New

York Times: April 13, 1994; Steppenwolf Theatre website: http://www.steppenwolf.org/backstage/article.aspx?id=118; Weber, Bruce. "Charming, Lying and Even Killing to Survive." *The New York Times:* May 28, 2003; Weber, Bruce. "Cruelties of Apartheid, Chronicled by a Child." *The New York Times:* September 21, 2000; Weber, Bruce. "Young in the Heartland, Seeking Video Salvation." *The New York Times:* April 18, 2003; Zinoman, Jason. "Lynn Nottage Enters Her Flippant Period." *The New York Times:* June 13, 2004.

ROBIN REESE

DYSTOPIAN FICTION

Definition. Dystopian literature describes an ideal society that has gone terribly wrong. Because dystopian literature was developed after the industrial revolution, advanced technology often plays an important role in the societies authors create. Typically, the imagined society was intended to feature a generally fair political system, but that system has instead created near-universal slavery. Conformity to this social system is enforced by a vigilant and brutal police force and a government-controlled media that bombards citizens with propaganda. Sometimes the dystopian societies authors create are plagued by shortages of food, fuel, and other essentials, while other dystopias are marked by a material abundance that serves to give the government ever-greater control over the dependant populace. Because dystopian literature developed in response to utopian literature, fictional dystopias often resemble fictional utopias. The inhabitants of both types of imagined societies are required to follow schedules, share meals, live in communal housing, or otherwise limit their personal choices.

Dystopian literature typically features a main character who is at first a satisfied—and sometimes prominent—citizen. Discomfort with the stifling regimentation of the totalitarian regime she or he lives under leads the protagonist to question the wisdom of the government. This questioning leads to violations of some of the many rules that govern daily life. Often, the protagonist will subsequently become involved with a resistance movement. The police typically then step in and force the protagonist to reform and commit to serving the interests of the state. Dystopian literature can also feature protagonists who are never aware that they live in a deeply flawed society. Authors create dystopian literature in order to make a comment about the society in which they themselves live. Sometimes authors create a dystopia as a warning about what their society may become. Under different circumstances, an author might create a dystopia to directly criticize the failings of the society in which he or she lives. *Dystopian* can also be used as an adjective to describe elements of otherwise non-dystopian texts that deal with an oppressive society or to describe political conditions that exist in the real world. This entry focuses on works of fiction that were deliberately created to depict a totalitarian society that governs through outright intimidation or the creation of false needs.

History. Although John Stuart Mill is reported to have used the term *dystopia* in a speech to Britain's parliament in 1868, the word was not directly associated with literary studies until Glenn Negley and Max J. Patrick made extensive use of the term in their 1952 book *Quest for Utopia.* Many scholars believe Jules Verne's *The Begum's Fortune,* published in 1879 as *Les Cinq cents millions de la Begum,* is the first novel to portray elements of a dystopian society, though it does not display all of the characteristics just discussed. Verne's book tells the story of two men who inherit a fortune from a distant relative who had married into Indian royalty. The Frenchman Dr. Sarrasin uses his share of the money to create a vaguely Fourierist utopian colony in Oregon. The German Professor Schultze uses his share of the money to create a totalitarian city-state dedicated to arms production just a few kilometers away from Sarrasin's colony. Schultze's high-tech Steel City is a heavily fortified police state, and its workers' lives are heavily regulated. But Verne's tale does not focus on the political awakening of an inhabitant of Schultze's city-state. Instead, Steel City eventually collapses because of Schultze's own carelessness with one of the superweapons he develops.

The first clearly articulated portrait of a dystopian society comes in Yevgeny Zamyatin's 1920 novel *We*. Zamyatin experienced the Russian revolution and the birth of the Soviet Union, and this could very well explain his invention of the disaffected citizen of the seemingly omnipotent totality that became so common in later dystopian fiction. Zamyatin created The One State, an outwardly benevolent society governed by The Benefactor that gives its citizens numbers instead of names and regulates every moment of their lives by means of the Book of Hours. Taking both Plato's description of the ideal society and Communist propaganda to their logical conclusion, Zamyatin creates a state that is ruled by reason and not passion. Even sexual intercourse is regulated by means of pink coupons.

Of course, the state does not trust that its citizens will always be rational, so the Secret Police keeps them under surveillance. This is easy to do because everyone literally lives in glass houses. The novel is presented as the diary of D-503, a prominent mathematician and designer of the rocket ship *Integral*. Though he begins the diary as a means to praise The One State, when D-503 begins an affair with I-330, a member of the resistance movement who is interested in stealing the *Integral*, D-503 realizes that he has been afflicted with an imagination. At novel's end, with the resistance fighting against the One State's security forces, D-503 submits to an operation designed to remove his imagination and help him accept the happiness that The One State offers.

Themes first developed in *We* were then taken up in two better known dystopias. In George Orwell's *1984*, published in 1948, readers meet Winston Smith, an insignificant bureaucrat in Oceania's Ministry of Truth. Winston also keeps a diary and begins to question his society after he begins an affair with a woman named Julia. Eventually, Winston is tricked into believing that he has joined the resistance by party member O'Brien. Captured, tortured, and forced to renounce his love for Julia, at the end of the novel, Winston has learned to love Big Brother in the same way that the semi-lobotomized D-503 learned to love The Benefactor. Orwell's unique contribution to the dystopian genre is his evocation of a totalitarian regime that has difficulty providing material comfort to its citizens and actively attempts to suppress its citizens' sexual experiences. This is very different from the comfortable world of The One State, where every citizen has plenty to eat, new clothes regularly delivered, and the right to request sexual favors from every other citizen.

Another descendant of *We* is Aldous Huxley's *Brave New World*, which was first published in 1932. Like Zamyatin's One State, Huxley's World State tries to give its citizens a happy existence through rationally planning their lives. The World State attempts to replace passion with reason by means of the Bokanovsky and Podsnap processes, scientific techniques that produce clones. Using state-produced clones to replace family-produced biological children helps do away with notions of private property and the sexual jealousy inherent in monogamy and creates a society where everyone is cared for by the state and where sexual play is encouraged. There is a rigid social structure, however, because the clones come in different grades. Alphas, the highest grade of clone, are destined to rule society, while Epsilons, the lowest of the grades, are fated to do society's dirty work. Huxley's innovation within the dystopian genre includes depicting the widespread use of a drug, Soma, to control emotional response and having the critique of the totalitarian society come from an outsider.

Bernard Marx, a low-level bureaucrat in the Central London Hatchery, returns from the savage reservation in New Mexico with John, the biological son of the hatchery's director. While this discovery forces the director to resign in disgrace, John quickly becomes a celebrity because of his parentage and because he has been raised in a traditional culture. This noble savage cannot tolerate the amoral World State, however, and eventually hangs himself. While Zamyatin's and Orwell's dystopias were primarily designed to critique political totalitarianism, Huxley's was intended to critique the loss of traditional values that occurs in a technological society.

American dystopian literature almost always strongly reflects the political and social questions facing the nation when the individual dystopian tales are written, though later works were also strongly influenced by themes developed by Zamyatin, Orwell, and Huxley. Initial dystopias were concerned with class struggles and the domination of government by corporate interests. Later dystopian fiction, while never abandoning these issues, modified the genre to address pressing concerns. In the 1930s, American dystopian fiction took on the rise of fascism, while in the 1950s it addressed the dangers that material abundance posed to democracy, and in the 1980s it speculatively depicted the consequences of the backlash against feminism by the religious right. The genre began in the United States with Populist political agitator and onetime Minnesota lieutenant governor Ignatius Donnelly's 1890 novel *Caesar's Column: A Story of the Twentieth Century*. Written in response to Edward Bellamy's 1888 utopian novel, titled *Looking Backwards, Caesar's Column* describes a working-class revolt that occurs in New York in 1988. Bellamy's book predicted that technological advancement would lead to a worker's paradise, but in 1890 many feared that class warfare would tear the country apart. In Donnelly's tale, working-class radical Caesar Lomellini leads a rebellion against the oppressive elite of a technologically sophisticated New York City. The uprising is very violent—the column referred to in the novel's title is a concrete monument filled with the bodies of those killed in the fighting. The wholesale destruction of the magnificent city fills Gabriel Weltstein, Donnelly's main character, with such despair that he is forced to flee to a Christian socialist utopian community in Africa.

The next significant fictional dystopia was Jack London's 1908 novel *The Iron Heel*. Written during a time of increasing concern about the power of corporate monopolies, London's novel is structured as the autobiography of socialist revolutionary Avis Everhard, who describes her battles with the Oligarchy, a combination of business interests that has run the Unites States for hundreds of years. London also includes commentary and footnotes written long after Avis's death by a scholar named Anthony Meredith. Meredith lived after the Oligarchy had been defeated by a popular uprising. While Meredith is ultimately a hopeful character, his commentary demonstrates how futile Avis's hopes were for a revolution that would free America from the power of the Oligarchy.

Political unrest caused by the Great Depression and the rise of fascism in Europe led Sinclair Lewis to portray the demise of democracy in America in his 1935 novel *It Can't Happen Here*. Lewis's tale focuses on Doremus Jessup, a moderate Republican and the editor of a small newspaper in Vermont. The editor grows more and more concerned as Buzz Windrip, who makes vague promises about ending the

Depression and returning America to its fundamental values, is elected president and gradually becomes a dictator. Windrip was modeled on the corrupt but popular Louisiana governor Huey Long, who attempted to arouse populist sentiment by means of a campaign he called Share Our Wealth. Windrip's campaign is assisted by Bishop Peter Paul Prang, who is modeled on the anti-Semitic and pro-fascist Father Charles Coughlin, who used his radio program to attack the policies of the Roosevelt administration. Over the course of the novel, Doremus is eventually imprisoned in a concentration camp and becomes a member of the resistance after fleeing to Canada.

During the postwar abundance of the 1950s, dystopian fiction expressed the fear that technology would lull America into dystopia through addiction to unnecessary conveniences. In Kurt Vonnegut's 1952 novel *Player Piano,* American society has become an enormous automated factory surrounded by legions of underemployed consumers. Only a few people have meaningful jobs, and a graduate degree is required for any paying employment—all real estate agents, for example, have PhDs. Everyone else lives in public housing and performs menial tasks such as street sweeping. Even though the standard of living is high, most people are dissatisfied because they do not have a meaningful role to play in society. Vonnegut's story focuses on Paul Proteus, head of industry in Illium, New York. Even though Paul is one of the very few people with an important job, and even though he is in line for a significant promotion, he becomes involved with the Ghost Shirt society, a resistance organization that takes its name from nineteenth-century Native American radicals who believed that if they wore "ghost shirts" they would be invulnerable to army bullets. The Ghost Shirt society channels very different class resentments than those found in *Caesar's Column* and *The Iron Heel.* In those stories, the working class was starved and beaten, exhausted and angry. In *Player Piano,* they miss having something important to do. Although the Ghost Shirt rebellion fails, Vonnegut presents the uprising as a gesture of resistance that allows the working class to maintain its dignity.

A darker variation on the theme of technological abundance leading to dystopian decadence and democratic decay is found in Ray Bradbury's 1953 novel *Fahrenheit 451.* In the near-future society Bradbury envisions, firemen burn books to prevent people from reading and developing the intellectual capacity to question the system— they never put out fires because houses are fireproof. This is soft dystopia at its best: people have plenty of consumer goods and television to keep them docile and entertained. There is a strong police force that uses a mechanical hound to track and kill deviants, but most people are quite content. Guy Montag, a fireman, is initially happy with his life and with his job. After having a few conversations with the nonconformist Clarisse McClellan, after an old woman who had been hiding books in her house is killed by firemen, and after his wife Mildred tries to kill herself by overdosing on tranquilizers, Montag begins to question his society. He starts reading books surreptitiously and eventually hatches a plot with a former English professor named Faber to plant books in firemen's homes. When Mildred turns him in, Beatty, the fire chief, forces Montag to burn down his own house. Montag then kills Beatty and is chased into the countryside by the mechanical hound. This is a fortunate move for Montag, however, because nuclear war destroys his city soon after he flees. The novel ends with Montag joining a group of people who live in the wilderness and attempt to keep the great books alive by memorizing them. Like Huxley, Bradbury uses his novel to question the impact that a consumerist, pleasure-seeking society has on more traditional vales such as literacy.

While fears of the downside of suburban affluence never entirely left American psyche, the 1960s and 1970s brought with them new concerns. For example, the emergence of feminism brought gender issues to the forefront of the cultural battle between conservatives and liberals. The environmental movement highlighted new concerns about the hazards of an affluent society. The latter movement began in earnest in 1962 with the publication of Rachel Carson's book *Silent Spring*. Because Carson's book employed dystopian imagery to depict the damage man-made chemicals could do to the environment, it encouraged other writers to imagine dystopia as polluted. Margaret Atwood's 1985 novel *The Handmaid's Tale* combines both issues, exploring both fears of genetic damage caused by pollution and the backlash against feminism generated by the religious right.

Atwood imagines the United States turning into the Republic of Gilead when fundamentalists foment a military coup against the federal government. Women are stripped of the right to vote and own property. Because pollution has greatly decreased fertility, members of the ruling elite often conceive children using fertile women known as handmaids. Because this is patterned after the relationship that Abraham had with his servant Hagar in the Old Testament, the handmaids live with the elite families in a form of polygamy. Atwood's novel is presented as the diary of Offred, a woman who had been married to a divorced man. This made her a second-class citizen in Gilead, but because she was fertile, she was given to a member of the ruling elite called the Commander. The Commander is not portrayed as a particularly evil person—he plays Scrabble with Offred and is reasonably kind to her—but her life in such an oppressive patriarchy is very difficult. Naturally, Gilead is a totalitarian nightmare even for its male inhabitants. Secret police known as the Eyes monitor citizens' every move, and public executions are common.

After the Commander fails to impregnate her, Offred begins an affair with Nick, the Commander's chauffer. This affair is condoned by the Commander's wife, Serena Joy, because children are very valuable in a society that is largely infertile. Eventually, at Nick's urging, Offred leaves with a group of men who could be members of either the Eyes or the Mayday underground. Readers do not know if Offred is being taken away to be shot or to be placed in the underground femaleroad and taken to Canada. Atwood concludes *The Handmaid's Tale* much like London concluded *The Iron Heel*: by having academics from a brighter future give commentary on the diary. Atwood uses a presentation given by a Professor Piexoto at an academic conference, held long after the Republic of Gilead fell, to explain some of the sociology of Gileadan society. Piexoto, however, has not been able to determine what happened to Offred.

Trends and Themes. Many of the themes found in earlier dystopian writing are present in contemporary texts. The gender dystopia found in Atwood's *The Handmaid's Tale* is revisited in Cheryl Bernard's *Turning on the Girls*, which satirically portrays a society where women are in charge, and in Patrick Califia's short story "Dolly," which introduces vigilante justice into a society similar to Gilead. The critique of affluent society first seen in Vonnegut and Bradbury has migrated away from the suburbs and toward various manifestations of an overstimulating entertainment industry. Corey Doctorow looks at a future world that has become a virtual Disneyland in *Down and Out in the Magic Kingdom*, and Robert Coover's *The Adventures of Lucky Pierre: Director's Cut* creates a dystopic America that is obsessed with pornographic movies. The United States is once again under the control of a falsely populist totalitarian government in Philip Roth's *The Plot Against*

America. And the corporate dystopia imagined by Donnelley and London finds updates in T.C. Boyle's "Jubilation," Margaret Atwood's *Oryx and Crake,* Lisa Lerner's *Just Like Beauty,* and David Allen Cates's *X Out of Wonderland.*

Context and Issues. Three major trends in American society have made the themes found in contemporary dystopian novels similar to themes found in the earlier novels discussed. The first trend is the disagreement over moral and political values between conservatives and liberals that has come to be know as the "culture wars." Often, the conservative position in the culture war is perceived as a backlash against progress by authors who respond by creating dystopian fiction that portrays the United States becoming a fascist Christian republic. The second trend has been the rapid advancement of entertainment technology. While the technological cocoon that the Internet, cell phones, and iPods have created makes authors like Vonnegut and Bradbury appear prophetic, our wired society has also encouraged contemporary writers to imagine technologies that create an even more disconnected and passive populace. Finally, Americans have long harbored a broad distrust of big government and big business. Contemporary authors have updated the fears that were first expressed in *Caesar's Column* and *The Iron Heel* with discussions of what new technologies can do to enhance government and corporate power.

Reception. It is difficult to accurately gauge the cultural impact of a work of fiction, especially one that has been in circulation for only a few years. Four criteria can be used to gain a broad idea of how a book has been received: (1) reviews give a good indication of the story's perceived literary value, (2) film adaptations and (3) sales figures demonstrate the popularity of a novel or story, and (4) the genre is historically popular. For example, a poorly selling self-help book is even more insignificant because that genre tends to regularly produce best sellers. All of the novels and stories discussed in this chapter continues to receive favorable reviews in mainstream media outlets such as *The New York Times.* No plans by major studios to turn any of these works into films have been announced. There are many sources for sales data, but the rankings provided by Amazon.com are useful because they give a reasonable idea of how many people are currently purchasing a given novel. It is important to remember, however, that Amazon.com lists millions of books, and therefore sales figures must be seen in relative terms. By this measure, both Philip Roth's *The Plot Against America,* with an Amazon.com sales ranking during January 2007 in the 4,800s, and Margaret Atwood's *Oryx and Crake,* with a ranking in the 6,600s, promise to have cultural impact. Corey Doctorow's *Down and Out in the Magic Kingdom* ranked in the 34,000s, and T.C. Boyle's *Tooth and Claw,* the collection of short stories in which "Jubilation" appears, ranked in the 35,000s, and they both also show some promise. The rest of the novels discussed have rankings above 100,000 but still make important contributions to the development of the genre.

The relative popularity of some of the new dystopian literature can be explained in part by the popularity of the genre. While not at the forefront of American culture, dystopian literature does have a solid appeal. Several of the major dystopian novels discussed previously have impressive sales rankings. Atwood's *The Handmaid's Tale* is in the top 600, Bradbury's *Fahrenheit 451* is in the top 500, Huxley's *Brave New World* is in the top 400, and Orwell's *1984* is in the top 300. Furthermore, many major dystopian novels have been made into films or television programs. *Brave New World* was on television in 1980 and 1998. *Fahrenheit 451* was put on the silver screen in 1966, *1984* appeared in theatres in 1984, and *The Handmaid's Tale* was made into a film in 1990. Soviet filmmakers even filmed an adaptation of *The Iron Heel* in 1919.

Selected Authors. Dystopian fiction is not like romance or mystery, with typical authors writing many short stories and novels in the genre they have chosen as their specialty. Instead, most dystopias are unique creations, exploring themes that authors have addressed in other kinds of fiction. Margaret Atwood and other authors do return to the genre, but dystopian fiction is usually a small part of their body of work. Dystopian authors come from many different places in the literary profession. Some are established, mainstream authors, and others are newcomers working in less visible genres such as children's literature.

Cheryl Bernard has an interesting professional background that makes her uniquely qualified to create a dystopia. Although she has also published *Moghul Buffet,* a murder mystery, Barnard's primary career is as a specialist in Middle Eastern political issues. She has a PhD in International Relations from the University of Vienna and is affiliated with the Rand Corporation, a think tank that has advised the U.S. government. Bernard brings this experience in comparative political analysis to her inverted dystopia *Turning on the Girls.* The novel turns *The Handmaid's Tale* on its head and presents a society that implicitly asks if one woman's paradise would be another man's prison. Bernard's near-future society depicts women in charge "of a fine, upstanding, democratic, justice-and-equality-oriented, security-minded, peace-seeking social order" (6). Yet while women may think that a world with a restaurant chain called Balls that focuses its double entendres on the male anatomy is a far better place than this one, men may not like having to wear wristbands that could stun or kill them at the whim of a female-dominated security apparatus. Bernard's novel tracks the adventures of Lisa, an employee of the *1984*-like Ministry of Thought who has been assigned to create politically correct sexual fantasies for women, and Justin, a man detailed to work as her assistant in order to complete his reeducation process. As is typical of dystopian narrative, Lisa and Justin become involved with the resistance and a plot to overthrow the government—though they remain loyal and work as spies. The plot is discovered, the government increases its security forces and places new restrictions on men, and, as Winston Smith does in *1984,* most of the male characters learn to love Big Sister. But Bernard's extensive use of irony makes the novel a genuine satire on political correctness and its opponents. Bernard is writing for readers who would find her playful questioning of gender-based social engineering and its discontents a refreshing change from the earnest political paranoia of *The Handmaid's Tale.*

Gender dystopias that portray a world very similar to that of Atwood's novel are still being written, however. Patrick Califia writes erotic fiction and criticism for the popular and scholarly gay press. In the short story "Dolly," Califia begins by introducing readers to Ro, a butch lesbian who works for a company that programs life-sized robotic sex slaves. America is under a fundamentalist military dictatorship reminiscent of the Republic of Gilead, and naturally the sex dolls are supposed to provide submissive female partners for heterosexual men. In an act of private rebellion, Ro programs the dolls to switch their loyalty to any woman they interact with sexually. One of the dolls is sold to Jason, a soldier who has recently returned from a war. He is married to Charlene, who has been laid off from her job because the government mandates that returned soldier's wives do not work. Charlene, who had an affair with a woman while Jason was away, quickly grows to hate her now very abusive husband. Because women cannot legally divorce their husbands, Charlene is stuck. Eventually, she finds Dolly, and the programming that Ro hid in the android's hard drive kicks in. When Jason attempts to beat Charlene after discovering their affair, Dolly ties him to a bed, and Charlene and Dolly leave together. In many ways, "Dolly" is an edgy reframing of the issues raised in *The Handmaid's Tale* for a gay, lesbian, and transgendered audience.

Cory Doctorow is very active in promoting Internet technology and has written for technology magazines such as *Wired* and *Popular Science* as well as *The New York Times*. As part of his exploration of the impact of technology on society, Doctorow wrote the cautionary dystopia *Down and Out in the Magic Kingdom*. Some commentators have suggested that Disney World has become the ideal to which American society is tending. Doctorow tries to imagine a future that best exemplifies the world that Imagineers would create. Unsurprisingly, the novel presents a net-enabled update of Vonnegut's *Player Piano*.

Doctorow's novel tells the story of Julius, a crowd-control specialist at Disney World, his girlfriend Lil, who maintains the robots in the Hall of Presidents, and their friend Dan. They live in a world without scarcity, where even the outcasts of society have access to all consumer goods. Largely speaking, it is a post-work society. People have heads-up displays implanted in their corneas, communication devices implanted in their cochleas, and continuous access to the Internet and telecommunications. When people die, a clone is prepared, and their existing memory is implanted into the clone's memory. Consequently, people do not have to worry about death, and age has become meaningless. Most choose to have an apparent age in the twenties or thirties. Government is based on the will of the popular, and the world has adapted a reputation economy, with the most popular people getting the best goods and services. This new social order is known as the Bitchun Society.

While this may sound good, Dan has become bored and longs for death. After serving as a missionary to the areas of the world that are not part of the Bitchun society and converting everyone he meets, he feels a lack of purpose and decides to commit suicide. He realizes that he is so unpopular, however, that no one would care if he died, so he goes to work at Disney World with Julius and Lil. Because of Disney World's popularity, people who work there command a great deal of attention, and in a reputation economy, this is a very good thing. Dan teams up with Julius's rival, Debra, and then has his friend assassinated—somewhat meaningless in a post-death environment but still not very nice. Debra wants to make the Disney experience completely virtual—dumping data directly into people's minds while they sit in the Hall of Presidents or the Haunted Mansion. Julius, on the other hand, wants to keep the analog elements of the experience intact. Although Dan eventually confesses his self-destructive, nihilistic plot and drives Debra away from Disney World in disgrace, it is clear that Debra's path is the way that the Bitchun society is headed. Dan decides to have himself cryogenically frozen and then unthawed when the universe implodes, while Julius leaves Disney World to live on a space station. This almost Jamesian renunciation suggests a critique of the lack of challenge that a Bitchun society would provide.

Fahrenheit 451 depicts television turning people into amoral zombies, and **Robert Coover**'s *The Adventures of Lucky Pierre* updates this theme by injecting America's contemporary fascination with pornography. Coover is a novelist and playwright whose experimental use of language has garnered him widespread recognition since the 1960s. His writing has taken up themes such as American political history in *Public Burning* and sports in *Universal Baseball Association*. To understand his dystopian novel, it is helpful to know that Coover is also the author of the screenplay for *The Babysitter*, an erotic film based on one of Coover's short stories. The film was released directly to video even though it starred Alicia Silverstone, who was at that time at the height of her popularity. In *Lucky Pierre*, Coover creates Cinecity, a town where pornographic movies are the primary industry and where the mayor's office is involved in making sure the industry stays viable. There are pornographic theatres on every corner, and people copulate in public. Lucky Pierre, the porn star at the center of Coover's tale, regularly walks city streets with his erect penis on display. Cinecity is not a love-in, however, but is instead a place where perpetual sexual gratification masks despair, where "suicides rain into the snow . . . as though the heavens were taking a dump" (118) and where pedestrians are often run over and killed as they attempt to cross the streets. There are energy shortages and hackers who shut down major systems. Making underground movies is a crime, and the police frequently beat protesters who demonstrate for better access to screen time. Pornography is no longer erotica, but merely one more way for a dystopian society to control its population.

Philip Roth is one of America's most prominent contemporary writers. During his almost 50-year career, he has dealt with issues including Jewish identity in works such as *Goodbye Columbus* and *Portnoy's Complaint* and American politics in novels such as *Our Gang*. Believing, like Sinclair Lewis did, that America has always been in peril of becoming a totalitarian state, Roth creates a dystopian tragicomedy that focuses on issues of Jewish identity in the 1940s. In *The Plot Against America*, unlike Sinclair Lewis's *It Can't Happen Here*, America stops short of becoming a fascist state. The totalitarian regime that almost takes control of the country is terrifying enough, however.

In his novel, Roth traces the impact on Newark's Jewish community of the hypothetical election of Charles Lindbergh as President of the United States in 1940. Lindbergh, a dupe of the Nazis since they kidnapped his child years earlier—in Roth's version of history, the Lindbergh baby was a Nazi hostage, and the killing was staged—implements a plan to resettle urban Jews in rural America, isolating them in small towns and destroying Jewish neighborhoods. He also creates an Office of American Absorption that is designed to remove Jewish ethnic identity from Jewish children. Typically, Lindbergh also suppresses all dissenting voices and arranges to have Walter Winchell, a prominent critic, fired from his radio show. World War II starts with America having signed a peace treaty with Nazi Germany, and it appears that the Allies will be defeated. But then, Lindbergh disappears, and his vice president, Burton K. Wheeler, arrests Franklin D. Roosevelt and attempts to become a dictator. Anne Lindbergh saves the day, however, when she escapes from the mental hospital she has been imprisoned in and has Wheeler removed from office. FDR wins a special election in 1942, and America enters war on the correct side after the Japanese bomb Pearl Harbor in 1942.

Most of the political commentary in contemporary dystopia focuses on fears of corporate domination. Sometimes, as in **T.C. Boyle**'s satirical short story "Jubilation," the domination is soft, and the dystopia created requires consumers to purchase shares in it. Boyle, who has written 19 books and numerous short stories, tells of the ultimate planned community, created by the Contash Corporation as an adjunct to their theme park. Boyle focuses on Jackson, a newly divorced man who has sold a medium-sized company to a larger one and is preparing for early retirement. He bribes his way into Jubilation, starts dating Vicki, an attractive single mother with attractive children, and seems to be well on the way to a pleasant if ready-made life. Unfortunately, Jubilation is not all it is supposed to be. The mosquitoes carry malaria, a redneck neighbor begins to rebuild a race car on his lawn, and there is a hurricane. The Contash Corporation has also forgotten to remove the alligators from the lake around which the town is built, and one of the alligators eventually eats Vicki's son Ethan while Jackson is squiring her family around the lake in a rowboat. Jackson, ever an optimist, stays on after the hurricane and after Vicki's departure. He begins dating a woman whose husband was killed in the hurricane and serving on Jubilation committees. Boyle's satire strongly argues that dystopia can be desirable if it is a commodity provided by corporate America.

Although she has written many novels, poems, and television scripts, **Margaret Atwood**'s intellectual reputation rests largely on her dystopia *The Handmaid's Tale*. This stature has allowed her to write for *The New York Times, The Washington Post,* and the liberal newsmagazine *The Nation*. In *Oryx and Crake,* her return to the dystopian genre, Atwood envisions a near-future dystopia that is a logical extension of trends in today's society. Corporations house not only their offices, research facilities, and plants inside compounds protected by armed security guards, but also their employees. Everyone else lives in the pleeblands, vast urban wastelands. Global warming has begun to drown coastal cities and create food shortages. Atwood begins the story shortly after society has been almost entirely wiped out by a plague and tells the story of the catastrophe in a series of flashbacks that initially appear to be the personal reminiscences of Jimmy, a plague survivor.

Jimmy has grown up in a compound run by a bioengineering firm that creates hybrid animals. While attending the compound's school, he meets Glenn, a new kid, and begins an unlikely friendship. Jimmy is a "word person," while Glenn is a scientific genius. As they go through high school together, Glenn develops an unusual interest in extinct animals and renames himself Crake. The two friends are parted by their careers, Jimmy going to an obscure college that specializes in the liberal arts and Crake attending the prestigious Watson-Crick institute. Jimmy takes a job writing advertising copy for a futuristic patent-medicine firm, while Crake takes a high-paying job with a biotech firm. Eventually, Crake recruits Jimmy to run the advertising campaign for BlyssPluss, a combination birth control/sexual enhancement product that Crake has designed. While working for Crake, Jimmy learns that his old friend has created a new race of humans via genetic engineering. They are docile, largely because the females go into estrus, and competition over lovers is therefore limited. They live for 30 years, and then their bodies shut down. Crake tells Jimmy that these new humanoids are for research purposes, but eventually Jimmy learns the truth. Crake has embedded a plague within BlyssPluss, and it soon spreads throughout the world. Crake has actually created replacements for humanity, reasoning that it is more moral to start over. Upon his friend's request, Jimmy kills Crake, ensuring that the government will not be able to force Crake to reveal the antidote for the plague. The novel ends with Jimmy, who has become a minor deity to Jimmy's new humans, debating whether to kill other plague survivors and keep Crake's Garden of Eden going. Unlike the hopeful ending of *The Handmaid's Tale, Oryx and Crake* provides no future voice telling readers of an eventual resolution. If Atwood is somewhat optimistic about gender relations, she is in a much darker mood about corporate interference with nature.

Not all environmental and anti-corporate dystopias present their arguments so grimly, however. **Lisa Lerner**'s eccentrically upbeat first novel *Just Like Beauty* uses a beauty pageant, a perennial target of satire, to provide a mirror of a monstrously dystopian society. Set in a generally recognizable near-future—people drive mini-wagons, live in the suburbs, and shop in identity malls—and focusing on the coming of age of 14-year-old Edie and her relationship with her dysfunctional family, the novel in many ways is a typical young adult tale. Indeed, a major subplot involves Edie getting her first period. Yet Edie is maturing in a society that has become the nightmare that both feminists and anti-corporate activists have been warning against. The economy is controlled by the Just Like corporation, a manufacturer of synthetic alternatives to everything from pharmaceuticals to clothing to food. Consequently, the rivers and rain smell foul, California has auctioned its redwood forests to a partner of the Just Like conglomerate, and housecat-sized grasshoppers are multiplying and mutating as they drink Just Like insecticide. Teachers torture students for being late to class, gangs of boys armed with oxy-acetylene torches terrorize attractive girls, and Edie and her peers are training to compete in the Feminine Woman of Conscience pageant, a droll satire of contemporary pageants that adds rabbit skinning, identifying chemical compounds, and sexually stimulating the Electric Polyrubber Man to evening gown and swimsuit competition. Consumerism keeps most of the citizens of Learner's dystopia appeased, but there are two countercultural movements. The first is Happy Endings, a group that promotes suicide as a means to heal the earth's problems. The second is the terrorist Lily Gates, who occupies herself with theatrical gestures such as blowing up Just Like Meat Planet fast food restaurants.

As difficult as adolescence is, Edie must grow into adulthood under these trying circumstances. Further angst is added to her life by the crush she has on her neighbor and classmate Lana. Even though Edie is one of the favorites to win the Feminine Woman of Conscience, she has trouble seeing how she can fit in to her society. Having cleverly set up the social and interpersonal conflicts in Edie's life, Lerner creates a problematic ending for her novel. At the pageant, Edie, who is poised to win, decides to pour insecticide around the stage and loose a plague of grasshoppers who are eagerly drawn to their favorite food. At that moment, a bomb-toting Lana reveals herself as Lily Gates, and the two girls ride off into the sunset in Lana's father's Triumph TR-3. Almost immediately, however, Edie decides to return home and patch things up with her family. This abrupt ending makes it seem like Edie has stopped worrying and learned to love Big Brother.

Many proponents of the free market speak of it in utopian terms. In **David Allen Cates**'s *X Out of Wonderland*, however, contemporary American faith in deregulation is portrayed as creating a dystopia that thinks it is a utopia. Cates, the Director of Missoula Medical Aid, is also a travel writer whose work has appeared in magazines such as *Outside*, and he has written extensively on poverty in America. Cates combines his journalistic experience and his political advocacy to create a cautionary tale about free-market fundamentalism modeled on Voltaire's *Candide*. Wonderland is a free-market paradise, at least according to the media and popular culture, which seem to be relying on the theories of the noted economist Dr. Fingerdoo for this information. The inhabitants of Wonderland, however, may see things differently.

Cates explores the distance between free-market utopianism and the lived experiences of the contemporary middle class by telling the story of X, who hosts a call-in radio show for home handymen and women on NPR. Although the Wonderlandian economy seems to be providing X with the goods and services he needs and desires, this is not to last. He is let go from his job when his show is privatized and the hardware store chain that purchases it decides to bring in its own host. Shortly thereafter, X's house is destroyed by a tornado, and his bankrupt insurance company is unable to make good on his claim. X's sudden poverty is much worse than it otherwise might have been because right before the tornado destroyed his house, X met C, the love of his life.

This begins X's lifelong quest to reestablish himself financially and make a life with C. While the various episodes are by turn funny and gut-wrenching, Cates's underlying theme is that the inherent instability of the free market makes it unable to create lasting human happiness. During the course of the novel, X peddles goods in an unregulated market with an unnamed woman in a pink lame dress until organized crime drives them out of business. He then works in a sweatshop making shoelaces, eventually rising to run the shoelace company with C, though a misunderstanding with the woman in pink lame drives X away from C. The star-crossed lovers eventually reunite, however, when C is dying of AIDS. X is also drafted into the Wonderlandian army to fight in a war designed to "keep the market free, a war against mean people who just plain 'didn't get it,' economically or culture-wise, and weren't good at making weapons, either" (137). He runs afoul of the Wonderlandian government and is accused of terrorism and imprisoned by Homeland Security. Through it all, however, he never loses faith in Dr. Fingerdoo and never bothers to question his assertions about the utopian nature of an unregulated market economy.

Bibliography

Atwood, Margaret. *Oryx and Crake*. New York: Doubleday, 2003.

———. *The Handmaid's Tale: A Novel*. New York: Anchor, 1998.

Bernard, Cheryl. *Turning on the Girls*. New York: Farrar, Straus, and Giroux, 2001.

Boyle, T.C. "Jubilation." In *Tooth and Claw*. New York: Viking, 2005.

Bradbury, Ray. *Fahrenheit 451*. New York: Del Ray, 1987.

Califia, Patrick. "Dolly." In *No Mercy*. San Francisco: Alyson, 2000.

Cates, David Allen. *X Out of Wonderland: A Saga*. New York: Random House, 2005.

Coover, Robert. *The Adventures of Lucky Pierre: Director's Cut*. New York: Grove, 2002.

Doctorow, Cory. *Down and Out in the Magic Kingdom*. New York: TOR, 2003.

Donnelly, Ignatius. *Caesar's Column: A Story of the Twentieth Century*. Middletown, CT: Wesleyan University Press, 2003.

Huxley, Aldous. *Brave New World*. New York: Harper Perennial, 1998.

Learner, Lisa. *Just Like Beauty*. New York: Farrar, Straus, and Giroux, 2002.

Lewis, Sinclair. *It Can't Happen Here*. New York: Signet, 2005.

London, Jack. *The Iron Heel*. New York: Penguin, 2006.

Orwell, George. *1984*. New York: Signet, 1950.

Roth, Philip. *The Plot Against America*. Boston: Houghton Mifflin, 2004.

Verne, Jules. *The Begum's Fortune*. Rockville, MD: Wildside Press, 2003.

Vonnegut, Kurt. *Player Piano*. New York: Dial Press, 1999.

Zamyatin, Yevgeney. *We*. New York: Eos, 1999.

Further Reading

Barash, Nanelle. "Biology, Culture, and Persistent Literary Dystopias." *Chronicle of Higher Education* 3 Dec. 2004: B10–B11; Beauchamp, Gorman. "Technology in the Dystopian Novel." *Modern Fiction Studies* 32.1 (1986): 53–63; Carson, Rachel. *Silent Spring*. New

York: Mariner, 2002; Culver, Stuart K. "Waiting for the End of the World: Catastrophe and the Populist Myth of History." *Configurations* 3.3 (1995): 391–413; Gottlieb, Erika. *Dystopian Fiction East and West: Universe of Terror and Trial.* Montreal: McGill-Queens University Press, 2001; Hintz, Carrie, and Elaine Ostrey. *Utopian and Dystopian Writing for Children and Young Adults.* New York: Routledge, 2003; Moylan, Tom. *Scraps of the Untainted Sky: Science Fiction, Utopia, Dystopia.* Boulder, CO: Westview-Perseus, 2000.

MARK T. DECKER